T0180730

IFIP Advances in Information and Communication Technology   **519**

IFIP – The International Federation for Information Processing

IFIP was founded in 1960 under the auspices of UNESCO, following the first World Computer Congress held in Paris the previous year. A federation for societies working in information processing, IFIP's aim is two-fold: to support information processing in the countries of its members and to encourage technology transfer to developing nations. As its mission statement clearly states:

IFIP is the global non-profit federation of societies of ICT professionals that aims at achieving a worldwide professional and socially responsible development and application of information and communication technologies.

IFIP is a non-profit-making organization, run almost solely by 2500 volunteers. It operates through a number of technical committees and working groups, which organize events and publications. IFIP's events range from large international open conferences to working conferences and local seminars.

The flagship event is the IFIP World Computer Congress, at which both invited and contributed papers are presented. Contributed papers are rigorously refereed and the rejection rate is high.

As with the Congress, participation in the open conferences is open to all and papers may be invited or submitted. Again, submitted papers are stringently refereed.

The working conferences are structured differently. They are usually run by a working group and attendance is generally smaller and occasionally by invitation only. Their purpose is to create an atmosphere conducive to innovation and development. Refereeing is also rigorous and papers are subjected to extensive group discussion.

Publications arising from IFIP events vary. The papers presented at the IFIP World Computer Congress and at open conferences are published as conference proceedings, while the results of the working conferences are often published as collections of selected and edited papers.

IFIP distinguishes three types of institutional membership: Country Representative Members, Members at Large, and Associate Members. The type of organization that can apply for membership is a wide variety and includes national or international societies of individual computer scientists/ICT professionals, associations or federations of such societies, government institutions/government related organizations, national or international research institutes or consortia, universities, academies of sciences, companies, national or international associations or federations of companies.

More information about this series at http://www.springer.com/series/6102

Lazaros Iliadis · Ilias Maglogiannis
Vassilis Plagianakos (Eds.)

Artificial Intelligence Applications and Innovations

14th IFIP WG 12.5 International Conference, AIAI 2018
Rhodes, Greece, May 25–27, 2018
Proceedings

 Springer

Editors
Lazaros Iliadis
School of Engineering
Democritus University of Thrace
Xanthi
Greece

Vassilis Plagianakos
University of Thessaly
Lamia
Greece

Ilias Maglogiannis
University of Piraeus
Piraeus
Greece

ISSN 1868-4238 ISSN 1868-422X (electronic)
IFIP Advances in Information and Communication Technology
ISBN 978-3-030-06347-4 ISBN 978-3-319-92007-8 (eBook)
https://doi.org/10.1007/978-3-319-92007-8

This Springer imprint is published by the registered company Springer International Publishing AG
part of Springer Nature
The registered company address is: Gewerbestrasse 11, 6330 Cham, Switzerland

Preface

It is a fact that the world is changing extremely fast. Technological advances in artificial intelligence (AI) are leading this change. We have already passed from theory and algorithmic approaches, to actual delivery with several real-life practical applications. We have entered the fourth "industrial revolution" era. AI will definitely rupture the human-centric status of our civilization. Many philosophical and ethical issues will arise mainly due to the challenge and fear that the machines might take over. However, the contribution of AI so far to the improvement of our quality of life is profound. The AIAI conference offers insight into all timely challenges related to intelligent systems-algorithms and their applications.

AIAI is a mature European conference, well established in the scientific area of artificial intelligence (AI). It has a very long and successful history, following and spreading the evolution of AI. The first event was organized in Toulouse, France, in 2004. Since then, it has had a continuous and dynamic presence as a major European scientific event. More specifically, it has been organized in China, Greece, Cyprus, and France.

Through the years it has always been technically supported by the International Federation for Information Processing (IFIP) and more specifically by the WG12.5.

Following a long-standing tradition, this Springer volume belongs to the IFIP AICT Springer series and it contains the papers that were accepted for oral presentation at the 14th AIAI conference. An additional volume comprises the papers that were accepted and presented at the workshops and were held as parallel events.

The event was held May 25–27, 2018, in the Aldemar Amilia Mare five-star Hotel in Rhodes, Greece.

Four scientific workshops on timely AI subjects were organized successfully during the 2018 event:

1. The 7th Mining Humanistic Data Workshop (MHDW) supported by the Ionian University and the University of Patras, Greece. The 7th MHDW was organized by Professor Christos Makris, Department of Computer Engineering and Informatics, University of Patras, Professor Phivos Mylonas Department of Informatics, Ionian University, Dr. Andreas Kanavos, Department of Computer Engineering and Informatics, University of Patras, and Georgios Drakopoulos, Department of Informatics, Ionian University Greece. The Steering Committee of MHDW 2018 comprised Dr. Ioannis Karydis, Department of Informatics, Ionian University, Professor Katia Lida Kermanidis Department of Informatics, Ionian University, and Professor Spyros Sioutas, Department of Informatics, Ionian University. We express our sincere appreciation to the committees of MHDW 2018 for organizing this important event for the seventh consecutive time.
2. The Third Workshop on 5G-Putting Intelligence to the Network Edge (5G-PINE 2018). The Third 5G-PINE was driven by the hard work of Dr. Ioannis P. Chochliouros (Hellenic Telecommunications Organization, OTE, Greece) Dr. Alexandros

Kostopoulos (OTE, Greece), Professors Oriol Sallent and Jordi Pérez-Romero (Universitat Politècnica de Catalunya UPC, Spain), Dr. Ioannis Neokosmidis (INCITES Consulting S.A.R.L, Luxembourg), Professor Fidel Liberal (Universidad del Pais Vasco/Euskal Herriko Unibertsitatea EHU, Spain), Dr. Emmanouil Kafetzakis (ORION Innovations Company, Greece), and Dr. Ioannis Giannoulakis, National Center for Scientific Research Demokritos, Greece). We would like to thank all of these colleagues for their hard work.

3. The Workshop on Semantics in the Deep: Semantic Analytics for Big Data (SEDSEAL 2018) supported by the University of Patras, Greece. The workshop was organized by Professor Spiridon D. Likothanasis, Department of Computer Engineering and Informatics, University of Patras, and Dr. Dimitrios Koutsomitropoulos, University of Patras, Greece. We wish to express our gratitude to these colleagues for their invaluable contribution.

4. The Intelligent Cloud and IOT Paradigms in EHealth (HEALTHIOT). This scientific event was organized by Professor Ilias Maglogiannis, Department of Digital Systems, University of Piraeus, Greece, Dimosthenis Kyriazis, Department of Digital Systems, University of Piraeus, Greece, and Vassilios Plagianakos, Department of Computer Science and Biomedical Informatics, University of Thessaly, Greece. We are very happy for the important contribution of this workshop to the success of the AIAI 2018.

The diverse nature of the papers presented demonstrates the vitality of neural computing and related soft computing approaches and proves the very wide range of ANN applications as well.

The Organizing Committee was delighted by the overwhelming response to the call for papers. All papers went through a peer-review process by at least two independent academic referees. Where needed, a third referee was consulted to resolve any conflicts. In total, 88 papers were submitted to the main event and 42 of them (around 47.7%) were accepted as full papers to be presented orally for 20 min each and to be included in the proceedings with 12 pages maximum. Owing to the high quality of the submissions, the Program Committee decided to accept an additional 12 short papers that were given 15 min for oral presentation and 10 pages each in the proceedings. The workshops also followed the same rules. More specifically, 5G-PINE accepted six full papers out of 14 submissions (42.85%) and one short, whereas the MHDW accepted seven full (46.6%) and four short papers of 15 submitted papers. HealthIOT accepted four full (44.5%) out of nine and SEDSEAL accepted two full papers out of five (40%).

The papers accepted for the 14th AIAI conference are related to the following thematic topics:

- Deep learning
- Genetic algorithms
- Constraints modeling
- ANN training algorithms
- Social media intelligent modeling
- Text mining/machine translation
- Fuzzy modeling
- Medical ANN

- Feature selection
- Emotion recognition
- Hybrid intelligent models
- Support vector machines
- Voice separation
- Classification-pattern recognition
- Greedy heuristics
- Intelligent security modeling
- Optimization
- Complex stochastic games
- Unsupervised machine learning
- ANN in industry
- Intelligent clustering
- Convolutional ANN
- Recommender systems
- Intelligent telecommunications modeling
- Intelligent hybrid systems using Internet of Things
- Intelligent systems simulation

The authors of submitted and of accepted papers came from 30 different countries from all over the globe, namely: Europe (Austria, Bulgaria, Czech Republic, Denmark, France, Finland, Germany, Greece, The Netherlands, Ireland, Italy, Norway, Romania, Russia, Spain, Slovakia, Turkey, UK), America (e.g., Brazil, Canada, USA), Asia (China, India, Japan, Pakistan, Iran), and Africa (Egypt, Algeria, South Africa).

Three keynote speakers were invited to give lectures in timely aspects of AI and ANN.

1. Plamen Angelov: "Empirical Approach to Learning from Data (Streams): Fast and Interpretable Deep Learning".
   Professor Angelov has 25+ years of professional experience in high-level research and holds a Personal Chair in Intelligent Systems at Lancaster University, UK. He leads the Data Science Groups at the School of Computing and Communications, which includes over 20 academics, researchers, and PhD students and is one of the eight groups of the school.
2. Georgios N. Yannakakis: "AI Designing Games for Us... with (or Without) Us".
   Georgios N. Yannakakis is Professor at the University of Malta (UoM) and Director of the Institute of Digital Games.
3. Anastasios Tefas: "Deep Learning and Robotics: Perception, Control, and Innovations".
   Anastasios Tefas is Associate Professor in the Department of Informatics of the Aristotle University of Thessaloniki, Greece.

A very interesting tutorial on the "Implementation of Hardware Accelerators for Machine Learning" was delivered by Professor Yannis Papaefstathiou, Technical University of Crete, Greece. Yannis Papaefstathiou has been Associate Professor at the ECE Department of the Technical University of Crete since June 2004.

We hope that these proceedings will help researchers worldwide to understand and to be aware of new AI aspects. We believe they will be of major interest for scientists from all over the globe and will stimulate further research in the domain of artificial intelligence in general.

May 2018   Lazaros Iliadis
                                                          Ilias Maglogiannis
                                                        Vassilis Plagianakos

Organization

Executive Committee

General Chairs

Lazaros Iliadis   Democritus University of Thrace, Greece
John MacIntyre   University of Sunderland, UK

Organizing Committee Co-chairs

Elias Pimenidis   University of West of England, UK
Yannis Manolopoulos   Aristotle University of Thessaloniki, Greece

Program Committee Co-chairs

Ilias Maglogiannis   University of the Piraeus, Greece
Vassilis Plagianakos   University of Thessaly, Greece

Honorary Committee

Plamen Angelov   University of Lancaster, UK
Nikola Kasabov   KEDRI Auckland University of Technology, New Zealand
Vera Kurkova   Czech Academy of Sciences, Czech Republic

Advisory Committee

Haralambos Mouratidis University of Brighton, UK

Publicity Chair

Simone Scardapane   Sapienza University, Italy

Publication Chair

Antonis Papaleonidas   Democritus University of Thrace, Greece

Tutorial Chairs

Bernardette Ribeiro   Universidade de Coimbra, Portugal
Costin Badica   University of Craiova, Romania

Workshop Chairs

Spyros Sioutas	Ionio University, Greece
Christos Makris	University of Patras, Greece

Web Admin

Kyriakos Georgiades	Easy Conferences, Cyprus

Program Committee

Michel Aldanondo	Toulouse-University, CGI, France
Athanasios Alexiou	Ionion University, Greece
Georgios Anastasopoulos	Democritus University of Thrace, Greece
Kostas Berberidis	University of Patras, Greece
George Caridakis	National Technical University of Athens, Greece
Mauro Gaggero	National Research Council of Italy
Christos Georgiadis	University of Macedonia, Greece
Denise Gorse	University College London, UK
Theodoros Iliou	Democritus University of Thrace, Greece
Petros Kefalas	City College Thessaloniki, Greece
Muhammad Khurram Khan	King Saud University, Saudi Arabia
Yiannis Kokkinos	University of Makedonia, Thessaloniki, Greece
Phivos Mylonas	Ionion University, Greece
Mihaela Oprea	Petroleum–Gas University of Ploiesti, Romania
Nikolaos Polatidis	University of Brighton, UK
Vassilis Plagianakos	University of Thessaly, Greece
Alexander Ryjov	Moscow State University, Russia
Spyros Sioutas	Ionion University, Greece
Andreas-Georgios Stafylopatis	National Technical University of Athens, Greece
Ioannis M. Stephanakis	Hellenic Telecommunication Organization S.A. (OTE), Athens, Greece
Xin-She Yang	Middlesex University, London, UK
Drago Žagar	University of Osijek, Croatia
Costin Badica	University of Craiova, Romania
Konstantinos Demertzis	Democritus University of Thrace, Greece
Giorgio Gnecco	Institute for Advanced Studies, Lucca, Italy
Petr Hajek	University of Pardubice, Czech Republic
Ioannis Hatzilygeroudis	University of Patras, Greece
Antonios Kalampakas	American University of the Middle East, Kuwait
Ryotaro Kamimura	Tokai University, Japan
Petia Koprinkova-Hristova	Bulgarian Academy of Sciences, Bulgaria

Konstantinos Koutroumbas	National Observatory of Athens, Greece
Ilias Maglogiannis	University of Piraeus, Greece
George Magoulas	Birkbeck College, London, UK
Kostas Margaritis	University of Makedonia, Thessaloniki, Greece
Nikolaos Mitianoudis	Democritus University of Thrace, Greece
Valeri Mladenov	Technical University Sofia, Bulgaria
Antonios Papaleonidas	Democritus University of Thrace, Greece
Elias Pimenidis	University of West of England, Bristol, UK
Bernadete Ribeiro	University of Coimbra, Portugal
Stefanos Spartalis	Democritus University of Thrace, Greece
Athanasios Tsadiras	Aristotle University of Thessaloniki, Greece
Nicolas Tsapatsoulis	Cyprus University of Technology, Cyprus
George Tsekouras	University of Aegean, Greece
Nikos Vassilas	TEI of Athens, Greece
Petra Vidnerova	Institute of Computer Science, AS CR, Czech Republic
Panagiotis Vlamos	Ionion University, Greece
Shigang Yue	University of Lincoln, UK
Ioannis Anagnostopoulos	University of Thessaly, Greece
Basil Papadopoulos	Democritus University of Thrace, Greece
Stavros Ntalambiras	Politecnico di Milano, Italy
Aristeidis Likas	University of Ioannina, Greece
Foteini Grivokostoloulou	University of Patras, Greece
Isidoros Perikos	University of Patras, Greece
Francesco Trovo	Politecnico di Milano, Italy
Rashid Bakirov	Bournemouth University, UK
Florin Leon	Technical University of Iasi, Romania
Turki Turki	King Abdulaziz University, Saudi Arabia
Ioannis Stephanakis	Hellenic Telecommunications Organisation SA, Greece
Andreas-Georgios Stafylopatis	National Technical University of Athens, Greece
Spyridon Lykothanasis	University of Patras, Greece
Dimitrios Koutsomitropoulos	University of Patras, Greece

Abstracts

Empirical Approach to Learning from Data (Streams): Fast and Interpretable Deep Learning

Plamen Angelov

Lancaster University, UK

Abstract. We are witnessing an explosion of data (streams) being generated and growing exponentially. Today, we carry in our pockets gigabytes of data in the form of USB flash memory sticks, smartphones, smartwatches etc. Extracting useful information and knowledge from these big data streams is of immense importance for society, the economy, and science. Deep learning has quickly become known as a powerful method for enabling items and processes with elements of AI in the sense that it makes possible human-like performance in recognizing images and speech. However, the currently used methods for deep learning that are based on neural networks (recurrent, belief, etc.) are opaque (not transparent), require a huge amount of training data and computing power (hours of training using GPUs), are offline and their online versions based on reinforcement learning have no proven convergence and do not guarantee the same result for the same input (lack repeatability).

The speaker recently introduced a new concept of empirical approach to machine learning and fuzzy sets and systems, which had proven convergence for a class of such models and used the link between neural networks and fuzzy systems; neuro-fuzzy systems are known to have a duality from the radial basis function (RBF) networks and fuzzy rule-based models and possess the key property of universal approximation proven for both. In this talk the author presents in a systematic way the basics of the newly introduced "Empirical Approach to Machine Learning, Fuzzy Sets, and Systems" and its applications to problems such as anomaly detection, clustering, classification, prediction, and control.

The major advantages of this new paradigm are the liberation from the restrictive and often unrealistic assumptions and requirements concerning the nature of the data (random, deterministic, fuzzy), the need to formulate and assume a priori the type of distribution models, membership functions, the independence of the individual data observations, their large (theoretically infinite) number, etc. From a pragmatic point of view, this direct approach from data (streams) to complex, layered model representation is automated fully and leads to very efficient model structures. In addition, the proposed new concept learns in a way similar to the way people learn – it can start from a single example. The reason why the proposed new approach makes this possible is because it is prototype based and non-parametric.

AI Designing Games for Us... with (or Without) Us

Georgios N. Yannakakis

University of Malta

Abstract. Can computational processes and machine-crafted artifacts be considered creative? When does this happen and who judges after all? What happens when we create together with a creative machine? Do we merely create together or can a machine truly foster our creativity as human creators? When does such co-creation foster the creativity of both humans and machines? In this talk these questions are addressed by positioning computer games as the ideal application domain for artificial intelligence because of the unique features they offer. Advanced methods for autonomous game design as well as procedural content generation and AI-assisted game design will be showcased via a plethora of projects running currently at the Institute of Digital Games.

Deep Learning and Robotics: Perception, Control, and Innovations

Anastasios Tefas

Aristotle University of Thessaloniki, Greece

Abstract. This keynote lecture focuses on deep learning methods and their use in robotics for increased perception, control, and other innovative tasks. Deep learning has emerged as one of the most promising research fields in artificial intelligence. The significant advancements that deep-learning methods have fostered for large-scale image classification tasks have generated a surge of excitement in applying the techniques to other problems in computer vision and more broadly to other disciplines of computer science, such as robotics. However, building deep-learning algorithms for highly non-linear real-world problems such as those encountered in computer vision and robotics is non-trivial and requires substantial expertise. Unmanned aerial vehicles (drones) are among the robotic units that have substantial needs for autonomous control and perception owing to their increasing use in several applications such as transportation, inspection, surveillance, and cinematography among others. Deep convolutional neural networks (CNNs) are among the state-of-the-art techniques for visual information analysis that can provide increased perception capabilities. CNNs can be used to perform several robotic perception tasks such as object detection and tracking, face detection and person identification, crowd detection for ensuring flight safety on drones, emergency landing point detection, etc. However, deploying such deep learning models on drones or other robotic units is not a straightforward task, since there are significant memory and model complexity constraints. To overcome these limitations several methodologies have been proposed: (a) training small lightweight CNNs, (b) using knowledge transfer techniques, such as neural-network distillation, layer hints, and similarity embeddings, to reduce the size of CNNs, and (c) using neural region proposals for fast object detection and classification (faster R-CNN, YOLO, SSD).

Furthermore, gathering training data suitable for training the deep learning models is also a challenging task. Learning by using dataset augmentation techniques, such as hard negative and positive sample mining, can help to partially overcome this limitation, while allowing us to further increase the performance of the trained models. Deep-learning techniques can be also used for end-to-end drone control, allowing the deep model to control every aspect of the flight, from the visual information analysis to the drone and camera controls. Using multiple drones (multidrone set-up) can increase the flexibility of drone cinematography. Such systems can be adaptive and evolving. Finally, there are several deep-learning frameworks that can be used for deploying the aforementioned deep-learning techniques on robotics (Tensorflow, Caffe, Theano, Darknet).

Tutorial

Yannis Papaefstathiou

Technical University of Crete, Greece

Abstract. Machine learning (ML) in general and deep-learning (DL) in particular have been widely accepted as the most prominent approaches for solving very complex problems in numerous application domains. However, their computational and power demands can be forbiddingly high when executed on general purpose CPUs. As a result, it is highly desirable to implement such schemes in reconfigurable hardware accelerators.

This tutorial provides an overview of the main ML and DL schemes that have been implemented in hardware to date. It focuses on how a software developer can utilize high-level synthesis so as to develop such an efficient accelerator in a modern reconfigurable hardware device (i.e., FPGA); this is illustrated in the design of a certain widely used DL module. Furthermore, a number of optimizations, applicable to most ML and DL schemes that allow the designer to explore in full the capabilities of the modern FPGAs, are presented.

Contents

Neural Networks

Medical Intelligence

Recommender Systems

Optimization

Learning - Intelligence

Human & Computer Interaction - Sound - Video - Processing

Social Media - Games - Ontologies

On Addressing the Challenges of Complex Stochastic Games Using *"Representative"* Moves

Armando H. Taucer, Spencer Polk[✉], and B. John Oommen

School of Computer Science, Carleton University, Ottawa, Canada
armando.h.taucer@gmail.com, andrewpolk@cmail.carleton.ca,
oommen@scs.carleton.ca

Abstract. The problem of achieving competitive game play in a board game, against an intelligent opponent, is a well-known and studied field of Artificial Intelligence (AI). This area of research has seen major breakthroughs in recent years, particularly in the game of Go. However, popular hobby board games, and particularly Trading Card Games, have unique qualities that make them very challenging to existing game playing techniques, partly due to enormous branching factors. This remains a largely unexamined domain and is the arena we operate in. To attempt to tackle some of these daunting requirements, we introduce the novel concept of *"Representative"* Moves (RMs). Rather than examine the complete list of available moves at a given node, we rather propose the strategy of considering only a *subset of moves* that are determined to be *representative* of the player's strategic options. We demonstrate that in the context of a simplified Trading Card Game, the use of RMs leads to a greatly improved search speed and an extremely limited branching factor. This permits the AI player to play more intelligently than the same algorithm that does not employ them.

1 Introduction

The problem of playing a competitive board game, intelligently and effectively, against a human player is canonical in AI. Over the years, a broad range of literature has been published addressing the problem of game playing, introducing a wide range of highly effective techniques, for many different types of games [7–9]. Historically, the literature has emphasized classical, deterministic, two-player board games, and in particular, *Chess* and *Go* [7,13]. AI systems for many such games are powerful enough to overwhelm even the best human players.

In recent years, perhaps influenced by their growing popularity in popular culture, card-based games such as Bridge and Poker have seen an increased emphasis in the literature [4,5]. However, there are still some categories of popular games (particularly amongst "hobbyist" game players), which have been the subject of proportionally

---

The third author Holds the positions of *Chancellor's Professor*; *Fellow: IEEE* and *Fellow: IAPR*. The third author is also an *Adjunct Professor* with the Dept. of ICT, University of Agder, Grimstad, Norway.

L. Iliadis et al. (Eds.): AIAI 2018, IFIP AICT 519, pp. 3–13, 2018.
https://doi.org/10.1007/978-3-319-92007-8_1

limited investigation within the field. One of these includes large-scale, complex, multi-player strategy board games, such as the popular Settlers of Catan and Carcassone [6, 12]. Another is the category of Trading Card Games (TCGs)[1], which are an interesting hybrid between classical board games and card games.

In TCGs, which include popular games such as *Yu-Gi-Oh!* and *Magic: The Gathering*, players typically construct their own decks, selecting a subset of potentially thousands of published cards, each with differing effects, and place them onto a dynamically constructed field of play, where they act as the pieces of the game. Despite their interesting qualities, they have seen almost no attention from AI researchers, and this can be primarily attributed to the fact that resolving them is far from trivial. Besides, they are not easily modeled using the traditional Mini-Max or Monte-Carlo sets of strategies.

Both large-scale, hobby board games and TCGs are characterized by extremely broad, complex game states, which are manipulated by players who are able to take *multiple* actions on their turn (often as many as their available resources allow), and consist of both deterministic and stochastic elements. These elements cause these games to have extremely complicated game trees. They, thus, pose a particular challenge to established game playing strategies applicable for deterministic/stochastic games. To address these challenges, in this work, we introduce the concept of *generalizing* available actions into *Representative Moves* (RMs), and consider *them* in our search. While this will necessarily lead to unrealistic look-ahead in the game tree, the impact in decision making is far surpassed by the benefits in execution time and available search depth.

The remainder of the paper is laid out as follows. Section 2 describes the established techniques upon which we base our work, and Sect. 3 describes the novel concept of RMs. Section 4 describes the simplified TCG that we will use in our model, and how RMs can be applied to it. Section 5 describes our experimental design, and Sects. 6 and 7 report our results and analysis. Lastly, Sect. 8 concludes the paper.

2   Background

The vast number of established search techniques for adversarial two-player and multiplayer games can be broadly divided into two paradigms, namely those of stochastic methods, such as the Monte-Carlo Tree Search (MCTS) algorithm and its many successful variants [1, 10, 12], and the deterministic methods, generally based on the well-known Mini-Max algorithm [7, 11]. Both paradigms are based upon an intelligent, efficient, and informed search of the game tree, which refers to the set of game states reachable by each player making legal moves to alter the board. Mini-Max based approaches generally search to a selected *ply* depth, pruning sections of the tree using methods such as the well-known alpha-beta strategy, which will not impact its end state, thus enabling a deeper and more effective search with available computational resources [7]. MCTS, and its many successful variants, such as the UCT algorithm, directs its search through random game playing, potentially weighted by learned or expert-provided strategies, and thus it determines the path to explore at each step *via* a bandit problem [1].

Both of these paradigms must adapt when they encounter cases of imperfect information. For example, if applied to the game of *Backgammon*, the search must account

---
[1] TCGs compose a market of over $600 million [2].

for the fact that the available moves to each player, and therefore the efficacy of specific strategies, are partly based upon a roll of the die. In both these paradigms, this can be handled by the incorporation of "chance" nodes, which represent the possible, weighted outcomes of a random event [7]. In the deterministic context, "chance" nodes are incorporated into the Mini-Max strategy in the Expectiminimax algorithm, where each node is assigned a score equal to its *expected value*, assuming players perform intelligently with the resources available to them [7]. MCTS schemes can also incorporate "chance" nodes in the manner employed by the Expectiminimax [3]. Intuitively, the incorporation of "chance" nodes can seriously impact the performance of the search, as they lead to a much larger functional branching factor, and effective tree pruning, particularly in the deterministic case, where it becomes a much greater challenge.

While relatively simple random elements, such as rolling a die, can transform a simple search problem into a far more challenging one, these problems are exacerbated in the context of "hobby" board games, such as *Settlers of Catan*, and TCGs, which often have very complex random events and player moves made from of a wide range of individual parts. Current applications of game playing strategies to hobby games generally require a great deal of bias and expert knowledge to perform competitively [12]. This requirement necessarily limits the development of a domain-*independent* approach. In the context of TCGs, while a number of attempts have been made to play subsets, or accomplish specific tasks, in popular TCGs, to the best of our knowledge, no attempt to create a competitive TCG player exists in the literature. This is possibly because the number of available moves and random components involved are too daunting for current strategies, which do not rely heavily on expert knowledge. In this work, we will refer to these types of games as Complex Stochastic Games (CSGs).

As the extremely large number of "chance" nodes and branching factor of TCGs are a major hurdle in achieving competitive play, we suggest that an effective method for tackling them could be to simplify the game tree in some way. While this would have the effect of considering an invalid or incomplete game state, it may not be as catastrophic to do so as one may intuitively believe. This is analogous to what happens in the context of multi-player games. In recent years, the Best-Reply Search (BRS) has been shown to achieve excellent, competitive play, even through it explores invalid game trees [8]. The BRS is based on an observation that in a multi-player board game, the moves of the other players are not as important as the moves of the perspective player, and simplifies the turn order and search by considering all opponents as if they were a single "super-opponent", and searching as if the game had only two players [8] – even though it considers invalid turn orderings. An example of this grouping in a single level of a BRS tree is shown in Fig. 1. We propose an analogous strategy for CGSs.

3   Representative Moves

While there are many difficult challenges to overcome in achieving competitive game play in the domains of TCGs and hobby board games, a critical concern that severely hampers state-of-the-art techniques is the extremely large branching factors of these games, due to the wide range of possible decisions available to the player, and the

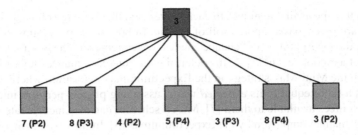

Fig. 1. The operation of a single level of the Best-Reply Search. The scores that are reported have the opponent's player number listed next to them (in parenthesis) to assist in the clarification.

presence of a substantial number of "chance" nodes in the game tree[2]. While traditional pruning methods can impact the branching factor, if there are hundreds of possible moves available to a player at each turn, their applicability will be limited. Therefore, it is worthwhile seeking out novel and radical methods for limiting the search space, to improve performance in these games. To achieve this, we propose the concept of *Representative Moves* (RMs).

The basic concept of RMs is as follows. In the scenario where a game, possibly, allows hundreds of moves, particularly when some are based on random chance, rather than considering all of these possible moves and their chance nodes, we, instead, consider a game model with only a much smaller set of moves. This smaller set of moves is "representative" of the total number available, standing in for "classes" of moves. They are either chosen representatives of their class, or some sort of average of the moves of that class. The classes of moves can be determined based on expert knowledge of the game's strategy, or potentially through unsupervised learning mechanisms. As a simple example, consider a game, similar to Backgammon, where during his turn, a player rolls two dice, and may advance two of his pieces by individual values shown on the pair of dice, towards a goal space. The player could move two different pieces, the same piece twice, reach the goal with one or two of his pieces, or perhaps, due to occupied spaces ahead, only move one, or even none of his pieces. These six types of moves could be the classes. Rather than consider all possibilities, we would consider these as RMs.

The main reason to do this is to limit the branching factor of the game. Instead of considering hundreds of available moves, we instead perform a search based upon distinct *strategies* available to the players at each level of the tree. Intuitively, by selecting only RMs at each level of the tree, we will be considering an incomplete version of the game tree, or, if averages are taken, potentially illegal board states. However, this is what the BRS does for multi-player games, and, despite this apparent weakness, it performs extremely well in the environments to which it applies [8]. When considering an exorbitantly large space, such as those associated with TCGs, this can potentially allow us to achieve a more substantial look-ahead, and faster search.

---

[2] As an example, in a TCG deck, there may be twenty or more possible cards, each with a different functional purpose, which the player could draw on any turn.

A disadvantage of using RMs is that a move, or random outcome, which is ignored, could be critical to formulating a winning strategy. Besides, it may not always be possible to properly select RMs. For example, in *Chess*, this technique would be unlikely to perform well, as it is difficult to strategically classify a player's available moves.

4   Game Model

The RMs paradigm was developed specifically to tackle the domain of TCGs, and therefore, it would be best to test its performance within the context of an actual TCG. However, due to the extreme complexity of these games, it is very difficult to implement an engine capable of fully capturing all their aspects. Therefore, in this exploratory work, we have created a custom TCG, designed to follow the conventions of the genre, while being a much simpler example than any on those available in market. TCG games generally represent a battle of some sorts, typically, in a fantasy or science fiction setting, with the names of cards, game mechanics, and so forth contributing to this story. Players draw cards from their own, customizable deck (with a unique set of rules for deck customization), and typically place these cards onto the "field of play", where they remain, functioning thereafter in a manner similar to game pieces, or have some effect and are then removed. For example, in a game like *Magic: the Gathering*, based on the concept of dueling wizards, a card could represent a dragon that could be summoned to battle, or a spell to destroy one of the opponents' summoned monsters. On each turn, a player can typically take as many actions as his cards would allow, plus some general-purpose acts, such as drawing a card from his deck.

In our custom TCG, each player has at their disposal a deck of twenty-five cards. As is typical of TCGs, each player has his own deck. However, in this case, the cards in each deck are identical. Two of these cards, when played, remove an opponent's card from the field immediately, and are then removed themselves; this is analogous to "Removal" cards in *Magic: the Gathering*. The other twenty-three represent "soldiers" of varying strength and quality, each having a value for "Fight", "Heal". and "Attack". Thus, each individual card can have different strengths and weaknesses. When played, these cards remain within the field of play, and afford the player additional actions on this turn and future turns, as is typical of TCG cards. The specific values of the "soldier" cards are chosen to provide an even spread of each value, with higher values being less common than lower values. The specific soldier cards are recorded in Table 1.

Each player begins with fifty "Health Points" (HP), conceptually representing his remaining vitality. To begin play, each player draws five cards. Unlike a normal TCG, for the sake of simplicity, each player's hand is visible. During each turn, the player must first draw a card, unless this would cause him to have more than five cards in his hand. The player may then place a card from his hand onto the field of play[3]. Then, for each of the player's cards on the field, he may take one of the following actions:

---

[3] In a typical TCG, the ability to put a card onto the field of play is limited by some form of resource, often obtained from other cards. Thus, careful deck construction is an important consideration, as powerful cards are of no strategic use if they cannot be played. As our game does not factor in deck construction, we have omitted resource cards from the game.

Table 1. Statistical values of cards in our custom TCG.

Fight	Heal	Attack	Fight	Heal	Attack	Fight	Heal	Attack
1	1	1	1	1	2	1	0	3
2	2	2	3	2	2	0	4	4
3	3	3	1	1	5	4	4	0
4	4	4	6	0	0	3	3	0
4	0	3	3	3	2	1	3	3
2	4	2	4	0	4	4	1	1
0	0	7	2	4	1	6	6	6
4	1	0	5	1	0	–	–	–

1. Do nothing.
2. Increase his HP by the card's "Heal" value.
3. Decrease his opponent's HP by the card's "Attack" value.
4. Have this card do battle with another on the field. The card with the lower "Fight" value is removed. In the event of a tie, both are removed.

The first player whose HP is reduced to zero loses the game, and his opponent wins.

5   Experimental Design

While the concept of defining and utilizing RMs has intuitive value, its performance must be gauged in a quantitative manner so to ensure that the balance between its benefits and drawbacks supports its use in real game playing engines. The task of performing a formal analysis of game playing algorithms [11] is well-known to possess extreme difficulties. Consequently, as is the accepted practice in the literature, we have chosen to verify its performance via experimentation. In this exploratory work, we will perform such an experimental verification using the custom TCG[4] described above.

Our goals in verifying the performance of RMs are twofold. Firstly, we seek to confirm that the use of RMs does, indeed, save substantial amounts of search time. Secondly, we seek to determine whether this benefit in performance is obtained at the cost of effective game play, or whether this even improves the play. To do this, we first measure the execution speed of both a basic Expectiminimax algorithm, and also that of an Expectiminimax algorithm that employs RMs. More specifically, in this regard, we measure both the execution time, and the total number of leaf nodes expanded, where the latter serves as a "platform agnostic" metric. We then measure their performance against each other, over a number of games, to examine the impact of RMs on the win rate. We conduct this experiment both to an equivalent move depth, and thereafter to a greater depth whenever RMs are employed, if the latter is found to work faster.

---

[4] We apologize for the detailed description of the game's moves, but it is necessary to clearly describe our work.

To apply RMs to our custom TCG, we must first have some concept of how the classes of moves, and their representatives, are selected. Observe that in our custom TCG, each card (except the "Removal" cards) has a total of three values ("Fight", "Heal", and "Attack"), each of which represents a distinct strategy. Thus, when determining which card to play next, we consider three possible RMs, one for each of the three values. Each of these three moves has a value equal to the average of "Fight", "Heal", or "Attack", of all remaining cards in the player's hand and deck, with the value doubled for cards in the hand. This produces three "representatives", roughly corresponding to the player's current capacity in each of the three aspects of the game.

This leaves us with the task of considering the "Removal" cards which function differently and which do not have three values. To factor them into our "representative" set, we observe that a "Removal" card has a purpose similar to a card with a high "Fight" value, that is, that of removing the opponent's cards from their field of play. We, therefore, consider each of the two "Removal" cards to be equivalent to a card with the values 5 "Fight", 0 "Heal", and 0 "Attack". Observe that this can "remove" almost anything from the field, but can do so only a single time. This is thus is not quite as good as the few cards which have 6 "Fight" values. This allows us to consider the "Removal" cards to be part of our three representatives.

For the sake of fairness, each of the players makes use of the same evaluation function. The evaluation function takes the player's "Health Points", and adds to it the total sum of all values, on all cards, on the player's field, divided by three. We subtract from this value a small factor which favours more "balanced" hands, thus encouraging the player to retain more strategic options. This factor is calculated by summing the three values on each card, and subtracting the lowest total value, from the highest (i.e., a card with "Fight" 3, "Heal" 1, and "Attack" 1 would have a sum of 5). The final value of the evaluation function is the difference between the perspective player's result, and his opponent's.

Our results are presented in the following section.

6 Results

Table 2 shows our execution time results for Expectiminimax when RMs were employed. In all cases, to ensure equivalent execution, each player had the starting hand 6/6/6, 2/1/1, 4/1/1, 2/3/2, and 1/3/3 ("Fight"/"Heal"/"Attack"). As expected from any game tree search algorithm, the runtime, and the number of leaf nodes examined, grow explosively as the *ply* depth is increased.

Table 2. Execution time when RMs are employed.

Depth	Runtime (ms)	Leaf nodes
3	108	3,100
4	246	62,400
5	2,200	238,100

Table 3 shows our execution time results for Expectiminimax when RMs were not employed. The same starting position was used, as with the previous experiments, to ensure consistency. As is immediately obvious, the use of RMs *vastly* cuts down the search space, with an Expectiminimax search to a *ply* depth of 3, taking much longer than one to a depth of 5 when RMs were not employed. At a greater depth, execution of the search showed no signs of halting after well over 30 min of execution time.

Table 3. Execution time when RMs are not employed.

Depth	Runtime (ms)	Leaf nodes
3	132,100	263,836,900
4	Inf.	Inf.

Table 4 shows our results when RM-enabled and Non-RM players faced each other, with equal search depths of 3. We found that, even when they were allowed only equivalent search depths, RMs achieved an 80% win rate over a non-RM search, winning with an average of 22.9 HP, and taking an average of 29.6 turns to finish the game.

Table 4. Games between RM and non-RM players at equivalent search depth.

Winner	RM final HP	Non-RM final HP	Number of moves
RM	25	−2	26
Non-RM	−3	28	24
RM	37	0	22
RM	59	−2	45
RM	6	−1	24
RM	21	−3	16
RM	20	−1	21
RM	40	−2	20
Non-RM	−5	11	42
RM	29	0	56

Table 5 shows our results when RM and Non-RM players faced each other, where the RM player was allowed to search to a depth of 5, given its proven efficiency. We found that, even allowed only equivalent search depth, RMs achieved an 72.7% win rate over a non-RM search, winning with an average of 19.9 HP, and taking an average of 26.2 turns to finish the game. The power of using RMs in the strategy is obvious!

7 Discussion

Our results very clearly demonstrate two things. First, the use of RMs significantly improves the speed and efficiency of the search. Secondly, despite considering only a

Table 5. Games between RM and non-RM players at differing search depths.

Winner	RM final HP	Non-RM final HP	Number of moves
RM	8	−1	16
Non-RM	0	16	32
RM	54	0	33
RM	18	−1	21
RM	29	−2	17
RM	24	0	24
RM	8	−5	25
Non-RM	−2	42	26
Non-RM	−5	15	26
RM	41	−1	36
RM	44	−1	32

small, representative portion of the complete game tree, not only does the use of RMs not hamper the strategic ability of the player in our custom TCG, but in fact, it achieves a noticeably higher win rate, compared to a player not using the RM technique.

Our first observation, about the speed of the search, is somewhat predictable. Indeed, the use of RMs converts a total of up to 25 possible cards that the player could place onto the field and which he must consider, into a total of three. However, it is still striking to observe how extreme the change is. Even comparing a search to a *ply* depth of five, using RMs, to a search to a depth of three, not using RMs, the RM-enabled search is two orders of magnitude faster. It also considers three orders of magnitude fewer leaf nodes. This result clearly demonstrates that the use of RMs can, indeed, enable a search to a much greater depth, in the same available processing time.

The second observation is far more interesting. Our original, stated goal was to demonstrate that the use of RMs does not *reduce* the strategic capabilities of the Expec-timinimax algorithm. However, we observed that it, in fact, regularly defeated a player who does not use it. More importantly, this effect was observed even when the primary predicted benefit of RMs, i.e., the faster search, was not factored in, to allow it to search deeper in the tree. This is a very interesting and unexpected, result. A possible expla-nation for this is that considering only the primary strategic factors of the game, rather than individually considering every possible card, RMs enabled a more focused search on the game's components. The RM technique did not perform better at a larger search depth, although given the restricted number of games we could play to completion (due to how slow the non-RM player was), this may easily be due to random chance.

We observed that in both experiments, the RM player would, on average, end the game with a similar (20–23) HP score, and that the game would take a similar (26–30) number of turns to complete. Examining individual cases, however, we observe some scenarios where the game took much longer, up to 56 turns, to finish, and some scenar-ios where the winning player would have a much higher, or lower, HP score. The highest winning HP score was 59, and the lowest was 6. Given that our custom TCG provides the ability for cards to "Heal" the player, it is likely that the cards drawn in games that either took a long time, or ended with high HP scores, had a much higher "Heal" value than other available cards. Conversely, whenever the winner won with a low HP score, it is likely that both opponents entered into a scenario where they had cards with high "Attack" values, and attempted to race to defeat each other. This balance of aggressive and defensive play is typical of real TCGs, such as *Magic: the Gathering*, and suggests that our custom TCG does, indeed, capture some of their strategic qualities.

8   Conclusions and Future Work

Our results in this paper very clearly demonstrate that, although it considers only a portion of the game tree, the use of RMs is capable of achieving competitive game play, with equivalent techniques that do not employ it. RMs are also capable of vastly improving the execution time of the search. Although we have done an examination of RMs in the context of Expectiminimax, it is also applicable to MCTS, and an examination of its capabilities in such settings is a possible avenue of future work.

In this work, we calculated the RMs based upon domain-specific knowledge of the game tree. However, as we briefly touched upon in Sect. 3, it would be possible to find classes of moves using an unsupervised learning technique, and elect specific representatives from the classes. Further, while our custom TCG replicates some of the strategic concerns of a real TCG, it is *much* simpler than the ones accessible in the market. It would be very interesting to examine the capacity of RMs in a real-world TCG, although significant work would need to be done in formalizing the game engine, before this would be possible. Finally, we believe that other non-TCG games, like *Settlers of Catan*, or *Backgammon*, could potentially benefit from the use of RMs.

References

1. Gelly, S., Wang, Y.: Exploration exploitation in go: UCT for monte-carlo go. In: Proceedings of NIPS 2006, the 2006 Annual Conference on Neural Information Processing Systems (2006)
2. Griepp, M.: Hobby games market nearly $1.2 billion. News article on hobby gaming's success, with notes on TCG market share (2016)
3. Jouandeau, N., Cazenave, T.: Monte-carlo tree reductions for stochastic games. In: Cheng, S.M., Day, M.Y. (eds.) Proceedings of TAAI 2014, The 2014 Conference on Technologies and Applications of Artificial Intelligence. LNCS, vol. 8916, pp. 228–238. Springer, Cham (2014)
4. Moravčík, M., Schmid, M., Burch, N., Lisý, V., Morrill, D., Bard, N., Davis, T., Waugh, K., Johanson, M., Bowling, M.: Deepstack: expert-level artificial intelligence in heads-up no-limit poker. Science, 508–513 (2017)
5. Onisawa, T., Yono, T.: Construction of poker playing system considering strategies. In: Proceedings of CyberGames 2006, The 2006 International Conference on Game Research and Development, pp. 121–128 (2006)
6. Pfeiffer, M.: Reinforcement learning of strategies for settlers of catan (2004)
7. Russell, S.J., Norvig, P.: Artificial Intelligence: A Modern Approach, 3rd ed., pp. 161–201. Upper Saddle River, New Jersey, Prentice-Hall Inc. (2009)

8. Schadd, M.P.D., Winands, M.H.M.: Best reply search for multiplayer games. IEEE Trans. Comput. Intell. AI Games **3**, 57–66 (2011)
9. Shannon, C.E.: Programming a computer for playing Chess. Phil. Mag. **41**, 256–275 (1950)
10. Silver, D., Huang, A., Maddison, C., Guez, A., Sifre, L., van den Driessche, G., Schrittwieser, J., Antonoglou, I., Panneershelvam, V., Lanctot, M., Dieleman, S., Grewe, D., Nham, J., Kalchbrenner, N., Sutskever, I., Lillicrap, T., Leach, M., Kavukcuoglu, K., Graepel, T., Hassabis, D.: Mastering the game of go with deep neural networks and tree search. Nature **529**, 484–489 (2016)
11. Sturtevant, N.: Multi-player games: algorithms and approaches. Ph.D. thesis, University of California (2003)
12. Szita, I., Chaslot, G., Spronck, P.: Monte-Carlo tree search in settlers of catan. In: van den Herik, H.J., Spronck, P. (eds.) ACG 2009. LNCS, vol. 6048, pp. 21–32. Springer, Heidelberg (2010). https://doi.org/10.1007/978-3-642-12993-3_3
13. Xiao, F., Liu, Z.: Modification of UCT algorithm with quiescent search in computer GO. In: Proceedings of TAAI 2010, The 2010 International Conference on Technologies and Applications of Artificial Intelligence, pp. 481–484 (2010)

Finding Influential Users in Twitter
Using Cluster-Based Fusion Methods
of Result Lists

Alexandros Georgiou, Andreas Kanavos$^{(\boxtimes)}$, and Christos Makris

Computer Engineering and Informatics Department,
University of Patras, Patras, Greece
{georgiua,kanavos,makri}@ceid.upatras.gr

Abstract. The topic of the paper is to present a novel methodology
in order to characterize influential users, such as members of Twitter,
as they arise in social networks. The novelty of our approach lies in
the fact that we incorporate a set of features for characterizing social
media authors, including both nodal and topical metrics, along with new
features concerning temporal aspects of user participation on the topic.
We also take advantage of cluster-based fusion techniques for retrieved
result lists for the ranking of top influential users.

Keywords: Cluster-based methods · Influential users
List fusion methods · Social networks · Temporal features · Twitter
Web mining

1 Introduction

The task of finding the most influential users in an online social networking
environment has gained a great amount of attention in recent years. Special
focus is given on social networking platforms called microblogging platforms.
These platforms allow only short messages to be published (usually ranging in
a few hundred characters), a fact that raises a wide range of problems against
text-based information retrieval techniques.

A prominent example of such microblogging platforms is the Twitter online
social network which only allows messages of 140 characters maximum. Twitter
is an internationally famous social networking platform with hundreds of millions of active users. Each user can create an unlimited circle of affiliated users to
whom they can publish updates (called *tweets*). Users are additionally presented
with a list of tweets by their affiliated users sorted by the latest, called *timeline*.
User relations in Twitter are not necessarily reciprocal: user a may *follow* user
b, without user b having to authorize it or to follow back. When user b chooses
to follow back user a, users a and b can be called *friends*. The Twitter platform allows users to repost content that they find interesting, an action called

L. Iliadis et al. (Eds.): AIAI 2018, IFIP AICT 519, pp. 14–27, 2018.
https://doi.org/10.1007/978-3-319-92007-8_2

retweet which is signified by the characters "RT" following the original content producer's username. A user is able to directly mention another user with the character "@" followed by the mentioned user's username. Topics of discussion can be initiated by any user and organized around user-specified keywords, called *hashtags* and signified by the character "#" followed by the desired keyword.

Recent studies [10, 23] have shown that groups of intermediate level users act as propagating nodes for the information flow on such networks, and users rely preferably on other users or special purpose user accounts for their information about certain topics. Taking into account the spread of such online social networks and the impact that they have on many aspects of everyday social, economic and political reality, identifying users with high influence around specified topics is of crucial importance for social media marketing agents, governments, policy makers, celebrities and communities.

The rest of the paper is structured as follows. Section 2 presents background topics while Sect. 3 presents our methodology followed and the system developed. In Sect. 4, details of the implementation of the system as well as the evaluation study conducted and the results gathered on both the sentiment analysis topic and the community detection topic are presented. Finally, Sect. 5 concludes our work and presents directions for future research.

2 Related Work

Recently, the identification of topical (or influential) authorities in microblogging has gained a lot of attention. In [19], the challenge of finding the most interesting and authoritative authors for any given topic in Twitter is reported. Authors provide a set of features for characterizing any social media author, including both nodal and topical metrics. Their experimental results show that a probabilistic clustering over a feature space, followed by a within-cluster ranking procedure, can yield to a final list of top authors for a given topic. More specifically, their technique uses a Gaussian Mixture Model to cluster users into two clusters over their feature space as the aim is to reduce the size of the target cluster; that is the cluster containing the most authoritative users. In addition in [11, 12], the notion of influence from users to networks is extended and in following, personality as a key characteristic for identifying influential networks is considered. The system creates influential communities in a Twitter network graph by considering user personalities where an existing modularity-based community detection algorithm is used. At a later point, the insertion of a pre-processing step that eliminates graph edges based on user personality is utilized. Moreover in [13], an efficient and innovative methodology for community detection that will also leverage users' behavior on emotional level is introduced.

Interesting is the work presented in [22], which employs Latent Dirichlet Allocation and a variant of the PageRank algorithm that clusters according to topics and finds the authorities of each topic; the proposed metric is called TwitterRank. The field of analysis in social networks is related to link analysis in the web with cornerstone the analysis of the significance of web pages in

Google using the PageRank citation metric [18], the HITS algorithm proposed by Kleinberg [15] as well as their numerous variants discussed in [16]. PageRank employs a simple metric based on the importance of the incoming links while HITS uses two metrics emphasizing the dual role of a web page as a hub and as an authority for information.

Historically, the above as well as other approaches and techniques have been harnessed throughout microblogging areas. In [8], an overall generative model for questions and answers in community-based Question Answering (cQA) services is developed, which is then altered to obtain a novel computationally tractable Bayesian network model. Initially, they seek to discover latent topics in the content of questions as well as the associated answers, and latent topic interests of users. Then, they recommend answer providers for new questions according to discovered topics as well as term-level information of queries and users. What is more, in [17], authors present an investigation dealing with user perceptions about credibility tweets, where they examined key elements of the information interface for their impact on credibility judgements. Their results indicate that users had difficulty determining the truthfulness of content and that their judgement was clouded and often based on heuristics (e.g. if a post has been retweeted) and biased systematically (e.g. topically-related user names seen as more credible).

Furthermore, the similar problem though in other platform (e.g. in Yahoo! Answers) was addressed in [5]. Their method automatically discriminates between authoritative and non-authoritative users through modeling the authority scores of users as a mixture of gamma distributions. The number of components in the mixture is estimated by the Bayesian Information Criterion (BIC) while the parameters of each component are estimated using the Expectation-Maximization (EM) algorithm. Concerning Yahoo! Answers, authors in [2] investigated methods for exploiting specific community feedback so as to automatically identify high quality content. More in detail, a general classification framework for combining the evidence from different sources of information, that can be tuned automatically for a given social media type and quality definition, is proposed and the experiments show an accurate separation of high-quality items from the rest, non-notable.

Finally, relative study with the current one is [3] by Anderson et al. in which it is investigated whether similarity in the characteristics of two users can affect the evaluation that one user provides to another. They analyze this problem under a range of natural similarity measures, demonstrating how the interaction between likeness and status can produce strong effects. Among these measures is a resemblance of interests using a distance metric capturing overlap in the types of content that users produce, as well as a similarity of social ties using a measure of the overlap in the sets of people they evaluated.

3   System Description

3.1   Modular Architecture

In the social media mining system we developed, the most authoritative users per topic are identified based on a variety of features that combine the quality of content they provide. Text similarity measures, social impact through retweets, ability to spike conversations considering the content provided (through conversational tweets), social graph relations and time-related variables measuring frequency and timezone span consist important characteristics as well.

Our system architecture consists of the following modules:

- A *Twitter access module*: Twitter database is accessed through Twitter API by this module, using the Twitter4j Java library for Twitter application development. This module receives topic name (#hashtag) as input, and returns user tweets from the specific topic as well as active user data and social graph relations from the total Twitter social graph.
- A *Parser module*: Output from the Twitter access module is parsed to create appropriate username searchable hashmaps which include all tweets, social graph data and time-related data. This stage is necessary as a preparation for the feature extraction process.
- *Feature extraction module*: Hashmaps containing username - tweet set pairs are given as input from the Parser module. Numbers of original tweets, retweets, conversational tweets are counted, social graph relations are measured, posting frequency for each user is reported and tweets are distributed into four 8-h time zones (morning, noon, evening, night) based on standard Twitter timestamps. These counts and measures are later combined to create the list of features for every user who participates in the specific topic. Hashmaps are restructured to contain username - feature value pairs.
- A *Clustering module*: the set of username - feature values hashmaps is given as input in a module responsible for the clustering algorithms. Using Fuzzy C-Means, data clusters are created.
- A *Ranking module*: Different types of ranking techniques are compared at the clustered user data. Gaussian ranking used by [19] is tested against a method described in [14].

This system operates nearly *on the fly*, in the sense that database read-write operations are used only for back-tracking reasons and result storage. Since the data size of specific topics is average and Twitter outputs its content in JSON form, an average computer system is able to execute hashmap counts and feature extraction in memory. There is an open window for parallelization at this point, discussed in Sect. 5. Direct access to the Twitter dataset queried by topic was used, through the requests documented in the Twitter API. Topic is user-defined at the beginning of the execution, but the Twitter API presents limitations on the maximum data transactions per hour.

3.2 Feature Extraction

This subsection describes the set of features we inherited from [19] (named "Basic Features") and our contribution to the feature set, which is named "Time-based Features".

3.2.1 Basic Features

User features are extracted by calculating and combining different measures, as proposed in [19]. Thus, we get measures of Original Tweets, meaning new content provided by the user, Conversational Tweets, meaning replies to user (signified by the "@username" string), Repeated Tweets, meaning content that the user provided and is then reproduced by other users (signified by the "RT" string), Mentions, meaning unique references to user's username by other users and Graph Characteristics, meaning measures of total and topic-active friends and followers of the specific user.

According to this method, for the given topic we calculate the following features:

- *Topical signal (TS)* indicates the percentage of participation in a given topic by a specific author, regardless of the type of tweets.
- *Signal strength (SS)* shows how strong an author's topical signal is based on how many tweets of this author have original content.
- *Non-Chat signal ($\sim CS$)* tries to capture how many of the author's tweets are not involved in a direct conversation with friends or followers. This is used to discard any conversations that the specific author participated in but were not initiated by them. This feature involves an λ parameter calculated approximately at 0.05 to satisfy the constraint mentioned above.
- *Retweet impact (RI)* demonstrates the impact of content generated by the author under measurement. The number of retweets is considered directly proportional to the impact this content has over the community around the specific topic. The calculations use multiplication by a logarithmic function to rule out the impact that may be generated by overly supportive followers of the specific author.
- *Mention impact (MI)* is counting how much an author is mentioned during the discussion of a certain topic, indicating that they are socially regarded as an authority in the topic. A log function is included here too, to ensure that the author is not mentioned due to their mentioning other authors (in a conversational manner).
- *Information Diffusion (ID)* is a social graph - based feature showing the ratio of number of users activated by the author on log-scale. We consider that an author is "activated" if they start tweeting on a topic after another user from the user's network that has tweeted on the topic before the author.
- *Network score (NS)* is a mere social graph - based feature which counts the number of users active on the topic that are in the social circle of the author.

For further details on the measurements and the calculations involved in the basic feature set, one should refer to [19].

3.2.2 Time-Based Features

A central point of motivation for this paper is that the dimension of time is absent from any measure extracted from Twitter topics. This type of topic analysis is based on a static idea about the topic data: it takes topic discussions as solid data, showing indifference for temporal distribution, namely the way that discussion data is spread through time. The reality of social media topic discussion is more dynamic than this. Sparks of "discussion traffic" can be recognized when the topic is "hot" meaning that at some time intervals, due to events of conjuncture, a lot of users get attracted by the specific topic. This can lead some users getting "authoritativeness" points for a short period of activity in the topic's lifecycle. Our claim is that a strongly authoritative user should provide content or be conversationally active throughout the total lifecycle of a topic. In addition, authoritative user tweets should be discoverable throughout the day, so that users active in different time zones could interact with the authoritative user content. This is true especially for topics with a lifecycle that lasts days or months and for topics that have global interest attracted to them, such as an economic or political crisis topic, sports organization topics, etc.

We consider zero time according to the timestamp of the first tweet containing the requested #hashtag and ending time according to the timestamp of the last such tweet by the time of query. We propose new features that put into consideration the above mentioned parameters:

– *Frequency* is a feature indicating the contribution of a specific author in a topic during the entire lifecycle of the topic. In our approach, high values of tweeting frequency increase the authority of the author. This may seem contrary to the burst of information in short time segments that usually emerge in social networks, but we claim that for a user to be more authoritative, their content generation must follow and span a large percentage of the topic lifecycle. In the example which motivates the research in [19], the *Gulf of Mexico Oil Spill*, Twitter accounts of environmental agencies considered authoritative for this topic should keep their followers informed as long as the topic is active. High frequency scores can rule out effects of posting burst. To calculate posting frequency, the ratio

$$freq = \frac{tweets_i}{endtime_{topic} - starttime_{topic}} \tag{1}$$

is used for every author active in the topic.

– *Part-of-day measure* captures the notion of users participating in a discussion from different time zones. This is especially interesting for topics with global effect and global audience. Due to the design of a platform such as Twitter, when a user logs in the platform, they see content in a newer-to-older fashion. To discover older content they have to scroll down, even if a search-by-topic approach is utilized. If time zones are taken into account, a user in East Asia should scroll down a lot to read original content from an author posting from the United States (taking into account that most users are not 24/7 online). For a global notion of authority, an author (such as an account registered by an institution or a news agency) should have a posting distribution that covers all day. This is an approximation feature; therefore dividing in four 6-h parts - of - day measures (morning, noon, evening, night) is enough to demonstrate such distribution. In each part - of - day, simple count of tweets is used and provided as a clustering dimension.

3.3   Clustering and Ranking

For the clustering and ranking process, used to derive possible authorative users, two methods were compared: *(i)* clustering and ranking with the use of Gaussian Mixture Models (GMM) and the Expectation - Maximization (EM) algorithm (the method used in [19], and *(ii)* our proposal, clustering and ranking with the use of cluster-based fusion of retrieved lists (as presented in [14]. Our proposal also contains the substitution of the simple K-means algorithm for primal clustering by the Fuzzy C-means (as found in [4,7]) algorithms because of the notion of similarity it points out which is well suited when one has to deal with user content on a specific topic.

3.3.1   Gaussian Mixture Model

A Gaussian Mixture Model (GMM) is a probability density function calculated as the weighted sum of Gaussian component densities. More specifically, a GMM is a weighted sum of M component Gaussian densities as given by the equation,

$$p(x|\lambda) = \sum_{i=1}^{M} w_i g(x|\mu_i, \sum i) \tag{2}$$

where x is a D-dimensional data vector of features, wi are the mixture weights and $g(x|\mu_i, \sum i)$ are the component Gaussian densities. Each is a D-variate Gaussian function with mean vector and covariance matrix.

GMMs are mostly used in continuous-value contexts, i.e. speaker recognition systems and biometric data. This raises a conceptual issue concerning the use of a GMM in the aspect of ranking authors in a microblogging environment. It is not proved that the set of features discussed in the previous section follows the normal (or Gaussian) distribution. Intuition and experiments show that a small cluster of authors around a specific topic achieves great scores, while a long tail of authors achieve low scores. Normal distribution implies that most of the authors should be at a $+ - s$ distance from the average score (where s is standard deviation), which is not the case especially for popular topics with thousands of followers. Most of the followers participate through a low activity of retweets or commentary tweets, while authorative users should have frequent multi-type contribution on the topic.

3.3.2   Using Cluster-Based Fusion of Retrieved Lists

The technique of cluster-based fusion is presented and evaluated in [14]. The key concept of this technique is that inter-similarity of documents presented in different query result lists should be rewarded. Given a query q, a document d and a corpus of documents C, one can get $L_1, \ldots, L_m$ result lists on m retrievals based on query q. In these lists, d may appear in a low position in a result list. Straightforward list fusion methods, such as the CombSum, CombMNZ and Borda methods use partial list rankings to build a final result list, which can lead to very low total ranking [14], of an important document d. Cluster-based fusion uses the *cluster hypothesis* to reward low-ranked documents with the condition that they belong in the same cluster with high ranked documents. Therefore, the cluster-based fusion method runs *some* clustering algorithm on the document set of documents appearing in the partial list and calculates the final ranking list based on partial list score plus cluster score.

In our proposal, we utilize this method using the fuzzy C-means algorithm for clustering documents. More specifically, the results are initially clustered into k lists using the fuzzy C-means algorithm, which permits an author to appear in more than one list. Each list is sorted with the Gaussian ranking method and then the cluster-based fusion method calculates the fusion score of the final ranking list. The cluster-based fusion method in our setting runs for the ClustFuseCombSUM, ClustFuseCombMNZ and ClustFuseBorda [14] best-performing versions of the algorithm.

4 Experimental Evaluation

In the next three subsections, the experimental setting for our approach is presented (Subsect. 4.1), followed by the results for the top-10 influential users of different versions of the algorithm (Subsect. 4.2) and results of anonymous user evaluation (Subsect. 4.3). The logic behind the experiments is to evaluate the quality of results between the GMM-based approach and the cluster-based fusion approach (with different versions of fusion strategies).

4.1 Dataset

For the construction of our test data set, we had to respect the current limitations of the Twitter API, together with the need to build a data set of topics that have differences in their temporal development. The Twitter database was queried for the hashtags: #blacklivesmatter, #bigdata and #germanwings.

The first hashtag, #blacklivesmatter, responds to a discussion topic about a social situation with duration in time and very different activity levels from time to time. The second hashtag, #bigdata, is reflecting a discussion topic with mostly scientific and business interest and quite sparse but also quite linear activity in time. The third hashtag, #germanwings had to do with an emerging tragic event and organized a discussion topic that demonstrated a burst of activity for the first few days but then faded to very low activity levels.

The construction of the data set was completed with a two-step repetitive process where firstly a tweet was returned as answer to the hashtag query and then a second query was performed to get the friends and followers list of the user that posted the tweet. That process resulted in 2.000 tweets and 49 user accounts (with a total of 50.622 followers) for the topic #blacklivesmatter, 2.000 tweets and 45 user accounts (with a total of 98349 followers) for the topic #bigdata and 1.860 tweets and 40 user accounts (with a total of 86.002 followers) for the topic #germanwings.

4.2   Top-K Users

For each topic and each tweet on the data set, two sets of experiments were conducted. The first set of experiments produced top-k ranked user lists by the execution of the GMM-based version of the algorithm as presented in [18] and three versions of cluster-based fusion algorithms using the ClustFuseCombMNZ, ClustFuseBorda and ClustFuseCombSUM strategies for list fusion, as presented in [14], without the addition of the proposed temporal features. In the four columns of Table 1, one can see the top-5 ranked user lists for the three different topics. The second set of experiments produced top-10 ranked user lists like the first set, but this time including the temporal features we proposed in Sect. 3.2.2. The four columns of Table 2 present the results of the four different algorithms for the top-5 ranked user accounts. It is important to note here that there are differences in the ranking produced by the algorithms after the addition of the temporal features, mostly affecting the methods based on the cluster hypothesis (e.g. ClustFuseCombSUM).

On the other hand, as previously mentioned, the average number of Followers per Community is slightly lower when the emotional methodology is followed. This is mainly a result of the way that Influential Metric is defined as it deals with an overall estimation of the impact of each user in the produced community.

4.3   User Evaluation

For the purposes of user evaluation of the different result sets, we organized an online survey and asked social media users to anonymously complete some web forms. A special occasion web application was developed linked to a database where answers where concentrated for later process. The evaluation scenario complied with the following assumptions: (1) evaluating users were anonymous (age and gender data where recorded for statistical reasons), (2) evaluating users were not presented with the results of the algorithms and are asked to rank usernames without guidance.

Users were presented with the whole data set and enabled to browse through the tweets, filter them by topic and query them by keyword or by username. After browsing through the data set, users were asked to choose the most influential username per topic, according to what they believe. That username was awarded by 10 extra points. After choosing the top username, users were presented with three forms, one for each topic, where they were asked to rank each of the

Table 1. Top-5 ranked users with temporal features

GMM	ClustFuseCombMNZ	ClustFuseBorda	ClustFuseCombSUM
#blacklivesmatter			
Shgamha	_PoeticRebel	Me_MrCool	Shelby_ville
newBREED_	pces	foodbruh_	chilllaxx_
ArtisMentis	I_Cant_Breathe	Shelby_ville	dmwwalker343
_PoeticRebel	Shgamha	chilllaxx_	AshhhG_
I_Cant_Breathe	newBREED_	dmwwalker343	newBREED_
#bigdata			
AnRcloudSoft	PyramidAnalytic	eberman007	revistadircom
revistadircom	bobehayes	GammaAnalytics	phatpenguin
danablouin	ThugMetricsNews	ThugMetricsNews	byod_news
METAMORF_US	aleson_es	KobbyDon1	BusinessNWSRM
phatpenguin	ymtreb	mallys_	BDUGUK
#germanwings			
GAABY	GAABY	DobleYouu	DobleYouu
WSJIndonesia	WSJIndonesia	FresaaChampagne	FresaaChampagne
KeystoneIDEAS	die_politik	EkoPardiyanto	EkoPardiyanto
mycomfor	mycomfor	adrianaeloca	adrianaeloca
EkoPardiyanto	lesatorr	nonotina	nonotina

usernames participating in the topics with a rank between 1 to 10 according to whether they are authoritative or not. The final rank for a username is the sum of ranks it has gained. A total number of 296 social media users from Facebook and Twitter took part in the evaluation survey with average age of 28.3 years and 37% of them were women. To understand the effectiveness of each method under evaluation, and also the effectiveness of the new time-based features we proposed, we used precision and Pearson - correlation metrics to measure the correctness of the algorithmic results and whether there is an agreement between method and user evaluation for the ranking order of users.

Precision and Pearson - correlation metrics are presented in Tables 3 and 4 for the two sets of experiments described in Subsect. 4.2. As we can see in both situations, the cluster-based methods score better than the GMM-based algorithm. The GMM-based algorithm seems to outrun the cluster-based fusion method only when ClustFuseCombMNZ strategy is used for fusion. Please notice that abbreviations have been used space wisely, i.e. #blac for #blacklivesmatter, #bigd for #bigdata and #germ for #germanwings.

Table 2. Top-5 ranked users without temporal features

GMM	ClustFuseCombMNZ	ClustFuseBorda	ClustFuseCombSUM
#blacklivesmatter			
Shgamha	pces	Me_MrCool	Shelby_ville
newBREED_	I_Cant_Breathe	foodbruh_	_PoeticRebel
ArtisMentis	_PoeticRebel	Shelby_ville	chilllaxx_
_PoeticRebel	Shgamha	_PoeticRebel	dmwwalker343
I_Cant_Breathe	newBREED_	chilllaxx_	AshhhG_
#bigdata			
AnRcloudSoft	NoSQLDigest	byod_news	NoSQLDigest
revistadircom	SocialNewsCorp	BusinessNWSRM	revistadircom
danablouin	KobbyDon1	BDUGUK	ThugMetricsNews
METAMORF_US	PyramidAnalytic	AnRcloudSoft	phatpenguin
phatpenguin	Paxata	eberman007	GammaAnalytics
#germanwings			
GAABY	flores_crespo	FresaaChampagne	FresaaChampagne
WSJIndonesia	tedmohs	lesatorr	lesatorr
KeystoneIDEAS	PhilDeCarolis	adrianaeloca	adrianaeloca
mycomfor	HInstMH	Peterotul97	Peterotul97
EkoPardiyanto	die_politik	HInstMH	HInstMH

Table 3. Precision and Pearson - correlation with temporal features

	GMM	ClustFuse CombMNZ	ClustFuse Borda	ClustFuse CombSUM
Precision				
#blac	0,7	0,6	0,85	0,8
#bigd	0,6	0,6	0,8	0,8
#germ	0,6	0,5	0,75	0,75
Pearson - correlation				
#blac	0,45	0,47	0,57	0,55
#bigd	0,49	0,47	0,62	0,64
#germ	0,51	0,48	0,55	0,59

In the case of adding temporal features, one can see a significant improvement in the precision of every method, and an average improvement in the Pearson - correlation. The algorithms based on the ClustFuseBorda and ClustFuseComb-SUM strategy seem to perform better in terms of recommendation quality.

Table 4. Precision and Pearson - correlation without temporal features

	GMM	ClustFuse CombMNZ	ClustFuse Borda	ClustFuse CombSUM
#blac	0,7	0,5	**0,8**	**0,8**
#bigd	0,6	0,6	0,8	**0,85**
#germ	**0,7**	0,5	**0,7**	**0,7**
Pearson - correlation				
#blac	0,43	0,44	**0,58**	0,52
#bigd	0,46	0,42	0,57	**0,66**
#germ	0,51	0,48	0,55	**0,59**

5   Conclusions and Future Work

In this paper, a novel approach to the problem of the discovery of topical influential users in a microblogging environment was presented and evaluated. The important advances of this research are the suggestion of fuzzy clustering and cluster-based fusion of user lists, together with the addition of time-based features that improve the overall precision and correlation scores. The list fusion approach circumvents possible drawbacks that the GMM-based methods have in cases that user features do not follow a normal distribution, a situation most common in social network environments. There is an open question of parallelization of the methods presented in this paper for the creation of a nearly real time authority discovery system.

The aspects of time in web and social network mining tasks are rather newly introduced but can gain potential due to the dynamic nature of these networks. Recent work on personalized user profile recommendation [1] and on event discovery in Twitter [20], expand the aspect of temporal dynamics in such environments.

For the discovery of influential users to be more accurate, one must comprehend the properties of the microblogging network and the behavior of the users, such as understanding collaborative behavior [9], analyzing why a tweet is likely to be retweeted [21] and decoding the social mechanism that explains why users with many followers are not necessarily the most influential [6].

References

1. Abel, F., Gao, Q., Houben, G.J., Tao, K.: Analyzing temporal dynamics in twitter profiles for personalized recommendations in the social web. In: Proceedings of the 3rd International Web Science Conference (WebSci), pp. 1–8 (2011)
2. Agichtein, E., Castillo, C., Donato, D., Gionis, A., Mishne, G.: Finding high-quality content in social media. In: Proceedings of the 2008 International Conference on Web Search and Data Mining (WSDM), pp. 183–194 (2008)
3. Anderson, A., Huttenlocher, D., Kleinberg, J., Leskovec, J.: Effects of user similarity in social media. In: Proceedings of the Fifth ACM International Conference on Web Search and Data Mining (WSDM), pp. 703–712 (2012)

4. Bezdek, J.C.: Pattern Recognition with Fuzzy Objective Function Algorithms. Kluwer Academic Publishers, New York (1981)
5. Bouguessa, M., Dumoulin, B., Wang, S.: Identifying authoritative actors in question-answering forums: the case of Yahoo! answers. In: Proceedings of the 14th ACM SIGKDD International Conference on Knowledge Discovery and Data Mining (KDD), pp. 866–874 (2008)
6. Cha, M., Haddadi, H., Benevenuto, F., Gummadi, P.K.: Measuring user influence in twitter: The million follower fallacy. In: Proceedings of the Fourth International Conference on Weblogs and Social Media (ICWSM) (2010)
7. Dunn, J.C.: A fuzzy relative of the isodata process and its use in detecting compact well-separated clusters. J. Cybern. **3**, 32–57 (1974)
8. Guo, J., Xu, S., Bao, S., Yu, Y.: Tapping on the potential of q&a community by recommending answer providers. In: Proceedings of the 17th ACM Conference on Information and Knowledge Management (CIKM), pp. 921–930 (2008)
9. Honeycutt, C., Herring, S.C.: Beyond microblogging: conversation and collaboration via Twitter. In: 2009 42nd Hawaii International Conference on System Sciences (HICSS), pp. 1–10 (2009)
10. Huberman, B.A., Romero, D.M., Wu, F.: Social networks that matter: Twitter under the microscope. First Monday **14**(1) (2008)
11. Kafeza, E., Kanavos, A., Makris, C., Chiu, D.: Identifying personality-based communities in social networks. In: Advances in Conceptual Modeling, pp. 7–13 (2014)
12. Kafeza, E., Kanavos, A., Makris, C., Vikatos, P.: T-PICE: Twitter personality based influential communities extraction system. In: IEEE International Congress on Big Data, pp. 212–219 (2014)
13. Kanavos, A., Perikos, I., Hatzilygeroudis, I., Tsakalidis, A.: Emotional community detection in social networks. Comput. Electr. Eng. **65**, 449–460 (2018)
14. Khudyak Kozorovitsky, A., Kurland, O.: Cluster-based fusion of retrieved lists. In: Proceedings of the 34th International ACM SIGIR Conference on Research and Development in Information Retrieval (SIGIR), pp. 893–902 (2011)
15. Kleinberg, J.M.: Authoritative sources in a hyperlinked environment. J. ACM **46**(5), 604–632 (1999)
16. Langville, A.N., Meyer, C.D.: Google's PageRank and Beyond: The Science of Search Engine Rankings. Princeton University Press, Princeton (2006)
17. Morris, M.R., Counts, S., Roseway, A., Hoff, A., Schwarz, J.: Tweeting is believing?: Understanding microblog credibility perceptions. In: Proceedings of the ACM 2012 Conference on Computer Supported Cooperative Work (CSCW), pp. 441–450 (2012)
18. Page, L., Brin, S., Motwani, R., Winograd, T.: The pagerank citation ranking: bringing order to the web. Technical report 1999–66 (1999)
19. Pal, A., Counts, S.: Identifying topical authorities in microblogs. In: Proceedings of the Fourth ACM International Conference on Web Search and Data Mining (WSDM), pp. 45–54 (2011)
20. Stilo, G., Velardi, P.: Time makes sense: event discovery in twitter using temporal similarity. In: 2014 IEEE/WIC/ACM International Joint Conferences on Web Intelligence (WI) and Intelligent Agent Technologies (IAT), vol. 2, pp. 186–193 (2014)
21. Suh, B., Hong, L., Pirolli, P., Chi, E.H.: Want to be retweeted? Large scale analytics on factors impacting retweet in Twitter network. In: Proceedings of the 2010 IEEE Second International Conference on Social Computing (SOCIALCOM), pp. 177–184 (2010)

22. Weng, J., Lim, E.P., Jiang, J., He, Q.: Twitterrank: finding topic-sensitive influ-
    ential Twitterers. In: Proceedings of the Third ACM International Conference on
    Web Search and Data Mining (WSDM), pp. 261–270 (2010)
23. Wu, S., Hofman, J.M., Mason, W.A., Watts, D.J.: Who says what to whom on
    Twitter. In: Proceedings of the 20th International Conference on World Wide Web
    (WWW), pp. 705–714 (2011)

Studying the Dissemination of the K-core Influence in Twitter Cascades

Sarah Elsharkawy[1]([⊠]), Ghada Hassan[2,3], Tarek Nabhan[1], and Mohamed Roushdy[3]

[1] Research and Development Department, ITWORX, Cairo, Egypt
{sarah.elsharkawy, tarek.nabhan}@itworx.com
[2] Faculty of Computer and Information Sciences,
The British University in Egypt, El Shorouk, Egypt
ghada.hassan@bue.edu.eg
[3] Faculty of Computer and Information Sciences,
Ain Shams University, Cairo, Egypt
mroushdy@cis.asu.edu.eg

Abstract. The k-core of an information graph is a common measure of a node connectedness in diverse applications. The k-core decomposition algorithm categorizes nodes into k-shells based on their connectivity. Previous research claimed that the super-spreaders are those located on the k-core of a social graph and the nodes become of less importance as they get assigned to a k-shell away from the k-core. We aim to evaluate the influence span of the social media super-spreaders, located at the k-core, in terms of the number of k-shells that their influence can reach. We base our methodology on the observation that the k-core size is directly correlated to the graph size under certain conditions. We explain these conditions and then investigate it further on real-life meme cascades extracted from Twitter. We utilize the correlation to assess the effectiveness of the k-core nodes for influence dissemination. The results of the carried-out experiments show that the correlation exists in our studied real-life datasets. A high correlation existed between the k-core size and the sizes of the inner k-shells in all the examined datasets. However, the correlation starts to decrease in the outer k-shells. Further investigations have shown that the k-shells that were less correlated exhibited a higher presence of spam accounts.

1 Introduction

The super-spreaders are the users capable of initiating a viral spread of a piece of information, a meme or an idea. Identifying a set of users as super-spreaders is an indication that they can influence a significantly large number of other users in the cascade. However, it does not indicate whether their influence spread is in the depth or breadth of the social network. For instance, a celebrity account or a news agency account that has thousands of followers could be a super-spreader because they influence many their direct followers, hence, the spread is in the cascade breadth. A depth effect, on the other hand, would signify their ability to influence the followers

L. Iliadis et al. (Eds.): AIAI 2018, IFIP AICT 519, pp. 28–37, 2018.
https://doi.org/10.1007/978-3-319-92007-8_3

of their followers. In this case, they can diffuse viral content to users outside the list of their direct followers.

Previous research [1, 15] has identified the users with largest spreading influence to be the users located in the k-core of the network. The k-core is a maximal subgraph, where all nodes are connected to some number (k) of other nodes in the same subgraph. The k-core decomposition analysis is used to find the k-core of a given graph by iteratively deleting nodes with degree less than k. The degree of a node is the number of edges connected to the node. A k-shell is the subgraph of nodes in the k-core but not in the (k + 1)-core. The work done in [9] proved that the most efficient spreaders are those located within the core of the network as identified by the k-shell decomposition analysis. The authors proved their observation by counting the total number of cascaded successors of each node and showing that the number of successors is correlated with the k-value of the k-shell where each user is located. However, their study did not differentiate between the users whose successors span a few k-shells from those whose successors span many k-shells.

In this paper, we propose a measure to estimate how far the influence of the super-spreaders located at the inner-most k-core of the cascade reaches other users located in further k-shells in the cascade. We differentiate between the datasets where the k-core users' influence is confined to the few neighboring k-shells, as opposed to where their influence is disseminating to the shallower k-shells of the cascade. In addition, we investigate whether the presence of spam accounts in the information cascade lessen the overall influence of the k-core users.

The paper is organized as follows: Sect. 2 gives an overview of research like this work. Section 3 studies the relationship between the k-core size and the graph size on synthetic graphs and discusses the meaning of such relationship in real-life datasets. Section 4 presents the conducted experiments and their results. Finally, Sect. 5 discusses and concludes this work.

2   Related Work

The virality of memes, as indicated by a large and/or quick growth in size, has been examined from various perspectives. A meme may become viral because it appeals to many [3], but virality of a meme also depends on other factors such as network structure, randomness, adoption patterns of influential users, timing, and many others [12]. Authors of [6] proposed an approach to judge the reliability of the cascade size in social networks by observing the k-core size. They argued that the size of the cascade, on its own, is a misleading indicator of the growth of popularity.

Other lines of research focused on identifying influential spreaders using different measures. Examples of such measures are the number of retweets, the number of followers, the number of mentions, betweenness centrality, and k-core [5, 9]. Authors in [11] found that the best spreaders are consistently located in the k-core across dissimilar social platforms such as Twitter and Facebook.

In [7], the authors evaluated communities based on the k-core concept, as means of evaluating their collaborative nature. In [8], the authors show that k-cores have an important role in counter-contagions in online social networks. They stated that to start a counter-contagion to an existing contagion, one needs to search for the most influential nodes to start with. k-cores was one of the methods they proposed to identify those influential nodes. Authors of [9] show that the most efficient spreaders are not necessarily the most connected people in the network, but rather are those located within the core of the network as identified by the k-core decomposition analysis.

3   Relationship Between K-core Size and Graph Size

In this section, we discuss the relationship between the inner k-core size and the graph size and its significance in meme cascades. Consider the following two scenarios for two different dynamic meme cascades: in the first cascade, as the k-core size increases, the graph size enlarges as well. And, as the k-core size gets smaller, the graph size decreases too. This synchronization between the k-core size and the graph size signifies that the core users are consistently spreading their influence to the whole community, and this relationship strengthens the criticality of the k-core users. In the second cascade, the k-core size increases and decreases regardless of the growth or shrinkage of the graph size. In this scenario, there is no noticeable relationship between the k-core size and the graph size, which indicates that the core users are not spreading their influence effectively. Therefore, we conclude that the correlation between the k-core size and the graph size is a projection for the real-life influence of the k-core on the rest of the cascade.

3.1   Conditions for the Presence of Correlation

Let G be a simple connected graph and k_d be the k value of the inner-most k-core of G; that is, no core exists at $k = k_d + 1$. Let S(G, k) be the k-core size measured as the number of nodes in the k-core of G. The size of the whole graph can be represented by S(G).

According to [14], the degrees of the nodes in the inner k-core represent an upper bound for the value k_d. Given the degree distribution (DD) of any simple connected graph, there is a percentage (P) of the graph nodes that have a degree larger than or equal to k_d, and a percentage $(100 - P)$ of nodes that have a degree less than k_d. Based on the k-core decomposition analysis, all the nodes in the k_d-core must have a degree larger than or equal to k_d, and hence they constitute a portion (P_{core}) of the (P) nodes. The k_d-core size is then calculated as:

$$S(G, k_d) = P_{core} \times P \times S(G) \tag{1}$$

Let the ratio of the k_d-core size to the graph size be denoted by r. Based on Eq. 1, a set of graphs $\{G_1, G_2, ..., Gn\}$ having equal percentages $\{P_1 = P_2 = ... = P_n\}$ and equal $\{P_{core_1} = P_{core_2} = ... = P_{core_n}\}$ would consequently have equal ratios $\{r_1 = r_2 = ... = r_n\}$. Hence, a direct correlation between the k_d-core size and the graph size exists within the given set of graphs.

3.2   Correlation on Synthetic Scale-Free Power-Law Degree Graphs

In this section, we focus on exploring the correlation on scale-free power-law synthetic graphs as it is the type of graphs found in social networks [2]. We generated thousands of scale-free synthetic graphs and used power-law curve fitting approaches to estimate the exponent of the power-law DD.

We used the Networkx Python package for graph generation and manipulation. Each synthetic graph is generated as follows:

1. A power-law sequence of degrees is generated (using the power law sequence method).
2. The graph is constructed based on the generated degrees (using the method configuration model).
3. Any self-loops and parallel-edges that may exist on the graph are removed and the largest connected component is extracted.
4. The DD of the graph is fitted to a power-law model, and the exponent of the fitted model is measured using the approach of [4].

Although we have created the graphs based on the power-law sequence of degrees (steps 1 and 2), there is a possibility that the DD of some graphs is not a power-law distribution due to applying step 3. A standard approach to check whether a given distribution follows a certain model is to use the goodness-of-fit test, such as the Kolmogorov-Smirnov (KS) [10], which generates a p-value that quantifies the plausibility of the hypothesis which, in our case, states that the observed data is drawn from a power-law distribution. The KS-test is applied to the graph relative to its fitted power-law model and the graph is disposed if its p-value is larger than 0.05. We ran the experiments using a variety of exponents and other parameters to ensure the variability of graph structures. We clustered the graphs into groups based on the power-law exponent of their fitted model.

We observed that the graphs having the same power-law exponent, also have the same P and P_{core} . For illustration, Fig. 1 plots two synthetic graphs that follow a power-law DD, where their k_d values lie on the 78th percentile of the degree range and

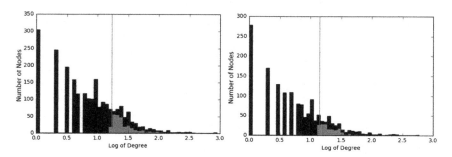

Fig. 1. Histograms representing the degree distributions of two synthetic graphs that follow a power-law DD. The vertical thin grey line is the k_d value. The black bars represent the number of graph nodes and the grey bars represent the number of k_d-core nodes.

the number of the k_d-core nodes is approximately 12% of the number of the total graph size.

Table 1 shows the exponents and the k_d-core size to graph size ratio of each group. We notice that, within each group, the k_d-core size to the graph size ratio varies minimally. This indicates a high positive correlation between the k_d-core size and the graph size when the graphs have similar power-law DD.

Table 1. Synthetic graphs grouped based on power-law exponent of node DD.

Exponent	k_d -core size to graph size percent
2.16 ± 0.023	(1.79 ± 0.66)%
2.35 ± 0.037	(1.45 ± 0.64)%
2.65 ± 0.073	(1.5 ± 1.12)%
2.82 ± 0.051	(2.37 ± 3.26)%
3.01 ± 0.051	(11.53 ± 13.58)%
3.2 ± 0.058	(20.88 ± 7.23)%
3.4 ± 0.058	(17.04 ± 3.95)%

3.3 DD Similarity in Real-Life Dynamic Cascades

In the previous section, we discussed the correlation on synthetic graphs. Synthetic graphs are constructed using specific rules and hence, they do not model the infinite patterns that occur in real-life datasets. In a real-life meme cascade, users are affected by one or more sources of influence that guide their adoption behavior towards a meme. To model a dynamic meme cascade, we take snap-shots of the cascade as it evolves over time. We found that the set of graphs representing the snapshots of a single meme cascade share similar structural properties, and their DD varies minimally. The mean and standard deviation of the power-law exponents of the snapshots in our datasets are shown in Table 2.

Table 2. Datasets description

Dataset Name		Tsunami	Royal Baby	P1	P2
Time span		10/3/2011 −10/4/2011	22/6/2013 −22/7/2013	1/6/2013 −1/7/2013	1/6/2013 −1/7/2013
Tweets Count		770,083	137,036	110,782	13,446
Users Count		415,642	130,788	42,760	7,821
Power-law exponent	Mean	3.06	4.63	3.03	3.69
	St. dev.	0.89	0.78	0.68	1.01
Spearman's rho for k_d - core to cascade size		0.767076	0.80355	0.54163	0.47127

To measure the K_d-core influence dissemination, in terms of k-shells, in a given meme cascade, we propose the following:

1. Taking consecutive snapshots of the meme cascade over periodic time steps.
2. Measuring the correlation between the inner k_d-core sizes and the graph sizes of the snapshots.
3. If the correlation is high: we conclude that the users located in the k_d-core of the given meme cascade are the most influential spreaders. They constitute the dominating source of influence that guides the propagation of the meme cascade.
4. If the correlation is low:
   (a) We propose to measure the correlation between the K_d-core size and each of the neighboring k-shells as an attempt to define the portion of the cascade that is being influenced by the K_d-core. The k-shells exhibiting a high correlation are the ones being influenced by the K_d-core.
   (b) One of the possible reasons behind the low correlation is the effect of other influential sources on the cascade propagation such as word-of-mouth, media channels, and/or spam. We recommend using a spam detection approach to detect the spam nodes, specifically within the nodes of the k-shells that are less correlated with the K_d-core due to the existence of a good indication that the nodes in these shells are not behaving like the rest of the graph nodes.

4 Experiments and Results

In this section, we present the conducted experiments and their results. In Sect. 4.1, we describe our datasets. Sections 4.2 and 4.3 present our findings.

4.1 Datasets Description

We collected four real-life Twitter datasets using the free Twitter API. The first is Tsunami dataset of tweets discussing the tsunami disaster of 2011 in Japan. The second is the Royal baby dataset which is the set of tweets discussing the birth of the son of Prince William of the UK. Two more datasets P1, P2 were collected that are tweets regarding two concurrent but competing political campaigns that ran during a constrained period. Table 2 shows the time span, the total number of tweets collected and the count of users in each dataset.

For each dataset, the set of information cascades representing the dynamics of the dataset were constructed. Each cascade represents a snapshot of the dataset information cascade with a 24-h time span between the cascades. For each cascade (snapshot in time), the node degree was fitted, the exponent determined, and the KS-test used to test the goodness-of-fit between the node degree curve and the power-law curve following the procedure described earlier in Sect. 3.2. Table 2 shows the mean and the standard deviation of the values of the fitted power-law curve exponents for each dataset.

4.2 Correlation on Twitter Datasets

In the first experiment, we measured the correlation between the k_d-core size and graph size of each dataset of snapshots. Table 2 shows the Spearman's correlation coefficients (ρ) between k_d-core size and graph size of each dataset. All the reported coefficients are statistically significant with a P-value < 0.05. We notice that the correlation is high in Tsunami (0.76) and Royal Baby (0.8) datasets, and it drops in the two political datasets, P1 (0.54) and P2 (0.47).

We conducted another experiment in which we correlate the k_d-core size with the size of each k-shell at $k < k_d$, to monitor at which k value the correlation would break. Table 3 shows how the correlation coefficient is high at inner shells and gradually

Table 3. Spearman's correlation coefficients between k_d -core size and each outer k-shell size measured on all snapshots of each dataset.

(k) of shell	Tsunami Shell to 13-core	Royal baby Shell to 29-core	P1 Shell to 29-core	P2 Shell to 28-core
1-shell	0.654	0.783	0.538	0.550
2-shell	0.750	0.789	0.545	0.532
3-shell	0.751	0.702	0.555	0.537
4-shell	0.721	0.782	0.571	0.656
5-shell	0.762	0.784	0.592	0.701
6-shell	0.815	0.784	0.655	0.849
7-shell	0.822	0.785	0.671	0.859
8-shell	0.819	0.821	0.728	–
9-shell	0.823	0.829	0.732	–
10-shell	0.877	0.831	0.739	–
11-shell	0.886	0.836	0.745	–
12-shell	0.890	0.835	0.752	–
13-shell	–	0.839	0.755	–
14-shell	–	0.842	0.757	–
15-shell	–	0.845	0.761	–
16-shell	–	0.845	0.767	–
17-shell	–	0.845	0.812	–
18-shell	–	0.851	0.861	–
19-shell	–	0.854	0.888	–
20-shell	–	0.855	0.895	–
21-shell	–	0.854	–	–
22-shell	–	0.855	–	–
23-shell	–	0.857	–	–
24-shell	–	0.860	–	–
25-shell	–	0.861	–	–
26-shell	–	0.866	–	–
27-shell	–	0.866	–	–
28-shell	–	0.872	–	–

decreases as we move to the outer shells. In Tsunami and Royal Baby datasets the correlation remains relatively high at all shells. However, in P1 and P2 political datasets, the correlation breaks at outermost shells.

4.3   The Spam Effect on the Correlation

The decrease of correlation is a direct indication of the disengagement of the growth or shrink of the k_d-core size and the graph size. One of the possible reasons of this disengagement is the effect of other influencing sources acting on the cascade. Due to the lack of ground-truth information about the other sources that affected our datasets, we are only able to use heuristic approaches that are found in literature to get an estimation of such an external effect on our cascades. After we have constructed all the cascades of our four datasets, we used Truthy's BotOrNot API [13] to check all user accounts in our graphs to determine how likely they are to be spam. We then spotted the location of each of them on the graph and measured the k-shell value at which each of them is located. Results are shown in Fig. 2.

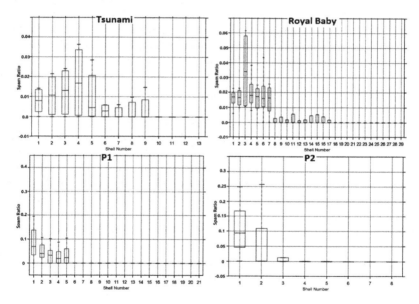

Fig. 2. Box plot representing the probability distribution of the percentage ratio be- tween the spam count in each k-shell to the shell size. The x-axis represents the (k) value of the k-shell, and the y-axis represents the percentage ratio of the number of spam accounts in a given k-shell to the number of nodes in the same k-shell.

The percentage of spam accounts relative to the cascade size is 0.02% in Tsunami, 0.05% in Royal Baby, 0.11% in P1 and 0.1% in P2. Figure 2 shows the amount of spam detected at each k-shell of the four datasets. We observe that no spam is found at inner k-shells while it increases at outer shells. The results match the values found in Table 3 which show how the correlation is significantly high at inner k-shells and decreases at outer shells.

From this experiment, we uncovered three main findings: first, the number of spam accounts found in each dataset is inversely proportional to the correlation between the K_d-core and the graph sizes of the snapshots of a given dataset. Where Tsunami has $\rho = 0.76$ and spam ratio of 0.02%, Royal baby has $\rho = 0.8$ and spam ratio of 0.05%, P1's $\rho = 0.54$ and spam ratio of 0.11 and finally P2 has $\rho = 0.47$ and spam ratio of 0.1. Second, the number of spam accounts in each k-shell is inversely proportional to the correlation between the k_d-core and k-shell sizes of the dataset as seen in Table 3 and Fig. 2. The third is that the number of spam accounts increases at outer k-shells and almost vanishes at the inner K_d-core.

5   Discussion and Conclusion

In this paper, we studied the relationship between the inner k-core size and the graph size and we tackled the question of how far the influence of the most influential spreaders located at the inner k-core reach users located in the outer k-shells.

We presented a novel approach to estimate the influence reach of the users located at the k-core inferred from the observed correlation between the k-core size and the graph size. We demonstrated that a correlation between the inner k-core size and the cascade size exist in sets of synthetic graphs under some constraints, and we identify such constraints.

We presented results of a case study on four real-life Twitter datasets. The datasets represented snapshots of the meme propagation graph every 24 h. We found that the correlation between the k-core and the neighboring k-shells decreases gradually towards the outer shells. We also found that in political datasets the correlation drops significantly at outer shells due to external influencing factors such as spam, while in the other two datasets the correlation remained consistent. Using Truthy BotOrNot API, we identified the spam ac-counts in our datasets. We found that the number of spam increases at outer shells and that the number of spam accounts in a shell is inversely proportional to the correlation of the size of that shell to the k-core size.

We conclude that the influence propagation of the super-spreaders located at the k-core of a meme cascade varies significantly from one dataset to another. In the datasets which exhibit other sources of influence such as spam accounts, the super-spreaders are notably unable to disseminate their influence to the shallower k-shells of the cascade. These datasets are signified by the low correlation between the inner k-core size and the graph size of snapshots captured over periodic time steps of the lifetime of the cascade. For those datasets, having low correlation, marketers need to pay more attention to other types of super-spreaders such as those having high betweenness centrality. Identifying the ideal super-spreaders that should be targeted in this case is still an area of investigation.

Another important conclusion is that the datasets that have a low correlation between its inner k-core size and graph size usually unveil a large number of spam accounts. Hence, the proposed correlation measure could be used for an early warning for spam. Moreover, we observed that the outer k-shells have a higher tendency for the presence of spam. This phenomenon could be used to speed up the spam detection algorithms by searching in the outer k-shells first.

References

1. Al-garadi, M.A., Varathan, K.D., Ravana, S.D.: Identification of influential spreaders in online social networks using interaction weighted k-core decomposition method. Phys.: Stat. Mech. Appl. **468**, 278–288 (2017)
2. Barabasi, A.-L., Albert, R.: Emergence of scaling in random networks. Science **286**(5439), 509–512 (1999)
3. Berger, J., Milkman, K.L.: What makes online content viral? J. Mark. Res. **49**(2), 192–205 (2012)
4. Clauset, A., Shalizi, C.R., Newman, M.E.: Power-law distributions in empirical data. SIAM Rev. **51**(4), 661–703 (2009)
5. Dorogovtsev, S., Goltsev, A., Mendes, J.: k-core organization of complex networks. Phys. Rev. Lett. **96**, 4 (2006)
6. Elsharkawy, S., Hassan, G., Nabhan, T., Roushdy. M.: On the reliability of cascade size as a virality measure. In: Proceedings of the European Conference on Electrical Engineering and Computer Science (EECS) (2017)
7. Giatsidis, C., Thilikos, D.M., Vazirgiannis, M.: Evaluating cooperation in communities with the k-core structure. In: Proceedings of the 2011 International Conference on Advances in Social Networks Analysis and Mining, pp. 87–93 (2011)
8. Guille, A., Hacid, H., Favre, C., Zighed, D.A.: Information diffusion in online social networks: a survey. ACM SIGMOD Rec. **42**(2), 17–28 (2013)
9. Kitsak, M., Gallos, L.K., Havlin, S., Liljeros, F., Muchnik, L., Stanley, H.E., Makse, H.A.: Identification of influential spreaders in complex networks. Nat. Phys. **6**, 888–893 (2010)
10. Massey, F.J.: The Kolmogorov-Smirnov test for goodness of fit. J. Am. Stat. Assoc. **46**(253), 68–78 (1951)
11. Pei, S., Muchnik, L., Andrade Jr., J.S., Zheng, Z., Makse, H.A.: Searching for superspreaders of information in real-world social media. Sci. Rep. **4**, 5547 (2014)
12. Pinto, H., Almeida, J.M., Goncalves, M.A.: Using early view patterns to predict the popularity of youtube videos. In: Proceedings of the Sixth ACM International Conference on Web Search and Data Mining, WSDM 2013, pp. 365–374. ACM, New York (2013)
13. Ratkiewicz, J., Conover, M., Meiss, M., Goncalves, B., Patil, S., Flammini, A., Menczer, F.: Truthy: mapping the spread of astroturf in microblog streams. In: Proceedings of the 19th ACM International Conference on Information and Knowledge Management, pp. 249–252. ACM (2011)
14. Shin, K., Eliassi-Rad, T., Faloutsos, C.: Corescope: graph mining using k-core analysis - patterns, anomalies and algorithms. In: Proceedings of the ICDM, pp. 469–478 (2016)
15. Zhang, F., Zhang, Y., Qin, L., Zhang, W., Lin, X.: Finding critical users for social network engagement: the collapsed k-core problem, pp. 245–251 (2017)

Spam Filtering in Social Networks Using Regularized Deep Neural Networks with Ensemble Learning

Aliaksandr Barushka and Petr Hajek[✉]

Institute of System Engineering and Informatics,
Faculty of Economics and Administration, University of Pardubice,
Studentska 84, 532 10 Pardubice, Czech Republic
aliaksandr.barushka@student.upce.cz,
petr.hajek@upce.cz

Abstract. Spam filtering in social networks is increasingly important owing to the rapid growth of social network user base. Sophisticated spam filters must be developed to deal with this complex problem. Traditional machine learning approaches such as neural networks, support vector machine and Naïve Bayes classifiers are not effective enough to process and utilize complex features present in high-dimensional data on social network spam. To overcome this problem, here we propose a novel approach to social network spam filtering. The approach uses ensemble learning techniques with regularized deep neural networks as base learners. We demonstrate that this approach is effective for social network spam filtering on a benchmark dataset in terms of accuracy and area under ROC. In addition, solid performance is achieved in terms of false negative and false positive rates. We also show that the proposed approach outperforms other popular algorithms used in spam filtering, such as decision trees, Naïve Bayes, artificial immune systems, support vector machines, etc.

Keywords: Neural network · Social networks · Regularization
Meta-learning

1 Introduction

Generally, spam can be defined as unwanted and unsolicited messages sent to usually a large number of recipients [1]. Spam message can be sent over multiple communication channels, such as e-mail, SMS, social networks, etc. Statistics show that a large proportion of all messages in social networks are spam messages. For instance, the study by Proofpoint, a major company specialized in cyber security, reported that during the first half of 2013 there has been a 355% growth of social spam. For every seven new social media accounts, five new spammers are detected [2].

The growing opportunities of social networks and their popularity have attracted many users. These days the base of social network users is steadily growing and considerable amount of communication is done through social networks. However, along with legitimate and useful information, inappropriate and unwanted content is also released on these networks. Indeed, spam senders target social network users as

L. Iliadis et al. (Eds.): AIAI 2018, IFIP AICT 519, pp. 38–49, 2018.
https://doi.org/10.1007/978-3-319-92007-8_4

well. Moreover, business social networks like Linkedin are also affected [3]. This has serious economic and social consequences. Spam messages decrease work productivity, increase IT support related resources (help desk) and may even result in security incidents. This is why a considerable attention is given to spam filtering.

Spam messages can be filtered either manually or automatically. Obviously, manual spam filtering by identifying spam message and removing it is a time consuming task. Moreover, spam messages may contain a security threat, such as links to phishing web sites or servers hosting malware. Therefore, over a number of decades researches and practitioners have worked on improving automatic spam filtering algorithms. Machine learning techniques are particularly known to be highly accurate in detecting spam messages. There is a number of existing machine learning algorithms applied to spam filtering, including neural networks [4], support vector machines (SVMs) [5], Naïve Bayes [6], random forest [7], etc.

Spam filtering task belongs to binary classification problem, each message should be identified either as spam or ham. Besides high accuracy algorithm should also perform well when it comes to false positive ratio (legitimate message is classified as spam) to avoid situations where legitimate message is not delivered to the intended receiver. The main concept of the machine learning algorithms is to build a word list and assign a weight to each word accordingly. However, spammers tend to include common legitimate messages into the spam message in order to decrease the probability of being detected. In social network spam filtering, additional attributes are therefore used, such as those related to sender's profile and behavior in the social network.

The state-of-the-art methods in social network spam filtering has recently been surveyed by [8]. According to the survey, ensemble learning methods, such as bagging and random forest, outperform traditional single classifiers. The ensemble methods combine the predictions of several base machine learning algorithms in order to improve accuracy and robustness over single algorithms. In previous studies, ensemble methods employed traditional classifiers like decision trees to effectively filter spam messages. However, surprisingly little attention has been paid to neural networks with ensemble learning. Recent evidence showed that neural networks equipped with regularization techniques may be highly accurate in detecting e-mail and SMS spam [4]. This can be attributed to better optimization convergence and resistance to overfitting. To take advantage of these qualities, here we integrate regularized neural networks with ensemble learning methods for social network spam filtering. Using the benchmark data from the Dutch social networking site Hyves, here we show that this approach can be more effective than state-of-the-art spam filtering methods in terms of accuracy.

The rest of this paper is organized in the following way. Section 2 briefly reviews recent development in social network spam filtering. Section 3 presents the benchmark dataset. In Sect. 4, we introduce the proposed spam filter. Section 5 shows the results of the experiments and a comparative analysis with several state-of-the-art methods used for social network spam filtering. In Sect. 6, we conclude this paper and discuss possible future research directions.

2 Social Network Spam Filtering – A Literature Review

User base of social networks is growing over the number of years. For instance, Facebook, one of the biggest social networks in the world, grew from one billion to two billion users just in 5 years [9]. Social network spam has become a major concern of industry and academia because it may include unwanted content, such as insults, hate speech, malicious links, etc. Such messages can be seen by the recipient's followers. Moreover, they may lead to confusions and misdirection in public discussions [10]. Fighting social network spam with traditional legal methods has serious limitation, since spam messages in social networks can be sent from different countries. It is important to note that spammers may use anonymisers, making it difficult to trace them. In order to overcome this problem, several social network spam filters have recently been developed [10–22].

A Naïve Bayes classifier was proposed by [11] to detect spam in Twitter. Features related to tweet content and user behaviour were identified and used in machine learning by [12]. A hybrid approach for identifying spam profiles was proposed by [13], combining social media analytics and firefly algorithm with chaotic maps for spam detection in Twitter marketing. In addition to spam messages detection, recent studies have also considered an alternative task of social spammer detection. A large Twitter dataset was used in [14] to demonstrate that feature distributions between spammers and legitimate users are different. These feature distributions were used in a social spammer detection framework that integrated this information with a social regularization term incorporate into a classification model. In [15], the so-called "social bridges" were identified to detect spammers in Twitter. These are reported as the major supporters of malicious users and a graph-topology based classifier was used to detect such bridge linkages. Another way to tackle the issue of detecting spammers in Twitter was described in [16]. A multilayer social network was defined and the identification of spammers was based on the existence of overlapping community-based features of users represented in the form of Hypergraphs, such as structural behaviour and URL characteristics. A unified approach was proposed in [17], utilizing the fact that social spammers tend to post more spam messages. Indeed, it was shown that combining social spammer filtering with spam message filtering improves the performance of both tasks.

Although Twitter represents the most frequently used source of data, alternative social networks have also been examined. For example, data from Sina Weibo were used to study features related to message content and user behaviour in [10]. The most important features were then used in the SVM classifier for spam detection. Extreme learning machines were used by [18] on a similar dataset. A semi-supervised social media spammer filtering approach was developed in [19]. This approach outperformed traditional supervised classifiers for the spammer detection task. Similar results were obtained by for spam message detection in Hyves social network [20]. Using the same dataset, significant improvements were achieved by combining data oversampling with regularized deep multi-layer perceptron neural networks [21].

Several researchers employed feature selection and extraction methodologies to identify the most important features for social network spam filtering. The concept of rough set theory was applied by [22], concluding that the used methodology selected a smaller subset of features than those of the baseline methodologies. By considering important features of the posts and their corresponding comments, and finally applying the feature selection techniques, the method proposed in [23] selected the most effective features to detect spam using machine learning techniques. A probabilistic generative model (latent Dirichlet allocation) was proposed by [24] to detect the latent semantics from user-generated comments. Incremental learning was then used to address the issue of the changing feature space.

In summary, previous related literature attempted to overcome the problem of high-dimensional data (the curse of dimensionality) by selecting the most important features, regardless of whether content-based features or user behaviour features. This was mainly due to the risk of overfitting or poor convergence of the used classification methods. However, useful information may be hidden in higher-order features that can be extracted by using deep neural networks [21]. In fact, additional hidden layers enable the recombination of features and thus to capture higher complexity and abstraction in high-dimensional datasets [25]. Moreover, ensemble methods have become popular in social network spam detection tasks due to their capacity to reduce the risk of overfitting and variance [8].

3   Dataset

In this study, we used the dataset from Hyves, the Dutch social networking site[1]. The original dataset contained both labelled and unlabelled messages. As we use a supervised learning approach here, we excluded the unlabelled (unannotated) messages from the dataset. Since the details on this dataset can be found in [20], we provide only a brief description in this study.

The dataset includes the following types of information: message content, spam report and user information. The messages were collected from publicly accessible profile or group pages. At least two spam reports were created for each message to obtain reliable categorization of messages into "spam" or "not spam". The user policy of Hyves was used to define spam messages. Specifically, unsolicited and promotional messages were labelled as spam.

The social network spam dataset contained 466 spam messages and 355 legitimate messages. The messages were represented as the arrays of json objects with the following fields: the annotation of the object (either spam or legitimate), anonymized IDs of the reporters of the message, anonymized ID of the author of the message, and bag of words representation of the message (an anonymized ID was assigned to each word). To represent the bag of words, we used $tf.idf$ weighting scheme. The weight v_{ij} for the i-the word in the j-th message can be calculated as follows:

$$v_{ij} = \left(1 + \log\left(tf_{ij}\right)\right) \times \log(N \, / \, df_i), \tag{1}$$

---

[1] http://ilps.science.uva.nl/framework-unsupervised-spam-detection-social-networking-sites/.

where tf_{ij} represents term frequency, df_i is document frequency, and N is the number of messages. We used top 2000 words according to their weights. This number was reported to be sufficient to perform document classification in previous studies [26].

4 Methods

Since the main interest of the paper is the proposal of a social network spam filter based on deep neural network with ensemble learning, we provide a brief description of these methods in this section.

The model of the deep neural network (DNN) used in this study is the multilayer perceptron neural network with multiple hidden layers that process complex relations between the input features and output categories. However, such a structure results in the large number of connections, leading to sampling noise. Therefore, intensive adaptation of training data may result in overfitting. To address this issue, we used dropout regularization. Indeed, increased accuracy may be achieved by dropping units from the neural network, including all their incoming and outgoing connections. The dropout regularization randomly changes the given ratio of the activations' values to zero while training is performed and therefore hidden units that produce the same result are ignored. In addition, we employed rectified linear units instead of traditional sigmoidal units in order to avoid poor local minima of training error and slow optimization convergence [27]. This is done by producing partial derivative equal to one, in case the rectified linear unit is activated. It is also worth to add that these units saturate when reaching one. This might be useful when hidden activations are selected as input features for the classifier. The mini-batch gradient descent was used as a training algorithm for the DNN. Connection weights are updated for every mini-batch of training data in the following way:

$$w_{t+1} = w_t - \eta \nabla_\theta J\left(w_t; x^{(i:i+n)}; y^{(i:i+n)}\right), \tag{2}$$

where w is connection weight, t denotes time, η is learning rate, J is an objective function, x^i and y^i are the inputs and output of the i-the data sample within every mini-batch, and n is the number of data samples in the mini-batch. By using the mini-batches a stable convergence can be achieved during the DNN learning.

The goal of ensemble learning algorithms is to combine the predictions of multiple base estimators constructed with the defined learning algorithm. This approach leads to better generalizability and robustness over single estimators. There are two main classes of ensemble learning algorithms, averaging and boosting. The fundamental concept of averaging is to construct several estimators independently from each other and calculate the average of their predictions. By reducing variance, the combined estimator is more accurate than single base estimator. By contrast, boosting builds the base estimators sequentially. Thus, several sequential weak models are combined to achieve a good ensemble. Here we used three conventional ensemble learning algorithms, namely Adaboost M1 [28], bagging [29] and random subspace [30].

The Adaboost M1 algorithm was developed to produce predictions with high accuracy utilizing a number of weak base learners. The algorithm keeps building the learners until there are no errors in training data predictions or the limit numbers of models is exceeded. This is done by increasing the weights of incorrectly predicted data. Finally, the predictions from all the models are combined by using a weighted majority vote to obtain the final predictions. The algorithm is defined as follows:

Algorithm 1: Adaboost M1

Input: The set T of training data $(x^i; y^i)$, i=1,2, ... ,n; the number B of base DNNs
Output: Ensemble of base DNNs $\{C_b\}$
For b=1 to B {
    Construct a base DNN C_b on weighted training data $T^* = (w_1 T^1{}_b, w_2 T^2{}_b, \ldots, w_n T^n{}_b)$;
    Calculate the probability estimates of the error $err_b = 1/n \; \Sigma \; w_{ib} \times \xi^i{}_b$ ($\xi^i{}_b$=0 if T^i classified correctly, $\xi^i{}_b$=1 otherwise);
    Set weight $c_b = 0.5 \times \log((1 - err_b)/err_b)$;
    If $err_b < 0.5$, set $w_{ib+1} = w_{ib} \times \exp(c_b \xi^i{}_b)$;
    Otherwise, set all weights w_{ib}=1 and restart the algorithm;
}
Combine base DNNs C_b, b=1,2,...,B into an ensemble $\{C_b\}$ by weighted majority voting;

The main idea behind bagging is to construct multiple instances of black-box estimator on the random subsets of the original training data. To produce an aggregated prediction, separate predictions are then combined by using the voting procedure. Thus, the variance of base estimator is reduced by applying randomization during the process of building ensembles. The bagging algorithm employed here can be defined as follows:

Algorithm 2: Bagging

Input: The set T of training data $(x^i; y^i)$, i=1,2, ... ,n; the number B of base DNNs
Output: Ensemble of base DNNs $\{C_b\}$
For b=1 to B {
    Create a bootstrapped replicate T_b of the training data set T;
    Construct a base DNN C_b on T_b;
}
Combine base DNNs C_b, b=1,2,...,B into an ensemble $\{C_b\}$ by simple majority voting;

Random subspace algorithm was proposed to handle the problem of trade-off between overfitting and achieving the highest accuracy. In fact, the random subspace algorithm is similar to bagging. The main difference is in the way they draw the random subsets of training data. In random subspace, these subsets are produced as the random subsets of the features. The random subspace algorithm applied here for social network spam filtering can be defined as follows:

Algorithm 3: Random subspace
Input: The set T of training data $(x^i; y^i)$, $i=1,2, \ldots ,n$; the number B of base DNNs
Output: Ensemble of base DNNs $\{C_b\}$
For $b=1$ to B {
$\quad$ Select an r-dimensional random subspace T_b from the original training data set T;
$\quad$ Construct a base DNN C_b in T_b;
}
Combine base DNNs C_b, $b=1,2,\ldots,B$ into an ensemble $\{C_b\}$ by simple majority voting;

5   Experimental Results

In this section, we first describe the setting of all experiments and then we present the results in terms of four prediction measures: accuracy, area under ROC (receiver operating characteristic) curve, FN (false negative) rate and FP (false positive) rate, and F1-score. FN rate represents the percentage of spam messages incorrectly predicted as legitimate, while FP rate is the percentage of legitimate messages incorrectly predicted as spam. F1-score combines precision and recall, where precision is a fraction of messages correctly classified as spam out of all the messages the algorithm classifies as spam, whereas recall is the fraction of messages correctly classified as spam out of all the spam messages. 10-fold cross-validation was used to avoid overfitting and evaluate the prediction performance.

The DNN with ensemble learning was trained with the following setting: number of hidden layers = $\{1, 2, 3\}$, number of units in hidden layers = $\{10, 20, 50\}$, and learning rate was set to $\eta = 0.1$, size of mini-batches = 100, dropout rate for input layer = 0.2; dropout rate for hidden layers = 0.5, and number of iterations = 1000. The best setting of the DNN structure (2 hidden layers with 50 and 20 units, respectively) was obtained by using grid search. Furthermore, 10 iterations were used in the learning of Adaboost M1 ensemble, the size of each bag in bagging was 100, and the size of each subspace was 50% of all attributes in the random subspace algorithm. The learning of bagging and random subspace was also performed in 10 iterations.

To demonstrate the effectiveness of the proposed social network spam filter, we compared its performance with several methods used in previous studies for spam filtering [4–8], namely the single DNN, CNN (convolutional neural network), Naïve Bayes, k-NN (k nearest neighbour), C4.5 decision tree, MLP (multilayer perceptron), SVM (support vector machine), AIRS (artificial immune recognition system), Adaboost M1 with decision stump as base learner, and random forest. The settings of these algorithms were as follows: single DNN (the same setting as for the DNN with ensemble learning); CNN (mini-batch gradient descent algorithm with patch size 5 × 5 and max pool size 2 × 2, the remaining parameters were the same as for the DNN); k-NN ($k = 3$); C4.5 (J48 implementation with the confidence factor of 0.25 and minimum instances per leaf = 2); MLP (backpropagation with {10, 20, 50, 100} units in the hidden layer (50 units worked best), learning rate = 0.1, momentum = 0.2, and iterations = 1000); SVM (sequential minimal optimization algorithm with $C = \{2^0, 2^1, ..., 2^6\}$ ($C = 2^2$ worked best) and polynomial kernel function); AIRS (AIRS2 parallel algorithm with affinity threshold = 0.2, clonal rate = 10, hyper-mutation rate = 2, $k = 3$ and stimulation threshold = 0.9); Adaboost M1 with 10 iterations and decision stump as base learner; and 100 random trees were used in random forest. All the experiments were performed in Weka 3.7.13 environment.

A brief description of the comparative methods is given as follows:

CNN uses layers together with convolving filters and filters are applied to the local features of adjacent layers. Each hidden layer consists of several feature maps (filters in a layer build a feature map sharing the same parametrization). Max-pooling is used to capture the most important features for each feature map. NB classifier utilizes information learnt from training data in order to calculate the probability of spam or legitimate class taking into consideration words found in the message. In k-NN, the message is classified based on the most common class in k neighbours. J48 algorithm generates a decision tree model, including variable classification rates built on cross-validation. MLP is a feed-forward neural network that consists of several layers of units, namely input, hidden and output layer. Each layer is directly connected to the next layer in the MLP. Backpropagation algorithm is commonly used to train this neural network. In contrast to empirical risk considered in the training of the MLP, SVM learning is based on structural risk minimization. Specifically, SVM finds the optimal separating hyperplane that represents the maximum margin between two classes and the corresponding decision boundaries are defined by the so-called support vectors. As a result, this algorithm can effectively handle high-dimensional data. AIRS is another artificial intelligence approach. This algorithm includes models resembling particular immunological processes. Finally, random forest consists of multiple tree predictors. Each of them is influenced by the values of an independently sampled random vector. Therefore, all the trees in the forest share the same distribution.

The results of the experiments are summarized in Tables 1 and 2. The results show that the DNN with bagging performed best in terms of accuracy and area under ROC curve. Besides the DNN with ensemble learning, the single DNN, CNN and random forest also performed well. Student's paired t-tests were performed to compare the results statistically. The results that are statistically similar to the best performer at $p = 0.05$ are in bold in Tables 1 and 2.

The results in Table 2 show that the DNN with ensemble learning performed well in terms of FN rate, while relatively poorly in terms of FP rate. Overall, however, the performance was well balanced for both spam and legitimate classes. This was also confirmed with the high values of the area under ROC curve. Moreover, the DNN with bagging and DNN with random subspace performed best in terms of F1-score, indicating a balanced performance in both the precision and the recall. Notably, we obtained better results than those reported in the original study using this dataset (ROC = 0.801) [20]. However, this original study was based on a simple spam score combining messages' own and neighbour characteristics. More precisely, the best performance in terms of accuracy was achieved by using the DNN with bagging. As presented in Table 2, this can be mainly attributed to the low value of FN rate. In other

Table 1. Results of the experiments – accuracy and area under ROC curve.

Method	Accuracy [%]	Area under ROC curve
Naïve Bayes	82.98 ± 7.08	**0.943 ± 0.026**
k-NN	88.37 ± 3.71	**0.946 ± 0.026**
C4.5	88.65 ± 3.84	0.912 ± 0.037
MLP	88.97 ± 3.86	**0.942 ± 0.027**
SVM	90.45 ± 3.25	0.907 ± 0.032
AIRS	80.42 ± 7.78	0.914 ± 0.033
Adaboost M1	89.10 ± 3.73	0.907 ± 0.034
Random forest	**91.94 ± 3.09**	**0.960 ± 0.023**
CNN	**91.11 ± 4.52**	**0.950 ± 0.051**
DNN	**92.27 ± 3.04**	**0.961 ± 0.021**
DNN with adaboost	**90.87 ± 2.87**	**0.940 ± 0.027**
DNN with bagging	**92.69 ± 2.82**	**0.962 ± 0.022**
DNN with random subspace	**92.45 ± 3.08**	**0.961 ± 0.023**

Table 2. Results of the experiments – FN and FP rates.

Method	FN rate [%]	FP rate [%]	F1-score
Naïve Bayes	**6.1 ± 3.8**	30.2 ± 19.5	0.8641 ± 0.0461
k-NN	16.1 ± 6.0	34.0 ± 3.0	0.8903 ± 0.0375
C4.5	14.0 ± 5.5	5.7 ± 4.3	0.8953 ± 0.0369
MLP	11.6 ± 17.0	6.8 ± 6.1	0.8978 ± 0.0364
SVM	10.8 ± 4.9	5.1 ± 3.8	0.9131 ± 0.0306
AIRS	25.4 ± 14.5	11.9 ± 18.5	0.8415 ± 0.0460
Adaboost M1	17.1 ± 6.0	**2.8 ± 2.5**	0.8952 ± 0.0388
Random forest	10.0 ± 4.7	5.1 ± 3.6	**0.9264 ± 0.0292**
CNN	**9.2 ± 4.6**	5.2 ± 4.2	**0.9211 ± 0.0338**
DNN	**9.2 ± 4.3**	3.4 ± 3.0	**0.9292 ± 0.0292**
DNN with adaboost	**8.8 ± 5.4**	9.6 ± 2.8	**0.9184 ± 0.0273**
DNN with bagging	**9.0 ± 3.6**	5.1 ± 2.9	**0.9338 ± 0.0258**
DNN with random subspace	10.1 ± 4.5	4.2 ± 2.4	**0.9308 ± 0.0211**

words, this method performs particularly well in predicting the spam class. The DNN with adaboost performed even better in terms of this criterion but it failed to classify the legitimate messages compared with the remaining ensemble methods. Finally, the DNN with random subspace performed reasonably well with respect to both classes, resulting in high accuracy and area under ROC curve. Regarding the other comparative methods, they were significantly outperformed by the best spam filter in terms of accuracy, except random forest, CNN and DNN. Although the improvement in accuracy might not seem substantial (e.g., less than one percent over random forest), real-life spam filters achieve up to 99.9% accuracy. Every improvement is therefore highly warranted. However, some of the comparative methods were good in detecting one of the classes. Specifically, Naïve Bayes was best in detecting the social network spam class, while Adaboost M1 performed best on the legitimate class of messages. On the other hand, Adaboost M1 cannot be recommended for spam filtering in social networks due to the low value of the area under ROC curve, reflecting the poor performance on the spam class.

6 Conclusion

In this study, we demonstrated that ensemble learning algorithms with DNN as the base learner is more accurate than state-of-the-art spam filtering methods. The results show that bagging algorithm trained with DNNs achieved best results, with a high accuracy on both classes. This can be attributed to the capacity of bagging in reducing the risk of overfitting. In fact, bagging performs best with complex base learners, just like DNNs. Note that this is different from boosting where weak base learners are preferred. Moreover, reducing the number of features with random subspace does not seem to be beneficial in case of DNNs. To sum up, the combination of complex DNNs trained on random subsets of high-dimensional data seems to be an effective method for social network spam filtering. On the other hand, ensemble learning algorithms with DNN performed relatively poorly when it comes to FN rate.

Several limitations of this study need to be mentioned. Here we used the content of the messages, together with the information about the author (the number of messages authored) and reporter (the number of messages reported). However, the content of the neighbouring messages could be utilized in future studies. This would require a larger dataset to be collected. This model could also be used to predict spammers in addition to spam messages. Recent studies showed that such a combination might significantly improve the accuracy of spam and spammer filters.

The results obtained here suggest that DNNs with ensemble learning might have great potential also in other text categorization tasks, such as web-page classification, e-mail spam filtering, sentiment classification and so forth. It would also be interesting to investigate the effect of different feature selection approaches and therefore further investigation and experimentation is highly recommended. Moreover, it would be beneficial to investigate whether described methods show similar performance for spam datasets from different countries in different languages from different social networking platforms and whether localization of classification algorithm is required.

Acknowledgments.. This article was supported by the by the grant No. SGS_2018_019 of the Student Grant Competition.

References

1. Cormack, G.V.: Email spam filtering: a systematic review. Found. Trends Inf. Retr. **1**(4), 335–455 (2006). https://doi.org/10.1561/1500000006
2. Nexgate: State of Social Media Spam (2013). http://nexgate.com/wp-content/uploads/2013/09/Nexgate-2013-State-of-Social-Media-Spam-Research-Report.pdf
3. Prieto, V.M., Alvarez, M., Cacheda, F.: Detecting Linkedin spammers and its spam nets. Int. J. Adv. Comput. Sci. Appl. (IJACSA) **4**(9), 189–199 (2013)
4. Barushka, A., Hájek, P.: Spam filtering using regularized neural networks with rectified linear units. In: Adorni, G., Cagnoni, S., Gori, M., Maratea, M. (eds.) AI*IA 2016. LNCS (LNAI), vol. 10037, pp. 65–75. Springer, Cham (2016). https://doi.org/10.1007/978-3-319-49130-1_6
5. Bhowmick, A., Hazarika, S.M.: E-mail spam filtering: a review of techniques and trends. In: Kalam, A., Das, S., Sharma, K. (eds.) Advances in Electronics, Communication and Computing. LNEE, vol. 443, pp. 583–590. Springer, Singapore (2018). https://doi.org/10.1007/978-981-10-4765-7_61
6. Almeida, T.A., Almeida, J., Yamakami, A.: Spam filtering: how the dimensionality reduction affects the accuracy of Naive Bayes classifiers. J. Internet Serv. Appl. **1**(3), 183–200 (2011). https://doi.org/10.1007/s13174-010-0014-7
7. Choudhary, N., Jain, A.K.: Towards filtering of SMS spam messages using machine learning based technique. In: Singh, D., Raman, B., Luhach, A.K., Lingras, P. (eds.) Advanced Informatics for Computing Research. CCIS, vol. 712, pp. 18–30. Springer, Singapore (2017). https://doi.org/10.1007/978-981-10-5780-9_2
8. Kaur, P., Singhal, A., Kaur, J.: Spam detection on Twitter: a survey. In: Proceedings of the 2016 3rd International Conference on Computing for Sustainable Global Development (INDIACom), pp. 2570–2573. IEEE, New Delhi (2016)
9. Statista. https://www.statista.com/statistics/264810/number-of-monthly-active-facebook-users-worldwide/
10. Zheng, X., Zeng, Z., Chen, Z., Yu, Y., Rong, C.: Detecting spammers on social networks. Neurocomputing **159**, 27–34 (2015). https://doi.org/10.1016/j.neucom.2015.02.047
11. Wang, A.H.: Don't follow me: spam detection in Twitter. In: Proceedings of the 2010 International Conference on Security and Cryptography (SECRYPT), pp. 1–10. IEEE (2010)
12. Benevenuto, F., Magno, G., Rodrigues, T., Almeida, V.: Detecting spammers on twitter. In: Proceedings of the 6th Collaboration, Electronic Messaging, Anti-Abuse and Spam Conference (CEAS), pp. 1–12 (2010)
13. Aswani, R., Kar, A.K, Ilavarasan, P.V.: Detection of spammers in twitter marketing: a hybrid approach using social media analytics and bio inspired computing. Inf. Syst. Front. 1–16 (2017). https://doi.org/10.1007/s10796-017-9805-8
14. Shen, H., Ma, F., Zhang, X., Zong, L., Liu, X., Liang, W.: Discovering social spammers from multiple views. Neurocomputing **225**, 49–57 (2017). https://doi.org/10.1016/j.neucom.2016.11.013
15. Gogoglou, A., Theodosiou, Z., Kounoudes, T., Vakali, A., Manolopoulos, Y.: Early malicious activity discovery in microblogs by social bridges detection. In: Proceedings of the 2016 IEEE International Symposium on Signal Processing and Information Technology (ISSPIT), pp. 132–137. IEEE, Limassol (2016). https://doi.org/10.1109/isspit.2016.7886022
16. Bindu, P.V., Mishra, R., Thilagam, P.S.:Discovering spammer communities in Twitter. J. Intell. Inf. Syst. 1–25 (2018). https://doi.org/10.1007/s10844-017-0494-z

17. Wu, F., Shu, J., Huang, Y., Yuan, Z.: Co-detecting social spammers and spam messages in microblogging via exploiting social contexts. Neurocomputing **201**, 51–65 (2016). https://doi.org/10.1016/j.neucom.2016.03.036

18. Zheng, X., Zhang, X., Yu, Y., Kechadi, T., Rong, C.: ELM-based spammer detection in social networks. J. Supercomput. **72**(8), 2991–3005 (2016)

19. Yu, D., Chen, N., Jiang, F., Fu, B., Qin, A.: Constrained NMF-based semi-supervised learning for social media spammer detection. Knowl.-Based Syst. **125**, 64–73 (2017). https://doi.org/10.1016/j.knosys.2017.03.025

20. Bosma, M., Meij, E., Weerkamp, W.: A framework for unsupervised spam detection in social networking sites. In: Baeza-Yates, R., de Vries, Arjen P., Zaragoza, H., Cambazoglu, B.Barla, Murdock, V., Lempel, R., Silvestri, F. (eds.) ECIR 2012. LNCS, vol. 7224, pp. 364–375. Springer, Heidelberg (2012). https://doi.org/10.1007/978-3-642-28997-2_31

21. Barushka, A., Hajek, P.: Spam filtering using integrated distribution-based balancing approach and regularized deep neural networks. Submitted to Applied Intelligence (2018)

22. Dutta, S., Ghatak, S., Dey, R., Das, A.K., Ghosh, S.: Attribute selection for improving spam classification in online social networks: a rough set theory-based approach. Soc. Netw. Anal. Min. **8**(7), 1–16 (2018). https://doi.org/10.1007/s13278-017-0484-8

23. Sohrabi, M.K., Karimi, F.: A feature selection approach to detect spam in the Facebook social network. Arabian J. Sci. Eng. **43**(2), 949–958 (2018)

24. Song, L., Lau, R.Y.K., Kwok, R.C.W., Mirkovski, K., Dou, W.: Who are the spoilers in social media marketing? Incremental learning of latent semantics for social spam detection. Electron. Commer. Res. **17**(1), 51–81 (2017). https://doi.org/10.1007/s10660-016-9244-5

25. Hinton, G., Srivastava, N., Krizhevsky, A., Sutskever, I., Salakhutdinov, R.: Improving neural networks by preventing co-adaptation of feature detectors (2012). arXiv:1207.0580

26. Dhillon, I.S., Mallela, S., Kumar, R.: A divisive information-theoretic feature clustering algorithm for text classification. J. Mach. Learn. Res. **3**, 1265–1287 (2003). https://doi.org/10.1162/153244303322753661

27. Maas, A.L., Hannun, A.Y., Ng, A.Y.: Rectifier nonlinearities improve neural network acoustic models. In: Proceedings of the 30th International Conference on Machine Learning, pp. 1–6 (2013)

28. Freund, Y., Schapire R.E.: Experiments with a new boosting algorithm. In: Thirteenth International Conference on Machine Learning, San Francisco, pp. 148–156 (1996)

29. Breiman, L.: Bagging predictors. Mach. Learn. **24**(2), 123–140 (1996). https://doi.org/10.1007/BF00058655

30. Ho, T.K.: The random subspace method for constructing decision forests. IEEE Trans. Pattern Anal. Mach. Intell. **20**(8), 832–844 (1998). https://doi.org/10.1109/34.709601

Sub-event Detection on Twitter Network

Chao Chen and Gabriel Terejanu[✉]

Department of Computer Science and Engineering, University of South Carolina,
Columbia, SC 29208, USA
chen288@email.sc.edu, terejanu@cse.sc.edu

Abstract. This work addresses the online detection of sub-events using Twitter stream data. We formulate the process of sub-event identification as an outlier detection problem using three statistical methods: Kalman Filter, Gaussian Process, and Probabilistic Principal Component Analysis. These methods are used to construct the probability distribution of percentage change in the number of tweets. Outliers are identified as future observations that do not fit these predicted probability distributions. Five real-world case studies are investigated to test the effectiveness of the methods. Finally, we discuss the limitations of the proposed frame-work and provide future directions for improvement.

Keywords: Outlier detection · Time-series analysis · Social media mining

1 Introduction

Launched in 2006, Twitter serves as a microblogging platform in which people can publish at most 140 character-long tweets or 10,000 character-long direct messages [1]. Due to its popularity, portability, and ease of use, Twitter quickly has grown into a platform for people sharing daily life updates, chatting, and recording or spreading news. As of September 2015, Twitter announced that there were more than 320 million monthly active users worldwide1[1]. In comparison to conventional news sources, Twitter favors real-time content and breaking news, and it thus plays an important role as a dynamic information source for individuals, companies, and organizations [2].

Since its establishment, Twitter has generously opened a portion of its data to the public and has attracted extensive research in many areas [3–5]. In many studies, the primary task is to identify the event-related tweets and then exploit these tweets to build domain knowledge-related models for analysis. As defined by Atefeh [2], events are generally considered as "real-world occurrences that unfold over space and time". Compared to many data sources, tweets serve as a massive and timely collection of facts and controversial opinions related to specific events [2]. Furthermore, events discussed on Twitter vary in both scale and category, while some may reach to global audiences such as presidential election [6], and others, such as wildfire [7, 8], appeal to local users. In general, studies of Twitter events can be categorized into natural events [3], political events [9], social events [10], and others [11].

---

[1] https://about.twitter.com/company

L. Iliadis et al. (Eds.): AIAI 2018, IFIP AICT 519, pp. 50–60, 2018.
https://doi.org/10.1007/978-3-319-92007-8_5

Originated from the Topic Detection and Tracking (TDT) program, detection of retrospective or new events has been addressed over two decades from a collection of news stories [12]. Historically, there exist a number of systems developed to automatically detect events from online news [13–15].

An event usually consists of many sub-events, which can describe various facets of it [7]. Furthermore, users tend to post new statuses of an event to keep track of the dynamics of it. Within an event, some unexpected situations or results may occur and surprise users, such as the bombing during the Boston Marathon and the verdict moment of the Zimmerman trial. By building an intelligent system, we can identify these sub-events to quickly respond to them, thus avoiding crisis situations or maximizing marketing impact.

2 Background

Traditionally, unsupervised models and supervised models have been widely applied to detect events from news sources. Clustering methods have been a classic approach for both Retrospective Event Detection (RED) and New Event Detection (NED) since 1990s. According to Allan et al. [12], they designed a single pass clustering method with a threshold model to detect and track events from a collection of digitalized news sources. Chen and Roy [16] also applied clustering approaches such as DBSCAN to identify events for other user-generated contents such as photos.

Additionally, supervised algorithms such as naive Bayes, SVM, and gradient boosted decision trees, have been proposed for event detection. Becker et al. [17] employed the Naive Bayes classifier to label the clustered tweets into event-tweets or non-events tweets with derived temporal features, social features, topical features, and Twitter-centric features, while the tweets are grouped using an incremental clustering algorithm. Sakaki et al. [3] applied the Support Vector Machine to classify tweets into tweets related to target events or not with three key features. Subsequently, they designed a spatial-temporal model to estimate the center of an earthquake and forecast the trajectory of a hurricane using Kalman filtering and particle filtering. Popescu and Pennacchiotti [18] proposed a gradient boosted decision tree based model integrated with a number of custom features to detect controversial events from Twitter streams.

Furthermore, ensemble approaches are also employed to address the event detection problem. Sankaranarayanan et al. [19] first employed a classification scheme to classify tweets into different groups, and then applied a clustering algorithm to identify events.

As argued by Meladianos et al. [1], sub-event detection has been receiving more and more attention from the event research community. For the time being, there are a number of studies dealing with sub-event detection in an offline mode [20]. Zhao et al. [21] adopted a simple statistical approach to detect sub-events during NFL games when tweeting rate suddenly rose higher than a prior threshold. Chakrabarti and Punera [22] developed a two-phase model with a modified Hidden Markov Model to identify sub-events and then derived a summary of the tweets stream. However, their approach has a severe deficiency because it fails to work properly under situations when unseen event types are involved. Zubiaga et al. [20] compared two different approaches for sub-event detection. The first approach measured recent tweeting activities and identified sub-events if there was a sudden increase of the tweeting rate by at least 1.7 compared to the previous period. The second approach relied on all previous tweeting activities and detected sub-events if the tweeting rate within 60 s exceeded 90% of all previously tweeting rates. As claimed by the authors, the latter outlier-based approach outperformed the first increase-based approach since it neglected situations when there existed low tweeting rates preceded by even lower rates [20].

Nichols et al. [23] provided both an online approach and an offline approach to detect sub-events as well as summarizing important events moments by comparing slopes of statuses updates with a specific slope threshold, which was defined as the sum of the median and three times the standard deviation (median + 3*standard deviation) in their experiment. Shen et al. [24] incorporated "burstiness" and "cohesiveness" properties of tweets into a participant-based sub-event detection framework, and developed a mixture model tuned by EM which yielded the identification of important moments of an event. Chierichetti et al. [25] proposed a logistic regression classifier, to capture the new sub-events with the exploration of the tweet and retweet rates as the features.

In this study, we formalize sub-event detection as an outlier detection problem, where a set of statistical models, Kalman filter (KF), Gaussian process (GP), and probabilistic principle component analysis (PPCA), are used to construct the probability distribution of future observables. Outliers are identified as observations that do not fit these predicted probability distributions. Three real-world case studies (2013 Boston marathon, 2013 NBA AllStar, Zimmerman trial) are investigated to test the effectiveness of the methods. Finally, we discuss the limitations of the proposed framework and provide future directions for improvement.

3 Methodology

Our goal is to model the evolution of the probability distribution of the tweeting change rate (increase/decrease) from period $t - 1$ to t as defined in the following equation. Each period t spans 30 min and #tweets represents the total number of tweets within that period and filtered for the particular event of interest.

$$v_t = \frac{\#tweets_t - \#tweets_{t-1}}{\#tweets_{t-1} + 1} \qquad (1)$$

Three methods (KF, GP, PPCA) described in the following subsections, are evaluated in constructing the probability density function $p(v_{t+1}|v_{1:t} = \{v_t^* \ldots v_1^*\})$. All three approximate the target using a Gaussian density function. This probability distribution is then used to determine whether an observation v_{t+1}^* is an outlier (*denotes the actual observation of percentage change). An observation is labeled as unexpected sub-event when it is identified as an outlier at the 0.025 significance test for the one-tail test.

$$p(v_{t+1} \geq |v^*_{t+1}| | v_{1:t}) < 0.025 \tag{2}$$

3.1 Kalman Filter (KF)

Kalman filter and its variants are widely applied in dynamic systems to estimate the state of a system [26, 27]. In this study, we assume that a latent variable h_t related to our quantity of interest - percentage change v_t, evolves with time using the following linear dynamical system.

$$h_t = Ah_{t-1} + \eta_t^h \tag{3}$$

$$v_t = Bh_t + \eta_t^v \tag{4}$$

$$h_1 \sim N(\mu_0, \sigma_0^2) \tag{5}$$

Here, η_t^h is the process noise and η_t^v is the measurement noise. They are as assumed to be independent of one another, temporally independent, and normally distributed according to $N(0, \Sigma_H)$ and $N(0, \Sigma_V)$ respectively. The model parameters $A, B, \Sigma_H, \Sigma_V, \mu_0, \sigma_0^2$ are learned from the data using the Expectation Maximization (EM) algorithm [28].

The initial mean μ_0 and variance σ_0^2 are obtained using data from a 12 h window, and the EM is run on a 12 h moving window to determine the rest of the parameters. After the parameters are obtained, we make a prediction for the next 30 min to compute the probability $p(v_{t+1} | v_{1:t} = \{v^*_t \ldots v^*_1\})$ and test whether the next incoming observation is a sub-event.

3.2 Gaussian Process (GP)

To better capture the non-linearity in the data, we have also tested Gaussian processes. GP is a generalization of a multivariate Gaussian distribution to infinitely many variables [29]. Specifically, a GP defines a distribution over functions, $p(f)$, and f is a mapping function. In this study we use GP to capture the nonlinear relation between several past observations of percentage change and future ones. Namely, we consider the following model.

$$v_t = f(v_{t-1}, v_{t-2}, v_{t-3}) + \epsilon_t \tag{6}$$

Here $f(\cdot) \sim GP(\cdot | 0, k)$ and $\varepsilon \sim N(\cdot | 0, \sigma^2)$, where $k(\cdot, \cdot)$ is the kernel function. Common choices for kernel function include the squared exponential kernel function, polynomial kernel functions, and sigmoid kernel functions. In this work we have used cubic covariance function, parameters of which are determined using maximum likelihood estimation for each 24 h moving window, where the training data consists of inputs $\{X = (v^*_t, v^*_{t-1}, v^*_{t-2})_{t=3\ldots47}, Y = (v^*_t)_{t=4\ldots48}\}$.

Once the training is completed, the probability density function corresponding to a new input $x_* = (v_t^*, v_{t-1}^*, v_{t-2}^*)$ is obtained via conditioning of the joint as follows.

$$p(v_{t+1}|x_*, X, y) = N(\mu_*, \sigma_*^2)$$
$$\mu_* = K_{*N}(K_N + \sigma^2 I)^{-1} y$$
$$\sigma_*^2 = K_{**} - K_{*N}(K_N + \sigma^2 I)^{-1} K_{N*} + \sigma^2$$

Here, K_N represents the Gram matrix whose entries are given by the kernel function evaluated at the corresponding pairs of inputs in the training data. K_{*N} is a row vector corresponding with kernel function evaluated between the new input x_* are all the training data points, and K_{**} is kernel function evaluated at the new input point.

3.3   Probabilistic Principle Component Analysis (PPCA)

A third model is tested by simply approximating the joint distribution $p(v_t, v_{t-1}, v_{t-2}, v_{t-3})$ using a Gaussian distribution based on 48 samples corresponding to each 24-h moving window. The prediction for the quantity of interest is obtained via conditioning the joint using the past three observations. Since we need to approximate the covariance in 4 dimensions using only 46 samples, we propose to use a more robust estimator such as PPCA than simply computing the sample covariance matrix.

PPCA model is defined as a linear relationship between the 4-dimensional observable $[v_t, v_{t-1}, v_{t-2}, v_{t-3}]^T$ and the M-dimensional latent variable z_n which follows a zero-mean normal distribution with unit covariance matrix [30]. In this study we have set $p = 2$.

$$[v_t, v_{t-1}, v_{t-2}, v_{t-3}]^T = W z_n + \mu + \epsilon_n \tag{7}$$

Here, W is a 4×2 matrix, μ is the data offset, and ϵ is the projection error, which assumed to follow isotropic Gaussian distribution $\varepsilon \sim N(0, \sigma^2 I)$. We can then obtain the joint distribution of the features by integrating out the latent variables:

$$p[v_t, v_{t-1}, v_{t-2}, v_{t-3}]^T \sim N(\mu, C) \tag{8}$$

Here, the covariance matrix $C = W W^T + \sigma^2 I$. The parameters W, μ, and σ^2 can be either estimated using the EM approach or by maximizing the following likelihood function [30].

$$L = -\frac{N}{2} d\ln(2\pi) + \ln|C| + \text{tr}(C^{-1} S) \tag{9}$$

$$S = \frac{1}{N} \sum_{n=1}^{N} (t_n - \mu)(t_n - \mu)^T \tag{10}$$

4 Experiments

Twitter data were collected from Jan. 2, 2013 to Oct. 7, 2014 using Twitter streaming APIs. Then we handpicked three national events during this period, including the 2013 Boston marathon event, the 2013 NBA AllStar event, and the Zimmerman trial event. For these events, we filtered out relevant tweets with pre-specified keywords and hashtags, and provided basic summary of the events shown in Table 1.

For two of the three events, we detected sub-events using data retrieved in one week. However, for the Zimmerman trial event, we missed partial data and thus used data collected in three days that were relevant to the event. Based upon the data, we developed an online detection system that could capture outliers. Figure 1 shows a daily pattern of the number of users and number of tweets for the collected tweets. As the figure indicates, there exist periodic patterns for both the number of tweets and the number of users.

5 Results

As shown in Figs. 2, 3 and 4, the upper sub-plot to the lower sub-plot are outliers identified by the KF, GP, and PPCA algorithms, respectively. Red color indicates actual percentage change of tweets, green color indicates the confidence interval, and cyan color indicates the identified outliers by each algorithm. For the Boston marathon event, as shown in Fig. 2, there were 90, 4, and 7 sub-events detected by the KF, GP, and PPCA algorithms, respectively. 4 of the 90 sub-events identified by KF were labelled as real sub-events, 2 sub-events identified by GP were labelled as real sub-events, and 3 sub-events identified by PPCA were labelled as real sub-events. For this particular event, GP yielded the best precision and 2 of the 4 identified sub-event were real sub-events. Meanwhile, KF achieved the best recall but with many false positives (Table 3).

Outliers of the Zimmerman trial event are visualized in Fig. 3. In terms of the recall value, both KF and PPCA captured 3 of the 10 sub-events, but PPCA achieved a slightly better precision value. In contrast, GP achieved the best precision value.

Figure 4 indicated the identified outliers of the NBA AllStar event. For this event, KF outperformed the other two methods and yielded slightly better recall and precision value. It captured 3 of the 12 sub-events and 3 of the 5 predicted sub-events were real.

A summary of the three picked events are provided in Table 3. Overall, GP and PPCA yield similar F1 score, while GP achieves better recall value and PPCA achieves better precision. KF, in compared to the other two methods, yields the best recall value. This performance is most affected by the Boston event, in which many false positives are identified. More interestingly, we notice that GP provides robust estimates of the uncertainty while the other two methods yield higher uncertainty estimates for time windows after outliers. This observation can be illustrated by the large green confidence bounds after the two spikes in Figs. 2 and 3.

Table 1. Basic information for the picked events

Event	Collection starting time	Event time	Collection ending time	Key words/ hashtags
2013 Boston marathon	04/12/2013 00:00:00	04/15/2013 14:49:00	04/18/2013 23:59:59	marathon, #marathon
2013 NBA AllStar	02/14/2013 00:00:00	02/17/2013 20:30:00	02/20/2013 23:59:59	allstar, all-star
Zimmerman trial	07/12/2013 11:30:00	07/13/2013 22:00:00	07/15/2013 11:30:00	trayvon, zimmerman

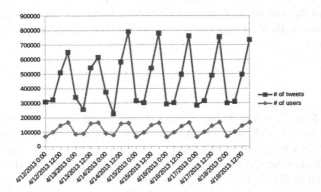

Fig. 1. Daily patterns of the collected tweets during 04/12/2013 and 04/18/2013.

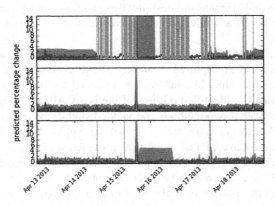

Fig. 2. Predicted sub-events with KF, GP, and PPCA, for the 2013 Boston marathon event. The cyan color indicates the sub-events identified by each algorithm. (Color figure online)

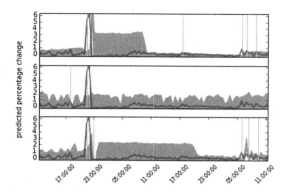

Fig. 3. Predicted sub-events with KF, GP, and PPCA, for the Zimmerman trial event. The cyan color indicates the sub-events identified by each algorithm. (Color figure online)

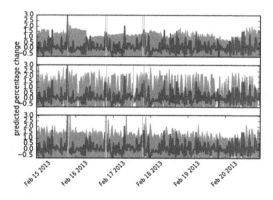

Fig. 4. Predicted sub-events with KF, GP, and PPCA, for the 2013 NBA AllStar event. The cyan color indicates the sub-events identified by each algorithm. (Color figure online)

Table 2. Evaluation metrics of the picked events

	Recall	Precision	F1
KF	0.34	0.10	0.15
GP	0.21	0.55	0.30
PPCA	0.28	0.42	0.33

Table 3. Evaluation metrics of the picked events

			Predicted	
			Sub-event	Non sub-event
KF	Real	Sub-event	10	19
		Non sub-event	92	552
GP	Real	Sub-event	6	23
		Non sub-event	5	639
PPCA	Real	Sub-event	8	21
		Non sub-event	11	633

6 Conclusion

In this study, we explore of building an intelligent system for sub-event detection with three probabilistic models. The sub-events of a point-of-interest event is captured by the system if a new observation is out of the confidence bound of the predictive distribution. We demonstrate the proposed system could capture sub-events with varying performance. The KF model is able to produce slightly better recall, while the GP model is most robust to outliers and yields the best precision. Compared to these two models, PPCA achieves a balanced performance on recall and precision, yielding the best overall F1 score. Nevertheless, we need to interpret the aggregated evaluation with caution because the performance is affected by individualized events, outliers, and the proper choice of parameters. In the future study, we will further tune the parameters, incorporate robust distributions (e.g. t distribution), and take content features into considerations.

References

1. Meladianos, P., Nikolentzos, G., Rousseau, F., Stavrakas, Y., Vazirgiannis, M.: Degeneracy based real-time sub-event detection in Twitter stream. In: Cha, M., Mascolo, C., Sandvig, C. (eds.) ICWSM, pp. 248–257. AAAI Press (2015)
2. Atefeh, F., Khreich, W.: A survey of techniques for event detection in Twitter. Comput. Intell. **31**(1), 132–164 (2015)
3. Sakaki, T., Okazaki, M., Matsuo, Y.: Earthquake shakes Twitter users: real-time event detection by social sensors. In: Proceedings of the 19th International Conference on World Wide Web, WWW 2010, pp. 851–860. ACM, New York (2010)
4. Guo, D., Chen, C.: Detecting non-personal and spam users on geo-tagged Twitter network. Trans. GIS **18**(3), 370–384 (2014)
5. Huang, Y., Guo, D., Kasakoff, A., Grieve, J.: Understanding us regional linguistic variation with Twitter data analysis. Comput. Environ. Urban Syst. **59**, 244–255 (2015)
6. Wang, H., Can, D., Kazemzadeh, A., Bar, F., Narayanan, S.: A system for real-time Twitter sentiment analysis of 2012 U.S. presidential election cycle. In: Proceedings of the ACL 2012 System Demonstrations, ACL 2012, pp. 115–120. Association for Computational Linguistics, Stroudsburg (2012)
7. Pohl, D., Bouchachia, A., Hellwagner, H.: Automatic sub-event detection in emergency management using social media. In: Proceedings of the 21st International Conference on World Wide Web, WWW 2012 Companion, pp. 683–686. ACM, New York (2012)
8. Palen, L., Starbird, K., Vieweg, S., Hughes, A.: Twitter-based information distribution during the 2009 red river valley flood threat. Bull. Am. Soc. Inf. Sci. Technol. **36**(5), 13–17 (2010)
9. Tumasjan, A., Sprenger, T.O., Sandner, P.G., Welpe, I.M.: Election forecasts with Twitter. Soc. Sci. Comput. Rev. **29**(4), 402–418 (2011)
10. Lee, R., Wakamiya, S., Sumiya, K.: Discovery of unusual regional social activities using geo-tagged microblogs. World Wide Web **14**(4), 321–349 (2011)
11. Mathioudakis, M., Koudas, N.: TwitterMonitor: trend detection over the Twitter stream. In: Proceedings of the 2010 ACM SIGMOD International Conference on Management of Data, SIGMOD 2010, pp. 1155–1158. ACM, New York (2010)

12. Allan, J. (ed.): Introduction to Topic Detection and Tracking, pp. 1–16. Kluwer Academic Publishers (2002)

13. Zhang, C., Zhou, G., Yuan, Q., Zhuang, H., Zheng, Y., Kaplan, L.M., Wang, S., Han, J.: GeoBurst: real-time local event detection in geo-tagged tweet streams. In: Perego, R., Sebastiani, F., Aslam, J.A., Ruthven, I., Zobel, J. (eds.) SIGIR, pp. 513–522. ACM (2016)

14. Li, R., Lei, K.H., Khadiwala, R., Chang, K.C.C.: TEDAS: a Twitter-based event detection and analysis system. In: Proceedings of the 2012 IEEE 28th International Conference on Data Engineering, ICDE 2012, pp. 1273–1276. IEEE Computer Society, Washington, DC (2012)

15. Ifrim, G., Shi, B., Brigadir, I.: Event detection in Twitter using aggressive filtering and hierarchical tweet clustering. In: Papadopoulos, S., Corney, D., Aiello, L.M. (eds.) SNOW-DC@WWW, CEUR Workshop Proceedings, vol. 1150, 33–40. CEUR-WS.org (2014)

16. Chen, L., Roy, A.: Event detection from Flickr data through wavelet-based spatial analysis. In: Proceedings of the 18th ACM Conference on Information and Knowledge Management, CIKM 2009, pp. 523–532. ACM, New York (2009)

17. Becker, H., Naaman, M., Gravano, L.: Beyond trending topics: real-world event identification on Twitter. In: Fifth International AAAI Conference on Weblogs and Social Media (2011)

18. Popescu, A.M., Pennacchiotti, M.: Detecting controversial events from Twitter. In: Proceedings of the 19th ACM International Conference on Information and Knowledge Management, CIKM 2010, pp. 1873–1876. ACM, New York (2010)

19. Sankaranarayanan, J., Samet, H., Teitler, B.E., Lieberman, M.D., Sperling, J.: TwitterStand: news in tweets. In: Proceedings of the 17th ACM SIGSPATIAL International Conference on Advances in Geographic Information Systems, GIS 2009, pp. 42–51. ACM, New York (2009)

20. Zubiaga, A., Spina, D., Amigó, E., Gonzalo, J.: Towards real-time summarization of scheduled events from Twitter streams. In: Proceedings of the 23rd ACM Conference on Hypertext and Social Media, HT 2012, pp. 319–320. ACM, New York (2012)

21. Zhao, S., Zhong, L., Wickramasuriya, J., Vasudevan, V.: Human as real-time sensors of social and physical events: a case study of Twitter and sports games. CoRR abs/1106.4300 (2011)

22. Chakrabarti, D., Punera, K.: Event summarization using tweets. In: ICWSM (2011)

23. Nichols, J., Mahmud, J., Drews, C.: Summarizing sporting events using Twitter. In: Proceedings of the 2012 ACM International Conference on Intelligent User Interfaces, IUI 2012, pp. 189–198. ACM, New York (2012)

24. Shen, C., Liu, F., Weng, F., Li, T.: A participant-based approach for event summarization using Twitter streams. In: Human Language Technologies: Conference of the North American Chapter of the Association of Computational Linguistics, Proceedings, 9–14 June 2013, Westin Peachtree Plaza Hotel, Atlanta, Georgia, USA, pp. 1152–1162 (2013)

25. Chierichetti, F., Kleinberg, J.M., Kumar, R., Mahdian, M., Pandey, S.: Event detection via communication pattern analysis. In: Proceedings of the Eighth International Conference on Weblogs and Social Media, ICWSM 2014, Ann Arbor, Michigan, USA, 1–4 June 2014 (2014)

26. Terejanu, G., Singh, T., Scott, P.D.: Unscented Kalman filter/smoother for a CBRN puff - based dispersion model. In: 11th International Conference on Information Fusion, Quebec City, Canada, July 2007

27. Ozbek, L., Ozlale, U.: Employing the extended Kalman filter in measuring the output gap. J. Econ. Dyn. Control 29(9), 1611–1622 (2005)

28. Fletcher, T.: The Kalman filter explained (2010). www.cs.ucl.ac.uk/sta/T.Fletcher/

29. Snelson, E., Ghahramani, Z.: Variable noise and dimensionality reduction for sparse Gaussian processes. In: UAI 2006, Proceedings of the 22nd Conference in Uncertainty in Artificial Intelligence, Cambridge, MA, USA, 13–16 July 2006 (2006)
30. Tipping, M.E., Bishop, C.M.: Probabilistic principal component analysis. J. Royal Stat. Soc. Ser. B **61**, 611–622 (1999)

Ontology-Based Spatial Pattern Recognition in Diagrams

Anitta Thomas[1(✉)], Aurona J. Gerber[2,3], and Alta van der Merwe[2]

[1] School of Computing, University of South Africa, The Science Campus, Florida Park, Johannesburg, South Africa
thomaa@unisa.ac.za
[2] Department of Informatics, University of Pretoria, Pretoria, South Africa
{aurona.gerber,alta.vdm}@up.ac.za
[3] Center for Artificial Intelligence Research (CAIR), CSIR Meraka, Pretoria, South Africa

Abstract. Diagrams are widely used in our day to day communication. A knowledge of the spatial patterns used in diagrams is essential to *read* and *understand* them. In the context of diagrams, spatial patterns mean accepted spatial arrangements of graphical and textual elements used to represent diagram-specific concepts. In order to assist with the automated understanding of diagrams by computer applications, this paper presents an ontology-based approach to recognise diagram-specific concepts from the spatial patterns in diagrams. Specifically, relevant spatial patterns of diagrams are encoded in an ontology, and the automated instance classification feature of the ontology reasoners is utilised to map spatial patterns to diagram-specific concepts depicted in a diagram. A prototype of this approach to support automated recognition of UML and domain concepts from class diagrams and its performance are also discussed in this paper. This paper concludes with a reflection of the strengths and limitations of the proposed approach.

Keywords: Spatial patterns · Diagrams · Ontology
Ontology reasoner · OWL · UML class diagrams · SVG

1 Introduction

Diagrams are widely used in our day to day communication, and different types of diagrams are used for various purposes in different domains. Prominent diagrams used in Computing include flow charts, state chart diagrams and Unified Modelling Language (UML) diagrams. A noticeable aspect of these diagrams is that they have generally accepted visual syntax, which are spatial patterns consisting of graphical and textual elements [15, 16] to indicate diagram-specific concepts in the diagrams. This study only considers diagrams that have established visual syntax irrespective of whether it is formally or informally specified. The knowledge of these visual patterns is essential to *read* and *understand* diagrams.

© IFIP International Federation for Information Processing 2018
Published by Springer International Publishing AG 2018. All Rights Reserved
L. Iliadis et al. (Eds.): AIAI 2018, IFIP AICT 519, pp. 61–72, 2018.
https://doi.org/10.1007/978-3-319-92007-8_6

Numerous approaches have been used to generate declarative specifications of various aspects of diagrams including their spatial patterns, and these specifications have been used to implement applications to either recognise or generate diagrams. The majority of these approaches are grammar-based approaches, and the prominence of these approaches stems from their success in natural language specifications [15]. However, the number of diagram specification techniques that have sufficient supporting literature, freely-available tools and literature that indicates their current use remains small.

Ontologies is a prominent knowledge representation technique, which has been successfully used to realise knowledge-based applications. An ontology, in general, is a model of domain knowledge designed for a specific purpose. Ontologies are used, in general, for two main purposes; as a formal vocabulary of concepts in a domain or as a knowledge source from which additional knowledge can be derived. Logic-based ontologies have the benefit of being able to use the automated reasoning capabilities of existing ontology reasoners to verify and infer additional information from them [5]. The Web Ontology Language (OWL), a logic-based ontology language, has a rich set of current literature, proven value in numerous application domains and freely-available tools [7,11].

In this paper, we present the results of a study that developed and evaluated an ontology-based approach to recognise spatial patterns in diagrams. In this approach, relevant spatial patterns of diagrams are encoded in an OWL ontology, and the automated instance classification feature of the ontology reasoners is utilised to map spatial patterns to diagram-specific concepts depicted in a diagram. The proposed approach is then instantiated in a prototype to recognise concepts from Scalable Vector Graphics (SVG) files of UML class diagrams using an ontology of relevant spatial patterns. Furthermore, the performance of the prototype in terms of its time usage and correctness is tested with a sample set of class diagrams. Automated recognition of concepts from diagrams can be a useful building block to generate automated summaries of diagrams, which can, for example, be useful for visually impaired users in reading the information depicted in diagrams.

The novel contributions of this study are three-fold; firstly a generic ontology-based approach to recognise diagram-specific concepts from diagrams is presented. Secondly an implementation, albeit a prototype, demonstrates the feasibility of the proposed approach, and thirdly, automated semantic interpretation of limited scope of class diagrams in SVG format using an ontology of spatial patterns is demonstrated.

This paper is structured into seven sections. In Sect. 2, the proposed ontology-based approach and a generic application design that uses this approach are presented. A prototype that follows this ontology-based approach to recognise UML and domain concepts in class diagrams of SVG format is presented in Sect. 3. Section 4 presents a discussion on the performance of the prototype. In Sect. 5, a discussion of the pros and cons of the proposed ontology-based approach is included. Section 6 includes a brief summary of related work and a conclusion is provided in Sect. 7.

2   Ontology-Based Spatial Pattern Recognition

Diagrams with established visual syntax consist of well-defined spatial patterns
for diagram-specific concepts. For example, Fig. 1 depicts (a) a *decision* (b) a
state (c) a *class* used in flow charts, state diagrams and UML class diagrams
respectively. In this example, *decision, state* and *class* are domain-specific concepts, which are represented using established spatial patterns, which consist of
spatial configurations of graphical and textual elements. For example, a *state* in
state diagrams can be represented using a circle and a text, where the text is
contained in the circle. Additionally the text in the circle is generally considered
as the description of the *state*, so in this case the string A will be read as *state A*.

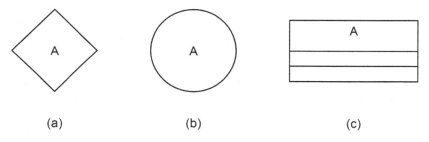

Fig. 1. Notations of (a) a *decision* (b) a *state* (c) a *class* used in flow charts, state
diagrams and UML class diagrams respectively

In our proposed approach, recognising domain-concepts in diagrams is
achieved using an ontology of visual patterns. The first step in this approach
is to create a ontology of visual patterns of diagrams. The model of visual patterns in the ontology should be aligned with the goals of the applications in which
it will be used. An application for diagram interpretation that uses this ontology
can then be realised using the generic design depicted in Fig. 2. In the generic
design, the component *Diagram processor* will process the diagram to extract
graphical and textual primitives as well as the spatial relationships between
these primitives, which is then amended to the ontology of visual patterns. The
ontology reasoner can then process, using instance classification, this amended
ontology to indicate the diagram-specific concepts depicted in the diagram. In
Sect. 3, the generic design given in Fig. 2 is modified to implement a prototype
that extracts UML and domain concepts from SVG files of class diagrams.

3   Prototype: Automated Extraction of UML Concepts from Class Diagrams in SVG Format

The aim of the prototype is to realise automated interpretation of a limited form
of class diagrams using a relevant spatial patterns ontology. The file format of
the class diagrams is restricted to SVG. The scope of interpretation is limited

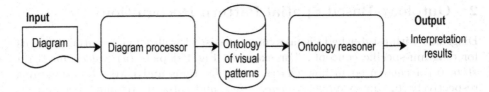

Fig. 2. The components of a generic diagram interpretation application that uses the spatial patterns ontology

to extract UML and domain concepts depicted in a given diagram. The concepts of interest are the nodes and links in the diagrams. Moreover, when links are identified in the diagram, the prototype should also extract the connecting nodes for each link. Examples of UML concepts that represent nodes are *class*es and *interface*s. On the other hand, *inheritance* and *dependency* are examples of concepts that are considered links in class diagrams.

A class diagram, in general, is a UML model that models a system or some aspect within some domain. The metamodel of class diagrams is defined in UML [18]. In the developed prototype, the concepts extracted automatically from class diagrams include elements from both the domain model and UML metamodel. For example, referring to Fig. 1(C), the notation can be seen as the UML concept (metaclass) *Class*, and the string *A*, representing the class name, can be seen as a concept from the domain model. The proposed approach of automated extraction of concepts is relevant when class diagrams do not contain explicit representations of models, for example, in the XML metadata interchange format XMI [24]. Any non-UML complaint tool, for example a general-purpose free sketching application, can generate class diagrams without explicit model information. One can find numerous class diagrams on web pages that are only available as images without explicit model information.

3.1 An Ontology of Spatial Patterns for Class Diagrams

The central component of the prototype is a dedicated ontology of spatial patterns to support recognition of concepts from class diagrams. In order to develop the ontology, decisions had to be made about how to model the spatial patterns, how to indicate which spatial patterns correspond to which UML concepts and which relevant spatial patterns need to be encoded in the ontology.

UML class diagrams are specified in the Classes package of the UML 2.4.1 specification [17]. This package includes fifty six concepts that can be used to represent an object oriented model in class, package and object diagrams. Moreover, a concept can have more than one spatial pattern. In other words, a concept can be illustrated in different ways. As the developed ontology is to be tested with a prototype, a finite set of UML concepts and spatial patterns was selected to be included in the ontology. This selection was based on which concepts and notations are typically used in class diagrams and also discussed in UML 2.4.1 specification [17].

The spatial patterns were modelled as spatial configurations of primitive elements and spatial relationships between these elements. This modelling approach was used because it aligns with the OWL constructs, classes and properties [9], where an OWL class represents a set of objects and a property describes a possible relationship between objects [8]. The developed ontology consists of numerous OWL classes and they are used to represent either a primitive element or a UML concept. For example, the graphical object rectangle is a graphical primitive used in class diagrams, so an OWL class named Rectangle is added in the ontology to represent all instances of rectangles in class diagrams. A set of spatial relationships were also selected, which were then added as properties in the developed ontology. The spatial pattern for a UML concept was then modelled as the class definition of the corresponding OWL class. If the selected UML concept had more than one spatial pattern, the OWL class corresponding to the concept encoded multiple spatial patterns. The OWL class (corresponding to UML concepts) definitions encoded spatial patterns in terms of existing OWL classes (corresponding to UML concepts and primitive elements) and properties (corresponding to spatial relationships).

Due to space limitations, the entire ontology cannot be included in this paper. Interested readers may refer to [21, 22] for details about the ontology. For illustrative purposes, consider the UML concept *class*, which has numerous spatial patterns - Fig. 3 depicts a few of them. In the developed ontology an OWL class, named *UMLClass* is created with its class definition encoding the spatial patterns of the UML concept *class*. The OWL class definition of *UMLClass* that contains the spatial pattern is listed below:

```
Class: UMLClass
EquivalentTo:
(Rectangle and (hasNonTangentialProperPartOf some String))
or
(Rectangle and (hasNonTangentialProperPartOf some String)
         and (hasTangentialProperPartOf some Line))
```

In the OWL code above, *Rectangle*, *Line* and *String* are the OWL classes in the ontology to represent graphical primitives rectangle and line, and textual primitive (one line of text) respectively. *hasNonTangentialProperPartOf* and *hasTangentialProperPartOf* are properties (corresponding to spatial relationships) encoded in the ontology, and they correspond to the spatial relationships $NTPP^{-1}$ and TPP^{-1} of RCC-8 [2] respectively. The spatial pattern encoded in the ontology for the concept class takes into account its different spatial patterns, especially those depicted in Fig. 3.

3.2 Prototype Design and Implementation

The prototype achieves automated interpretation of class diagrams in several steps. The first step involves extracting primitives and spatial relationships between the primitives from an input diagram, which is used to generate OWL code specific for the input diagram. In the second step, the generated OWL code is added to the ontology described in Sect. 3.1. In the third step, the ontology reasoner performs instance classification on the updated ontology. In the fourth step, the results of the instance classification and the reasoner justifications for the results of instance classification are processed to extract the desired interpretation for the given diagram.

The prototype has a design with three main components namely *SVG processor*, *OWL code generator and writer* and *Interpretation processor* to realise automated interpretation of class diagrams. The inputs to the prototype are class diagrams in SVG format and the ontology described in Sect. 3.1, and the final output is the interpretation, which in this case is a list of nodes and links in the diagram. The overall design of the prototype is given in Fig. 4. The functionality of each component is described below.

SVG Processor: The aim of this component is to extract relevant graphical and textual primitives, and the spatial relationships between these primitives in the input class diagram. Relevant primitives are graphical and textual elements visible to the user and also specified in the ontology. When extracting relevant graphical and textual primitives, their relevant geometric features are also extracted in order to calculate relevant spatial relationships specified in the ontology.

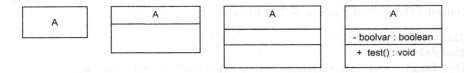

Fig. 3. Different depictions of the UML concept *class*

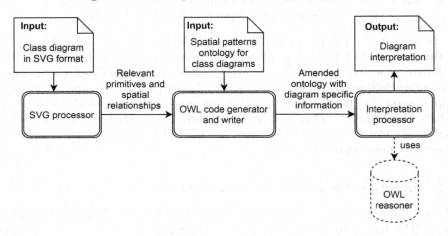

Fig. 4. Prototype design

Different SVG files can generate visibly same image, which is attributed to different ways to encode graphics in SVG. Due to differences in SVG modelling, the models of SVG were restricted for this prototype. However, the chosen models require processing, both XML and geometrical, of SVG elements to determine visible graphical primitives and the spatial relationships between the primitives.

OWL Code Generator and Writer: The *OWL code generator and writer* component consists of two sub-components; one to generate OWL code relating to the input diagram and the second one to write this generated OWL code to the ontology described in Sect. 3.1. The output from *SVG processor* is used to create the OWL code, which includes unique names, types of all the primitives and spatial relationships between them. The generated OWL code is then written to a copy of the .owl file containing the visual patterns ontology, which means each input diagram has a unique ontology file.

Interpretation Processor: *Interpretation processor* invokes the ontology reasoner with the visual patterns ontology output of *OWL code generator and writer* to produce the interpretation. There are two steps taken by *Interpretation processor* to obtain the desired interpretation.

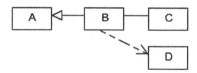

Fig. 5. A simple class diagram

The first step is to use the instance classification feature of the reasoner to obtain the instances of OWL classes that represent relevant UML concepts in the ontology. Specifically, lists of all primitives encoded in the ontology that are classified as instances of OWL classes of interest are obtained. For example, *Interpretation processor* obtains the list of all rectangles that are classified as instances of the OWL class *UMLClass* meaning that these rectangles form part of spatial patterns that represent the UML concept *class*.

In the second step, *Interpretation processor* processes the *justifications* of the results of instance classification from the first step to obtain relevant *node* pairs that satisfy relevant *links*. In particular, *justifications* of the results of instance classification of OWL classes that correspond to only UML concepts that represent *links* are selected for further processing. This selection is because UML concepts that represent *links* are modelled in terms of *nodes* in the class diagrams. For example, the spatial pattern encoded for the UML concept inheritance consists of graphical primitives, triangle and line(s), as well as *node*(s) (examples of nodes include classes and interfaces). If the reasoner inferred that an instance of OWL class *triangle* is an instance of the OWL class *inheritance*, the *justifications* for this instance classification would contain the information about the *node*(s) that led to this inference. Thus by processing these *justifications* one can extract the node pairs that satisfy relationship links.

Input and Output: The inputs to the prototype are class diagrams in SVG format, and the spatial patterns ontology for class diagrams. An intermediate output of the prototype is a modified spatial patterns ontology that contains input diagram-specific information in addition to the spatial patterns. The final output is a textual summary of the interpretation, i.e. lists of all relevant nodes and links in the input diagram.

   To illustrate the output produced by the prototype, consider the simple class diagram depicted in Fig. 5. The textual interpretation produced for this diagram is $Class[A, B, C, D]$, $Inheritance[(A, B)]$, $Association[(B, C)]$ and $Dependency[(D, B)]$. Note that the textual interpretation contains a summary of the domain model in terms of UML concepts; A, B, C and D refer to domain concepts and *Class*, *Inheritance*, *Association* and *Dependency* refer to UML concepts.

Implementation: *SVG processor* and *OWL code generator and writer* are written in C++ without the use of any external libraries. *Interpretation processor* is written in Java because the OWL API is a Java API [7], and it makes use of the OWL API version 3.5.0 and the OWL reasoner HermiT [6]. Additionally, *Interpretation processor* makes use of the clarkparsia library to obtain *justifications* from the OWL reasoner.

4   Prototype Performance

An initial evaluation of the prototype was conducted using fifteen class diagrams. The SVG file sizes of the class diagrams varied from 2 kB to 59 kB. As expected the larger files have larger number of SVG elements and graphical representations in the diagrams than smaller files. The number of XML elements varied from 15 to 640 in the sample SVG files and the number of actual graphical and textual primitives visible in the diagrams varied from 2 to 205.

   For the initial evaluation, precision, recall and processing times of the prototype for the sample class diagrams were noted. The average precision and recall of the final interpretation results were 0.95 and 0.98 respectively. However, the lowest precision of 0.78 and recall of 0.76 were recorded for certain class diagrams. The main cause for mistakes in diagram interpretation was incorrect modelling of spatial patterns for certain UML concepts, which led to certain UML concepts identified incorrectly as well as certain UML concepts not identified in the diagrams.

   The average time used by the prototype was under a minute for the sample class diagrams. However, the longest time taken was approximately 7 min for the sample set. Based on the times recorded for each process in the prototype, it was noted that accessing justifications from the reasoner using the clarkparsia library was the most time-intensive process, taking up to an average of 97% of the total time used by the prototype.

The prototype demonstrates high precision and recall, which is highly desirable even though the sample set was relatively small. However, the time taken for accessing justifications of reasoner seems unreasonably high in comparison to the times taken by other processes in the prototype. Overall, the performance of the prototype is deemed satisfactory and it encourages further evaluation with larger number of diagrams, and improvements to the prototype. Improvements to the prototype will include modifications to the spatial patterns ontology to improve precision and recall, as well as the use of other available libraries to obtain justifications from the ontology reasoner to improve its time usage.

5   Discussion

The ontology-based approach presented in this paper can be applied to any type of diagrams with well-established spatial patterns, and thus the design in Fig. 2 can be reused in other diagram interpretation applications. This paper also showed an example of how the general design in Fig. 2 was adapted and instantiated in an interpretation application for class diagrams with promising results.

It should be noted that the scope of interpretation of diagrams using this approach is dependent on how the spatial patterns are modelled in the ontology. Similarly, the content of the spatial patterns ontology influences all the processes in the design in Fig. 2. For example, which primitives should be extracted in *Diagram processor* is directed by the model encoded in the ontology. This tight coupling between the spatial patterns ontology and all the components in the general design may limit the reusability of program codes from one diagram interpretation application to another.

Diagram processor tries to extract graphical and textual primitives from the input diagram, which is indeed a form of mapping from raster or scalar data to semantic concepts of graphical shapes and text. Thus it may be possible to use a different type of ontology to support the functionality of *Diagram processor*.

Use of *justifications* from the ontology reasoner seems to be a feasible way to obtain necessary information for the diagram interpretation scope of the developed prototype. However, it is possible that using *justifications* may not work for other diagram interpretation scopes. Although processing *justifications* was a bottle neck in the prototype, there are other ways to access *justifications* from the reasoners. One possibility is to use the Protégé [19] API instead of clarkparsia library to access the *justifications*.

Currently the prototype provides a textual summary of the class diagram. However, it is possible to format the summary in XMI since it is the recommended format for model exchange among UML tools [18].

6   Related Work

In [13], an ontology-based approach to recognise design patterns in program codes is proposed, where the ontology consists of models of design patterns and the reasoner is used to identify design patterns from an input program. The approaches in [13] and in this paper are similar but the difference is that the former is applied to the analysis of program codes in text and the latter is applied to the analysis of diagrams.

In [20], a framework to realise domain-based Resource Description Framework (RDF) annotation of SVG images is presented. In this framework, the SVG image is initially processed to extract relevant graphical features, which is used to create a layer of RDF data. In order to provide semantic annotation, the application uses a RDF database relevant for the domain in order to compute similarities between the given image and the semantic concepts in the database. The semantic annotation generated by the application is also checked by a domain expert, which is fed back into the RDF domain database. Comparing the prototype discussed in this paper and the annotation framework presented in [20], it is evident that both approaches use declarative domain knowledge to assist with the interpretation of SVG images. However, the approach in this work is focussed on spatial patterns in diagrams, and how an ontology of such patterns can be used for diagram interpretation.

Ontology-based approaches have been successfully used in the field of image analysis - see examples of such studies in [3,10,14]. In the field of image analysis, single to multiple ontologies are used in an application, and what is modelled in the ontology differs from domain knowledge to generic knowledge relevant for describing images in general. The ontology-based approaches used in image analysis may be adapted for semantic interpretation of diagrams, or generic ontologies used in image processing may be applied in *Diagram processor* or *SVG processor* in Figs. 2 and 4 respectively. The primary focus of ontologies in the current work is to model spatial patterns in diagrams, and to reuse the automated reasoning features of ontology reasoners for diagram interpretation.

There are numerous works that combine UML and OWL, which can be roughly classified into two categories. The first category deals with model translations from UML to OWL or RDF (examples of such studies include [4,23,25]) and the second category focuses on reasoning about the models represented in UML diagrams (examples of such studies include [1,12]). These two categories of works assume that the models represented in diagrams are easily accessible, so that they can focus on the translation of UML models into OWL. However, the prototype presented in this work is useful when the models have to be *read* from the class diagrams. In other words, the developed prototype *reads* the models in the class diagrams using a visual syntax ontology. Thus an OWL ontology is used to infer the model specified in the class diagram. Once the models in the class diagrams have been *read*, then the approaches specified in [1,4,12,23,25] can be used to translate these models into OWL, and to reason about class diagrams, if required.

7   Conclusion

This paper presented an approach to represent spatial patterns of diagrams in an ontology, which is then used for diagram interpretation using the instance classification feature of ontology reasoners. This ontology-based approach was used to realise a prototype to interpret UML class diagrams in SVG format. The performance of the prototype was evaluated with a small set of sample class diagrams, which showed promising results that support the need for further improvements to and evaluations of the prototype.

References

1. Berardi, D., Cali, A., Calvanese, D., Giacomo, G.D.: Reasoning on UML class diagrams. Artif. Intell. **168**, 70–118 (2005)
2. Cohn, A., Bennett, B., Gooday, J., Gotts, N.: Qualitative spatial representation and reasoning with the region connection calculus. GeoInformatica **1**(3), 275–316 (1997)
3. Fiorini, S.R., Abel, M., Scherer, C.M.: Semantic image interpretation of gamma ray profiles in petroleum exploration. Exp. Syst. Appl. **38**(4), 3724–3734 (2011)
4. Gašević, D., Djurić, D., Devedžić, V., Damjanović, V.: Converting UML to OWL ontologies. In: Proceedings of the 13th International World Wide Web Conference on Alternate Track Papers & Posters, WWW Alt. 2004, pp. 488–489. ACM, New York (2004)
5. Halland, K., Britz, K., Gerber, A.: Investigations into the use of SNOMED CT to enhance an OpenMRS health information system. South Afr. Comput. J. **47**, 33–46 (2011)
6. HermiT OWL Reasoner. http://www.hermit-reasoner.com/. Accessed 16 Oct 2017
7. Hitzler, P., Krötzsch, M., Rudolph, S.: Foundations of Semantic Web. CRC Press, Taylor & Francis Group, Boca Raton (2009)
8. Horridge, M., Drummond, N., Jupp, S., Moulton, G., Stevens, R.: A Practical Guide to Building OWL Ontologies using Protégé 4 and CO-ODE Tools. University of Manchester (2009)
9. Horrocks, I., Parsia, B., Sattler, U.: OWL 2 Web Ontology Language: Direct Semantics (Second Edition). World Wide Web Consortium (2012)
10. Hudelot, C.: Towards a cognitive platform for semantic image interpretation; application to the recognition of biological organisms. Ph.D. thesis, University of Nice - Sophia Antipolis (2005)
11. Kashyap, V., Bussler, C., Moran, M.: The Semantic Web: Semantics for Data and Services on the Web. Springer, Heidelberg (2008). https://doi.org/10.1007/978-3-540-76452-6
12. Khan, A.H., Porres, I.: Consistency of UML class, object and statechart diagrams using ontology reasoners. J. Vis. Lang. Comput. **26**, 42–65 (2015)
13. Kirasić, D., Basch, D.: Ontology-based design pattern recognition. In: Lovrek, I., Howlett, R.J., Jain, L.C. (eds.) KES 2008. LNCS (LNAI), vol. 5177, pp. 384–393. Springer, Heidelberg (2008). https://doi.org/10.1007/978-3-540-85563-7_50
14. Maillot, N., Thonnat, M., Boucher, A.: Towards ontology-based cognitive vision. Mach. Vis. Appl. **16**(1), 33–40 (2004)

15. Marriott, K., Meyer, B., Wittenburg, K.B.: A survey of visual language specification and recognition In: Marriott, K., Meyer, B. (eds.) Visual Language Theory, pp. 5–85. Springer, New York (1998). https://doi.org/10.1007/978-1-4612-1676-6

16. Minas, M.: Syntax definition with graphs. Electr. Notes Theoret. Comput. Sci. **148**(1), 19–40 (2006)

17. Object Management Group: Information Technology - Object Management Group Unified Modeling Language (OMG UML), Superstructure, April 2012

18. Object Management Group: Object Management Group Unified Modeling Language (OMG UML) Version 2.5, March 2015

19. Protégé. https://protege.stanford.edu/. Accessed 16 Mar 2018

20. Salameh, K., Tekli, J., Chbeir, R.: SVG-to-RDF image *Semantization*. In: Traina, A.J.M., Traina, C., Cordeiro, R.L.F. (eds.) SISAP 2014. LNCS, vol. 8821, pp. 214–228. Springer, Cham (2014). https://doi.org/10.1007/978-3-319-11988-5_20

21. Thomas, A., Gerber, A.J., van der Merwe, A.: Visual syntax of UML class and package diagram constructs as an ontology. In: Fred, A., Dietz, J., Aveiro, D., Liu, K., Filipe, J. (eds.) Proceedings of the 7th International Joint Conference on Knowledge Discovery, Knowledge Engineering and Knowledge Management (IC3K 2015), vol. 2, pp. 17–28. SCITEPRESS (2015)

22. Thomas, A., Gerber, A.J., van der Merwe, A.: An investigation into OWL for concrete syntax specification using UML notations. In: Jamnik, M., Uesaka, Y., Elzer Schwartz, S. (eds.) Diagrams 2016. LNCS (LNAI), vol. 9781, pp. 197–211. Springer, Cham (2016). https://doi.org/10.1007/978-3-319-42333-3_15

23. Tong, Q., Zhang, F., Cheng, J.: Construction of RDF(S) from UML class diagrams. J. Comput. Inf. Technol. **22**(4), 237–250 (2014)

24. About the XML Metadata Interchange Specification Version 2.5.1. http://www.omg.org/spec/XMI. Accessed 15 Mar 2018

25. Zedlitz, J., Jörke, J., Luttenberger, N.: From UML to OWL 2. In: Lukose, D., Ahmad, A.R., Suliman, A. (eds.) KTW 2011. CCIS, vol. 295, pp. 154–163. Springer, Heidelberg (2012). https://doi.org/10.1007/978-3-642-32826-8_16

Deep Learning

Improving Deep Models of Person Re-identification for Cross-Dataset Usage

Sergey Rodionov[1,2], Alexey Potapov[1,3(✉)], Hugo Latapie[4],
Enzo Fenoglio[4], and Maxim Peterson[2,3]

[1] SingularityNET Foundation, Amsterdam, The Netherlands
pas.aicv@gmail.com, astroseger@gmail.com
[2] Novamente LLC, Rockville, USA
maxim.peterson@gmail.com
[3] ITMO University, Kronverkskiy pr. 49, 197101 St. Petersburg, Russia
[4] Chief Technology and Architecture Office, Cisco, San Jose, USA
{hlatapie,efenogli}@cisco.com

Abstract. Person re-identification (Re-ID) is the task of matching humans across cameras with non-overlapping views that has important applications in visual surveillance. Like other computer vision tasks, this task has gained much with the utilization of deep learning methods. However, existing solutions based on deep learning are usually trained and tested on samples taken from same datasets, while in practice one need to deploy Re-ID systems for new sets of cameras for which labeled data is unavailable. Here, we mitigate this problem for one state-of-the-art model, namely, metric embedding trained with the use of the triplet loss function, although our results can be extended to other models. The contribution of our work consists in developing a method of training the model on multiple datasets, and a method for its online practically unsupervised fine-tuning. These methods yield up to 19.1% improvement in Rank-1 score in the cross-dataset evaluation.

Keywords: Person re-id · Deep learning · Metric embedding · Triplet loss
Cross-dataset evaluation

1 Introduction

Person tracking is one of the most typical tasks in visual surveillance. A great deal of methods for tracking within one camera has been developed. However, it is usually necessary to track a person using multiple cameras with non-overlapping fields of view. Here, traditional tracking techniques cannot be used, and the task of person re-identification (Re-ID) should be stated. This task is challenging because of high variations in background, illumination, viewpoint, human poses, etc., and absence of tight space-time constraints on candidate IDs like in tracking. Although some constraints do exist, and they should be used in a practical system.

Many attempts to solve this task exist [1], but it is far from being completely solved yet. Currently, deep convolutional neural networks (CNNs) are replacing traditional hand-crafted methods [2] that became possible due to both the progress in deep

© IFIP International Federation for Information Processing 2018
Published by Springer International Publishing AG 2018. All Rights Reserved
L. Iliadis et al. (Eds.): AIAI 2018, IFIP AICT 519, pp. 75–84, 2018.
https://doi.org/10.1007/978-3-319-92007-8_7

learning and the availability of larger public datasets like Market-1501 [3] and MARS [4], CUHK03 [5], DukeMTMC-reID [6], and others. Different deep learning models have been developed to solve the person Re-ID task including classification CNNs used for feature learning as in [7], Siamese CNNs that use image pairs [8], metric embedding CNNs trained with the triplet loss [9].

However, most of the existing deep learning models for Re-ID that show state-of-the-art results on different benchmarks are trained and tested on each of these benchmarks separately (e.g. [8, 9]). At the same time, in practice, it is usually necessary to deploy a person Re-ID system to a new camera set, for which a large labeled training set is expensive or impossible to acquire, so pre-trained models should be used. Unfortunately, as it is shown in [7], if a model is trained on one dataset and tested on another dataset, its performance drops significantly (seemingly below the level of hand-crafted features), because changes between datasets are rather large (see Fig. 1). For example, Rank-1 score can decrease from 0.762 to 0.361 on the Market-1501 test set if the training was performed on the Duke training set instead of the Market-1501 training set.

Fig. 1. Pairs of images of same IDs from different cameras from different datasets: Market-1501 [3], CUHK03 [5], Duke [6], Viper [14], WARD [15]

Few works address the problem of unsupervised fine-tuning of pre-trained models on new datasets, and even less of them report improvements achieved by unsupervised fine-tuning in comparison with corresponding pre-trained models, not just the final performance that depends both on the base model and unsupervised fine-tuning algorithm. One such recent work is [7], in which improvements in Rank-1 accuracy from 1.2% for the model trained on Duke and tested on CUHK03 to 11.9% for the model trained on CUHK03 and tested on Market-1501 are reported. While this can be useful in practice, the achieved accuracy is still far below supervised learning results. Also, the Progressive Unsupervised Learning (PUL) algorithm proposed in [7] assumes the known number of IDs in new dataset, which is usually unknown in practice. So, further progress in this task is needed.

In our work, we use one of the state-of-the-art models, namely, metric embedding network trained with the use of the triplet loss function [9] as the base model. The contribution of our paper is two-fold:

(1) We develop the novel method to train the metric embedding network using the triplet loss function on multiple datasets resulting in the increased invariance (and corresponding cross-dataset scores) of the embedding w.r.t. cameras.
(2) We develop a novel fine-tuning method for the person re-id task, which relies on easily accessible information to collect negative samples, so we call it practically unsupervised. It yields up to 10% improvement in Rank-1 score.

2   Metric Embedding Learning for Person Re-ID

2.1   Loss Function

In the task of person Re-ID, it is usually assumed that bounding boxes (BBs) around humans are already extracted. These BBs are usually resized to a certain fixed size. Each resized BB yields a pattern (image) in an initial space of raw features (color values in resized BBs) $\mathbf{x} \in R^F$.

BBs containing certain IDs can also be tracked within each camera forming the so-called tracklets, and in practice it is better to compare not separate BBs, but tracklets. But since it is usually enough to simply average over features calculated for BBs in a tracklet, and compare these averaged features, usage of tracklets doesn't influence on the rest functionality of a Re-ID system.

Each image $\mathbf{x}$ corresponds to a certain ID y, and the task is to identify which images from different cameras have same IDs. These IDs can be considered as classes, but it should be noted that the number of such classes is large and unknown while the number of images in each class is small. Thus, it is inefficient to cast the Re-ID task as the traditional pattern recognition problem.

One way to solve the task is to train a model (e.g. a Siamese Network) that accepts two images as input and infers if they correspond to same ID or not. The problem with this approach is that it requires running the model for one query image with each gallery image that is computationally expensive, especially in the case of deep neural networks.

Another possibility is to train a classification model (e.g. based on CNNs) for a fixed set of IDs known for a training set, and then to cut off the classification layer and compare images using high-level convolutional features, which were useful for classification. Similarity between images can be calculated directly as distance between these latent features, and the performance of such approach is acceptable in practice. However, images with the same ID will not be necessarily closer to each other than images with different IDs in the space of features useful for classification. Thus, additional step of metric learning is added to improve the overall performance.

In fact, what we want to learn is a metric embedding, i.e. a mapping $f(\mathbf{x}|\theta):R^N \to R^M$ that transforms semantically similar images onto metrically close points in R^M (and semantically dissimilar images onto metrically distant points). That is, $D_{i,j} = D$ $(f(\mathbf{x}_i|\theta), f(\mathbf{x}_j|\theta))$ is small if $y_i = y_j$ and large otherwise, where D is some distance measure (e.g. Euclidean). One can try to learn this mapping directly without learning surrogate classification model, if an appropriate loss function is specified.

The following triplet loss function can be used [9]

$$L_{tri}(\theta) = \sum_{\substack{a,p,n \\ y_a = y_p \neq y_n}} [m + D_{a,p} - D_{a,n}]_+ , \qquad (1)$$

where m is some margin by which positive and negative examples should be separated. That is, different triplets of images are considered – one is anchor image with index a, another one is a positive example $y_p = y_a$ with index p, and the last one is a negative example $y_n \neq y_a$ with index n, and we want distance $D_{a,p}$ be smaller than distance $D_{a,n}$ by m.

Softplus $\ln(1 + \exp(x))$ is proposed to be used in place of the hidge function $[m + \cdot]_+$ in [9], since in Re-ID we want to pull images with the same ID further even after the margin m is reached.

However, distances to similarly looking positives are easy to minimize and distances to arbitrary negatives are easy to maximize. Since triplets in (1) are mostly *weak* examples and all of them are also computationally demanding to use, *hard positive samples* and *hard negative samples* should be somehow selected to make embedding learning with the triplet loss successful. Computationally efficient selection of such hard samples can be done with the use of *Batch Hard* loss function [9]. The idea is to form batches using P randomly selected classes (IDs) with randomly sampled K images per class, and to select the hardest positive and negative samples within the batch to form the triplets for the loss function (see details in [9]).

Here, we also use soft margin and batch hard loss.

2.2   Model

We implemented the same network architecture as in [9] with few differences. Instead of ResNet-50, we used MobileNet [10], since we found that performance is very similar while MobileNet is much faster. We also discarded the last classification layer and added two fully connected layers to map high-level convolutional features to the embedding space. Similar to [9], we used the first dense layer with 1024 units with ReLU activation function [11], while the second (output) layer had 128 units corresponding to the embedding dimension. We also used batch normalization [12] between layers. Additionally we used dropout [13] after batch normalization, but in one experiment we found it beneficial to switch it off.

For the usual training, we used ADAM optimizer with default parameters ($beta_1 = 0.9$, $beta_2 = 0.999$). The learning rate was set to 10^{-4} during first 100 epochs. During next 300 epochs we exponentially decay the learning rate till 10^{-7}. The number of steps per epoch was somewhat arbitrarily defined as N_{total}/N_{batch}, where N_{total} is total the number of images in all used datasets, and $N_{batch} = KP$ is the batch size. We used $K = 4$ and $P = 18$ in all experiments.

In our online fine-tuning method (described below), we used RMSProp optimizer with default parameters. The initial learning rate was set to 10^{-5}, and the final learning rate after decay was 10^{-6}. The number of steps per epoch was defined as N_{pos}/K, where N_{pos} is total number of images in all positive samples. Since fine-tuning it was applied to the pre-trained model MARS is much larger, the number of epochs was taken smaller (20 epochs for Market-1501, and 2 epochs for MARS).

3   Improvements

3.1   Embedding Learning on Multiple Datasets

Usually the difference between different Re-ID datasets (for example between Duke and CUHK03) is quite significant. This is the source of the problem with using on one dataset a model trained on another dataset. The obvious idea is to train a model on several datasets simultaneously to force it to learn dataset-invariant embedding, which will be better transferrable to new datasets.

However, large difference between datasets means that it would be quite easy for the model to distinguish images from different sources. One can argue that it will prevent the model from learning invariant features. Instead, the model will focus on pushing different datasets apart in the embedding space, and on learning features more specific for individual datasets, which will be less useful in general setting.

In the case when we use the batch hard triplet loss, we can try to prevent this problem. Our approach is to train an embedding in such a way that network never "sees" images from different datasets simultaneously. We do it by forming each batch with images from only one dataset and we continuously switch between them during training. As we expect, this should prevent the model from simply pushing images from different datasets apart. Instead this should force it to search for invariant features, which, as we hope, will be useful for other datasets. We call this algorithm *BH-switch*. We will compare this algorithm with straightforward approach for training on multiple datasets where we just simply merge datasets together. We call this straightforward algorithm *BH-merge*.

3.2   Practically Unsupervised Fine-Tuning

We can hope that the model trained on multiple datasets will be more dataset-invariant, and thus easier transferrable to new cameras. However, the model still needs to be tuned to achieve higher performance on new data distributions. This tuning should be done unsupervisingly. To apply the triplet loss directly, one should somehow guess positive and negative samples, i.e. which pairs of images correspond to same ID, and which correspond to different IDs.

3.2.1 Extracting Positive Samples

We propose the following method for extracting positive samples from unlabeled set of images (or tracklets) from two cameras. We can assume that we have a pre-trained model, which has a reasonable Re-ID performance for these two cameras. Using this model we calculate features for all images in our unlabeled training set. Then, the distance in the feature space is calculated between each possible pair of images from different cameras. We can except that pairs with minimal distance will be, with high probability, positive samples. We select first N_p pairs with minimal distance and we will use them as presumable positive samples, where N_p is a parameter.

Appropriate choice of N_p can be important. If it is too small, there will be not enough training data to tune the model. If it is too high, the fraction of false positives among selected N_p pairs will higher, and the model drift will take place. It is clear that N_p should be proportional to the number of available images, but the coefficient of proportionality depends on two unknown factors, namely, on how well the pre-trained model suits these new data, and on the fraction of images (or tracklets) which belong to IDs which presented on both cameras (some IDs can be presented only on one camera). For example, the latter varies considerably for different pairs of cameras in MARS (from 0.24 to 0.92).

Our experiments showed that the dataset-dependent choice of N_p influences the performance of fine-tuning. However, if we simply use $N_p = \alpha \min(N_1, N_2)$, where $N_{1,2}$ are the numbers of images (or tracklets) from two cameras, and α is a constant (we used $\alpha = 0.1$), then the final performance drops no more than by 0.5%. Thus, we used this simple method without assuming the availability of additional information.

3.2.2 Extracting Negative Samples

Now we turn to the extraction of negative samples since we need them in the triplet loss. When the positive samples are defined, the negative sample can be extracted in a practically unsupervised manner. The simplest way is to take images, which were observed together with one of presumably positive images at the same time on the same camera. Even more negative samples can be gathered if two cameras have strictly non-overlapping field of view. In this case, we can use all images observed simultaneously on both cameras as negatives for each other. Thus, in the following experiments we will assume that we can obtain e.g. 10 negative samples for each positive pair.

3.2.3 Batch Hard Modification

Previously described Batch Hard loss should be adapted to the usage with our method for selecting positive and negative samples, since we don't have complete information about positive and negatives samples for each image in the batch.

We also form $P \times K$ batches, but each of them contains K mutually positive samples (corresponding to one ID) and $(P-1)K$ images of other IDs, which are negative samples for first K samples (but we don't know, what images have same IDs among these $(P-1)$

K images). While the original Batch Hard averages over all $P \times K$ images in the batch, here we average over first K images, for each of which the hardest positive and negative samples are found. Consequently, this modified loss will be much noisier. In the following experiments with unsupervised fine-tuning, RMSProp optimizer (instead of ADAM which we used in Multiple datasets training) and a smaller learning rate appeared to be more efficient, since this modified loss is more difficult to optimize.

4 Experiments

4.1 Multiple Datasets

Let us start with testing the embedding training on multiple datasets with the following details. All the scores were computed without test-time data augmentation on MARS dataset. From the Duke dataset, we removed IDs, which belong to images only from a single camera. We found that such IDs only decrease the cross-camera Re-ID performance.

We underline that the models were trained on datasets which do not include MARS or Market-1501, but all scores are given for MARS dataset. So, we are focusing on the cross-base performance here. Table 1 shows Rank-1 and mAP scores for *BH-merge* and *BH-switch*.

Table 1. Rank-1 (mAP) scores on MARS for the embedding trained on different datasets

Method	*BH-merge*	*BH-switch*
Training sets		
Duke	0.401 (0.204)	
CUHK03	0.358 (0.189)	
Duke + CUHK03	0.427 (0.243)	0.455 (0.266)
Duke + CUHK + WARD	0.437 (0.247)	0.468 (0.269)
Duke + CUHK + WARD + VIPER	0.444 (0.252)	0.483 (0.296)

As can be seen, training the embedding on multiple datasets without fine-tuning results in better performance even in the case of *BH-merge*. Even if the embedding shows an inferior performance on some dataset (e.g. CUHK03 in comparison to Duke), adding this dataset to the united training set improves the cross-base performance. Adding VIPER [14] and WARD [15] datasets also improved the performance. One can also see, that our *BH-switch* method is better then *BH-merge* (by almost 4%).

4.2 Unsupervised Fine-Tuning

We used the model trained on CUHK03 + DUKE + WARD + VIPER as the pre-trained model for further fine-tuning. Its performance before fine-tuning was 0.483/0.296 (Rank-1/mAP). The tests were conducted on MARS dataset, which contains tracklets from 6 cameras.

We extracted presumably positive samples for each combination of cameras (15 possible combinations in total). Each of our "presumably positive" sample is a pair of tracklets from different cameras. We expect that most of our "presumably positive" pairs are indeed belong to the same ID, but of course we will have some fraction of errors. For each positive sample we choose 10 negative samples (random tracklets from the selected pair of cameras, which do not belongs to the ID of the first tracklet from our "positive" pair), which are easily available in practical situations. One should note that if a "presumably positive" pair is identified mistakenly, there is some possibility that negative samples will also contain errors (some negative samples can belong to ID of the second tracklet from the "presumably positive" pair).

First of all, we checked the fraction of real positive samples among selected "presumably positive" samples. This fraction varies from 0.6 to 0.99 for different pairs of cameras. For most of them, it is larger than 0.8, and the average value is 0.83.

The Rank-1/mAP scores after fine-tuning with our method appeared to be 0.566/0.355 meaning +8.3% improvement in Rank-1 over the model pre-trained on multiple datasets and +16.5% improvement over the best embedding model pre-trained on a single dataset. These results were obtained using the training set of MARS for fine-tuning. Since the goal is online unsupervised fine-tuning, both training and test sets are acceptable to use. So, we performed an additional step: we took the model fine-tuned on the training set and additionally fine-tuned it on the test set. The final scores increased to 0.592/0.380, so the overall improvement in Rank-1 is +19.1%.

Although our method is developed for real situations, in which tracklets are usually available, in many datasets they are absent, so we compare our results with [7] on Market-1501 dataset without tracklets. We also note that we didn't use dropout in our model here, because it leads to slightly worse results (unlike on MARS, because MARS contains incorrect labels). Here, we also used test-time data augmentation (see [9] for details). The comparison results are shown in Table 2.

Table 2. Rank-1 (mAP) scores on Market-1501 for the embedding and PUL trained on different datasets

Method	PUL (no fine-tuning)	PUL	Our (no fine-tuning)	Our
Training sets				
CUHK03	0.300 (0.115)	0.419 (0.180)	0.337 (0.143)	0.397 (0.183)
Duke	0.361 (0.142)	0.447 (0.201)	0.417 (0.175)	0.509 (0.238)
Multiple datasets	0.400 (0.170)	0.455 (0.205)	0.518 (0.208)	0.608 (0.350)

It should be noted that the baseline model for PUL was pre-trained on Duke + CUHK03 in the case of "multiple datasets". The authors [7] point out "we find that initialization using more labeled datasets does not noticeably improve re-ID accuracy. Sometimes, multi-dataset initialization yields even worse results than single dataset initialization". Thus, we consider the pre-training of our model on more datasets as an improvement.

It should also be noted that we performed fine-tuning of our model on a united test and training sets of Market-1501, because no labels are used, and in a real situation one is interested in the online fine-tuning. If we use only the training set for fine-tuning, the scores are somewhat lower 0.586 (0.333).

Since we and [7] use different baseline models, not the absolute scores, but improvements are of interest. From Table 2 it can be seen that the embedding baseline model is better (and thus actually more difficult for improvements), but also relative increase in scores are higher in our method both for multiple dataset pre-training, and for online fine-tuning. Indeed, PUL gains only +0.8% in Rank-1 due to the use of more datasets (in addition to Duke) during pre-training, and +5.5% due to fine-tuning on several datasets (with overall +9.4% in Rank-1 when switching from Duke-baseline to Multiple datasets-PUL). Our fine-tuned model gains +9.9% thanks to the pre-training on several datasets and +9.0% due to fine-tuning on several datasets (with overall +19.1% in Rank-1), which is considerably larger improvement in comparison to PUL (although PUL has superior improvement in the case of CUHK03 only).

5   Conclusion

In this paper, we have proposed two practical techniques, which help to improve performance of Re-ID systems in real situations, in which these systems should be applied to unlabeled images taken by new cameras placed at new locations. We model this situation by the cross-dataset testing using different public datasets, and take the metric embedding learning with the triplet loss function as a baseline model.

The first technique consists in a special formation of batches using images from several datasets. The main idea is not to feed images from different datasets to the embedding network simultaneously, so the model will learn to distinguish different IDs from the same dataset, but not to distinguish datasets. As a result, we achieved +8.2% increase in Rank-1 score on MARS dataset due to the training on 4 datasets (Duke, CUHK03, WARD, VIPER) instead of using one best dataset (Duke). At the same time, simple merging of datasets yields only +4.3%.

The second technique consists in selecting presumably positive and negative samples to perform fine-tuning from the target unlabeled dataset, for which the Re-ID system should be applied. The main idea is to supplement best positive samples guessed by the model with samples, which appear with presumably positive pairs simultaneously in the video frames and which thus should be negative samples. Our fine-tuning algorithm results in +9% improvement in Rank-1 score on MARS and Market datasets (with the assumption that we can obtain 10 negative examples for each presumably positive pair).

The overall improvement in Rank-1 on MARS and Market-1501 achieved by switching from the baseline embedding model trained on Duke to the fine-tuned model pre-trained on several datasets was +19.1%, which is much higher than +9.4% achieved by PUL [7].

References

1. Bedagkar-Gala, A., Shah, S.K.: A survey of approaches and trends in person re-identification. Image Vis. Comput. **32**, 270–286 (2014)
2. Zheng, L., Yang, Y., Hauptmann, A.G.: Person re-identification: past, present and future. arXiv:1610.02984 [cs.CV] (2016)
3. Zheng, L., Shen, L., Tian, L., Wang, S., Wang, J., Bu, J., Tian, Q.: Scalable person re-identification: a benchmark. In: IEEE International Conference on Computer Vision (2015)
4. Zheng, L., Bie, Z., Sun, Y., Wang, J., Su, C., Wang, S., Tian, Q.: MARS: a video benchmark for large-scale person re-identification. In: Leibe, B., Matas, J., Sebe, N., Welling, M. (eds.) ECCV 2016. LNCS, vol. 9910, pp. 868–884. Springer, Cham (2016). https://doi.org/10.1007/978-3-319-46466-4_52
5. Li, W., Zhao, R., Xiao, T., Wang, X.: DeepreID: deep filter pairing neural network for person re-identification. In: 2014 IEEE Conference on Computer Vision and Pattern Recognition (CVPR), pp. 152–159 (2014)
6. Zheng, Z., Zheng, L., Yang, Y.: Unlabeled samples generated by GAN improve the person re-identification baseline in vitro. In: CoRR (2017)
7. Fan, H., Zheng, L., Yang, Y.: Unsupervised person re-identification: clustering and fine-tuning. arXiv:1705.10444 [cs.CV] (2017)
8. Varior, R.R., Haloi, M., Wang, G.: Gated siamese convolutional neural network architecture for human re-identification. arXiv:1607.08378 [cs.CV] (2016)
9. Hermans, A., Beyer, L., Leibe, B.: In defense of the triplet loss for person re-identification. arXiv:1703.07737v3 [cs.CV] (2017)
10. Howard, A.G., et al.: MobileNets: efficient convolutional neural networks for mobile vision applications. arXiv:1704.04861 [cs.CV] (2017)
11. Glorot, X., Bordes, A., Bengio, Y.: Deep sparse rectifier neural networks. In: AISTATS (2011)
12. Ioffe, S., Szegedy, C.: Batch normalization: accelerating deep network training by reducing internal covariate shift. In: ICML (2015)
13. Hinton, G.E., Srivastava, N., Krizhevsky, A., Sutskever, I., Salakhutdinov, R.: Improving neural networks by preventing co-adaptation of feature detectors. arXiv:1207.0580 [cs.NE] (2012)
14. Gray, D., Tao, H.: Viewpoint invariant pedestrian recognition with an ensemble of localized features. In: Forsyth, D., Torr, P., Zisserman, A. (eds.) ECCV 2008. LNCS, vol. 5302, pp. 262–275. Springer, Heidelberg (2008). https://doi.org/10.1007/978-3-540-88682-2_21
15. Martinel, N., Micheloni, C.: Re-identify people in wide area camera network. In: 2012 IEEE Computer Society Conference on Computer Vision and Pattern Recognition Workshops, pp. 31–36 (2012)

Keywords-To-Text Synthesis Using Recurrent Neural Network

Nikolaos Kolokas[✉], Anastasios Drosou, and Dimitrios Tzovaras

Center for Research and Technology Hellas, Thermi, Thessaloniki, Greece
{nikolokas,drosou,dimitrios.tzovaras}@iti.gr
pitygonos@gmail.com

Abstract. This paper concerns an application of Recurrent Neural Networks to text synthesis in the word level, with the help of keywords. First, a Parts Of Speech tagging library is employed to extract verbs and nouns from the texts used in our work, a part of which are then considered, after automatic eliminations, as the aforementioned keywords. Our ultimate aim is to train a Recurrent Neural Network to map the keyword sequence of a text to the entire text. Successive reformulations of the keyword and full text word sequences are performed, so that they can serve as the input and target of the network as efficiently as possible. The predicted texts are understandable enough, and their performance depends on the problem difficulty, determined by the percentage of full text words that are considered as keywords (ranging from 1/3 to 1/2), and the training memory cost, mainly affected by the network architecture.

Keywords: Deep machine learning · Sequence modeling
Natural language processing · Text mining

1 Introduction

Keywords-to-text synthesis appertains to the general field of the well known Natural Language Processing (NLP). NLP regards the understanding of a human language by the computer, and also, conversely, the ability of the computer to synthesize text or speech. Examples of applications include speech recognition, machine translation, text-to-speech synthesis, Parts Of Speech (POS) tagging and text summarization [1].

NLP research generally started in the 1950's, but machine learning techniques for NLP were firstly employed in the 1980's, when the tasks started to be solved by statistical inference instead of the former disadvantageous handwritten rules. Even more especially, deep learning was involved very recently [1, 2]. Most approaches are supervised, but recently semi-supervised and unsupervised approaches are investigated as well. In this paper the supervised option is preferred, because it demands less data to achieve desirable performance.

In this work the problem of keywords-to-text synthesis is addressed. Especially, our main goal is to provide a tool which, taking a keyword sequence as input, is able to produce a full text containing the keywords, or synonyms of them, in the same order. This synthesis facilitates the text composition, since it demands less typing by the user. The Recurrent Neural Network (RNN) is chosen as such a tool, since RNNs are

Published by Springer International Publishing AG 2018. All Rights Reserved
L. Iliadis et al. (Eds.): AIAI 2018, IFIP AICT 519, pp. 85–96, 2018.
https://doi.org/10.1007/978-3-319-92007-8_8

particularly appropriate for sequence modeling problems and they have many applications related to NLP, knowledge representation, reasoning and question answering [1, 3]. This paper concerns a supervised learning method and some full texts are used as a data set. As for the keywords, here they are defined as the least necessary words from which a unique full text can be inferred. Since such words are almost always verbs and nouns, the verbs and nouns are extracted from the texts using an available POS tagging algorithm. Finally, for the automatic synonym matching, a library containing a dictionary which includes synonyms for each of its words is used.

In this paper a relatively simple family (among those presented in [1, 2]) of an RNN is eventually employed. It is empirically confirmed that our text synthesis goal does not demand gated RNNs [e.g. Long Short-Term Memory (LSTM), Gated Recurrent Unit (GRU)], which deal with long-term dependencies, something rather irrelevant to this problem, where for a word production the present and a few neighboring input keywords and full text predicted words obviously suffice, as also shown by the results.

The remainder of the paper is organized as follows. In Sect. 2 related work is cited and the uniqueness of ours is briefly described. In Sect. 3 the preprocessing of our data set before training is presented, and in Sect. 4 our experimental results from several training approaches are shown and discussed. Finally, Sect. 5 summarizes our work and proposes possible next steps.

2   Previous Work and Motivation

In this section previous work is presented, related to the two coarse phases of ours: the keywords extraction from texts and the reproduction of the texts (text synthesis) from these keywords.

Considerable work on keywords extraction and text summarization is found in the bibliography, e.g. in [4–8]. The criteria of defining/selecting keywords, or even the goal, differ among references, so the methodologies are not directly linked and comparable with each other and with ours. The work of [4] is somehow relevant to ours, because in that paper the keywords are considered as the nouns (as characterized by a POS tagging algorithm) that imply many other nouns in the same sentence. However, the final aim in that work is not the text synthesis from the extracted keywords, which constitute a percentage of the total word number that is too small to serve such a goal. Thus, despite our inspiration by the cited keywords extraction methodology, it needed to be modified in our work. In [5] the purpose of keyword extraction is the classification (annotation) of texts, so words are evaluated by the number of families in which they appear and their mean frequency in them. In [6] keywords are defined according to their frequency and extracted from abstracts and titles. Finally, in [7, 8] keywords [7] or whole key-sentences [8] are extracted from texts according to several criteria, with the purpose of summarization. Particularly, in [7] a supervised and an unsupervised approach (both graph-based) are introduced for the extraction.

References about text synthesis regard mainly text-to-speech, speech-to-text and text-to-image synthesis. Regarding keywords-to-text synthesis, there is some work found about text generators based on keywords [9–11], where the meaning of the keywords or a categorization of them is necessary for their appropriate mapping to the full texts. Also, in those works the input of the text generator is either too complex for manual assignment [9, 10] or domain-specific [11]. In this paper the mapping model has been defined with the help of neural network (especially RNN) training, so that the manual specification of the meaning, category or part of speech of the input keywords is not necessary. In our methodology the input used for text synthesis is very simple; just a sequence of keywords, from the domain used in training, which may be any desired. So, a user may benefit from the provided tool even by assigning the input manually. Also, it is experimentally observed that our goal cannot be addressed by a standard encoder-decoder sequence-to-sequence architecture [1, 2, 12], which is too complex for our problem and not well-suited enough to it. (This is discussed more extensively in Sect. 3.5.) Other pieces of work on RNNs (some of which regard NLP) appear in [1].

3 Preprocessing Methodology

Apparently, the first step of the experiment is the definition of the data set. It should consist of texts of similar content, for the sake of sufficient training and appropriate evaluation. A family of steak recipes is constructed according to [13] and considered as such a data set, but any other content could have been selected. The used texts are 15, with a total length of 761 words. The first 9 of them are treated as the training set and the rest 6 as the test set. Two examples are shown below. Observe similarities and dissimilarities.

- "Mix garlic and oil in a bowl. Pour marinade into a resealable plastic bag over the steaks. Later squeeze excess air and seal bag. Afterwards marinate beef in the refrigerator for 4 h. Preheat grill for medium-high heat and bribe grate. Then remove meat from the marinade and shake off excess. Later discard marinade and afterwards cook steaks on preheated oven to desired degree for about 8 min."
- "In a bowl combine garlic, oil, sauce and sugar. Pour marinade into a resealable plastic bag over the beef. Later in the fridge marinate meat for 8 h. Preheat grill for high heat and then bake steaks to desired degree for about 60 min."

In the following, the dot and the comma are considered as separate words and all letters are treated as capitals.

In the rest of this section all preprocessing steps, included also in Fig. 1, are described in detail, as executed for our recipes data set. As mentioned above, first the verbs and nouns from all texts are extracted with POS tagging [14]. Afterwards, synonyms are detected and unified using an appropriate library containing a dictionary [15], and then some of the remaining verbs/nouns are automatically selected as keywords. Later, according to the extracted keywords, the texts are (also automatically) separated into chunks. Finally, the data are reformulated in a form acceptable by the network, which is taught using the training set. Our trained model is evaluated using mainly the test set.

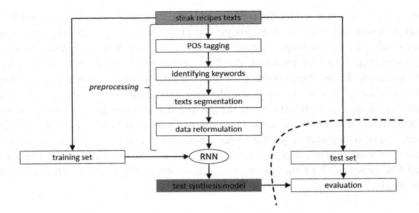

Fig. 1. Architecture of our work

3.1 Detecting Verbs and Nouns with Parts of Speech Tagging

In any of the employed texts the predicted nouns and verbs by the POS tagging algorithm (which was already available in [14]) plus the adjectives "high", "medium-high" and the numerical adjectives are initially treated as keywords. The participles with suffix "-ing" or "-ed" and the indefinite article "a" are prohibited from being considered as keywords, because it has been observed that they do not play a key role in a sentence. Therefore, no stemming by unifying words with the same prefix has been performed.

3.2 Unifying Synonyms

The elimination of the vocabulary to be used in the RNN not only may reduce the number of its parameters (weights), but it also decreases the size of the training set that is required for satisfactory results. Furthermore, by reducing the percentage of full text words that are considered as keywords, the mapping tool is rendered smarter, since less words suffice for the full text synthesis. Thus, only one word is attempted to be used for every group of synonyms, both in input and output/target. (The output is the prediction of the target.) The automatic identification of synonyms for the sake of training is subject to a library [15], which consists of a language dictionary providing meanings, translations, synonyms and antonyms of words. In the training scope two words are initially defined as synonyms when at least one of them is proposed by the library as one of the (up to 5) synonyms of the other one. However, this procedure leads to several wrong matches, so then the user is proposed to confirm which of the suggested pairs of words (s)he desires to be considered as synonyms (something subjective and dependent on the context, which is not taken into account by the library). This manual verification is practical only for a small training text corpus. Also, there are pairs of synonyms that are not identified, but this is not faced manually for training. For each finally considered group of synonyms, a representative is automatically selected to be used in training.

3.3   Other Keyword Elimination Measures

The preprocessing steps of the current and the following sections are programmed mainly from scratch, i.e. without employing some package.

For the further decrease of the number of keywords with respect to the sizes of the full texts, further elimination measures are taken for keywords. Particularly, it has been accepted that when two or more verbs or nouns always coexist in the same sentence, then only one of them implies the existence of the others. (An example is obvious in Fig. 2.) So only the first one is considered as keyword. Also, when the presence of a verb/noun always implies the presence of another verb/noun, even without the reverse holding, and the pair of these two words appears at least 5 times (in order to avoid cases of random coexistences), then optionally the second word is not considered as keyword (see also the term "degree of inclusion" in [4]). After this last optional measure, the non-distinct keywords constitute 31.8% of the total number of non-distinct words of the full texts. In case it is not applied, the keyword rate is 47.7%. Of course, the above implications depend on the data set. The remaining keywords are inserted into a single list (which will generate the RNN input during the data reformulation), and the extra keyword "." is introduced to separate adjacent recipes.

3.4   Segmentation of Texts

In the scope of preprocessing and training all words are replaced by their synonym group representative, and they appear in this way in the next figures.

Definition 1. A"chunk" is defined in this paper as a sequence of words (text segment) ending at a keyword and starting at the word after the previous keyword (or, if not any, at the first word).

According to this definition, a chunk may be seen as a part of a full text which is generated by a single keyword.

Fig. 2. Segmentation of a part of the first recipe shown in the beginning of the section into chunks according to the extracted keywords (colored). The noun "air" is not considered as keyword, because it always coexists with the verb "squeeze" in the same sentence. The word "excess" is an adjective in this context, but it has been mistakenly recognized as noun.

The full texts are divided into chunks. An example is depicted in Fig. 2. Our goal is to teach the RNN to map each input keyword to its chunk (with the additional help of the neighboring keywords and the predicted context), so that the full texts are automatically produced by concatenating the learned chunks.

3.5   Data Reformulation

Another interesting phase is to reformulate the data so that they suit an RNN.

The keywords and the corresponding full texts have to serve as input and output respectively in this work. Sequence-to-sequence models with and without attention [1, 12] were initially employed, but the result was fully unsatisfactory (worse predicted texts than the empty text, according to the measures of Sect. 4.2). A major mistake of such a model was that it was predicting many words multiple times, although these words were related to the respective chunks. This fact indicates that the sequence-to-sequence model is improper for word-to-word mappings, maybe due to the intervention of the context variable between the input and output. Therefore, a more appropriate, tailored idea has been implemented to resolve our problem. The model family used in this paper demands the input and output data sequences to have the same size. However, the keywords of each text are apparently less than all of its words, and also the chunks do not have fixed number of words. The consideration of a chunk as an undivided entity would not be a solution, because then the fact that same words appear in different chunks would not have been taken into account. That is, the output needs to be predicted in the word and not in the chunk level. The above issues are overcome by reformulating the keyword and text sequences, according to the first of the following steps. The second step regards the appending of the previous and the next keyword to each keyword, and the third one converts the words to vectors, so that they can be inserted in the network. All these steps are also executed automatically. The effect of the first two is clear in Fig. 3.

1. All training chunks are stored in groups according to their keyword, and empty words are inserted where needed such that all chunks of the same keyword have the same length, and same words are at the same position of the text segment (so that their alignment with the input is more appropriate). Then, the reformulated chunks compose the extended full texts (with the empty words inserted), which are con-catenated, forming an undivided sequence, that will be called "verbal target", since it is the verbal form of the network target sequence. In the RNN input the keywords are replicated in order to fit their chunk length. In our application the texts are artificial, and thus there was the possibility to construct a training set containing all the words of the test set. Auxiliary ordinal keywords are also created, indicating the serial numbers of the positions of each chunk, so that the prediction of every word of a chunk at the correct position is facilitated. Optionally, these numbers are bonded with the keywords, forming new words [e.g. the pair (oil, 2) becomes oil2].

2. As soon as the extended keyword list(s) resulting from the previous step has/have been constructed, two other auxiliary lists of the same length are created for the network's input, informing about the keyword of the previous and the next chunk. This step is based on our observations about the dependence between the current chunk and the neighboring keywords. Its advantage has also been inferred with trials.

3. The words are converted to vectors, so that they can be used by the network. In this step two approaches are examined and compared [1, 2] for the input and/or target words; a. a one-hot and b. a word embedding conversion.

   a. In the first one, the words are converted to one-hot vectors, (i.e. vectors with all their entries equal to 0 except one, which equals 1). This is applied for every

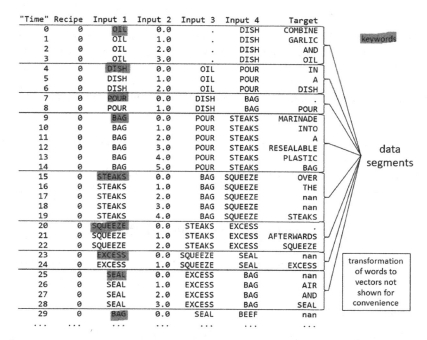

"Time"	Recipe	Input 1	Input 2	Input 3	Input 4	Target
0	0	OIL	0.0	.	DISH	COMBINE
1	0	OIL	1.0	.	DISH	GARLIC
2	0	OIL	2.0	.	DISH	AND
3	0	OIL	3.0	.	DISH	OIL
4	0	DISH	0.0	OIL	POUR	IN
5	0	DISH	1.0	OIL	POUR	A
6	0	DISH	2.0	OIL	POUR	DISH
7	0	POUR	0.0	DISH	BAG	.
8	0	POUR	1.0	DISH	BAG	POUR
9	0	BAG	0.0	POUR	STEAKS	MARINADE
10	0	BAG	1.0	POUR	STEAKS	INTO
11	0	BAG	2.0	POUR	STEAKS	A
12	0	BAG	3.0	POUR	STEAKS	RESEALABLE
13	0	BAG	4.0	POUR	STEAKS	PLASTIC
14	0	BAG	5.0	POUR	STEAKS	BAG
15	0	STEAKS	0.0	BAG	SQUEEZE	OVER
16	0	STEAKS	1.0	BAG	SQUEEZE	THE
17	0	STEAKS	2.0	BAG	SQUEEZE	nan
18	0	STEAKS	3.0	BAG	SQUEEZE	nan
19	0	STEAKS	4.0	BAG	SQUEEZE	STEAKS
20	0	SQUEEZE	0.0	STEAKS	EXCESS	.
21	0	SQUEEZE	1.0	STEAKS	EXCESS	AFTERWARDS
22	0	SQUEEZE	2.0	STEAKS	EXCESS	SQUEEZE
23	0	EXCESS	0.0	SQUEEZE	SEAL	nan
24	0	EXCESS	1.0	SQUEEZE	SEAL	EXCESS
25	0	SEAL	0.0	EXCESS	BAG	nan
26	0	SEAL	1.0	EXCESS	BAG	AIR
27	0	SEAL	2.0	EXCESS	BAG	AND
28	0	SEAL	3.0	EXCESS	BAG	SEAL
29	0	BAG	0.0	SEAL	BEEF	nan
...	...	...	...	...	...	...

keywords

data segments

transformation of words to vectors not shown for convenience

Fig. 3. Data reformulation corresponding to the first part of the first recipe shown in the beginning of the section. First auxiliary words are added to both the target and the first input column, so that they have the same length. (Empty words are represented as "nan".) Then, the serial numbers of the positions of the data segments defined by the chunks are appended as the second input column, and finally two other input columns are created (3, 4), giving information about the precedent and the upcoming keyword.

column (i.e. list) separately. Only the empty word is represented as zero vector instead of one-hot.

b. In the second approach, the words are represented as vectors of floats instead of one-hot vectors, as obtained by a word embedding (word-to-vector) algorithm [16]. In this way, not only the dimension of vectors may be reduced in comparison with the one-hot conversion, but also the distance of representations of all word pairs is determined by the degree of their context relevance. For the training of the word embedding model, the chunks of the training recipes have been used (since the training set contains all the words of the test set). Another option was to use a pre-trained word embedding model. This was examined with GloVe, which is considered as the most preferred by NLP practitioners [16]. As expected, the text synthesis results were remarkably worse, since the word-to-vector training was not based on the domain context. In case the keywords of the first input columns are not bonded with the serial numbers, every input word is also an output word, so word embedding may be applied both to the whole input and to the output/target.

With the above reformulation steps, the sequences of the RNN input ($x(t)$) and target ($y(t)$) are created. That is, $y(t)$ is the vector representation of the $(t + 1)$-th word of the verbal target sequence (assuming that t starts from 0), and $x(t)$ is the concatenation of the representations of the $(t + 1)$-th words of the input sequences. Although the argument t does not really stand for time in our case, it will be mentioned as such, because the data are sequential. The examined RNN predictive models belong to the family

$$y_{\text{pred}}(t) = f\big(\{x(t - i) \; : \; i \in I\}, \{y_{\text{pred}}(t - j) \; : \; j \in J\}\big),\tag{1}$$

where I, J are finite subsets of $\{0,1,\ldots\}$, $\{1,2,\ldots\}$ respectively. Particular assumptions have been made for the multidimensional function f [17, 18].

4 Recurrent Neural Network Training and Results

After the preprocessing of the data so that they suit the network architecture, training is ready to start.

4.1 Training Details

The Mean Square Error is used as cost function. It is proportional to the Sum of Square Errors, i.e.

$$SSE = \sum_{t \in T_{train}} \big[y(t) - y_{\text{pred}}(t)\big]^2 \tag{2}$$

where T_{train} denotes the set of "time points" of the training set.

A 2nd order iterative optimization algorithm (e.g. Levenberg-Marquardt, Broyden-Fletcher-Goldfarb-Shanno) is practical in our problem only in case of sufficient word embedding, due to its usually extreme memory cost (resulting from the Hessian approximations and the big input and output dimensions). Thus, a 1st order algorithm is employed otherwise.

Better results are achieved by setting the initial values of the model parameters to 0 than with random initialization. This is explained rather in the one-hot approach by the sparsity (big percentage of zeros) of the optimal model, which is anticipated due to the one-hot (or zero) encoding of the input and target.

4.2 Evaluation

As follows by the above, this work aims to resolve a classification problem using a regression model, so the continuous output has to be converted to a class (a word of the target vocabulary in our case). In the one-hot approach the output is converted to a one-hot vector by setting the maximum value of the output vector to 1 if the output vector's sum exceeds 0.5 (which indicates that possibly a non-empty word corresponds to that position), and to the zero vector otherwise. In the word embedding approach the output is converted to the closest vector representation of the target vocabulary.

The modified output is then compared to the target for the sake of evaluation and text production.

For vocabulary diversity in predictions, each predicted word is randomly mapped to one of its synonyms or itself. For the sake of evaluation, the pairs of synonyms that have not been identified by the library have been manually defined as synonyms.

For the evaluation of the model's performance, the following measures are used for each of the training and the test set. Both aim at quantifying the quality/correctness of the predicted texts, which are compared to the ground truth (i.e. actual) ones. However, these metrics do not consider the case of multiple correct syntaxes of a sentence, so they may admit a bit worse quality than real.

- Mean Word Error Rate (MWER): The widely known Word Error Rate (WER), common for NLP problems, is computed for each text (recipe) separately and the mean is taken as the evaluation measure. The WER equals the also well known Levenshtein distance between the ground truth and the predicted text divided by the number of ground truth non-empty text words.
- Mistake Rate (MR): This is a simple, heuristic measure similar to WER, but it never rewards the prediction of the correct word in the false position, even if the non-empty words are predicted in the correct order. It is the number of wrong predictions (in terms of time) for all texts divided by the number of ground truth non-empty words of all texts. A mistake is considered as single when an empty word is predicted as non-empty or vice versa, and as double when a non-empty word is predicted as another non-empty word. Apparently, the empty predicted text corresponds to an error of 1, as in the WER case.

4.3   Selecting Recurrent Neural Network Mapping Model

With intuitive trial and error and after search of several shallow and deep architectures (including also LSTM and GRU [17]), there is a general conclusion that one of the best models is the linear simple RNN with input delay 0 and output (direct) delays from 1 to 5, i.e. the shallow model

$$y_{\text{pred}}(t) = Ux(t) + \sum_{j=1}^{5} V_j y_{\text{pred}}(t - j) + b, \tag{3}$$

where U, V_j, b contain the weights. (The first 5 predictions are set as equal to the target values.) This intuition results from the fact that a word of a full text is dependent on the present and the neighboring keywords, as well as a few previous full text words. The use of even one hidden layer has proven to be completely helpless, since it leads to training and test errors comparable with those of the empty text. Consequently, the best architecture is found very easily. As for shallow gated RNNs, LSTM has comparable, but often slightly poorer performance, whereas GRU is even worse. Maybe LSTM would be the best if the average chunk length were higher (or, in other words, if the keyword rate were smaller).

4.4 Results and Discussion

In Table 1 the results of training the selected simple RNN of (3) [18] are summarized and compared to the best of LSTM [17] (shallow, stateful network with dropout and recurrent dropout equal to 0.01 and no feedforward activation), according to all possible approaches discussed above. In each case, one of the best numbers of iterations has been chosen. The optimization time of these executions ranges from a few seconds to a few minutes, and depends on the RNN type and dimensionality, the optimizer and the chosen number of iterations. It is worth mentioning that there are 66 distinct non-empty full text words after the unification of synonyms among the initial 73 distinct non-empty full text words. Word embedding, especially on the output/target, reduces the number of weights significantly. For example, all shallow simple RNNs have $O(n^2 + nm)$ parameters, where m, n are the input and the output/target dimensions respectively. This would be particularly important in case that more (and more complex) texts were used, where the need to save memory and computational time would emerge.

Table 1. Evaluation of best RNNs with test errors. IE/OE = Input/Output Embedding (+size), ICB = Input Columns 1 & 2 bonded, SRNN = Simple RNN with direct delays of orders from 1 to 5. The percentages in the headings denote keyword rate.

IE	OE	ICB	MWER 31.8% SRNN	MWER 31.8% LSTM	MWER 47.7% SRNN	MWER 47.7% LSTM	MR 31.8% SRNN	MR 31.8% LSTM	MR 47.7% SRNN	MR 47.7% LSTM
10	10	no	0.608	0.640	0.375	0.410	0.924	0.892	0.605	0.680
no	10	no	0.697	0.619	0.285	0.351	1.042	0.917	0.483	0.573
no	10	yes	0.319	0.311	0.111	0.168	0.378	0.373	0.203	0.220
20	20	no	0.354	0.489	0.262	0.342	0.479	0.627	0.407	0.515
no	20	no	0.378	0.501	0.233	0.325	0.484	0.651	0.400	0.494
no	20	yes	0.239	0.273	0.106	0.163	0.265	0.295	0.186	0.195
10	no	no	0.340	0.403	0.157	0.211	0.423	0.427	0.233	0.203
no	no	no	0.295	0.461	0.060	0.212	0.357	0.477	0.075	0.199
no	no	yes	0.229	0.335	0.017	0.069	0.232	0.357	0.017	0.071

A general remark is that the results worsen as the problem requirements (in terms of keyword rate -resulting from Sect. 3.3- and number of weights) strengthen. It can be subjectively inferred that when the keyword rate is 31.8% (which is the most useful and challenging scenario), the best choice is to apply embedding only on the output and not on the input, so that the first two input columns can be bonded (6th row of the table).

Word embedding training with the skip-gram instead of Continuous-Bag-Of-Words algorithm and use of hierarchical softmax yield the best results here.

The results with a Mean WER of about 0.3 can be characterized as quite satisfactory, because the meaning of the text is almost understandable. For an illustrative example, the prediction. "Preheated oven bake meat to desired extent for about 30 min." of the text "Preheat oven and then bake beef to desired extent for about 30 min." has WER = 0.29.

The variety of the keywords' order in some input sequence among recipes not only does not cause significant problem in training, but also results to an aesthetically appealing variety in the chunks order, which changes correspondingly.

5 Conclusion and Future Work

In this work a tailored and quite simple algorithm which, with a sequence of known keywords as input, is able to produce full text containing these keywords, or synonyms of them, in the same order, has been developed. This automatic mapping relies on an RNN model, based on some training texts, from which the keywords are automatically extracted with the help of a POS tagging algorithm and a dictionary library. The results, which depend on the problem difficulty, are rather satisfactory, because the meaning of the predicted text is almost clear.

So far it seems that the proposed methodology is applicable to any domain/ vocabulary, although the used texts have to be quite similar (maybe after deliberate editing), especially if they are few. A basic limitation is that when the test set contains words neither included in the training set nor synonymous of a training word, then the word embedding may be based only on a pre-trained word-to-vector model, which is then necessary to determine the chunk length of a new keyword as that of a training neighboring one. The new words need to belong to the domain of the training texts for effective training as well.

The text synthesis work done for steak recipes is going to be repeated for a data set from another domain, containing much more distinct and non-distinct words. By increasing the amount and diversity of texts, it will be interesting to examine the necessary word embedding size to yield fairly good results. Furthermore, there is an ambition that our program will be useful for everyday applications, like news production.

Acknowledgements. This work has been partially supported by the European Commission through project Scan4Reco funded by the European Union Horizon 2020 programme under Grant Agreement No. 665091.

References

1. Goodfellow, I., Bengio, Y., Courville, A.: Deep Learning. MIT Press, Cambridge (2016). http://www.deeplearningbook.org
2. Goldberg, Y.: A Primer on neural network models for natural language processing. J. Artif. Intell. Res. **57**, 345–420 (2016). https://www.jair.org/media/4992/live-4992-9623-jair.pdf
3. Sutskever, I., Martens, J., Hinton, J.: Generating text with recurrent neural networks. In: Proceedings of the 28th International Conference on Machine Learning, Bellevue, WA, USA (2011). http://machinelearning.wustl.edu/mlpapers/paper_files/ICML2011Sutskever_524. pdf
4. Shah, P., Perez-Iratxeta, C., Andrade, M.: Information extraction from full text scientific articles: where are the keywords? BMC Bioinform. BioMed Central **4**, 20 (2003). https://doi. org/10.1186/1471-2105-4-20

5. Andrade, M.A., Valencia, A.: Automatic extraction of keywords from scientific text: application to the knowledge domain of protein families. Bioinformatics **14**(7), 600–607 (1998). https://doi.org/10.1093/bioinformatics/14.7.600

6. HaCohen-Kerner, Y.: Automatic extraction of keywords from abstracts. In: Palade, V., Howlett, R.J., Jain, L. (eds.) KES 2003. LNCS (LNAI), vol. 2773, pp. 843–849. Springer, Heidelberg (2003). https://doi.org/10.1007/978-3-540-45224-9_112

7. Litvak, M., Last, M.: Graph-based keyword extraction for single-document summarization (2008). https://dl.acm.org/citation.cfm?id=1613178

8. Al-Hashemi, R.: Text summarization extraction system (TSES) using extracted keywords. Int. Arab J. e-Technol. **1**(4), 164–168 (2010). https://core.ac.uk/download/pdf/25749874.pdf

9. Kasper, R.: A flexible interface for linking applications to Penman's sentence generator. In: Proceeding HLT 1989, Proceedings of the workshop on Speech and Natural Language, pp. 153–158 (1989) https://doi.org/10.3115/100964.100979

10. Feiner, S., McKeown, K.: Automating the generation of coordinated multimedia explanations. Computer, **24**(10), 33–41 (1991). https://doi.org/10.1109/2.97249. http://ieeexplore.ieee.org/abstract/document/97249/

11. Bernauer, J., Gumrich, K., Kutz, S., Lindner, P., Pretschner, D.P.: An interactive report generator for bone scan studies. In: Proceedings of the Annual Symposium on Computer Application in Medical Care, pp. 858–860 (1991). https://www.ncbi.nlm.nih.gov/pmc/articles/PMC2247652/pdf/procascamc00004-0868.pdf

12. Brownlee, J.: How to develop an encoder-decoder model for sequenceto-sequence prediction in keras. https://machinelearningmastery.com/develop-encoder-decoder-model-sequence-sequence-prediction-keras/

13. allrecipes - Beef Steak Recipes. http://allrecipes.com/recipes/475/meat-and-poultry/beef/steaks/

14. Natural Language Toolkit (NLTK). http://www.nltk.org

15. PyDictionary 1.3.4. https://pypi.python.org/pypi/PyDictionary/1.3.4

16. Brownlee, J.: How to develop word embeddings in python with gensim. https://machinelearningmastery.com/develop-word-embeddings-python-gensim/

17. Keras Documentation - Models - Sequential. https://keras.io/models/sequential/

18. Atabay, D.: pyrenn: a recurrent neural network toolbox for python and matlab. Institute for energy economy and application technology, Technische Universität, München. http://pyrenn.readthedocs.io/en/latest/

Attention-Based Temporal Weighted Convolutional Neural Network for Action Recognition

Jinliang Zang[1], Le Wang[1(✉)], Ziyi Liu[1], Qilin Zhang[2], Gang Hua[3], and Nanning Zheng[1]

[1] Xi'an Jiaotong University, Xi'an 710049, Shannxi, People's Republic of China
lewang@xjtu.edu.cn
[2] HERE Technologies, Chicago, IL 60606, USA
[3] Microsoft Research, Redmond, WA 98052, USA

Abstract. Research in human action recognition has accelerated significantly since the introduction of powerful machine learning tools such as Convolutional Neural Networks (CNNs). However, effective and efficient methods for incorporation of temporal information into CNNs are still being actively explored in the recent literature. Motivated by the popular recurrent attention models in the research area of natural language processing, we propose the Attention-based Temporal Weighted CNN (ATW), which embeds a visual attention model into a temporal weighted multi-stream CNN. This attention model is simply implemented as temporal weighting yet it effectively boosts the recognition performance of video representations. Besides, each stream in the proposed ATW frame- work is capable of end-to-end training, with both network parameters and temporal weights optimized by stochastic gradient descent (SGD) with backpropagation. Our experiments show that the proposed attention mechanism contributes substantially to the performance gains with the more discriminative snippets by focusing on more relevant video segments.

Keywords: Action recognition · Attention model
Convolutional neural networks · Video-level prediction · Temporal weighting

1 Introduction

Action recognition and activity understanding in videos are imperative elements of computer vision research. Over the last few years, deep learning techniques dramatically revolutionized research areas such as image classification, object segmentation [7–9] and object detection [1–6]. Likewise, Convolutional Neural Networks (CNNs) and Recurrent Neural Networks (RNNs) have been popular in the action recognition task [6, 10–17]. However, various network architectures have been proposed with different strategies on the incorporation of video temporal information. However, despite all these variations, their performance improvements over the finetuned image classification network are still relatively small.

© IFIP International Federation for Information Processing 2018
Published by Springer International Publishing AG 2018. All Rights Reserved
L. Iliadis et al. (Eds.): AIAI 2018, IFIP AICT 519, pp. 97–108, 2018.
https://doi.org/10.1007/978-3-319-92007-8_9

Unlike image classification, the most distinctive property of video data is the variable-length. While Images can be readily resized to the same spatial resolution, it is difficult to subsample videos temporally. Therefore, it is difficult for the early 3D ConvNet [1] to achieve action recognition performance on par with the sophisticated hand-crafted iDT [18] representations.

In addition, some of the legacy action recognition datasets (e.g., KTH [19]) only contain repetitive and transient actions, which are rarely seen in everyday life and therefore have limited practical applications. With more realistic actions included (with complex actions, background clutter and long temporal duration), the more recent action recognition dataset, e.g., YouTube's sports, daily lives videos (UCF-101 [20]) and isolated activities in movies (HMDB-51 [21]), offer much more realistic challenges to evaluate modern action recognition algorithms. Therefore, all experimental results in this paper are based on the UCF-101 and HMDB-51 datasets.

Previous multi-stream architecture, such as the two-stream CNN [10], suffers from a common drawback, their spatial CNN stream is solely based on a single image randomly selected from the entire video. For complicated activities and relatively long action videos (such as the ones in the UCF-101 and HMDB-51 datasets), viewpoint variations and background clutter could significantly complicate the representation of the video from a single randomly sampled video frame. A recent remedy was proposed in the Temporal Segment Network (TSN) [12] with a fusion step which incorporates multiple snippets[1].

Inspired by the success of the attention model widely used in natural language processing [22] and image caption generation [23, 24], the Attention-based Temporal Weighted CNN (ATW) is proposed in this paper, to further boost the performance of action recognition by the introduction of a benign competition mechanism between video snippets. The attention mechanism is implemented via temporal weighting: instead of processing all sampled frames equally, the temporal weighting mechanism automatically focuses more heavily on the semantically critical segments, which could lead to reduced noise. In addition, unlike prior P-CNN [15] which requires additional manual labeling of human pose, a soft attention model is incorporated into the proposed ATW, where such additional labeling is eliminated. Each stream of the proposed ATW CNN can be readily trained end-to-end with stochastic gradient descent (SGD) with backpropagation using only existing dataset labels.

The major contributions of this paper can be summarized as follows. (1) An effective long-range attention mechanism simply implemented by temporal weighting; (2) each stream of the proposed ATW network can be optimized end-to-end, without requiring additional labeling; (3) state-of-the-art recognition performance is achieved on two public datasets.

---

[1] Snippets are multi-modal data randomly sampled from non-overlapping video segments, see Fig. 1. Typically, a video is divided into 1 to 8 segments. Segments are typically much longer than "clips" used by 3D CNN literature, e.g., the 16-frame clip in C3D [14].

2   Related Works

Human action recognition has been studied for decades, which were traditionally based on hand-crafted features, such as dense trajectories [18, 25] and sparse space-time interest points [26]. In the past few years, CNN based techniques have revolutionized the image/video understanding [1, 2, 4, 6, 10–13, 16, 27]. Per the data types used for action recognition, deep neural networks based methods can be categorized into two groups: (1) RGBD camera based action recognition, usually with skeleton data and depth/3D point clouds information [15, 28, 29]; (2) conventional video camera based action recognition.

RGBD camera based action recognition offers 3D information, which is a valuable addition to the conventional RGB channels. Such datasets are usually captured by the Microsoft Xbox One Kinect Cameras, such as The Kinetics dataset [15]. Despite its obvious advantage, there are some limiting factors which restrict such model from wide applications. RGBD video datasets are relatively new and labelled ones are not always readily available. A huge backlog of videos captured by conventional RGB camcorders cannot be parsed by such methods due to modality mismatch [30]. In addition, pure pose/skeleton based pipelines rarely achieve recognition accuracy on par with RGB video frame based pipelines [31, 32], making them more suitable for an auxiliary system to existing ones.

Inspired by the success of computer vision with still RGB images, many researchers have proposed numerous methods for the conventional RGB video camera based action recognition. Ji et al. [1] extend regular 2D CNN to 3D, with promising performances achieved on small video datasets. Simonyan and Zisserman [10] propose the two-stream CNN, with each steam being a regular 2D CNN. The innovation is primarily in the second CNN steam, which parses a stack of optical flow images that contain temporal information. Since then, optical flow is routinely used as the secondary modality in action recognition. Meanwhile, 3D CNN has evolved, too. Tran et al. [14] modified traditional 2D convolution kernels and proposed the C3D network for spatiotemporal feature learning. Feichtenhofer et al. [16] discovered one of the limiting factors in the two-stream CNN architecture, only a single video frame is randomly selected from a video as the input of the RGB image stream. They proposed five variants of fusing spatial CNN stream and two variants for the temporal steam. Additionally, Donahue et al. [13] developed a recurrent architecture (LRCN) to boost the temporal discretion. Consecutive video frames are loaded with redundant information and noises, therefore, they argue that temporal discretion via LRCN is critical to action recognition. Some recent literature also proposed new architectures with special considerations for temporal discretion [12, 17, 33, 34].

3   Formulation

Firstly, the temporally structured video representation is introduced, followed by the temporal attention model and the proposed ATW framework.

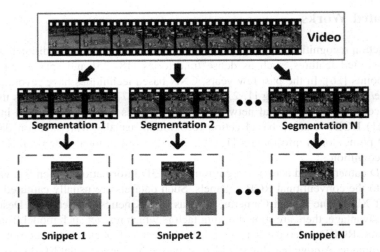

Fig. 1. Snippet generation with a fixed target number (*N*) of chunks. A video is evenly portioned into N non-overlapping segments. Each segment contains approximately the same number of video frames. As shown above, 2 additional modalities derived from RGB video frames are also included, i.e., optical flows and warped optical flows. RGB, optical flow and warped optical flow images sampled from the same segment are grouped in a snippet.

3.1 Temporally Structured Representation of Action

How do various CNN based architectures incorporate the capacity to extract se- mantic information in the time domain? According to the previous two-stream CNN [10] literature, there are generally 3 sampling strategies: (1) dense sampling in time domain, the network inputs are consecutive video frames covering the entire video; (2) spare sampling one frame out of τ ($\tau \geq 2$) frames, *i.e.*, frames at time instants $0, t, t + \tau$, $t + 2\tau,..., t + N\tau$ are sampled; (3) with a target number of N segments[2], non-overlapping segments are obtained by evenly partition the video into N such chunks, as illustrated in Fig. 1.

As noted by [12, 13, 16], the dense temporal sampling scheme is suboptimal, with consecutive video frames containing redundant and maybe irrelevant information, recognition performance is likely to be compromised. For the sparse sampling strategy with τ intervals, the choice of τ is a non-trivial problem. With τ too small, it degrades to the dense sampling; with τ too large, some critical discriminative information might get lost. Therefore, the third sampling scheme with fixed target segments is arguably the advisable choice, given the segment number N is reasonably chosen.

Suppose a video V is equally partitioned into N segments, *i.e.*, $V = \{S_k\}_{k=1}^{N}$, where S_k is the k-th segment. Inspired by [10, 12, 35], multi-modality processing is beneficial.

---

[2] Typical N values are from 1 to 8.

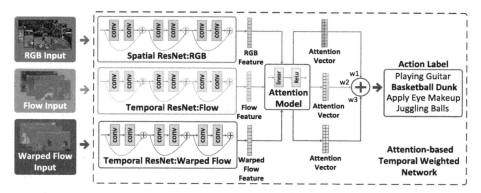

Fig. 2. Proposed ATW network architecture. Three CNN streams are used to process spatial RGB images, temporal optical flow images, and temporal warped optical flow images, respectively. An attention model is employed to assign temporal weights between snippets for each stream/modality. Weighted sum is used to fuse predictions from the three streams/modalities.

Therefore, three modalities (RGB video frame, optical flow image and warped optical flow image[3]) are included in our proposed ATW network.

One RGB video frame, five optical flow image and five warped optical flow images are randomly sampled from each segment S_k, as illustrated in Fig. 1, and respectively used as the inputs to the spatial RGB ResNet stream, temporal flow ResNet stream, and temporal warped flow ResNet stream, as shown in Fig. 2. RGB, optical flow and warped optical flow images sampled from the same video segment are grouped in a snippet. Each snippet is processed by the proposed 3-stream ATW network and a per-snippet action probability is obtained. After processing all snippets, a series of temporal weights are learned via the attention model, which are used to fuse per-snippet probabilities into video-level predictions.

3.2   Temporal Attention Model

The proposed ATW network architecture is presented in Fig. 2. Our base CNN is the ResNet [36] or BN-Inception [37], which are both pre-trained on the ImageNet dataset [38]. During the training phase, every labeled input video V is uniformly partitioned into N segments, *i.e.*, $V = \{M_i^{RGB}, M_i^{F}, M_i^{RWF}, y\}_{1=1}^{N}$, where $M_i^{RGB}, M_i^{F}, M_i^{RWF}$ represent the RGB, optical flow and warped optical flow images from the i-th snippet, with y being the corresponding action label. The 3 CNN stream ($C_{RGB}, C_F,$ and C_{WF}) map each input to corresponding feature vector as

$$C_{RGB}\left(M_i^{RGB}\right) = \mathbf{a}_i^{RGB}$$

---

[3] As in [18], warped optical flow is obtained by compensating camera motion by an estimated homography matrix.

$$C_F\left(M_i^F\right) = \mathbf{a}_i^F,\tag{1}$$

$$C_{WF}\left(M_i^{WF}\right) = \mathbf{a}_i^{WF},$$

$$i = 1,\ldots,N,$$

where we call these $a_{att}^{RGB}, a_{att}^F, a_{att}^{WF}$ action feature vectors, and use $\mathbf{a}_i$ to represent any given one from the 3 modalities. Note that w_i is the expected importance value of the ith snippet relative to the entire video. Evidently, if $w_i \equiv \frac{1}{N}$, the attention model degrades to naive averaging. The weight w_i is computed by the attention model f_{att} by a multi-layer perceptron conditioned on the previous fully-connected hidden state (*i.e.*, $\mathbf{w}_{att}$). The value of weight w_i decides which part of the segments should to pay attention to. Formally, the attention model f_{att} is defined as

$$e^i = f_{att}(\mathbf{w}_{att}, \mathbf{a}_i) = \mathbf{w}_{att}^{\mathbf{T}}\mathbf{a}_i.\tag{2}$$

The weight w_i of each action vector is computed by

$$w_i = \frac{\exp e_i}{\sum_j \exp e_j}\tag{3}$$

where each w_i are normalized by passing through a softmax function, which guarantees they are positive with $\sum_i w_i = 1$. Finally, the attention mechanism φ is implemented with a linear layer followed by a rectifier (ReLu), which serve as a temporal weighting function that aggregates all the per-snippet prediction probabilities into a per-video prediction. After training, the attention model obtains a set of non-negative weights $\{w_i\}_{i=1}^N$, so the weighted attention feature is obtained by

$$A_{att}^{RGB} = \varphi\left(\mathbf{a}_1^{RGB},\ldots,\mathbf{a}_N^{RGB}\right) = \sum_i w_i\mathbf{a}_i^{RGB},$$

$$A_{att}^F = \varphi\left(\mathbf{a}_1^F,\ldots,\mathbf{a}_N^F\right) = \sum_i w_i\mathbf{a}_i^F,\tag{4}$$

$$A_{att}^{WF} = \varphi\left(\mathbf{a}_1^{WF},\ldots,\mathbf{a}_N^{WF}\right) = \sum_i w_i\mathbf{a}_i^{WF}$$

For better readability, we give this new action feature vector $\mathbf{A}_{att}$ a name as attention vector. To emphasize, the attention model directly computes a soft alignment, so that the gradient of the loss function is trained by backpropagation.

3.3   Implementation Details

During the training phase, images from all three modalities (RGB, optical flow and warped optical flow) are cropped to 224×224. We employ cross modality pre-training [12]. Firstly, the spatial stream (ResNet or BN-Inception) is pre-trained on the

ImageNet image dataset. Subsequently, these pre-trained weights are used to initialize all 3 streams in the ATW. Each stream of the proposed ATW is trained independently. We use a single frame (1) and a stack of (5) consecutive (warped) optical flow frame as inputs. Based on the standard cross-entropy loss function, the SGD algorithm is used with a mini-batch size of 128 videos. We use an initial learning rate of 0.001 for the spatial stream and 0.005 for both temporal streams. For spatial stream, the learning rate is multiplied by a factor of 0.1 every 2000 iterations. For both temporal streams, the learning rate decay is divided into stages. Learning rates are multiplied by 0.1 at iterations 12000 and 18000. All momentums are fixed at 0.9.

During the testing phase, with each testing video, a fixed number of snippets (80 in our experiments) are uniformly sampled. We use weighted average fusion (1, 1, 0.5 for the spatial stream, optical flow stream, and warped optical flow stream, respectively) to generate a per-video prediction.

Pytorch [39] is used in our experiments with optical flow and warped optical flow extracted via OpenCV with CUDA 8.0. To speed up training, 2 NVIDIA Titan Xp GPUs are used.

4 Experiments

Trimmed Action Datasets. We evaluate our approach on two popular action recognition benchmarks, namely UCF-101 [20] and HMDB-51 [21]. The UCF- 101 dataset is one of the biggest action datasets containing 13320 videos clips distributed in 101 classes. HMDB-51 dataset is a very challenging dataset with 6766 videos (3570 training and 1530 testing videos) in 51 classes. Evaluation on these two trimmed datasets is performed using average accuracy over three training/testing splits.

Baselines. Throughout the following section, we compare our proposed ATW network with the standard base architecture, mostly two-stream with the single segment of a video ($N = 1$). For network architecture, we choose the traditional BN-Inception [37] for comparison in experiments.

Comparison with Different Consensus Functions. Firstly, we focus on comparing the attention model from two optional consensus functions: (1) max segmental consensus; (2) average segmental consensus. The max and weighted average consensus function is injected at last fully-connected layer, whereas, average consensus can be used after softmax layer. On the other hand, our attention model is set before softmax layer. The experimental performance is summarized in Table 1. We implement these four segmental consensuses with the BN-Inception ConvNet [37] on the first split of UCF-101. The number of segmentation N is set to 4. We use the weighted average fusion of three-stream outputs to generate the video-level prediction. Average segmental consensus performs slightly better than max function. The best result is obtained by the proposed attention model. Thus it can be seen the usage of attention model significantly improves temporal structure for action recognition

Multi-segment. Specially, in Table 3, we use RGB modality for training on multi-segment temporal structure with BN-Inception ConvNet [37]. Note that if $N < 3$,

Table 1. Exploration of different segmental consensus functions on the UCF-101 dataset (split1).

Consensus function	Spatial ConvNets	Temporal ConvNets	Two-Stream
Max	85.0%	86.0%	91.6%
Average	85.0%	87.9%	94.4%
Attention model	**86.7%**	**88.3%**	**94.6%**

Table 2. Experiments of different initialization strategies for initializing the attention layer's parameters and several traditional activation functions on the UCF-101 dataset (split1). Specifically, $weight = 1/N$ ($N = 4$) equivalent to average consensus.

Initialization	Spatial-Stream	Activation function	Spatial-Stream
$weight = 1/N$	84.44%	tanh	84.91%
$weight = 1$	85.17%	sigmoid	85.29%
random Gaussian	**85.80%**	relu	**85.80%**

Table 3. Exploration of ATW CNN with more number of segments on the UCF-101 dataset and HMDB-51 dataset (split1).

Datasets	Spatial-Stream accuracy							
	$N = 1$	$N = 2$	$N = 3$	$N = 4$	$N = 5$	$N = 6$	$N = 7$	$N = 8$
UCF-101	83.33%	83.89%	84.80%	**85.80%**	85.29%	85.21%	85.04%	85.55%
HMDB-51	50.07%	53.33%	53.01%	**53.88%**	53.33%	55.36%	53.20%	53.14%

the model is oversimplified, and the performance on UCF-101 (split1) has seriously degraded. The attention model boosts the mAP with 85.80% on the UCF-101 dataset and 53.88% on HMDB-51 dataset ($N = 4$), resulting from the successfully reduced training error. This comparison verifies the effectiveness of the soft attention mechanism on long-range temporal structure.

Parameters Initialization and Activation Function. As we train the pro- posed ATW CNN, an appropriate initialization of the attention layer's parameters is crucial. We compare different initialization strategies: (1) the weight w_i is set to 1, bias is 0; (2) the weight w_i is set to $\frac{1}{N}$ bias is 0; (3) random Gaussian distribution initialization. In addition, on behalf of finding the most fitting activation functions, we tested several traditional activation functions in the attention layer. As shown in Table 2, on the UCF-101 dataset, 1 for weight and 0 for bias initialization achieves 85.80% on the top of the three.

Comparison with State-of-the-Arts. We present a comparison of the performance of Attention-based Temporal Weighted CNN and previous state-of-the-art methods in Table 4, on UCF-101 and HMDB-51 datasets. For that we used a spatial ConvNet pre-trained on ImageNet, the temporal ConvNet was trained by cross-modality pre-training. We choose ResNet [36] for network architecture. As can be seen from Table 4, both our spatial and temporal nets alone out- perform the hand-crafted

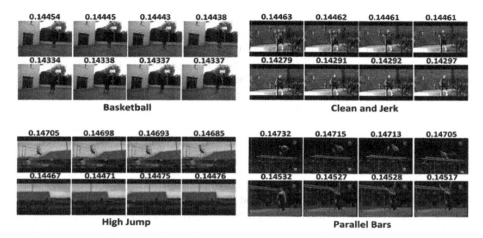

Fig. 3. Visualization of the focus of attention on four videos from UCF-101 dataset over temporal dimension. The model learns to focus on the relevant parts. The attention weight is given on top of each image. The higher the attention weight (w_i) of the frame, the more critical to classify the action.

Table 4. Comparison of our method with other state-of-the-art methods on the UCF- 101 dataset and HMDB-51 dataset.

HMDB-51		UCF-101	
Model	Accuracy	Model	Accuracy
DT [40]	55.9%	DT [40]	83.5%
iDT [18]	57.2%	iDT [18]	85.9%
BoVW [41]	61.1%	BoVW [41]	87.9%
MoFAP [42]	61.7%	MoFAP [42]	88.3%
Two Stream [10]	59.4%	Two Stream [10]	88.0%
VideoDarwin [47]	63.7%	C3D [14]	85.2%
MPR [48]	65.5%	2 stream +LSTM [11]	88.6%
FCN [43]	59.1%	FCN [43]	88.1%
TDD + FV [44]	63.2%	TDD + FV [44]	90.3%
LTC [45]	64.8%	LTC [45]	91.7%
KVMF [46]	63.3%	KVMF [46]	93.1%
TSN [12]	69.4%	TSN [12]	93.4%
Proposed ATW	**70.5%**	Proposed ATW	**94.6%**

architectures of [18, 40–42] by a large margin. The combination of attention improves the results and is comparable to the very recent state-of-the-art deep models [10, 12, 14, 43–48].

Visualization. To analyze the ability of the proposed attention model and to select key snippets from long-range temporal multi-segment, we visualize what the proposed model has learned on frame-level, which can help to understand the operation of attention interpreting the feature activity. We test our model on several videos to acquire the expected value of the action feature, which can map this attention back to the input temporal dimension. Figure 3 presents what input images originally caused an attention value. The first row shows the top ranked four frames with their corresponding attention weights, and the second row shows the lowest ranked four frames. The attention model pays more attention to the relevant frames than irrelevant frames, and this means that the attention model always focuses on the foreground over time.

5   Conclusion

We presented the Attention-based Temporal Weighted Convolutional Neural Network (ATW), which is a deep multi-stream neural network that incorporates temporal attention model for action recognition. It fuses all inputs with a series of data-adaptive temporal weights, effectively reducing the side effect of redundant information/noises. Experimental results verified the advantage of the proposed method. Additionally, our ATW can be used for action classification from untrimmed videos, and we will test our proposed method on other action datasets in our future work.

Acknowledgment. This work was supported partly by NSFC Grants 61629301, 61773312, 91748208 and 61503296, China Postdoctoral Science Foundation Grant 2017T100752, and key project of Shaanxi province S2018-YF-ZDLGY-0031.

References

1. Ji, S., Xu, W., Yang, M., Yu, K.: 3D convolutional neural networks for human action recognition. IEEE T-PAMI 35(1), 221–231 (2013)
2. Karpathy, A., Toderici, G., Shetty, S., Leung, T., Sukthankar, R., Fei-Fei, L.: Large- scale video classification with convolutional neural networks. In: CVPR, pp. 1725–1732 (2014)
3. Zhang, Q., Abeida, H., Xue, M., Rowe, W., Li, J.: Fast implementation of sparse iterative covariance-based estimation for source localization. J. Acoust. Soc. Am. 131(2), 1249–1259 (2012)
4. Ran, L., Zhang, Y., Zhang, Q., Yang, T.: Convolutional neural network-based robot navigation using uncalibrated spherical images. Sensors 17(6), p. 1341 (2017)
5. Abeida, H., Zhang, Q., Li, J., Merabtine, N.: Iterative sparse asymptotic minimum variance based approaches for array processing. IEEE Trans. Sig. Process. 61(4), 933–944 (2013)
6. Carreira, J., Zisserman, A.: Quo vadis, action recognition? a new model and the kinetics dataset. In: 2017 IEEE Conference on Computer Vision and Pattern Recognition (CVPR), pp. 4724–4733. IEEE (2017)
7. Le, W., Jianru, X., Nanning, Z., Gang, H.: Automatic salient object extraction with contextual cue. In: ICCV, pp. 105–112 (2011)
8. Wang, L., Hua, G., Sukthankar, R., Xue, J., Zheng, N.: Video object discovery and co-segmentation with extremely weak supervision. T-PAMI 39(10), 2074–2088 (2017)
9. Long, J., Shelhamer, E., Darrell, T.: Fully convolutional networks for semantic segmentation. In: CVPR, pp. 3431–3440 (2015)

10. Simonyan, K., Zisserman, A.: Two-stream convolutional networks for action recog-nition in videos. In: NIPS, pp. 568–576 (2014)
11. Yue-Hei, Ng, J., Hausknecht, M., Vijayanarasimhan, S., Vinyals, O., Monga, R.: Beyond short snippets: deep networks for video classification. In: CVPR, pp. 4694–4702 (2015)
12. Wang, L., Xiong, Y., Wang, Z., Qiao, Y., Lin, D., Tang, X., Van Gool, L.: Temporal segment networks: towards good practices for deep action recognition. In: ECCV, pp. 20–36 (2016)
13. Donahue, J., Anne Hendricks, L., Guadarrama, S., Rohrbach, M., Venugopalan, S., Saenko, K., Darrell, T.: Long-term recurrent convolutional networks for visual recognition and description. In: CVPR, pp. 2625–2634 (2015)
14. Tran, D., Bourdev, L., Fergus, R., Torresani, L., Paluri, M.: Learning spatiotemporal features with 3D convolutional networks. In: ICCV, pp. 4489–4497 (2015)
15. Chéron, G., Laptev, I., Schmid, C.: P-cnn: pose-based cnn features for action recognition. In: ICCV, pp. 3218–3226 (2015)
16. Feichtenhofer, C., Pinz, A., Zisserman, A.: Convolutional two-stream network fusion for video action recognition. In: CVPR, pp. 1933–1941 (2016)
17. Huang, J., Zhou, W., Zhang, Q., Li, H., Li, W.: Video-based sign language recog-nition without temporal segmentation. arXiv preprint arXiv:1801.10111 (2018)
18. Wang, H., Schmid, C.: Action recognition with improved trajectories. In: ICCV, pp. 3551–3558 (2013)
19. Schuldt, C., Laptev, I., Caputo, B.: Recognizing human actions: a local SVM approach. In: ICPR, vol. 3, pp. 32–36 (2004)
20. Soomro, K., Zamir, A.R., Shah, M.: Ucf101: a dataset of 101 human actions classes from videos in the wild. arXiv preprint arXiv:1212.0402 (2012)
21. Kuehne, H., Jhuang, H., Stiefelhagen, R., Serre, T.: Hmdb51: a large video database for human motion recognition. In: High Performance Computing in Science and Engineering, pp. 571–582 (2013)
22. Luong, M.T., Pham, H., Manning, C.D.: Effective approaches to attention-based neural machine translation. arXiv preprint arXiv:1508.04025 (2015)
23. Xu, K., Ba, J., Kiros, R., Cho, K., Courville, A., Salakhudinov, R., Zemel, R., Bengio, Y.: Show, attend and tell: neural image caption generation with visual attention. In: ICML, pp. 2048–2057 (2015)
24. Mnih, V., Heess, N., Graves, A., et al.: Recurrent models of visual attention. In: NIPS, pp. 2204–2212 (2014)
25. Wang, H., Kläser, A., Schmid, C., Liu, C.L.: Action recognition by dense trajectories. In: CVPR, pp. 3169–3176 (2011)
26. Laptev, I.: On space-time interest points. IJCV **64**(2–3), 107–123 (2005)
27. Ran, L., Zhang, Y., Wei, W., Zhang, Q.: A hyperspectral image classification framework with spatial pixel pair features. Sensors **17**(10), p. 2421 (2017)
28. Wang, J., Liu, Z., Wu, Y., Yuan, J.: Mining actionlet ensemble for action recognition with depth cameras. In: CVPR, pp. 1290–1297 (2012)
29. Du, Y., Wang, W., Wang, L.: Hierarchical recurrent neural network for skeleton based action recognition. In: CVPR, pp. 1110–1118 (2015)
30. Zhang, Q., Hua, G.: Multi-view visual recognition of imperfect testing data. In: Proceedings of the 23rd Annual ACM Conference on Multimedia Conference, pp. 561–570. ACM (2015)
31. Zhang, Q., Hua, G., Liu, W., Liu, Z., Zhang, Z.: Can visual recognition benefit from auxiliary information in training? In: Cremers, D., Reid, I., Saito, H., Yang, M.-H. (eds.) ACCV 2014. LNCS, vol. 9003, pp. 65–80. Springer, Cham (2015). https://doi.org/10.1007/978-3-319-16865-4_5

32. Zhang, Q., Hua, G., Liu, W., Liu, Z., Zhang, Z.: Auxiliary training information assisted visual recognition. IPSJ Trans. Comput. Vis. Appl. **7**, 138–150 (2015)
33. Yao, L., Torabi, A., Cho, K., Ballas, N., Pal, C., Larochelle, H., Courville, A.: Describing videos by exploiting temporal structure. In: ICCV, pp. 4507–4515 (2015)
34. Gaidon, A., Harchaoui, Z., Schmid, C.: Temporal localization of actions with actoms. IEEE T-PAMI **35**(11), 2782–2795 (2013)
35. Zhang, Q., Abeida, H., Xue, M., Rowe, W., Li, J.: Fast implementation of sparse iterative covariance-based estimation for array processing. In: 2011 Conference Record of the Forty Fifth Asilomar Conference on Signals, Systems and Computers (ASILOMAR), pp. 2031–2035. IEEE (2011)
36. He, K., Zhang, X., Ren, S., Sun, J.: Deep residual learning for image recognition. In: CVPR, pp. 770–778 (2016)
37. Ioffe, S., Szegedy, C.: Batch normalization: accelerating deep network training by reducing internal covariate shift. In: ICML, pp. 448–456 (2015)
38. Deng, J., Dong, W., Socher, R., Li, L.J., Li, K., Fei-Fei, L.: Imagenet: a large-scale hierarchical image database. In: CVPR, pp. 248–255 (2009)
39. Paszke, A., Gross, S., Chintala, S., Chanan, G.: Pytorch (2017)
40. Cai, Z., Wang, L., Peng, X., Qiao, Y.: Multi-view super vector for action recognition. In: CVPR, pp. 596–603 (2014)
41. Peng, X., Wang, L., Wang, X., Qiao, Y.: Bag of visual words and fusion methods for action recognition: comprehensive study and good practice. CVIU **150**, 109–125 (2016)
42. Wang, L., Qiao, Y., Tang, X.: Mofap: a multi-level representation for action recognition. IJCV **119**(3), 254–271 (2016)
43. Sun, L., Jia, K., Yeung, D.Y., Shi, B.E.: Human action recognition using factorized spatio-temporal convolutional networks. In: ICCV, pp. 4597–4605 (2015)
44. Wang, L., Qiao, Y., Tang, X.: Action recognition with trajectory-pooled deep- convolutional descriptors. In: CVPR, pp. 4305–4314 (2015)
45. Varol, G., Laptev, I., Schmid, C.: Long-term temporal convolutions for action recognition. In: IEEE T-PAMI (2017)
46. Zhu, W., Hu, J., Sun, G., Cao, X., Qiao, Y.: A key volume mining deep framework for action recognition. In: CVPR, pp. 1991–1999 (2016)
47. Fernando, B., Gavves, E., Oramas, J.M., Ghodrati, A., Tuytelaars, T.: Modeling video evolution for action recognition. In: CVPR, pp. 5378–5387 (2015)
48. Ni, B., Moulin, P., Yang, X., Yan, S.: Motion part regularization: improving action recognition via trajectory selection. In: CVPR, pp. 3698–3706 (2015)

Content-Aware Attention Network
for Action Recognition

Ziyi Liu, Le Wang$^{(\boxtimes)}$, and Nanning Zheng

Institute of Artificial Intelligence and Robotics,
National Engineering Laboratory for Visual Information Processing and Applications,
Xi'an Jiaotong University, Xi'an, Shaanxi, People's Republic of China
lewang@xjtu.edu.cn

Abstract. This paper presents a content-aware attention network (Cat-Net) for action recognition task, which can leverage attention mechanism to aggregate frame-level features into a compact video-level representation. Unlike most previous methods that consider every video frame equally, our CatNet contains an attention module which can adaptively emphasize the representative frames, and thus can benefit the action recognition task. Moreover, the CatNet can take an action video with arbitrary length yet produce a compact video representation with fixed length. The attention module consists of two cascaded blocks, an adaptive attention weighting block and a content-aware weighting block. The experiments are carried on two challenging video action datasets, *i.e.*, the UCF-101 dataset and HMDB-51 dataset. Our method achieves significantly improvements on both datasets compared with existing methods. The results show that our proposed CatNet is able to focus on the representative frames corresponding to a specific action category, and meanwhile significantly improve the recognition performance.

Keywords: Action recognition · Attention mechanism
Content-aware

1 Introduction

Recognizing human actions in various videos is a challenging task, and has received significant attention in the computer vision community [1–12]. From hand-crafted features based methods [4,5], to deep learning based methods [6–12], impressive progresses have been achieved in recent years. Similar with other computer vision tasks, the performance of action recognition has been significantly improved due to the emerging deep learning, especially the convolutional neural networks (CNN), based methods.

However, compared with the successes achieved by CNN in still image classification field [13–15,17], the action recognition task has not been fully explored yet. There still remains many challenges need to be further addressed. In order to

© IFIP International Federation for Information Processing 2018
Published by Springer International Publishing AG 2018. All Rights Reserved
L. Iliadis et al. (Eds.): AIAI 2018, IFIP AICT 519, pp. 109–120, 2018.
https://doi.org/10.1007/978-3-319-92007-8_10

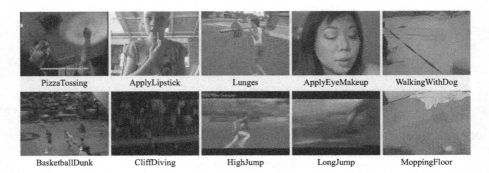

| PizzaTossing | ApplyLipstick | Lunges | ApplyEyeMakeup | WalkingWithDog |

| BasketballDunk | CliffDiving | HighJump | LongJump | MoppingFloor |

Fig. 1. Some example frames alone with their action category labels that are not suited for the action recognition task. In these cases, it is very difficult to predict the video category by a single frame. The first row consists of frames with semantic ambiguity, which can be easily mistaken for PlayingDaf, BrushingTeeth, CleanAndJerk, ApplyLipstick and Skiing from left to right. The second row consists of frames in poor condition, such as motion blur and poor illumination.

better recognize the action categories inside a variety of videos, the action/video representation should be discriminative and, more importantly, compact. Thus, one of the key issues is *how to construct a discriminative and compact video-level representation*. Hand-crafted feature based methods usually employ encoding methods, such as Fisher Vectors [16], to aggregate local hand-crafted descriptors into a global video representation [4]. With the benefit from the deep CNN, early CNN based methods propose to use a single frame to represent the whole video [6], or feed multiple frames into CNN and aggregate them with average or max pooling strategy [9,18]. In addition, [19] proposed to employ a long short-term memory (LSTM) network upon the CNN, which can model the temporal correlations among frames into a fixed-length representation. To further explore both the spatial and temporal correlations among video frames simultaneously, [20] first proposed the 3D convolution pipeline to handle related tasks in videos.

We argue that to effectively aggregate frame-level descriptors and construct a compact video-level representation, an adaptive content-aware aggregation method is vital. The motivation behind this idea is quite intuitive, *i.e.*, there should exist a subset of the video frames, which are more tightly related to the action category. Thus, we should emphasize these representative frames when aggregating the frame-level descriptors, in order to make the aggregated video-level representation discriminative. Figure 1 gives some example frames alone with their action category labels that are not suitable for the recognition task, due to semantic ambiguity or motion blur. These "bad" samples will introduce noisy information into the inference stage of the neural network [21]. These ambiguities should be suppressed during the inference process. Therefore, it is a natural sense to utilize the attention mechanism for action recognition, which can enable the whole network to focus on the representative frames and suppress the noises.

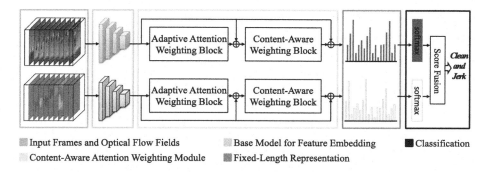

Fig. 2. Content-aware attention network. The inputs are video frames and optical flows. First, they are embedded by a CNN (base model). Then, the extracted features are aggregated by the proposed content-aware attention weighting module, and a fixed-length representation can be obtained. Finally, we use this representation to classify the input video, and adopt score fusion to obtain the prediction of the video.

We propose a content-aware attention network (CatNet) embedding an effective attention module to identify the representative frames from the noisy ones. The framework of the CatNet is illustrated in Fig. 2. The attention module consists of two cascaded blocks, *i.e.*, an adaptive attention weighting block which can adaptively weight all frames fed into the CatNet based on their extracted features, and a content-aware weighting block which is added to constrain the aggregation weights to be more consistent with the video content. To capture both the appearance and motion information, a standard two-stream structure is adopted, where each stream can be trained in an end-to-end manner.

The main contributions of this paper are:

- We propose a novel structure, namely CatNet, for action recognition, which achieves state-of-the-art performance.
- We introduce the attention mechanism to action recognition and validate it is beneficial for the action recognition task.

The rest of the paper is organized as follows. Section 2 reviews previous work related to action recognition. Section 3 presents the content-aware attention network for action recognition. Section 4 introduces the experiments and discussions. Section 5 presents the conclusion and future work.

2 Related Work

In this section, we review the related work in action recognition, mainly including hand-crafted feature based methods, and deep learning based methods.

2.1   Hand-Crafted Feature Based Methods

Before the prevalent of deep learning, hand-crafted feature based methods have dominated the action recognition filed [4,22–24]. Plenty of image local descriptors have been extended to the video domain, such as 3D-sift [25], HOG3D [26], and motion boundary histograms (MBH) [27]. The improved Dense Trajectory (iDT) [4] achieves state-of-the-art performance among these hand-crafted feature based methods. The iDT consists of multiple local descriptors extracted along with the dense trajectories where camera motion is compensated. To perform action recognition, the descriptors are then aggregated into a video-level representation by using encoding methods, such as Fisher vector [16].

2.2   Deep Learning Based Methods

Aggregating Frame-Level Features. Recently, the CNN based image descriptors have emerged as the state-of-the-art generic descriptors for visual recognition. To obtain a discriminative frame-level representation, the recent work on action recognition almost always extract the CNN feature as the frame-level descriptor, and then aggregate them into a global video-level representation. The aggregation methods can be roughly divided into two categories. The first one is to employ recurrent neural network (RNN) upon a frame-level feature extractor, such as LSTM [19]. By plugging RNN on top of CNN, temporal correlations within the action video can be easily captured, and a compact fixed-length video representation is then obtained. The other one aims to aggregate the frame-level features via different pooling methods, such as the average or max pooling over time [9], the vector of locally aggregated descriptors (VLAD) [10,28], and the temporal pyramid pooling (TPP) [29]. All these methods treat the frame-level features equally during aggregation, which may inevitably over-weight the noisy frames. To eliminate the negative influence from noisy frames, we propose to embed an attention module into action recognition, which can adaptively emphasize the representative frames while suppressing the influence from noisy frames.

Spatio-temporal CNN. The spatio-temporal CNN was first proposed in [20] and named 3D CNN, and later a number of its variants were proposed [8,11, 30,31]. The 3D CNN based action recognition methods take the video clip as input, and aim to model both the spatial and temporal correlations among the video content. Considering the 3D convolution brings extra kernel parameters, to fully train 3D CNN model usually requires massive video data and is time consuming, and thus 3D CNN is unsuitable to handle small dataset [11,18].

3   Content-Aware Attention Network

This section details the proposed content-aware attention network (CatNet). As shown in Fig. 2, our proposed CatNet takes a video with arbitrary length as input, and outputs a fixed-length video representation for subsequent action recognition task. The frame-level feature embedding is based on the CNN model, which is followed by an adaptive attention weighting block and a content-aware weighting block. These two blocks enable the CatNet to adaptively emphasize the representative frames and meanwhile suppress the noisy ones.

3.1 Frame-Level Feature Embedding

The frame-level features are extracted using the deep CNN, which embeds each frame of an action video to a fixed-length vector. Here, we adopt the Inception with Batch Normalization [32] as the feature extractor (base model). Note that our proposed attention module is not limited to a specific CNN model, other CNN models can also be used. The extracted d-dimension CNN features are first normalized by $L2$ norm and then fed into the attention module. Formally, given a video $\mathbf{V} = \{f_t\}_{t=1}^T$ with T frames, where f_t denotes the tth frame, the feature embedding can be formulated as

$$\mathbf{x}_t = \mathcal{F}(f_t; \mathbf{W}), \tag{1}$$

$$\bar{\mathbf{x}}_t = \frac{\mathbf{x}_t}{||\mathbf{x}_t||}, \tag{2}$$

where $\mathcal{F}$ denotes the base model and $\mathbf{W}$ denotes the parameters of $\mathcal{F}$. $\mathbf{x}_t \in R^d$ represents the extracted d-dimensional feature of f_t. $\bar{\mathbf{x}}_t$ is a normalized feature.

3.2 Adaptive Attention Weighting Block

As obtained the feature $\mathbf{x}_t$ of each frame f_t by feature embedding, our goal is to obtain a fixed-length video representation for video $\mathbf{V}$ by aggregating its frame-level descriptors $\mathbf{X} = \{\mathbf{x}_t\}_{t=1}^T$. Our adaptive attention weighting block first computes a corresponding weight w_t for each frame f_t, and then aggregates the frame-level descriptors into a fix-length video-level representation by

$$\mathbf{v} = \sum_{t=1}^T w_t \bar{\mathbf{x}}_t. \tag{3}$$

Here, the key is how to compute an appropriate weight w_t for $\mathbf{x}_t$ according to its importance. If $w_t = \frac{1}{T}$, then this block will degrade to average pooling.

There are two issues need to be considered when building the adaptive attention weighting block. First, the block should be able to handle videos with arbitrary lengths. Second, the block should be differentiable, *i.e.*, can be easily plugged into the current networks to perform an end-to-end training. Our proposed solution is to introduce a learnable kernel $\mathbf{k}$ with the same dimension as $\mathbf{x}$. Then, w_t can be calculated by

$$w_t = \mathbf{k}^T \bar{\mathbf{x}}_t. \tag{4}$$

Here, $\mathbf{k}$ actually serves as a scoring function. It is expected that if $\mathbf{x}_t$ is discriminative, w_t will be larger, and vice versa. In this way, the video representation $\mathbf{v}$ calculated by Eq. (3) will adaptively emphasize the representative frames and suppress the noisy frames during aggregation.

3.3   Content-Aware Weighting Block

To leverage context information, which is popular in image segmentation field [33,34], a content-aware weighting block is introduced to let the attention module select the discriminative features by considering the content throughout the video instead of single frames. Inspired by [35] for language modeling, we borrow the ideas from [35,36] and adjust it to the action recognition task. The content-aware weighting block can be formulated as

$$\mathbf{k}_c = \mathcal{C}(\mathbf{v}; (\mathbf{W}_c, \mathbf{b})) = \sigma(\mathbf{W}_c \mathbf{v} + \mathbf{b}), \tag{5}$$

$$w_t^c = \mathbf{k}_c^T \mathbf{x}_t, \tag{6}$$

$$\mathbf{v}_c = \sum_{t=1}^{T} w_t^c \mathbf{x}_t, \tag{7}$$

where σ denotes the sigmoid function and $\mathbf{k}_c$ serves as a new weighting kernel which is content-aware. $\mathbf{W}_c \in R^{d \times d}$ and $\mathbf{b} \in R^d$ are trainable parameters of this block. $\mathbf{v}_c$ is the final fixed-length representation of the input video.

3.4   Two-Stream Structure

It is critical to capture temporal information for action recognition. A common way to capture temporal information is adopting the two-stream structure [6,37]. We also employ this validated effective structure to combine the spatial and temporal features. Each of the two streams is constructed as described above, and can be trained in an end-to-end way. To fuse the scores from these two streams, the simplest weighted average fusion strategy is utilized.

4   Experiments and Discussions

We evaluate the performance of the proposed CatNet on two challenging action datasets, including UCF-101 dataset [38] and HMDB-51 dataset [39]. The UCF-101 dataset contains 13320 action videos in 101 action categories. Our evaluation on UCF-101 dataset follows the scheme of the THUMOS-13 challenge [40]. We use all the three training/testing splits, and report the average accuracy on them. The HMDB-51 dataset contains 6766 videos in 51 action categories. We follow the standard evaluation scheme with three training/testing splits, and report the average accuracy on them. We proceed to introduce the implementation details of our method, and then explore the efficacy of our attention module and compare with baseline method. Finally, our CatNet is compared with the state-of-the-art methods.

4.1 Implementation Details

We use the stochastic gradient descent optimizer to train the network, by setting momentum to be 0.9 and batch size to be 32. We implement a two-stream CNN framework with the spatial stream for RGB image inputs and temporal stream for optical flow inputs, as multi-modality inputs offer more information [9,41, 43,45]. We choose the Inception with Batch Normalization (BN-Inception) [32] as the building block for both spatial and temporal stream, because of its good balance between accuracy and efficiency. We adopt the partial BN with extra dropout layer proposed in [9] to avoid over-fitting. For the spatial stream, the weights are initialized by pre-trained models from ImageNet [42]. While for the temporal stream, we use the cross modality pre-training proposed in [9]. As to data augmentation, we employ the scale jittering technique [44] and random horizontal flipping. For the computation of optical flow, we use the TVL1 optical flow algorithm [46], which is implemented in OpenCV with CUDA. When fusing the scores from the two streams, we average the final prediction score of each stream with a weight 1 for spatial stream and a weight 1.5 for temporal stream.

4.2 Evaluation of the Proposed Attention Module

To validate the efficacy of the proposed attention module, we compared it with a baseline aggregation strategy, *i.e.* average pooling. The average accuracies for action recognition of them are summarized in Table 1. They showed that our aggregation strategy outperforms the average pooling on both of the UCF-101 dataset [38] and HMDB-51 dataset [39]. This clearly manifests that the proposed attention module can improve the action recognition performance.

It can be also seen that the performance improvement on HMDB-51 is larger than that on UCF-101. This is mainly because the videos in HMDB-51 contain more noisy frames that should be suppressed. Note that the improvement on temporal stream is less than that on spacial stream. This is because the optical flow fields contain less noise and are more discriminative than RGB images, especially for the action recognition task.

Table 1. The average accuracies by using average pooling and our aggregation strategy on the UCF-101 dataset [38] and HMDB-51 dataset [39].

Stream	UCF-101	HMDB-51	Stream	UCF-101	HMDB-51
Spacial (Avg)	85.5	50.9	Spacial (Ours)	**86.1**	**51.6**
Temporal (Avg)	87.9	61.1	Temporal (Ours)	**88.0**	**61.4**
Fusion (Avg)	93.4	67.8	Fusion (Ours)	**93.8**	**68.6**

Besides, to further verify the efficacy of the proposed attention module, we visualize what has been learnt by the attention module. Figure 3 presents some example frames sorted by their attention weights. They showed that the proposed

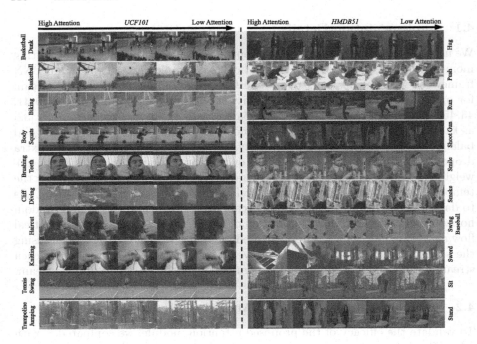

Fig. 3. Some example frames sorted by their attention weights from high (left) to low (right) along with their action category labels. The frames of the left part are from the UCF-101 dataset, and the frame of the right part are from the HMDB-51 dataset. We can see that the representative frames are assigned with higher attention weights compared with frames in poor conditions, such as motion blur (*e.g.*, Biking and Knitting), shot changing (*e.g.*, Smile), irrelevant clips (*e.g.*, Shoot Gun and Run), partial observation (*e.g.*, Brushing Teeth and Haircut), and semantic ambiguity (*e.g.*, Tennis Swing and Hug).

attention module can automatically pay more attention to the representative frames while suppressing the frames in poor condition, without providing any extra supervision during training. For example, in video "Hug", it is difficult to judge it is either hugging or hand shaking by the frames with low attention. However, the frames with higher attention can clearly reveal the hugging action. Similar examples can be found in other videos shown in Fig. 3.

Moreover, it is interesting to observe that our attention module assigns high attention to frames containing action "Stand" in the video labelled as "Stand", while it assigns low attention to frames containing similar action in other videos (as shown in "Sit" and "Stand" videos in Fig. 3). This validates that our attention module is content-aware.

4.3   Evaluation of the Proposed CatNet for Action Recognition

After comparing with baseline methods to validate the efficacy of our proposed attention module, it is also very important to compare our CatNet with other

Table 2. The average accuracies of our CatNet and other state-of-the-art methods on the UCF-101 dataset [38] and HMDB-51 dataset [39].

Method	UCF101	HMDB51
iDT+FV [4]	85.9	57.2
Spatio-Temporal ConvNet [18]	65.4	-
LRCN [19]	82.9	-
C3D [8]	85.2	-
Factorized ConvNet [30]	88.1	59.1
Two-Stream ConvNet [6] (VGG-M)	88.0	59.4
Two-Stream + LSTM [7] (GoogLeNet)	88.6	-
Two-Stream Fusion [37] (VGG-16)	92.5	65.4
Transformations [47]	92.4	62.0
TPP [29]	89.1	63.1
ActionVLAD [10]	92.7	66.9
LTC [31]	92.7	67.2
CatNet Spacial-Stream	86.1	51.6
CatNet Temporal-Stream	88.0	61.4
CatNet Two-Stream	**93.8**	**68.6**

state-of-the-art methods for action recognition. We present the average accuracies of CatNet and a variety of recently proposed action recognition methods on both UCF-101 dataset [38] and HMDB-51 dataset [39] in Table 2.

The results showed that, the two-stream version of CatNet significantly outperforms other state-of-the-art methods, although we adopt the simplest weighted average fusion strategy. Moreover, both the single stream versions of our method can achieve competitive performances, when comparing with the hand-crafted based methods (*e.g.*, [4]), LSTM based methods (*e.g.*, [19]), and 3D CNN based methods (*e.g.*, [8]).

5   Conclusion and Future Work

This paper proposed a content-aware attention network for action recognition, which leverages an attention module to aggregate the frame-level features into a compact video-level representation. Experimental results on the UCF-101 dataset and HMDB-51 dataset validated the efficacy of the proposed attention module and also the whole action recognition method, and demonstrated that the attention module can lead the content-aware attention network to adaptively emphasize the representative frames while suppressing the noisy frames.

For future work, we aim to extend our content-aware attention network to handle untrimmed action videos, where we argue that the attention module can play a more significant role. We will conduct extensive experiments on untrimmed videos to fully explore the efficacy of the attention module. Moreover, we only validate that the attention module can help improving the action recognition performance in this paper. In future work, we will extend the attention module to action localization or action segmentation task.

Acknowledgments. This work was supported partly by NSFC Grants 61629301, 61773312, 91748208, and 61503296, China Postdoctoral Science Foundation Grant 2017T100752, and key project of Shaanxi province S2018-YF-ZDLGY-0031.

References

1. Poppe, R.: A survey on vision-based human action recognition. Image Vis. Comput. **28**(6), 976–990 (2010)
2. Cheng, G., Wan, Y., Saudagar, A.N., Namuduri, K., Buckles, B.P.: Advances in human action recognition: a survey. arXiv:1501.05964 Computer Vision and Pattern Recognition (2015)
3. Herath, S., Harandi, M.T., Porikli, F.: Going deeper into action recognition. Image Vis. Comput. **60**, 4–21 (2017)
4. Wang, H., Schmid, C.: Action recognition with improved trajectories. In: ICCV, pp. 3551–3558 (2013)
5. Lan, Z., Lin, M., Li, X., Hauptmann, A.G., Raj, B.: Beyond Gaussian pyramid: multi-skip feature stacking for action recognition. In: CVPR, pp. 204–212 (2015)
6. Simonyan, K., Zisserman, A.: Two-stream convolutional networks for action recognition in videos. In: NIPS, pp. 568–576 (2014)
7. Yue-Hei Ng, J., Hausknecht, M., Vijayanarasimhan, S., Vinyals, O., Monga, R., Toderici, G.: Beyond short snippets: deep networks for video classification. In: CVPR, pp. 4694–4702 (2015)
8. Tran, D., Bourdev, L., Fergus, R., Torresani, L., Paluri, M.: Learning spatiotemporal features with 3D convolutional networks. In: CVPR, pp. 4489–4497 (2015)
9. Wang, L., Xiong, Y., Wang, Z., Qiao, Y., Lin, D., Tang, X., Van Gool, L.: Temporal segment networks: towards good practices for deep action recognition. In: Leibe, B., Matas, J., Sebe, N., Welling, M. (eds.) ECCV 2016. LNCS, vol. 9912, pp. 20–36. Springer, Cham (2016). https://doi.org/10.1007/978-3-319-46484-8_2
10. Girdhar, R., Ramanan, D., Gupta, A., Sivic, J., Russell, B.: ActionVLAD: learning spatio-temporal aggregation for action classification. In: CVPR (2017)
11. Carreira, J., Zisserman, A.: Quo vadis, action recognition? A new model and the kinetics dataset. In: CVPR (2017)
12. Huang, J., Zhou, W., Zhang, Q., Li, H., Li, W.: Video-based sign language recognition without temporal segmentation. arXiv preprint arXiv:1801.10111 (2018)
13. Krizhevsky, A., Sutskever, I., Hinton, G.E.: Imagenet classification with deep convolutional neural networks. In: NIPS, pp. 1097–1105 (2012)
14. He, K., Zhang, X., Ren, S., Sun, J.: Deep residual learning for image recognition. In: CVPR, pp. 770–778 (2016)
15. Ran, L., Zhang, Y., Wei, W., Zhang, Q.: A hyperspectral image classification framework with spatial pixel pair features. Sensors **17**(10) (2017)
16. Perronnin, F., Dance, C.: Fisher kernels on visual vocabularies for image categorization. In: CVPR, pp. 1–8. IEEE (2007)
17. Ran, L., Zhang, Y., Zhang, Q., Yang, T.: Convolutional neural network-based robot navigation using uncalibrated spherical images. Sensors **17**(6) (2017)

18. Karpathy, A., Toderici, G., Shetty, S., Leung, T., Sukthankar, R., Fei-Fei, L.: Large-scale video classification with convolutional neural networks. In: CVPR, pp. 1725–1732 (2014)
19. Donahue, J., Anne Hendricks, L., Guadarrama, S., Rohrbach, M., Venugopalan, S., Saenko, K., Darrell, T.: Long-term recurrent convolutional networks for visual recognition and description. In: CVPR, pp. 2625–2634 (2015)
20. Ji, S., Xu, W., Yang, M., Yu, K.: 3D convolutional neural networks for human action recognition. IEEE Trans. Pattern Anal. Mach. Intell. **35**(1), 221–231 (2013)
21. Lan, Z., Zhu, Y., Hauptmann, A.G., Newsam, S.: Deep local video feature for action recognition. In: 2017 IEEE Conference on Computer Vision and Pattern Recognition Workshops (CVPRW), pp. 1219–1225. IEEE (2017)
22. Laptev, I.: On space-time interest points. Int. J. Comput. Vision **64**(2–3), 107–123 (2005)
23. Dollár, P., Rabaud, V., Cottrell, G., Belongie, S.: Behavior recognition via sparse spatio-temporal features. In: 2nd Joint IEEE International Workshop on Visual Surveillance and Performance Evaluation of Tracking and Surveillance, 2005, pp. 65–72. IEEE (2005)
24. Sadanand, S., Corso, J.J.: Action bank: a high-level representation of activity in video. In: CVPR, pp. 1234–1241 (2012)
25. Scovanner, P., Ali, S., Shah, M.: A 3-dimensional sift descriptor and its application to action recognition. In: Proceedings of the 15th ACM International Conference on Multimedia, pp. 357–360. ACM (2007)
26. Klaser, A., Marszałek, M., Schmid, C.: A spatio-temporal descriptor based on 3D-gradients. In: BMVC, pp. 275–1. British Machine Vision Association (2008)
27. Dalal, N., Triggs, B., Schmid, C.: Human detection using oriented histograms of flow and appearance. In: Leonardis, A., Bischof, H., Pinz, A. (eds.) ECCV 2006. LNCS, vol. 3952, pp. 428–441. Springer, Heidelberg (2006). https://doi.org/10.1007/11744047_33
28. Arandjelovic, R., Gronat, P., Torii, A., Pajdla, T., Sivic, J.: NetvLAD: CNN architecture for weakly supervised place recognition. In: CVPR, pp. 5297–5307 (2016)
29. Wang, P., Cao, Y., Shen, C., Liu, L., Shen, H.T.: Temporal pyramid pooling-based convolutional neural network for action recognition. IEEE Trans. Circuits Syst. Video Technol. **27**(12), 2613–2622 (2017)
30. Sun, L., Jia, K., Yeung, D.Y., Shi, B.E.: Human action recognition using factorized spatio-temporal convolutional networks. In: CVPR, pp. 4597–4605 (2015)
31. Varol, G., Laptev, I., Schmid, C.: Long-term temporal convolutions for action recognition. IEEE Trans. Pattern Anal. Mach. Intell. (2017)
32. Ioffe, S., Szegedy, C.: Batch normalization: accelerating deep network training by reducing internal covariate shift. In: ICML, pp. 448–456 (2015)
33. Wang, L., Xue, J., Zheng, N., Hua, G.: Automatic salient object extraction with contextual cue. In: ICCV, pp. 105–112 (2011)
34. Wang, L., Hua, G., Sukthankar, R., Xue, J., Zheng, N.: Video object discovery and co-segmentation with extremely weak supervision. IEEE Trans. Pattern Anal. Mach. Intell., 2074–2088 (2017)
35. Dauphin, Y.N., Fan, A., Auli, M., Grangier, D.: Language modeling with gated convolutional networks. arXiv preprint arXiv:1612.08083 (2016)
36. Miech, A., Laptev, I., Sivic, J.: Learnable pooling with context gating for video classification. arXiv:1706.06905 (2017)
37. Feichtenhofer, C., Pinz, A., Zisserman, A.: Convolutional two-stream network fusion for video action recognition. In: CVPR, pp. 1933–1941 (2016)

38. Soomro, K., Roshan Zamir, A., Shah, M.: UCF101: a dataset of 101 human actions classes from videos in the wild. In: CRCV-TR-12-01 (2012)
39. Kuehne, H., Jhuang, H., Garrote, E., Poggio, T., Serre, T.: HMDB: a large video database for human motion recognition. In: ICCV, pp. 2556–2563. IEEE (2011)
40. Jiang, Y.G., Liu, J., Roshan Zamir, A., Laptev, I., Piccardi, M., Shah, M., Sukthankar, R.: THUMOS challenge: action recognition with a large number of classes (2013). http://crcv.ucf.edu/ICCV13-Action-Workshop/
41. Zhang, Q., Hua, G.: Multi-view visual recognition of imperfect testing data. In: Proceedings of the 23rd Annual ACM Conference on Multimedia Conference, pp. 561–570. ACM (2015)
42. Deng, J., Dong, W., Socher, R., Li, L.J., Li, K., Fei-Fei, L.: Imagenet: a large-scale hierarchical image database. In: CVPR, pp. 248–255. IEEE (2009)
43. Zhang, Q., Hua, G., Liu, W., Liu, Z., Zhang, Z.: Auxiliary training information assisted visual recognition. IPSJ Trans. Comput. Vision Appl. **7**, 138–150 (2015)
44. Simonyan, K., Zisserman, A.: Very deep convolutional networks for large-scale image recognition. In: ICLR (2015)
45. Zhang, Q., Hua, G., Liu, W., Liu, Z., Zhang, Z.: Can visual recognition benefit from auxiliary information in training? In: Cremers, D., Reid, I., Saito, H., Yang, M.-H. (eds.) ACCV 2014. LNCS, vol. 9003, pp. 65–80. Springer, Cham (2015). https://doi.org/10.1007/978-3-319-16865-4_5
46. Zach, C., Pock, T., Bischof, H.: A duality based approach for realtime TV-L1 optical flow. In: Pattern Recognition, pp. 214–223 (2007)
47. Wang, X., Farhadi, A., Gupta, A.: Actions transformations. In: CVPR (2016)

Cognition-Based Deep Learning: Progresses and Perspectives

Kai Yi[1,2], Shitao Chen[1,2], Yu Chen[1,2], Chao Xia[1,2],
and Nanning Zheng[1,2(✉)]

[1] Institute of Artificial Intelligence and Robotics, Xian Jiaotong University,
Xian, Shaanxi, People's Republic of China
{yikai2015, chenshitao, alan19960212,
xc06210417}@stu.xjtu.edu.cn, nnzheng@mail.xjtu.edu.cn
[2] National Engineering Laboratory for Visual Information Processing
and Applications, Xi'an Jiaotong University,
Xi'an, Shaanxi, People's Republic of China

Abstract. The human brain is composed of multiple modular subsystems, with a unique way interacting among each other. These subsystems have their own unique characteristics and interact to support cognitive functions such as memory, attention and cognitive control. Nowadays, deep learning methods based on the above-mentioned functions accompanied with knowledge are widely used to design more dynamic, robust and powerful systems. We first review and summarize the progresses of cognition-based deep neural networks, and how cognitive mechanisms can be applied to more brain-like neural networks. Then we propose a general framework for the design of cognition-based deep learning system. Although great efforts have been made in this field, cognition-based deep learning is still in its early age. We put forward the potential directions towards this field, such as associative memory in deep learning, interpretable network with cognitive mechanisms, and deep reinforcement learning based on cognitive science.

Keywords: Cognitive mechanisms · Deep learning · Attention
Memory · Knowledge · Decision-making

1 Introduction

In recent years, deep learning, characterized by learning large neural-network-style models with multiple layers of representations, has received lots of attention. Those models based on deep learning have achieved remarkable gains in many domains, including image classification [1, 2, 3], control and decision-making [4, 5]. [1] trained a deep convolutional neural network that nearly halved the error rate of the previous state-of-the-art methods on the typical image classification dataset. In recent years, [2] even surpass the human-level performance on several challenging classification datasets. In the field of decision-making, deep learning in combination with reinforcement learning, have been widely used to play games. [5] achieved several human even superhuman level performance on several games, illustrating that computer can master

L. Iliadis et al. (Eds.): AIAI 2018, IFIP AICT 519, pp. 121–132, 2018.
https://doi.org/10.1007/978-3-319-92007-8_11

go learning from scratch by trial-and-error strategies. These accomplishments have helped Deep Neural Networks (DNNs), the core of deep learning, to regain their status as a leading paradigm in machine learning. Nowadays, deep learning has shown more and more interests on how our brain works and how to develop a cognitive science inspired artificial intelligence system. The human brain doesn't learn through a unified undifferentiated neural network. It is composed of multiple modular subsystems, with a unique way interacting among. These subsystems have their own unique characteristics, and interact to support cognitive functions, such as memory, attention, language and cognitive control. What's more, the brain can combine knowledge (including internal knowledge from self-experience, environment knowledge by interacting with objects around, global knowledge extracted from the universe), with different cognitive functions to conduct complicated tasks with a few data. In this article, we review the latest progresses and future perspectives of deep learning systems based on the cognitive core elements, especially memory, attention and knowledge. In section two, we will review the fundamental concepts of deep learning, cognitive mechanism, and what deep neural networks can benefit from cognitive science. In section three to section five, we review and summarize the latest progresses of deep learning methods based on memory, attention and knowledge respectively. In section six, we propose a general framework of cognition-based deep learning and make assumptions of the essential future directions towards this field. In the last section, we'll make conclusions about all above-mentioned issues concerning cognition-based deep learning.

2 Fundamental Concepts

In this section, we will review the basic concepts of deep learning, cognitive mechanism, as well as the reason and the way that the former two are combined. We first introduce the core concepts of deep learning and it's foundations (i.e., two kind of neural works). Then, the major mechanisms of cognitive science, especially those that have been applied to more powerful deep learning systems will be presented. Further, we give some directions on how to build deep learning systems inspired or based on important elements of cognitive science.

2.1 Deep Learning

Deep learning is a kind of computational methods. It is composed of multiple processing layers which learn and represent the feature and the distribution of input data with multiple levels of abstraction, (i.e., different depth of feature map). Nowadays, the success of deep learning can own to two branches of well-designed neural networks: Convolutional Neural Networks (CNNs or ConvNets) and Recurrent Neural Networks (RNNs).

ConvNets are feature extractor indeed. They are very excellent at dealing with structured 2D arrays in areas like image processing. ConvNets achieved a state-of-the-art performance on image classification [1, 2, 3], image segmentation [6], and object detection [7, 8]. RNNs are excellent at dealing with sequence inputs, such as speech and language [9, 10]. RNNs process an input sequence one element at a time, maintaining in their hidden units a "state vector" that implicitly contains information about the history of all the past elements of the sequence. For more detailed explanations, please refer to [11].

2.2 Cognitive Mechanisms

Cognitive science is a discipline and a recognition of a fundamental set of common concerns shared by psychology and artificial intelligence [12]. The key point of cognitive science is the way we reflect to our environment and the effect of our brain activities. Our brain is composed of several subsystems, which interact with each other in a very complicated way. And they communicate to support cognitive functions, including attention, memory, language and cognitive control. The combination of the above-mentioned functions with knowledge extracted from self-experience, environments, intuitive psychology and physical worlds are among the key characteristics of human.

2.3 Combination

The most important elements of cognitive science are attention, memory and knowledge. The last one can be classified to internal knowledge, environment knowledge and global knowledge. Deep learning system can benefit from every element separately or together by increasing dynamics and target-oriented accuracy with fewer training data. Further, the cognitive science mechanisms are derived from human brains. Deep learning, which is regarded as the "black box", can be interpreted at the aspect of cognitive science, such as the view of decision tree [13] and the view of shape bias [14].

3 Deep Learning Inspired by Memory Mechanism

From the perspective of cognitive science and our intuitions, humans can learn in a continuous spatial sequence and memorize the pattern and characteristics. Therefore applying this mechanism to deep learning systems is of vital importance. How to guide those systems to memorize sequences of input and memorize according to the relative importance are two topics that will be reviewed next.

3.1 RNNs-Based Memory Model

RNNs is a type of artificial neural network where connections between units form a directed cycle. This creates an internal state of the network which allows it to exhibit dynamic behavior. Unlike feed forward neural networks, RNNs can use their internal memory to process and work on arbitrary sequences of inputs. This makes deep neural networks applicable to handle the data with rich structures, especially the sequences. It has been widely used in speech recognition [15, 16], natural language processing [10, 17] and object detection [18, 19].

Traditional RNNs structures have been used to deal with sequences of input mentioned above, but [20] found it is difficult to train RNNs to capture long-term dependencies because the gradient tends to either vanish or explode, which can cause severe effects. Long Short-Term Memory (LSTM) [21] and Gated Recurrent Units (GRU) [22] are two of the well-designed recurrent neural networks which can elevate this problem. The idea of those two RNNs is to design a more sophisticated activation function than an usual one, consisting of affine transformation followed by a simple element-wise nonlinearly part by using gating units.

3.2 Memory Model with Importance

In the process of human learning, the old stored information that we stored will be overwritten by new incoming information [23]. However, what we memorized are rarely with equal importance: frequently used and important knowledge is often prevented from being erased. Inspired by the memory mechanism, we think evaluating what is important and what is not behind the structure of a deep neural network is very meaningful. Elastic Weight Consolidation [24] used an approximation of the diagonal term of the Fisher information matrix to identify the important parameters for the task. While training a new task, a regularizer is used to prevent those important weights from being overwritten by the new task. The Fisher information matrix needs to be computed in a separate phase after each task and also needs to be stored for each task for later use when learning a new task. Thus, this model stores a large number of parameters that grows with the number of executed tasks. To avoid this, Improved multi-task learning through synaptic intelligence [25] adopts an online way of computing the importance of the network parameters. [26] formulates the importance of memorized information as the absolute gradient of the parameters in deep neural network based on the sensitivity of the predicted output to a change in this parameter. When learning a new task, changes to important parameters are penalized. The memory-based deep learning method shows the ability to adapt the importance of the parameters towards what the network needs (not) to forget.

4 Attention Mechanism Applied to Deep Learning

Human attention is a built-in mechanism for deciding how to apply their brain- power from moment to moment, (e.g., decide where to see in saliency visual object detection [27]). Attention mechanism is a reasonably well studied subject within the field of cognitive psychology and is known to be a key feature of human artificial intelligence [28]. Nowadays, attention-based deep learning methods are active especially in dealing problems concerning sequence prediction or control, including object detection, natural language processing, and deep reinforcement learning.

4.1 Natural Language Processing

The seminal work of natural language processing with attention was proposed by [29] for English-to-French translation. They used a novel neural machine translation model that implements an attention mechanism in the decoder, which achieved much better performance than traditional phrase-based models. In order to allow parallelization,

[30] proposed a highly parallelizable multi-hop attention module with convolutional neural network, which takes multiple glimpses at the sentence to determine what will be translated next, and a separate attention module in each decoder layer. Moreover, the attention mechanisms have been widely used in other language processing fields, like text classification [31, 32] and text understanding [33].

4.2   Object Detection

Attention mechanism in object detection decides which object or which field we need to see. Recurrent attention models are widely used to deal with the problem. [34] represented how an attention mechanism can be applied to ignore irrelevant objects in a scene and how an object can be "seen" by the system with the help of the attention mechanism. [35] proposed a deep recurrent neural network trained with reinforcement learning to detect multiple objects automatically. [36] found the attention models with deep neural networks are the insights gained by approximately visualizing where and what the attention focused on (i.e., what the model "sees") after feeding a sequence of data. Besides, attention models with deep learning are hot methods in several topics related to object detection, including saliency detection [37, 38] (detecting the most salient object and segmenting the accurate region of that object), eye fixation [39, 40, 41] (maintaining the visual gaze on a single location).

4.3   Deep Reinforcement Learning

Deep reinforcement learning is widely used in decision-making and control. Deep Q-Network (DQN) proposed by [4] showed a single algorithm that can outperform human or even superhuman performance on Atari 2600 games. By combining the attention mechanisms into DQN, [42] proposed the Deep Attention Recurrent Q-Network (DARQN). By combining what they called "soft" and "hard" attention mechanisms, the model greatly outperformed the traditional DQN. The attention network takes the current game state as input and generates a context vector based on the features observed. Then a typical LSTM network takes the context vector with a previous hidden state and the memory state to evaluate the action that an agent can take. Further, [43] improved on DARQN by implementing a multi-focus attention network where the agent has the ability to attend to multiple important elements. They proposed a novel model by using multiple parallel attention to attend to entities concerning the problem instead of just one attention layer in DARQN.

5   Deep Neural Networks with Knowledge

Humans can combine different kinds of knowledge in a complicated manner to solve very difficult problems without being trained with plenty of data. On the one hand, our brains use knowledge accompanied with other elements (e.g. attention, reasoning) to realize associative memory and build high-level concepts. On the other hand, the logical and physical constraints derived from our knowledge can be used to build a more robust model, especially towards solving natural problems as it can be influenced by too many factors. Briefly speaking, our knowledge originated from three different parts: self-experience (i.e., internal knowledge), surrounding objects (i.e., environment knowledge) and universe (i.e., global knowledge). Human brains process and summarize that knowledge into three categories: intuitive originates psychology knowledge, intuitive derives from physical knowledge and domain specific knowledge.

5.1 Intuitive Psychology

Humans gain plenty of psychology knowledge by interacting with the environment. Infants can understand mental states of other people like beliefs and goals, and this understanding strongly guides and constraints decisions that they make [44]. Besides, humans tend to assign the same name to similarly shaped items rather than to items with similar color, texture, or size by psychological experiments [45]. Those psychology intuitions can help create more interpretable neural networks and create a new area of one-shot learning. [14] found that several well-performed one-shot learning models trained on ImageNet exhibit a similar bias to that observed in humans: they prefer to categorize objects according to shape rather than color. Inspired by cognitive psychology, [46] proposed shape Matching Network (MN) with inception network, which has the state-of-the-art one-shot learning performance on ImageNet.

5.2 Intuitive Physics

Deep learning can learn features and patterns not only from plenty of labeled data, but also from physical laws. The limitation and constraints can help neural networks learn from fewer labeled data, even without any labeled data (i.e., un-supervised learning). Further, deep learning methods with physical constraints can help build high-level structural models and solve complicated scientific problems. In many fields, labeled data and long-time training is scarce and obtaining more labels is expensive. Constraint learning with physical knowledge is another active field of machine learning, which is aimed at uncover the hidden structure of models. By using physical knowledge, [47] trained a convolutional neural network to detect and track objects without any labeled examples.

5.3 Domain Knowledge

Regulating deep neural networks (DNNs) with human structured domain knowledge has been confirmed to be of great benefit for improved accuracy and interpretability with fewer training data. Recently, [48] proposed a general distillation framework that transfers knowledge into neural networks by combining first-order logic (FOL), where FOL constraints are integrated via posterior regularization [49]. Further, [50] used a generalized framework that makes it possible to learn procedure for knowledge representations and adapt their weights jointly with the help of the regulated DNN models. [50] proposed to transfer logical knowledge information into neural networks with diverse architectures such as recurrent networks and convolutional networks.

6 Perspectives

Cognition-based deep learning has become one hot research topic, and some of the most important functions of our human brains like memory and attention associated with knowledge extracted from experience and the universe, have been widely used in the design of a more human-like deep learning system. Meanwhile, the brain does not learn through a unified undifferentiated neural network. The brain is composed of multiple modular subsystems, with an unique and complicated way interacting among. Although deep neural network can process structural data well, it can't deal with dynamic clouds of data. What's more, data is very scarce in some fields. Deep learning systems can get a lot of inspirations from cognitive science, to alleviate and even eliminate those problems.

In this section, we will discuss the essential trend to apply more elements of cognitive science to build more dynamic, robust and intelligent deep learning systems. We are going to give a general framework of cognition-based learning firstly. Then we will discuss the key problems of fusing deep neural network with cognitive mechanisms and essential solutions.

6.1 General Framework of Cognition-Based Deep Learning

We suggest the general framework of designing cognition-based deep learning systems. This framework use cognitive mechanisms in a particular way. It can help build more dynamic, robust and intelligent systems. More accurately speaking, it can process unstructured data as constructed one with the help of our memory with concepts, especially associative memory. Further, the system based on the proposed framework can reasoning and infer based on the knowledge by gaining structural feature map with hierarchical knowledge sets in the top-down manner. Every layer in hierarchical knowledge sets is corresponding to each layer in the structural feature maps. As feedback is also very essential in our human brains, we can monitor this mechanism by designing two feedback loops.

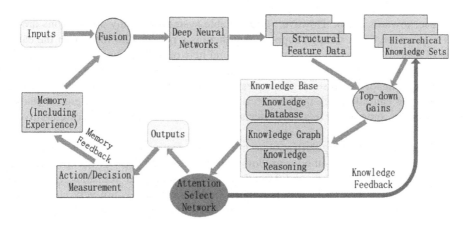

Fig. 1. General framework of cognition-based deep learning

One is knowledge feedback loop, to update our knowledge based on attention select network, which is aimed at deciding what we need to see. Another is memory feedback loop, to update our memory (especially the experience), and gains high-level concepts after measuring actions/decisions the system make. The general framework is shown in Fig. 1. The model based on this framework can be suitable for plenty domains such as image processing and nature language processing.

6.2 Key Problems and Potential Solutions

This part will discuss the future directions of cognition-based deep learning. It is organized by current problems and essential solutions.

6.3 Associative Memory

Human brains can associate patterns similar to the input patterns when being stimulated. Associative memory model was once prevailing in 1980s and 1990s, accompanied with the popularity of Hopfield Neural Network [51], a typical network that can store patterns and realize associative memory. Due to the potential chaos state of network evolution, HNNs alone is difficult to handle natural real-world problems well. However, it has the potential as it is an important kind of brain-like neural network. Besides, synesthesia is a typical perceptual phenomenon in cognitive science. That is, a person can activate a sensory when stimulated by another sensory (e.g., grapheme-color synesthesia means a person can directly associate a colorful image when listening to music). The proposition of an effective associative memory model by combining human-like neural network and synesthesia with deep learning is a promising direction. A recent successful attempt was Dense Associative Memory [52], which combined associative memory with deep learning and achieved a good result on MNIST dataset.

6.4 Interpretable Network with Cognitive Mechanisms

For we human, it's difficult to understand how deep neural networks work and how they react towards a task. However, interpretable systems in many applications are of vital importance. For example, suppose that there is a person who may be in the early stage of cancer, the system based on deep neural networks needs to infer whether he is suffering from cancer. We can gather all features of the person as the input of DNNs, such as age, history of disease. The question is why we can trust the output of this system as we can not check the correct- ness. What if the process of inference can be understood or monitored (e.g., the decision tree) by an expert? Interpretability is important in these fields.

[13] proposed a tree regularization to interpret the neural network in the perspective of decision tree. This method can not train towards the typical backpropagation learning rule as the tree is undifferentiated. They suggested replacing trees with multi-layer perceptrons in the training phase, but this solution is not very elegant and does not create a interpretable network indeed. According to psychological experiments

[45], humans tend to assign the same name to similarly shaped items instead of items with similar color, texture or size. [46] proposed shape MN with inception network, which achieved better performance than several state-of-the-art methods in the field of one-shot learning on ImageNet. And [14] found that this kind of networks that exhibits a similar shape bias to that observed in humans. Cognitive mechanisms like shape bias, decision and inference can help design more interpretable neural networks.

6.5 Cognition-Based Deep Reinforcement Learning

Deep reinforcement learning has raised a lot of interests nowadays. However, due to the uncertainty of the state space and the complexity of the reward function, it is difficult for the traditional trial-and-error strategies to associate continuous actions with reward. Imagination is utilized to make use of the knowledge embedded in the model. However, deep reinforcement learning is still in its early stage.

As decision making and feedback mechanism are very similar to that of humans, there is a trend to apply cognitive mechanisms to reinforcement learning. As for attention mechanism, [42] proposed the Deep Attention Recurrent Q-Network (DARQN), which greatly outperformed the traditional Deep Q-Network (DQN) on Atari 2600 games by combining what they called "soft" and "hard" attention mechanisms. Besides, [43] used a multi-focus attention network where the agent can give attention to multiple important elements. This model achieved better performance than the traditional DARQN. Further, [53] extended the typical LSTM-based memory network to choose more sophisticated addressing schemes over the past k frames by using memory mechanism. [54] proposed a spatially structured 2D memory image that is capable of learning to store arbitrary information about the environment over long time lags. As for our human knowledge mechanism, in which field we call usually transfer learning. What's more, a novel policy distillation (i.e., knowledge-based reinforcement learning policy) architecture was proposed by [55] for deep reinforcement learning. This architecture was well organized by implementing task-specific high-level convolutional features as the inputs to the multi-task policy network. However, how to hierarchically reconstruct the knowledge and uncover the hidden characteristics, how to abstract our knowledge and experience for the feasibility to deal with unstructured data by fusion, how to design a generalized attention selection network, may remain issues that lead the future research direction in this field.

7 Conclusion

Cognition-based deep learning has gained widely interests recent years. Several core functions of cognitive science (i.e. attention, memory) and knowledge, are used to design more dynamic and robust systems based on deep neural network. We reviewed the recent progress related to this field. Meanwhile, deep neural networks are not interpretable to our human brains. We can design a more interpretable neural network in the perspective of cognitive science. Finally, we proposed a general framework of cognition-based deep learning and made assumptions of the essential future directions towards this field.

Acknowledgment. This research was partially supported by the Programme of Introducing Talents of Discipline to University (No. B13043), the National Natural Science Foundation of China (No. 61773312, 61790563).

References

1. Krizhevsky, A., Sutskever, I., Hinton, G.E.: Imagenet classification with deep convolutional neural networks. In: Advances in Neural Information Processing Systems, pp. 1097–1105 (2012)
2. He, K., Zhang, X., Ren, S., Sun, J.: Deep residual learning for image recognition. In: Proceedings of the IEEE Conference on Computer Vision and Pattern Recognition, pp. 770–778 (2016)
3. Szegedy, C., Liu, W., Jia, Y., Sermanet, P., Reed, S., Anguelov, D., Erhan, D., Vanhoucke, V., Rabinovich, A., et al.: Going deeper with convolutions. In: CVPR (2015)
4. Mnih, V., Kavukcuoglu, K., Silver, D., Graves, A., Antonoglou, I., Wierstra, D., Riedmiller, M.: Playing atari with deep reinforcement learning. arXiv preprint arXiv:1312.5602 (2013)
5. Mnih, V., Kavukcuoglu, K., Silver, D., Rusu, A.A., Veness, J., Bellemare, M.G., Graves, A., Riedmiller, M., Fidjeland, A.K., Ostrovski, G., et al.: Human-level control through deep reinforcement learning. Nature **518**(7540), 529 (2015)
6. Long, J., Shelhamer, E., Darrell, T.: Fully convolutional networks for semantic segmentation. In: Proceedings of the IEEE Conference on Computer Vision and Pattern Recognition, pp. 3431–3440 (2015)
7. Ren, S., He, K., Girshick, R., Sun, J.: Faster R-CNN: towards real-time object detection with region proposal networks. In: Advances in Neural Information Processing Systems, pp. 91–99 (2015)
8. Liu, W., Anguelov, D., Erhan, D., Szegedy, C., Reed, S., Fu, C.-Y., Berg, Alexander C.: SSD: single shot MultiBox detector. In: Leibe, B., Matas, J., Sebe, N., Welling, M. (eds.) ECCV 2016. LNCS, vol. 9905, pp. 21–37. Springer, Cham (2016). https://doi.org/10.1007/978-3-319-46448-0_2
9. Graves, A., Mohamed, A., Hinton,G.: Speech recognition with deep recurrent neural networks. In: 2013 IEEE International Conference on Acoustics, Speech and Signal Processing (ICASSP), pp. 6645–6649. IEEE (2013)
10. Yin, W., Kann, K., Yu, M., Schütze, H.: Comparative study of CNN and RNN for natural language processing. arXiv preprint arXiv:1702.01923 (2017)
11. LeCun, Y., Bengio, Y., Hinton, G.: Deep learning. Nature **521**(7553), 436 (2015)
12. Simon, H.A.: Cognitive science: the newest science of the artificial. Cogn. Sci. **4**(1), 33–46 (1980)
13. Wu, M., Hughes, M.C., Parbhoo, S., Zazzi, M., Roth, V., Doshi-Velez, F.: Beyond sparsity: tree regularization of deep models for interpretability. arXiv preprint arXiv:1711.06178 (2017)
14. Ritter, S., Barrett, D.G.T., Santoro, A., Botvinick, M.M.: Cognitive psychology for deep neural networks: a shape bias case study (2017)
15. Sak, H., Senior, A., Beaufays, F.: Long short-term memory recurrent neural network architectures for large scale acoustic modeling. In: Fifteenth Annual Conference of the International Speech Communication Association (2014)
16. Miao, Y., Li, J., Wang, Y., Zhang, S.-X., Gong, Y.: Simplifying long short-term memory acoustic models for fast training and decoding. In: 2016 IEEE International Conference on Acoustics, Speech and Signal Processing (ICASSP), pp. 2284–2288. IEEE (2016)

17. Prakash, M., Ohno-Machado, L., Chapman, W.W.: Natural language processing: an introduction. J. Am. Med. Inform. Assoc. **18**(5), 544–551 (2011)
18. Liang, M., Hu, X.: Recurrent convolutional neural network for object recognition. In: Proceedings of the IEEE Conference on Computer Vision and Pattern Recognition, pp. 3367–3375 (2015)
19. Tripathi, S., Lipton, Z.C., Belongie, S., Nguyen, T.: Context matters: refining object detection in video with recurrent neural networks. arXiv preprint arXiv:1607.04648 (2016)
20. Bengio, Y., Simard, P., Frasconi, P.: Learning long-term dependencies with gradient descent is difficult. IEEE Trans. Neural Netw. **5**(2), 157–166 (1994)
21. Hochreiter, S., Schmidhuber, J.: Long short-term memory. Neural Comput. **9**(8), 1735–1780 (1997)
22. Cho, K., Van Merriënboer, B., Gulcehre, C., Bahdanau, D., Bougares, F., Schwenk, H., Bengio, Y.: Learning phrase representations using RNN encoder-decoder for statistical machine translation. arXiv preprint arXiv:1406.1078 (2014)
23. Jonides, J., Lewis, R.L., Nee, D.E., Lustig, C.A., Berman, M.G., Moore, K.S.: The mind and brain of short-term memory. Annu. Rev. Psychol. **59**, 193–224 (2008)
24. Kirkpatrick, J., Pascanu, R., Rabinowitz, N., Veness, J., Desjardins, G., Rusu, A.A., Milan, K., Quan, J., Ramalho, T., Grabska-Barwinska, A., et al.: Overcoming catastrophic forgetting in neural networks. Proc. Natl. Acad. Sci. **114**(13), 3521–3526 (2017)
25. Zenke, F., Poole, B., Ganguli, S.: Improved multitask learning through synaptic intelligence. arXiv preprint arXiv:1703.04200 (2017)
26. Aljundi, R., Babiloni, F., Elhoseiny, M., Rohrbach, M., Tuytelaars, T.: Memory aware synapses: learning what (not) to forget. arXiv preprint arXiv:1711.09601 (2017)
27. Liu, T., Yuan, Z., Sun, J., Wang, J., Zheng, N., Tang, X., Shum, H.-Y.: Learning to detect a salient object. IEEE Trans. Pattern Anal. Mach. Intell. **33**(2), 353–367 (2011)
28. Helgason, H.P.: General attention mechanism for artificial intelligence systems (2013)
29. Bahdanau, D., Cho, K., Bengio, Y.: Neural machine translation by jointly learning to align and translate. arXiv preprint arXiv:1409.0473 (2014)
30. Gehring, J., Auli, M., Grangier, D., Yarats, D., Dauphin, Y.N.: Convolutional sequence to sequence learning. arXiv preprint arXiv:1705.03122 (2017)
31. Yang, Z., Yang, D., Dyer, C., He, X., Smola, A.J., Hovy, E.H.: Hierarchical attention networks for document classification. In: HLT-NAACL (2016)
32. Chaplot, D.S., Sathyendra, K.M., Pasumarthi, R.K., Rajagopal, D., Salakhutdinov, R.: Gated-attention architectures for task-oriented language grounding. arXiv preprint arXiv: 1706.07230 (2017)
33. Dhingra, B., Liu, H., Yang, Z., Cohen, W.W., Salakhutdinov, R.: Gated-attention readers for text comprehension. arXiv preprint arXiv:1606.01549 (2016)
34. Mnih, V., Heess, N., Graves, A., et al.: Recurrent models of visual attention. In: Advances in Neural Information Processing Systems, pp. 2204–2212 (2014)
35. Ba, J., Mnih, V., Kavukcuoglu, K.: Multiple object recognition with visual attention. Computer Science (2014)
36. Xu, K., Ba, J., Kiros, R., Cho, K., Courville, A., Salakhudinov, R., Zemel, R., Bengio, Y.: Show, attend and tell: neural image caption generation with visual attention. In: International Conference on Machine Learning, pp. 2048–2057 (2015)
37. Kuen, J., Wang, Z., Wang, G.: Recurrent attentional networks for saliency detection. arXiv preprint arXiv:1604.03227 (2016)
38. Li, G., Yu, Y.: Visual saliency based on multiscale deep features. arXiv preprint arXiv:1503.08663 (2015)

39. Liu, N., Han, J., Zhang, D., Wen, S., Liu, T.: Predicting eye fixations using convolutional neural networks. In: 2015 IEEE Conference on Computer Vision and Pattern Recognition (CVPR), pp. 362–370. IEEE (2015)

40. Kruthiventi, S.S.S., Ayush, K., Babu, R.V.: Deepfix: a fully convolutional neural network for predicting human eye fixations. IEEE Trans. Image Process. **26**(9), 4446–4456 (2017)

41. Cornia, M., Baraldi, L., Serra, G., Cucchiara, R.: Predicting human eye fixations via an LSTM-based saliency attentive model. arXiv preprint arXiv:1611.09571 (2016)

42. Sorokin, I., Seleznev, A., Pavlov, M., Fedorov, A., Ignateva, A.: Deep attention recurrent q-network. arXiv preprint arXiv:1512.01693 (2015)

43. Choi, J., Lee, B.-J., Zhang, B.-T.: Multi-focus attention network for efficient deep reinforcement learning. arXiv preprint arXiv:1712.04603 (2017)

44. Lake, B.M., Ullman, T.D., Tenenbaum, J.B., Gershman, S.J.: Building machines that learn and think like people. CoRR, abs/1604.00289 (2016)

45. Landau, B., Smith, L.B., Jones, S.S.: The importance of shape in early lexical learning. Cogn. Dev. **3**(3), 299–321 (1988)

46. Vinyals, O., Blundell, C., Lillicrap, T., Wierstra, D., et al.: Matching networks for one shot learning. In: Advances in Neural Information Processing Systems, pp. 3630–3638 (2016)

47. Stewart, R., Ermon, S.: Label-free supervision of neural networks with physics and domain knowledge. In: AAAI, pp. 2576–2582 (2017)

48. Hu, Z., Ma, X., Liu, Z., Hovy, E., Xing, E.: Harnessing deep neural networks with logic rules. arXiv preprint arXiv:1603.06318 (2016)

49. Ganchev, K., Gillenwater, J., Taskar, B., et al.: Posterior regularization for structured latent variable models. J. Mach. Learn. Res. **11**(Jul), 2001–2049 (2010)

50. Hu, Z., Yang, Z., Salakhutdinov, R., Xing, E.: Deep neural networks with massive learned knowledge. In: Conference on Empirical Methods in Natural Language Processing, pp. 1670–1679 (2016)

51. Hopfield, J.J.: Neural networks and physical systems with emergent collective computational abilities. Proc. Natl. Acad. Sci. **79**(8), 2554–2558 (1982)

52. Krotov, D., Hopfield, J.J.: Dense associative memory for pattern recognition. CoRR, abs/1606.01164 (2016)

53. Oh, J., Chockalingam, V., Singh, S., Lee, H.: Control of memory, active perception, and action in minecraft. arXiv preprint arXiv:1605.09128 (2016)

54. Parisotto, E., Salakhutdinov, R.: Neural map: structured memory for deep reinforcement learning. arXiv preprint arXiv:1702.08360 (2017)

55. Yin, H., Pan, S.J.: Knowledge transfer for deep reinforcement learning with hierarchical experience replay. In: AAAI, pp. 1640–1646 (2017)

A Novel Camera Based Approach for Automatic Expiry Date Detection and Recognition on Food Packages

Liyun Gong[1(✉)], Miao Yu[1], Wenting Duan[1], Xujiong Ye[1],
Kjartan Gudmundsson[2], and Mark Swainson[2]

[1] School of Computer Science, University of Lincoln, Lincoln LN6 7TS, UK
{lgong,myu,wduan,xye}@lincoln.ac.uk
[2] National Centre for Food Manufacturing, University of Lincoln,
Holbeach PE12 7PT, UK
{kgudmundsson,mswainson}@lincoln.ac.uk

Abstract. There is abundant of information on food packages, which include the food name, the expiry date and the ingredients. These information, especially the expiry date needs to be coded correctly before the products can be released into the market/supply chains. Failure of printing the correct expiry date can lead to both the health issues to the public and financial issues for recalling product back and even reimbursement. In this paper, we develop an automatic system that can achieve the expiry date region detection and recognition in an efficient and effective way. A deep neural network (DNN) based approach is firstly applied to find the expiry date region on the food package. The date characters are then extracted and recognized through the image processing and machine learning methods from the expiry date region. The system is the first camera based automatic system for recognizing expiry date on food packages. And the results tested on different types of food packages show that the system can achieve good performance on both detection and recognition of the expiry date.

Keywords: Fully convolutional network · Stroke width transform
Maximally stable extremal regions · Tesseract OCR

1 Introduction

In the European Union food production is the largest manufacturing sector where it accounts for 13.3% of the total EU-28 manufacturing sector with a reported turnover of 945 billion [1]. Whilst food availability is a primary concern in developing nations and food quality (value) is a focal point in more affluent societies, food safety is a requirement that is common across all food supply chains. Food safety in the sector is typically underpinned by food science and technology and assured by a combination of operational control systems and procedures including Good Manufacturing Practice (GMP) and Hazard Analysis Critical Control Point (HACCP) [2].

The food product information printed on the food package is a vital for the food safety. Pre-packaged food product information which are incorrectly labelled, especially the expiry date results in product recalls as the fault/issue could cause a food

L. Iliadis et al. (Eds.): AIAI 2018, IFIP AICT 519, pp. 133–142, 2018.
https://doi.org/10.1007/978-3-319-92007-8_12

safety incident such as food poisoning due to the consumption of product which is past its actual safe Use-by date. These recalls are usually at very high financial and reputational cost to food manufacturers.

The reasons/root causes for issues or mistakes resulting in label faults on food packaging are many and varied. They include human error and equipment faults. For example, a label printer on a production line can break down and the line carries on running. The faulty packaging therefore needs to be identified and the production line stopped. A common current process line Use-by check approach is to use a human operator to read and verify the packaging label. This check is conducted by either manually picking a pack from the line for inspection or verifying it through an image captured of the pack. However, these methods create mundane and repetitive tasks and therefore place the operator in an error-prone working environment.

Another common approach to control date codes is to use Optical Character Verification (OCV). This involves a supervisory system holding the correct expiry date string and transferring it to both the printer and the vision system. The latter will then verify its read and actions are taken depending on the result. However, OCV systems rely on consistency in expiry date format, packaging and camera view angle. This consistency tends to be hard to achieve in the food and drink manufacturing environment and therefore there is a great need for a more robust solution.

In this work, we have developed an automatic system based on a camera, which can efficiently and effectively recognize the expiry date information printed on different types of food packages. Food packages with wrong expiry date printed on will be picked up. This system will enable far greater control over the accuracy and legibility of critical 'Use-by'/'Best Before' dates and also key traceability information in food and drink manufacturing operations, resulting in significantly increased food safety and compliance with related legislation.

To develop such a system, the first step is to identify expiry date regions as the region of interest (ROI) on a recorded food package image. And the expiry date recognition task is then performed within the ROI instead of the whole image. In this way, the computational costs can be saved to a large extent. One straightforward method to determine ROI is applying the text detection method for detecting text regions as ROI on a food package. For text detection, a number of traditional image processing based techniques have been applied, examples include Stroke Width Transform (SWT) based approach [3] and Maximally Stable Extremal Regions (MSER) based approach [4]. With the deep learning techniques having become mainstream in the image processing, computer vision and machine learning communities, different types of deep neural networks have been applied for the text detection [5, 6] with better results being obtained.

However, if the food package contains too much other text information in addition to the expiry date (that is the usual situation on the food package), the obtained ROI will still be tremendous. Instead of the text region detection for the ROI identification, in our work we apply a deep neural network approach for directly identifying the expiry date region as ROI. The fully convolutional network (FCN) in [5], which is originally developed for text detection, is fine-tuned by our dataset for expiry date region detection. By adopting such an approach, only the expiry date region can be extracted while other texts on the food package are excluded. The most precise ROI is directly obtained and computational costs can then be further reduced by performing the recognition on only the ROI of the expiry date region.

Based on the extracted ROI, the date characters blobs in the ROI can be directly extracted. Related shape features are then extracted for classification by an efficient nearest neighbour method. In our experiment, we have tested our system for both expiry date region detection and classification on different types of food packages in different captured image formats (colour/grayscale), with good results being obtained.

2 Method

In this section, we present the methodology for expiry date recognition on the food package, which is divided into two parts: expiry region identification and recognition. The block diagram of the proposed methodology is shown in Fig. 1. Details of every block are presented as follows.

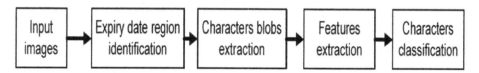

Fig. 1. The block diagram of the proposed system.

2.1 Date Code Region Identification

For effectively identifying the expiry date region on the food package which contains different types of pictures/texts contents with different colours, a deep neural network based approach is applied. The deep neural network structure is a fully convolutional network (FCN) as described in [5], which was originally developed for detecting texts. The network is fine-tuned on our food package dataset for detecting the date expiry region.

The FCN structure is shown in Fig. 2, which is decomposed into three parts: feature extractor stem, feature-merging branch and output layer.

The stem part is a PVANet [7], with interleaving convolution and pooling layers. Four levels of feature maps, denoted as f_i are extracted from the original input image, whose sizes are $\frac{1}{32}, \frac{1}{16}, \frac{1}{8}$ and $\frac{1}{4}$ of the original input image. Features from different scale levels meet the requirements of detecting text regions with different sizes.

In the feature-merging branch, features are merged in the following strategy:

$$g_i = \begin{cases} unpool(h_i) \, if \, i \leq 3 \\ conv_{3\times3}(h_i) \, if \, i = 4 \end{cases}$$

$$h_i = \begin{cases} f_i & if \, i = 1 \\ conv_{3\times3}(conv_{1\times1}([g_{i-1};f_i])) & if \, i = 4 \end{cases} \tag{1}$$

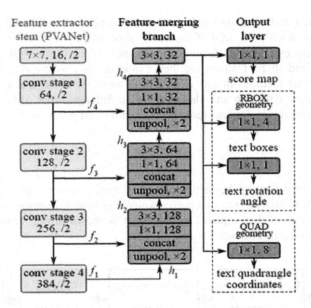

Fig. 2. The FCN structure for the expiry date identification.

where g_i is the merge based as in [5] and h_i is the merged feature map. And the operator [;]. represents concatenation along the channel axis. In each merging stage, the feature map from the last stage is first fed to an unpooling layer to double its size, and then concatenated with the current feature map. A $conv_{1\times1}$ bottleneck cuts down the number of channels to reduce computation, followed by a $conv_{3\times3}$ that fuses the information to finally produce the output of this merging stage. Following the last merging stage, a $conv_{3\times3}$ layer produces the final feature map of the merging branch and feed it to the output layer.

The final output layer contains several $conv_{1\times1}$ operations to project 32 channels of feature maps into 1 channel of score map F_s, which gives the likelihood that a pixel belong to the expiry date region as well as a multi-channel geometry map F_g, which could be either rotated box (RBOX) or quadrangle (QUAD) representing different geometries. RBOX geometry map contains a 4-channel map representing 4 distances from every pixel location to the top, right, bottom, left boundaries of a rectangle enclosing the candidate expiry date region, as well as a 1-channel map representing the angle of the related rectangle. QUAD geometry map is a 8-channel map, which contains the coordinate shift from four corner vertices of a quadrangle (representing candidate expiry date region) to every pixel position.

FCN Training and Testing. For obtaining the network parameters, firstly, a loss function is defined as:

$$L = L_s + \lambda L_g \tag{2}$$

where L_s and L_g represent losses for score and geometry maps respectively, while λ is a balancing parameter.

The term L_s is defined as:

$$L_s = -\beta Y^* log \hat{Y} - (1 - \beta)(1 - Y^*)log(1 - \hat{Y}) \tag{3}$$

where $\hat{Y}$ and Y^* represent the predicted and groundtruth score maps respectively. β is a balancing parameter. While the L_g is defined as scale-invariant IoU loss for RBOX geometry map and scale-normalized smoothed-L1 for the QUAD one as [5]. Based on the defined loss function, the network is trained end-to-end using ADAM optimizer until performance stops improving.

To determine the final expiry date region, first a threshold is set to find positions at which score map values are larger than it. The geometries associated with those positions on the geometry map will then be merged by the locality aware Non-Maximum Suppression (NMS) to determine the final expiry date region, which can achieve lower computational costs compared with the basic NMS algorithm. Under the assumption that the geometries from nearby pixels tend to be highly correlated, the locality-aware NMS is proposed to merge the geometries row by row. And while merging geometries in the same row, the geometry currently encountered will be merged with the last merged one. In this way, the computational costs could be reduced from O(n2) of the original NMS to O(n), where n is the number of candidate geometries. Figure 3 shows the results of different parts the expiry date region detection procedure.

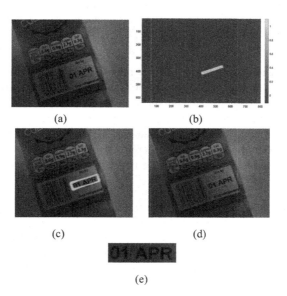

(a)　　　　　　　　(b)

(c)　　　　　　　　(d)

(e)

Fig. 3. The expiry date region detection procedure. (a) Original image (b) Score map output by the FCN (c) Candidate expiry date region results before NMS (d) Expiry date region results after NMS (e) Expiry date patch output

2.2 Expiry Date Recognition

Expiry date will then be recognized based on the identified region by Tesseract OCR [10]. The Maximally Stable External Regions (MSER) algorithm will firstly be applied, to make a binarization of the extracted date code region with characters being differentiated from the background (Fig. 4 (b)). Component connected analysis [9] is then made to find blobs representing different characters, with small noisy blobs being filtered out (Fig. 4 (c)).

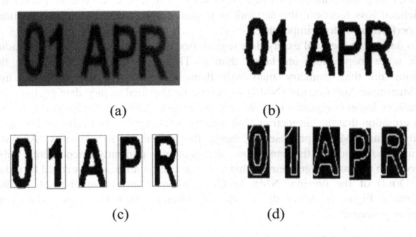

(a)   (b)

(c)   (d)

Fig. 4. Extracted expiry date region and related processing. (a) Original date code region (b) Binarization for differentiating character regions from the background (c) Character blobs extraction (d) boundary extraction

As in [8], for each candidate blob, the boundary will be extracted as in Fig. 4 (d) (here the Canny edge extraction operator is applied) and the corresponding shape features, such as topological and polynomial approximation can be extracted for characters classification. In this work, a simple but effective nearest neighbour (NN) approach is applied for the classification. The features of every blob will be compared with prototypes representing different characters. A blob will be classified as the character for which the related distance is the smallest.

3 Experimental Results

The proposed system is trained and tested on different types of food packages, with representative examples being shown in Fig. 5. We have collected 800 images from stores, among which 70% (560 images) are used for training and 30% (240 images) are used for testing.

Fig. 5. Examples of food package pictures containing date code information.

3.1 Expiry Date Region Detection Evaluation

The FCN as mentioned in the previous section is fine tuned for identifying the expiry date region on the food package. We have manually masked the ground truth expiry date regions in the training dataset for tuning the FCN, to transfer it from a text detection network to a date code region detection one. We train the network in the GPU-supported tensorflow environment, with two PASCAL GPUs. The input image patches are resized to 512×512. Mini-batch training is applied with the batch size is 14 per GPU and the learning rate is set to be 0.0001 in the ADAM optimizer.

Figure 6 shows the comparison results between FCN before and after fine tuning. We can see that after fine-tuning, the original text detection network transfers from a text detection network to a expiry date detection one. The transferred network is tested on captured images of different food packages, with both colour and grayscale formats. Related results are presented in Fig. 7, we can see that the date code regions on different food packages can be successfully identified. For a qualitative analysis, we test the developed FCN on the aforementioned testing dataset containing 240 images. The testing results show that 236 out of 240 images, the date region is correctly identified with 4 out of 240 are missing. A total detection rate of 98% is obtained.

3.2 Expiry Date Recognition Evaluation

Based on the detected expiry date region, the characters within it are extracted and classified. We have applied the Tesseract OCR [10] for classification, which has implemented the characters extraction, feature extraction and classification steps as mentioned in the Sect. 2.2. Some initial results are presented that in Fig. 8. It is shown that the characters on the extracted expiry date region can be successfully recognized; however, some classification mistakes may happen when characters are blurred.

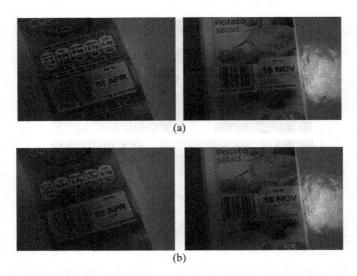

Fig. 6. FCN detection results before/after the fine tuning. (a). Text region detection results before the fine-tuning (b). Date code regions detection results by the FCN after the fine tuning

Fig. 7. FCN detection results of the date code on different packages.

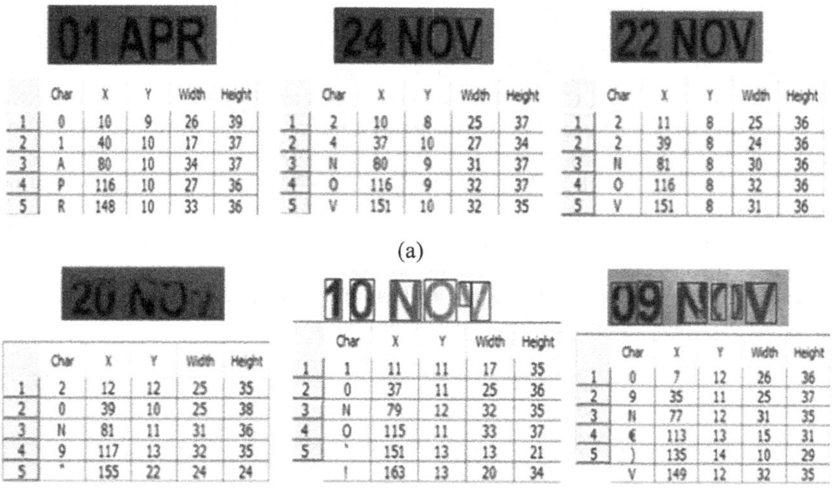

01 APR

Char	X	Y	Width	Height
1	0	10	9	26	39
2	1	40	10	17	37
3	A	80	10	34	37
4	P	116	10	27	36
5	R	148	10	33	36

24 NOV

Char	X	Y	Width	Height
1	2	10	8	25	37
2	4	37	10	27	34
3	N	80	9	31	37
4	O	116	9	32	37
5	V	151	10	32	35

22 NOV

Char	X	Y	Width	Height
1	2	11	8	25	36
2	2	39	8	24	36
3	N	81	8	30	36
4	O	116	8	32	36
5	V	151	8	31	36

(a)

20 NOV

Char	X	Y	Width	Height
1	2	12	12	25	35
2	0	39	10	25	38
3	N	81	11	31	36
4	9	117	13	32	35
5	"	155	22	24	24

10 NOV

Char	X	Y	Width	Height
1	1	11	11	17	35
2	0	37	11	25	36
3	N	79	12	32	35
4	O	115	11	33	37
5	'	151	13	13	21
	!	163	13	20	34

09 NOV

Char	X	Y	Width	Height
1	0	7	12	26	36
2	9	35	11	25	37
3	N	77	12	31	35
4	€	113	13	15	31
5	)	135	14	10	29
	V	149	12	32	35

(b)

Fig. 8. Texts classification results by Tesseract OCR. (a). Classification results on clear date characters (b). Classification results on blurred characters

4 Conclusions

In this work, we have developed a novel food package expiry date recognition system based on the camera. A FCN deep neural network approach is applied to detect the expiry date region. Based on the detection results, the date character blobs will be extracted. Related features will be extracted and classified to particular characters. Such a system will potentially advance the assurance of food quality and safety. The experimental results show that the proposed method can achieve very good performance in identifying the expiry date region and classifying characters correctly when they are clear. However, if the characters are blurred, misclassifications can be made and that will be the future researches which will be investigated.

References

1. Eurostat: Manufacturing statistics - NACE Rev. 2 (2014). http://ec.europa.eu/eurostat/statistics-explained/index.php/
2. WHO FAO (2009). http://www.fao.org/docrep/012/a1552e/a1552e00.htm
3. Epshtein, B., Ofek, E., Wexler, Y.: Detecting text in natural scenes with stroke width transform. In: 2010 IEEE Conference on Computer Vision and Pattern Recognition (CVPR), San Francisco, CA, USA (2010)
4. Chen, H., Tsai, S., Schroth, G., Chen, D., Grzeszczuk, R., Girod, B.: Robust text detection in natural images with edge-enhanced maximally stable extremal regions. In: 18th IEEE International Conference on Image Processing (ICIP), Brussels, Belgium (2011)

5. Zhou, X., Yao, C., Wen, H., Wang, Y., Zhou, S., He, W., Liang, J.: EAST: an efficient and accurate scene text detector. In: International Conference on Computer Vision and Pattern Recognition, Honolulu, Hawaii, USA (2017)
6. Zhang, Z., Shen, W., Yao, C., Bai, X.: Symmetry-based text line detection in natural scenes. In: International Conference on Computer Vision and Pattern Recognition, Boston, Massachusetts, USA (2015)
7. Kim, K., Hong, S., Roh, B., Cheon, Y., Park, M.: PVANET: deep but lightweight neural networks for realtime object detection. In: arXiv preprint arXiv:1608.08021 (2016)
8. Smith, R.: An overview of the tesseract OCR engine. In: Ninth International Conference on Document Analysis and Recognition, Parana, Brazil (2007)
9. Gonzalez, R.: Digital Image Processing. Third Edition, Pearson Education (2008)
10. Tesseract-ocr. https://github.com/tesseract-ocr/tesseract

Spatial-Temproal Based Lane Detection Using Deep Learning

Yuhao Huang, Shitao Chen, Yu Chen, Zhiqiang Jian,
and Nanning Zheng[✉]

Institute of Artificial Intelligence and Robotics, Xi'an Jiaotong University, Xi'an,
Shaanxi, People's Republic of China
{hyh950623,chenshitao,alan19960212,
flztiii}@stu.xjtu.edu.cn, nnzheng@mail.xjtu.edu.cn

Abstract. Lane boundary detection is a key technology for self-driving cars. In this paper, we propose a spatiotemporal, deep learning based lane boundary detection method that can accurately detect lane boundaries under complex weather conditions and traffic scenarios in real time. Our algorithm consists of three parts: (i) inverse perspective transform and lane boundary position estimation using the spatial and temporal constraints of lane boundaries, (ii) convolutional neural networks (CNN) based boundary type classification and position regression, (iii) optimization and lane fitting. Our algorithm is designed to accurately detect lane boundaries and classify line types under a variety of environment conditions in real time. We tested our proposed algorithm on three open-source datasets and also compared the results with other state-of-the-art methods. Experimental results showed that our algorithm achieved high accuracy and robustness for detecting lane boundaries in a variety of scenarios in real time. Besides, we also realized the application of our algorithm on embedded platforms and verified the algorithm's real-time performance on real self-driving cars.

Keywords: Lane detection · Inverse perspective transform
Convolutional neural network · Spatial-temporal correlation

1 Introduction

In recent years, autonomous driving has received widespread attention. Identifying traffic scenes around autonomous vehicles is a key step in autonomous driving. Besides, the identification of traffic markings in traffic scenes, especially lane boundaries, provides the necessary information for decision making in autonomous driving modules like path planning. We all know that human drivers rely mainly on vision when driving cars and the vision sensors are low-cost in the market. Therefore, the vision-based lane detection algorithm is the mainstream direction of lane detection. While there already exist plenty of vision-based lane detection algorithms, several tough challenges remain to be handled in practice. Firstly, poor lighting conditions makes it difficult to recognize lane markings at night or in other bad weather conditions like rain, snow, fog, etc. Secondly, com- plex traffic environments, including wear and tear of lane boundaries, congestion of urban roads and lane boundaries being partially

© IFIP International Federation for Information Processing 2018
Published by Springer International Publishing AG 2018. All Rights Reserved
L. Iliadis et al. (Eds.): AIAI 2018, IFIP AICT 519, pp. 143–154, 2018.
https://doi.org/10.1007/978-3-319-92007-8_13

obscured, have increased the difficulty of lane detection. The last is the boundary type recognition. Compared to Advanced Driver Assistance Systems (ADAS), autonomous driving requires not only accurate lane boundary location but also precise boundary type classification.

Lane boundary detection is generally divided into three parts [6, 11]: prepro- cessement of the image and segmentation of the region of interest (ROI), extraction of lane boundary features, and finally lane fitting. Traditionally, lane detection has been performed by using hand-crafted features like gradient information and intensity change information [8, 12, 16]. These algorithms achieve high accuracy on highways with well-lit scenes while having a comparatively bad performance on finding lane markings when lane boundaries are obscured or the experiments are run in bad weather conditions. This is because that lane boundaries have different features in different traffic scenarios, while the hand-crafted features cannot meet the requirements of multiple scenes at the same time.

With the development of artificial intelligence, deep learning is widely used in various fields. AlexNet, VggNet [18], GoogleNet [19] and ResNet [5] achieved good results in the ImageNet Challenge from 2012 to 2015 respectively. CNN- based object detection methods like Faster R-CNN [15], YOLO [14] and SSD [9] have gained high accuracy in object detection task. Some algorithms utilized CNN as a feature extractor to identify lane boundaries and also achieved high accuracy in data sets of different conditions [8, 13, 4]. However, they are computationally complex and are difficult to be applied to driverless systems with limited computing resources.

To deal with the above challenges, we propose a real-time, robust and accurate lane detection approach. We use CNN to accurately extract the features of lane boundaries and obtain the lane boundary position in different traffic scenes, instead of the tradi- tional lane detection algorithm which uses image processing. In order to reduce the computational complexity, we combine the constraints of spatial and temporal infor- mation of lanes to reduce the scale of CNN network structure and to ensure that our algorithm can run accurately and robustly on a self-driving platform in real time.

2 Related Work

Lane detection algorithms can be divided into two types, one includes traditional methods which use hand-crafted features like the gradient information and the color space for lane detection. Another one contains CNN-based methods that are more frequently used by researchers because of the rise of deep learning.

Since lane boundaries have color and shape informations that are different from that of the road, there are many gradient-based approaches developed to extract lane boundary features by calculating the gradient information in images and also to determine lane boundary locations. Aly et al. [1] used Hough trans- form to detect lane boundaries. In [17], hierarchical Hough transform was used by authors to detect lane boundaries with the corresponding intensity variations.

Because of CNN's powerful feature extraction capabilities, many researchers use CNN for lane boundary detection. He et al. [4] used lane boundary detection based on the front view and the top view. It first extracted lane boundary candidates using weighted hat-like filtering in the top view and then classified lane boundary candidates according to Dual-View Convolutional Neutral Network (DVCNN). Lee et al. [9] proposed VPGNet based on multi-task learning to accomplish lane detection and ground traffic identification. In the process of lane detection, VPGNet first divided the image into 8 × 8 grids and determined if each grid belongs to a lane boundary class, and then they used sub-sampling and clustering algorithm to extract lane boundaries from the VPGNet's output. Pan et al. [14] proposed a novel network structure called SCNN, which introduced spatial information into the network structure and accurately identified lane boundaries, even in the case of lane boundary obstructions. However, the CNN network structures in these three methods are complicated and require a large amount of computing resources, making it difficult to use them in actual autonomous vehicle applications. Chen et al. [3] also used regression to do lane boundary detection. This article proposed an end-to-end method which used front view images as input and got the lane boundaries position directly from the CNN. However, it was greatly influenced by the environment.

3   Spatial and Temporal Based Lane Boundary Detection

The workflow of our algorithm is shown in Fig. 1: first, we use inverse perspective transform to get top view images and use the temporal and spatial relevance of a lane to get its estimated location. Then we cut the image into 10–20 sub-images centering on the estimated position of the lane boundary, each sub-image contains local lane boundary information. We then use CNN to classify and regress sub-images to get the exact location and category of local lane boundaries. Finally, we combine the local lane boundary location with the linear information and through the spline fitting, we can get the lane boundary information for the entire image.

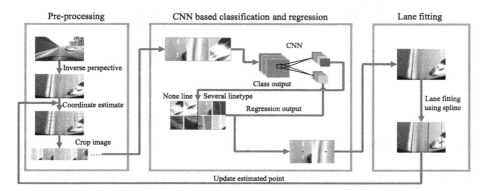

Fig. 1. Our method's workflow consists of three parts. First we perform the inverse perspective transform and estimate the rough position of lane boundaries. Next we use CNN to classify the boundary type and regress the lane boundaries position. Finally, we optimize the output of CNN and perform lane fitting.

3.1 Spatial-Temporal Based Lane Boundary Position Estimation in Top View

Inverse Perspective Transform: It is common sense that images taken by a camera have perspective effects which will destroy the original geometry of lane boundaries. Therefore, the first step in our algorithm is to convert the front view to the top view by inverse perspective mapping. Inverse perspective transform can eliminate the distortion caused by perspective effects in the picture. Through this transform step, we can get the top-down projection of the road. We select the top view as the basis for lane detection. Then we utilize the inverse perspective transform method proposed in [7]:

$$
\begin{bmatrix} u \\ v \\ 1 \end{bmatrix} = \frac{1}{z} \begin{bmatrix} f & 0 & u_c \\ 0 & f & v_c \\ 0 & 0 & 1 \end{bmatrix} \begin{bmatrix} 1 & 0 & 0 & 0 \\ 0 & cos\theta_x & -sin\theta_x & y_c \\ 0 & sin\theta_x & cos\theta_x & 0 \end{bmatrix} \begin{bmatrix} x \\ y \\ z \\ 1 \end{bmatrix} \tag{1}
$$

(x, y, z) is the world coordinates and (u, v) is the pixel coordinates of the image. The camera tilt is θx and the focal length is f. (uc, vc) is the camera optical center and yc is camera height. Figure 2(a) is an image of the real physical scale obtained by the transformation. For convenience, we have resized the image to 1280 × 1024. The image we used is shown in Fig. 2(b).

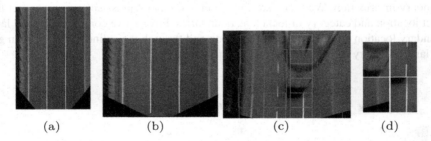

(a)   (b)   (c)   (d)

Fig. 2. (a) Is the top view image of real physical scale. (b) is the resized image. (c) shows the searching area, where the rectangles are the searching area and the estimated lane boundary positions are in the center of the rectangles. (d) illustrates some sub-images extracted from the whole image.

Coordinate Estimate: Both Lee et al. [9] and Pan et al. [13] used the single-frame lane detection methods. The benefit is that these methods don't require any prior information in the process of lane detection task, which can be completed only by inputting the image of a single frame. However, single-frame algorithms have high time and space complexity and redundancy. In application, lane boundaries have strong spatial and temporal constraints, especially in the top view. A lane boundary is a continuous ground road marking for dividing different lanes. In practice, the camera typically samples the pavement information at 30 frame per second (FPS). By combining these two points, it is not difficult to conclude that the lane boundary position between upper and lower frame images does not change much, which means that the lane boundary in the next frame image is near the lane boundary of the previous frame. Generally, speaking, the lane width is the same for multi-lane roads, and the space constraints are obvious in the top view.

Based on the above considerations, we propose to use the temporal and spatial constraints of lane boundaries to reduce the range of searching area (shown in Fig. 2 (c)). The main difference between our detection algorithm and the algorithm in [13] is that ours is based on multi-frame image lane detection. We use the historical lane boundary information of the previous frame image as a priori knowledge to estimate the lane boundary position of the current frame. We then use CNN to accurately detect the position of the boundary based on the estimated lane boundary position with the time constraints of the lane bound- aries discussed above. The mean value of the former 10 frames' lane boundary positions is utilized as the estimated position of the current frame.

Sub-image Extraction: In our algorithm, we use control points to represent lane boundaries and a lane boundary is usually represented by five control points. Typically, we select 10–20 control points according to the boundary type classification result. These control points represent the lane information of the current lane and the lane beside the current lane. After we obtain the estimated position of the lane boundary through the above steps, both the lane boundary regression and the boundary type classification are performed in the neighbor- hood of the estimated position. So at this step we will divide the image into 10–20 sub-images centered on the estimated location and pass them to CNN (as shown in Fig. 2(d)). We use the estimated position of the lane as a priori information and cut the sub-image centered on the estimated position. After obtaining the exact location of the lane boundary through CNN, we use the exact position we get as the control point for the current frame and also as a reference for the next frame. The sub-image size needs to be determined by the camera's internal and external parameters. We consider the following rules when determining the sub-image size: first, each sub-image can only contain one lane which needs to be as large as possible. Second, sub-images should be long enough in the vertical direction to avoid lane misdetection of the white dotted boundary. However, an excess of vertical length will result in a decline in the accuracy of the curve section. In experiments, the size of the sub-image in our algorithm is 220 × 300.

3.2 CNN for Boundary Type Classification and Lane Boundary Regression

Network Structure: Inspired by the network structures in [2, 15], we proposed a novel convolutional neural network based on multitasking, which can accurately track the lane boundary position while classifying lane boundary types. For each task of classification and regression, the network consists of 9 layers, including 5 convolutional layers and 4 fully connected layers. Before entering CNN, we normalized the input image. The feature of our network structure is that the sub-tasks share the 5 convolutional layers and a fully connected layer, thus compressing the parameter space. Experiments show that our CNN based on multitasking can improve the performance of line boundary classification and lane regression tasks during training and eventually converges well. Our CNN is structured as follows: The first 3 convolutional layers we use the 5×5 kernel with 2×2 stride, and it followed with 2 convolutional layers which have 3×3 kernel and non-stride. The last convolutional layer is connected with a fully connected (FC) layer which has 4096 neurons. Then the network is divided into two parts (for the two sub-tasks of linetype classification and lane boundary regression), for each contains the same scale of 3 FC layers. The 3 FC layers have 1000, 500, 100 neurons respectively. We added a softmax layer for the sub networks which we used as the linetype classifier.

In our algorithm, we use a multitasking learning mechanism to learn and predict simultaneously the lane boundary type and the lane boundary position. Our loss function is defined as follows:

$$loss = \begin{cases} L_{cls}, boundarytype = Noneline \\ \alpha L_{cls} + (1 - \alpha)L_{loc}, boundarytype \neq Noneline \end{cases} \quad (2)$$

where α is a factor to balance the classification loss and regression loss. L_{cls} and L_{loc} are respectively the classification loss function and regression loss function. In this paper, we use the cross-entropy loss as the classification loss function and the mean square error loss as the regression loss function.

Linetype Classification and Lane Boundary Regression: In autonomous vehicles, linetype classification is necessary since self-driving cars need to change lanes and sometimes even at a high frequency. Traditional methods are not good at boundary classification while CNN can realize it easily with its powerful classification capabilities. Based on lane categories, we classify lane boundaries into double yellow lines, white solid lines, white dashed lines, single yellow lines, Noneline, etc. The Noneline category is designed to improve the robustness of the system, as lane boundary information for lane boundaries, especially for adjacent lanes, tends to be obstructed by moving vehicles in a realistic traffic environment. In this case, the control point of the corresponding position will be set to Noneline type. We will not refer to the CNN coordinate regression value of this control point. Generally, the lane boundaries are occluded 1–2 control points, so we can still get the lane information accurately by using lane fitting.

Different from the methods which transform the regression problems into classification task, we predict the exact value of the lane boundary location directly from the CNN. There are two main benefits of using lane boundary regression: a high regression accuracy which can reach pixel level and a direct regression which requires low space and time costs with a small amount of computation. The CNN output is shown in Fig. 3(a).

(a)   (b)

Fig. 3. (a) The regression and classification outputs from CNN. The red points are the regression output and the rectangles refer to the boundary type classification output, where blue, yellow and green ones represent the white solid line, yellow line and white dashed line respectively. (b) Experiment platform. (Color figure online)

3.3   Lane Fitting and Optimization

Lane Fitting: The algorithm of the previous step gives information about the control points of the current lane and its adjacent lane, including the boundary type and the exact location of the lane boundary. In this step, we fit the lane boundary through control points with the Catmull-Rom (CR) spline [20]. The CR spline is also known as Overhauster spline, which is one kind of cubic interpolation spline. It is calculated as follows:

$$P(s) = \begin{bmatrix} 1 & u & u^2 & u^3 \end{bmatrix} \begin{bmatrix} 0 & 1 & 0 & 0 \\ -\tau & 0 & \tau & 0 \\ 2\tau & \tau - 3 & 3 - 2\tau & -\tau \\ -\tau & 2 - \tau & \tau - 2 & \tau \end{bmatrix} \begin{bmatrix} P_{i-2} \\ P_{i-1} \\ P_i \\ P_{i+1} \end{bmatrix} \tag{3}$$

where P_i, P_{i-1}, P_{i+1} are the current point, the previous point and next point on the spline respectively. τ is the tension parameter which affects the spline's sharpness. The value of u is set in the interval (0, 1), which represents the points between P_i and P_{i-1}.

Optimization: Searching for lane boundary information throughout the whole image is unnecessary. In our algorithm, we will verify the linetype of the adjacent right and left lanes. If the left lane or the right lane cannot be changed, we will cancel the lane boundary position estimation of the adjacent lane, and in the next frame If the current lane can be changed lanes (e.g. the left lane is white dashed boundary), we will initialize the corresponding adjacent lanes based on the lane constraints. We noticed that multi-lane roads have the same lane width in general. Therefore, by calculating the deviation between the current lane's boundaries on each side, we can estimate the lane's position relative to the adjacent lane. Then in the next frame's prediction we can detect lane information for the corresponding adjacent lane. In this way the amount of computation will also be minimized.

4   Experiments

In this section, we have performed a series of contrast experiments for verifying the effectiveness of our proposed algorithm. These experiments are mainly executed on three different open-source datasets containing various traffic scenarios as well as different data:

1. Road Vehicle Dataset (RVD). This dataset contains images taken in different traffic scenarios and weather conditions, which were collected by our autonomous vehicle research group about one year ago.
2. Caltech lane dataset. This dataset contains 1224 tabbed images taken in four different places with the weather condition, however, limited to sunny days.
3. Tusimple benchmark dataset. The Tusimple benchmark dataset contains 6408 labeled images, but again lacks lane boundary data for different traffic or weather conditions.

In the three above-mentioned datasets, RVD contains mainly data of highway or urban roads in China, while most of the other two datasets' data was collected on Americans roads. Except for evaluations of algorithm quantitative tests on these open-source datasets, we have also compared our experiment results with that of other state-of-the-art methods. Besides, we also implemented our proposed algorithm on embedded platforms (i.e., Nvidia TX2) to verify the capability of its real-time performance in real autonomous vehicles, along with algorithm migration and application on a real self-driving car named Pioneer in our research group. Our experiment platform is shown in Fig. 3(b).

4.1   Model Training

The input of our proposed model contains images with a resolution of 1280×1024 pixels. In order to speed up the operation and reduce the computational complexity, a set of pre-processing and transforms of original image input are needed before sending these images to the core CNN network. The final resolution of CNN input image patches is 110×150 pixels. Due to the special structure of our CNN network, there is no pre-training model available, which means that we need to train CNN from scratch. We first train the lane boundary classifier. Next, we change the CNN learning rate, batch size and dropout rate for training the lane boundary regression as well as classification tasks in the same time. After that use the Adaptive Moment Estimation optimization (Adam) and adjust the proportion of regression loss to classification loss to 4:1. We then use the Rectifier neural networks (ReLU) activation function and add the softmax layer to the output of the classification network.

4.2   Evaluation

To estimate our model's effectiveness, we evaluated our algorithm by using precision and recall. Since we did the boundary type classification and lane boundary regression simultaneously, only samples with the correct classification and regression results will be set as True Positive (TP). As for the measurement of the regression result, we set the threshold to a value which is supposed to be accurate when it is larger than the deviation of the predicted lane boundary coordinates and the ground-true. In the experiment we set the threshold to 5 pixels. Table 2 shows the accuracy of our algorithm in various traffic scenarios.

Road Vehicle Dataset (RVD): Since RVD contains images collected from different weather conditions and traffic scenarios, we can evaluate our methods' robustness on it. There are some visualized results, which are shown in Fig. 4. And also we measured precision and recall which are shown in Table 1. The performance on RVD shows that our method can accurately recognize the lane boundaries in several environments especially in bad weather conditions.

Fig. 4. Visualization result on RVD

Caltech Lane Dataset: We compared our methods with Lee's [9] on Caltech lane dataset. Table 2 shows that our methods outperformed Lee's method in such scenario. Since Caltech lane dataset only contains 1224 labeled images, this result represent that our method can extract the lane boundaries' features from a relative small scale of dataset efficiently.

Tusimple Benchmark Dataset: Tusimple benchmark dataset evaluates the methods performance on highway. We also tested our methods on it. Our methods only achieved about 90% accuracy. Although the images in Tusimple dataset are collected from undulated roads, which seriously impact the quality of the top view image, our methods show the robustness in this situation. Some of the visualized results on Caltech lane dataset and Tusimple benchmark dataset shown in Fig. 4.

4.3   Implementation on Embedded System

Since self-driving platforms have limited computing resources, it is meaningful to implement the lane boundary detection algorithm on the embedded platform.

Table 1. Evaluation on RVD dataset.

Scenario	Total image	Precision [%]	Recall [%]	F_1 [%]
Highway	5066	97.067	95.389	96.221
Rainy and snowy	3802	93.127	94.864	93.987
Night	3566	92.376	91.272	91.821
Urban	3467	98.261	96.246	97.192
Heavy urban	3257	93.491	92.341	92.912
Nonline	1237	95.912	94.366	95.133
Curve	1520	96.491	92.231	94.312
Complex illumination	1382	94.821	93.412	94.112

Table 2. Comparison with Lee's [9] work on Caltech dataset.

Traffic	Methods	Precision [%]	Recall [%]	F_1 [%]
Cordova1	Ours	97.326	96.651	**96.987**
	Lee's	–	–	88.4
Washington1	Ours	98.067	97.129	**97.596**
	Lee's	–	–	86.9

We choose the GPU-based embedded platform Nvidia TX2, which has 256 CUDA cores and low power consumption as the experiment's platform. After implemented and optimized proposed algorithm on Nvidia TX2, the frame rate has achieved 30 FPS on embedded system (Fig. 5).

Fig. 5. Visualization result on Caltech lane dataset and Tusimple benchmark dataset

5   Conclusion and Future Work

In this paper, we proposed a lane detection algorithm based on deep learning and spatial-temporal information. We used the spatial and temporal constraints of a lane to estimate the position of the lane and also applied CNN to predict the lane boundary type and the exact location of a lane. Based on the reorganization of boundary types, we propose a lane detection framework that corresponds to human driving habits, which reasonably reduces the computational complexity of the algorithm and improves the robustness of it. Experiments showed that our algorithm can accurately and quickly detect lane boundary information. In the future work, we hope to combine laser sensor information with our algorithm to further improve the accuracy and robustness of lane boundary inspection.

Acknowledge. This research was partially supported by the National Natural Science Foundation of China (No. 61773312, 61790563), the Programme of Introducing Talents of Discipline to University (No. B13043). We are grateful to the reviewers for taking the time to read this article.

References

1. Aly, M.: Real time detection of lane markers in urban streets. In: Intelligent Vehicles Symposium, pp. 7–12. IEEE (2008)
2. Bojarski, M., Del Testa, D., Dworakowski, D., Firner, B., Flepp, B., Goyal, P., Jackel, L.D., Monfort, M., Muller, U., Zhang, J.-A., et al.: End to end learning for self-driving cars. arXiv preprint arXiv:1604.07316 (2016)
3. Chen, S., Zhang, S., Shang, J., Chen, B., Zheng, N.: Brain inspired cognitive model with attention for self-driving cars. arXiv preprint arXiv:1702.05596 (2017)
4. He, B., Ai, R., Yan, Y., Lang, X.: Accurate and robust lane detection based on dual-view convolutional neutral network. In: Intelligent Vehicles Symposium (IV), 2016 IEEE, pp. 1041–1046. IEEE (2016)
5. He, K., Zhang, X., Ren, S., Sun, J.: Deep residual learning for image recognition. In: Proceedings of the IEEE Conference on Computer Vision and Pattern Recognition, pp. 770–778 (2016)
6. Hillel, A.B., Lerner, R., Levi, D., Raz, G.: Recent progress in road and lane detection: a survey. Mach. Vis. Appl. **25**(3), 727–745 (2014)
7. Hoiem, D., Efros, A.A., Hebert, M.: Putting objects in perspective. Int. J. Comput. Vis. **80**(1), 3–15 (2008)
8. Krizhevsky, A., Sutskever, I., Hinton, G.E.: Imagenet classification with deep convolutional neural networks. In: Advances in Neural Information Processing Systems, pp. 1097–1105 (2012)
9. Labayrade, R., Douret, J., Laneurit, J., Chapuis, R.: A reliable and robust lane detection system based on the parallel use of three algorithms for driving safety assistance. IEICE Trans. Inf. Syst. **89**(7), 2092–2100 (2006)
10. Lee, S., Kweon, I.S., Kim, J., Yoon, J.S., Shin, S., Bailo, O., Kim, N., Lee, T.-H., Hong, H. S., Han, S.-H.: VPGNet: Vanishing point guided network for lane and road marking detection and recognition. In 2017 IEEE International Conference on Computer Vision (ICCV), pp. 1965–1973. IEEE (2017)

11. Liu, W., Anguelov, D., Erhan, D., Szegedy, C., Reed, S., Fu, C.-Y., Berg, A.C.: SSD: single shot MultiBox detector. In: Leibe, B., Matas, J., Sebe, N., Welling, M. (eds.) ECCV 2016. LNCS, vol. 9905, pp. 21–37. Springer, Cham (2016). https://doi.org/10.1007/978-3-319-46448-0_2

12. Narote, S.P., Bhujbal, P.N., Narote, A.S., Dhane, D.M.: A review of recent advances in lane detection and departure warning system. Pattern Recogn. **73**, 216–234 (2018)

13. Nieto, M., Salgado, L., Jaureguizar, F., Arróspide, J.: Robust multiple lane road modeling based on perspective analysis. In: 15th IEEE International Conference on Image Processing, ICIP 2008, pp. 2396–2399. IEEE (2008)

14. Pan, X., Shi, J., Luo, P., Wang, X., Tang, X.: Spatial as deep: spatial cnn for traffic scene understanding. arXiv preprint arXiv:1712.06080 (2017)

15. Redmon, J., Divvala, S., Girshick, R., Farhadi, A.: You only look once: unified, real-time object detection. In: Proceedings of the IEEE Conference on Computer Vision and Pattern Recognition, pp. 779–788 (2016)

16. Ren, S., He, K., Girshick, R., Sun, J.: Faster R-CNN: towards real-time object detection with region proposal networks. In: Advances in Neural Information Processing Systems, pp. 91–99 (2015)

17. Samadzadegan, F., Sarafraz, A., Tabibi, M.: Automatic lane detection in image sequences for vision-based navigation purposes. In: ISPRS Image Engineering and Vision Metrology (2006)

18. Satzoda, R.K., Sathyanarayana, S., Srikanthan, T., Sathyanarayana, S.: Hierarchical additive hough transform for lane detection. IEEE Embed. Syst. Lett. **2**(2), 23–26 (2010)

19. Simonyan, K., Zisserman, A.: Very deep convolutional networks for large-scale image recognition. arXiv preprint arXiv:1409.1556 (2014)

20. Szegedy, C., Liu, W., Jia, Y., Sermanet, P., Reed, S., Anguelov, D., Erhan, D., Vanhoucke, V., Rabinovich, A., et al.: Going deeper with convolutions. In: CVPR (2015)

Support Vector Machines

An Investigation into the Effects of Multiple Kernel Combinations on Solutions Spaces in Support Vector Machines

Paul Kelly[1] and Luca Longo[2]([✉])

[1] National College of Ireland, Dublin, Ireland
x15006956@student.ncirl.ie
[2] School of Computing, College of Health and Sciences,
Dublin Institute of Technology, Dublin, Ireland
luca.longo@dit.ie

Abstract. The use of Multiple Kernel Learning (MKL) for Support Vector Machines (SVM) in Machine Learning tasks is a growing field of study. MKL kernels expand on traditional base kernels that are used to improve performance on non-linearly separable datasets. Multiple kernels use combinations of those base kernels to develop novel kernel shapes that allow for more diversity in the generated solution spaces. Customising these kernels to the dataset is still mostly a process of trial and error. Guidelines around what combinations to implement are lacking and usually they requires domain specific knowledge and understanding of the data. Through a brute force approach, this study tests multiple datasets against a combination of base and non-weighted MKL kernels across a range of tuning hyperparameters. The goal was to determine the effect different kernels shapes have on classification accuracy and whether the resulting values are statistically different populations. A selection of 8 different datasets are chosen and trained against a binary classifier. The research will demonstrate the power for MKL to produce new and effective kernels showing the power and usefulness of this approach.

1 Introduction

Support Vector Machines are one of the many methods in Machine Learning used as a discriminative classification algorithm. They are a form of supervised learning that allows the categorisation of inputs based on their position in a feature space. They traditionally address binary classification problems by separating data points in the solution hyperspace by means of a hyperplane. The goal is to generate the maximal margin between the hyperplane and the closest points of each category being classified. When a hyperplane cannot be found, which can adequately separate the data points, a kernel can be used [16]. Kernels are used in SVMs to allow non-linearly separable data points to be mapped to a

© IFIP International Federation for Information Processing 2018
Published by Springer International Publishing AG 2018. All Rights Reserved
L. Iliadis et al. (Eds.): AIAI 2018, IFIP AICT 519, pp. 157–167, 2018.
https://doi.org/10.1007/978-3-319-92007-8_14

higher, and potentially infinitely higher dimensional space [22]. Using the kernel trick this can be done with relatively low computation cost as the simple inner product of vectors. In the case of Mercer compliant kernels [16], which are the focus of this study, the kernels have the property of being positive semi-definite (PSD) that guarantees a convex solution space. A PSD matrix is defined as one that has only positive eigenvalues. It's resultant convex space guarantees a search minimum and it reduces the search requirements of non-convex solution spaces associated with methods such as Artificial Neural Networks (ANNs). Multiple Kernel Learning is an expansion on these base kernels and used when the traditional kernels, such as Radial Based Functions or Polynomial expansions, are insufficient. Properties of PSD kernels is that the product of two will always produce another semi-definite kernel. This allows for a broad range of combinations and shapes of kernel to be used against data that is difficult to classify. Previous studies on Multiple Kernel Learning have focused on a few themes, the use of a genetic algorithm for hyperparameters selection [8], genetic algorithms for kernel selection, the weighted combination of multiple kernels to determine kernel shape [23], and large scale kernel combinations [1,6]. These approaches focus on specifics of the MKL implementation for a chosen task such as image identification [21] or landslide detection [13]. They are also generally more specific in the choice of kernel combinations and commonly focus on combinations of two different base kernel types. The computation time of constructing the kernels and testing them against the data is a prohibitive feature of the MKL research and the sparse knowledge around global kernel shape approaches makes the scope of research quite broad. The fundamental question of whether the MKL kernel will produce novel results is not explicitly addressed and that is the goal of this research.

This paper is structured as follows. Section 2 will address the previous work done in this field and the varying approaches used in relation to their strength and weaknesses regard computation time and performance. Section 3 will detail the approach put forward in the paper and address the choice for experimental design, evaluation methods used, and datasets chosen. Sections 4 and 5 will deal with the results, and what conclusions can be drawn from them, respectively.

2   Related Work

SVM optimisation is based on the configuration and adjustment of hyperparameters along with the kernel choice when the data is non-linearly separable. Additional hyperparameters also come into play regarding the kernels themselves with specific values needed based on type. Multiple approaches to tuning these hyperparameters have been used to overcome what was originally described by Boser [2] as needing direct configuring and altering. This problem of tuning is described by Diosan [5] as an empirical one and should be treated in similar ways to other problems of scale. As an example, the weight of any one hyperparameter, such as the slack variable, has a direct effect on the influence of each support vector [20]. Slack in SVMs is the allowance given to the algorithm to accept misclassified or anomalous data points in the training data. Similarly, the gamma value for the kernel defines the nonlinear mapping to the higher feature space [14]. Weighting these vital parameters, and avoiding over-weighting, then becomes a trade-off between maximising the support vector width and reducing errors in classification [4]. The following sections will describe the different approaches used to tackle the tuning of hyperparameters, the use of genetic algorithms in previous MKL work, and what considerations computational complexity plays in the implementation of MKLs.

2.1 Hyperparameter Tuning

One approach used by both Shermeh [20] and Lessmann [12] to find optimal hyperparameter values for a kernel is the grid search approach where a range of values are iterated through to find the best solution. Alternatively, Genetic Algorithms (GA) whereby a fitness measure is used to assess a population of randomly chosen parameter sets applied to the SVM is also popularly used to determine the best values. The computation cost, however, of Genetic Algorithm Support Vector Machines (GASVMs) makes them less useful, particularly over larger datasets, as the execution time for all the permutations becomes high. While GASVM approaches have gained popularity in recent years, they have not addressed general rules for the effectiveness or differentiation from base kernel outcomes that the specific kernel combinations produce. While SVM and kernel specific hyperparameter tuning are needed to ensure robust modeling, the use of which kernel combinations determines what shape and eventual properties the MKL kernel will have.

2.2 Genetic Algorithm Approach to Kernel Weights

The question of which kernels to combine and their effect on robust models is another important decision after hyperparameter selection and can also use GA-SVMs to solve for more effective combinations. Polynomial and Radial Based Function(RBF) kernels were combined by Howley [10] to identify hand-written characters, which is an extremely well-studied problem, to see the effect of their different weighting. The RBF kernel, or Gaussian Kernel, is known for its effectiveness at handling small, high dimensionality datasets which are both notoriously difficult properties for a classification algorithm. Li [13] demonstrated the RBF's ability to perform well at nonlinear mapping while Diosan [5] highlights its effectiveness at nonparametric classification functions. Both papers, however, point out the conflicting trade-off that optimisation brings in gains of training accuracy over the complexity of the model. Other approaches have also used a weighted method to determine the role that each of the component kernels has in the resulting MKL kernel. For example, Deng took this approach to include higher weight based on individual features of the dataset but highlighted the resultant search space as being a prohibitive factor [3]. Similarly to the previous approaches, they suggested a possible approach being the use of a GASVM (Genetic Algorithm SVM) to calculate the optimal solution for kernels as opposed to hyperparameter choice, but again this comes with the high cost of computation expense and time required. Weighting can be counter productive also as strong weighting of less optimal kernels in the MKL arrangement can undermine performance, as documented by Li et al. [13] in their EEG classification MKL-SVM, and Hao's [9] research into primal MKL.

2.3 Computational Cost

Computational cost is not only restricted to the choice of kernel combinations or hyperparameter settings but also in either maintaining Mercer compliance to allow simple gradient descent search or employing a more advanced search algorithm to account for the non-convex solution space that non-Mercer kernels produce. Ensuring the Mercer compliance can be maintained easily by making kernels the inner product of existing Mercer compliant kernels and removing the need for these tests that prove positive semi-definiteness. This combination always results in a continuous, positive semi-definite kernel and due to the commutative property of Mercer kernels the order of base kernels has no bearing on the output. MKL kernels can be tested to ensure that the combinations of kernels are compliant with the positive semi-definite properties of a Mercer kernel as highlighted by Howley et al. in their use of GASVMs [10].

3   Design and Methodology

The approach for this paper is to show that over a broad range of configurations, MKL kernels are valid and novel in shape. To take in a large range of possibilities, a broad range of parameters for the individual kernels will be selected. These will be a choice of kernel specific parameters and tested against the various datasets. Each of the starting, or base, kernels will be first tested against the datasets and then each combined to give the new MKL kernels. This combination will be guaranteed PSD, as discussed earlier, as the base kernels will be chosen from preexisting PSD kernels. The aim will be to test the outputs of the base kernels compared to that of the MKL kernels derived from those specific base kernels. The goal is to move beyond most MKL approaches which use fixed or heuristic based techniques identified by Gonen et al. [7] and demonstrate the power of combinations.

The approach used will be the CRISP DM method (Cross Industry Standard Process for Data Mining) [19] and involves six major stages: (1) Business understanding, (2) Data understanding, (3) Data preparation, (4) Modelling, (5) Evaluation, and (6) Deployment.

3.1   Business Understanding

The research hypothesis behind this study is that the accuracy of models induced by SVM classifiers by employing base kernels is statistically significantly less than the accuracy of models induced by employing multiple base kernels, at a 95% confidence level. Formally: $H : acc(SVM - baseKernel) <> acc(SVM - MKL)$, with alpha $= 0.05$.

3.2   Data Understanding

To test the research hypothesis 8 testing datasets have been taken from the UCI repository and are exclusively binary output variables. The datasets selected are the Prognosis, Heart, Ionosphere, Student Math, Diagnosis, Indian Liver, Student Portuguese, and Pima Indian sets. The datasets were chosen to be relatively small binary sets that have a been previously used in SVM papers and could be run against the full range of hyperparameters and kernels within the allotted time. Variation of the dimensionality, post normalised ranges for standard deviation and variance, and proportion of nominal to categorical variables were also selected for to give a more diverse range of datasets. The focus will be on the individual dataset responses to the different kernel structures and not the specifics of the data.

3.3   Data Preparation

All of the datasets were formatted in the following ways to maintain consistency and to make them suitable for the SVM implementation.

- Formatted to CSV file type to allow for import and to standardise to a common file type.
- Column values added from Metadata description files for easier referencing.
- Categorical and non-numeric fields encoded to numeric values representing each unique entry. This is done to allow them to be used by the SVM.
- Normalised between values of 0 and 1 across all dimension excluding on the output/classification variable to minimise the influence of large number fields.
- The output variable is converted to a −1 and 1 encoding which will be used as factors in the R code.
- Training and testing datasets are both merged as the k-fold method described later will construct multiple training and testing groups later in the process to ensure the quality of accuracy measurement.

3.4   Modeling

The 10-fold cross validation technique has been adopted to induce models using the original Support Vector Machine learning algorithm. This validation technique has been chosen because it will ensure a measure of accuracy that prevents over-fitting and maximises the variation in the relatively small datasets used.

Base Kernel Details

1. Linear Kernel
   Inner product of [x,y] and c value for offset

$$[k(x,y) = x * y + c]$$

2. Polynomial Kernel (Degrees 2, 3, and 4)
   Polynomial kernels expand the examination of similarity between entries in the data. The hyperparameters for the polynomial kernel are the slope, the constant C, as in the Linear Kernel, and the degree, d, of the Polynomial used against the combined transposed x and y input vectors.

$$[k(x,y) = (x^T y + c)^d]$$

3. Gaussian Kernel
   The Gaussian Kernel, also known as the Radial Based Function Kernel, is essentially a weighted linear combination that results in a smooth function of the Hilbert space that is defined as a Euclidean space which is complete, separable and infinitely-dimensional.

$$[k(x,y) = e^{\frac{-\|x-y\|^2}{2\sigma^2}}]$$

The sigma parameter determines the width from the classifying points with smaller sizes trending towards local classification and larger sigma for more general classification. It is specifically important for an effective implementation as if underestimated the model becomes particularly susceptible to noise in the training data whereas, if overestimated, it reduces the non-linear power that is associated with Gaussian kernels.

4. Hyperbolic Tangent (Sigmoid) Kernel
   The Hyperbolic Tangent, or Sigmoid Kernel, has its origins in Artificial Neural Networks (ANNs) where the sigmoid function is used by neurons in the ANN for an activation function. It is also referred to as the Multilayer Perceptron Kernel.

$$[k(x,y) = tanh(\alpha x^T y + c)]$$

The Sigmoid Kernel is very effective but is not guaranteed to be positive semi definite at higher levels. These higher levels will be avoided for the purposes of this study in order not to affect Mercer conditions.

Hyperparameter Ranges. Hyperparameters used across the kernels are:

- Slack: it determines the cost of improperly labelled data points. Range: (0.1, 1, 10, 100, 1000)
- Tolerance: required for termination of SVM. Range:(0.1, 0.01, 0.001, 0.0001, 0.00001)
- Sigma: parameter for Gaussian kernel. Range: (.01, 0.1, 0.2, 0.5, 0.7, 0.9).
- Offset: add an additional offset to data points. Range: (1, 2, 3)
- Scale: used by the Sigmoid and Polynomial. Range: (1, 2, 3)
- Degree: used as the power for the Polynomial kernel. Range: (2, 3, 4)

Novel kernels will be named based on their basic kernel components and will total 11 unique combinations all tested again every configuration of hyperparameters. They will be referred to going forward as LinSigGauPoly(LSGP), LinSigGau (LSG), LinSigPoly(LSP), LinGauPoly(LGP), SigGauPoly(SGP), LinSig(LS), LinGau(LG), LinPoly(LP), SigGau(SG), SigPoly(SP), and GauPoly(GP).

3.5   Evaluation

Due to the fact that 10-fold cross validation has been used in the training phase, 10 surrogate models have been produced. Therefore, a distribution of 10 classification accuracies for each combination of dataset, hyper-parameters and kernel, is available for comparison purposes [17]. The Kruskal Wallis test has been chosen to compare obtained distributions of accuracies and to test the research hypothesis. In particular, the distributions obtained when using combination of multiple simple kernels is compared against the distributions of accuracies obtained when employing these individual kernels alone. This method allows for an analysis of variance that is not restricted to normal distributions of equal size. The Kruskal Wallis technique allows for non-parametric analysis of variance [11]. This means that the distribution of values does not need to be normal and also accommodates differing sample sizes for comparison. Both characteristics are needed in the case of the SVM outputs as there are non-normal, and occasionally bimodal, distributions of cross validation results for certain kernels across the hyperparameter range. The range of hyperparameters themselves are also kernel specific which will result in differing population sizes that need to be compared. As an example the Linear/Vanilla kernel doesn't take in kernel specific hyperparameters but instead just requires the slack and tolerance values to be tested which totals only 24 combinations. Other kernels, however, such as Lin, Sig, Gau, Poly will require the entire range of combinations resulting in over 4000 results per dataset. The Kruskal Wallis test is run across each of the 8 datasets and compares each base kernel with the kernels that have it as a component part. An example would be all the result for Polynomial Kernel against the Ionosphere dataset compared to those of the LinPoly kernel which is composed, in part, by the Polynomial kernel. A threshold of 95% confidence is required to establish if the distributions match and therefore show a lack of a novel solution space.

4   Results

4.1   Cross Validation

Results show (Table 1) the classification accuracies obtained across selected datasets, base kernels and combined kernels. It also placed these accuracies in context by comparing them with those obtained in another similar studies in the literature (GMKL) [15]. The SimpleMKL [18] package, which is very popular method, has also been included with comparable results although over a different set of hyperparameters and completion criteria.

Cross validation is used as it gives an indication of a kernels tendency to overfit. Within our results we see multiple 'error' values for the SVM that represent the best outcome achieved in fitting to the dataset which return a zero value. This represents one hundred percent classification accuracy for the training values. The cross validation being much higher than this zero value indicated that

Table 1. Base kernel and MKL kernel performance

Dataset	GMKL	SimpleMKL	Base kernel	MKL
WPBC	79.0	76.7	Gaussian	SigGau
			83.9	82.9
Iono	93.0	91.5	Gaussian	SigGauPoly
			96.2	96.2
Liver	72.7	65.9	Polynomial	LinGau
			72.5	72.0
Pima	77.2	76.5	Polynomial	LinPoly
			78.4	78.4

the kernel shape has been over fitted to the training set and therefore underperforms when presented with novel data. The role of particular kernels and hyperparameters is not in the scope of this specific research but there are trends visible in the data showing a tendency to overfit when the slack value is set too high. This makes intuitive sense as a high punishment for incorrect value will tend to force the SVM to over accommodate mislabels or outliers. The cross validated SVMs results will be using the second evaluation stage as the populations, per kernel and dataset, that need to be compared to the base kernel values.

4.2 Kruskal Wallis Analysis

The Kruskal Wallins test is performed against each kernel/dataset combination to determine statistically significant differences in the combined kernels output results and that of the base kernels used in their creation

$$H = (N-1) \frac{\sum_{i=1}^{g} n_i (\bar{r}_{i \cdot} - \bar{r})^2}{\sum_{i=1}^{g} \sum_{j=1}^{n_i} (r_{ij} - \bar{r})^2},$$

This method allows for an analysis of variance (ANOVA) that is not restricted to normal distributions of equal size. The test will result in a p_value which will allow a rejection or acceptance of the null or alternate hypothesis set out in the business understanding section.

Of the 224 results there were only 8 populations which show a distribution unchanged through the addition of another kernel. The 8 ranges of accuracies, produced by the new kernels, that didn't show a new distribution are highlighted in **bold** below (Table 2). This shows that for the Maths dataset the gaussian kernel was the only one unchanges in some MKl instance. For the Iono, Liver, and Pima the Sigmoid base kernel was the one without changes in some cases and for the Diag dataset the Polynomial had this property. All other 216 combinations produced a new solution space as a result of being combined with another Mercer Kernel.

Table 2. Base kernel and MKL kernel performance

	Base	LSGP	LSG	LGP	SGP	LG	SG	GP
Math	Gau	<0.01	**0.66685**	0.01632	**0.73788**	**0.80290**	0.03859	**0.73731**
		LSGP	LSG	LSP	SGP	LS	SG	SP
Iono	Sig	<0.01	<0.01	**0.86221**	<0.01	<0.01	<0.01	<0.01
Liver	Sig	0.02753	**0.05394**	<0.01	0.01759	**0.21516**	0.01934	**0.08873**
Pima	Sig	0.02017	<0.01	0.01120	<0.01	**0.08193**	<0.01	<0.01
		LSGP	LSP	LGP	SGP	LP	SP	GP
Diag	Poly	<0.01	<0.01	<0.01	<0.01	<0.01	<0.01	**0.12087**

4.3   Summary of Findings, Strengths and Limitations

The findings of the study means that the expansion of the base kernels using additional base kernel(s) does result in a unique range of cross validated results in the vast majority of cases. Most of the p-values related to the comparison of models trained with a base kernels and models trained by adding another base kernel were less than 0.00001. Despite findings strongly support the research hypothesis, these do not give any insight on the impact of multiple kernel on the enhancement of classification accuracies. The confidence in the results can only be stated for the small datasets used relatively balanced target variables. While characteristics of the dataset were noted at the start phase for dimensionality, proportion of categorical fields, and range of values pre and post normalisation, these factors have not been analysed as part of this research and a further investigation is needed to understand how the classification accuracies change and whether dataset properties have a predictable response to the MKL expansions. However, this empirical study does have an impact in validating kernels as viable and distinct kernels for use in SVMs.

5   Conclusion

The conclusion of this study finds that for the vast majority of base kernel result across the varying datasets, the combination with an additional base kernel or base kernel combination resulted in a statistically significant different range of cross validated accuracies. This helps to further validate the use of multiple kernel learning as a solution to inseparable data through the use of combined conventional kernels. It further opens up investigation into how certain data sets might respond to different kernel shapes based on the dataset properties. Future work should be around investigating the specific hyperparameters role, alongside the dataset characteristics. While this study concentrated on accuracy as the measure of the populations of output, additional work could investigate the ways in which the distributions were altered, positively or negatively, to determine patterns and trends that could help with future MKL creation. The datasets in this study were also relatively small, however, later implementations should address the computational cost using higher performing machines to incorporate larger datasets. Differing proportions of output variables should also be tested and, with it, an examination into the role of kernel shape in accommodating datasets with high sensitivity and specificity requirements. As noted before, when increasing the data size and the balance of outcomes, seed values should be set in the code to ensure the SVM runs against the same partitions of data when using the k-fold cross-validation approach. The scale parameter can also be ignored in future work as the data was pre-normalised but was included for completeness. Finally, the number of base kernels should be expanded to add to the diversity of MKL kernels along with a weighting approach that can consider multiple additions of a specific kernel type rather than MKL kernel composed of just one instance of a particular base kernel.

References

1. Aiolli, F., Donini, M.: Easy multiple kernel learning. In: Proceedings of European Symposium on Artificial Neural Networks, ESANN 2014, Computational Intelligence and Machine Learning, pp. 23–25, April 2015
2. Boser, B.E., Guyon, I.M., Vapnik, V.N.: A training algorithm for optimal margin classifiers. In: Proceedings of the Fifth Annual Workshop on Computational Learning Theory, pp. 144–152 (1992)
3. Deng, S., Sakurai, A.: Integrated model of multiple kernel learning and differential evolution for EUR/USD trading. Sci. World J. **2014**, 12 (2014)
4. Deng, S., Yoshiyama, K., Mitsubuchi, T., Sakurai, A.: Hybrid method of multiple kernel learning and genetic algorithm for forecasting short-term foreign exchange rates. Comput. Econ., pp. 1–41 (2013)
5. Diosan, L., Rogozan, A., Pecuchet, J.P.: Improving classification performance of support vector machine by genetically optimising kernel shape and hyper-parameters. Appl. Intell. **36**(2), 280–294 (2012)
6. Duvenaud, D., Lloyd, J.R., Grosse, R., Tenenbaum, J.B., Ghahramani, Z.: Structure discovery in nonparametric regression through compositional kernel search. In: Proceedings of the 30th International Conference on Machine Learning, vol. 28, pp. 1166–1174 (2013)
7. Gonen, M., Alpaydin, E.: Multiple kernel learning algorithms. J. Mach. Learn. Res. **2011**, 2211–2268 (2011)
8. Gupta, A.K., Guntuku, S.C., Desu, R.K., Balu, A.: Optimisation of turning parameters by integrating genetic algorithm with support vector regression and artificial neural networks. Int. J. Adv. Manufact. Technol. **77**(1–4), 331–339 (2014)
9. Hao, Z., Yuan, G., Yang, X., Chen, Z.: A primal method for multiple kernel learning. Neural Comput. Application. **23**(3–4), 975–987 (2012)
10. Howley, T., Madden, M.: The genetic evolution of kernels for support vector machine classifiers. In: 15th Irish Conference on Artificial Intelligence, pp. 445–453 (2004)
11. Kruskal, W.H., Wallis, W.A.: Use of ranks in one-criterion variance analysis. Am. Stat. Assoc. **47**, 583–621 (1952)
12. Lessmann, S., Stahlbock, R., Crone, S.: Genetic algorithms for support vector machine model selection. In: Proceedings of The 2006 IEEE International Joint Conference on Neural Network, pp. 3063–3069 (2006)

13. Li, X.Z., Kong, J.M.: Application of GA-SVM method with parameter optimization for landslide development prediction. Nat. Hazards Earth Syst. Sci. **14**(3), 525–533 (2014)
14. Lu, D., Qiao, W.: A GA-SVM hybrid classifier for multiclass fault identification of drivetrain gearboxes. In: Proceedings of 2014 IEEE Energy Conversion Congress and Exposition, ECCE 2014, pp. 3894–3900 (2014)
15. Varma, M., Babu, R.R.: More generality in efficient multiple kernel learning, pp. 1065–1072 (2009)
16. Mercer, J.: Functions of positive and negative type, and their connection the theory of integral equations. Philos. Trans. R. Soc. Lond. A: Math. Phys. Eng. Sci. **209**(441–458), 415–446 (1909)
17. Mosteller, F., Tukey, J.W.: Data analysis, including statistics. In: Lindzey, G., Aronson, E. (eds.) Handbook of Social Psychology. Addison-Wesley, New York (1968). ICML 2011
18. Rakotomamonjy, A., Bach, F.R.: SimpleMKL. J. Mach. Learn. Res. **9**, 2491–2521 (2008)
19. Shearer, C.: The CRISP-DM model: the new blueprint for data mining. J. Data Warehous. **5**, 13–22 (2000)
20. Shermeh, A.E., Ghazalian, R.: Recognition of communication signal types using genetic algorithm and support vector machines based on the higher order statistics. Digit. Signal Process. **20**(6), 1748–1757 (2010)
21. Siddiquie, B., Vitaladevuni, S.N., Davis, L.S.: Combining multiple kernels for efficient image classification. In: Applications of Computer Vision WACV 2009 Workshop, pp. 1–8 (2009)
22. Vladimir Vapnik, C.C.: Support-Vector Networks. Kluwer Academic Publishers, Boston (1995)
23. Xu, Z., Jin, R., Yang, H., King, I., Lyu, M.R.: Simple and efficient multiple kernel learning by group lasso. In: International Conference on Machine Learning (ICML), pp. 1191–1198 (2010)

A Dynamic Early Stopping Criterion for Random Search in SVM Hyperparameter Optimization

Adrian Cătălin Florea[1](✉) and Răzvan Andonie[2]

[1] Electronics and Computers Department,
Transilvania University of Braşov, Braşov, Romania
acflorea@unitbv.ro
[2] Computer Science Department,
Central Washington University, Ellensburg, WA, USA
andonie@cwu.edu

Abstract. We introduce a dynamic early stopping condition for Random Search optimization algorithms. We test our algorithm for SVM hyperparameter optimization for classification tasks, on six commonly used datasets. According to the experimental results, we reduce significantly the number of trials used. Since each trial requires a re-training of the SVM model, our method accelerates the RS optimization. The code runs on a multi-core system and we analyze the achieved scalability for an increasing number of cores.

1 Introduction

Most Machine Learning (ML) models are described by two sets of parameters. The first set consists in regular parameters that are learned through training. The other set, called *hyperparameters* or meta-parameters, consists of parameters which are set before the learning starts. It is essential to identify the combination of hyperparameter values which produce the best (or closed to the best) generalization performance. This is done by re-training multiple models with different combinations of hyperparameter values and evaluating their performance. We call this re-training + evaluation for one set of hyperparameter values a *trial*. Since training a model can be very resource intensive, it is important to reduce the number of trials.

In the specific case of SVM classifiers, the algorithm performance depends on several parameters and it is quite sensitive to changes in any of those parameters [1]. The choice of the *kernel*, for example, can have a dramatic influence on the classification performance [2]. The cost parameter (C), controlling the trade-off between margin maximization and error minimization is also highly important as, for the non-separable case, the algorithm must allow training errors. For a polynomial kernel, a wrong choice of the *degree* can easily lead to over-fitting [3].

The most commonly used hyperparameter optimization strategy is a combination of Grid Search (GS) and manual tuning[1] [4–6]. More elaborate techniques are: Nelder-Mead [7], simulated annealing [8], evolutionary algorithms [9], and Bayesian methods [10].

Random Search (RS) is another standard technique for hyperparameter optimization. A nice feature of RS is the possibility of adaptive early stopping. The key is to define a good stopping criterion, representing a trade-off between accuracy and computation time. The rise of the randomized methods begun with the work of Bergstra and Bengio [11, 12]. Using the same number of trials, RS generally yields better results than GS or more complicated hyperparameter optimization methods. Especially in higher dimensional spaces, the computation resources required by RS methods are significantly lower than for GS [13]. Also, RS methods are relatively simple and easy to implement on parallel computer architectures.

Several software libraries dedicated to hyperparameter optimization exist, some of them being autonomous, while others being built on top of existing ML software. LIBSVM [14] and scikit-learn [15] come with their own implementation of GS, with scikit-learn also offering support for RS. Spearmint [16] and Bayesopt [17] are software packages dedicated to Bayesian optimization. Auto-WEKA [18] is also able to perform Bayesian optimization but, unlike the previous two which are standalone libraries, it is built on top of Weka [19]. Hyperopt [20] and Optunity [21] are currently two of the most advanced libraries for hyperparameter optimization.

Our contribution is an improved RS optimization technique, which reduces the number of trials, without a significant impact on the prediction performance. The key is a new dynamically calculated early stopping condition for RS. The method is implemented in parallel and achieves a good scalability. Our experiments are on the SVM classification problem applied to six commonly used datasets and five hyperparameters. According to them, our method accelerates the RS optimization.

The paper proceeds as follows. Section 2 describes our algorithm and the dynamic stopping condition, with an emphasis on the algorithm's parallel nature. Section 3 presents the experimental results and the paper is concluded with Sect. 4.

2 Proposed Algorithm and Probabilistic Properties

A highly simplified version of a hyperparameter optimization algorithm is characterized by an objective fitness function f and a generator of samples g. The fitness function returns a classification accuracy measure of the target model, computed either through cross-validation or on a separate validation set. The generator g is in charge of providing the next set of values that will be used to compute the model's fitness. A *hasNext* method implemented by the generator offers the possibility to terminate the algorithm before the maximum number of N evaluations is reached, if some convergence criteria is satisfied.

---

[1] https://github.com/jaak-s/nips2014-survey - 82 out of 86 optimization related papers presented at the NIPS 2014 conference used GS.

In the particular case of RS, the generator g simply draws samples from the specific distribution of each of the hyperparameters to be optimized. Our goal is to reduce the computational complexity of the RS method in terms of number of trials. In other words, we aim to compute less than N trials, without a significant impact on the value of the fitness function.

For this, we introduce a dynamic stopping criterion, included in a randomized optimization algorithm (Algorithm 1). The algorithm is a two step optimizer. First, it iterates for a predefined number of steps n, $n < < N$, and finds the optimal combination of hyperparameter values, *temp_opt*. Then, it searches for the first result better than *temp_opt*. The optimal result, *opt*, is either the first result better than *temp_opt* or *temp_opt* if N is reached.

Algorithm 1. Parametric stop optimizer

```
func Maximize(f, g, n, N){
    index = -1; tmp_opt = -math.MaxFloat64;   opt = tmp_opt
    for i := 0; i <= n; i++ {
        rndPoint := g.Next(); f_rnd, _ := f(rndPoint)
        if (f_rnd > tmp_opt) {
            index = i; p = rndPoint; tmp_opt = f_rnd
        }
    }
    for i := n+1; i < N; i++ {
        rndPoint := g.Next(); f_rnd, _ := f(rndPoint)
        if (f_rnd > tmp_opt) {
            index = i; p = rndPoint; opt = f_rnd
            break
        }
    }
    return index, p, opt
}
```

The following problems arise: (*i*) Can we determine a value for n that maximizes the probability of obtaining the best results?; and (*ii*) Can the algorithm be parallelized without impacting the probability of obtaining an optimal value?

2.1 Sequential Execution

Algorithm 1 finds the optimum under the assumption that *opt* is in any position i, $i > n$, and no result better than *temp_opt* is in the range $[n+1, i-1]$.

We denote by $E1_i$ the event that *opt* is reached on the i-th trial, and by $E2_i$ the event that no value better than *temp_opt* is obtained between the n-th and the i-th trial. The probability of $E1_i$ is

$$P(E1_i) = 1/N \tag{1}$$

The probability that all values in the range $[n+1, i-1]$ are worse than *temp_opt* is the same as the probability that the best result among the first $i-1$ attempts lays in the range $[1, n]$:

$$P(E2_i) = n/(i-1) \tag{2}$$

Since the two events are independent, the probability that we hit *opt* after $i > n$ attempts is:

$$P_i = P(E1_i) \cdot P(E2_i) = n/(N(i-1)) \tag{3}$$

The event E of finding *opt* after at most m trials, $n < m < N$ (where $m = N/2$ is a reasonable target), has probability

$$P(E) = \sum_{i=n+1}^{m} P_i = \frac{n}{N} \sum_{i=n+1}^{m} \frac{1}{(i-1)} = \frac{n}{N} \sum_{i=n}^{m-1} \frac{1}{i} \tag{4}$$

Since $1/i$ is monotonically decreasing, the right term of Eq. (4) has a lower bound:

$$\frac{n}{N} \int_{n}^{m} \frac{1}{x} dx \leq \frac{n}{N} \sum_{i=n}^{m-1} \frac{1}{i} \tag{5}$$

We differentiate the left term of Eq. (5):

$$\frac{d}{dn} \left(\frac{n}{N} (ln\ m - ln\ n) \right) = \frac{1}{N} (ln\ m - ln\ n - 1), \tag{6}$$

equate to zero and solve for n obtaining:

$$n = m/e \tag{7}$$

Choosing for n a value larger than the optimal one increases the probability of finding the combination of values that yields the optimal result but with an increased risk of a greater number of trials. The result from Eq. (7) can be used to implement an improved version of the Algorithm 1 that can automatically set the value of n to N/e. For example, in order to maximize the chances to obtain the best value, after a target maximum of 150 attempts, we must set n to $150/e$ (≈ 55). For a target maximum of 100 attempts, n should be 37, and so on. Figure 1 shows the lower bound heatmap of the probability to obtain the best results while stopping earlier with respect to the values of m and n.

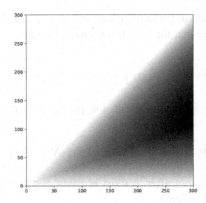

Fig. 1. Lower bound heatmap of the probability to obtain best result from a target space of maximum 300 attempts while terminating faster, depending on the values of m (x axis) and n (y axis). Darker shades correspond to greater probability.

2.2 Parallel Execution

We generate a parallel implementation of our method as follows:

- Split the work between W workers (can be anything from lightweight threads of execution, OS threads, CPU cores or even different servers). We decided to use the GOLANG [22] support for goroutines[2], which are basically lightweight threads managed by the GO run-time.
- Each worker w executes N/W trials using the same early stopping criterion. In this case, $n_w = n/W$, signifying that on average, with $m = N/2$, W workers will terminate after $N/(2W)$ trials, with N/W being the worst case.
- The manager gathers the results from all workers and selects the best candidate.

Algorithm 2 implements the above steps. The random values are generated and distributed by the manager, or each worker generates its own random sequence. Any of the following parallel pseudo-random number generation strategies can be selected [23]: Manager-Worker (MW), Sequence Splitting (SS), Leapfrog (LF), and Parametrization (P).

---

[2] https://tour.golang.org/concurrency/1.

Algorithm 2. Parallel stop optimizer

```
func PMaximize(f, g, N, W) {
    // channels used by workers to communicate their results
    resultsChans := make(chan fn.Sample, W)
    for w := 0; w < W; w++ {
        go func(w int) {
            // index, point, function value, global optim, k
            i, p, v, gv, k := Maximize(f, g, N/W, w )
            resultsChans <- fn.Sample{i, p, v, gv, k}
        }(w)
    }
    // Collect results
    results := make([]fn.Sample, W)
    for i := 0; i < W; i++ {
        results[i] = <-resultsChans
    }
}
```

2.3 The Inverse Problem

Given a restricted computational budget, expressed by a target number of trials m, we obtained the optimal value for n. We are now interested in solving the reverse problem: Given an acceptable probability P to achieve the best result among the N trials, which is the optimal value for n?

For the RS algorithm without the dynamic stopping criterion, if all trials are independent, the required number of trials needed to identify the optimum with a probability P_0 is given by $m = N \cdot P_0$ The problem becomes interesting in the context of our stopping criterion when we are willing to compromise, by accepting a lower probability $P < P_0$, for a further reduction of the number of trials.

In case of Algorithm 2, according to Eq. (5), probability P has a lower bound:

$$P \geq \frac{n}{N}\left(1 + \int_n^m \frac{1}{x}dx\right) = \frac{n}{N}\ln\frac{em}{n} \tag{8}$$

This, together with Eq. (7) gives:

$$P \geq \; = m/(eN) \cdot \ln e^2 = 2P_0/e \approx 0.7357P_0 \tag{9}$$

The value from Eq. (9) represents the probability to identify the optimum regardless of the activation of the stopping criterion - *opt* might also be among the first n trials in which case the algorithm will test all the N possible combinations. The probability to find the optimum after a number of trials strictly lower than N has a lower bound given by relation (5), which translates to:

$$P \geq m/(eN) = P_0/e \approx 0.3678 P_0 \tag{10}$$

The value of n in Eq. (8) can be adjusted in the interval $[m/e, m]$ to increase the probability of identifying the optimal value, but at the same time increase the computational cost (the number of trials).

3   Experiments

We use our method to optimize the following five hyperparameters of a SVM [1] classifier: kernel type (RBF, Polynomial or Linear chosen with equal probability), γ (drawn from an exponential distribution with $\lambda = 10$); cost (C, drawn from an exponential distribution with $\lambda = 10$); degree (chosen with equal probability from the set $\{2, 3, 4, 5\}$) and $coef0$ (uniform on $[0, 1]$).

We run our experiments on six of the most popular datasets from UCI Machine Learning Repository[3]: Adult (a1a), Adult (a6a), Breast Cancer, Diabetes, Iris and Wine. Adult (a1a) and Adult (a6a) are variations of the same dataset but with different number of samples; the second one is around six times larger. Details of the datasets are presented in Table 1.

Table 1. Details on used datasets

Dataset	Instances	Features	Classes #
Adult (a1a)	1,605	123	2
Adult (a6a)	11,220	123	2
Breast cancer	683	10	2
Diabetes	768	8	2
Iris	150	4	3
Wine	178	13	3

We apply ten fold cross-validation to evaluate the classification accuracy [24] and compare the obtained results, both in terms of classification performance and number of trials. We use the following optimizers (all implemented in the Optunity library): GS, RS, Particle Swarm, and Nelder-Mead. We also use the Weka SVM, with its implicit hyperparameters.

We run the Algorithm 2 with $W = 8$ and $N = 250$, which leads to $n = 92$. We also run the four optimizers in Optunity, for a maximum number of 250 trials.

---

[3] http://archive.ics.uci.edu/ml/index.php.

3.1 Accuracy Estimation

Table 2 presents the results of applying Algorithm 2 for four parallelization strategies, compared with the results obtained with Optunity (RS, GS, Particle Swarm and Nelder-Mead) as well as with the results obtained using Weka with each of the three kernels (RBF, Polynomial and Linear) and the implicit values for the other parameters ($C = 1.0$, $\gamma = 1/number\_of\_features$, $degree = 3$, $coef0 = 0.0$). The best results are marked in bold.

Table 2. Accuracy and number of trials for Algorithm 2 using different parallelization strategies (MW, SS, LF, P), compared with Optunity (RS, GS, Particle Swarm and Nelder-Mead) and Weka's SVM.

Dataset	GO MW		GO SS		GO LF		GO P		Optunity RS	Optunity GS	Optunity PS	Optunity NM		Weka RBF	Weka Poly	Weka Linear
	Acc	Runs	Acc	Runs	Acc	Runs	Acc	Runs	Acc	Acc	Acc	Acc	Runs	Acc	Acc	Acc
Adult (a1a)	0.837	164	0.836	194	0.837	194	0.837	148	0.837	0.835	0.838	0.833	108	0.828	**0.839**	0.754
Adult (a6a)	0.844	169	0.844	133	0.844	203	**0.845**	138	0.844	0.844	0.845	0.843	142	0.838	0.760	0.760
Cancer	0.975	172	0.975	167	0.975	214	0.975	187	0.975	0.975	**0.975**	0.968	17	0.969	0.974	0.969
Diabetes	0.776	223	0.776	203	**0.780**	220	0.779	130	0.777	0.777	0.776	0.651	6	0.775	0.686	0.777
Iris	0.973	224	0.980	156	0.980	189	0.973	158	0.980	**0.987**	0.967	0.940	6	0.953	0.727	0.960
Wine	**0.989**	194	**0.989**	215	**0.989**	162	**0.989**	177	**0.989**	0.984	**0.989**	0.956	62	0.983	0.404	0.972
Average	0.899	191	0.900	178	**0.901**	197	0.900	156.334	0.900	0.900	0.898	0.865	**56.834**	0.891	0.732	0.865
STDEV	0.091	27.188	0.092	31.241	0.091	**20.746**	0.090	22.223	0.092	0.092	0.090	0.120	57.711	**0.088**	0.190	0.112

Since we compare multiple classifiers on multiple datasets, we have to use additional statistical tests for further investigation, as suggested in [25].

We calculate the Friedman [26] and the Iman-Davenport [27] statistics using Eq. (11), respectively Eq. (12), with N being the number of datasets, k the number of algorithms and R_j the average rank of algorithm j from Table 3, and obtain $\chi_F^2 = 32.826, F_F = 6.04$.

$$\chi_F^2 = \frac{12N}{k(k+1)} \left[\sum_{j=1}^{k} R_j^2 - \frac{k(k+1)^2}{4} \right] \tag{11}$$

$$F_F = \frac{(N-1)\chi_F^2}{N(k-1) - \chi_F^2} \tag{12}$$

With 11 algorithms and six data sets, F_F is distributed according to the F distribution with $11 - 1 = 10$ and $(11 - 1) \times (6 - 1) = 50$ degrees of freedom. The critical value of $F(10, 50)$ for $\alpha = 0.05$ is 2.03, so we reject the null-hypothesis, which means the algorithms are not equivalent in terms of prediction performance.

The critical difference [25, 28] is given by:

$$CD_\alpha = q_\alpha \sqrt{\frac{k(k+1)}{6N}} \tag{13}$$

Table 3. Algorithms' accuracy ranking on the used datasets.

Dataset	GO MW	GO SS	GO LF	GO P	Optunity RS	Optunity GS	Optunity PS	Optunity NM	Weka RBF	Weka Poly	Weka Linear
Adult (a1a)	6	7	3.5	3.5	5	8	2	9	10	1	11
Adult (a6a)	3	4	7	1	5	6	2	8	9	10.5	10.5
Cancer	5.5	5.5	5.5	5.5	2.5	2.5	1	11	9.5	8	9.5
Diabetes	8	7	1	2	5	4	6	11	9	10	3
Iris	5.5	3	3	5.5	3	1	7	10	9	11	8
Wine	2.5	2.5	2.5	2.5	5.5	7	5.5	10	8	11	9
Average	5.083	4.833	3.750	3.333	4.333	4.750	3.917	9.833	9.083	8.583	8.500

where critical values q_α are based on the Studentized range statistic divided by $\sqrt{2}$. At significance level of $\alpha = 0.05$, the critical difference is $CD_{0.05} = 6.163$.

This clearly rules out the Nelder-Mead algorithm, which is significantly worse than the Parametrization based implementation of our RS ($9.833 - 3.333 > 6.163$). At significance level $\alpha = 0.1$, the critical difference is $CD_{0.1} = 5.701$ and we observe that Optunity - NM is significantly worse than GO - LF and GO - P and also that GO - P is significantly better than Optunity - NM and Weka - RBF.

3.2   Efficiency of the Stopping Condition

Based on the above results, we exclude Nelder-Mead (due to its significantly worse classification performance) and the Weka SVM (since is it does not perform a real hyperparameter optimization) from the analysis. Table 4 depicts the rank across all datasets in terms of number of trials.

Table 4. Algorithms ranking in terms of number of runs.

Dataset	GO MW	GO SS	GO LF	GO P	Optunity RS	Optunity GS	Optunity PS
Adult (a1a)	2	3.5	3.5	1	6	6	6
Adult (a6a)	3	1	4	2	6	6	6
Cancer	2	1	4	3	6	6	6
Diabetes	4	2	3	1	6	6	6
Iris	4	1	3	2	6	6	6
Wine	3	4	1	2	6	6	6
Average	3.000	2.083	3.083	1.833	6.000	6.000	6.000

We perform another Friedman test and, using formulas (11) and (12), and obtain: $\chi_F^2 = 28.554$ and $F_F = 19.173$. The critical value for $F(6, 30)$ ($7 - 1$ and respectively $(7 - 1)(6 - 1)$) is 2.420. This means that we can rule out the null-hypothesis and state that the algorithms are not equivalent with respect to the number of trials. We compute the critical difference according to formula (13) and obtain $CD_{0.05} = 3.678$.

Table 5 shows the difference in the average rank values for each pair of algorithms. The values greater than $CD_{0.05}$ are marked in bold font. We can identify two groups of algorithms, the first group (GO - SS and GO - P) performs significantly better than the second group (Optunity - GS, Optunity - RS and Optunity - PS). It is not clear to which of the two groups GO - MW and GO - LF belong to. One possible explanation for the better results obtained by GO - SS and GO - P may be related to the superior parallel implementation of the random generators. However, since the number of random values generated in our tests is relatively small, this difference in performance is most probably coincidental.

Table 5. Algorithms ranking difference in terms of number of runs.

	GO MW	GO SS	GO LF	GO P	Optunity RS	Optunity GS	Optunity PS
GO MW	–	−0.917	0.084	−1.167	3	3	3
GO SS		–	1	−0.25	**3.917**	**3.917**	**3.917**
GO LF			–	−1.25	2.917	2.917	2.917
GO P				–	**4.167**	**4.167**	**4.167**
Optunity RS					–	0	0
Optunity GS						–	0
Optunity PS							–

Finally, since the main goal of our work is to obtain an improved version of RS, we compare our method directly with Optunity RS, using the Holm [29] test. The standard error for our experiment is $SE = \sqrt{k(k+1)/(6N)} = 1.247$. Table 6 shows the results of the Holm rejection test.

Table 6. Performance in terms of number of trials required for GO - MW, GO - P, GO - SS and GO - LF against Optunity - RS in terms of the Holm test.

	i	$z = (R0 - Ri)/SE$	p	α/i
GO P	1	3.341	0.00084	0.0084
GO SS	2	3.140	0.00043	0.01
GO MW	3	2.405	0.00808	0.0125
GO LF	4	2.339	0.009668	0.0167

The Holm test rejects all four hypotheses, since the corresponding p values are smaller than the adjusted α's, leading to the conclusion that all four versions of our algorithm are significantly more efficient in terms of number of trials than the standard RS implementation.

3.3   Scalability

Besides the accuracy and the number of runs we also measure the algorithm's speedup (the ratio of the sequential execution time to the parallel execution time) as a measure of its scalability. The values are depicted in Table 7.

Table 7. Algorithm speedup with increasing number of cores.

Dataset/Cores	2	3	4	6	8
Adult(a1a)	1.37	2.96	3.48	4.13	4.52
Adult (a6a)	1.97	2.71	3.02	3.35	3.70
Cancer	1.98	2.91	3.53	3.91	4.09
Diabetes	1.86	2.72	3.34	3.70	3.88
Iris	1.94	2.75	3.10	3.43	3.54
Wine	1.99	2.81	3.28	3.96	4.11
Average	1.85	2.81	3.29	3.75	3.97

4   Conclusions

We introduced a new dynamic stopping condition for RS based hyperparameter optimization, together with its parallel implementation. In the context of SVM classification, on six of the most commonly used datasets, we obtained on par accuracy values with the existing mainstream hyperparameter optimization techniques. With all four of the parallel random generators used, the algorithm terminates after a significantly reduced number of trials compared to the standard implementation of RS, which leads to an important decrease in the computational budget required for the optimization.

The present work opens further research directions in terms of optimizing the hyperparameters for other ML algorithms where the search space has a larger number of dimensions and the required computational budget is currently a major issue. The algorithm implementation is flexible enough to allow a gradient-free optimization of any function.

References

1. Cortes, C., Vapnik, V.: Support-vector networks. Mach. Learn. **20**(3), 273–297 (1995). https://doi.org/10.1023/A:1022627411411
2. Chapelle, O., Vapnik, V., Bousquet, O., Mukherjee, S.: Choosing multiple parameters for support vector machines. Mach. Learn. **46**(1), 131–159 (2002). https://doi.org/10.1023/A:1012450327387
3. Bishop, C.M.: Pattern Recognition and Machine Learning (Information Science and Statistics). Springer-Verlag, New York Inc., Secaucus (2006)
4. LeCun, Y.A., Bottou, L., Orr, G.B., Müller, K.-R.: Efficient backprop. In: Montavon, G., Orr, G.B., Müller, K.-R. (eds.) Neural Networks: Tricks of the Trade. LNCS, vol. 7700, pp. 9–48. Springer, Heidelberg (2012). https://doi.org/10.1007/978-3-642-35289-8_3

5. Hinton, G.E.: A practical guide to training restricted boltzmann machines. In: Montavon, G., Orr, G.B., Müller, K.-R. (eds.) Neural Networks: Tricks of the Trade. LNCS, vol. 7700, pp. 599–619. Springer, Heidelberg (2012). https://doi.org/10.1007/978-3-642-35289-8_32
6. Smusz, S., Czarnecki, W.M., Warszycki, D., Bojarski, A.J.: Exploiting uncertainty measures in compounds activity prediction using support vector machines. Bioorg. Med. Chem. Lett. **25**(1), 100–105 (2015)
7. Nelder, J.A., Mead, R.: A simplex method for function minimization. Comput. J. **7**, 308–313 (1965)
8. Kirkpatrick, S.: Optimization by simulated annealing: quantitative studies. J. Stat. Phys. **34** (5), 975–986 (1984)
9. Hansen, N., Muller, S.D., Koumoutsakos, P.: Reducing the time complexity of the derandomized evolution strategy with covariance matrix adaptation (CMA-ES). Evol. Comput. **11**(1), 1–18 (2003). https://doi.org/10.1162/106365603321828970
10. Thornton, C., Hutter, F., Hoos, H.H., Leyton-Brown, K.: Auto-WEKA: combined selection and hyperparameter optimization of classification algorithms. In: Proceedings of the 19th ACM SIGKDD International Conference on Knowledge Discovery and Data Mining, KDD 2013, pp. 847–855. ACM, New York (2013). http://doi.acm.org/10.1145/2487575.2487629
11. Bergstra, J., Bardenet, R., Bengio, Y., Kgl, B.: Algorithms for hyper-parameter optimization. In: Shawe-Taylor, J., Zemel, R.S., Bartlett, P.L., Pereira, F.C.N., Weinberger, K.Q. (eds.) NIPS 2011, pp. 2546–2554 (2011). http://dblp.uni-trier.de/db/conf/nips/nips2011.html
12. Bergstra, J., Bengio, Y.: Random search for hyper-parameter optimization. J. Mach. Learn. Res. **13**, 281–305 (2012)
13. Lemley, J., Jagodzinski, F., Andonie, R.: Big holes in big data: a monte carlo algorithm for detecting large hyper-rectangles in high dimensional data. In: 2016 IEEE 40th Annual Computer Software and Applications Conference (COMPSAC), vol. 1, pp. 563–571, June 2016
14. Chang, C.-C., Lin, C.-J.: LIBSVM: a library for support vector machines. ACM Trans. Intell. Syst. Technol. **2**, 27:1–27:27 (2011), Software. http://www.csie.ntu.edu.tw/cjlin/libsvm
15. Pedregosa, F., Varoquaux, G., Gramfort, A., Michel, V., Thirion, B., Grisel, O., Blondel, M., Prettenhofer, P., Weiss, R., Dubourg, V., Vanderplas, J., Passos, A., Cournapeau, D., Brucher, M., Perrot, M., Duchesnay, E.: Scikit-learn: machine learning in python. J. Mach. Learn. Res. **12**, 2825–2830 (2011)
16. Snoek, J., Larochelle, H., Adams, R.P.: Practical bayesian optimization of machine learning algorithms. In: Pereira, F., Burges, C.J.C., Bottou, L., Weinberger, K.Q. (eds.) Advances in Neural Information Processing Systems, vol. 25, pp. 2951–2959. Curran Associates, Inc. (2012). http://papers.nips.cc/paper/4522-practical-bayesian-optimization-of-machine-learning-algorithms.pdf
17. Martinez-Cantin, R.: Bayesopt: a bayesian optimization library for nonlinear optimization, experimental design and bandits. CoRR, abs/1405.7430 (2014). http://arxiv.org/abs/1405.7430
18. Kotthoff, L., Thornton, C., Hoos, H.H., Hutter, F., Leyton-Brown, K.: Auto-WEKA 2.0: automatic model selection and hyperparameter optimization in WEKA. J. Mach. Learn. Res. **18**(25), 1–5 (2017). http://jmlr.org/papers/v18/16-261.html
19. Hall, M., Frank, E., Holmes, G., Pfahringer, B., Reutemann, P., Witten, I.H.: The WEKA data mining software: an update. SIGKDD Explor. Newsl. **11**(1), 10–18 (2009). http://doi.acm.org/10.1145/1656274.1656278
20. Bergstra, J., Komer, B., Eliasmith, C., Yamins, D., Cox, D.D.: Hyperopt: a python library for model selection and hyperparameter optimization. Comput. Sci. Discov. **8**(1), 014008 (2015). http://stacks.iop.org/1749-4699/8/i=1/a=014008

21. Claesen, M., Simm, J., Popovic, D., Moreau, Y., Moor, B.D.: Easy hyperparameter search using optunity. CoRR, abs/1412.1114 (2014). http://arxiv.org/abs/1412.1114
22. Google: The Go Programming Language (2007). https://golang.org/project/
23. Quinn, M.J.: Parallel Programming in C with MPI and OpenMP. McGraw-Hill Education Group (2003)
24. Sokolova, M., Lapalme, G.: A systematic analysis of performance measures for classification tasks. Inf. Process. Manage. **45**(4), 427–437 (2009). https://doi.org/10.1016/j.ipm.2009.03.002
25. Demsar, J.: Statistical comparisons of classifiers over multiple data sets. J. Mach. Learn. Res. **7**, 1–30 (2006). http://www.jmlr.org/papers/volume7/demsar06a/demsar06a.pdf
26. Friedman, M.: A comparison of alternative tests of significance for the problem of m rankings. Ann. Math. Statist. **11**(1), 86–92 (1940). https://doi.org/10.1214/aoms/1177731944
27. Iman, R., Davenport, J.: Approximations of the critical region of the Friedman statistic. Commun. Stat.-Theo. Meth. **9**, 571–595 (1980)
28. Nemenyi, P.: Distribution-free Multiple Comparisons. Thesis Princeton University (1963). https://books.google.ro/books?id=nhDMtgAACAAJ
29. Holm, S.: A simple sequentially rejective multiple test procedure. Scand. J. Stat. **6**, 65–70 (1979)

Constraints

Constraints

Greedy Heuristics for Automatic Synthesis of Efficient Block-Structured Scheduling Processes from Declarative Specifications

Amelia Bădică[1], Costin Bădică[1(✉)], Daniela Dănciulescu[1],
and Doina Logofătu[2]

[1] University of Craiova, Craiova, Romania
ameliabd@yahoo.com, cbadica@software.ucv.ro
[2] University of Applied Sciences, Frankfurt, Germany
logofatu@fb2.fra-uas.de

Abstract. This paper introduces a new Greedy heuristic algorithm for the automatic synthesis of block-structured scheduling processes that satisfy a given set of declarative ordering constraints, as well as basic theoretical results that support the correctness of this algorithm. We propose two heuristics that can be used with this algorithm: hierarchical decomposition heuristic and critical path heuristic. We also present initial experimental results supporting the effectiveness and efficiency of our proposed algorithm and heuristics.

Keywords: Greedy algorithm · Process model · Ordering constraints
Optimization

1 Introduction

There are many formalisms for the specification of business process models. Block-structured models have certain advantages compared with other approaches [3].

It is useful and quite intuitive to declaratively specify desired properties of process models. We are interested in constructing process models that are consistent with the given declarative specification [6]. This problem has practical applications in scheduling tasks encountered in manufacturing systems [4].

Manual construction of large process models satisfying a set of ordering constraints is almost impossible or at least not scalable. Automatic generation based on exhaustive exploration of the space of possibilities is difficult because of the huge number of potential candidates. The only feasible solution is to design automatic approaches based on efficient heuristic algorithms that are able to drastically prune the huge search space.

© IFIP International Federation for Information Processing 2018
Published by Springer International Publishing AG 2018. All Rights Reserved
L. Iliadis et al. (Eds.): AIAI 2018, IFIP AICT 519, pp. 183–195, 2018.
https://doi.org/10.1007/978-3-319-92007-8_16

In this paper we focus on scheduling processes. In this case, the declarative specification defines the scheduling constraints. We are interested in determining optimal or at least, as efficient as possible, block-structured scheduling processes that satisfy the scheduling constraints. The optimization criterion requires the minimization of the total completion time. Optionally, we can add other constraints, like for example imposing upper bounds for the amount of parallel work. This constraint may result from the practical restriction regarding the limited availability of certain resources. In particular: (i) our processes are defined only using sequential and parallel composition; (ii) each activity must have exactly one instance in the schedule.

Our work was mainly influenced by previous results of [4,5]. Nevertheless, our results are different in many aspects. Most important, our heuristics are deterministic and different. We are using the hierarchical decomposition of a graph, while [4,5] are based on the more complex modular decomposition. We also provide theoretical results to support our work. Finally, we performed experiments with larger graphs, and our preliminary results suggest that our algorithm might be faster.

Note that there are many theoretical studies on evolutionary algorithms and randomized (meta/hyper) heuristics applied to combinatorial optimization algorithms [1]. Such works could be considered for the further expansion of our results by comparison of our method with different, but related approaches.

2   Process Models

Let us consider a finite nonempty set of activities Σ. A *trace* $t \in \Sigma^*$ is a sequence of zero or more activities[1]. The length of a trace $t = a_1 a_2 \ldots a_n$ is n and this is denoted as $|t| = n$. The empty trace is denoted by ε and $|\varepsilon| = 0$. For each nonempty trace $t = a_1 a_2 \ldots a_n$ we define: (i) the head of t as $head(t) = a_1$, and (ii) the tail of t as $tail(t) = a_2 \ldots a_n$.

A *language* $L \subseteq 2^{\Sigma^*}$ is defined as a set of traces. We can define certain operations with languages. The *sequential composition* of two languages L_1 and L_2 denoted by $L_1 \to L_2$, is defined as follows:

$$L_1 \to L_2 = \{w = l_1 l_2 \mid l_1 \in L_1 \text{ and } l_2 \in L_2\}$$

This notation can be extended for a trace t and a language L as: $t \to L = \{t\} \to L$.

The *parallel composition* of two traces t_1 and t_2, denoted by $t_1 \parallel t_2$, is defined as:

– For each nonempty trace t we have: $t \parallel \varepsilon = \varepsilon \parallel t = \{t\}$
– For each nonempty traces t_1 and t_2 we have:

$$t_1 \to t_2 = (head(t_1) \to (tail(t_1) \parallel t_2)) \cup (head(t_2) \to (t_1 \parallel tail(t_2)))$$

---

[1] Σ^* is the set of all sequences consisting of zero or more elements of Σ.

The *parallel composition* $L_1 \parallel L_2$ of two languages L_1 and L_2 is now defined as:

$$L_1 \parallel L_2 = \cup_{t_1 \in L_1, t_2 \in L_2} t_1 \parallel t_2$$

Let us consider the set $\{\rightarrow, |, \parallel\}$ of three binary operators used for constructing block-structured processes. The operator $\rightarrow$ denotes *sequential composition*, the operator $|$ denotes the *nondeterministic choice*, and the operator $\parallel$ denotes *parallel composition*.

Let us denote with $a, b, c, \ldots$ the activities of Σ and with $P, Q, R, \ldots$ process terms. Process terms can be defined recursively as follows:

$$P ::= a \mid P \rightarrow Q \mid P \mid Q \mid P \parallel Q$$

The language $L(P)$ of process P is recursively defined as follows:

- $L(a) = \{a\}$
- $L(P \rightarrow Q) = L(P) \rightarrow L(Q)$
- $L(P \mid Q) = L(P) \cup L(Q)$
- $L(P \parallel Q) = L(P) \parallel L(Q)$

Operator $\parallel$ has higher precedence, operator $\rightarrow$ has middle precedence, and operator $|$ has lower precedence. All operators are associative, while $\parallel$ and $|$ are also commutative.

Process terms represent models of processes and they can be graphically depicted as trees or as block-structured flowcharts, as shown in Fig. 1.

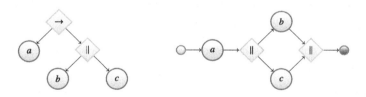

Fig. 1. Tree model of process $a \rightarrow b \parallel c$ (left) and its equivalent block-structured model (right)

In what follows we focus on process models with the following particularities:

- They represent sets of possible activity schedules. A schedule must contain exactly one instance of each activity.
- They use sequential ($\rightarrow$) and parallel ($\parallel$) operators. Scheduling processes are deterministic, explaining why nondeterministic choice is not used in their definition.

Rigorously defining scheduling processes requires the introduction of the support set $supp(P)$ of a process P that denotes the set of activities that occur in process P.

A *block-structured scheduling process* is recursively defined as follows:

- If a is an activity then a is also a process such that $supp(a) = \{a\}$.
- If P and Q are processes such that $supp(P) \cap supp(Q) = \emptyset$ then $P \to Q$ and $P \parallel Q$ are processes with $supp(P \to Q) = supp(P \parallel Q) = supp(P) \cup supp(Q)$.

For example, processes $a \parallel c \to b$ and $a \parallel (c \to b)$ are well-formed, and:

- $supp(a \parallel c \to b) = supp(a \parallel (c \to b)) = \{a, b, c\}$
- $L(a \parallel c \to b) = \{acb, cab\}$
- $L(a \parallel (c \to b)) = \{acb, cab, cba\}$

It is not difficult to observe that if P is a well-formed block-structured scheduling process then all its traces $t \in L(P)$ have the same length $|t| = |supp(P)|$.

3   Declarative Specification of Ordering Constraints

3.1   Activity Ordering Graph

Based on domain-specific semantics, one can impose ordering constraints of the activities of a process. For example if two activities are independent and there are enough resources to be allocated to each of them then those activities can be scheduled for parallel execution. However, if an activity depends on the output produced by another activity, then the first activity can be scheduled for execution only after the completion of the second activity, i.e. there is a sequencing constraint between their execution order. Finally, if two activities define distinct action options then their execution is incompatible, so it cannot occur within the same schedule, i.e. they are mutually exclusive.

The ordering constraints imposed on each trace of a scheduling process are declaratively specified using an *activity ordering graph* $\mathcal{G} = \langle V, E \rangle$ [5] such that:

- V is the set of nodes and each node represents an activity.
- $E \subseteq V \times V$ is the set of edges. Each edge represents an ordering constraint. Set E is partitioned into two disjoint sets $E_{\to}$ and $E_{\neq}$ with the following meaning:
  - Set $E_{\to}$ specifies sequential ordering constraints. If $(u, v) \in E_{\to}$ then activity v cannot occur in a schedule without being preceded by activity u. $E_{\to}$ is a partial ordering, i.e. it is transitive and antisymmetric, so it cannot define cycles.
  - Set $E_{\neq}$ specifies mutual exclusion constraints. If $(u, v) \in E_{\neq}$ then activities u and v are incompatible, so they cannot occur within the same schedule. Set $E_{\neq}$ defines a symmetric relation.

Intuitively, satisfaction of mutual exclusion constraints requires the availability of nondeterministic choice operator in process definition. As we assumed that this operator is not available for scheduling processes, we will now focus only on sequential ordering constraints, i.e. we assume that $E_{\neq} = \emptyset$ so $E = E_{\to}$. This means that the ordering graph is a directed acyclic graph with arcs defining sequential ordering constraints.

If $t = a_1 a_2 \ldots a_n$ is a trace of a scheduling process and u, v are two activities of t then u precedes v in t, i.e. $u \xrightarrow{t} v$ if there are $1 \leq i < j \leq n$ such that $a_i = u$ and $a_j = v$.

Let $\mathcal{G} = \langle V, E \rangle$ be an ordering graph and let t be a trace containing all the activities of V with no repetition. Then t *satisfies* $\mathcal{G}$, written as $t \models \mathcal{G}$, if and only if $E_{\rightarrow} \subseteq \xrightarrow{t}$. This means that trace t cannot contain activities ordered differently than as specified by $\mathcal{G}$.

The language $L(\mathcal{G})$ of an ordering graph $\mathcal{G}$ is the set of all traces that satisfy $\mathcal{G}$, i.e.:

$$L(\mathcal{G}) = \{t \mid t \models \mathcal{G}\}$$

Let P be a scheduling process and let $\mathcal{G} = \langle V, E \rangle$ be an ordering graph. P *satisfies* $\mathcal{G}$ written as $P \models \mathcal{G}$, if and only if:

- $L(P) \subseteq L(\mathcal{G})$, i.e. each trace of P satisfies $\mathcal{G}$, and
- $supp(P) = V$, i.e. all the activities of V are relevant and occur in P.

The set of processes P such that $P \models \mathcal{G}$ is nonempty, as it contains at least one sequential process defined by the topological sorting of $\mathcal{G}$.

3.2   Optimal Scheduling Processes

Each activity has an estimated duration of execution that is represented using a function $d : \Sigma \to \mathbb{R}^+$. The duration of execution $d(P)$ of a process P is defined as follows:

- If $P = a$ then $d(P) = d(a)$.
- $d(P \to Q) = d(P) + d(Q)$.
- $d(P \parallel Q) = \max \{d(P), d(Q)\}$.

The *minimum duration of execution* of a process that satisfies a given ordering graph $\mathcal{G}$, denoted with $d_{MIN}(\mathcal{G})$, is defined as:

$$d_{MIN}(\mathcal{G}) = \min_{P \models \mathcal{G}} \{d(P)\}$$

An *optimal scheduling process* that satisfies a given ordering graph $\mathcal{G}$ is a process P^* with a minimum duration of execution, i.e. it satisfies:

- $P^* \models \mathcal{G}$, and
- $d(P^*) = d_{MIN}(\mathcal{G})$.

There is a finite and nonempty set of processes that satisfy an ordering graph $\mathcal{G}$, so the optimal scheduling process trivially exists. Moreover, as there is an exponential number of candidate processes satisfying $\mathcal{G}$, we postulate that the computation of the optimal scheduling process is generally an intractable problem. Therefore, we will be focusing on developing efficient heuristic algorithms that are able to produce "suboptimal" or "good enough" scheduling processes using a reasonable computational effort.

4   Heuristics for Suboptimal Processes

We introduce two heuristics that are used to derive an efficient Greedy heuristic algorithm for computing a suboptimal scheduling process satisfying an ordering graph.

4.1   Hierarchical Decomposition Heuristic

Let $\mathcal{G} = \langle V, E \rangle$ be an ordering graph. Remember that $\mathcal{G}$ is a directed acyclic graph defining the sequential ordering constraints imposed on a scheduling process.

– For each node $v \in V$ we define the set $I(v)$ of *input neighbors* of v as follows: $I(v) = \{u \in V \mid (u, v) \in E\}$.
– For each node $v \in V$ we define the *level* $l(v)$ of v as a function $l : v \to \mathbb{N}$ such that:
  • If $I(v) = \emptyset$ then $l(v) = 0$.
  • If $I(v) \neq \emptyset$ then $l(v) = 1 + \max\limits_{u \in I(v)} \{l(u)\}$.
– The *height* $l(\mathcal{G})$ of graph $\mathcal{G}$ is defined as $l(\mathcal{G}) = \max\limits_{v \in V} \{l(v)\}$.
– If $m = l(\mathcal{G}) \geq 0$ then the family of $m + 1$ sets $\{V_0, V_1, \ldots, V_m\}$ defined as $V_i = \{v \mid l(v) = i\}$ for all $0 \leq i \leq m$ is a partition of V. If $\mathcal{G}_i$ is the subgraph of $\mathcal{G}$ induced by V_i then the family of graphs $\{\mathcal{G}_0, \mathcal{G}_1, \ldots, \mathcal{G}_m\}$ is known as the *hierarchical decomposition* of $\mathcal{G}$.

Proposition 1. *(Hierarchical Decomposition Process) Let $\mathcal{G} = \langle V, E \rangle$ be an ordering graph. The* hierarchical decomposition process $P_{HD}(\mathcal{G})$ *associated to $\mathcal{G}$ is defined as:*

– $P_i = \|_{v \in V_i} v$ *for all $0 \leq i \leq m$.*
– $P_{HD}(\mathcal{G}) = P_0 \to P_1 \to \cdots \to P_m$.

Then $P_{HD}(\mathcal{G}) \models \mathcal{G}$. Moreover, the duration of execution of the hierarchical decomposition process associated to an ordering graph, denoted as $d_{HD}(\mathcal{G}) = d(P_{HD}(\mathcal{G}))$, represents a non-trivial upper bound of the duration of execution of the optimal scheduling process $d_{MIN}(\mathcal{G})$, i.e. $d_{HD}(\mathcal{G}) \geq d_{MIN}(\mathcal{G})$.

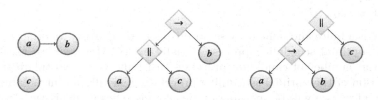

Fig. 2. Ordering graph $\mathcal{G}_1$ (left), process P_1 (middle) and process P_2 (right)

Figure 2 shows an ordering graph $\mathcal{G}_1$, and two processes P_1 and P_2 such that $\mathcal{G}_1 \models P_1$ and $\mathcal{G}_1 \models P_2$. The hierarchical decomposition of $\mathcal{G}_1$ is induced by the partition of its vertices $\{\{a, c\}, \{b\}\}$, so we can easily notice that P_1 is the hierarchical decomposition process of $\mathcal{G}_1$. Observe that:

- $d_{HD}(\mathcal{G}_1) = d(P_1) = \max\{d(a), d(c)\} + d(b)$
- $d(P_2) = \max\{d(a) + d(b), d(c)\}$

Clearly $d(P_1) \geq d(P_2)$ and P_2 is optimal (other satisfying processes are strictly sequential, incurring a higher duration of execution). But note that if $d(a) \geq d(c)$ then $d(P_1) = d(P_2) = d(a) + d(b)$ so the optimal scheduling process has duration $d_{HD}(\mathcal{G}_1)$ which shows that we can have equality in the inequality resulted from Proposition 1. However, if $d(a) < d(c)$ the optimal scheduling process has duration $d(P_2) = \max\{d(a) + d(b), d(c)\} < d_{HD}(\mathcal{G}_1) = d(c) + d(b)$.

4.2   Critical Path Heuristic

Observe that an activity u cannot start unless all the neighboring activities from the input set $I(u)$ are finished. This time point is denoted with $start(u)$. Activity u that started at $start(u)$ will finish at time $finish(u) = start(u) + d(u)$. The values $start(u)$ and $finish(u)$ for each activity $u \in V$ can be computed using the *critical path method* [2], as follows:

- If $I(u) = \emptyset$ then $start(u) = 0$ and $finish(u) = d(u)$.
- If $I(u) \neq \emptyset$ then $start(u) = \max_{v \in I(u)}\{finish(v)\}$ and $finish(u) = start(u) + d(u)$.

The maximum value of the finishing time of each activity, known as *critical path length*, is a lower bound for the duration of execution of the optimal scheduling process.

Proposition 2. *(Critical Path) Let $\mathcal{G} = \langle V, E \rangle$ be an ordering graph and let $d_{CP}(\mathcal{G})$ be its critical path length. Then $d_{CP}(\mathcal{G})$ is a lower bound of the duration of execution of the optimal scheduling process $d_{MIN}(\mathcal{G})$, i.e. $d_{MIN}(\mathcal{G}) \geq d_{CP}(\mathcal{G})$.*

Figure 3 shows an ordering graph $\mathcal{G}_2$ and its hierarchical decomposition process P_3. The critical path length of $\mathcal{G}_2$ is trivially $d_{CP}(\mathcal{G}_2) = \max\{d(a) + d(b), d(a) + d(d), d(c) + d(d)\}$, while $d(P_3) = \max\{d(a), d(c)\} + \max\{d(b), d(d)\} = \max\{d(a) + d(b), d(a) + d(d), d(c) + d(b), d(c) + d(d)\} = \max\{d_{CP}(\mathcal{G}_2), d(c) + d(b)\} \geq d(\mathcal{G}_2)$. Note that:

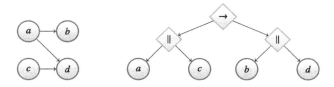

Fig. 3. Ordering graph $\mathcal{G}_2$ (left) and process P_3 (right)

- If $d(c) + d(b) \leq \max\{d(a) + d(b), d(a) + d(d), d(c) + d(d)\}$ then $d_{CP}(\mathcal{G}_2) = d(P_3)$, i.e. the hierarchical decomposition process has a duration of execution equal to the critical path length. This clearly shows that $d_{MIN}(\mathcal{G}_2) = d_{CP}(\mathcal{G}_2)$.
- If $d(c) + d(b) > \max\{d(a) + d(b), d(a) + d(d), d(c) + d(d)\}$ then we infer that $d(c) > d(a)$, $d(b) > d(d)$, and $d(P_3) = d(b) + d(c)$. However, we do not know yet if in this case $d_{MIN}(\mathcal{G}_2)$ is equal to or strictly higher than $d_{CP}(\mathcal{G}_2)$. This depends on the other processes that satisfy $\mathcal{G}_2$. Two such processes are P_4 and P_5 (see Fig. 4). Observe that if we choose $d(c) + d(d) > d(b)$ and $d(a) + d(b) > d(c)$ then $d_{CP}(\mathcal{G}_2) = \max\{d(a) + d(b), d(c) + d(d)\}$, while $d_{MIN}(\mathcal{G}_2) = \min\{d(P_3), d(P_4), d(P_5)\} = \min\{d(b) + d(c), d(a) + d(c) + d(d), d(a) + d(b) + d(d)\}$, that clearly shows that $d_{MIN}(\mathcal{G}_2) > d_{CP}(\mathcal{G}_2)$, i.e. the inequality from Proposition 2 is strict.

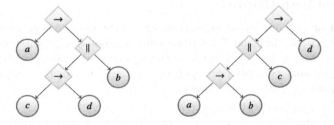

Fig. 4. Two other processes P_4 (left) and P_5 (right) that satisfy the ordering graph $\mathcal{G}_2$

4.3   Reducing the Duration of Execution

Analyzing Fig. 2, we can observe that the duration of execution of the hierarchical decomposition process can be reduced by doing a transformation that pushes the parallel composition operations upper in the process tree. However, this transformation is not always possible. We now provide sufficient conditions that enable the transformation and guarantee that the duration of execution of the resulted process is lower than of the original process. Referring at Fig. 2, the key observation is that the set of nodes of graph $\mathcal{G}_1$ can be partitioned in two subsets $U_0 = \{a, b\}$ and $U_1 = \{c\}$ such that there are no arcs cross-linking nodes in U_0 to nodes in U_1 or nodes in U_1 to nodes in U_0. Note that such a decomposition is not possible for the graph $\mathcal{G}_2$ from Fig. 2.

We consider the most general situation of reducing the duration of execution of a process $(P_1 \parallel P_2) \rightarrow (Q_1 \parallel Q_2)$. Similar results can be obtained for the processes of the form $(P_1 \parallel P_2) \rightarrow Q$ and $P \rightarrow (Q_1 \parallel Q_2)$.

Proposition 3. *(Reducing the Duration of Execution) Let $P = (P_1 \parallel P_2) \rightarrow (Q_1 \parallel Q_2)$ and let $\mathcal{G} = \langle V, E \rangle$ be an ordering graph such that $P \models \mathcal{G}$. Let us also assume that $((supp(P_1 \rightarrow Q_1) \boxtimes supp(P_2 \rightarrow Q_2)) \cap E = \emptyset^2$. Then it follows that:*

---

[2] Operator $\boxtimes$ denotes the symmetric cartesian product defined as $A \boxtimes B = (A \times B) \cup (B \times A)$.

- *Process* $P' = (P_1 \rightarrow Q_1) \parallel (P_2 \rightarrow Q_2)$ *is well-formed,*
- $P' \models \mathcal{G}$, *and*
- $d(P) \geq d(P')$.

4.4   Automatic Synthesis Algorithm

Let $\mathcal{G} = \langle V, E \rangle$ be an ordering graph and let $\mathcal{U}$ be the undirected graph obtained by removing the orientation of arcs of graph $\mathcal{G}$. We denote with $\mathcal{G}(W)$ and $\mathcal{U}(W)$ the subgraphs of $\mathcal{G}$ and $\mathcal{U}$ induced by a subset $W \subseteq V$ of nodes.

Let $\{V_0, V_1, \ldots, V_m\}$ be the partition of node set V defined by the hierarchical decomposition of $\mathcal{G}$. We define the following sets of nodes:

- $W_0 = V_0$
- $W_1 = W_0 \cup V_1$

$\ldots$

- $W_m = W_{m-1} \cup V_m = V$

Let $\mathcal{U}_i = \mathcal{U}(W_i)$ and $\mathcal{G}_i = \mathcal{G}(W_i)$ for each $0 \leq i \leq m$. Each undirected graph $\mathcal{U}_i$ can be partitioned into connected components that induce the partition $\{U_1, U_2, \ldots, U_{k_i}\}$ of the set W_i of nodes such that $k_i > 1$. This situation is intuitively described in Fig. 5.

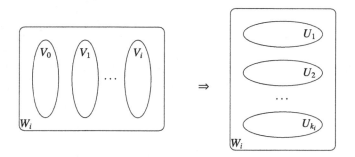

Fig. 5. Transformation to reduce duration of execution.

Following the result of Proposition 3, the hierarchical decomposition process P defined for subgraph $\mathcal{G}_i$ can be transformed into process P' such that:

- $P' = \parallel_{j=1}^{k_i} P_j$
- $supp(P_j) = U_j$ for all $1 \leq j \leq k_i$
- $d(P) \geq d(P')$

Consider for example the sample ordering graph $\mathcal{G}_3$ from Fig. 6. The partition of nodes corresponding to the hierarchical decomposition of $\mathcal{G}_3$ is $\{V_0, V_1, V_2\} = \{\{a, c\}, \{b, d\}, \{e\}\}$ and its height is $m = 2$. The hierarchical decomposition process of $\mathcal{G}_3$ is $P_6 = (a \parallel c) \rightarrow (b \parallel d) \rightarrow e$. Its duration of execution is 46.

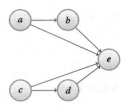

Fig. 6. Ordering graph $\mathcal{G}_3$. Activity durations: $d(a) = 10$, $d(b) = 18$, $d(c) = 20$, $d(d) = 7$, $d(e) = 8$.

We observe that for $i = 1$ the set $W_1 = V_0 \cup V_1 = \{a, b, c, d\}$ can be partitioned into $\{\{a, b\}, \{c, d\}\}$, so $k_1 = 2$. Using this observation we determine the transformed process $P_7 = ((a \to b) \parallel (c \to d)) \to e$. This process has the duration of execution of $36 < 46$. It follows that by applying our proposed transformation we were able to significantly reduce the duration of execution of process P_6 from $d(P_6) = 46$ to $d(P_7) = 36$.

We can combine this transformation with the hierarchical decomposition heuristic d_{HD} provided by Proposition 1 or with the critical path heuristic d_{CP} provided by Proposition 2 to design an efficient Greedy algorithm for the automatic synthesis of a suboptimal scheduling process that is consistent with a declarative specification.

Let $\mathcal{G} = \langle V, E \rangle$ be an ordering graph. The algorithm can be defined as a function $proc(W, \mathcal{G}(W))$ that takes a subset of nodes $W \subseteq V$, the subgraph $\mathcal{G}(W)$ of $\mathcal{G}$ induced by W and returns a suboptimal process that satisfies $\mathcal{G}(W)$.

Let $\{V_0, V_1, \ldots, V_m\}$ be the partition of node set V defined by the hierarchical decomposition of $\mathcal{G}$. Function $proc(V, \mathcal{G}(V))$ is recursively defined as follows:

- If $m = 0$ then $proc(V, \mathcal{G}(V)) = \parallel_{v \in V} v$.
- If $m > 0$ and $V_0 = \{v\}$ is a singleton set then $proc(V, \mathcal{G}(V)) = v \to proc(V \setminus \{v\}, \mathcal{G}(V \setminus \{v\}))$.
- If $m > 0$ and V_0 has at least two elements then for each $0 \leq i \leq m$ determine the number k_i of the sets of the partition of set W_i induced by the connected components of the undirected graph $\mathcal{U}_i$ obtained from the directed graph $\mathcal{G}_i$. We have $k_0 \geq k_1 \geq \cdots \geq k_m \geq 1$. Let i be the largest index for which $k_i > 1$. Such an index always exists as $k_0 = |V_0| > 1$. Select an index $0 \leq j \leq i$ for which the estimated duration of execution of the "synthesized process" (to be defined in what follows) is minimized.

We now recursively define the "synthesized process" and its estimated duration of execution, in terms of function $proc$. Let $\mathcal{G} = \langle V, E \rangle$ be an ordering graph, let $\{V_0, V_1, \ldots, V_m\}$ be the partition of node set V defined by the hierarchical decomposition of $\mathcal{G}$, and let us assume that $m > 0$ and $|V_0| > 1$. The "synthesized process" P_j and its estimated duration of execution $d_{G-EST}(P_j)$ with $EST \in \{HD, CP\}$ is:

- If $j = 0$ then $P_0 = \|_{v \in V_0} \to proc(V \setminus V_0, \mathcal{G}(V \setminus V_0))$ and is duration of execution is estimated to $d_{G-EST}(P_0) = \max_{v \in V_0}\{d(v)\} + d_{G-EST}(\mathcal{G}(V \setminus V_0))$.
- If $0 < j < m$ then let us consider the partition $\{Y_1, Y_2, \ldots, Y_{k_j}\}$ of W_j. Then $P_j = (\|_{i=1}^{k_j} proc(Y_i, \mathcal{G}(Y_i))) \to proc(V \setminus W_j, \mathcal{G}(V \setminus W_j))$ and is duration of execution is estimated to $d_{G-EST}(P_j) = \max_{i=1}^{k_j}\{d_{G-EST}(Y_i)\} + d_{G-EST}(V \setminus W_j)$.
- If $j = m$ then let us consider the partition $\{Y_1, Y_2, \ldots, Y_{k_m}\}$ of $W_m = V$. Then $P_m = \|_{i=1}^{k_m} proc(Y_i, \mathcal{G}(Y_i))$ and is duration of execution is estimated to $d_{G-EST}(P_m) = \max_{i=1}^{k_m}\{d_{G-EST}(Y_i)\}$.

Proposition 4. *(Duration of Execution of Greedy Suboptimal Processes) Let $d_{G-EST}(\mathcal{G})$ be the duration of execution of the suboptimal process that was computed with the Greedy algorithm using heuristic $EST \in \{HD, CP\}$. Then this process satisfies ordering graph $\mathcal{G}$ and $d_{HD}(\mathcal{G}) \geq d_{G-EST}(\mathcal{G}) \geq d_{MIN}(\mathcal{G}) \geq d_{CP}(\mathcal{G})$.*

5   Experimental Evaluation

We implemented our algorithm in Standard C using the 64-bit GCC compiler, version 5.1.0 and tested it on a x64-based PC with Intel(R) Core(TM) i7-5500U CPU at 2.40 GHz running Windows 10. In this section we present the experimental results that we obtained with this implementation. The experiment was organized as follows:

- We randomly generated a number of directed acyclic graphs of increasing sizes representing ordering constraints, as well as random durations of execution for each activity of the graph. The parameters of a data set are: number n of graph nodes, number ng of generated graphs, minimum and maximum durations $dmin$ and $dmax$ of each activity, and the density factor $f \in [0,1]$ of the graph. The higher is this factor the more dense is the graph. Value of f is given as a percentage.
- For each graph $\mathcal{G}$ we estimated the basic metrics given by the hierarchical decomposition heuristic $d_{HD}(\mathcal{G})$ and by the critical path heuristic $d_{CP}(\mathcal{G})$.
- For each graph $\mathcal{G}$ we computed the suboptimal scheduling process that satisfies $\mathcal{G}$ using the Greedy heuristic algorithm proposed in Sect. 4.4, in two variants: using the hierarchical decomposition heuristic and respectively using the critical path heuristic, to confirm the result claimed by Proposition 4, and to compare the results obtained for d_{G-HD} and d_{G-CP}.

The graph data sets were generated for the following values of the parameters: $ng = 100$, $n \in \{10, 50, 150, 300, 500, 700\}$, $dmin = 1$, $dmax = 20$, and density factor $f \in \{15\%, 30\%, 45\%, 60\%, 75\%\}$. For each test we recorded the total execution time and the values of the metrics of interest. We labelled each data set to reflect its number of nodes and density. For example if $n = 500$ and $f = 30\%$ then the label is 500-30.

Table 1. Total execution time in seconds for processing each data set

# nodes/density	15%	30%	45%	60%	75%
10	0.019	0.009	0.012	0.010	0.012
50	0.191	0.202	0.186	0.208	0.198
150	1.813	1.898	2.057	2.157	2.295
300	7.883	9.358	10.552	10.482	12.435
500	26.200	31.889	36.889	41.378	46.221
700	65.121	75.967	90.575	104.268	116.500

Table 1 presents the total execution time of running the synthesis algorithm for each data set. We observe that increasing the number of nodes, as well as the density, determines the increase of the execution time. Note that these times cover the processing of batches of 100 graphs. This means for example that the average time to process one graph of the 700-75 data set is approximately 1 second, i.e. our algorithm is quite fast.

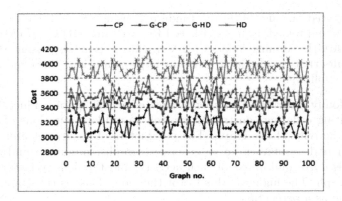

Fig. 7. Comparison of costs for the 700-30 data set

Figures 7 and 8 illustrate the values of the cost metrics for each graph of each data set 700-30 and 700-60. Three observations are drawn from these figures. Firstly, these experimental results are consistent with the theoretical results stated by Proposition 4. Secondly, that results of both experiments show that CP heuristic performs better than HD heuristic for almost all the graphs of the data set (there are few exceptions difficult to observe on the figures). Thirdly, the heuristics CP and HD tend to give closer results for higher density ordering graphs, as can be noticed by comparing the "closeness" of the cost values obtained for G-CP and G-HD for each data set 700-30 and 700-60.

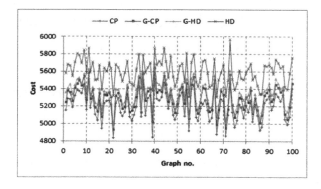

Fig. 8. Comparison of costs for the 700-60 data set

6 Conclusions

We proposed a new Greedy algorithm for the automatic synthesis of block structured scheduling processes that satisfy given declarative ordering constraints. We
presented basic theoretical results that support the correctness of this algorithm.
We proposed two heuristics that can be used with this algorithm: hierarchical
decomposition and critical path. Our initial experimental results support the
effectiveness of our proposals and suggest that the critical path heuristic performs better.

References

1. Demertzis, K., Iliadis, L.: Adaptive elitist differential evolution extreme learning
machines on big data: intelligent recognition of invasive species. In: Angelov, P.,
Manolopoulos, Y., Iliadis, L., Roy, A., Vellasco, M. (eds.) INNS 2016. AISC, vol. 529,
pp. 333–345. Springer, Cham (2017). https://doi.org/10.1007/978-3-319-47898-2_34
2. Kelley Jr., J.E.: Critical-path planning and scheduling: mathematical basis. Oper.
Res. **9**(3), 296–320 (1961). https://doi.org/10.1287/opre.9.3.296
3. Leemans, S.J.J., Fahland, D., van der Aalst, W.M.P.: Discovering block-structured
process models from event logs - a constructive approach. In: Colom, J.-M., Desel,
J. (eds.) PETRI NETS 2013. LNCS, vol. 7927, pp. 311–329. Springer, Heidelberg
(2013). https://doi.org/10.1007/978-3-642-38697-8_17
4. Mrasek, R., Mülle, J., Böhm, K.: Automatic generation of optimized process models
from declarative specifications. In: Zdravkovic, J., Kirikova, M., Johannesson, P.
(eds.) CAiSE 2015. LNCS, vol. 9097, pp. 382–397. Springer, Cham (2015). https://
doi.org/10.1007/978-3-319-19069-3_24
5. Mrasek, R., Mülle J., Böhm, K.: Process synthesis with sequential and parallel
constraints. In: Debruyne, C., et al. (eds.) OTM 2016. LNCS, vol 10033, pp. 43–60.
Springer, Cham (2016). https://doi.org/10.1007/978-3-319-48472-3_3
6. Pesic, M., van der Aalst, W.M.P.: A declarative approach for flexible business processes management. In: Eder, J., Dustdar, S. (eds.) BPM 2006. LNCS, vol. 4103,
pp. 169–180. Springer, Heidelberg (2006). https://doi.org/10.1007/11837862_18

Corpus Based Machine Translation
for Scientific Text

Irsha Tehseen[1](✉) ⓘ, Ghulam Rasool Tahir[2] ⓘ, Khadija Shakeel[1] ⓘ,
and Mubbashir Ali[1] ⓘ

[1] University of Lahore, Gujrat, Pakistan
IrshaTehseen@gmail.com
[2] National Language Promotion Department, Islamabad, Pakistan

Abstract. From many years, machine translation and computational linguistic research community has given immense attention towards the development of machine translation techniques. In order to fulfill the goal of machine translation "translation without losing meaning", a lot of translation methods have been proposed. All of these translation methods differ in their theories and implementation strategies. Although some basic rules of translation are same but many of them vary with the selection of language pair. While concerning with the scientific text, every science domain has thousands of terminologies. Translation of these terminologies according to the domain boosts the performance of translation. Translation of scientific text is ignored in the literature, as it needs more effort and expertise of both domain and language are required. In this research, we have proposed an effective scientific text translator for English to Urdu to cope with the challenge of scientific text translation. This method tags and translate the terms according to the domain. We have introduced a term tagger for tagging terms. The system can work for any domain but for experimental purpose we have selected the domain of computer science. System is evaluated on self-generated corpus of computer science. It is also compared with the existing translators to demonstrate the dominance of proposed translator as compared to the competitor. The comparative results of proposed approach and existing are shown in the form of tables.

Keywords: Machine translation · Corpus based machine translation
Scientific text translation · Term tagger

1 Introduction

Language is the main medium for humans to communicate. Whenever humans need to communicate, having different languages, they have to face issues. This arises the demand to translate. This demand is as old as the human [1]. Human experts in multiple languages are offering their services of translation from many decades. The demand of translation is increasing with the growth of cross-regional communication. Different sources of data are accessed worldwide. They cannot be written or translated in every language manually. They need to be written in one language and automatically translated in user preferred. This demands to cover the barrier of the language [2]. Due

L. Iliadis et al. (Eds.): AIAI 2018, IFIP AICT 519, pp. 196–206, 2018.
https://doi.org/10.1007/978-3-319-92007-8_17

to increase of translation demand humans are not able to fulfill the needs of the society, in response the automate process of translation is generated [3]. This idea fascinated the researchers. This research area is known as Machine Translation.

1.1 Machine Translation

Machine Translation (MT) is the process of translation from one language to another by the use of computing devices [1]. MT is an automatic process in which all the translation jobs are done with the help of programming languages and software [1, 4]. All materials needs to be translated, this includes commercial, business and scientific documents, instruction manuals, text books, World Wide Webs [3, 5].

Machine Translators are serving for multiple languages. Quality of MT also varies with language pairs. Two languages for instance English to French may have high quality of translation, some other pair may have translation of low quality. Currently none of the language pairs are translated accurately. The main difficulty in automated translation of one language to another is varied written scripts and multiple lexical choices for a single idea. A single world may have various meanings, in different situations it is used for different purposes. At the current level of research, a single level of representation of every language is almost impossible. Every language needs to be considered separately with its scripting choices for automatic translation [6].

1.2 English to Urdu Machine Translation

English and Urdu both are Indo-European languages but differ in written scripts and morphology. Urdu is a right to left scripted language and Eng. is left to right. Eng. follows the same order while Urdu is a free order language. English always follows the subject-verb-object order, Urdu mostly follows subject-object-verb pattern but not always [7]. Although a lot of work is done for MT but still English to Urdu MT is in its early stage. This pair of language is considered a low resource language because enough standard translated text is not available for the training of the system [8].

1.3 Machine Translation Service for Scientific Text

The number of scientific texts other than English keeps increasing quickly as compared to past, as the scientific communities in non-English countries grow [9]. However, majority of high impact journals are published in English [9]. For translating scientific text, considering only the semantic representation is not enough.

Different terminologies have various meanings in multiple domains. A single word may give a total different concept in various fields. Terms are different in every subject, while translating from one language to another these terms should be considered according to the scenario. For the true sense of data all of the terms should be translated with true meaning of the domain. None of the translator is working on the translation of scientific text in true meaning. While translating scientific text accuracy is a major issue [10]. We can get more advantage by using MT for translating these scientific text in local language or from local language to English language.

1.4 Problems in Automated Translation of Scientific Text

Translation of scientific text is not as simple as it seems. There are approx. 10 main branches of science and each branch is followed by many sub branches so approx. there are more than 100 fields of sciences [11]. Each field has different terms and meaning of terms, so a single generic system for all these sciences is not easy.

Translation of scientific text requires domain and translator expert. These texts are written by using Languages for Special Purposes (LSP). Translation of scientific text not only requires the knowhow of the language but it also requires the deep understanding of the field. For the translation of scientific text both of the skills: translation skill and domain skill are compulsory [12, 13].

Although there are many translators doing the job but translation of scientific text is still ambiguous. Translators are not trained for domain skills. Translators are working only with the translation. There is need to develop a MT system which can be a benchmark for translating scientific text while considering domain of the text.

2 Shortfalls in Existing MT Techniques for Scientific Text

Various terminologies are overlapped in multiple fields but their meaning is different in ever field. Such as the word "monitor" is a device in the field of Computer Science (CS), but in classroom environment it is used for a student. The word "Python", in CS is the name of a programming language, outside of the CS it is considered a snake. Both examples shows generic words may have different meanings in various field.

Existing translators are translating data in generic meanings. They are not able to translate scientific text in real sense. These systems do not distinguish between domains. Above mentioned are the few samples of basics sentences of CS. Translating a whole book or a research paper is more pathetic, humorous.

So far no such benchmark is available for translating scientific text. People have to make extra effort in understanding scientific text because have to understand the language also. So there is need of a study, to identify different techniques which should be used for better translation of scientific text. It is to decrease the effort in learning language skills or translating manually. Existing work do not bridge this gap to translate the scientific text with correct sense. There is a need to develop a customized translator which can effectively bridge this gap. Domain specific translators are tend to give better results as compared to the translation of generic systems [14–16].

3 Methodology

Terms of any field plays an important role in the translation of the text. It enables to understand the meaning or idea correctly. For quality translation a term tagger can play an important role in translation. It is complex to create single term tagger for all the fields together. This section focuses on the development of a scientific text translator and a term tagger for the field of CS. This translator and term tagger can be trained for any domain of science. The main contribution of the proposed work is term corpus of

CS, translation of that corpora and, a term tagger of scientific text and translation of text according to the meaning of the domain.

3.1 Overview of Proposed Scientific Text Translator

The development of a quality translator is a challenging and tricky task in MT research community. This is mainly due to the diversity of the languages. We have proposed a customized domain specific translator for scientific text. A complete overview of the system is given in the Fig. 1. The process of generating scientific text translation is comprised of following steps:

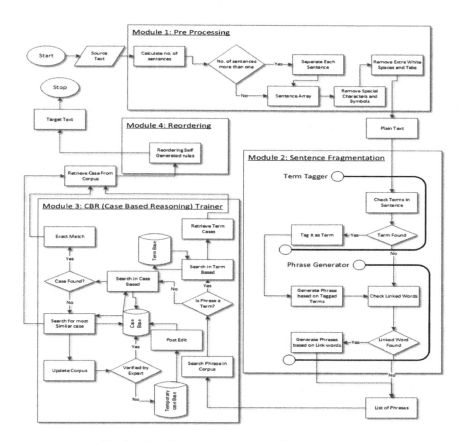

Fig. 1. Overview of proposed scientific text translator

Proposed Algorithm Overview:

1. Check number of sentences entered
2. If sentence is more than one, separate each sentence
3. Create a list of sentences

4. Select a sentence
   a. Remove special characters, symbols, white-spaces and tabs
5. Check for term in the sentences
   a. If term found, tag the term and also generate phrases based on tagged term
      (1) Repeat step 5a for all the terms in the sentence
   b. If linked word found, generate phrases based on linked words
      (1) Repeat step 5b for all the linked words in the phrase
6. List of phrases generated
7. Pick a phrase, if phrase is tagged as a term; search phrase in term base
   a. Retrieve term case b. Repeat step 7 for all the terms
8. If phrase is not a term, check in case base
   a. Compute similarity of the phrase in case base
   b. If similarity is 1, retrieve the case c. If similarity is less than 1
9. search for most similar case
10. Retrieve most similar case
11. Repeat step 8 for all the non-term phrase cases
12. Generate list of phrases
13. Reorder the retrieved cases as
14. Repeat step 4 to 11 for all the sentences and present solutions of the reordered case

It is composed of 4 modules. In module 1, inputted text is converted into plain text. The module 2 tag the terms and divide the sentences into phrases. CBR (Case Based Reasoning) Trainer is used for the searching and retrieving case from case base in 3rd module. At the end, module 4 is used to reorder the phrases to make the translation quality a bit better and readable.

3.2   Module 1: Preprocessing

All the formatted characters, special numbers, tags, images are removed from the text. At the end of this step text is totally normalized, only readable English characters is present in the text. Translation of any character, special symbol or syntax is ignored.

Preprocessing Algorithm: Input: English Text   Output: Plain text of English
   Check no. of sentences entered
      If sentence is more than one separate each sentence
   For each sentence, in the list of sentences
      If special character or symbol is found
         Remove special characters, symbols, and whitespaces   If ends Loop ends

3.3   Module 2: Sentence Fragmentation

There are two ways to keep the sentences into the corpus. One is to keep whole sentence. It will decrease the scope of the sentence as one sentence is equal to only one example. The second choice is to fragment it into multiple phrases. Each sentence is divided into two or more phrases. Scope of the sentences is increased with this. A broader range of sentences is covered by using genetic algorithm [17]. This module is divided into the following submodules: Term Taggers, Phrase Generator.

Term Tagger: Terms are used to express a concept, mainly in a particular domain of the study. A list of terms is developed to handle the terms of the computer science. Term Tagger tag and checks whether the terms are present in the sentence or not. If it found one or more terms in the sentence, it tags the terms are T1, T2 ... Tn.

Phrase Generator: Generating phrases is a required and vital module [18]. More phrases leads to more accurate results. Our phrase generator is based on tagged terms and linking words. Linking words are available at [19]. These words are used for further fragmentation.

Fragmentation Algorithm: Input: English sentence   Output: Set of English phrases
For each term, in the list of terms
Find term in the input sentence
If term is found tag it as a term
             Separate the sentences into new sentences   If ends   Loop ends
Find linked words
For each linked word separate the fragments of sentences

3.4   Module 3: CBR (Case Based Reasoning) Trainer

CBR Trainer is responsible of searching, measuring similarity and retrieving the solution of new case based on the old cases or training.

Searching in Corpus: Searching is checking whether the input phrase is available. If exact match is available its translation is presented. If it's not available the most similar solution is presented. Similarity of the case is checked in two ways: exact match and most similar case.

Searching Algorithm: Input: Phrase   Output: Case ID
     For each phrase in the list of phrases check it is tagged as a term or not
          If phrase is a term
             Compare the term in the term base and return ID of the term case
          Else
             Compare the phrase in case base
             If exact match found return matched case ID from case base
          Else
             Search most similar case in case base
             If similarity of the case is ≥ 0.8 return the ID of the selected case
          Else
             Tag the case as approx. solution
             add the case in update corpus and return the ID of selected case
          If ends   If ends   If ends   Loop ends

Retrieving from Corpus: The exact match or the most similar case is retrieved and its corresponding translation is presented. If a sentence is based on a single phrase its translation is presented directly. If sentence is based on two or more than two phrases, translation of every phrase is retrieved individually. Later on they are combined to formulate a single sentence.

Retrieving Algorithm: Input: Case ID   Output: Solution of all cases in Urdu
       Set a=1   For each case en_a
     If case is a term case
         Find the case en_a in the term base and make a set Ur_a
         Find the translation solutions of en_a and add it to Ur_a and add 1 to a
     Else
         Find the case en_a in the case base and make a set Ur_a
         Find the translation solutions of en_a and add it to Ur_a and add 1 to a
     If ends   Loop ends   Find the union of all Ur_a's

Note: *a* is a counter variable for counting number of phrases
en is a set of English Computer Science (CS) phrases
ur is the set of Urdu CS Translation phrases
for each e_a there is an equivalent part Ur_a. It is considered as follows:
En = Set of English CS phrases = $\{en_1, en_2, en_3 \ldots en_n\}$
Ur = Union of all the Urdu CS Translation phrases = $Ur_1 + Ur_2 + Ur_3 \ldots Ur_n$
Here number of phrases of a particular sentence is not specific and cannot be known before the actual program executes. These phrases are constructed at the run time. Solution of the cases are also only available at the run time.

Updating Corpus: New solved cases are saved for future use. Case base is updated but these cases are kept separate until they are post-edited and verified by expert.

3.5   Module 4: Reordering

Union of *Ur* is presented as output. Reordering of the sentence is a separate issue. Here we only consider it to some extent, just to make the translation a bit readable.

Reordering Rules: If $en_1 \ldots en_n$ are the CS phrases in English whose equivalent phrases are $Ur_1 + Ur_2 \ldots Ur_n$, then the translation of $[en_1, en_2, en_3 \ldots en_n]$ is $[Ur_1 + Ur_n + Ur_{n-1} \ldots + Ur_3 + Ur_2]$.

4   Experimental Studies

Here we present self-generated corpora, its translation and results. The accuracy results of our system are presented and compared with existing translators.

4.1   Experimental Corpus

We used self-generated corpus. Generating corpus is a weighty research extraction. There are two corpus: Term Corpus; Base Corpus.

Term Corpus: It is our first corpus, for this corpus the terms are picked from multiple sources [3, 21–24]. Many resources have same terms, overlapped terms are cleaned and discarded automatically, later they are checked manually.

Base Corpus: It is our second corpora. It consists on CS phrases. These phrases are constructed from multiple sentences. Sentences are selected from CS books, research papers and Wikipedia page of CS. These sentences have various length and terms in it. Sentences are fragmented into phrases by using proposed fragmentation algorithm. All the duplicate phrases and special symbols are removed.

Translation of Corpora: It is another major issue. As there are very few standard translated text of CS is available in Urdu language. Text is translated as accurate as it can. Translation of term requires a careful and persistent effort [25]. How we translated these terminology is also a separate issue. Translation of Term corpora is done according to the meanings of CS and it is also revised twice. The second step is translating Base corpora into equivalent Urdu translation. These translations still can be improved by expert. A concise overview of the above explained corpora is given in the Table 1.

Table 1. A concise overview of our experimental datasets

Sr#	Corpora	Dataset description	Total	Unique
1	Term Base	A Bilingual Corpus (English to Urdu) of unique CS terms	14002 Terms	10156 Terms
2	Case Base	A Bilingual Corpus (English to Urdu) of unique CS text phrases	1500 sentences/18982 Phrases	14232 Phrases

4.2 Experiments

In this section, we presented the experiments to evaluate the performance of our system. These experiments are performed by using datasets discussed in Table 1. The accuracy results of our proposed system are shown in Table 2.

Table 2. A concise overview of our experimental datasets

#	Translator	Type	Sentences test	Terms in sentences	Successfully translated terms	Accuracy %
1	Proposed system	Domain specific	500	379	301	79%
2	Google	Generic	500	379	102	26%
3	Being	Generic	500	379	153	40%
4	Babylon	Generic	500	379	77	20%
5	Dictionary translator	Generic	500	379	46	12%

Experiment 1: Evolution of Proposed Scientific Text Translator

The purpose of this experiment is to evaluate the translation accuracy of proposed system. The experiment has been conducted on above mentioned datasets. After giving the text, first step performed is preprocessed the text according to the algorithm proposed. Second step performed is to tag the terms in the given sentence and generate phrases fragmentation algorithm. Third step is to search and retrieve solution cases. At the end of the translation process reordering is done.

Experiment 2: Comparison of Proposed Translator with competitor

Purpose of Experiment: The aim to conduct this experiment is to compare the proposed system's accuracy with existing systems. The experiment is performed on our internally generated datasets. This experiment is performed in three different steps. In first step, 500 sentences of CS are selected from the corpora and CS books, 50% sentences are selected from corpus, 25% from different text books and rest 25% is from Wikipedia page of CS. Second step is to check translation of selected sentences one by one and verify those translations on famous existing systems and analyzed how much of them are translated correctly.

Comparison of Existing and Proposed Scientific text translation: Experimental results of competitors for scientific text translation are given in Table 2. We can observe that the existing systems are giving very less translation accuracy and very less terms are translated correctly. These sentences are tested on different famous translation systems. Results are given below in the table. It can be clearly seen that proposed system gives more accuracy as compared to the existing system.

5   Conclusion

We have introduced an effective scientific text translator. The proposed translation method is based on tagging terms of sciences and corpus based MT approach by using CBR. To meet the challenges of terminologies translation of scientific text, a term tagger for scientific text is proposed. It tags the terms of sciences and then translate with the help of self-generated Term Corpora. The performance of proposed technique has been evaluated by performing experiment on self-generated English to Urdu parallel bilingual dataset of CS. Both corpus are developed and translated. Experiment has also been conducted to provide a comparison between proposed technique and existing translation services. From the comparative results we concluded that, the proposed translator accuracy results are significantly better as compared to existing translator approaches. It gives considerable accuracy rate. Our proposed technique is also capable of handling other fields of sciences, all we need is to train the system for that domain. The current training of the system is done on the domain of CS. If we change its training, it can effectively work for every domain of life.

References

1. Homiedan, A.H.: Machine translation. J. King Saud Univ. (1998)
2. Callison-Burch, C., Koehn, P., Monz, C., Zaidan, O.F.: Findings of the 2011 workshop on statistical machine translation. In: Proceedings of the Sixth Workshop on Statistical Machine Translation, pp. 22–64. Association for Computational Linguistics (2011)
3. Hutchins, W.J., Somers, H.L.: An Introduction to Machine Translation. vol. 362. Academic Press London (1992)
4. Khan, S., Mishra, R.: Translation rules and ANN based model for English to Urdu machine translation. INFOCOMP J. Comput. Sci. **10**(3), 36–47 (2011)
5. Khan, N.A., Ansari, L.. Mahmud, S.R., Sultana, M., Muntaheen, A., Huda, M.N.: Bangla to English machine translation
6. Garcia, I.: Beyond translation memory: computers and the professional translator. J. Specialised Transl. **12**(12), 199–214 (2009)
7. Jawaid, B., Kamran, A., Bojar, O.: English to urdu statistical machine translation: establishing a baseline. In: COLING 2014, p. 37 (2014)
8. Salam, K.M.A., Yamada, S., Nishino, T.: Example-based machine translation for low-resource language using chunk-string templates. In: 13th Machine Translation Summit, Xiamen, China (2011)
9. Altbach, P.G.: The imperial tongue: english as the dominating academic language. Econ. Political Weekly, pp. 3608–3611 (2007
10. Olohan, M., Salama-Carr, M.: Science in Translation. Taylor & Francis (2014)
11. Sandstrom, G.: How many 'sciences' are there? Soc. Epistemology Rev. Reply Collective I **10**, 4–15 (2012)
12. Wright, S.E., Wright, L.: Editors' Preface: Technical Translation and The American Translator. In: Scientific and Technical Translation. John Benjamins, Amsterdam/Philadelphia, pp. 1–7 (1993)
13. Byrne, J.: Scientific and Technical Translation Explained. Taylor & Francis (2015)
14. Micher, J.C.: Improving domain-specific machine translation by constraining the language model. Technical report, DTIC Document (2012)
15. Xu, J., Deng, Y., Gao, Y., Ney, H.: Domain dependent statistical machine translation. MT Summit (2007)
16. Hatim, B., Mason, I.: Discourse and the Translator. Routledge (2014)
17. Echizen-ya, H., Araki, K., Momouchi, Y., Tochinai, K.: Machine translation method using inductive learning with genetic algorithms. In: Proceedings of the 16th Conference on Computational Linguistics, vol. 2, pp. 1020–1023. Association for Computational Linguistics (1996)
18. Mallinson, J., Sennrich, R., Lapata, M.: Paraphrasing revisited with neural machine translation. In: Proceedings of the 15th Conference of the European Chapter of the Association for Computational Linguistics, vol. 1. Long Papers (2017)
19. Linking words and phrases. https://www.dlsweb.rmit.edu.au/lsu/content/4_writingskills/writing_tuts/linking_LL/linking3.html. Accessed 26 June 2016
20. Oţăt, D.: Corpus-based training to build translation competences and translators' self-reliance. Romanian J. Engl. Stud. **14**(1) (2017)
21. Knight, K.: Machine translation glossary. http://www.isi.edu/natural-language/people/dvl.html. Accessed 02 May 2016
22. Henderson, H.: Encyclopedia of Computer Science and Technology. Infobase Publishing (2009)

23. Koehn, P.: Statistical Machine Translation. Statistical Machine Translation. Cambridge University Press (2010)
24. Microsoft Press, Microsoft Computer Dictionary. CPG Series. Microsoft Press (2002)
25. Olohan, M.: Scientific and Technical Translation (2016)

Machine Learning - Regression - Classification

The Regularization of CSPs for Rostering, Planning and Resource Management Problems

Sven Löffler[✉], Ke Liu, and Petra Hofstedt

Brandenburg University of Technology Cottbus-Senftenberg, Cottbus, Germany
Sven.Loeffler@b-tu.de

Abstract. This paper presents a new approach to solve rostering, planning and resource management problems. This is achieved by transforming several kinds of finite domain constraints of a given constraint satisfaction problem (CSP) into a set of regular membership constraints; and then these regular membership constraints are combined together to a more specific regular membership constraint. The purpose of this approach is to improve the speed of CSPs resolution and to remove undesirable redundant constraints (constraints which slow down the resolution speed) by replacing part of or all constraints of a CSP with a set of regular membership constraints followed by the combination of multiple regular membership constraints into a new, more precise regular membership constraint. A concise rostering example has demonstrated that our approach enables a significant improvement of the performance of the CSP resolution due to the pruning of the search tree.

Keywords: Constraint programming · CSP · Refinement · Planning
Resource management · Scheduling

1 Introduction

Constraint programming is a powerful method to model and solve NP-complete problems in a declarative way. Typical problems in constraint programming are planning, scheduling, resource management, graph coloring and satisfiability (SAT) problems [9].

Mostly, a CSP in practical can be described in various ways; and consequently, the problem can be modeled by different combinations of constraints, which results in the diversity of resolution speed and behavior. This phenomenon mainly caused by different propagators used by different constraints. Hence, the diversity of models and constraints for a given CSP offers us an opportunity to improve the problem solving by using another model in which a certain type of constraints can be replaced by a faster alternative or combined together to form more specific constraints.

This paper presents a way to model planning, scheduling and resource management problems using a regular CSP and discusses the use of the transformation from a CSP to a regular CSP. Because of the size of such planning, scheduling and resource management problems solving them is mostly very time consuming. The goal is to improve the resolution speed of CSPs, remove redundancy, strengthen propagation, and avoid unnecessary backtracks (or failed backtracks). We reach this goal by

© IFIP International Federation for Information Processing 2018
Published by Springer International Publishing AG 2018. All Rights Reserved
L. Iliadis et al. (Eds.): AIAI 2018, IFIP AICT 519, pp. 209–218, 2018.
https://doi.org/10.1007/978-3-319-92007-8_18

replacing some or all constraints of a CSP with regular membership constraints followed by the combination of such created multiple regular membership constraints into a new, more precise regular membership constraint. The regular membership constraint (in the following: regular constraint) and its propagation algorithm [6, 10, 11] provide the basis of this approach. In [8] was shown that this approach can improve the solving speed of a CSP by reducing the number of backtracks and fails. In this paper we focus more on the question how we can transform special constraints (especially the count constraint) into regular constraints.

This paper is structured as follows: In Sect. 2 the basics of constraint satisfaction problems (CSPs) are explained and the notion of a regular CSP is presented. In Sect. 3 we show that every CSP can be transformed into a regular CSP, theoretically, and we present a selection of effective constraint transformations for practical use. Section 4 is dedicated to a discussion of the advantages and disadvantages and shows an example of this new approach. Finally, we give an outlook on the directions of future research in Sect. 5.

2   Basic Principles of Constraint Programming

This paper will consider constraint satisfaction problems (CSPs) which are defined as follows.

Definition 1 CSP [2]. A constraint satisfaction problem (CSP) is defined as a 3-tuple $P = (X, D, C)$ with $X = \{x_1, x_2, ..., x_n\}$ is a set of variables, $D = \{D_1, D_2, ..., D_n\}$ is a set of finite domains where D_i is the domain of x_i, $C = \{c_1, c_2, ..., c_m\}$ is a set of primitive or global constraints on the subsets of X.

We distinguish primitive and global constraints. Primitive constraints are simple relations like $x_1 = x_2$, $x_1 \neq x_2$ or $x_1 + x_2 < x_3$. Global constraints [14] are more complex and mostly employed with efficient dedicated propagation algorithms to solve a problem faster than counterpart primitive constraints. Examples of global constraints are the *allDifferent*, *globalCardinality*, *cumulative*, *count*, *sum* and *regular* constraints, described in [13].

Definition 2 Global constraint [13]. A global constraint is a restriction which describes a relationship between a non-fixed number of variables.

Furthermore, we define a solution of a CSP, local consistency and global consistency.

Definition 3 Solution. A value valuation $\sigma = d_1 \times \cdots \times d_n$, $\forall i \in \{1, ..., n\} : d_i \in D_i$ of the variables $X = \{x_1, x_2, ..., x_n\}$ in which the value d_i is assigned to the variable x_i, is a solution of P if all constraints C are satisfied.

Definition 4 Local consistency (Hyper-Arc consistency) [1]. A constraint $c \in C$ where $c \subseteq D_1 \times \cdots \times D_k$ is locally consistent if $\forall i \in \{1, ..., k\}$, $\forall d \in D_i, \exists (d_1, ..., d_{i-1}, d_{i+1}, ..., d_k) \in D_1 \times \cdots \times D_{i-1} \times D_{i+1} \times \cdots \times D_k$ such that $(d_1, ..., d_{i-1}, d, d_{i+1}, ..., d_k)$ satisfies c.

Definition 5 Global consistency [2]. Let $P = (X, D, C)$ be a CSP with the variables $X = \{x_1, ..., x_n\}$, the domains $D = (D_1, ..., D_n)$ and the set of constraints $C = \{c_1, ..., c_k\}$ over X. The CSP P is globally consistent, if $\forall i \in \{1, ..., n\}$, $\forall d_i \in D_i : \exists d_1 \in D_1, ...,$ $\exists d_{i-1} \in D_{i-1}$, $\exists d_{i+1} \in D_{i+1}$, ..., $\exists d_n \in D_n$ such that the valuation σ with $\sigma(x_k) = d_k$, $k \in \{1, ..., n\}$ is a solution for P, i.e. satisfies the conjunction of all constraints in C.

To find a solution of a CSP, a certain level of consistency-enforcing algorithm is interleaved with backtrack search. The consistency-enforcing algorithm (e.g., local or global consistency) removes the illegal values that cannot occur in any solutions of the CSP in the domain of the variables.

It is important to differentiate between local consistency and global consistency in this paper. Local consistency guarantees that each value of a variable in the scope of the constraint is at least part of one solution of this constraint. In contrast, global consistency implies that each value of the variable of the CSP can be extended to at least one solution of the entire CSP. Therefore, global consistency is much strong enforcement of consistency. In particular, the search interleaved with global consistency is backtrack free. We introduce regular CSPs as CSPs (as defined in Definition 1), where all constraints must be regular membership constraints.

Definition 6 Regular CSP. A regular constraint satisfaction problem (RCSP) is defined as a 3-tuple $P = (X, D, C)$ with $X = \{x_1, x_2, ..., x_n\}$ is a set of variables, $D = \{D_1, D_2, ..., D_n\}$ is a set of finite domains where D_i is the domain of x_i $\forall i \in \{1, 2, ..., n\}$ and $C = \{c_1, c_2, ..., c_m\}$ is a set of regular constraints on the subsets of X.

The only difference between a CSP and an RCSP is that a CSP allows all kinds of constraints while an RCSP only allows regular constraints. Because every regular constraint is hyper arc consistent, an RCSP with only one (regular) constraint is globally consistent. This means no backtracking will be necessary when solving such a problem.

3   Transformation from a CSP into a RCSP

In this section, we briefly show that for every CSP exists at least one equivalent RCSP (theoretically), and then we present a selection of effective constraint transformations for the practical use.

3.1   Theoretical Considerations

According to Definition 1 a CSP P has a fixed number n of variables $X = \{x_1, ..., x_n\}$ and their respective domains $D = \{D_1, ..., D_n\}$ are finite, it follows that the potential solution space of the CSP P is limited by l (1).

$$l = \prod_{i=1}^{n} |D_i| \tag{1}$$

If the number of solutions is finite, then these can be enumerated by a regular language; besides, for every regular language exists at least one automaton which describes this language (Myhill-Nerode theorem [7]). It follows that for every CSP

P exists at least one regular CSP P_{reg} which is declaratively equivalent to P and contains only one regular constraint.

Such a RCSP $P_{reg} = (X, D, C_{reg})$ can obviously be generated if all solutions of P are known, because, given the language L, we can easily create an appropriate deterministic finite automaton (DFA) M. In practice, however, this is not useful because we intend to use the RCSP P_{reg} to find one, all or the best solutions of P faster than with the original CSP. For this reason, we consider the direct transformation from multiple types of constraints to regular constraints. For several global constraints (see Sect. 3.2), we defined corresponding efficient transformations, among them count, global cardinality constraint, and table constraints.

3.2 Transformations from Special Global Constraints into Regular Constraints

Nevertheless, there is a gap between theory and practice because finding all solutions for the fast transformation from CSP to RCSP can hardly be used in practice. Thus, we seek an efficient transformation method for global constraints. In the following, we are going to present the transformations for several global constraints defined and implemented in [12].

The Count Constraint. The count constraint is defined as $count(X', occ, v)$, where $X' = \{x_1, x_2, ..., x_n\}$ is a set of variables ($X' \subseteq X$, X is the set of Variables in the CSP) and $occ \in X$ with $D_{occ} = \{occ_{min}, ..., occ_{max}\}$ is a variable to denote admissible numbers of occurrences of the value $v \in N$ in X'.

In order to transform a count constraint into a regular constraint, we take into consideration the following two different cases:

Case 1: The occ variable is not used in other constraints.

In this case, the occ variable can be implicitly represented in the DFA. We create a DFA $M = (Q, \Sigma, \delta, q_0, F)$ with

- $Q = \{q_0, q_1, ..., q_{occ_{max}}\}$,
- $\Sigma = \cup_{i=1}^{n} D_i$
- q_0 is the initial state,
- $F = \{q_i \mid i \in D_{occ}\}$
- $\delta(q_i, v) = q_{i+1} \mid \forall i \in \{0, ..., occ_{max-1}\}$
- $\delta(q_i, v_2) = q_i \mid \forall i \in \{0, ..., occ_{max}\}, \forall v_2 \in \Sigma \backslash v$.

The regular constraint $regular(X', M)$ is equivalent to the original count constraint, and can be used to replace the count constraint.

Example 1. Given the count constraint $count(\{x_1, x_2, x_3, x_4, x_5\}, occ, 2)$ with $D_i = \{1, 2, 3\}$ $\forall i \in \{1, 2, ..., 5\}$ and $D_{occ} = \{1, 3\}$. The legal assignments for variables of count constraint must contain value 2 with 1 or 3 occurrences. Our transformation yields the automaton M:

$M = (\{q_0, q_1, q_2, q_3\}, \{1, 2, 3\}, \delta, q_0, \{q_1, q_3\})$ with
$\delta = \{ ((q_0, 1) \to q_0), ((q_0, 2) \to q_1), ((q_0, 3) \to q_0),$
$((q_1, 1) \to q_1), ((q_1, 2) \to q_2), ((q_1, 3) \to q_1),$

a) Case 1   b) Case 2

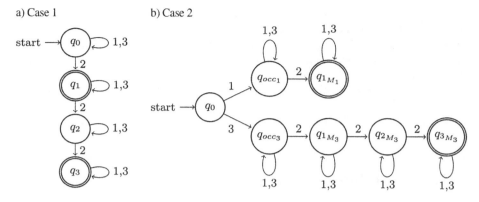

Fig. 1. Automaton representations of the *count* constraint from Example 1 (both cases).

$((q_2, 1) \rightarrow q_2)$, $((q_2, 2) \rightarrow q_3)$, $((q_2, 3) \rightarrow q_2)$, $((q_3, 1) \rightarrow q_3)$, $((q_3, 3) \rightarrow q_3)\}$.

A graphical presentation of M is depicted in Fig. 1a.

Case 2: The *occ* variable is used by other constraints.

In this case, we perform as follows: First, we create an automaton M with set of states $Q = \{q_0\} \cup (q_{occ_t} | \forall t \in D_{occ})$. We let q_0 be the initial state, all other states are labelled with occ_t, $t \in D_{occ}$. In the next step, we create $|occ|$ successor automata M_t, $t \in D_{occ}$ as described for case 1 with variables X_0, value v and $occ = t$ as input. We combine these automata M_t with the automaton M such that the initial state of each M_t is replaced with the state q_{occ_t} from M. The original count constraint can replace by the regular constraint $regular(\{occ, x_1, ..., x_{|X'|}\}, M)$ with the resulting DFA M. A graphical presentation of M for the previous example is depicted in Fig. 1b.

The *global cardinality constraint*. The *global cardinality constraint* can be interpreted as several count-constraints for which an efficient transform into regular constraints is given above.

The *stretch* constraint. A good description of the *stretch* constraint and its transformation into a regular constraint is given in [10].

The *table*-constraint. The table constraint is defined as *Table(X', A, b)*, where $X' = \{x_1, x_2, ..., x_n\} \subseteq X$ is a set of variables, and the Matrix $A^{m \times n}$ list all tuples extensionally. If boolean variable b is true, any allowed assignment of X' for the table constraint must be limited among the rows of matrix A, otherwise not.

Without loss of generality, we only sketch the automaton construction for b is true. For each table constraint with b is false an equivalent table constraint with b is true can be found. The idea here is to create m DFAs M_j, $j \in \{1, ..., m\}$ which only accept the words $w_j = A_{j,1}A_{j,2}...A_{j,n}$. We build M as the union of these m automata M_j. This DFA M can be used as a replacement of the *table* constraint with $regular(X', M)$.

We have presented examples of possible replacements of constraints with regular constraints. However, there exist more, e.g., cumulative constraint, which, however, is beyond the scope of this paper. Please note that a regular constraint created directly from another constraint might be slower than the original constraint. Thus, this transformation is, fairly often, useful if it is possible to combine several regular constraints into one new regular constraint. This can be done by the intersection of automata in which several regular constraints are combined together into one new regular constraint so that fewer backtracks and failures will be encountered. The next section will show more details about this.

4 The Use of Regular CSPs

In this section, we discuss advantages and disadvantages of the transformation of a general CSP P into an equivalent regular CSP P_{reg}, and use a rostering problem as an example.

4.1 Advantages and Disadvantages

There are some obvious disadvantages: a transformation for every constraint is necessary (not trivial for some global constraints) and it may be time-consuming to transform a constraint to a regular constraint. Furthermore, the newly created regular constraints might even reduce the performance of the solver.

To illustrate the advantages we briefly repeat how a final domain solver finds solutions. The solver uses depth-first search (DFS) nested with consistency enforcement. In contrast to some other constraints (e.g. sum or cumulative constraint), the regular constraint enforces hyper arc consistency (local consistency) over its variables. Therefore, transforming constraints with a lower consistency level into regular constraints, can (while potentially in-/decreasing the complexity for consistency enforcement) reduce the number of fails and backtracks in DFS in the solution process.

Furthermore, an important advantage is that several constraints can be combined into one new constraint by means of automata intersection. This reduces the number of overlapping constraints and, if we reach a single (hyper-arc consistent) constraint, then the whole CSP has global consistency and no backtracking is necessary any more. Similarly, this idea will often use to substitute pairwise inequality constraints with one allDifferent [3, 12] constraint.

A great advantage is that the transformation into regular constraints allows combining constraints of originally different types into a new constraint with joint propagation function. This happens by generating the automata, building their intersection (create product automata), and minimizing the resulting DFAs. This, furthermore, leads to a removal of redundancy and, in general, to a reduction of fails and backtracking steps in the depth-first search process. This preprocessing algorithm happens before other algorithms like common parallelization algorithms will be used. This means that the performance improvements of both approaches (regularization and parallelization) can be used simultaneously.

4.2 A Rostering Example

In this section, an example is shown to demonstrate the power of regular constraints. We use the same example as [8] but the results are summarized. The study [8] states that regular constraints can improve the performance of CSPs; however, the regular constraints were created directly by the developer requiring domain knowledge about DFAs and regular languages. In this paper we added some automatic transformations by the solver so that the designer of the CSP can model the problem by normal constraints without additional knowledge about regular languages.

CSP 1. Consider a rostering problem, CSP $P = (X, D, C)$, with $X = \{x_1, x_2, ..., x_n \mid n \bmod 7 = 0\}$, $D = \{D_1, D_2, ..., D_n\}$, where $i \in \{1, ..., n\}:D_i = \{0,1,2,3\}\}$ and $C = \{C_{shiftRequirements}, C_{shiftRepetitions}, C_{shiftOrder}, C_{equalDays}\}$.

Based on the constraints *count, stretch, table* and *arith* which are defined in [3, 12] the constraints C can be modeled as follows:

- $C_{shiftRequirements}^{1} = \{count(X_i, occ, j) \, \forall i \in \{1, 2, ..., 7\}, j \in \{0, 1, 2, 3\}\}$ where $X_i = \{x_i, x_{7+i}, x_{14+i} ...\} \subset X$ and $occ = \{\frac{n}{7*4}, \frac{n}{7*4}\}\}$
- $C_{shiftRepetitions} = stretch(X, \{2, 2, 2, 2\}, \{4, 4, 4, 3\}, \{0, 1, 2, 3\})$
- $C_{shiftOrder} = \{table(x_i, x_{i+1}, \begin{pmatrix} 3 & 1 \\ 3 & 2 \\ 2 & 1 \end{pmatrix}, false) \, \forall i \in \{1, 2, ..., n-1\}\}$
- $C_{equalDays} = \{arith(x_i, "=", x_{i+1}) \, \forall i \in \{6, 13, ..., n-1\}\}$

We consider n ($n \in N$, $n \bmod 7 = 0$) days, i.e. several weeks. A variable x_i, $i \in \{1, 2, ..., n\}$ represents the shift of a person A_1 at day i, where we have four possible shifts: 0, 1, 2, and 3 represent a day off, an early shift, a late shift, and a night shift respectively.

As typical for many rostering problems, we just consider the plan of one person A_1 and assume, that the plan for further staff is received by rotating A_1s plan by e.g. a week. For example given a shift plan $sol_{A1} = (v_1, v_2, ..., v_7, v_8, ..., v_{14}, v_{15}, ..., v_n)$ (as a solution of the CSP P) for A_1, the plan for a person A_2 would be $sol_{A2} = (v_8, ..., v_{14}, v_{15}, ..., v_n, v_1, v_2, ..., v_7)$. The constraints C are explained in the following:

- The $C_{shiftRequirements}$ constraints guarantee that for each day for each shift are exactly as many staff persons as needed. For example there must be between 3 and 4 employees each Monday in morning shift.
- The $C_{shiftRepetitions}$ constraints guarantee that the same shift in consecutive days is limited by a lower and an upper bound. This is necessary because in some countries (i.e. Germany) ergonomic knowledge must be respected [4].
- The $C_{shiftOrder}$ constraints restrict the order of shifts. We consider a forward rotation of shifts which guarantees conformance with the regulations on rest periods in the German labor time law [5, Sect. 5].

---

[1] The use of *global cardinality constraints* would be an alternative here, but, in performance measurements yields worse results in our experiments.

- $C_{equalDays}$ are constraints which guarantee that on Saturday a person always has the same shift as on the following Sunday, which is recommended in [4].

Remark: Of course, for real rostering problems, further restrictions and recommendations must be considered.

Evaluation. A series of tests with different values for n (28, 35, 42, 49, 56) days and four different search strategies, a combination of the variable selectors *Smallest* and *FirstFail* and the value selectors *IntDomainMin* and *IntDomainMedian* was investigated. We applied variable and value selection strategies as defined by Charles Prud'homme for the Choco 4 solver (for details see [12]).

We compare the solution behavior of the original version of the CSP P and its regular version CSP P_{reg}, as a result of the intersection of the automatons created with the presented transformations. In the regular version P_{reg} all constraints have been transformed as described in the previous sections and then all automata - except the $C_{shiftRequirements}$ - were intersected and minimized to a new constraint $c_{regular}$ as described before. We omitted the intersection of the automatons which represents the $C_{shiftRequirements}$ constraints with the other automata because this requires more time as available. The presented transformations in our example have a time requirement in double-digit micro seconds, which is negligible in comparison to the needed solution time.

Table 1 shows the average improvements of the constructed regular CSP P_{reg} in comparison to the original CSP P over all four search strategies and for the respective values of n. For example, for $n = 28$ days the regular approach was in average 4.546 times faster to find the first solution and 2.413 times faster to find all solutions in comparison to the original approach. For $n = 42$ and $n = 49$ there exist no solutions. The regular approach was *3.950* respectively more than *2.780* times faster than the original approach to come to this conclusion. Because problems can need a lot of time, we limited the solution time. The original approach for $n = 49$ doesn't find a solution in this time limit but the time limit was *2.780* times over the time which the regular approach needed. So the regular approach was at least *2.780* times faster as the original approach.

Table 1. Statsitics for n = 28, ..., 56.

Criteria \n	28	35	42	49	56
1st solution	4.546	5.774	–	–	>6.278
All solutions	2.413	6.146	–	–	–
No solution	–	–	3.950	>2.780	–

For $n = 56$ not all solutions were found in the time limit, but the first solution was found more than six times faster in average and within the limited time more than nine times so many solutions were found. Furthermore Table 2 shows the reduction factor of the number of nodes (fails resp. backtracks) of the original approach divided by the number of nodes (fails resp. backtracks) of the regular approach. You can see that the full search tree of the regular approach has at least two times less nodes, fails and backtracks as the original approach which is also an indication for the faster solution speed. For the reason of the time limit the whole search tree was not created for $n = 56$ so that it cannot be said how much smaller the search tree for this RCSP is.

Table 2. Statsitics for n = 28, ..., 56.

Criteria \n	28	35	42	49	56
Nodes	3.018	2.501	4.538	>2.385	–
Fails	3.043	3.636	4.538	>2.385	–
Backtracks	3.069	11.824	4.538	>2.385	–

5 Conclusion and Future Work

We are going to give a brief summary of this paper, a conclusion, and we explain our next steps.

Summary and Conclusion. We presented a new approach for the modelling and optimization of general CSPs using the regular constraint.

It was explained how a set of selected global constraints can be transformed into a regular CSP. A regular constraint can be minimized by the use of automata intersection and minimization. By employing a rostering example we have demonstrated that this approach allows to reduce the size of the search tree and to significantly improve the solution speed. For practical problems the execution time for the transformation must be taken into consideration.

Our investigations support that our approach can be applied successfully when considering sub-problems of a potentially large CSP P and, thus, subsets of its variables X. Transforming only sub-problems (instead of P completely) is, thus, much faster and, still, leads to a reduction of the number of constraints (also the number of backtracks) and of redundancy which, altogether, improves the solution speed.

Future Work. Future work will be finding more direct transformations for global constraints, finding an automated transformation algorithm, investigating promising variable orderings to optimize the size of the DFAs. Furthermore we would like to study variable and value orderings for the regular constraint, research on potential benefits of decomposition of automata, general (static) criteria to decide when to apply the approach as well as extracting promising application areas in general.

References

1. Apt, K.: Principles of Constraint Programming. Cambridge University Press, New York (2003)
2. Dechter, R.: Constraint processing. Elsevier Morgan Kaufmann (2003)
3. Demassey, S.: Global Constraint Catalog, 05 June 2016. http://sofdem.github.io/gccat/. Accessed 24 Oct 2017

4. German Federal Institute for Occupational Safety and Health (BAuA) - Design of night and shift work (2013). http://www.baua.de/. Accessed 10 May 2017
5. German working time law from 6. June 1994, (BGBl.IS.1170,1171), last updates by Art. 3 para. 6 of the Law of 20 April 2013 (BGBl.IS.868) (1994). http://www.gesetze-im-internet. de/arbzg. Accessed 10 May 2017
6. Hellsten, L., Pesant, G., van Beek, P.: A domain consistency algorithm for the stretch constraint. In: Wallace, M. (ed.) CP 2004. LNCS, vol. 3258, pp. 290–304. Springer, Heidelberg (2004). https://doi.org/10.1007/978-3-540-30201-8_23
7. Hopcroft, J.E., Ullman, J.D.: Introduction to Automata Theory, Languages and Computation. Addison-Wesley, Reading (1979)
8. Löffler, S., Liu, K., Hofstedt, P.: The power of regular constraints in CSPs. In: Eibl, M., Gaedke, M. (ed.) Lecture Notes in Informatics (LNI), INFORMATIK 2017, pp. 603–614. Society for Computer Science, Bonn (2017)
9. Marriott, K.: Programming with Constraints - An Introduction. MIT Press, Cambridge (1998)
10. Paltzer, N.: Regular Language Membership Constraint. Saarland University, Germany, Seminararbeit (2008)
11. Pesant, G.: A filtering algorithm for the stretch constraint. In: Walsh, T. (ed.) CP 2001. LNCS, vol. 2239, pp. 183–195. Springer, Heidelberg (2001). https://doi.org/10.1007/3-540-45578-7_13
12. Prud'homme, C., Fages, J.G., Lorca, X.: Choco Documentation. TASC, INRIA Rennes, LINA CNRS UMR 6241, COSLING S.A.S. (2016). http://www.Choco-solver.org/. Accessed 20 June 2017
13. Rossi, F., Beek, P.V., Walsh, T.: Handbook of Constraint Programming, 1st edn. Elsevier, Amsterdam (2006)
14. Van Hoeve, W. J., Katriel, I.: Global Constraints, Chap. 6. Elsevier (2006)

An Evaluation of Regression Algorithms Performance for the Chemical Process of Naphthalene Sublimation

Silvia Curteanu[1], Florin Leon[2(✉)], Andrei-Ştefan Lupu[3],
Sabina-Adriana Floria[2], and Doina Logofătu[4]

[1] Department of Chemical Engineering and Environmental Protection,
"Gheorghe Asachi" Technical University of Iaşi, Iaşi, Romania
scurtean@ch.tuiasi.ro
[2] Department of Computer Science and Engineering,
"Gheorghe Asachi" Technical University of Iaşi, Iaşi, Romania
{florin.leon, sabina.floria}@tuiasi.ro
[3] School of Electronics and Computer Science, University of Southampton,
Southampton, UK
asllul2@soton.ac.uk
[4] Faculty of Computer Science and Engineering,
Frankfurt University of Applied Sciences, Frankfurt, Germany
logofatu@fb2.fra-uas.de

Abstract. Different regression algorithms are applied for predicting the sublimation rate of naphthalene in various working conditions: time, temperature, trainer rate and shape of the sample. The original Large Margin Nearest Neighbor Regression (LMNNR) algorithm is applied and its performance is compared to other well-established regression algorithms, such as support vector regression, multilayer perceptron neural networks, classical k-nearest neighbor, random forest, and others. The experimental results obtained show that the LMNNR algorithm provides better results than the other regression algorithms.

Keywords: Regression · Large margin · Nearest neighbor
Naphthalene sublimation

1 Introduction

Machine learning is a subdomain of artificial intelligence whose popularity and success are constantly growing [1, 2]. Its main goal is to extract high-level patterns, i.e. knowledge, from large amounts of raw information, patterns that can provide more abstract and useful insight into the data under study. Many problems in science and social science can be expressed as classification or regression problems, where one does not know an analytical model of some underlying phenomenon, but sampled data is available through experiments or observations, and the aim is to define a predictive model based on those samples. To date, many such algorithms have been proposed, which belong to different paradigms, e.g. neural networks, nearest neighbor, decision trees, support vector machines, Bayesian approaches, etc.

© IFIP International Federation for Information Processing 2018
Published by Springer International Publishing AG 2018. All Rights Reserved
L. Iliadis et al. (Eds.): AIAI 2018, IFIP AICT 519, pp. 219–230, 2018.
https://doi.org/10.1007/978-3-319-92007-8_19

Unfortunately, there is no single best algorithm that can handle the large variety of situations encountered in practice. Each method has its own advantages and disadvantages. They are mainly related to the flexibility or complexity of the models and their generalization capabilities. For a non-trivial pattern, using a very simple model may result in poor performance, whereas using an overly complex model can result in overfitting, i.e. very good results for the training set and poor results for the test set or prediction, in general. Therefore, one must make several choices when dealing with such a problem: first, to establish the most appropriate learning method and, second, to control the complexity of the model generated with that learning method by changing its specific parameters.

In the present paper, we investigate the performance of some well-established algorithms in comparison to an original regression algorithm, namely the *Large Margin Nearest Neighbor Regression* (LMNNR), which combines the idea of nearest neighbors with that of a large separation margin, typical of support vector machines. The sublimation of naphthalene was chosen to illustrate these methodologies based on the difficulties involved due to the toxicity of the process, in which case predictions on the model become recommended and useful.

We organize our paper as follows. Section 2 presents a selection of related work about regression algorithms applied for the modeling of chemical processes. Section 3 describes the dataset used for the experiments and Sect. 4 presents the algorithms employed to model it. Section 5 describes some experimental results, while Sect. 6 contains the conclusions of our work.

2 Related Work

There are many applications of artificial intelligence and soft computing methods in the domain of chemical engineering, especially for modeling and optimization. In this section, we review several applications of regression algorithms for chemical processes.

Article [3] proposes a combination of online support vector regression with an ensemble learning system to adapt to nonlinear and time-varying changes in process characteristics and various process states in a chemical plant. [4] uses a probabilistic combination of local independent component regression in order to assess the quality of chemical processes with multiple operation modes. [5] addresses a non-linear, time-variant problem of soft sensor modeling for process quality prediction using locally weighted kernel principal component regression. [6] uses multiple linear regressions and least squares support vector regression to model and optimize the dependency of methyl orange removal with various adsorption influential parameters. [7] compares the performance of support vector regression, neural network and random forest models in predicting and mapping soil organic carbon stocks.

In [8], the authors make a thorough presentation of neural networks used for bioprocessing and chemical engineering, with applications in process forecasting, modeling, control of time-dependent systems, and the hybridization between neural networks and expert systems.

The issue of predicting sublimation thermodynamics, such as enthalpy, entropy, and free energy of sublimation using machine learning methods was addressed in [9].

Semi-empirical models were used to model systems of solids and supercritical fluids in order to determine sublimation pressures and sublimation enthalpies, and then to model different multiphasic equilibriums [10].

Some of the recent research of the authors of the present paper addressed a performance comparison of different regression methods for a polymerization process with adaptive sampling [11], a comparison between simulation and experiments for phase equilibrium and physical properties of aqueous mixtures [12], an experimental analysis and mathematical prediction of cadmium removal by biosorption [13] and the prediction of corrosion resistance of some dental metallic materials with an original adaptive regression model based on the k-nearest-neighbor regression technique [14].

3   The Naphthalene Sublimation Dataset

Our case study is naphthalene sublimation – a physical process of solids that transition directly into vapors. This technique is one of the most convenient methods to study heat and mass transfer. In addition, the rate of sublimation, the amount of solid converted to vapor per time unit and solid area unit is used to study problems related to environment protection, health protection, transportation safety and security, meteorology, by determining the concentration of various substances in the environment and the dynamical properties in a wind tunnel.

In a previous approach [15], a series of experiments were performed to investigate the sublimation of the naphthalene samples under atmospheric pressure in air as entrainer, without recycle. Our experimental data fulfill a necessary condition for empirical modeling: a sufficient number of data was obtained which uniformly cover the investigated domain.

The sample weight was measured continuously as a function of time, at different air flow characteristics. The experimental data is then used to calculate the mass transfer rate, the degree of sublimation, the sublimation front position; the influence of air flow characteristics was also evaluated.

More details on experiments and data processing can be found in [15], where neural network modeling was performed. In the current work, a more efficient algorithm, LMNNR, was applied, comparatively with other algorithms: linear regression, support vector regression, neural networks, k-Nearest Neighbors, K*, and Random Forest. In addition, a large dataset was used here (1323 instances) including different shapes of the samples, while in [15] only spherical samples were considered (150 instances).

The data gathered from experiments contains four variables as inputs: the shape of the sample (i.e. pallets, small pills, large pills and rods), time, air speed (the trainer) and temperature, and one output: the speed of naphthalene sublimation.

Consequently, the modeling purpose was to evaluate the performance of the process, quantified by the sublimation rate depending on process time, entrainer temperature, and entrainer flow rate.

In order to apply the instance-based methods, the data is normalized between 0 and 1, independently for each numerical attribute.

Figure 1 presents some statistics regarding the distribution of the data before normalization: the histogram for the first discrete input and a box plot for each numerical

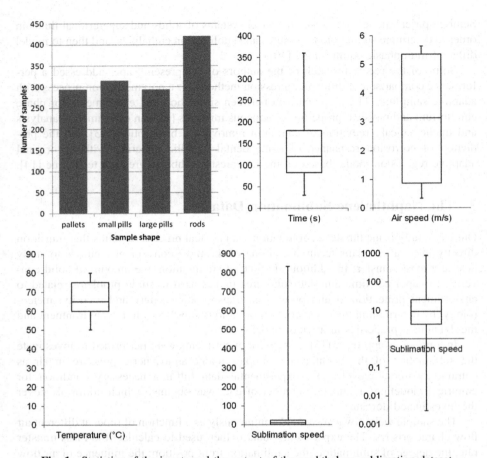

Fig. 1. Statistics of the inputs and the output of the naphthalene sublimation dataset

input, showing the minimum value, the first quartile, the median, the third quartile and the maximum value. For the output, two box plots are included, with a linear and a logarithmic scale. The output has values between 0.003 and 832.98, with the mean of 34.95 and the median of 9.24. There are a few greater values far from the median, but they are not outliers; they are important results of the process, difficult to learn, and which need to be handled accordingly by the regression models.

4 Regression Algorithms

The goal of the paper was to find a good model for the naphthalene sublimation data. The first step was to apply classical methods, with known good performance, implemented in *Weka* [16]. This was intended to constitute a basis for comparison with the original LMNNR algorithm. From the large number of algorithms in Weka, a few were selected which, in previous studies, were noticed to yield good performance for a large number of regression problems. Thus, neural networks, support vector machines, nearest neighbor, K-Star and random forest were selected. The details about their structure and operation are given below.

It must be emphasized that these techniques have very different nature and assumptions, and, by comparing the LMNNR results with the best results obtained with either of these classical algorithms, we can underline that the algorithm proposed by the authors is, in fact, a good alternative for regression.

4.1 Classical Algorithms

Neural networks in the form of *multilayer perceptrons* (MLP) are often used in classification and regression problems. The structure of an MLP contains an input layer, an output layer and one or more hidden layers of neurons. Each neuron sums the weighted input data of the neurons in the previous layer, to which another term (bias) is added, and the result is sent to the neurons in the next layer through a nonlinear transformation called an activation function. Each connection has an associated weight. In the training process, the weights and biases are adjusted such that the output of the network should match the desired output of the vectors from the training set. The training algorithm used most often is back-propagation [17]. It aims to minimize the mean-squared error between the desired output and the computed one using the gradient descent method.

The *Epsilon-Support Vector Regression* (ε-SVR) algorithm tries to approximate the desired continuous output within a tolerating error ε while using the idea of the large margin characteristic of support vector machines [18]. When the data is not linearly separable, the ε-SVR algorithm uses kernels to transform them into a higher-dimensional space. There are several types of functions that can be used as kernels, e.g. polynomial or radial basis functions (RBF). If some training instances still do not satisfy the constraints, slack variables are introduced to allow some errors (soft margin). The number of these erroneous instances can be controlled with a cost parameter C. If the value of C is decreased, a larger number of incorrectly classified training instances is allowed, which can however lead to better generalization.

The *k-Nearest Neighbor* (kNN) algorithm is based on the choice of k nearest neighbors using a distance function as a criterion and the output is computed by aggregating the outputs of those k training instances. As a distance function, one can use Euclidian or Manhattan distance, usually particularizations of the Minkowski distance. Choosing the value of k is important. If k is too small, then the classification can be affected by the noise in the training data, and if the value of k is too large, then distant neighbors can affect the correctness of the results. To avoid the difficulty of finding an optimum value for k, one can weight the neighbor influence. The neighbors have a greater weight as they are closer to the instance, while those farther apart have a smaller weight.

The *K-Star* algorithm [19] is an instance-based classifier that very much resembles the k-Nearest Neighbor algorithm presented before. Its novelty comes from the usage of an entropy metric in its similarity function, rather than the usual distance metric. It has been shown in the literature that such an approach has beneficial outcomes for certain industry-related problems [20]. The K-Star algorithm can also be used for regression purposes, similarly to how k-Nearest Neighbor is used.

A *random forest* [21] is composed of a collection of classification or regression trees. Each tree is generated using random split tests on slightly different training set generated using bagging. The output of a new instance is computed by aggregating the outputs of the individual trees.

4.2 The Large Margin Nearest Neighbor Regression Algorithm

The performance of the above algorithms was compared to that of an original algorithm, *Large Margin Nearest Neighbor Regression* (LMNNR) [22, 23].

The support vector machines, in a classification context, rely on the idea of finding a large margin between classes by solving an optimization problem. This idea was used in conjunction with the k-Nearest Neighbor method, also for classification [24]. Its main assumption is to change the distance metric of the kNN space by using a matrix:

$$d_M(\mathbf{x}_i, \mathbf{x}_j) = (\mathbf{x}_i - \mathbf{x}_j)^T \mathbf{M}(\mathbf{x}_i - \mathbf{x}_j).$$ (1)

If **M** is a diagonal matrix, the weights of the neighbors are:

$$w_{d_M}(\mathbf{x}, \mathbf{x}') = \frac{1}{d_M(\mathbf{x}, \mathbf{x}')} = \frac{1}{\sum_{i=1}^{n} m_{ii} \cdot (x_i - x_i')^2}.$$ (2)

Equation (2) involves a single, global matrix **M** for all the instances. However, it is possible to have different distance metrics for the different instances or groups of instances. Thus, *prototypes* can be used which are defined as special locations in the input space of the problem, and each prototype P has its own matrix $\mathbf{M}^P$. When computing the distance weight to a new point, an instance uses the weights of its nearest prototype, i.e. m_{ii}^P instead of m_{ii} in Eq. (2).

Finding the appropriate matrices is achieved by solving an optimization problem. In a simplified formulation, the objective function F, which is to be minimized, takes into account two criteria with equal weights, F_1 and F_2, described below. In order to briefly explain the expressions of these functions, the following notations were made, where d_M means the weighted square distance function using the weights we search for: $d_{ij} = d_M(x_i, x_j)$, $d_{ik} = d_M(x_i, x_k)$, $g_{ij} = |f(x_i) - f(x_j)|$, $g_{ik} = |f(x_i) - f(x_k)|$.

The first criterion is:

$$F_1 = \sum_{i=1}^{n} \sum_{j \in N(i)} d_{ij} \cdot (1 - g_{ij}),$$ (3)

where $N(i)$ is the set of the nearest k neighbors of instance i, e.g. $k = 3$. Basically, this criterion says that the nearest neighbors of i should have similar values to the one of i, and more distant ones should have different values.

The second criterion is expressed as follows:

$$F_2 = \sum_{i=1}^{n} \sum_{j \in N(i)} \sum_{l \in N(i)} \max\left(1 + d_{ij} \cdot \left(1 - g_{ij}\right) - d_{ik} \cdot \left(1 - g_{il}\right),\ 0\right).$$ (4)

Here, the distance to the neighbors with close values (the positive term) is minimized, while simultaneously trying to maximize the distance to the neighbors with distant values (the negative term). An arbitrary margin of at least 1 should be present between an instance with a close value and another with a distant value.

For optimization, both an evolutionary algorithm and an approximate differential method following the central difference definition of the derivative can be used.

The estimated output of a new query instance $\mathbf{x}_q$ is computed as follows. Its k nearest neighbors are identified using the distance metric from Eq. (1). The weights of these neighbors are computed with Eq. (2) and then normalized:

$$w_{d_M}^{n}(\mathbf{x}_i, \mathbf{x}_q) = \frac{w_{d_M}(\mathbf{x}_i, \mathbf{x}_q)}{\sum_{j=1}^{k} w_{d_M}(\mathbf{x}_j, \mathbf{x}_q)}.$$ (5)

Finally, the output is computed as a weighted average of the neighbor outputs:

$$\tilde{f}(\mathbf{x}_q) = \sum_{i=1}^{k} w_{d_M}^{n}(\mathbf{x}_i, \mathbf{x}_q) \cdot f(\mathbf{x}_i).$$ (6)

5   Results and Discussion

In this section, the choice of parameters for different regression methods is explained. For each algorithm, multiple experiments with different parameter values were performed. The tables containing the results only display those with the best performance in terms of correlation coefficient (r) and root mean square error ($RMSE$).

In order to compare the performance of the various algorithms, the cross-validation method with 10 folds was used. Also, since an objective comparison was intended, the data set was randomly divided into 10 groups (iteratively one for test and the rest for training) and the same groups were used by all the algorithms. It was considered that this methodology is particularly important to compare the algorithms implemented in Weka with the original implementation of the LMNNR algorithm. The results obtained for individual test groups, although interesting, were omitted in the results section, and only the aggregated results are displayed in the following tables.

5.1   Parameters of Regression Methods

Multilayer Perceptron Neural Network (MLP). For the problem at hand, repeated experiments showed that a neural network produces best results when given a low learning rate. The momentum parameter also has a great impact on learning. Its optimal value tends to be around 0.4 or 0.5. The number of hidden layers was automatically chosen by Weka. This option yielded the best outcomes because the optimal number of hidden layers tends to vary between cross-validation sets, making it hard to achieve similar performance with manually chosen values. The encoding for the discrete input is "one-hot", leading to 7 inputs and 1 output. The best network architecture was the one with one hidden layer containing 4 neurons with sigmoid activation functions, and with the output neuron with a linear activation function. 1000 epochs for training were found to be an acceptable compromise between the quality of the resulting model and the overall training time.

Support Vector Regression (SVR). The Epsilon-SVR algorithm achieved a very good overall fit if the kernel used was based on radial basis functions. The kernel type choice was vastly influential on the outcome. RBF, therefore, yielded a correlation that was at least 20% better than all of the other options (linear, polynomial and sigmoid). The best results were obtained with relatively large values of the parameters: $\gamma = 14$, $C = 10$, whereas ε was best kept at a low value, i.e. $\varepsilon = 0.001$. Fine-tuning these parameters helped improve the algorithm performance significantly, such that the final correlation was the best out of all the algorithms tested with Weka.

***k*-Nearest Neighbor (*k*-NN).** The optimal number of neighbors used in this algorithm is in this case 2. The correlation dropped significantly if the number of neighbors was increased above this value. The search method used was the linear nearest neighbor search. A slight improvement was achieved by using the Manhattan distance as metric, instead of the Euclidean distance.

K-Star (K*). The only numeric parameter that this algorithm takes, the global blending index, was optimal at low values. In the experiments, the value 3 was used. The parameter, however, influenced the outcome in a slight manner ($\sim 5\%$ correlation improvement). The entropic auto blend functionality provided by Weka was turned off for these experiments.

Random Forest (RF). In the case of this algorithm, the number of trees parameter plays an important role in the overall performance. Several tests were conducted to determine the optimal value of this parameter and the best outcome was recorded with a value of approximately 200 trees. Although the difference in performance obtained by optimizing this parameter was only around 3%, it allowed Random Forest algorithm to yield one of the best correlations for the data.

Large Margin Nearest Neighbor Regression (LMNNR). For this algorithm, the parameters are the number of prototypes, the number of optimization neighbors and the number of regression neighbors. Different combinations of values for these parameters were attempted. Since the LMNNR results are not deterministic, because the initialization of the matrices is random and then optimized, the best results were included out of 100 algorithm runs for each configuration.

5.2   A Comparison Between Algorithm Performance

In Tables 1 and 2, one can see the best results achieved with the use of the regression algorithms presented in the previous section.

Table 1. The best results obtained for optimized configurations by algorithms in Weka

Algorithm	Parameters	r	RMSE
ε-SVR	C: 10; ε: 0.001; γ: 14; kernel: RBF	0.91514	0.04022
Random forest	Number of features: 1; number of trees: 200	0.91332	0.03965
k-NN	k: 2; Manhattan distance	0.90639	0.04022
K*	Global blend: 3	0.89025	0.04450
MLP	Learning rate: 0.1; momentum: 0.4; number of training epochs: 1000	0.88344	0.04615
Linear regression		0.64395	0.07277

Table 2. The best results obtained with the original LMNNR algorithm

Number of prototypes	Number of regression neighbors	Number of optimization neighbors	r	RMSE
1	3	3	0.93151	0.036118
1	5	5	0.93052	0.036276
1	10	10	0.92426	0.03825
2	3	3	0.94097	0.033554
2	5	5	0.9365	0.035707
2	10	10	0.93416	0.037173
3	3	3	0.94067	0.033251
3	5	5	0.93698	0.036821
3	10	10	0.93428	0.036797
5	3	3	0.94185	0.033915
5	5	5	0.94425	0.034913
5	10	10	0.93614	0.036856

Five out of the six algorithms tested show a very good correlation of the data (~ 0.9) and come in a very short range from one another. Linear regression, which is included only for comparative reasons, achieves a low total correlation. This emphasizes the nonlinearity of the problem at hand. ε-SVR and Random Forest yield the best, almost identical, predictions. kNN and K-star present similar results, despite the different metrics they use in their similarity functions.

From Table 2, it can be seen that the LMNNR results are clearly better than the results obtained by other well-established regression algorithms.

Unlike the problems studied in previous works [22, 23], it can be seen that more prototypes are needed for this particular problem. 5 prototypes provide the best results in terms of correlation coefficient. This shows that this dataset is more difficult to learn using a unique distance metric and that different regions of its input space have different characteristics with can be properly addressed with the use of prototypes.

Figure 2 shows a comparison between the predictions of the model and the desired data, for the case with 5 prototypes, 5 regression neighbors and 5 optimization neighbors from Table 2, which yields the highest correlation coefficient r. One can see that the two datasets are quite close. An exception is e.g. the data point with the value of 1. Since Fig. 2 presents the results for the 10 testing sets of the cross-validation process put together, the data point with a maximum value in the test set cannot be correctly approximated by the model relying on the rest of the data in the training set. The LMNNR algorithm is based on the nearest neighbor paradigm, and therefore it cannot extrapolate to a value that is larger than any value in the training set. Furthermore, one can see that most of the data has small output values, and only 0.8% of the normalized data has output values above 0.5. This contributes to the difficulty of the model to approximate higher output values.

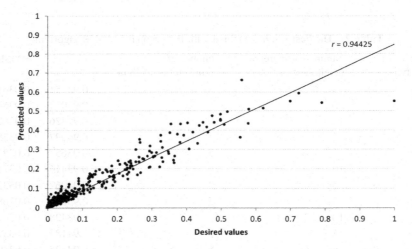

Fig. 2. Comparison between the predictions of the model and the desired data

6   Conclusions

The results obtained by the LMNNR algorithm proposed by the authors are better than those provided by other classical regression algorithms. These predictions are important for the chosen process, avoiding or, at least, minimizing the number of experiments made in toxicity conditions, and saving materials and energy. In addition, the developed modeling methodologies can be easily adapted and applied to other chemical engineering processes.

The promising results of LMNNR determine the planning of other applications and methodologies that include this algorithm. As a future direction of investigation, one can consider its further refinement in order to automatically detect the optimal values of its parameters, namely the number of prototypes, the number of regression neighbors and the number of optimization neighbors.

Acknowledgments. This work was supported by the "Program 4, Fundamental and Border Research, Exploratory Research Projects" financed by UEFISCDI, project no. 51/2017.

References

1. Goodfellow, I., Bengio, Y., Courville, A.: Deep Learning. The MIT Press, Cambridge (2016)
2. Witten, I.H., Frank, E., Hall, M.A., Pal, C.J.: Data Mining: Practical Machine Learning Tools and Techniques, 4th edn. Morgan Kaufmann, Cambridge (2016)
3. Kaneko, H., Funatsu, K.: Adaptive soft sensor based on online support vector regression and Bayesian ensemble learning for various states in chemical plants. Chemometr. Intell. Lab. Syst. **137**, 57–66 (2014)
4. Ge, Z., Song, Z., Wang, P.: Probabilistic combination of local independent component regression model for multimode quality prediction in chemical processes. Chem. Eng. Res. Des. **92**(3), 509–521 (2014)
5. Yuan, X., Ge, Z., Song, Z.: Locally weighted kernel principal component regression model for soft sensing of nonlinear time-variant processes. Ind. Eng. Chem. Res. **53**(35), 13736–13749 (2014)
6. Ghaedi, M., Rahimi, M.R., Ghaedi, A.M., Tyagi, I., Agarwal, S., Gupta, V.K.: Application of least squares support vector regression and linear multiple regression for modeling removal of methyl orange onto tin oxide nanoparticles loaded on activated carbon and activated carbon prepared from *Pistacia atlantica* wood. J. Colloid Interface Sci. **461**, 425–434 (2016)
7. Were, K., Bui, D.T., Dick, Ø.B., Singh, B.R.: A comparative assessment of support vector regression, artificial neural networks, and random forests for predicting and mapping soil organic carbon stocks across an Afromontane landscape. Ecol. Ind. **52**, 394–403 (2015)
8. Baughman, D.R., Liu, Y.A.: Neural Networks in Bioprocessing and Chemical Engineering. Academic Press, San Diego (1992)
9. McDonagh, J.L., Palmer, D.S., van Mourik, T., Mitchell, J.B.O.: Are the sublimation thermodynamics of organic molecules predictable? J. Chem. Inf. Model. **56**(11), 2162–2179 (2016)
10. Tabernero, A., Martín del Valle, E.M., Galán, M.A.: On the use of semiempirical models of (solid + supercritical fluid) systems to determine solid sublimation properties. J. Chem. Thermodyn. **43**(5), 711–718 (2011)
11. Leon, F., Curteanu, S.: Performance comparison of different regression methods for a polymerization process with adaptive sampling. Int. J. Comput. Electr. Autom. Control Inf. Eng. **10**(10), 1515–1519 (2016)
12. Pirdashti, M., Movagharnejad, K., Mobalegholeslam, P., Curteanu, S., Leon, F.: Phase equilibrium and physical properties of aqueous mixtures of poly (vinyl pyrrolidone) with trisodium citrate, obtained experimentally and by simulation. J. Mol. Liq. **223**, 903–920 (2016)
13. Hlihor, R.M., Diaconu, M., Leon, F., Curteanu, S., Tavares, T., Gavrilescu, M.: Experimental analysis and mathematical prediction of Cd(II) removal by biosorption using support vector machines and genetic algorithms. New Biotechnol. **32**(3), 358–368 (2015)

14. Chelariu, R., Suditu, G.D., Mareci, D., Bolat, G., Cimpoesu, N., Leon, F., Curteanu, S.: Prediction of corrosion resistance of some dental metallic materials with an adaptive regression model. J. Miner. Met. Mater. Soc. (JOM) 67(4), 767–774 (2015)
15. Curteanu, S., Smarandoiu, M., Horoba, D., Leon, F.: Naphthalene sublimation. experiment and optimisation based on a neuro-evolutionary methodology. J. Ind. Eng. Chem. 20(4), 1608–1611 (2014)
16. Hall, M., Frank, E., Holmes, G., Pfahringer, B., Reutemann, P., Witten, I.H.: The WEKA data mining software: an update. ACM SIGKDD Explor. 11(1), 10–18 (2009)
17. Rumelhart, D.E., Hinton, G.E., Williams, R.J.: Learning internal representations by error propagation. In: Parallel Distributed Processing: Explorations in the Microstructure of Cognition, vol. 1. MIT Press, Cambridge (1986)
18. Smola, A.J., Schölkopf, B.: A tutorial on support vector regression. Stat. Comput. 14(3), 199–222 (2004)
19. Cleary, J.G., Trigg, L.E.: An instance-based learner using an entropic distance measure. In: 12th International Conference on Machine Learning, pp. 108–114 (1995)
20. Painuli, S., Elangovan, M., Sugumaran, V.: Tool condition monitoring using K-star algorithm. Expert Syst. Appl. 41(6), 2638–2643 (2014)
21. Breiman, L.: Random forests. Mach. Learn. 45(1), 5–32 (2001)
22. Leon, F., Curteanu, S.: Evolutionary algorithm for large margin nearest neighbour regression. In: Núñez, M., Nguyen, N.T., Camacho, D., Trawiński, B. (eds.) ICCCI 2015. LNCS (LNAI), vol. 9329, pp. 305–315. Springer, Cham (2015). https://doi.org/10.1007/978-3-319-24069-5_29
23. Leon, F., Curteanu, S.: Large margin nearest neighbour regression using different optimization techniques. J. Intell. Fuzzy Syst. 32, 1321–1332 (2017)
24. Weinberger, K.Q., Saul, L.K.: Distance metric learning for large margin nearest neighbor classification. J. Mach. Learn. Res. 10, 207–244 (2009)

Using Decision Trees to Extract Patterns for Dairy Culling Management

M. Lopez-Suarez[1], E. Armengol[2(✉)], S. Calsamiglia[1],
and L. Castillejos[1]

[1] Animal Nutrition and Welfare Service, Department of Animal
and Food Sciences, Universitat Autonoma de Barcelona, Bellaterra, Spain
{Montserrat.Lopez.Suarez,Sergio.Calsamiglia,
Lorena.Castillejos}@uab.cat
[2] Artificial Intelligence Research Institute (IIIA - CSIC),
Campus UAB, 08193 Bellaterra, Catalonia, Spain
eva@iiia.csic.es

Abstract. The management of a dairy farm involves taking difficult technical and economic decisions such as the replacement of some cows to either maintain or increase the productivity of the farm. However, there is not a standard method supporting the selection procedure of which animals need to be culled. In the present study we used decision trees to develop a model able to classify a cow according to the average herd productivity. This model, obtained from a data base around 98000 cows, predicts the average milk production of the first lactation of a cow based on the monthly milk controls corresponding to the lactation peak. Our goal is to identify poor productive cows during her first lactation in order to make more accurate selections of which cows should be culled.

Keywords: Veterinary · Dairy farms · Milk production · Voluntary culling
Artificial intelligence · Machine learning · Decision trees

1 Introduction

To be highly productive a dairy farm needs good management. There are many complex technical and economic decisions that have to be taken in order to maintain or increase the productivity. Direct benefits of a dairy are those coming from either milk or animal sales. However, raising a cow has also many costs that should be discounted from these benefits (feeding, labor, veterinary care, depreciation of facilities, utilities, etc.).

Culling is the departure of cows from the herd due to sale, slaughter or death. The main reasons to cull a cow are infertility, mastitis and poor milk production. Commonly, culling reasons have been classified as voluntary or involuntary or, as suggested by Fetrow et al. [4], economic or biologic. Biological culls are those cows for which no possible productive future exists due to disease, injury or infertility. Thus, this class of culls are mainly involuntary as most of the times are "forced" decisions. Economic culls mean that a cow is removed because a replacement is expected to produce greater

L. Iliadis et al. (Eds.): AIAI 2018, IFIP AICT 519, pp. 231–239, 2018.
https://doi.org/10.1007/978-3-319-92007-8_20

profit. In this case, farmer has freedom of choice over which cows are removed from the herd, although they are healthy [1, 4]. Hence, the farmer can do a voluntary selection of cows to cull based in the herd size and herd production level. Therefore, herd profitability can be improved by minimizing the proportion of the herd culled for involuntary or biological reasons and maximizing the proportion culled for voluntary or economic reasons [1]. Because it is important to know as soon as possible if a cow will be poorly productive, we propose to analyze first lactation production data to identify those animals in a herd which are candidates to be culled following milk yield improvement criteria.

For such a purpose, in the present paper, we used Decision Trees (DT) [9], an Artificial Intelligence technique that allows the classification of objects, to extract patterns for making decision support during the culling process. This is our main contribution since the use of these patterns is an easy and understandable way to support the farmer in culling decision making. A DT represents a model of a given domain that can be used for classification tasks. Thus, given the description of a cow, a DT could classify her as *Good* or *Bad*, supporting in this way the culling process. In Sect. 2 we briefly revise some works that use Artificial Intelligence technologies for dairy management. Section 3 explains how we have modelled the culling task, and the data base we used in our experiments (Sect. 3.1). Section 4 explains our results, and in Sect. 5 these results are discussed. Finally, Sect. 6 is devoted to conclusions.

2   Related Work

Most of the work focused on modelling the culling task or aspects related to it, try to construct statistical models based on the analysis of past cases of a dairy [2]. The use of artificial intelligence techniques is still not widely used for managing the culling although they have been used for other purposes. For instance, Cavero et al. [3] developed a fuzzy logic model for mastitis detection; [13, 15] are some examples of using neural networks for classification and control of mastitis in cows milked using an automatic milking system; Shainfar et al. [10] used fuzzy neural networks to predict breeding values for dairy cattle; Grzesiak et al. [6] also used neural networks to predict milk production; Sugiono et al. [12] built an adaptive system (BPNN) to predict performance of dairy cattle based on environmental and physical data; and Sitkowska et al. [11] used decision trees to predict the increment of the levels of somatic cells in milk. Thus, to our knowledge, Artificial Intelligence techniques and, particularly, decision trees, have not been used to support the decision of culling the herd.

Also the multi-agent technology has been used in dairy farms to support the process of decision making in several aspects of a dairy farm. For instance, Parrot et al. [8] investigated the feasibility of using a multi-agent system for heifer management; Thangaraj et al. [14] used a multi-agent system to make integrated decisions taking into account pasture availability, nutrients, and herd economic aspects. Goel et al. [5] also developed a multi-agent system to implement electronic contracting of food grains integrating various millers and producers in a food supply chain for better negotiations to reach a mutually acceptable price.

The approach we propose uses decision trees, a technique that, as far as we know, has not been used before in dairy management although Kamphuis et al. [7] used decision trees to improve the detection of clinical mastitis with sensor data from automatic milking systems.

Most of the mentioned studies using Artificial Intelligence technologies employed neural networks and fuzzy logic. This is mainly due to real time needs, since they deal with problems that need to be solved in a short time. However, we considered that, for the objective of this study, the use of inductive learning methods to construct a domain model could be a better approach. Inductive models, differently than neural networks, can explain the results they provide since the descriptions used to classify an object can be interpreted as an explanation of the result. This is an interesting characteristic as it enables the final user to completely understand how an automatic system has reached the solution it proposes. For this reason, our approach can contribute to support the farmer in taking more informed decisions when he needs to cull his herd.

3   Modelling the Culling Task

In this paper we propose the use of inductive learning methods to construct a model able to predict and explain why a cow should be culled during her first lactation. The goal of inductive learning algorithms is the construction of a domain theory from the known data. Commonly this domain theory is further used to predict the classification of unseen objects.

To characterize each one of the classes of the domain by means of discriminatory descriptions we have to solve the so-called *discrimination task*. Given a solution class C_i, the *discrimination task* for inductive learning methods is defined as follows:

- Given: a set E of positive E^+ and negative E^- examples of a class c_i.
- Find: a description D_i such that it is satisfied by elements in E^+ and it is not satisfied by any of the elements of E^-.

The discrimination task produces discriminatory descriptions, i.e., descriptions satisfied only by objects of one of the classes. A class C_i can be described by more than one discriminatory description D_i. To build a model of a domain we have to perform the discrimination task over each one of the classes. In that way, the model is composed of descriptions that can classify univocally an object as belonging to a class. One of the widely used inductive learning methods are the *Decision Trees (DT)*.

The goal of using DT is to create a domain model predictive enough to classify future unseen domain objects. The leaves of a tree determine a partition of the original set of examples, since each domain object only can be classified following one of the paths of the tree. The construction of a decision tree is performed by splitting the source set of examples into subsets based on an attribute-value test. This process is repeated on each derived subset in a recursive manner. Figure 1 shows the ID3 algorithm [9] commonly used to construct decision trees. The path from the root to each one of the leaves of a decision tree can be seen as a description of a class. When all the examples of a leaf belong to the same class the description is *discriminatory*, otherwise it is *non-discriminatory*. In our experiments we implemented our own version of the algorithm in Fig. 1 in order to control overfitting and also to construct the patterns from the tree paths.

Decision trees can be useful for our purpose because their paths give us patterns describing classes of objects (cows in our approach) in a user-friendly manner. One shortcoming of decision trees is *overfitting*, meaning that there are few objects in most of the leaves of the tree. In other words, paths are actually descriptions that poorly represent the domain. The main procedure to either avoid or reduce overfitting is by pruning the tree, i.e., under some conditions, a node is no longer expanded. However, this means that leaves can contain objects belonging to several classes and, therefore, paths do not represent discriminatory descriptions of classes, i.e., these descriptions are satisfied by objects of more than one class. In our approach, we managed overfitting by controlling the percentage of elements of each class. Let S_N be the set of objects associated with an internal node N, the stopping condition in expanding N (the *if* of the ID3 algorithm) holds when the percentage of objects in S_N that belong to the majority class decreases in one of the children nodes. In such a situation, the node N is considered as a leaf.

3.1 The Data Base

We used a data base containing 97987 objects. These objects are descriptions of Holstein-Frisian cows which lived from 2006 to 2016, belonging to dairy farms within the CONAFE register system[1]. Nowadays, most of farms have automatic systems to collect data, so there is a lot of information about each cow (genetics, production, morphology, reproductive indexes, disease control, etc.). In addition, most of farms pass a monthly control in which, for every lactating cow, the day milk yield is registered and a milk sample for analyses is taken. Therefore, the first step we carried out was to select which pieces of this information could be useful to detect as soon as possible poorly productive cows. To reach this goal, we decided to use only information relative to the first lactation. The attributes we considered for every cow were the following one:

- **BirthMonth:** Month (season) in which the cow was born.
- **Month1Calving:** Month (season) of the first calving of a cow.
- **Kl:** Milk production genetic index.
- **ICO:** Official cattle breeding index in Spain.
- **Morpho:** Morphologic qualification of a cow.
- **KgMilkPeak:** Average test-day milk yield (kg/day) of the second and third control of the first lactation (lactation peak).
- **Fat:** Fat average percentage from the second and third controls of the first lactation.
- **Protein:** Protein average percentage from the second and third control of the first lactation.
- *SCC*: Somatic cell count in the milk. It is an indicator of the quality of milk as it expresses the likeliness to contain harmful bacteria.

---

[1] The Confederacion Nacional de la Raza Frisona (CONAFE) is a Spanish entity whose goal is to develop programs oriented to the improvement and selection of the Holstein-Frisian herd.

```
ID3 (examples, attributes)
        create a node
        if all examples belong to the same class return class as the label for the node
        otherwise
                A ← best attribute
                for each possible value vᵢ of A
                        add a new tree branch below node
                        examplesᵥᵢ ← subset of examples such that A = vᵢ
                        ID3(examplesᵥᵢ, attributes - {A})
        return node
```

Fig. 1. ID3 algorithm for growing a decision tree.

- **OpenDays:** Days from calving to conception.
- **Calving1stAI:** Interval of days between the first calving and the first insemination after it.
- **AI:** Number of artificial insemination attempts to conceive after the first calving.
- **Production/DIM:** Average daily milk production of the first lactation (kg/day) calculated dividing total amount of milk produced by a cow during the whole lactation by the total days in milk (DIM).

For the attributes **BirthMonth** and **Month1Calving** we divided the months according to seasons. All the remaining attributes have numerical values and we have discretised them. For all of them, we calculated the quartiles and divided the whole interval of values in four according to these quartiles. We associated to each of the 4 quartile interval the labels: *VeryLow (VL), Low (L), High (H)*, and *VeryHigh (VH)*. Table 1 shows the quartiles of the attributes **KgMilkPeak** and **Production/DIM**. For instance, for the attribute **KgMilkPeak**, the interval from 5 to 28 of milk average during the lactation peak, means that the cow has had very low milk production (*VL*). We considered **Production/DIM** as the solution class, i.e., the decision tree will model and predict the first lactation milk production performance of a cow (kg/day).

4   Results

We used the whole data base as input for a decision tree algorithm to obtain patterns (the tree paths) describing the classes of cows according to the values of the attribute **Production/DIM**. The resulting tree was formed by patterns that are discriminatory and by patterns that are not (due to the stopping condition explained in previous section). Figure 2 shows an example of discriminatory pattern formed by 6 attributes (**KgMilkPeak, Kl, Morpho, Month1Calving, AI**, and **Fat**). This pattern is satisfied by 104 cows, where the 93.27% of them have a very low **Production/DIM** and the 6.73% of them have a low **Production/DIM**. None of the cows satisfying this pattern has **Production/DIM** high or very high. For model evaluation purposes, we decided to consider two final solution classes: *Good* formed by cows with **Production/DIM** high or very high; and *Bad* formed by cows with **Production/DIM** low or very low. This is

Table 1. Intervals corresponding to each quartile of the attributes **KgMilkPeak** and **Production/DIM**

Attribute	VL	L	H	VH
KgMilkPeak	(5, 28]	(28, 32]	(32, 36]	(36, 65]
Production/DIM	(6, 25]	(25, 29]	(29, 32]	(32, 60]

because the actual goal is to identify the less productive cows of the herd, Therefore, the pattern in Fig. 2 classifies all the cows that satisfy it as *Bad* with a 100% of predictability. Once the good cows have been separated, a more fine procedure could be used to select which of the bad cows are the worst. In fact, this procedure could depend on factors different for each dairy.

We evaluated the model using 10-fold cross-validation. Therefore, the whole data base has been divided in 10 parts. In each experiment we taken 9 of these parts to generate the patterns and the remaining part has been used as test on which we estimated the accuracy of the model. After the 10 experiments we obtained a mean accuracy of 84.10% in classifying a cow as *Bad* or *Good*.

We also tested the developed model using a different data base to check if the set of patterns shown in Table 2 could be used to classify the cows, using the same criteria, on any farm. For this test, we took a data base with information about 5474 cows different from the ones used during the construction of the model. In fact, these cows were alive from 1999 to 2006. We divided the data base in subsets of around 500 cows, and each subset was discretised according to the quartiles of the own subset. Then we used the patterns in Table 2 to classify the cows of each subset simulating, in that way, the difference between dairies. The mean accuracy of classification in this test was 82.72%. Comparing both this accuracy with the one from the 10-fold cross-validation (84.10%) we can conclude that it is feasible to use the model obtained from the data base of around 98000 since it provides good patterns for the classification of cows coming from different farms.

5   Discussion

All the patterns composing the model in Table 2 explain that milk production (kg/day) in the lactation peak of the first lactation (**KgMilkPeak**) of a cow is directly related to the average milk production (kg/day) of the whole first lactation (**Production/DIM**). This result is very interesting as the performance of a cow in her first lactation can be predicted in early lactation stages instead of having to wait until the end of the lactation (after 9 to 14 months). This is especially interesting to take early decisions about culling since, with around a 97% of predictability, poorly productive cows of a herd can be early detected. Therefore, the model composed by patterns that take into account only the attribute **KgMilkPeak** is a good predictor of the first lactation production of a cow.

We also performed a statistical analysis to compare the results of the DT model with the statistical one. Table 3 shows that all the variables included in the model were significant ($p < 0.05$). The most relevant variable is **KgMilkPeak** as in the DT model.

Pattern : [[KgMilkPeak, VL], [Kl, VL], [Morpho, VL],
[Month1Calving, FirstTrim], [Al, VH], [Fat, VH]]

Classes of the cows satisfying the pattern: [[VL, 93.27], [L, 6.73]]
Final class: Bad (100 %)
Satisfied by 104 cows

Fig. 2. Discriminatory pattern satisfied by 104 cows having **Production/DIM** *low* or *very low*. According to this pattern, all these cows will be classified as Bad.

Table 2. Model formed by non-discriminatory patterns. For each pattern it is shown the number of cows that satisfy it, and the percentage of them that are *VeryLow (VL), Low (L), High (H),* and *VeryHigh (VH)*. In addition, column *Bad* shows the sum of both bad and very bad cows, and column *Good* shows the sum of both good and very good cows.

Pattern	Cows	VL	L	H	VH	Bad	Good
[[**KgMilkPeak**, *VL*]]	27179	75.16	22.02	2.36	0.46	97.18	2.82
[[**KgMilkPeak**, *L*]]	25571	22.04	55.21	19.16	3.58	77.25	22.74
[[**KgMilkPeak**, *H*]]	23651	4.57	31.71	41.18	22.54	36.28	63.72
[[**KgMilkPeak**, *VH*]]	21586	0.65	7.66	21.55	70.14	8.31	91.69

Other variables, although significant, are much less important in the statistical model. This result can be interpreted as that the production of the first lactation can be predicted from the records of the milk control from the 3–4 months of lactation with a determination coefficient of 0.7176, i.e., the variable **KgMilkPeak** explains the 71.76% of the variability of the variable Production/DIM. By adding Kl, the model explains the 74.36%.

Therefore, the statistical model confirms the results we obtained with the DT model. However, whereas the statistical model only shows the high correlation between both **KgMilkPeak** and **Production/DIM**, the patterns of the DT model show explicitly the relation between certain values of both attributes. For instance, a Low value of **KgMilkPeak** corresponds to a Low value of **Production/DIM**.

The model in Table 2 supports to split the herd in two groups corresponding to *Good* and *Bad* cows, regarding first lactation production. Once the *Good* cows have been separated, a next step to take could be the addition of more specific patterns to select which of the *Bad* cows are the worst. We could use, for instance, patterns including the next more relevant attribute which, as in the statistical model, is **Kl**. An example of such a pattern is [[**KgMilkPeak**, L], [**Kl**, VL]] satisfied by 7145 cows, the 89.85% of them are *Bad* and the remaining 10.15% are *Good*. This example shows the advantage of the DT model compared to the statistical model since the latter only shows that both **KgMilkPeak** and **Kl** explain the 74.36% of **Production/DIM**, whereas by using the patterns from the DT model, we know the range of values in both **KgMilkPeak** and **Kl** (L and VL respectively) that support the decision of culling a cow.

Table 3. Statistical model obtained using Multiple Regression Model using Stepwise Selection Method (SAS 9.4).

Step	Variable	Partial R^2	Model R^2	C(p)	F-value	Pr > F
1	**KgMilkPeak**	0.7176	0.7176	12984.4	248933	<.0001
2	**Kl**	0.0260	0.7436	2757.89	9948.78	<.0001
3	**Morpho**	0.0045	0.7481	995.217	1747.00	<.0001
4	**Month1Calving**	0.0019	0.7500	239.494	755.91	<.0001
5	**Protein**	0.0003	0.7503	111.662	129.69	<.0013
6	**Age1Calving**	0.0002	0.7506	20.8978	92.75	<.0026
7	**SCC**	0.0000	0.7506	13.8943	9.00	<.0001
8	**BirthMonth**	0.0000	0.7506	11.1981	4.70	<.0001
9	**ICO**	0.0000	0.7506	0.7506	4.17	<.0001

6   Conclusions

In the present work we used decision trees to obtain patterns supporting the culling decision process of a dairy farm. From a data base with around 98000 cows, we obtained a model formed by 4 patterns that predicts the milk production of a cow on her first lactation (**Production/DIM**). By using this model, **Production/DIM** can be predicted based on milk yield records from first lactation peak (**KgMilkPeak**) with an 84% of accuracy after one trial of 10-fold cross-validation, and 83% of accuracy on different dairy farms. This result is consistent with the statistical model constructed from the same data base, which shows a high correlation between both variables (**Production/DIM** and **KgMilkPeak**). Thus, the model could be a helpful tool for the decision of culling a cow in early stages of her lactation since, poorly productive cows can be identified using a pattern that has a predictability of around 97%.

Acknowledgments. The authors acknowledge data support from CONAFE (Confederacion Nacional de la Raza Frisona). This research is partially funded by the projects (Project AGL2015-67409-C2-01-R) from the Spanish Ministry of Economy and Competitiveness; RPREF (CSIC Intramural 201650E044); and the grant 2014-SGR-118 from the Generalitat de Catalunya. Authors also thank to Àngel García-Cerdaña his helpful comments.

References

1. Ansari-Lari, M., Mohebbi-Fani, M., Rowshan-Ghasrodashti, A.: Causes of culling in dairy cows and its relation to age at culling and interval from calving in Shiraz, Southern Iran. Vet. Res. Forum **3**, 233–237 (2012)
2. Calsamiglia, S., Castillejos, L., Astiz, S., Lopez-DeToro, C., Baucells, J.: A dairy farm simulation model as a tool to explore the technical and economical consequences of management decisions. In: Buiatrics, W.A. (ed.) Proceedings of the World Buiatrics Congress 2016, p. 406 (2016)
3. Cavero, D., Tölle, K., Buxadé, C., Krieter, J.: Mastitis detection in dairy cows by application of fuzzy logic. Livestock Sci. **105**, 207–213 (2006)

4. Fetrow, J., Nordlund, K.V., Norman, H.D.: Culling: nomenclature, definitions, and recommendations. J. Dairy Sci. **89**, 1896–1905 (2006)
5. Goel, A., Zobel, C.W., Jones, E.C.: A multi-agent system for supporting the electronic contracting of food grains. Comput. Electr. Agric. **48**(2), 123–137 (2005). http://www. sciencedirect.com/science/article/pii/S016816990500058X
6. Grzesiak, W., Blaszczyk, P., Lacroix, R.: Methods of predicting milk yield in dairy cows: Predictive capabilities of wood's lactation curve and artificial neural networks (ANNs). Comput. Electron. Agric. **54**(2), 69–83 (2006)
7. Kamphuis, C., Mollenhorst, H., Heesterbeek, J., Hogeveen, H.: Detection of clinical mastitis with sensor data from automatic milking systems is improved by using decision-tree induction. J. Dairy Sci. **93**(8), 3616–3627 (2010)
8. Parrott, L., Lacroix, R., Wade, K.M.: Design considerations for the implementation of multi-agent systems in the dairy industry. Comput. Electr. Agric. **38**(2), 79–98 (2003). http:// www.sciencedirect.com/science/article/pii/S0168169902001394
9. Quinlan, J.R.: Induction of decision trees. Mach. Learn. **1**(1), 81–106 (1986)
10. Shahinfar, S., Mehrabani-Yeganeh, H., Lucas, C., Kalhor, A., Kazemian, M., Weigel, K.A.: Prediction of breeding values for dairy cattle using artificial neural networks and neuro-fuzzy systems. Comput. Math. Methods Med. (ID 127130) (2012)
11. Sitkowska, B., Piwczyński, D., Aerts, J., Kolenda, M., Özkaya, S.: Detection of high levels of somatic cells in milk on farms equipped with an automatic milking system by decision trees technique. Turkish J. Vet. Anim. Sci. **41**, 532–540 (2009)
12. Sugiono, S., Soenoko, R., Riawati, L.: Investigating the impact of physiological aspect on cow milk production using artificial intelligence. Int. Rev. Mech. Eng. **11**(1), 30–36 (2017)
13. Sun, Z., Samarasinghe, S., Jago, J.: Detection of mastitis and its stage of progression by automatic milking systems using artificial neural networks. J. Dairy Res. **77**, 168–175 (2009)
14. Thangaraj, A., Patricia, A., Samarasingh, S.: Modelling a multi agent system for dairy farms for integrated decision making. In: 22nd International Congress on Modelling and Simulation, Hobart, Tasmania, Australia (2017)
15. Wang, E., Samarasinghe, S.: On-line detection of mastitis in dairy herds using artificial neural networks. In: Proceedings of the International Congress on Modelling and Simulation (MODSIM 2005), Melbourne, Australia (2005)

Wind Energy Forecasting at Different Time Horizons with Individual and Global Models

R. Martín-Vázquez[✉], R. Aler, and I. M. Galván

EVANNAI, Carlos III University of Madrid,
Avda. Universidad, 30, 28911 Leganés, Spain
ruben.martin@uc3m.es

Abstract. In this work two different machine learning approaches have been studied to predict wind power for different time horizons: individual and global models. The individual approach constructs a model for each horizon while the global approach obtains a single model that can be used for all horizons. Both approaches have advantages and disadvantages. Each individual model is trained with data pertaining to a single horizon, thus it can be specific for that horizon, but can use fewer data for training than the global model, which is constructed with data belonging to all horizons. Support Vector Machines have been used for constructing the individual and global models. This study has been tested on energy production data obtained from the Sotavento wind farm and meteorological data from the European Centre for Medium-Range Weather Forecasts, for a 5 × 5 grid around Sotavento. Also, given the large amount of variables involved, a feature selection algorithm (Sequential Forward Selection) has been used in order to improve the performance of the models. Experimental results show that the global model is more accurate than the individual ones, specially when feature selection is used.

Keywords: Wind power forecasting · Machine learning · Forecasting horizons

1 Introduction

The correct forecast of the energy obtained from the wind is still one of the main challenges of renewable energies. To predict the wind power generated in a wind farm is a difficult task although there is a wide literature on this area. Currently, to forecast the power there are mainly three approaches: physical methods, statistical methods and methods based on artificial intelligence [1, 2].

Physical methods collect values measured in the lower atmosphere to build mathematical models, named Numerical Weather Prediction (NWP), that are used to make predictions of the weather [3]. These methods have the drawback that they require long operation time and a large amount of computational resources.

Statistical methods use historical data from wind farms to find a relationship between the input variables and the power. These models are faster than physical methods but they have the disadvantage that they have large error for long horizons. Time series [4], Autoregressive Moving Average (ARMA) [5], Autoregressive

L. Iliadis et al. (Eds.): AIAI 2018, IFIP AICT 519, pp. 240–248, 2018.
https://doi.org/10.1007/978-3-319-92007-8_21

Integrated Moving Average (ARIMA) [6] or Modified Taylor Kriging (MTK) [7], are examples of these techniques.

Artificial intelligence methods use mainly, but not exclusively, machine learning techniques. They use information from NWP variables and/or historical data to predict power wind, trying to find the relationship between these variables. Some of these artificial intelligence techniques are Fuzzy Logic [8], Genetic Algorithms [9], Artificial Neural Networks (ANN) [10], Support Vector Machines (SVM) [11] or ensemble methods [12].

Some of these approaches can be hybridized. The growing popularity of renewable energies has led to the search for new alternatives by combining existing methods to try to make more reliable predictions. Time series and boosting with historical data [13], ANN and time series with wind speed [14] and Gaussian Process with NWP and historical data [15] are some of the combinations that can be found.

In this work, machine learning methods using Support Vector Machine models (SVM) are proposed to predict wind power at different time horizons (or steps), from 3 h until 15 h, using meteorological variables (from a NWP model) in a grid centered at the Sotavento wind farm. With this purpose two approaches has been studied: individual models and global models. Individual models are made for working in a single time horizon, building up a different model for each horizon. The motivation for using individual models is to train them under the same situation that they will be used operationally. When used operationally, the only inputs available to the model are the meteorological variables forecasts. Therefore, for training the individual models, forecasts carried out in the past (historical forecasts) will also be used. This has the advantage that both training and operation use the same kind of data, but it has two drawbacks. First, forecasts contain prediction errors that might affect negatively the training process. Second, each individual model can only be trained with data belonging to its time horizon. Thus, a second approach is proposed, the global model, where a single model is trained using the data from all horizons put together. In this case, the model can be trained using reanalysis data, that contains observations/ measurements, rather than forecast records. In operation mode, the same global model can be used for making predictions at any horizon.

On the other hand, using a grid of meteorological variables implies that the number of attributes can be very large, which can reduce the model generalization capability, specially for the individual models, which are trained with fewer data. In a previous work [16] three different attribute selection methods were evaluated to estimate wind energy at Sotavento. It was concluded that Sequential Forward Selection (SFS) reduced significantly the number of attributes while obtaining very accurate results. In this work, SFS has also been used for both the individual and global models. In the case of the individual models, different attributes can be selected for different horizons.

The rest of the paper is organized as follows. In Sect. 2 data sets are explained. Section 3 describes the individual and global approaches that are studied in the present work. Experimental results are presented in Sect. 4. Finally, Sect. 5 draws the conclusions learned from this study.

2 Data

As in the previous work [16], data is obtained from a 5×5 grid, with a distance between coordinates of 0.125 degrees, centered at Sotavento experimental wind farm between 2005 and 2010. 19 meteorological variables are selected for each grid point, and they have been obtained from the ERA-20C dataset made available by the European Centre for Medium-Range Weather Forecasts (ECMWF)[1].

This results in a total of 475 attributes (19 * 5 * 5). The 19 meteorological variables are shown in Table 1. For the same period, there is a reanalysis data set and a forecasting data set. As its name indicates, forecasting datasets contain forecasts, while reanalysis datasets contain information obtained to observations. The forecast datasets provide predictions at different steps (or horizons). All the forecasts are made every day at 06:00UTC and predictions are provided for steps 3, 6, 9, 12, and 15 h ahead. The reanalysis dataset contains a time series for each meteorological variable, with observations provided at 06:00UTC+3h, 06:00UTC+6h ... 06:00UTC+15h. Generated wind power has been obtained from the Sotavento website[2]. Table 2 displays the number of instances for each data set.

3 Individual and Global Approaches for Energy Forecasting

In this work, two different approaches are used for predicting wind energy: individual models and a global model. Individual models are built to be used for specific time horizons while the global model can be used for any time horizon. Next, the process used for training and using the individual and global models will be described:

Individual models follow Eq. 1, where t_0 is the time at which the predictions are made (06:00UTC), h = 3, 6, 9, 12, 15 are the steps, and $v_i(t_0 + h)$ are the forecasted meteorological variables. Each F_h model is trained using the data for that particular step from the forecast dataset (see Table 2, so that every individual model is specialized in a particular step.

$$E_h^{(0)}(t_0 + h) = F_h(\widehat{v_1}(t_0 + h), \ldots, \widehat{v_n}(t_0 + h)) \tag{1}$$

In order to study the influence on the forecast of the energy measured at prediction time t_0, a new input variable is added (see Eq. 2) with the energy value at 06:00 UTC ($E(t_0)$).

$$E_h^{(1)}(t_0 + h) = F_h(\widehat{v_1}(t_0 + h), \ldots, \widehat{v_n}(t_0 + h), E(t_0)) \tag{2}$$

The **global model** is trained using reanalysis data, according to Eq. 3, where $v_i(t)$ are the reanalysis meteorological variables. In this case, the data size is larger than the ones used with individual models (see Table 2).

---

[1] https://www.ecmwf.int/en/forecasts/datasets/reanalysis-datasets/era-20c.

[2] http://www.sotaventogalicia.com/en/real-time-data/historical.

Table 1. Meteorological variables used as input to the models.

Variables	
2 m temperature (K)	10 m U wind component (ms^{-1})
10 m V wind component (ms^{-1})	100 m U wind component (ms^{-1})
100 m V wind component (ms^{-1})	Convective available potential energy (Jkg^{-1})
Forecast logarithm of surface roughness for heat	Forecast surface roughness (m)
Instantaneous eastward turbulent surface stress (Nm^{-2})	Instantaneous northward turbulent surface stress (Nm^{-2})
Leaf area index, high vegetation (m^{2}m^{-2})	Leaf area index, low vegetation (m^{2}m^{-2})
Neutral wind at 10 m u-component (ms^{-1})	Neutral wind at 10 m v-component (ms^{-1})
Soil temperature level 1 (K)	Soil temperature level 2 (K)
Soil temperature level 3 (K)	Soil temperature level 4 (K)
Surface pressure (Pa)	

Table 2. Number of instances for each data set.

Data Set	Instances
Forecast step 3	1445
Forecast step 6	1446
Forecast step 9	1543
Forecast step 12	1550
Forecast step 15	1468
Reanalysis	8347

$$E^{(0)}(t) = F(v_1(t), \ldots, v_n(t)) \tag{3}$$

Equation 4 shows how to use the global model for making predictions at time t_0 for different horizons (h = 3, 6, 9, 12, 15). In this case, forecasts $\widehat{v_i}(t_0 + h)$ must be used because observations are not available at prediction time. It is important to remark that, differently to individual models, the same global model is used for all steps.

$$E^{(0)}(t_0 + h) = F(\widehat{v_1}(t_0 + h), \ldots, \widehat{v_n}(t_0 + h)) \tag{4}$$

Similarly to individual models, the influence of wind energy measured at prediction time ($E(t_0)$) is studied, with models trained according to Eq. 5.

$$E^{(1)}(t) = F(v_1(t), \ldots, v_n(t), E(t_0)) \tag{5}$$

Similarly to model $E^{(0)}$, in order to use $E^{(1)}$ for making predictions, Eq. 6 must be used.

$$E^{(1)}(t_0 + h) = F(\widehat{v_n}(t_0 + h), \ldots, \widehat{v_n}(t_0 + h), E(t_0)) \tag{6}$$

4 Experimental Results

In this section the results obtained in the experiments are shown. To measure the performance the Mean Absolute Error (MAE) is used. A methodology similar to cross validation has been used to evaluate both individual and global models. Given that data is available for six years (2005 to 2010), each year is used as a test set, and the remaining five years are used to construct the model. That means that the process of model construction and model evaluation has been repeated six times (6 folds) and then the average number of inputs and test MAE have been obtained. Data reserved for model construction is further divided into training and validation datasets by choosing, every three days, the first two days for training and the third one for validation. The validation partition will be used for hyper-parameter tuning and to select the most relevant attributes with the SFS algorithm. The final model is trained joining the training and validation data, using the hyper-parameters and attributes selected previously. This model is finally evaluated on the test set.

SVM hyper-parameter tuning has been carried out by means of grid search, for Gamma = {0, 0.01, 0.1, 0.1, 0.25, 0.5, 0.75, 1} and C = {0.1, 1, 10, 100, 500}. Grid search returned the same parameter values for all folds: C = 1 and Gamma = 0.01 for individuals and global models.

Because of the large number of input attributes, and taking into account the results of the previous work, SFS has been used to reduce the number of input features. In the case of the global model, the 26 attributes selected are the same as in the previous work, where also the Sotavento reanalysis dataset was used [16]. In the case of the individual models, SFS was run for each of the steps, so that the attributes selected are specialized for every step.

The average results of the 6 folds are shown in Table 3. The first half of the table displays results for the individual models and the second half for the global one. For each of them, the MAE is provided for the model without feature selection (second column), with SFS selection (third column), and with SFS selection plus the $E(t_0)$ input (last column). All results have been broken down by step (first column), but average and standard deviation results are also included. When SFS selection is used, the average number of inputs selected is also given.

With respect to the individual models, it can be seen that using SFS (third column) reduces significantly the number of inputs (from 475 to 8.54 on average). MAE is also improved for all steps except the last one. Adding $E(t_0)$ as input to the model ($E_h^{(1)}$ in the fourth column) does not improve results, except for the first step (3 h) (see Fig. 1). For the global model, SFS selection improves MAE for all steps and adding $E(t_0)$ as input decreases MAE for the two first steps (see Fig. 2). This should be expected, because the longer the horizon, the less relevant is the power measured at prediction time t_0.

Table 3. Results for the individual global approaches.

Individual models

Step	$E_h^{(0)}$, 475 Inputs	$E_h^{(0)}$, SFS Inputs		$E_h^{(1)}$, SFS Inputs
	MAE	MAE	Number Inputs	MAE
Step 3	266.15	261.34	7.33	246.79
Step 6	291.42	272	11.17	273.34
Step 9	280.06	275.32	11.17	306.81
Step 12	259.32	257.5	6.67	295.41
Step 15	288.64	303.21	6	356.82
Average	277.12	274.07	8.47	295.83
Std.	13.99	17.94	2.51	41.08

Global models

Step	$E^{(0)}$, 475 Inputs	$E^{(0)}$, SFS Inputs		$E^{(1)}$, SFS Inputs
	MAE	MAE	Number Inputs	MAE
Step 3	268.86	256.61	26	238.8
Step 6	282.88	259.74	26	251.3
Step 9	273.42	247.71	26	252.46
Step 12	260.53	237.13	26	242.6
Step 15	295.72	281.33	26	303.43
Average	276.28	256.5	26	257.72
Std.	13.54	16.43	0	26.2

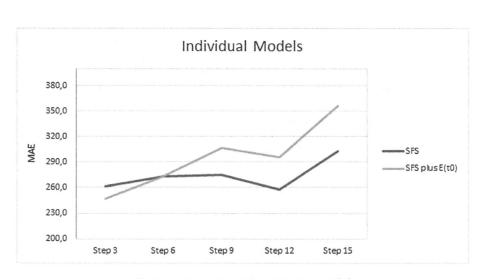

Fig. 1. Individual models with/without $E(t_0)$

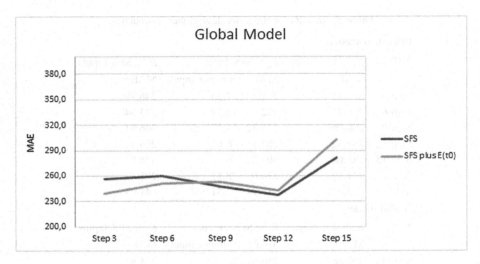

Fig. 2. Global model with/without $E(t_0)$

Comparing the individual and global models, it can be seen in Table 3 that the global models outperform the individual ones on average in the three cases studied: without feature selection, with SFS, and with SFS plus $E(t_0)$. In the first case, the improvement of the global model is small (277.12 vs. 276.28), but the difference increases for the other two cases (274.07 vs. 256.50 and 295.83 vs. 257.72, respectively). In fact, for the last two cases, the global model is more accurate than the individual ones, not only on average, but for each step.

In order to assess the significance of the comparisons between global and individual models, the number of folds where each model is better will be given. $E^{(0)}$ global model is better in 5 out of 6 folds for every step than individual models. For $E^{(1)}$ models with SFS variables, results are better for global model than individual models in step 3 for 5 folds. In the following steps, the global model is better than the individual models in all of the folds.

In order to provide some baseline results, the persistence method has also been used. Persistence uses the current value of wind power as forecast for the next time step. The 6-fold average MAE obtained for each time horizon can be seen in Table 4.

Table 4. Results for the persistence method.

Step	MAE
Step 3	305.85
Step 6	395.20
Step 9	427.57
Step 12	450.34
Step 15	494.20
Average	414.63
Std.	25.8

It can be observed that the different approaches studied in this work are better than persistence for all the steps.

5 Conclusions

Two different approaches, individual and global, for predicting wind power in different time horizons have been studied and compared. Individual models are specific for each step. Therefore, they are trained with data belonging to the step and with forecasting dataset. The global model is trained with data from all steps and using the reanalysis dataset. This results in a unique model that can be used for making predictions in the different steps.

Although it could be expected that individual models performed better because they are specific for each horizon, the fact that fewer data is used to train each of them, and the need to use the forecasted input meteorological variables, rather than the reanalysis dataset, makes the global model perform more accurately, at least in this study.

Regarding the use of the SFS algorithm for feature selection, results show that both individual and global improve accuracy, but it is the global approach which specially takes advantage from it. Finally, adding the wind power measurement available at prediction time as input to the models, benefits mainly the global model and only the forecasting horizons close to prediction time. The improvement for short time horizons (steps 3 and 6) should be expected, because long time horizons depend much less on observations at prediction time.

Acknowledgements. The authors acknowledge financial support granted by the Spanish Ministry of Science under contract ENE2014-56126-C2-2-R.

References

1. Tascikaraoglu, A., Uzunoglu, M.: A review of combined approaches for prediction of short-term wind speed and power. Renew. Sustain. Energy Rev. **34**(Suppl. C), 243–254 (2014)
2. Jung, J., Broadwater, R.P.: Current status and future advances for wind speed and power forecasting. Renew. Sustain. Energy Rev. **31**, 762–777 (2014)
3. Roulston, M.S., Kaplan, D.T., Hardenberg, J., Smith, L.A.: Using medium-range weather forcasts to improve the value of wind energy production. Renew. Energy **28**(4), 585–602 (2003)
4. Croonenbroeck, C., Ambach, D.: A selection of time series models for short- to medium-term wind power forecasting. J. Wind Eng. Ind. Aerodyn. **136**, 201–210 (2015)
5. Liu, H., Erdem, E., Shi, J.: Comprehensive evaluation of ARMA-GARCH(-M) approaches for modeling the mean and volatility of wind speed. Appl. Energy **88**, 724–732 (2011)
6. Kavasseri, R.G., Seetharaman, K.: Day-ahead wind speed forecasting using f-ARIMA models. Renew. Energy **34**(5), 1388–1393 (2009)
7. Liu, H., Shi, J., Erdem, E.: Prediction of wind speed time series using modified Taylor Kriging method. Energy **35**(12), 4870–4879 (2010)

8. Zhu, B., Chen, M., Wade, N., Ran, L.: A prediction model for wind farm power generation based on fuzzy modeling. Procedia Environ. Sci. **12**, 122–129 (2012)
9. Damousis, I.G., Alexiadis, M.C., Theocharis, J.B., Dokopoulos, P.S.: A fuzzy model for wind speed prediction and power generation in wind parks using spatial correlation. IEEE Trans. Energy Convers. **19**(2), 352–361 (2004)
10. Mohandes, M.A., Halawani, T.O., Rehman, S., Hussain, A.A.: Support vector machines for wind speed prediction. Renew. Energy **29**(6), 939–947 (2004)
11. Heinermann, J., Kramer, O.: Precise wind power prediction with SVM ensemble regression. In: Wermter, S., Weber, C., Duch, W., Honkela, T., Koprinkova-Hristova, P., Magg, S., Palm, G., Villa, Alessandro E.P. (eds.) ICANN 2014. LNCS, vol. 8681, pp. 797–804. Springer, Cham (2014). https://doi.org/10.1007/978-3-319-11179-7_100
12. Ren, Y., Suganthan, P.N., Srikanth, N.: Ensemble methods for wind and solar power forecasting—a state-of-the-art review. Renew. Sustain. Energy Rev. **50**, 82–91 (2015)
13. Jiang, Y., Chen, X., Yu, K., Liao, Y.: Short-term wind power forecasting using hybrid method based on enhanced boosting algorithm. J. Mod. Power Syst. Clean Energy **5**(1), 126–133 (2017)
14. Doucoure, B., Agbossou, K., Cardenas, A.: Time series prediction using artificial wavelet neural network and multi-resolution analysis: application to wind speed data. Renew. Energy **92**, 202–211 (2016)
15. Chen, N., Qian, Z., Nabney, I.T., Meng, X.: Wind power forecasts using Gaussian processes and numerical weather prediction. IEEE Trans. Power Syst. **29**(2), 656–665 (2014)
16. Martín-Vázquez, R., Aler, R., Galván, Inés M.: A study on feature selection methods for wind energy prediction. In: Rojas, I., Joya, G., Catala, A. (eds.) IWANN 2017. LNCS, vol. 10305, pp. 698–707. Springer, Cham (2017). https://doi.org/10.1007/978-3-319-59153-7_60

Entropy-Assisted Emotion Recognition of Valence and Arousal Using XGBoost Classifier

Sheng-Hui Wang[✉], Huai-Ting Li, En-Jui Chang,
and An-Yeu (Andy) Wu

Graduate Institute of Electronics Engineering, National Taiwan University,
Taipei, Taiwan
{harry,wesli,enjui,andywu}@access.ee.ntu.edu.tw

Abstract. Emotion recognition is an essential function to realize human-machine interaction devices. Physiological signals which can be collected easily and continuously by wearable sensors are good inputs for emotion analysis. How to effectively process physiological signals, extract critical features, and choose machine learning model for emotion classification has been a big challenge. In this paper, an entropy-based processing scheme for emotion recognition framework is proposed, which includes entropy domain feature extraction and prediction by XGBoost classifier. We experiment on AMIGOS database and the experimental results show that the proposed scheme for multi-modal analysis outperforms conventional processing approaches. It achieves approximately 80% and 68% accuracy of prediction for two affect dimensions, valence and arousal. For one modality case, we found that galvanic skin response (GSR) channel is the most potential modality for prediction, which leads to best performances.

Keywords: Affective computing · Emotion recognition
Physiological signal processing · Entropy domain features · XGBoost

1 Introduction

Affective computing is a key technology for human–computer interaction (HCI) in the future era of Internet of thing (IoT) [1], which makes it possible for machines and computers to realize human's emotion and mentality in real time. Furthermore, it can give appropriate responses and services based-on human's current mental status. Related databases have been developed for related researches on affective computing. Among the open-source databases available on the Internet, FEEDTUM [2] and Berlin Database of Emotional Speech (EmoDB) [3], released in 2005, used facial video and speech for emotion recognition, respectively. They predicted basic emotion of people, such as anger and happy, by single type of signal.

As intelligent IoT develops, more and more wearable devices are equipped with different kinds of sensors. We can effectively get various signals sensed from subjects and have the access for continuously monitoring. For this scenario, physiological signals can be good inputs for affective computing framework, since we do not express

L. Iliadis et al. (Eds.): AIAI 2018, IFIP AICT 519, pp. 249–260, 2018.
https://doi.org/10.1007/978-3-319-92007-8_22

our emotions on faces and make sounds every time. Integrating multiple-channel of physiological signals for emotion recognition and aggregating machine learning classifiers for ensemble learning have gain attention in recent years. DEAP database [4] proposed in 2012 has been experimented in many works [5, 6], it contains several types of physiological signals which were recorded when subjects were watching music videos. In DEAP, emotions perceived by subjects are self-assessed on two affect dimensions, valence and arousal. Valence tells how positive or negative the emotion is and arousal indicates the intensity of emotion. In 2016, ACERTAIN database [7] was proposed that first used commercial wearable sensor to collect data and added personality into experiments. AMIGOS database [8] proposed in 2017 contains stable data, several types of videos, and elements for other related research, such as social context and mood. These all indicate that multi-modality analysis of physiological signals is a trend of affective computing. Therefore, how to effectively process different physiological signals and further extract critical features from different channels for emotion classification have been a big challenge.

The aim of this paper is to establish reliable emotion recognition framework based on physiological signals. To improve the accuracy of emotion recognition, we firstly extract the entropy domain features to quantify the regularity and randomness of signal, which has high potential to represent the different levels of emotion. Next, we apply the XGBoost [9] to enhance the performance of classification which has high scalability and efficiency for training and has the ability to learn from high dimension data without using high complexity feature selection algorithms.

The rest of the paper is organized as follows. Section 2 describes common methods for emotion recognition task. Section 3 illustrates the enhanced methods for feature extraction and machine learning engine. Section 4 shows the experimental results and Sect. 5 concludes.

2   Common Approaches of Emotion Recognition Framework

The flow chart of the emotion recognition framework in this study is shown in Fig. 1. Three kinds of physiological signals are inputs and the output is the prediction for high or low of affect dimensions. Three other blocks including pre-processing, feature extraction, and machine learning engine will be introduced as below.

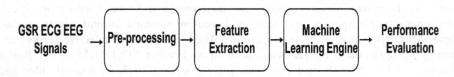

Fig. 1. Flow chart of general emotion recognition framework.

2.1 Pre-processing

We use the processed data provided by the official website of AMIGOS dataset. In AMIGOS database, each subject watched both long and short videos as stimulus for emotion. Because long-length video data contain multiple values for valence and arousal, only short-length video data are used in this work to reduce the uncertainty. There are total 40 subjects and 16 short-length videos in database. Each video of each subject is seen as one data. Each of data has 14 channels for Electroencephalography (EEG), 2 channels for Electrocardiography (ECG), and 1 channel for galvanic skin response (GSR). 7 subjects whose physiological signals of videos contain some missing values are removed (ID number: 9, 12, 21, 22, 23, 24, 33). Therefore, there are totally (40–7) (subjects) × 16 (videos) = 528 data. We further checked the data stability. First Channel of ECG signals suffer from fewer noises compared to second channel and are used for further analyzing. In addition, GSR signals are filtered by the low-pass filter with cut-off frequency 3 Hz to remove abnormal high frequency noises.

In this work, we do binary classification for valence and arousal. Self-assessments of each subject on two affect dimensions provided in AMIGOS database is used for labels. They are originally values between [1, 9] and needed to be transformed to either positive class or negative class label, which represents high and low, respectively. Figure 2 shows two different ways to process. Directly cut by threshold 5 is intuitive, but hard to distinguish one's relative high and low emotion. In this way, values may highly accord to personal tendency to rate high or low scores, which results in imbalance of labels and decrease in performances. Our method is to define labels by subject-dependent mean value among all 16 videos of each person. Using mean value instead of median value can avoid ambiguity whether the median is labeled positive class or negative class.

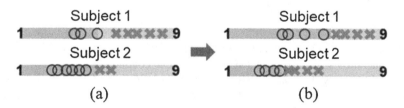

(a)   (b)

Fig. 2. (a) Define labels by comparing with threshold score 5. (b) Define labels by comparing with subject-dependent mean among all videos.

2.2 Feature Extraction

Feature extraction is implemented on all three kinds of signals with different ways to reduce the input dimension before using machine learning methods. Features illustrated in this Section are slightly different from the feature set in AMIGOS database. Features extracted among physiological signals are shown in Table 1.

GSR Signal: Partly follow methods in [8, 10], skin response (SR) related features (18) are first extracted and skin conductance (SC) signal is got by computing SR

Table 1. Features extracted among physiological signals

Modality	Features extracted
GSR signal (32 features)	**SR features (18)**: mean, mean of derivative, mean of negative derivative, proportion of negatives in derivative, number of local minimum, mean of each rise time series, spectral power 0–2.4 Hz (12, per 0.2 Hz). **SC features (4)**: mean, standard deviation, mean of derivative, mean of second derivative. **SCSR features (4)**: mean, standard deviation, mean of derivative, mean of second derivative. **SCSR & SCVSR features (6)**: zero crossing rate of SCSR, zero crossing rate of SCVSR, average magnitude of SCSR occurrences, average magnitude of SCVSR occurrences, average magnitude of all SCSR and SCVSR occurrences, ratio of number of SCSR occurrences to SCVSR.
ECG signal (77 features)	**Features from raw ECG (60)**: spectral power 0–6 Hz (per 0.1 Hz) **HRV features (10)**: mean, standard deviation, skewness, kurtosis, root mean square, root mean square of the successive differences, percentage of points higher than mean + standard deviation, percentage of points lower than mean − standard deviation, low frequency spectral power (0.01–0.08 Hz), middle frequency spectral power (0.08–0.15 Hz), high frequency spectral power (0.15–0.50 Hz). **HR features (6)**: mean, standard deviation, skewness, kurtosis, percentage of points higher than mean + standard deviation, percentage of points lower than mean − standard deviation
EEG signal (105 features)	**PSD features (70)**: average 5 bands (theta, slow alpha, alpha, beta, and gamma) PSD in 14 channels. **Asymmetry features (35)**: difference of 5 bands PSD between 7 pairs of channel.

signal's reciprocal. SC signal is then normalized and used to extract features (4). Next, skin conductance slow response (SCSR) and skin conductance very slow response (SCVSR) is got by low-pass filtering normalized SC signal at 0.2 and 0.08 Hz, respectively. Afterwards, some SCSR related features are extracted (4). Last, after de-trending SCSR and SCVSR by using empirical mode decomposition (EMD) methods [11] to remove the last half intrinsic mode functions (IMFs), some related features are extracted.

ECG Signal: Partly follow methods in [8, 10], 0–6 Hz spectral power features are first extracted (60, per 0.1). Then, R-R interval (RRI) series is calculated after detecting R peaks in ECG. Heart rate variability (HRV) and heart rare (HR) time series can be computed by using RRI. Finally, HRV related features (11) and HR related features (6) are extracted.

EEG Signal: Follow the methods in [4], average power spectral density (PSD) of theta band (4–7 Hz), slow alpha band (8–10 Hz), alpha band (8–13 Hz), beta band (14–30 Hz), gamma band (31–47 Hz) of each EEG channel are extracted (5 × 14 = 70).

Also, asymmetry of PSD of 5 bands between 7 pairs of EEG channel are extracted (5 × 7 = 35).

2.3   Machine Learning Engine

This block consists of a feature selection method and a machine learning classifier, as shown in Fig. 3a. Feature space which contains 214 features is comparatively big while we only have 528 (16 subjects * 33 videos) data in AMIGOS database. Thus, feature selection is applied to eliminate redundant features and reduce the model complexity of machine learning algorithm in next stage. This is helpful for enhancing overall performance and sparing lots of computation resources.

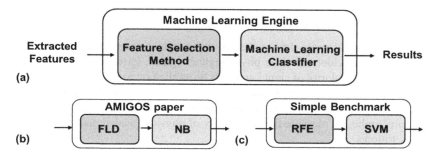

Fig. 3. (a) Overview of machine learning engine block. (b) Machine learning engine block in AMIGOS paper. (c) Machine learning engine block of simple benchmark.

In Fig. 3b, overview of machine engine block in AMIGOS database is shown. For feature selection method in original paper of Amigos database [8], Fisher's linear discriminant (FLD) J [12] is calculated over each feature, which is defined as

$$J(f) = \frac{|\mu_1 - \mu_0|}{\sigma_1^2 + \sigma_0^2}. \tag{1}$$

Afterward, user can decide how much discriminant features they would like to select based on validation sets and pick up features with the highest J values. For machine learning classifier, Gaussian Naïve Bayes (GaussianNB) classifier is used. Assuming features are independent and Gaussian distributed, GaussianNB is given as

$$G(f_1,\ldots,f_n) = argmax_c \; p(C = c) \prod_{i=1}^{n} p(F_i = f_i | C = c), \tag{2}$$

and calculate the probability of each sample for each class, where F is feature set and C is the classes set. These two methods are not powerful and lead to relatively low f1-score shown in [8].

In this work, we first implement support vector machine (SVM) [13, 14] based approach as the benchmark, as shown in Fig. 3c. SVM is a famous tool in the field of machine leaning and it has good performance on classification and prediction over many applications. Compared with other classifier, SVM can deal with small-size datasets well, since it uses only support vectors to construct hyperplane. When it comes to feature selection, recursive feature elimination (RFE) algorithm [15] can efficiently remove irrelevant features and be suit for SVM. RFE-SVM eliminates features with smallest weight in SVM model on a sequential backward selection (SBS) based process. The progress continues until one feature is left and the features combined with SVM model with the highest performance is outputted.

3 Proposed Framework with Entropy Domain Features and XGBoost Classifier

3.1 Entropy Domain Features

Non-linear entropy domain features, such as sample entropy, permutation entropy based features, are widely used on physiological signals. Extracted entropy value can help quantify the regularity of signal and thus be applied on medical diagnosis. For this emotion recognition work, three types of entropy domain features, including refined composite multiscale entropy (RCMSE), turning point ratio (TRP), and Shannon entropy, are applied to measure the complexity of physiological signals. The details are shown as follows.

Refine Composite Multiscale Entropy (RCMSE) [16]: Multiscale entropy (MSE) [17] has been used widely to evaluate physiological control mechanisms, such as atrial fibrillation and Alzheimer's disease [18]. RCMSE is an improved version of MSE. It reduces the possibility of undefined value problem when the signal length is short and has a better accuracy for entropy estimation. The concept of RCMSE is using different scales of local matching pattern to compute the regularity of the signal. There are two steps of RCMSE. First step: time series of signal is coarse-grained into multiscale series. For each scale factor τ, τ series are generated by average τ points in non-overlapping windows and each of series overlap $\tau-1$ points with neighbor series. The j-th point of k-th coarse-grained series, $y_k^{(\tau)} = \left\{ y_{k,1}^{(\tau)} y_{k,2}^{(\tau)} y_{k,3}^{(\tau)} \ldots y_{k,p}^{(\tau)} \right\}$, with scale factor τ of signal x is defined:

$$y_{k,j}^{(\tau)} = \frac{1}{\tau} \sum_{i=(j-1)\tau+k}^{j\tau+k-1} x_i, \quad 1 \leq j \leq \frac{N}{\tau}, \quad 1 \leq k \leq \tau. \tag{3}$$

In the conventional MSE algorithm, output of coarse graining is only first series of each scale factor. Second step: averaged sample entropy of each τ is calculated as below:

$$RCMSE(x, \tau, m, r) = -ln\left(\frac{\sum_{k=1}^{\tau} n_{k,\tau}^{m+1}}{\sum_{k=1}^{\tau} n_{k,\tau}^{m}}\right), \tag{4}$$

where m is the matching pattern length and r is the similarity criterion. In (4), $n_{k,\tau}^{m}$ is the number of two sets of simultaneous data points of length m in kth series have the difference $< r$. When the ratio of $\sum_{k=1}^{\tau} n_{k,\tau}^{m+1}$ and $\sum_{k=1}^{\tau} n_{k,\tau}^{m}$ is small, sample entropy would be large, which means high complexity of signal. Value of RCMSE is undefined only when $\sum_{k=1}^{\tau} n_{k,\tau}^{m+1} = 0$, which means $n_{k,\tau}^{m}$ of k series are all zero. By summation of matching pattern of multiple series, RCMSE has less probability to be undefined than conventional MSE.

In this work, RCMSE is applied to RRI series of ECG signals. Because the length of ECG signals are relatively short (each video 55 s–155 s), the scale factor τ s set up to be 3. In addition, we set the matching pattern m up to be three and the similarity criterion r is set to be 0.2 of standard deviation.

Turning Points Ratio (TPR): TPR is proposed on the basis of nonparametric "Runs Test" to evaluate the randomness in a time-series [19] and the idea was used in RRI of ECG signal [20]. The concept of TPR is to measure the complexity of the signal by number of turning points compared to total points. Turning point is found by comparing each point with left and right neighbor points and TPR is calculated as follows:

$$TPR = \frac{\sum_{i=2}^{N-1} [(x_i - x_{i-1})(x_i - x_{i+1}) > 0]}{N - 2}, \tag{5}$$

where N is the length of the signal x. Besides original TPR, we extracted modified TPR (MTPR) on signals. The procedure of MTPR is to use EMD methods to extract trend of the signal first, in order to remove trivial peaks of the signal. Next, compute TPR as (3) on the extracted trend.

In this work, TPR and MTPR are calculated on RRI of ECG signals and GSR signals. EEG signal has less information on time series and is skipped.

Shannon Entropy: Shannon entropy is commonly calculated in the domain of information theory. It is defined for a given discrete probability distribution, using probability of each symbol to measure the uncertainty or randomness of the data. However, almost every point has different values. We can't see each of different points as a new symbol, otherwise almost the same value of Shannon entropy we would get from different signals. In other way, we classify every points into one group of the group set. First, outliers that have larger differences than three standard deviations with mean are removed. Second, we sort rest data points into N groups, which are equally divided between max and min value. Last, p_i of each ith group is calculated and Shannon entropy we can get by:

$$Shannon\, Entropy = -\sum_{i=1}^{N} p_i \log{(p_i)}. \tag{6}$$

The concept of Shannon entropy is to observe the complexity of the signal by overall distribution. Each group is seen as a symbol.

In this work, Shannon entropy is calculated on RRI of ECG signals and GSR signals. Since the optimal group number is data dependent, we apply total 4, 8, 16, 32, 64 groups for simulation.

For these three enhanced feature extraction methods, total 26 features are added into original feature space. The details are listed in Table 2.

Table 2. Enhanced features extracted among physiological signals

Modality	Features Extracted
GSR signal (7 features)	**TPR (2):** TPR, MTPR. **Shannon Entropy (5):** number of groups: 4, 8, 16, 32, 64
ECG signal (19 features)	**RCMSE (12):** m = 0: τ = {1, 2, 3}, sum of τ = {1, 2, 3} m = 1: τ = {1, 2, 3}, sum of τ = {1, 2, 3} m = 2: τ = {1, 2, 3}, sum of τ = {1, 2, 3} **TPR (2):** TPR, MTPR. **Shannon Entropy (5):** number of groups: 4, 8, 16, 32, 64

3.2 Extreme Gradient Boosting (XGBoost)

In this part, we would like to change the content of the machine learning blocks mentioned before in Sect. 2.3, where RFE based SVM approach was used. Among all the machine learning algorithms, gradient boosting tree based model [21] has shown in many applications in different domains. XGBoost [9] is an efficient and scalable gradient boosting machine, which has won lots of machine competitions in recent years [22, 23]. It is an ensemble model consisting of sets of classification and regression tree (CART). While XGB is used for supervised learning problems and we use training data x_i to predict a target variable y_i, the model can be described in the form:

$$\hat{y}_i = \sum_{k=1}^{K} f_k(x_i), f_k \in F, \tag{7}$$

where K is the total number of trees, f_k for kth tree is a function in the functional space F, and F is the set of all possible CARTs. In the training, each of new-trained CART will try to complement the so-far residual. Objective function been optimized at $(t + 1)$th CART is described:

$$obj = \sum_{i=1}^{n} l(y_i, \hat{y}_i^{(t)}) + \sum_{i=1}^{t} \Omega(f_i), \tag{8}$$

Where $l()$ denotes the training loss function, y_i the is ground truth, and $\hat{y}_i^{(t)}$ is the prediction value at step t. $\Omega()$ given by

$$\Omega(f) = \gamma T + \frac{1}{2}\lambda \sum_{j=1}^{T} w_j^2 \qquad (9)$$

is the regularization term, where T are the number of leaves and w_j is the score on jth leaf. When (9) is optimized, Taylor's expansion is used so that gradient descent can be used for different loss functions. Furthermore, feature selection is no need when we use XGBoost approach. During training period of XGBoost, good features would be chosen as node in trees, which means features not used are abandoned.

In this work, we use the scikit-learn API for XGBoost classification. The inputs of XGBoost are total 240 features (214 traditional features + 26 entropy domain feature) and the outputs are prediction results for valence or arousal. For loss function in (8), logistic loss function is set. The details of used features and performances are shown in next Section.

4   Experimental Settings and Results

Single trial classification for two affect dimensions, arousal and valence, is experimented and the flow is shown in Fig. 1. After signal is pre-processed and transformed into features, all features are normalized to [1]. Leave-one-subject-one approach is conducted to evaluate performance. That is, every time one of the 33 subjects is leaved as test set and machine learning engine is trained using remaining 32 subjects' features. When the procedure is repeated 33 times, final performance is calculated by averaging 33 values in each procedure.

There are 3 processing schemes that are compared.

- Scheme_1: Using the feature set and the method described in original AMIGOS database [8], where FLD and GaussianNB were used for machine learning engine block.
- Scheme_2: Using the feature set illustrated in Sect. 2.2 and RFE-SVM for machine learning engine block.
- Scheme_3: Using new feature set with entropy domain features and XGBoost for machine learning engine block.

Table 3 shows the comparison of f1-score and accuracy over three schemes, F1-score is the harmonic mean of precision and recall and here we average f1-scores of positive and negative class as final value. Four scenarios were experimented: using only GSR, ECG, EEG, and using all modalities. Table 4 shows the features used in trees of XGBoost classifier for classification of valence and arousal.

F1-score for Scheme_1 is directly obtained from [8]. For dimension valence and arousal, best accuracy is about 80% and 68%, respectively. Scheme_3 outperforms Scheme_1 and Scheme_2 in almost every scenario on both affect dimensions, especially in valence dimension, outperforms by more than 10% of accuracy.

Table 3. Performance of scheme_1 - scheme_3 on emotion recognition framework. (F1-score is mean for positive and negative class. Red value indicates the highest accuracy or f1-score in each affect dimension. Scheme_1: Amigos feature set + FLD + GaussianNB; Scheme_2: commom feature set + RFE-SVM; Scheme_3: new feature set + XGBoost)

		Accuracy				F1-score			
		GSR	ECG	EEG	All	GSR	ECG	EEG	All
V	Scheme_1	-	-	-	-	0.531	0.535	0.576	0.570
	Scheme_2	0.640	0.615	0.589	0.680	0.610	0.588	0.556	0.666
	Scheme_3	0.776	0.634	0.581	0.801	0.774	0.630	0.577	0.800
A	Scheme_1	-	-	-	-	0.548	0.550	0.592	0.585
	Scheme_2	0.644	0.623	0.566	0.663	0.643	0.612	0.557	0.660
	Scheme_3	0.682	0.542	0.579	0.684	0.707	0.566	0.604	0.698

Table 4. Features selected in XGBoost classifier for classification of two affect dimensions. (Entropy domain features are marked in red color)

Dimension	Features
Valence	**GSR**: spectral power 0-0.2 0.4-0.6 0.6-0.8 0.8-1.0 1.4-1.6, SC_mean of derivative, SCSR_mean, SR_MTPR **ECG**: spectral power 1.2-1.3 2.5-2.6, HRV_ root mean square, HRV_ low frequency spectral power, HRV_ high frequency spectral power, HRV_percentage of points lower than mean - standard deviation, TPR, Shannon group4, RCMSE_m=2 sum **EEG**: T8_gamma, O2_gamma, T7_gamma, O2_beta, T7-T8_slow alpha, T7-T8_beta, , T7-T8_theta, O1-O2_beta
Arousal	**GSR**: spectral power 0-0.2 1.6-1.8, SC_mean of derivative, SC_mean of second derivative, SCSR_number of local minimum **ECG**: spectral power 1.8-1.9 1.9-2.0 3.0-3.1, HRV_percentage of points lower than mean - standard deviation, HRV_ low frequency spectral power, RCMSE_m=1, τ=1 **EEG**: FC6_alpha

Using all-modalities for prediction can have highest performances except for f1-score in arousal. In our experiments (Scheme_2 and Scheme_3), using GSR channel to predict can have the best performance for both valence and arousal dimensions, when only one channel is used. However, the features extracted in GSR channel is the least among three modalities, which indicates that the quality but not the quantity of features lead to better prediction ability.

5   Conclusion

In this paper, we proposed the scheme including both entropy domain features and XGBoost. We enhance feature extraction methods which are entropy domain and helpful for evaluating the complexity of physiological signals. On the other hand, XGBoost classifier which gains popularity in recent years is used for learning and prediction. The proposed scheme can reach the performance of approximately 80% and 68% accuracy on valence and arousal dimension, respectively. It outperforms the processing scheme in original paper of AMIGOS database and the scheme that contains common features and traditional SVM model.

Acknowledgements. This work was supported by the Ministry of Science and Technology of Taiwan (MOST 106-2221-E-002-205-MY3 and MOST 106-2622-8-002-013-TA), National Taiwan University and Pixart Imaging Inc.

References

1. Picard, R.: Affective computing for HCI. In: International Conference on Human-Computer Interaction, pp. 829–833. Lawrence Erlbaum Associates Inc., Munich, Germany (1999)
2. Wallhoff, F.: Facial expressions and emotion database (2005). http://www.mmk.ei.tum.de/_waf/fgnet/feedtum.html
3. Burkhardt, F., Paeschke, A., Rolfes, M., Sendlmeier, W., Weiss, B.: A database of german emotional speech. In: Proceedings of Interspeech, pp. 1517–1520 (2005)
4. Koelstra, S., et al.: DEAP: a database for emotion analysis; using physiological signals. IEEE Trans. Affect. Comput. 3(1), 18–31 (2012)
5. Chen, M., Han, J., Guo, L., Wang, J., Patras, I.: Identifying valence and arousal levels via connectivity between EEG channels. In: 2015 International Conference on Affective Computing and Intelligent Interaction (ACII), Xi'an, pp. 63–69 (2015)
6. Wu, S., Xu, X., Shu, L., Hu, B.: Estimation of valence of emotion using two frontal EEG channels. In: 2017 IEEE International Conference on Bioinformatics and Biomedicine (BIBM), Kansas City, MO, pp. 1127–1130 (2017)
7. Subramanian, R., Wache, J., Abadi, M., Vieriu, R., Winkler, S., Sebe, N.: ASCERTAIN: emotion and personality recognition using commercial sensors. IEEE Trans. Affect. Comput. **PP**(99), 1 (2016)
8. Miranda-Correa, J.A., Abadi, M.K., Sebe, N., Patras, I.: AMIGOS: a dataset for mood, personality and affect research on individuals and groups. ArXiv e-prints (2017)
9. Chen, T., Guestrin, C.: XGBoost. In: Proceedings of the 22nd ACM SIGKDD International Conference on Knowledge Discovery and Data Mining, KDD 2016, pp. 785–794 (2016)
10. Kim, J., Andr, E.: Emotion recognition based on physiological changes in music listening. IEEE Trans. Pattern Anal. Mach. Intell. 30(12), 2067–2083 (2008)
11. Huang, N.E., Shen, Z., Long, S.R., Wu, M.C., Shih, H.H., Zheng, Q., Yen, N.-C., Tung, C. C., Liu, H.H.: The empirical mode decomposition and the hilbert spectrum for nonlinear and non-stationary time series analysis. Proc. Roy. Soc. Lond. A Math. Phys. Eng. Sci. **454** (1971), 903–995 (1998)
12. Song, F., Mei, D., Li, H.: Feature selection based on linear discriminant analysis. In: 2010 International Conference on Intelligent System Design and Engineering Application (ISDEA), vol. 1, pp. 746–749 (2010)

13. Cristianini, N., Shawe-Taylor, J.: An Introduction to Support Vector Machines and Other Kernel-based Learning Methods. Cambridge University Press, Cambridge (2000)
14. Luts, J., Ojeda, F., van de Plas, R., de Moor, B., van Huffel, S., Suykens, J.A.K.: A tutorial on support vector machine-based methods for classification problems in chemometrics. Anal. Chim. Acta **665**, 129–145 (2010)
15. Guyon, I., Weston, J., Barnhill, S., Vapnik, V.: Gene selection for cancer classification using support vector machines. Mach. Learn. **46**(1), 389–422 (2002)
16. Wu, S., Wu, C., Lin, S., Lee, K., Peng, C.K.: Analysis of complex time series using refined composite multiscale entropy. Phys. Lett. A **378**(20), 1369–1374 (2014)
17. Costa, M., Goldberger, A.L., Peng, C.K.: Multiscale entropy analysis of biological signals. Phys. Rev. E **71**, 1–17 (2005)
18. Tsai, P.H., Lin, C., Tsao, J.: Empirical mode decomposition based detrended sample entropy in electroencephalography for Alzheimer's disease. J. Neurosci. Methods **210**, 230–237 (2012)
19. Wallis, W.A., Moore, G.H.: A significance test for time series analysis. J. Am. Stat. Assoc. **36**, 401–409 (1946)
20. Dash, S., Raeder, E., Merchant, S., Chon, K.: A statistical approach for accurate detection of atrial fibrillation and flutter. In: Proceedings of the Annual Computers in Cardiology Conference (CinC), pp. 137–140 (2009)
21. Friedman, J.: Greedy function approximation: a gradient boosting machine. Ann. Stat. **29**(5), 1189–1232 (2001)
22. Adam-Bourdarios, C., Cowan, G., Germain-Renaud, C., Guyon, I., Kégl, B., Rousseau, D.: The higgs machine learning challenge. J. Phys: Conf. Ser. **664**, 072015 (2015)
23. Phoboo, A.E.: Machine learning wins the higgs challenge. CERN Bull. (2014). http://cds.cern.ch/journal/CERNBulletin/2014/49/News%20Articles/1972036. Accessed 24 Apr 2016

Evaluating Sequence Discovery Systems in an Abstraction-Aware Manner

Eoin Rogers$^{(\boxtimes)}$, Robert J. Ross, and John D. Kelleher

Applied Intelligence Research Centre, Dublin Institute of Technology, Dublin, Ireland
eoin.rogers@student.dit.ie, {robert.ross,john.d.kelleher}@dit.ie

Abstract. Activity discovery is a challenging machine learning problem where we seek to uncover new or altered behavioural patterns in sensor data. In this paper we motivate and introduce a novel approach to evaluating activity discovery systems. Pre-annotated ground truths, often used to evaluate the performance of such systems on existing datasets, may exist at different levels of abstraction to the output of the output produced by the system. We propose a method for detecting and dealing with this situation, allowing for useful ground truth comparisons. This work has applications for activity discovery, and also for related fields. For example, it could be used to evaluate systems intended for anomaly detection, intrusion detection, automated music transcription and potentially other applications.

1 Introduction

Activity discovery (AD) refers to the unsupervised discovery of plausible human activities in unannotated datasets composed of sensor readings of human subjects. AD is itself a sub-field of *activity recognition*, the recognition of activities from sensor readings in a supervised manner. These technologies have potential applications in the automatic labelling of activity recognition datasets and building profiles of normal and abnormal behaviour.

Evaluating activity discovery systems in a fair manner is a major challenge for the field. A major reason for this is that pre-annotated ground truths, often used to evaluate the performance of such systems on existing datasets, may exist at different levels of abstraction to the output of the output produced by the system. We propose a method for detecting and dealing with this situation, allowing for useful ground truth comparisons.

Activity discovery is equivalent to a number of challenging problems that are known in the wider computing literature. One good example would be anomaly detection algorithms used for such applications as intrusion detection in the field of computer security. Security practitioners have already made use of machine learning algorithms for this task [1], and our work could help evaluate such systems fairly.

© IFIP International Federation for Information Processing 2018
Published by Springer International Publishing AG 2018. All Rights Reserved
L. Iliadis et al. (Eds.): AIAI 2018, IFIP AICT 519, pp. 261–272, 2018.
https://doi.org/10.1007/978-3-319-92007-8_23

The layout of this paper is as follows. Section 2 investigates prior work in this area. Section 3 discusses in detail the general problem with ground truth-based methods being applied to this problem. We introduce the concept of *activity abstraction* in more detail in Sect. 4, before utilising it to produce an activity discovery evaluation metric presented in Sect. 5. We detail experiments carried out to evaluate the metric in Sect. 6, and present the results of these before concluding in Sect. 7.

2   Prior Work

A number of existing approaches to evaluating activity discovery systems have already been proposed in the literature. Cook and Krishnan [2] provide a good overview of existing approaches, and we refer the interested reader to this reference, rather than repeat its contents in detail here.

Our notation for this section will be relatively standard: we assume the input dataset $D = \langle d_1, d_2, \ldots, d_L \rangle$ is an ordered sequence of *sensor events* drawn from an alphabet Σ. An activity discovery system is modelled as a mathematical function g, which takes the dataset (or a subset of the dataset) as input and returns a set of activities $Y = g(D)$. There are a number of forms that Y could take, and in order to keep our discussion as general as possible, we refrain from privileging one over the other. In the simplest case, each element of Y may only be a non-contiguous subset of the events in D. Alternatively, each element of Y may in fact be an ordered non-contiguous sequence of events, or even a grammar- or state machine-like object that could allow for the learning of complex activities with optional and mandatory elements, complex rules relating to the allowed ordering of elements within activities, or even probabilistic activity rules.

2.1   Stability-Based Metrics

When we evaluate any machine learning system, we are usually interested in determining the degree to which the learned model is *generalised* (that is, the degree to which it can be applied to similar but unseen data). Many authors propose the use of similar criteria for the evaluation of activity discovery systems. These take the form of measures of *stability*, where the dataset D is split into training and test subsets, B and C respectively, such that $D = B \cap C$, and the system is evaluated by demonstrating that some property of the system is stable across both subsets. For example, the Cook and Krishnan book [2] mentioned previously outlines two stability-based metrics: *predictive* and *compressive* stability. Predictive stability measures that the activities seen in the training set are also observed in the test set with about the same frequency. By contrast, compressive stability measures the degree to which the compression ratio achieved on the training and test set is roughly equivalent. The idea of evaluating activity discovery (and related) systems via the use of compression ratios is an idea that shows great promise, and has already seen use in the wider ML community in the form of *perplexity* [5]. A related concept, although one we will skip over here due to space constraints, is *minimum description length* [8].

2.2   Ward et al.'s Error Analysis Technique

Moving away from Cook & Krishnan's proposals, we feel that the contents of [10] could be relevant to the task of evaluating activity discovery systems. This paper does not propose an evaluation metric, but rather an *error analysis method*, in other words a means to detect the types of errors a system under analysis seems to make consistently. The core mechanism proposed in the paper is presented in Fig. 1, which is a figure taken from the paper itself. The three sub-figures correspond to three stages in the method itself. Here, the ground truth is depicted as pale dotted lines, and the prediction output as darker bold lines.

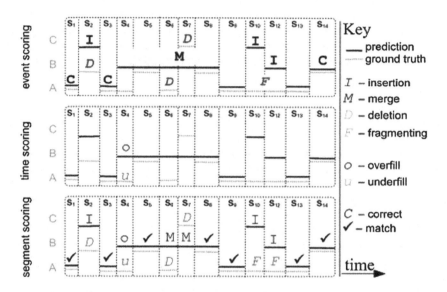

Fig. 1. An illustration, taken from [10], of the three stages involved in the proposed error analysis method. The first stage evaluates segments according to whether they match with an activity in the ground truth, irrespective of how accurately they may do this. The second evaluates segments according to the precision of the start and end of activities, and the fourth combines these into a finished per-segment evaluation.

The first stage (which the authors of the paper call *event scoring*) looks at each event/ground truth pair, and counts the amount of event insertions, deletions, merges and fragmentations that are observed. The second stage, *time scoring*, computes the temporal correspondence between the system output and the ground truth by counting overfills and underfills. Finally, the output from the two previous steps are combined to create the final output, which is called the *segment scoring*, and can be seen at the bottom of Fig. 1. Although simple, this error analysis technique is a major inspiration behind the metric that will be proposed later in this paper.

3   Ground Truth-Based Metrics

While reading Sect. 2, one thing that may strike some readers as unusual is the fact that most of the metrics proposed (Ward's is an exception) seem to refrain from using ground truths as a gold standard with which to compare the output of the activity discovery system under evaluation. Although a perfectly valid way of evaluating machine learning models in the general case, there are two major reasons why one might be suspicious of ground truth comparisons for activity discovery. The first of these is that, by definition, and activity discovery system must be *unsupervised*, that is it trains without making use of any sort of output data in the dataset. The entire point of the *discovery* of activities is to provide a way for the detection of plausible activities in *unannotated datasets* without any ground truth. In a real-world use case, it is quite possible that the model will therefore be trained on a dataset for which no ground truth to compare against exists, and so we have to find a means of evaluation that can be used even in these kinds of situations.

The second issue with ground truth-based evaluation is the *subjectivity inherent in the output of any activity discovery process*. Although the behaviours reflected in the sensor stream may be objective and leave no room for subjective interpretation, the same cannot be said for the activities detected in the stream. For example, the point at which an activity can be said to start and end is arbitrary. Consider the hypothetical case of a sensor stream in a house where an activity corresponding to *making dinner* takes place every evening. One could say that this activity begins when the resident(s) of the house enter the kitchen to cook, or when they turn on the oven, or when they first put food into the oven. Different activity discovery systems (and indeed human annotators) may well use different boundaries for their activities in this manner, and one cannot privilege one annotation over the other. By extension, it is also possible for entire activities to be (in a sense) subjective. For instance, what if one argues that the resident entering the kitchen to cook does not constitute part of the *making dinner* activity, but rather an activity in its own right, perhaps called *preparing to make dinner*? This issue provides major challenges for the evaluation of these systems. Note that we are speaking of a very particular kind of subjectivity. Intuitively, any system which fails to find a consistent activity every evening around dinner time in our hypothetical house seems to be objectively wrong in some way, since it cannot pick up a real pattern that exists in the data. But aspects of the pattern (its size, constitution, cardinality and so forth) are subjective in a way that makes comparison to a ground truth seem like an inherently unfair approach to evaluation.

Any proposed activity discovery evaluation metric must take these issues into consideration. Failure to do so could result in an unfair evaluation that biases in favour of certain systems and against others without justification. Nonetheless, if a ground truth is available, it would be sensible to make use of it, even if only in addition to, rather than instead of, the unsupervised evaluation metrics mentioned in Sect. 2.

4   Instances, Types and Abstractions

Many of the subjective differences noted in Sect. 3 can be *attributed to differences in the level of abstraction that the various systems we are looking at are outputting*. Say g and h are activity discovery models, Y_g is the set of activities output by g (where each $y \in Y_g$ is a subset of D), and likewise Y_h is the set of activities output by h (where each $z \in Y_h$ is a subset of D). Note that since we don't annotate these activities as instances or types we presume they could be either. We formally represent this scenario as:

$$g(D) = Y_g \tag{1}$$

$$h(D) = Y_h \tag{2}$$

Suppose that for a particular $y \in Y_g$ and a particular $z \in Y_h$, we find that $y \subset z$, in other words y is strictly a subset of z (i.e. $\forall i (i \in y \Rightarrow i \in z)$, but $\exists i (i \in z \wedge i \notin y)$). We say that z is thus a *more abstract* version of the activity y: everything in y is also in z, but the reverse is not true. To make this more concrete, we can imagine y being an activity like *making dinner*, and z being a more abstract version of the same activity like *having dinner*, which contains *making dinner* in its entirety, in addition to other sensor events covering the consumption of the dinner, and perhaps cleaning up after. Notationally, we represent this scenario as $y \prec z$, which can be read as "y is less abstract than z", or "y precedes z".

To complicate matters further, we have to resist the temptations we may have at this point to claim that activity discovery model g is less abstract than h, simply because it output a less abstract activity in one instance. It is entirely possible that multiple levels of abstraction are interleaved in the output of our models, i.e. it may be possible to find activities for which g finds a more abstract version than h. Unless all activities found by g are less abstract than or equal to all activities found by h, we should refrain from talking about the abstraction of entire models. We will later use this concept in Sect. 5 as a component in our metric.

5   A Proposal for a New Metric

By combining the insights from Sect. 4 with the error analysis from [10] (see Sect. 2.2), we believe that we can propose an evaluation metric for activity discovery systems using ground truths that (at least to some extent) bypasses the second issue discussed in Sect. 3. The idea is to use abstraction to get around the issue of subjectivity. Suppose our dataset D has an associated ground truth G, and our discovered activities Y contain an activity called *making dinner*, but the ground truth only recognises an activity called *having dinner*. The intuition is that if *making dinner* $\prec$ *having dinner*, we can mark each instance of *making dinner* as correct if it overlaps with an instance of *having dinner* in the ground truth.

This is similar to Ward et al.'s proposal of marking merges, fragmentations, over-fills and underfills, but rather than treating these as a sort of error, we instead allow them to be seen as correct once the types of the activities match.

We will formalise this intuition by first proposing a simple means for evaluating an activity discovery system, which will have the flaws described in Sect. 3. We will then modify the definition to match our proposal. Recall that D is a dataset, and G is the associated ground truth. We assume $|G| = |D|$, and that each element $g \in G$ is a sequence of k Boolean values, where k is the number of activities in the ground truth. Thus, G_{ij} is true iff activity j is true or active for the ith event in the dataset. We will also commit to a specific structure for the output Y, since not doing so would make our formalism needlessly abstract. We feel that the formalism can be easily adapted for other output structures and formats, although we will not attempt to prove this here. We model Y as a matrix, such that each value Y_{ij} represents the probability that activity j is true or active for the ith event. This maps closely to the probabilistic output of the topic modelling based system we will be using for our experiments, yet to be discussed in Sect. 6 below. Given a particular ground activity g, an index into the output activities y, and a real-valued threshold value t, we can define the true positives of our AD system to be:

$$TP_{gyt}(G, Y) = \sum_{i=1}^{L} \mathbb{1}(g \in G_i \wedge Y_{iy} \geq t_y) \tag{3}$$

Where $\mathbb{1}$ is an indicator function that evaluates to 1 if the Boolean formula passed to it is true, and 0 if it is false. The threshold t is a meta-parameter, and we compute a different value of t_y for each proposed activity in Y. It will hopefully be clear to the reader how this could be extended to compute false positives and true and false negatives also. From here, we can obviously calculate F-measures for the system.

A diagrammatic example of our proposal is shown in Fig. 2. Here, each of the horizontal lines labelled A to E represent a single channel of information. Channel A is a ground truth, as found in an annotated dataset. Channel B represents the *raw output* of an activity discovery system for a particular event type. The output overlaps to a degree with the ground truth. We are proposing extending the length of channel B to match channel A, as shown in channel C (which is the *extended output*). We can formalise this by modifying Eq. 3 as follows:

$$TP_{gyt}(G, Y) = \sum_{i=1}^{L} \mathbb{1}((g \in G_i \vee g \in G_{i-1} \vee g \in G_{i+1})$$
$$\wedge (Y_{iy} \geq t \vee Y_{(i+1)y} \geq t_y \vee Y_{(i-1)y} \geq t_y)) \tag{4}$$

Now, rather than strictly requiring that the probability of activity y during event i at least meet our threshold, we look to the events immediately before and after the current (ith) event, and we will also accept event i as a valid true positive if one of its neighbours are also a true positive. The ground truth is similarly extended in the same manner. We actually repeat this computation *as many times as needed for the true positive value to stop increasing.* Thus, we are willing to extend the length of both the ground truth (channel A in our diagram) and the output until their respective lengths match.

Fig. 2. If channel A is an output, and channel B is the output from a system under evaluation, we propose extending B to match A (*extended output*, channel C), optionally making the extensions values less than 1. In channel D (*staircase output*) we use a small value for the extensions, and we use a reducing gradient for channel E (*gradient output*).

Some people may object to the presented proposal on the basis that it is making the evaluation *too easy* for the activity recognition system. For this reason, channels D and E can be used as alternatives to C for comparison to the ground truth (channel A). In these cases, the darkness of the colour corresponds to its magnitude, with the number 1 being as dark as channels B and C, and lower numbers (closer to zero) being represented with a lighter number. Most evaluation metrics (raw similarity, F-measures and so on) work by counting the number of matches between two binary channels. For example, F-measures build a confusion matrix, and match a False from both the ground truth and output channels as a true negative, a False from the ground truth and True from the output as a false positive and so on. We are proposing to use non-binary, fuzzy values instead of these binary comparisons, so that we would increment the counts for the confusion matrix by a number between zero and one. For channel D (the *staircase output*), we use a value of 1 for the true overlaps, and a smaller value (0.4, or $\frac{2}{5}$ in our experiments, see below) for the extensions. Formally, this becomes:

$$TP_{gyt}(G,Y) = \sum_{i=1}^{L} \mathbb{1}(g \in G_i \wedge Y_{iy} \geq t) +$$

$$\frac{2}{5}(G_{i-1} \vee g \in G_{i+1} \vee Y_{(i+1)y} \geq t \vee Y_{(i-1)y} \geq t) \tag{5}$$

Here, we now have 2 indicator functions: the $\mathbb{1}$ function from previously, and a new $\frac{2}{5}$ function, which returns a value of $\frac{2}{5}$ if its input is true, and false otherwise.

Finally, in channel E (the *gradient output*), the extensions don't have a fixed value, but rather have a value of $1 - (0.001 \times n)$, where n is the number of events away from the true overlaps, but cannot have a value below zero. Again, we define an indicator function which is suitable for this purpose, but rather than calling it $\mathbb{1} - (.001 \times \mathbb{n})$, we instead give it the more succinct (but less descriptive) name $\mathbb{f}$.

$$TP_{gyt}(G,Y) = \sum_{i=1}^{L} \mathbb{f}((g \in G_i \vee g \in G_{i-1} \vee g \in G_{i+1}) \tag{6}$$
$$\wedge (Y_{iy} \geq t \vee Y_{(i+1)y} \geq t_y \vee Y_{(i-1)y} \geq t_y))$$

Note that in Fig. 2, we are only showing the extensions applied to the output channels. The ground truth channels should also be extended according to the above process.

At this point, the usual performance metrics used to evaluate ground truth-based systems can be employed. This could include raw percentage accuracy measures, or preferable a more sophisticated metric like F-measures.

6   Experiments and Results

In order to try to determine if our proposed metric is useful, we used an activity discovery system that was presented previously by the same authors [6]. We refer the interested reader to the cited paper for a detailed explanation of how this system works, but in summary we split the dataset D up into $L-w+1$ subsets using a sliding window of length w and run each window through a topic modelling algorithm as if it was a single document. This allows us to compute a probability distribution over topics for all events in the dataset. We threshold these values to assign each event to zero or more activities, using the t_y threshold previously mentioned in Sect. 5. In effect, this threshold is the prior over activities. For each ground truth activity g and output activity y, we compute the candidate threshold value t_{gy} that comes closest to making $c_{gy} = \|P(g \in G_i) - P(Y_{iy} \geq t_{gy})\|$ (the difference between the ground truth and output activity probabilities) equal to zero. The final threshold t_y is then simply the threshold that has the minimal c_{gy} value over all gs, i.e. $t_y = argmin_{t_{gy}} c_{gy}$. This thresholding gives us a dataset of 10 channels, consisting of 5 ground truths and 5 discovered topics (outputs). We then compute the F1 score for each (*ground truth, topic*) pair for each of the 4 types of evaluation shown in Fig. 2. Each ground truth is then associated *with the single topic that scores highest with it according to the extended F1 score.*

We present here the result of the experiment described above on two different datasets. The first of these datasets was generated by the author using a state machine probabilistically moving from state to state and emitting events, with some events being more common than others for each state. The results of this experiment are shown in Table 1 below. The first two columns show the (*ground truth, topic*) pairs, and the remaining columns show the raw F1 score (i.e. the score calculated *without* using our method), the extended F1, the staircase F1 and the gradient F1 respectively. The results show an interesting pattern: for each row, the raw F1 score is substantially lower than the equivalent scores computed with our proposed method. Bearing in mind that the only difference between these metrics are that the latter three take the concept of abstraction into account in the manner described above, we take this as evidence that our metrics are a fairer way to evaluate such systems. The raw F1 score is unfairly penalising the system for what could actually be valid disagreements over abstraction levels and the start and end times of activities, while our method does not do so.

Table 1. Performance metrics gathered by our experiment on an artificial dataset

Topic	Label	F1	Extended F1	Staircase F1	Gradient F1
Activity A	Topic 2	0.6385	0.9521	0.9865	0.9896
Activity B	Topic 3	0.2269	0.9211	0.9834	0.9853
Activity C	Topic 1	0.3159	0.876	0.9619	0.977
Activity D	Topic 4	0.1146	0.8426	0.8923	0.8994
Activity E	Topic 0	0.01835	0.1428	0.8053	0.8192

In order to evaluate the metric on a more challenging dataset, we repeated the experiment on the SCARE corpus [9]. SCARE is an annotated corpus of human actions in a 3D game-like environment. This dataset has already been converted to the necessary binary-event-based format that our system expects [7], so we used this version of the dataset. The results of this experiment are presented in Table 2. Again, one can see a substantial improvement in performance when our metric is employed. Note that the SCARE corpus is extremely challenging: it is unusual for activity recognition systems to obtain a score greater than about 0.6, let alone activity discovery systems, which must produce their output without access to the ground truth. This metric could not only give a fairer means to evaluate activity discovery systems, but potentially a fairer means to evaluate corpora used also, by highlighting excessively narrowly defined activities in a corpus's ground truth.

Before moving on to the conclusion, we also present Fig. 3. This consists of a selection of visualisations of the output of our system (shown as red bars in the upper half of the images) compared to the associated ground truth (shown as blue bars in the lower half of the images) running on the SCARE corpus. The complete images are of course extremely wide, and cannot therefore be reproduced in full here. However, the extracts show real-world examples of the issues that we were highlighting in this paper. Figure 3(a) shows a typical example of a length mismatch between the output and ground truth events. Here, the output is more conservative than the ground truth, and assumes that the activity both starts

Table 2. Performance metrics gathered by our experiment on an artificial dataset

Topic	Label	F1	Extended F1	Staircase F1	Gradient F1
goal_move_box	Topic 1	0.1349	0.6441	0.6831	0.8309
goal_move_rebreather	Topic 5	0.3057	0.9484	0.9575	0.9589
goal_move_quad	Topic 2	0.1111	0.623	0.5625	0.5472
goal_move_silencer	Topic 4	0.05674	0.5812	0.8176	0.8444
goal_move_picture	Topic 3	0.07292	0.5128	0.6491	0.6379
null_goal	Topic 0	0.0	0.0	0.0	0.0

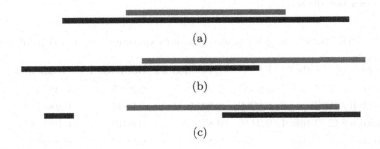

(a)

(b)

(c)

Fig. 3. A sample of a side-by-side comparison of an output and the ground truth. This illustrates some of the issues that we have discussed in this paper. (Color figure online)

later and ends sooner. As noted in Sect. 3, a human directly annotating this dataset could have a legitimate disagreement with the annotator of the ground truth, which would lead to the system being given an unreasonably poor score. Figure 3(b) shows an example of the output activity starting later, but ending later also. Again, most metrics would penalise a system which did this, which is unfair, since the sensor event that allowed the system to recognise that the activity has started may occur after the ground truth annotation declares the onset of the activity. One interesting aspect of this is that one could argue that the quality of the output should depend on how far to the left the ground truth continues for. If the ground truth activity is very long, but was only picked up for a short while, that could indicate that the output activity was a spurious co-incidence, rather than the system finding the activity at all. This presents a case to use the staircase or gradient based versions of the metric that we have discussed. Another interesting scenario is shown in Fig. 3(c). Here the ground truth shows a strange pattern: an activity comes to an end, there is a short pause, and then it resumes. This presents some questions about the annotation of the dataset: would it be fair to just bridge the gap, and say that there was simply one long instance of the activity rather than two short instances? If the output from the system was to bridge the gap, would it be fair to give it a poorer or better score for doing that? Ones view on these issues could lead one to therefore argue *against* using the staircase or gradient variants of the metric. Again, it pays to be aware that there is in fact a degree of subjectivity on this evaluation problem, and assuming something is set in stone can lead to unreasonable conclusions.

7 Conclusion

This paper has presented an argument as to why current means of evaluating the performance of existing activity discovery systems by comparison of outputs to ground truth may be construed as unfair and misleading, due to valid disagreements in abstraction level. We have proposed an extension to existing methods that we feel remedies this issue. Our experiments show that an existing activity discovery system gets a better result from our metrics. Since our metric only aims to resolve the abstraction issue, we feel that there is an argument to be made that our metrics are a fairer way to evaluate activity discovery systems, and thus help progress the state-of-the-art in the field. We are not, however, claiming that our metric is a one-size-fits-all panacea to the activity discovery evaluation problem: rather, it would be better served by using it in conjunction with other metrics (for instance, the stability-based metrics detailed in Sect. 2.1). We advocate the use of a suite a disparate metrics to illuminate the strengths and weaknesses of activity discovery systems.

References

1. Buczak, A.L., Guven, E.: A survey of data mining and machine learning methods for cyber security intrusion detection. IEEE Commun. Surv. Tutor. **18**(2), 1153–1176 (2016)
2. Cook, D.J., Krishnan, N.C.: Activity Learning: Discovering, Recognizing, and Predicting Human Behavior from Sensor Data, pp. 121–124. Wiley, New York (2015). ISBN 978-1-119-01024-1
3. Heinz, J., Rogers, J.: Estimating strictly piecewise distributions. In: Proceedings of the 48th Annual Meeting of the Association for Computational Linguistics, pp. 886–896. Association for Computational Linguistics (2010)
4. Heinz, J., Rogers, J.: Learning subregular classes of languages with factored deterministic automata. In: Proceedings of the 13th Meeting on the Mathematics of Language (MoL 2013), pp. 64–71 (2013)
5. Jelinek, F., Mercer, R.L., Bahl, L.R., Baker, J.K.: Perplexity-a measure of the difficulty of speech recognition tasks. J. Acoust. Soc. Am. **62**(S1), S63–S63 (1977)
6. Rogers, E., Kelleher, J.D., Ross, R.J.: Using topic modelling algorithms for hierarchical activity discovery. Ambient Intelligence-Software and Applications – 7th International Symposium on Ambient Intelligence (ISAmI 2016). AISC, vol. 476, pp. 41–48. Springer, Cham (2016). https://doi.org/10.1007/978-3-319-40114-0_5
7. Ross, R., Kelleher, J.: A comparative study of the effect of sensor noise on activity recognition models. In: O'Grady, M.J., Vahdat-Nejad, H., Wolf, K.-H., Dragone, M., Ye, J., Röcker, C., O'Hare, G. (eds.) AmI 2013. CCIS, vol. 413, pp. 151–162. Springer, Cham (2013). https://doi.org/10.1007/978-3-319-04406-4_15

8. Rissanen, J.: Modeling by shortest data description. Automatica **14**(5), 465–471 (1978)
9. Stoia, L., Shockley, D., Byron, D., Fosler-Lussier, E.: SCARE: a situated corpus with annotated referring expressions. In: Proceedings of the Sixth International Conference on Language Resources and Evaluation (LREC 2008) (2008)
10. Ward, J.A., Lukowicz, P., Tröster, G.: Evaluating performance in continuous context recognition using event-driven error characterisation. In: Hazas, M., Krumm, J., Strang, T. (eds.) LoCA 2006. LNCS, vol. 3987, pp. 239–255. Springer, Heidelberg (2006). https://doi.org/10.1007/11752967_16

PIDT: A Novel Decision Tree Algorithm Based on Parameterised Impurities and Statistical Pruning Approaches

Daniel Stamate[1], Wajdi Alghamdi[1(✉)], Daniel Stahl[2],
Doina Logofatu[3], and Alexander Zamyatin[4]

[1] Data Science & Soft Computing Lab, Department of Computing, Goldsmiths,
University of London, London, UK
{d.stamate,mapO1wa}@gold.ac.uk
[2] Department of Biostatistics & Health Informatics, Institute of Psychiatry,
Psychology and Neuroscience, King's College London, London, UK
[3] Department of Mathematics and Computer Science,
Frankfurt University of Applied Sciences, Frankfurt, Germany
[4] Faculty of Informatics, Department of Applied Informatics,
National Research Tomsk State University, Tomsk, Russia

Abstract. In the process of constructing a decision tree, the criteria for selecting the splitting attributes influence the performance of the model produced by the decision tree algorithm. The most well-known criteria such as Shannon entropy and Gini index, suffer from the lack of adaptability to the datasets. This paper presents novel splitting attribute selection criteria based on some families of parameterised impurities that we proposed here to be used in the construction of optimal decision trees. These criteria rely on families of strict concave functions that define the new generalised parameterised impurity measures which we applied in devising and implementing our PIDT novel decision tree algorithm. This paper proposes also the S-condition based on statistical permutation tests, whose purpose is to ensure that the reduction in impurity, or gain, for the selected attribute is statistically significant. We implemented the S-pruning procedure based on the S-condition, to prevent model overfitting. These methods were evaluated on a number of simulated and benchmark datasets. Experimental results suggest that by tuning the parameters of the impurity measures and by using our S-pruning method, we obtain better decision tree classifiers with the PIDT algorithm.

Keywords: Machine learning · Decision trees
Parameterised impurity measures · Concave functions · Optimisation
Preventing overfitting · Statistical pruning · Permutation test · Significance level

1 Introduction

The decision tree algorithm is a highly efficient algorithm used in machine learning and data mining; the model the algorithm produces is easy to understand and interpret, and the algorithm offers accurate results in abbreviated time. Different versions of the

© IFIP International Federation for Information Processing 2018
Published by Springer International Publishing AG 2018. All Rights Reserved
L. Iliadis et al. (Eds.): AIAI 2018, IFIP AICT 519, pp. 273–284, 2018.
https://doi.org/10.1007/978-3-319-92007-8_24

decision tree algorithm have been introduced in the last few decades, and it remains an attractive research domain within the field of machine learning. Such algorithms are useful in numerous contexts within pattern recognition and machine learning applications. In the medical field, for instance, decision trees have been employed to diagnose heart disease patients [1] and to predict patients who may suffer from psychosis [2].

A decision tree algorithm simulates a tree assembly [3]. A decision tree consists of nodes that are connected via branches. The decision tree begins with a single root node and ends with a number of leaf/decision nodes; the nodes in between are the internal nodes.

In classification trees, each leaf node is labelled with a particular class. Each node that is not a leaf node applies a test on a certain attribute, and each branch represents a result of the test. The nodes are selected from the top level based on the attribute-selection measure [4]. For example, ID3 algorithm [5] and its extended version C4.5 [4] use information gain (which is based on Shannon entropy) to construct the decision tree; the element with the highest gain is taken as the root node, and the dataset is divided based on the root element values. Again, the information gain is calculated for all the internal nodes separately, and the process is repeated until leaf nodes are reached.

Unlike most machine learning algorithms, decision trees perform local feature selection on different sets of features. The selected feature should be the feature that reduces the uncertainty at the node the most [6]. The dataset may then be partitioned accordingly into sub-nodes. This procedure is applied recursively until it meets any stopping criterion, such as the minimum number of instances or the maximum tree depth. Choosing the splitting and stopping criteria are two open problems in decision tree algorithms.

To address the first issue, many decision tree algorithms have proposed different impurity measures as a splitting criterion. Most decision tree algorithms are based on the information gain function for choosing the best attribute for splitting the data at each node that is not a leaf node. For instance, the ID3 and C4.5 algorithms are based on Shannon entropy [6], while the classification and regression tree CART algorithm is based on the Gini index [7]. However, one drawback in this kind of approach is that these types of impurity measures are only based on one fixed concave function for assessing the impurity in the datasets' class distributions, which means they suffer from a lack of adaptability to various datasets.

Many studies have investigated the importance of the split criterion [8, 9]. These studies have concluded that the choice of impurity measure does have some influence on the decision tree's efficacy. Inspired by these studies, we have proposed several novel splitting criteria based on parameterised families of strict concave functions that may be used as impurity measures. As such, we propose new parameterised impurities including parameterised entropy (PE), parameterised Gini (PG), parameterised Tsallis (PT), parameterised Renyi (PR), as well as parameterised AlphaBeta impurity (ABI) and parameterised GiniEntropy (GE) impurity. Their purpose will consist of being mostly reduced in a node after a split, which will dictate the choice of the most suitable attribute in that node. These methods indeed provide an innovative approach to improved decision tree performance, as this work shows.

As for the second problem, most practical decision tree implementations use a 'greedy' approach to grow the tree. Such algorithms would usually suffer from over-fitting the dataset [3], and additional mechanisms are needed to be put in place to prevent this. Several stopping criteria have been introduced to overcome this issue, such as setting the minimum value of the information gain to grow the tree with a C4.5 algorithm for instance [4]. A number of recent papers have used permutation tests for different machine learning problems, such as studying the classifier performance [10], or in the feature selection process [11]. With the model overfitting problem in mind, we proposed in this paper the S-condition based on statistical permutation tests, whose purpose is to ensure that the reduction in impurity, or gain, for the selected attribute in a node of the decision tree is statistically significant, and that the observed gain is unlikely to be at least that high just by chance. Moreover, we implemented the S-pruning procedure based on the S-condition, to prevent model overfitting.

We integrate the use of our novel families of parameterised impurities for the attribute selection, with the S-pruning procedure, and with the optimisation of the parameters of the impurity via cross-validation according to the accuracy performance, in a new decision tree algorithm that we call PIDT, whose name stands for Parameterised Impurity Decision Tree.

The rest of this paper is organised as follows. Section 2 introduces the mathematical formulations and the general requirements for the impurity measures, as well as the novel parameterised impurity measures that we propose to be used in selecting the splitting attributes in our PIDT algorithm. Section 3 introduces our S-condition and S-pruning procedure based on permutation tests, which enhance the PIDT algorithm to prevent model overfitting. Section 4 experimentally investigates the proposed parameterised impurity measures and compares them with conventional impurity functions, based on the performances obtained by the PIDT and conventional decision tree algorithms on a number of benchmarks and generated datasets. Finally, Sect. 5 presents conclusions and offers directions for future work.

2   Impurity Measures

As mentioned above, a decision tree algorithm splits the dataset sample (at each node that is not a leaf node) into two or more sets based on the attribute that scores the highest gain (i.e. reduction in impurity) [12]. In the previous section, we mentioned two conventional impurities mostly used in decision tree algorithms, namely Shannon entropy and Gini index. But there are also other impurities which are presented in the literature such as Tsallis [13], and Renyi [12]. A different work proposed also a generalisation of the conditional entropy [14]. Considering these different studies based on various impurity measures suggests that the choice of the impurity measure influences the decision tree's effectiveness. In the following sub-sections, we provide the mathematical formulations of and the criteria for functions defined on discrete probabilistic distributions, to be impurity measures.

2.1 Mathematical Formulations

Let X be an $n \times m$ data matrix. We denote the r-th row vector of X by X_r, and the c-th column vector of X by X^c. Rows are also called *records* or *data points*, while columns are also called *attributes* or *features*. Since we do not restrict the data domain of X, the scale of this domain's features can be categorical or numerical. For each data point X_r, we have a class label y_r. We assume a set of known class labels Y, so $y_r \in Y$. Let D be the set of labelled data $D = \{(X_r, y_r)\}_{r=1}^{n}$. During the classification task, the goal is to predict the labels of new data points by training a classifier on D. Now, let k be the total number of data entries in a node, and k_i be the number of data entries classified as class i. Then $p_i = k_i/k$ is the ratio of instances classified as i and estimates the probability of class i in the dataset in that node.

The primary purpose of the impurity measures is to express the degree of mixture of various classes in a dataset and then to help to define how well the classes are separated via a split in a node. As such, in general, an impurity measure should satisfy specific requirements. Breiman [7] suggested that an impurity measure is a function *Imp* whose argument is a vector of probabilities from a discrete probability distribution (given by the class proportions in a dataset), which satisfies the following properties:

Property A: Strict concavity $Imp'' < 0$.
Property B: Maximality $Imp' = 0$ for $(p_i = 1/k)$ for $i = 1, \dots, k$.
Property C: Minimality $Imp = 0 \leftrightarrow \exists i | pi = 1$.

These properties state that the impurity function should be a strictly concave function; they also express what the maximum and minimum points of the function are. Both Shannon entropy and Gini index, which are defined below, meet the impurity-based criteria:

$$Entropy(D) = E(D) = -\sum\nolimits_{i=1}^{k} p_i * \log(p_i) \tag{1}$$

$$Gini(D) = G(D) = 1 - \sum\nolimits_{i=1}^{k} p_i^2 \tag{2}$$

Several authors compared the behaviour of Gini index and Shannon entropy to determine which performs better; they concluded that it is not possible to decide which one leads to higher accuracies of the produced decision trees since the two measures have only about 2% disagreement in most cases [9]. Note that both Gini index and Shannon entropy are based on one strict concave function each, and as such they might not have the flexibility in adapting to various datasets. We have also considered Renyi entropy and Tsallis entropy, both of which generalising Shannon entropy. They are described by the following formulas, respectively:

$$Renyi(D) = R(D) = \frac{1}{1 - \gamma} * log\left(\sum\nolimits_{i=1}^{k} p_i^\gamma\right) \quad where\, \gamma > 0\, and\, \gamma \neq 1 \tag{3}$$

$$Tsallis(D) = T(D) = \frac{1 - \sum_{i=1}^{k} p_i^\gamma}{1 - \gamma} \quad where\, \gamma > 0\, and\, \gamma \neq 1 \tag{4}$$

In the next subsection, we propose several families of generalised parameterised impurity measures based on the requirements suggested by Breiman [7] and outlined above, and we introduce our new PIDT algorithm employing these impurities.

2.2 Parameterised Impurity Measures

As mentioned, the novel parameterised impurity measures that we propose in what follows, are used to select the attribute that mostly reduces the impurity by splitting the dataset in a node of the decision tree.

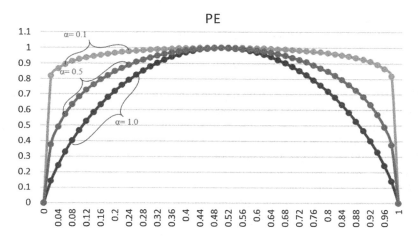

Fig. 1. Parameterised entropy (PE) with different values for α.

Our first proposed family of parameterised impurities is the parameterised entropy PE, which is formulated below, and is illustrated in Fig. 1 for the case of the 2 class problems (the x-axis represents the probability of one class).

$$PE(D) = E(D)^{\alpha} \quad where \, \alpha \in (0, 1] \tag{5}$$

The interval of variation for the parameter α, i.e. (0,1], was chosen to allow, on the one hand, a large diversity of shapes of the graph of the impurity PE, and on the other hand, to mathematically ensure the concavity of the impurity (proof not included here due to lack of space). The other requirements inspired by Breiman's work [7], to which we referred in the previous subsection, are also met.

Figure 1 illustrates the impact of α on the shape of the PE curve. In particular, α = 1 corresponds to the conventional Shannon entropy, while smaller positive values for α have an effect of diminishing the curvature of the PE curve around its middle (the second derivative's absolute value tends to decrease in that area), and of gradually transforming the curve and make it tends to a plateau for small values of the parameter (for illustration see the curve for α = 0.1 in Fig. 1). Intuitively, these changes in the shape of the PE curve suggest potential changes in choosing attributes in a split node of the decision tree, and this was confirmed experimentally when we implemented our framework. This situation happens because the process may give preference to different class probability distributions in the data subsets that are issued from the split. Parameter α clearly influences which splits will be created in the decision tree, and as such it influences the model learnt from the data and allowed it to have more flexibility in adapting to the data than in the case of a fixed impurity such as the conventional Shannon entropy.

In the same manner, parameterised Gini, parameterised Renyi, and parameterised Tsallis are defined by using the following formulas:

$$PG(D) = G(D)^\alpha \quad where \, \alpha \in (0, 1] \tag{6}$$

$$PR(D) = R(D)^\alpha \quad where \, \alpha \in (0, 1] \tag{7}$$

$$PT(D) = T(D)^\alpha \quad where \, \alpha \in (0, 1] \tag{8}$$

Note that since the concave functions that define the conventional Shannon entropy and Gini index are generalised by the proposed families of parameterised impurities PE and PG respectively, the use of these families of impurities is expected, roughly speaking, to produce comparable or better decision trees in most cases than those based on the conventional entropy and Gini index.

We now define two more families of parameterised impurities based on two parameters α and β this time.

$$GE(D) = G(D)^\alpha + E(D)^\beta \quad where \, \alpha \, and \, \beta \in (0, 1] \tag{9}$$

$$ABI(D) = \sum_{i=1}^{k} p_i^\alpha * (1 - p_i)^\beta \quad where \, \alpha \, and \, \beta \in (0, 1] \tag{10}$$

Note that GE combines arbitrary positive and not larger than 1 powers of the Gini index and of the conventional Shannon entropy, generalising these impurities, and offering further flexibility by using two parameters. By the use of the two parameters, ABI family generalises the Gini index and also offers further flexibility in expressing various shapes of impurity. Note also that both GE and ABI fulfil, mathematically speaking, the requirements of impurity inspired by Buntine and Niblett [8] (proof omitted here due to lack of space).

Figure 2 illustrates, for the case of 2 class problems, the parameterised families of impurities PE and PG for various values of parameter α (see the top half), and the parameterised family of impurities GE for various values of parameters α and β (see the bottom half).

The above parameterised impurity families are used in our novel decision tree algorithm which we call PIDT, whose name stands for Parameterised Impurity Decision Trees. In particular, the impurities define the criterion for selecting the best attributes in the nodes of the decision tree, based on the largest decrease in impurity from the dataset in the parent node to the datasets in the child nodes. This difference is the so-called gain, and will be precisely defined in the next section when the statistical S-condition will be introduced. The PIDT algorithm uses one single selected family of

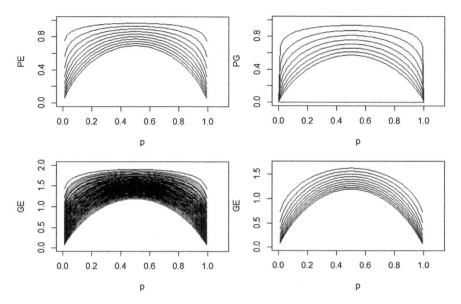

Fig. 2. Novel parametrised impurity measures PE, PG (top), and GE (bottom)

parameterised impurities for a tree induction, and optimises the parameters of the impurity in a cross-validation fashion with respect to the accuracy performance.

In the next section, we develop an enhancement of the process of growing the decision tree with the PIDT algorithm, based on a novel statistical pruning procedure S-pruning that we introduce here as a useful tool to prevent overfitting problems.

3   S-pruning

Roughly speaking, the novel S-pruning procedure we describe here terminates some of the branches of the decision tree based on the outcome of a statistical test. In particular, this pruning method only allows the attributes that have a significant predictive power to split the node and grow the tree. Stopping the development of a branch is based on a certain condition, named here the S-condition.

S-condition:

Let X^c be the attribute with the highest gain G in a node N. Roughly speaking, G is expressed by the reduction in impurity after the split with attribute X^c in the node N. More precisely, the gain is defined in the same way as the information gain for the conventional Shannon entropy in C4.5 algorithm [4]. The impurity is measured in the dataset before the split, and in the resulting data subsets for each child after the split. The impurities in all these data subsets are averaged with weights derived as the fractions represented by the data subsets out of the dataset before the split. The impurity weighted average is then subtracted from the impurity of the dataset before the split, and the result defines the gain G mentioned above. The gain is non-negative for all attributes due to the concavity property of the impurity. Moreover, a higher gain may indicate a higher predictive power for an attribute. However, we want to ensure that a higher gain does not occur by chance. The S-condition defined here is a statistical mechanism to check this.

Let D be the dataset in node N. Shuffle (i.e. randomly permute) the labels in dataset D and measure again the gain for X^c. Do this t times so that a vector V of t gain values is built. *The S- condition is satisfied if and only if G is smaller than the q quantile of vector V.* When the S-condition is satisfied, the branch in node N stops growing and N becomes a terminal node. *This defines the S-pruning procedures.*

Overall, the logic behind the S-condition is that if the gain G is smaller than the q quantile (for instance for a value q such as 0.95 or 0.9) of a vector V of t gain values (for instance $t = 1000$) obtained for X^c using random labels (since they are shuffled or randomly permuted), then X^c is not considered to have predictive power according to the data D in that node N. The values of t and $s = 1 - q$ must be specified by the user, where t is the number of label permutations (and thus equal to the number of gain values collected), and the value of s is the significance level (such as in the statistical tests). A smaller s will encourage more pruning. Intuitively, s indicates how likely the gain of the selected attribute X^c would have been acceptably high just by chance. Another relevant quantity here is the p-value, defined experimentally as the fraction of cases in which the gain obtained with the random labels was higher than or equal to the gain obtained with the original labels of the records in D. Therefore, if the p-value is small enough (e.g. the p-value is smaller than or equal to the significance level $s = 0.1$ or 0.05), then we can say that the gain of the selected attribute in the original data is indeed significantly better and, in consequence, that the gain is too high to have occurred just by chance. That is, the null hypothesis of the permutation test is rejected in this case. As such the attribute X^c is considered to have significant predictive power, and the split takes place. Note that the S-condition does not hold in this case.

On the other hand, if the p-value is larger than the significance level s, or in other words the S-condition holds, this means that the gain for the selected attribute is not large enough to indicate predictive power, so the development of that branch is stopped.

Note also that higher q (or equivalently smaller s) results in oversimplified trees, whereas the opposite results in reduced pruning and larger trees. As a result of using the S-pruning procedure, fewer nodes are expanded during the building phase, and thus constructing the decision tree is simplified. In addition, the decision tree has the advantage of avoiding overfitting while it is being built.

4   Comparison of Decision Tree Classifiers with Various Impurity Measures

We now compare several impurity measures with respect to their impact on the decision tree induction, including the conventional impurities such as Shannon entropy and Gini index, and also the new parameterised families of impurities introduced here. We argue that the conventional impurities mentioned above have their flexibility limitations when used with various datasets. We also argue that, due to their flexibility, the parameterised families of impurities are better suited for the purpose of class separation. We also test our novel S-pruning procedure introduced in the previous section. Finally, we demonstrate empirically that the proposed PIDT algorithm indeed produces better decision trees than the algorithms that use simply the conventional entropy and Gini index impurity measures.

This section also investigates the performance of decision trees as a result of parameter optimisation. In order to investigate the usefulness of the novel parameterised impurity functions, we tested them on different datasets and compared them with the conventional impurities mentioned above. In order to optimise the parameters of an impurity family, a grid search over a parameter space with 5-fold cross-validation, were used to select the best parameters' values.

4.1 Experimental Analysis

We chose the open-source library Weka (Waikato Environment for Knowledge Analysis) [15] as a starting point in implementing our PIDT algorithm with the S-pruning method option, and parameter optimisation for the families of parameterised impurities above. In particular, the tree builder code was modified and extended to support the conventional impurities Shannon entropy, Gini index, as well as Tsallis, and Renyi, and of course we implemented also the new families of parameterised impurity measures introduced in this paper. The S-pruning method was also added. The PIDT software allows users to specify the family of impurities and values for their relevant parameters, or choose the optimisation of these parameters. It also allows specifying the significance level s and the number of permutations t when the S-pruning method is enabled.

Each experiment used 5-fold cross-validation and was performed with and without the S-pruning method. Finally, the minimum number of nodes was set to 7 in all experiments. Each of the techniques was applied to 7 datasets, of which 5 were real datasets and 2 were simulated datasets with different characteristics.

The real datasets from the University of California–Irvine (UCI) machine learning repository [16] that were provided to illustrate the performance of different impurity measures, included the diagnostic Wisconsin breast cancer dataset, the diabetes dataset, the glass identification dataset, and a medical dataset for hepatitis and primary tumours [17]. Two datasets were also generated using simulation techniques, in particular based on Guyon's proposed approach employed in various researches [17–20]. The simulated datasets contain a few thousand samples and different numbers of classes.

The PIDT algorithm was run for different impurity measures and values for α, β, γ parameters (whichever apply), and significance level s. The parameter space for α and β was 0.05, 0.1, ..., 0.95, 1.0; for γ the values were 0.1, 0.2, ...,0.9,1.5, 2.0, ..., 5.0; and the considered significance level s values were 0.01, 0.05, and 0.1. Finally, the best-performing models with their parameters were chosen for the final comparison on the separate test datasets. Table 2 shows a summary of the models built with the chosen optimised parameters, while Table 1 provides the summary of the models built by using conventional impurities. Bold fonts in Table 2 show the best results scored regarding the chosen dataset. The results demonstrate that the parameterised entropy

(PE) could be used to construct more efficient decision trees compared with the conventional entropy impurity and Gini index impurity. In particular, PE led to better results when it was applied with the S-pruning method on most datasets. By looking at Tables 1 and 2, we observe that the accuracy generally improved, and the number of nodes decreased for the models produced by the PDIT algorithm.

Table 1. Assessing decision trees built with conventional impurity performances

Dataset	Decision tree with entropy		Decision tree with Gini	
	Accuracy	No. nodes	Accuracy	No. nodes
Breast cancer	0.654	67	0.654	76
Pima diabetes	0.736	119	0.724	135
Hepatitis	0.807	21	0.794	25
Primary tumour	0.434	60	0.363	57
Glass	0.626	39	0.556	55
Simulated data 1	0.721	33	0.668	67
Simulated data 2	0.612	188	0.601	157

Table 2. Assessing decision trees built with the PIDT algorithm with parameter optimisation, and with and without S-pruning procedure activated. "-" means values do not apply.

Dataset	PIDT								
	Accuracy	No. nodes	Parameters						
			Impurity	α	β	γ	S-pruning	s	Permutations
Breast cancer	**0.731**	91	PG	0.5	-	-	No	-	-
	0.720	**29**	PR	1	-	0.5	Yes	0.05	1000
Pima diabetes	0.734	**11**	PE	0.5	-	-	Yes	0.05	1000
Hepatitis	**0.839**	23	PE	0.3	-	-	No	-	-
	0.807	**7**	PE	0.3	-	-	Yes	0.05	1000
Primary tumour	0.434	60	PE	1	-	-	No	-	-
Glass	**0.636**	**27**	PE	0.6	-	-	No	-	-
Simulated data 1	0.721	**7**	PE	0.8	0	0	Yes	0.05	1000
Simulated data 2	**0.693**	**157**	GE	1	0.4	-	No	-	-

In particular, it is interesting to observe that the accuracy tended to improve depending on the dataset, thus confirming that this performance could be affected by the method used for selecting attributes during the tree construction. In terms of tree size, this was diminished for most datasets. The best reduction was achieved for the Pima diabetes database, where the size of the tree was reduced ten times compared to the standard tree algorithm – which used entropy (as shown in Table 1) – and was comparable to the tree size discussed in [14]. We also note that our results for the hepatitis dataset produced more accurate and smaller tree compared to the results presented in [14]. Overall, PE and PR impurities, in conjunction with activating the S-pruning procedure, produce more accurate results and yield much smaller trees for most of the datasets.

5 Conclusion and Directions for Future Work

This paper proposed and tested an approach to building optimised classification trees using novel parameterised impurity measures which generalise conventional impurities such as Shannon entropy and Gini index. The experiments were conducted on five real datasets as well as on two simulated datasets. The results show that by building decision trees using parameterised impurity measures with optimal values for their parameters, the predictive models primarily led to better performance in terms of accuracy, than those built with traditional entropy impurity and Gini impurity.

A novel S-pruning method based on permutation tests was also introduced here to overcome the overfitting problem and to produce smaller decision trees. The proposed impurity measures gained significance and produced much smaller trees when they were applied with the S-pruning procedure enabled. However, if the significance level s for S-pruning is set too small, it may result in oversimplified trees.

One direction of extending this work is related to investigating novel impurity measures with flexibility capabilities in adapting to and working well with class-unbalanced problems. This direction is currently under investigation.

References

1. Shouman, M., Turner, T., et al.: Using decision tree for diagnosing heart disease patients. In: Proceedings of 9th Australasian Data Mining Conference, pp. 23–30 (2011)
2. Alghamdi, W., Stamate, D., et al.: A prediction modelling and pattern detection approach for the first-episode psychosis associated to cannabis use. In: Proceedings of 15th IEEE International Conference on Machine Learning and Applications, Anaheim, CA, pp. 825–830 (2016)
3. Han, J., Kamber, M., Pei, J.: Data Mining Concepts and Techniques, pp. 279–328 (2011)
4. Witten, I., Frank, E., et al.: Data mining: Practical Machine Learning Tools and Techniques. Morgan Kaufmann Publisher, San Francisco (2016)
5. Quinlan, J.: Induction of decision trees. Mach. Learn. **1**, 81–106 (1986)
6. Tan, P., Michael, S., Vipin, K.: Introduction to Data Mining (2005)
7. Breiman, L., Friedman, J., et al.: Classification and regression trees (1984)
8. Buntine, W., Niblett, T.: A further comparison of splitting rules for decision-tree induction. Mach. Learn. **8**, 75–85 (1992)
9. Liu, W., White, A.: The importance of attribute selection measures in decision tree induction. Mach. Learn. **15**, 25–41 (1994)
10. Ojala, M., Garriga, G.: Permutation tests for studying classifier performance. J. Mach. Learn. Res. **11**, 1833–1863 (2010)

11. Good, P.: Permutation Tests: A Practical Guide to Resampling Methods for Testing Hypotheses. Springer Series in Statistics, vol. 2. Springer, New York (2000). https://doi.org/10.1007/978-1-4757-2346-5

12. Maszczyk, T., Duch, W.: Comparison of Shannon, Renyi and Tsallis Entropy used in decision trees. In: Rutkowski, L., Tadeusiewicz, R., Zadeh, L.A., Zurada, J.M. (eds.) ICAISC 2008. LNCS (LNAI), vol. 5097, pp. 643–651. Springer, Heidelberg (2008). https://doi.org/10.1007/978-3-540-69731-2_62

13. Raileanu, L., Stoffel, K.: Theoretical comparison between the gini index and information gain criteria. Ann. Math. Artif. Intell. **41**, 77–93 (2004)

14. Tsallis, C., Mendes, R., et al.: The role of constraints within generalised non-extensive statistics. Physica **261A**, 534–554 (1998)

15. Frank, E., Hall, M., Witten, I.: The WEKA workbench. In: Online Appendix for Data Mining: Practical Machine Learning Tools and Techniques, Fourth Edition. Morgan Kaufmann (2016)

16. UCI machine learning repository: Datasets. https://archive.ics.uci.edu/ml/datasets.html. Accessed 1 Jan 2017

17. Guyon, I., Li, J., Mader, T.: Competitive baseline methods set new standards for the nips 2003 feature selection benchmark. Pattern Recogn. Lett. **28**(12), 1438–1444 (2007)

18. Guyon, I.: Design of experiments of the nips 2003 variable selection benchmark (2003)

19. Guyon, I., Gunn, S., et al.: Result analysis of the NIPS 2003 feature selection challenge. In: Advances in Neural Information Processing Systems, pp. 545–552 (2005)

20. Guyon, I., Elisseeff, A.: An introduction to feature extraction. In: Guyon, I., Nikravesh, M., Gunn, S., Zadeh, L.A. (eds.) Feature Extraction. Studies in Fuzziness and Soft Computing, vol. 207. Springer, Heidelberg (2006). https://doi.org/10.1007/978-3-540-35488-8_1

Smoothness Bias in Relevance Estimators for Feature Selection in Regression

Alexandra Degeest[1,2(✉)], Michel Verleysen[2], and Benoît Frénay[3]

[1] Haute-Ecole Bruxelles Brabant - ISIB, 150 Rue Royale,
1000 Brussels, Belgium
adegeest@he2b.be
[2] Machine Learning Group - ICTEAM, Université catholique de Louvain, Place
du Levant 3, 1348 Louvain-La-Neuve, Belgium
michel.verleysen@uclouvain.be
[3] Faculty of Computer Science, NADI Institute - PReCISE Research Center,
Université de Namur, Rue Grandgagnage 21, 5000 Namur, Belgium
benoit.frenay@unamur.be

Abstract. Selecting features from high-dimensional datasets is an important problem in machine learning. This paper shows that in the context of filter methods for feature selection, the estimator of the criterion used to select features plays an important role; in particular the estimators may suffer from a bias when comparing smooth and non-smooth features. This paper analyses the origin of such bias and investigates whether this bias influences the results of the feature selection process. Results show that non-smooth features tend to be penalised especially in small datasets.

Keywords: Feature selection · Smoothness · Filter methods
Mutual information · Noise variance

1 Introduction

High-dimensional datasets are now ubiquitous. Selecting a subset of the most relevant features is useful to ease the learning process, to alleviate the curse of dimensionality, to increase the interpretability of features, to visualise data, among others. Many works focus on methods to reduce the number of features in datasets [1–7]. These methods can be roughly categorised into filter methods, wrappers and embedded methods that all have their respective advantages and drawbacks [1]. This paper focuses on filter methods, which have the advantage to be fast because they do not require to train any model during the feature selection process, contrarily to wrappers [6] and embedded methods [8].

Filters use a relevance criterion during the feature selection process. Three popular relevance criteria used to select features in regression tasks are the correlation, the mutual information and the noise variance. This paper focuses on mutual information and noise variance because of their property to be able to detect features that have nonlinear relationships with the variable to predict. It shows that the statistical estimators of mutual information and of noise variance both suffer from a bias, mostly

L. Iliadis et al. (Eds.): AIAI 2018, IFIP AICT 519, pp. 285–294, 2018.
https://doi.org/10.1007/978-3-319-92007-8_25

when small samples are considered, and that this bias may affect the selection of the features. The paper also shows that this bias disappears in large datasets, but faster when using noise variance than when using mutual information.

The remaining of the paper is organised as follows. Feature selection in regression with filters is detailed in Sect. 2. Section 3 analyses the behaviour of mutual information and Delta Test, and discusses the potential bias for small sample datasets. In order to confirm the bias and its consequences, simple experiments are described in Sect. 4 and their results are shown in Sect. 5. Finally, conclusions are given in Sect. 6.

2 Feature Selection with Filters

In the context of filter methods for feature selection, a relevance criterion is necessary to select the most relevant features among all the available ones. The relevance criterion aims at measuring the existing relationship between a feature or a set of features and the variable to predict. There exist several relevance criteria. Correlation is the simplest one, but it is only able to detect linear relationships between random variables, and it is restricted to the univariate case (sets of features can only be evaluated individually, which prevents to take into account the possible relations between the features themselves). In this paper, we focus on nonlinear and multivariate relationships between a set of random input variables and one random output variable. For this type of relationships, mutual information (MI) and noise variance are both popular measures used as relevance criteria for filter methods. Both need to be estimated in practice on a finite set of data: traditional estimators are the Kraskov estimator for the former and the Delta Test for the latter. These criteria have been repeatedly used for feature selection in regression problems [9, 10].

This section reviews the mutual information (MI) and noise variance criteria, and their Kraskov and Delta Test estimators. Both estimators are based on k-nearest neighbours. The next sections show that these estimators implicitly take into account a measure of smoothness (Sect. 3), which could lead to a bias in the choice of features during the feature selection process (Sects. 4 and 5).

2.1 Feature Selection with Mutual Information

Mutual information (MI) is a popular criterion for filter methods [5, 11–14]. Based on entropy, it is a symmetric measure of the dependence between random variables, introduced by Shannon in 1948 [15]. MI measures the information contained in a feature, or in a group of features, with respect to another one. It has been shown to be a reliable criterion to select relevant features in classification [16] and regression [9, 10, 17, 18]. This paper focuses on regression problems.

Let X and Y be two random variables, where X represents the features and Y the target. MI measures the reduction in the uncertainty on Y when X is known

$$I(X;Y) = H(Y) - H(Y|X) \qquad (1)$$

Where

$$H(Y) = -\int_Y p_Y(y) \log p_Y(y) dy \qquad (2)$$

is the entropy of Y and

$$H(Y|X) = \int_X p_X(x) H(Y|X = x) dx \qquad (3)$$

is the conditional entropy of Y given X. The mutual information between X and Y is equal to zero if and only if they are independent. If Y can be perfectly predicted as a function of X, then $I(X; Y) = H(Y)$.

In addition to the criterion, feature selection needs a search procedure to find the best feature subset among all possible ones. Given the exponential number of possible subsets, search procedures such as greedy search or genetic algorithms are used to find the best subset of features without having to compute the selection criterion between all subsets of variables and the output. Among these subsets, the one maximising the MI with the output is selected.

In practice, MI cannot be directly computed because it is defined in terms of probability density functions. These probability density functions are unknown when only a finite sample of data is available. Therefore, MI has to be estimated from the dataset. The estimator introduced by Kraskov et al. [19] is based on a k-nearest neighbour method and results from the Kozachenko-Leonenko entropy estimator [20]

$$\hat{H}(X) = -\psi(k) + \psi(N) + \log c_d + \frac{d}{N} \sum_{i=1}^{N} \log \epsilon_k(i), \qquad (4)$$

where k is the number of neighbours, N is the number of instances in the dataset, d is the dimensionality, $c_d = (2\pi^{d/2})/\Gamma(d/2)$ is the volume of the unitary ball of dimension d, $\epsilon_k(i)$ is twice the distance from the ith instance to its kth nearest neighbour and ψ is the digamma function.

Kraskov estimator (4) of the mutual information is then

$$\hat{I}(X; Y) = \psi(N) + \psi(K) - \frac{1}{k} - \frac{1}{N} \sum_{i=1}^{N} (\psi(\tau_x(i)) + \psi(\tau_y(i))) \qquad (5)$$

where $\tau_x(i)$ is the number of points located no further than the distance $\epsilon_X(i, k)/2$ from the ith observation in the X space, $\tau_y(i)$ is the number of points located no further than the distance $\epsilon_Y(i, k)/2$ from the ith observation in the Y space and where $\epsilon_X(i, k)/2$ and $\epsilon_Y(i, k)/2$ are the projections into the X and Y subspaces of the distance between the ith observation and its kth neighbour.

2.2 Feature Selection with Noise Variance

Noise variance is another filter criterion used for feature selection. Its definition is even more intuitive than mutual information. With this filter criterion, the noise represents the error in estimating the output variable by a function of the input variables, under the hypothesis that this function could be built (by a machine learning regression model). It is a filter criterion because it does not require building a regression model, but it is close to the idea of a wrapper method because the goal is to evaluate how good a model could be.

Let us consider a dataset with N instances, d features X_j, a target Y and N input-output pairs $(\mathbf{x}_i, y_i)$. The relationship between these input-output pairs is

$$y_i = f(\mathbf{x}_i) + \epsilon_i \quad i = 1, \ldots, N \tag{6}$$

where f is the unknown function between $\mathbf{x}_i$ and y_i, and ϵ_i is the noise or prediction error when estimating f. The principle is to select the subsets of features which lead to the lowest prediction error, or lowest noise variance [17].

In practice the noise variance has to be estimated, e.g. with the Delta Test [18]. The Delta Test δ is defined as

$$\delta = \frac{1}{2N} \sum_{i=1}^{N} \left[y_{NN(i)} - y_i \right]^2 \tag{7}$$

where N is the size of the dataset, $y_{NN(i)}$ is the output associated to $x_{NN(i)}$, $x_{NN(i)}$ being the nearest neighbour of the point x_i.

Similarly to the use of mutual information for feature selection, when using the Delta Test the relationships between several subsets of features and Y are computed, again with a search procedure such as a greedy search. Among these subsets of features, the one minimising the value of δ with Y will be selected. The Delta Test has also been widely used for feature selection [21, 22].

3   Behaviour of kNN-Based Estimators of Relevance Criteria in Small Sample Scenarios

This section analyses the behaviour of the mutual information and noise variance estimators in small datasets.

3.1   Mutual Information Analysis

The Kraskov estimator (5) can be used to estimate MI in regression. However, as a kNN-based estimator of $I(X; Y) = H(Y) - H(Y|X)$, it is affected by the degree of smoothness of the relationship between the target and the considered features. Indeed, the Kraskov estimator assumes that the conditional distribution $p(Y|X)$ is stationary in the k-neighbourhood of x. However, if the neighbourhood of x is large, which is the case when the sample is small, this hypothesis does not hold anymore and the interval of observed values for Y will widen. The Kraskov estimator will consequently overestimate the conditional entropy $H(Y|X)$ and underestimate $I(X; Y)$. This underestimation will be more severe for non-smooth functions, as the interval of Y in the neighbourhood of x is larger in this case. Consequently, when two features will be compared, the one that has the smoother relation to Y will tend to be favoured in the feature selection.

3.2 Delta Test Analysis

To estimate the variance of the noise in regression problems, the Delta Test uses a 1-nearest neighbour method by looking for the nearest neighbour of each point of the dataset and by computing a variation in target values between the point and its nearest neighbour.

The Delta Test, already defined in (7), can be rewritten with (6) as

$$\delta = \frac{1}{2N} \sum_{i=1}^{N} [f(\mathbf{x}_{NN(i)}) + \epsilon_{NN(i)} - f(\mathbf{x}_i) - \epsilon_i]^2 \tag{8}$$

where noise ϵ_i is i.i.d. The average behaviour of the Delta test can be characterised using a first order approximation $f(\mathbf{x}) \approx f(\mathbf{x}_i) + \nabla f(\mathbf{x}_i)^T (\mathbf{x} - \mathbf{x}_i)$, based on the assumption that the nearest neighbour is close enough to make this approximation sufficiently accurate. The expected value of the Delta Test is then approximated as

$$
\begin{aligned}
\mathrm{E}[\delta] &= \mathrm{E}\left[\frac{1}{2N} \sum_{i=1}^{N} [f(\mathbf{x}_{NN(i)}) + \epsilon_{NN(i)} - f(\mathbf{x}_i) - \epsilon_i]^2\right] \\
&\approx \mathrm{E}\left[\frac{1}{2N} \sum_{i=1}^{N} [\nabla f(\mathbf{x}_i)^T (\mathbf{x}_{NN(i)} - \mathbf{x}_i) + \epsilon_{NN(i)} - \epsilon_i]^2\right] \\
&= \mathrm{E}[\epsilon^2] + \frac{1}{2} \mathrm{E}\left[[\nabla f(\mathbf{x})^T (\mathbf{x}_{NN} - \mathbf{x})]^2\right].
\end{aligned}
\tag{9}
$$

The first term of (9) is the noise variance, but the second term is related to the smoothness of f and is independent from the noise variance: it measures how much f changes on average from an instance $\mathbf{x}$ to its closest neighbour $\mathbf{x}_{NN}$. This second term is affected by two factors. First, if the gradient is small (i.e. the function is smooth), the second term remains small. Second, if instances and their closest neighbours are close (i.e. the dataset is quite large), the second term also remains small. Hence, for small datasets, the second term penalises non-smooth functions.

3.3 Discussion

In small datasets, smooth relations between features and output will have, on average, a smaller Delta Test or a higher MI result. On the opposite, a nonsmooth relation will have, on average, a larger Delta Test or smaller MI result, even with the same level of target noise. As discussed above, estimators based on k-nearest neighbours methods seem to be biased by the smoothness of functions. The two estimators make the assumption that the function does not vary too much in the proximity of the neighbours. However, in small sample and with non-smooth functions, this assumption is violated, which introduces a bias in the estimators. It is thus anticipated that smooth features will tend to be selected first when comparing two features that have the same level of information content to predict output Y. However, this short analysis does not answer the question whether this estimation bias has a real influence during the feature selection process, nor if the problem is more severe with MI or with noise variance. The next section evaluates these questions by experiments.

4   Experimental Settings

In order to study how much the smoothness can be a bias for selection criteria such as the mutual information or Delta Test in regression, experiments performed in this paper consider several functions with various smoothnesses and several sizes of datasets. These experiments are conducted to give some insights to the questions raised in the previous section, i.e. does the estimation bias has an influence while comparing features, and is the problem more severe with MI or with noise variance.

Six different periodic functions have been generated with different frequencies and different levels of noise:

$$
\begin{aligned}
y_1 &= f_1(\mathbf{x}) = sin(\mathbf{x}) + \epsilon & \text{where } \epsilon \sim N(0, 0.05) \\
y_2 &= f_2(\mathbf{x}) = sin(3\mathbf{x}) + \epsilon & \text{where } \epsilon \sim N(0, 0.05) \\
y_3 &= f_3(\mathbf{x}) = sin(9\mathbf{x}) + \epsilon & \text{where } \epsilon \sim N(0, 0.05) \\
y_4 &= f_4(\mathbf{x}) = sin(\mathbf{x}) + \epsilon & \text{where } \epsilon \sim N(0, 0.3) \\
y_5 &= f_5(\mathbf{x}) = sin(3\mathbf{x}) + \epsilon & \text{where } \epsilon \sim N(0, 0.3) \\
y_6 &= f_6(\mathbf{x}) = sin(9\mathbf{x}) + \epsilon & \text{where } \epsilon \sim N(0, 0.3)
\end{aligned}
\tag{10}
$$

Figures 1(a), (b), (c), (d), (e) and (f) represent the six functions f_1, f_2, f_3, f_4, f_5 and f_6, respectively. In theory, features associated to f_1, f_2 and f_3 (resp. f_4, f_5, f_6) should be selected equally in a feature selection process, as prediction errors (or levels of noise) are identical.

The experiments have been performed with various sizes of samples, from extremely small to large ones. For each size of the sample, an estimator of the two decision criteria, the mutual information and the noise variance, has been used to drive the selection process, in order to show the influence of the bias introduced by the smoothness of the function on both criteria. For the noise variance, the estimator used is the Delta Test, based on a k-NN method with 1-nearest neighbour, and described in Sect. 2.2. For the mutual information, the estimator used is the one introduced by Kraskov et al. and described in Sect. 2.1, also based on a k-NN method (with k = 6 as suggested in [19]). All experiments have been repeated 10 times; averages are reported.

5   Experimental Results

Figure 2 represents the average value (on 10 repetitions) of the mutual information estimator (Fig. 2(a) and (c)) and the Delta Test estimator (Fig. 2(b) and (d)), for increasing sizes of the dataset.

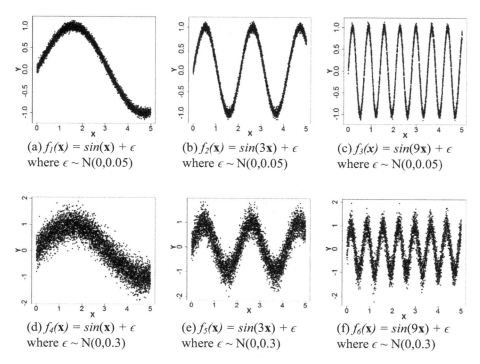

(a) $f_1(x) = sin(x) + \epsilon$
where $\epsilon \sim N(0,0.05)$

(b) $f_2(x) = sin(3x) + \epsilon$
where $\epsilon \sim N(0,0.05)$

(c) $f_3(x) = sin(9x) + \epsilon$
where $\epsilon \sim N(0,0.05)$

(d) $f_4(x) = sin(x) + \epsilon$
where $\epsilon \sim N(0,0.3)$

(e) $f_5(x) = sin(3x) + \epsilon$
where $\epsilon \sim N(0,0.3)$

(f) $f_6(x) = sin(9x) + \epsilon$
where $\epsilon \sim N(0,0.3)$

Fig. 1. Experimental data generated with various frequencies and different levels of noise variance.

All figures show a clear effect in overestimating the noise variance and underestimating the mutual information in small datasets. The over- and underestimations are much more severe for non-smooth functions (f_3 and f_6). It is also clear that when the size of the dataset increases, the biases tend to disappear. What is more interesting to see is that the asymptotic values of the Delta Test are reached in this experiment when the dataset includes a few hundreds of instances, while for the MI a few thousands of instances are necessary, in the same experiment (the horizontal logarithmic scales with the number of instances are different in the left and right figures). This is an argument in favour of using the noise variance rather than the mutual estimation.

When comparing the upper and lower parts of Fig. 2 (both left -MI- and right -noise variance-), it is also interesting to see that for small samples, the order of selection between features can be inverted. For example, let us consider the Delta Test values in Figs. 2(b) and (d) for three cases. First, for 40 instances, the 6 functions will be ranked in the following order: f_1, f_2, f_4, f_5, f_3 and f_6, given that the features with the lower Delta values are selected first. Without the bias effect shown in this paper, it would have been expected that f_1, f_2 and f_3 would be selected first, as their capacity to predict Y is higher (or their noise is lower) than for f_4, f_5 and f_6. Second, for 70 instances, the 6 functions will be ranked in the following order f_1, f_2, f_3, f_4, f_5 and f_6. In this case, the order of selection between features is not inverted anymore but the bias still remains. Finally,

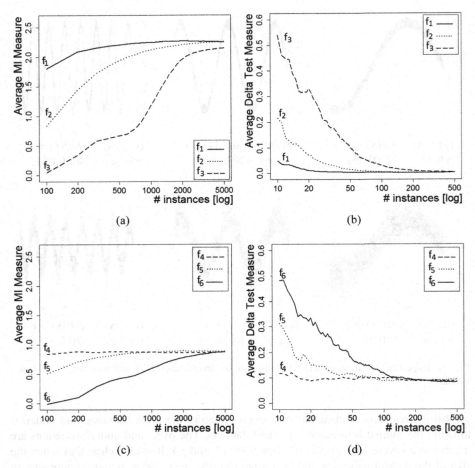

Fig. 2. Average values of MI measures for 3 functions with a low level of noise (a) and for 3 functions with a higher level of noise (c), and of Delta Test for 3 functions with a low level of noise (b) and 3 functions with a higher level of noise (d).

for approximately 300 instances, the bias disappears, the 3 functions f_1, f_2, f_3 obtain the same Delta value and the 3 functions f_4, f_5, f_6 obtain another unique Delta value, higher than the one for f_1, f_2, f_3. These cases show that, for small samples, the bias has an influence on the order of selection between features and that it disappears with a larger dataset. A similar behaviour can be observed for MI in Figs. 2(a) and (c).

6 Conclusion

To the best of our knowledge, no work in the literature focuses on the bias explicitly associated to the smoothness in a feature selection context. Wookey and Konidaris [23] use smoothness as a prior knowledge during feature selection, but only for data regularization.

This paper shows that an overestimation of the noise variance and an underestimation of the mutual information can occur in small datasets when the function to estimate is not smooth. Experiments have been conducted with both criteria on functions with various smoothnesses and levels of noise, for different sizes of datasets. They confirm the theoretical discussion and show that the biases in the estimations are much more severe when using mutual information than when using the noise variance; this is an argument in favour of using the latter rather than the former.

The experiments also confirm that in a feature selection process, where a decision to select a feature is taken by comparing values of the criteria between different possible features or groups of features, the order of selection may be affected (a smooth feature with a low dependency to the output could be selected before a non-smooth with a high dependency). This is a serious shortcoming that should be taken into account when designing a feature selection algorithm. For example the noise variance could be explicitly estimated and used to remove the bias, or the selection process could be improved to favour non-smooth features.

References

1. Guyon, I., Elisseeff, A.: An introduction to variable and feature selection. J. Mach. Learn. Res. **3**, 1157–1182 (2003)
2. François, D., Rossi, F., Wertz, V., Verleysen, M.: Resampling methods for parameter-free and Robust feature selection with mutual information. Neurocomputing **70**(7–9), 1276–1288 (2007)
3. Verleysen, M., Rossi, F., François, D.: Advances in feature selection with mutual information. In: Similarity-Based Clustering, pp. 52–69 (2009)
4. Frénay, B., van Heeswijk, M., Miche, Y., Verleysen, M., Lendasse, A.: Feature selection for nonlinear models with extreme learning machines. Neurocomputing **102**, 111–124 (2013)
5. Gomez-Verdejo, V., Verleysen, M., Fleury, J.: Information-theoretic feature selection for functional data classification. Neurocomputing **72**(16–18), 3580–3589 (2009)
6. Kohavi, R., John, G.H.: Wrappers for feature subset selection. Artif. Intell. **97**, 273–324 (1997)
7. Paul, J., D'Ambrosio, R., Dupont, P.: Kernel methods for heterogeneous feature selection. Neurocomputing **169**, 187–195 (2015)
8. Efron, B., Hastie, T., Johnstone, I., Tibshirani, R.: Least angle regression. Ann. Stat. **32**, 407–499 (2004)
9. Frénay, B., Doquire, G., Verleysen, M.: Is mutual information adequate for feature selection in regression? Neural Netw. **48**, 1–7 (2013)
10. Doquire, G., Frénay, B., Verleysen, M.: Risk estimation and feature selection. In: Proceedings of the 21th International Symposium on Artificial Neural Networks, Computational Intelligence and Machine Learning (ESANN 2013) (2013)

11. Degeest, A., Verleysen, M., Frénay, B.: Feature ranking in changing environments where new features are introduced. In: 2015 International Joint Conference on Neural Networks (IJCNN), pp. 1–8, July 2015
12. Brown, G., Pocock, A., Zhao, M., Lujan, M.: Conditional likelihood maximisation: a unifying framework for mutual information feature selection. J. Mach. Learn. Res. **13**, 27–66 (2012)
13. Battiti, R.: Using mutual information for selecting features in supervised neural net learning. IEEE Trans. Neural Netw. **5**, 537–550 (1994)
14. Vergara, J.R., Estévez, P.A.: A review of feature selection methods based on mutual information. Neural Comput. Appl. **24**, 175–186 (2014)
15. Shannon, C.E.: A mathematical theory of communication. Bell Syst. Tech. J. **27**(379–423), 623–656 (1948)
16. Frénay, B., Doquire, G., Verleysen, M.: Theoretical and empirical study on the potential inadequacy of mutual information for feature selection in classification. Neurocomputing **112**, 64–78 (2013)
17. Guillén, A., Sovilj, D., Mateo, F., Rojas, I., Lendasse, A.: New methodologies based on delta test for variable selection in regression problems. In: Workshop on Parallel Architectures and Bioinspired Algorithms, Toronto, Canada (2008)
18. Yu, Q., Séverin, E., Lendasse, A.: Variable selection for financial modeling. In: Proceedings of the CEF 2007, 13th International Conference on Computing in Economics and Finance, Montréal, Quebec, Canada, pp. 237–241 (2007)
19. Kraskov, A., Stögbauer, H., Grassberger, P.: Estimating mutual information. Phys. Rev. E **69**, 066138 (2004)
20. Kozachenko, L.F., Leonenko, N.: Sample estimate of the entropy of a random vector. Probl. Inform. Transm. **23**, 95–101 (1987)
21. Eirola, E., Liitiäinen, E., Lendasse, A., Corona, F., Verleysen, M.: Using the delta test for variable selection. In: Proceedings of ESANN 2008 (2008)
22. Eirola, E., Lendasse, A., Corona, F., Verleysen, M.: The delta test: the 1-NN estimator as a feature selection criterion. In: Proceedings of the 2014 International Joint Conference on Neural Networks (IJCNN), pp. 4214–4222, July 2014
23. Wookey, D.S., Konidaris, G.D.: Regularized feature selection in reinforcement learning. Mach. Learn. **100**(2), 655–676 (2015)

Neural Networks

The Random Neural Network with a Genetic Algorithm and Deep Learning Clusters in Fintech: Smart Investment

Will Serrano[(⊠)]

Intelligent Systems and Networks Group, Electrical and Electronic Engineering,
Imperial College London, London, UK
g.serrano11@imperial.ac.uk

Abstract. This paper presents the Random Neural Network in a Deep Learning Cluster structure with a new learning algorithm based on the genetics according to the genome model, where information is transmitted in the combination of genes rather than the genes themselves. The proposed genetic model transmits information to future generations in the network weights rather than the neurons. The innovative genetic algorithm is implanted in a complex deep learning structure that emulates the human brain: Reinforcement Learning takes fast local current decisions, Deep Learning Clusters provide identity and memory, Deep Learning Management Clusters take final strategic decisions and finally Genetic Learning transmits the information learned to future generations. This proposed structure has been applied and validated in Fintech; a Smart Investment application: an Intelligent Banker that performs Buy and Sell decisions on several Assets with an associated market and risk. Our results are promising; we have connected the human brain and genetics with Machine Learning based on the Random Neural Network model where biology; similar as Artificial Intelligence is learning gradually and continuously while adapting to the environment.

Keywords: Genetic learning · Deep Learning clusters
Reinforcement Learning · Random Neural Network · Smart Investment
Fintech

1 Introduction

Biology is gradually and continuously learning while adapting to the environment using genetic changes to generate new complex structures in organisms [1], the current structure of the organisms defines the type and level of future genetic variation that will provide a better adaption to the environment or increased reward to a goal function. Random genetic changes have more probability to be successful in organisms that change in a systematic and modular manner where the new structures acquire the same set of sub goals in different combinations; therefore they not only remember their reward evolution but also generalize goal functions to successfully adapt future environments [2]. The adaptations learned from the living organisms affect and guide evolution even though the characteristics acquired are not transmitted to the genome [3], however, its

© IFIP International Federation for Information Processing 2018
Published by Springer International Publishing AG 2018. All Rights Reserved
L. Iliadis et al. (Eds.): AIAI 2018, IFIP AICT 519, pp. 297–310, 2018.
https://doi.org/10.1007/978-3-319-92007-8_26

gene functions are altered and transmitted to the new generation; this enables learning organisms to evolve much faster.

The genome is the genetic material of an organism; it consists of 23 pairs of chromosomes (1-22, X and Y) for a human cell formed of genes (approximately 21,000 in total) that code for a molecule that has a function or instruction to make proteins [4], furthermore genes are formed of base pairs (approximately 3 billion in total). The DNA is a double helix formed by the combination of only four nucleotides (cytosine [C], guanine [G], adenine [A] or thymine [T]) where each base pair consists of the combination of two nucleoids G-C and A-T. The genetic code is formed of codons, a sequence consisted of three nucleotides or three-letter words. Proteins that have similar combination of base pairs tend to have a related functionality determination of protein functions from genetic sequences [5].

Successful Machine Learning and Artificial Intelligence models have been purely based on biology emulating the structures provided by nature during the learning, adaptation and evolution when interacting with the external environment. Neural networks and deep learning are based on the brain structure which is formed of dense local clusters of same neurons performing different functions which are connected between each other with numerous very short paths and few long distance connections [6]. The brain retrieves a large amount of data obtained from the senses; analyses the material and finally selects the relevant information [7] where the cluster of neurons specialization occurs due to their adaption when learning tasks.

This paper proposes a new genetic learning algorithm on Sect. 3 based on the genome and evolution; where the information transmitted to new generations is learned when interacting and adapting to the environment using reinforcement and deep learning respectively. Information in the proposed genetic algorithm is transmitted in the network weights through the different combinations of four different nodes (C, G, A, T) rather than the value of nodes themselves where the output layer of nodes replicates the input layer as the genome. This innovative genetic algorithm is inserted in a complex deep learning structure that emulates the human brain on Sect. 4: Reinforcement Learning takes fast local current decisions, Deep Learning clusters provide identity and memory, Deep Learning Management Clusters takes final strategic decisions and finally Genetic Learning transmits the information learned to future generations. This innovative model has been applied and validated in Fintech, a Smart Investment application on Sect. 5; an Intelligent Banker that performs Buy and Sell decisions on several assets with an associated market and risk. The results shown on Sect. 6 are promising; the Intelligent Banker takes the right decisions, learns the variable asset price, makes profits on specific markets at minimum risk and finally it transmits the information learned to future generations.

2   Related Work

Artificial Neural Networks have been applied to make financial predictions. Leshno et al. [8] evaluate the bankruptcy prediction capability of several neural network models based on the firm's financial reports. Chen et al. [9] uses Artificial Neural Networks for a financial distress prediction model. Kara et al. [10] apply an Artificial Neural Network to predict the direction of Stock Market index movement. Guresen [11] evaluates the effectiveness of neural network models in stock market predictions. Zhang et al. [12] analyse Artificial Neural Networks in bankruptcy prediction. Kohara et al. [13] investigate different ways to use prior knowledge and neural networks to improve multivariate prediction ability. Sheta et al. [14] compares Regression, Artificial Neural Networks and Support Vector Machines for predicting the S&P 500 Stock Market Price Index. Tung et al. [15] includes Artificial Neural Networks and Fuzzy Logic for market predictions. Pakdaman et al. [16] use a feed forward multilayer perceptron and an Elman recurrent Network to predict a company's stock value. Iuhasz et al. [17] create a hybrid system based on a multi Agent Architecture to analyse Stock Market behaviour to improve the profitability in a short or medium time period investment. Nicholas et al. [18] examine the use of neural networks in stock performance modelling.

Several survey papers haven been published. Bahrammirzaee [19] presents a comparative survey of Artificial Intelligence Applications in Finance: Artificial Neural Networks, Expert System and hybrid intelligent systems. Coakley et al. [20] reviews the use of Artificial Neural Networks in Accounting and Finance including modeling issues and guidelines. Fadlalla et al. [21] analyses the applications of Neural Networks in Finance. Huang et al. [22] reviews the use of neural networks in finance and economics forecasting. Li et al. [23] summarize different applications or artificial intelligence technologies in several domains of business administration including finance, retail, manufacturing and management consultancy.

Machine learning has been applied to solve nonlinear models in continuous time in economics and finance by Duarte [24] and forecasting the volatility of asset prices by Stefani et al. [25]. Deep Learning has also recently incorporated in long short term memory Neural Networks for financial market predictions by Fischer et al. [26] and Hasan et al. [27].

Genetic Algorithms have been proposed as method to increase learning. Arifovic [28] analyses genetic algorithms in inflationary economies. Kim et al. [29] uses a genetic Algorithm to feature discretization in artificial neural networks for the prediction of stock market index. Ticona et al. [30] applies a hybrid model based on Genetic algorithm and Neural Networks to forecast Tax Collection. Hossain et al. [31] present a Genetic Algorithm based Deep Learning Method. Tirumala [32] and David et al. [33] review of the latest deep learning structures and evolutionary algorithms that can be used to train them.

3 The Random Neural Network Genetic Deep Learning Model

3.1 The Random Neural Network

The RNN [34–36] represents more closely how signals are transmitted in many biological neural networks where they travel as spikes or impulses, rather than as analogue signal levels. The RNN is a spiking recurrent stochastic model for neural networks. Its main analytical properties are the "product form" and the existence of the unique network steady state solution. The Random Neural network has been Genetics [37–46] (Fig. 1).

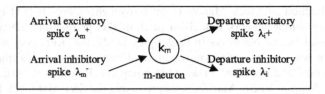

Fig. 1. The Random Neural Network

3.2 The Random Neural Network with Multiple Clusters

Deep Learning with Random Neural Networks is described by Gelenbe and Yin [47–49]. This model is based on the generalized queuing networks with triggered customer movement (G-networks) where customers are either "positive" or "negative" and customers can be moved from queues or leave the network. G-Networks are introduced by Gelenbe [50, 51]; an extension to this model is developed by Gelenbe et al. [52] where synchronised interactions of two queues could add a customer in a third queue (Fig. 2).

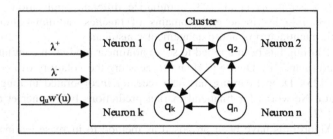

Fig. 2. Clusters of Neurons

3.3 Deep Learning Management Cluster

The Deep Learning management cluster was proposed by Serrano et al. [53–56]. It takes management decisions based on the inputs from different Deep Learning clusters.

3.4 Genetic Learning Algorithm Model

The proposed Genetic learning algorithm is based on the auto encoder presented by Gelenbe and Yin [47–49] based on two instances of the Network shown on Fig. 3, the auto encoder models the genome as it codes the replica of the organism that contains it. Network 1 is formed of U input neurons and C clusters and Network 2 has C input neurons and U clusters. The organism is represented as a set of data X which is a U vector $X \in [0, 1]^{U}$. The proposed Genetic learning algorithm fixes C to 4 neurons that represent the four different nucleoids G, C, A and T and it also fixes W_1 to generate 4 different types of neurons rather than random values.

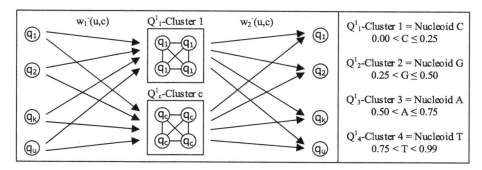

Fig. 3. Genetic Learning Algorithm

Network 1 encodes the organism, it is defined as:

- $q_1 = (q_1^1, q_2^1, \ldots, q_u^1)$, a U-dimensional vector $q_1 \in [0, 1]^U$ that represents the input state q_u for neuron u;
- W_1 is the $U \times C$ matrix of weights $w_1^-(u, c)$ from the U input neurons to the neurons in each of the C clusters;
- $Q^1 = (Q_1^1, Q_2^1, \ldots, Q_c^1)$, a C-dimensional vector $Q^1 \in [0, 1]^C$ that represents state q_c for the cluster c where $Q^1 = \zeta(W_1 X)$.

Network 2 decodes the genome, as the pseudo inverse of Network 1, it is defined as:

- $q_2 = (q_1^2, q_2^2, \ldots, q_c^2)$, a C-dimensional vector $q_2 \in [0, 1]^C$ that represents the input state q_c for neuron c with the same value as $Q^1 = (Q_1^1, Q_2^1, \ldots, Q_c^1)$;
- W_2 is the $C \times U$ matrix of weights $w_2^-(u, c)$ from the C input neurons to the neurons in each of the U cells;
- $Q^2 = (q_1^2, q_2^2, \ldots, q_u^2)$, a U-dimensional vector $Q^2 \in [0, 1]^U$ that represents the state q_u for the cell u where $Q^2 = \zeta(W_2 Q^1)$ or $Q^2 = \zeta(W_2 \zeta(X W_1))$.

The learning algorithm is the adjustment of W_1 to code the organism X into the four different neurons or nucleoids and then calculate W_2 so that resulting decoded organism Q_2 is the same as the encoded organism X:

$$\min \|X - \zeta(W_2 \zeta(X W_1))\| \text{ s.t. } W_1 \geq 0 \qquad (1)$$

Following the Extreme Learning Machine on [57]; W_2 is calculated as:

$$W_2 = \text{pinv}(\zeta(X W_1)) X \qquad (2)$$

Where pinv is the Moore-Penrose pseudoinverse:

$$\text{pinv}(x) = (x^T x) x^T$$

4 Smart Investment Model

The Smart Investment model, called "GoldAI Sachs", combines there different learn-ings: Reinforcement Learning, Deep Learning and Genetic Learning. "GoldAI Sachs" is formed of clusters of Intelligent Bankers that take local fast local binary decisions "Buy or Sell" on a specific assets based on Reinforcement Learning through the interactions and adaptations with the environment where the Reward is the profit made. Each Asset Banker has an associated Deep Learning cluster that memorizes asset identity such as price and reward properties. Asset bankers are dynamically clustered to different properties such as investment reward, risk or market type and managed by a Market Banker Deep Learning Management Cluster that selects the best performing Asset Bankers. Finally, a CEO Banker Deep Learning Management Cluster manages the different Bankers and takes the final investment decisions based on the Market Reward and associated Risk prioritizing markets that generate more reward at a lower Risk as every banker would do. This approach enables decisions based on shared information where Intelligent Bankers work collaborative to achieve a bigger reward (Fig. 4).

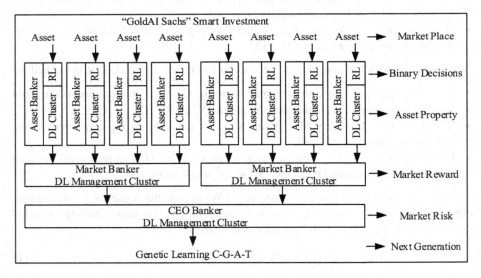

Fig. 4. "GoldAI Sachs" Smart Investment Model

4.1 Asset Banker Reinforcement Learning

The Reinforcement Learning algorithm is used to take fast binary investment decisions "Buy or Sell", it is based on Cognitive Packet Network presented by Gelenbe [11–15]. The Intelligent Banker is formed of two interconnected neurons "q_0 or Buy" and "q_1 or Sell" where the investment decision is taken according to the neuron that has the maximum potential. The state q_0 and q_1 is the probability that it is excited [11–15], these quantities satisfy the following system of non linear equations:

$$q_0 = \frac{\lambda^+(0)}{r(0) + \lambda(0)} \quad q_1 = \frac{\lambda^+(1)}{r(1) + \lambda(1)} \tag{3}$$

where:

$$\begin{aligned}
\lambda^+(0) &= q_1 w_{10}^+ + \Lambda_0 & \lambda^+(1) &= q_0 w_{01}^+ + \Lambda_1 \\
\lambda^-(0) &= q_1 w_{10}^- + \lambda_0 & \lambda^-(1) &= q_0 w_{01}^- + \lambda_1 \\
r(0) &= w_{01}^+ + w_{01}^- & r(1) &= w_{10}^+ + w_{10}^-
\end{aligned} \tag{4}$$

On the above equations, w_{ij}^+ is the rate at which neuron i transmits excitation spikes to neuron j and w_{ij}^- is the rate at which neuron i transmits inhibitory spikes to neuron j in both situations when neuron i is excited. Λ_i and λ_i are the rates of external excitatory and inhibitory signals respectively (Fig. 5).

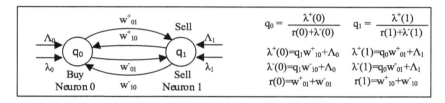

Fig. 5. Asset Banker Reinforcement Learning

The Reward R is based on the economic profit that the Asset Bankers achieve with the decisions they make, successive measured values of the R are denoted by R_l, $l = 1, 2\ldots$ these are used to compute the Predicted Reward:

$$PR_l = \alpha\,PR_{l-1} + (1 - \alpha)R_l \tag{5}$$

where α represents the investment reward memory.

If the observed measured Reward is greater than the associated Predicted Reward; Reinforcement Learning rewards the decision taken by increasing the network weight that point to it, otherwise; it penalises it.

5   Experimental Results

"GoldAI Sachs" is evaluated with eight different assets to assess the adaptability and performance of our proposed Smart Investment solution for eleven days. The assets are split into the Bond Market with low risk and slow reward and the Derivative Market with high risk and fast reward. Experiments are carried with very reduced memory $\alpha = 0.1$ where the Reinforcement Learning is first initialized with a Buy Decision (Fig. 6).

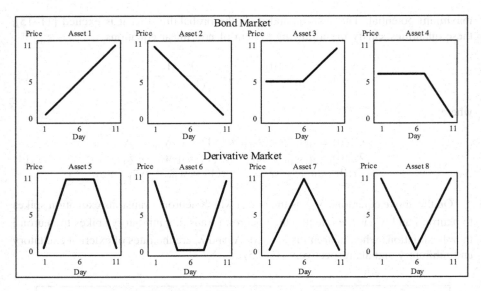

Fig. 6. "GoldAI Sachs" Smart Investment Model assets

5.1 Asset Banker Reinforcement Learning Validation

Table 1 represents the Profit that each Asset Banker makes when buying or selling 100 Assets for 11 days with the Maximum Profit, the number of winning decisions against the losing ones and the number of buy decisions against the sell.

The Profit made in assets that start downwards such as Asset 2, Asset 4, Asset 6 and Asset 8 is worse than the upwards ones because the Asset Bankers are initialized with a buy decision. The Reinforcement Learning Algorithm adapts very quickly to variable asset prices.

Table 1. Asset Banker Reinforcement Learning Validation

Asset	Profit	Maximum Profit	Win	Loss	Buy	Sell
1	1000	1000	10	0	10	0
2	800	1000	9	1	1	9
3	600	600	6	0	10	0
4	300	500	4	1	6	4
5	2000	2000	8	0	4	6
6	1200	2000	6	2	4	6
7	1600	2000	9	1	6	4
8	800	2000	7	3	4	6

5.2   Market Banker Deep Learning Management Cluster Validation

The profits the Market Bankers can make are shown in Tables 2 and 3. The Market Bankers take market decisions rather than individual asset decisions form the Asset Bankers. Market Bankers invests 400 assets which is the combination of the four Asset Bankers purchasing power.

Table 2. Bond Market Banker Profits

Day	Total Asset Banker	Bond Market	I	Maximum Asset	Maximum Market	I
2	0	400	400.00%	200	400	100.00%
3	200	400	100.00%	200	400	100.00%
4	200	400	100.00%	200	400	100.00%
5	200	400	100.00%	200	400	100.00%
6	300	400	33.33%	300	400	33.33%
7	200	400	100.00%	400	400	0.00%
8	400	400	0.00%	400	400	0.00%
9	400	400	0.00%	400	400	0.00%
10	400	400	0.00%	400	400	0.00%
11	400	400	0.00%	400	400	0.00%
Total	2700	4000	48.15%	3100	4000	29.03%

Table 3. Derivative Market Banker Profits

Day	Total Asset Banker	Derivative Market	I	Maximum Asset	Maximum Market	I
2	0	800.0	400.00%	800	800.0	400.00%
3	1000	1200	20.00%	1000	1200	20.00%
4	1000	1200	20.00%	1000	1200	20.00%
5	800	800	0.00%	800	800	0.00%
6	400	0	−100.00%	400	0	−100.00%
7	−400	−800	100.00%	400	800	100.00%
8	0	800	800%	800	800	0.00%
9	1000	1200	20.00%	1000	1200	20.00%
10	1000	1200	20.00%	1000	1200	20.00%
11	800	800	0.00%	800	800	0.00%
Total	5600	7200	28.57%	8000	8800	10.00%

5.3   CEO Banker Deep Learning Management Cluster Validation

Table 4 represents the CEO Banker, "AI Morgan" profits at different Risks ratios with a total of investment of 800 assets. A risk value $\beta = 0.2$ represents 640 assets in the Bond Market and 160 is the Derivative Market whereas a risk value $\beta = 0.8$ is 160 assets in the Bond Market and 640 in the Derivative Market respectively.

Table 4. CEO Banker Profits

Day	Risk β = 0.2			Risk β = 0.5			Risk β = 0.8			Max profit
	B	D	Total	B	D	Total	B	D	Total	
2	640	320	960	400	800	1200	160	1280	1440	1440
3	640	480	1120	400	1200	1600	160	1920	2080	2080
4	640	480	1120	400	1200	1600	160	1920	2080	2080
5	640	320	960	400	800	2800	160	1280	1440	1440
6	640	0	640	400	0	400	160	0	160	640
7	640	−320	320	400	−800	−400	160	−1280	−1120	320
8	640	320	960	400	800	1200	160	1280	1440	1440
9	640	480	1120	400	1200	1600	160	1920	2080	2080
10	640	480	1120	400	1200	1600	160	1920	2080	2080
11	640	640	1280	400	800	1200	160	1280	1440	1440
Total	6400	2880	9280	4000	7200	11200	1600	11520	13120	15040

5.4   Genetic Algorithm Validation

The Genetic Algorithm validation for the four different Nucleoids (C, G, A, T) during the 11 different days is shown in Table 5 with the Genetic Algorithm Error.

Table 5. Genetic Algorithm Validation

Day	Error	Nucleoid-C	Nucleoid-G	Nucleoid-A	Nucleoid-T
2	3.05*10E−31	0.2048	0.3893	0.6295	0.9268
3	5.85*10E−31	0.2026	0.3861	0.6263	0.9259
4	6.78*10E−32	0.2025	0.3859	0.6262	0.9259
5	1.17*10E−31	0.2029	0.3865	0.6267	0.9260
6	4.44*10E−31	0.2033	0.3870	0.6272	0.9262
7	1.29*10E−31	0.2049	0.3894	0.6296	0.9269
8	3.61*10E−31	0.2031	0.3868	0.6271	0.9261
9	2.96*10E−31	0.2021	0.3852	0.6255	0.9257
10	6.90*10E−31	0.2020	0.3851	0.6254	0.9256
11	1.36*10E−31	0.2023	0.3856	0.6259	0.9258

6   Conclusions

This paper has presented a new learning Genetic Algorithm based on the Genome where the information is transmitted in the network weights rather than the neurons. The algorithm has been incremented in an Smart Investment model that simulates the human brain with reinforcement learning for fast decisions, deep learning to memorize properties to create asset identity, deep learning management clusters to make global decisions and genetic to transmit learning into future generations.

In the Smart Investor Model, "GoldAI Sachs" Asset Banker Reinforcement Learning Algorithm takes the right investment decisions; with great adaptability to asset price changes whereas Asset Banker Deep Learning provides asset properties and identity. Market Bankers success to increase the profit by selecting the best performing Asset Bankers and the CEO Banker, "AI Morgan" increases the profits considering the associated market risks, prioritizing low risk investment decision at equal profit. Genetic learning algorithm has a minimum error and it exactly codes and encodes the CEO Banker, "AI Morgan".

Future work will validate our model in a Fintech cryptocurrency environment with real market values. In addition the relevance of memory in investment with its optimum value will be analyzed.

Appendix: Smart Investment Model - Neural Schematic

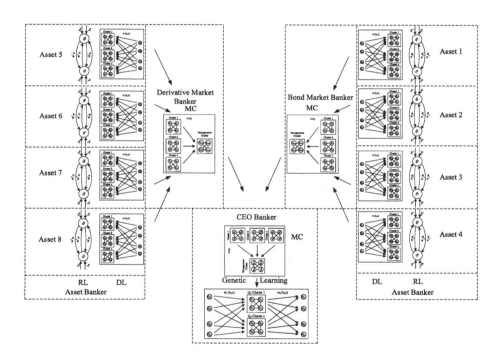

References

1. Kirschner, M., Gerhart, J.: The Plausibility of Life Resolving Darwin's Dilemma. Yale University Press, New Haven (2005)
2. Parter, M., Kashtan, N., Alon, U.: Facilitated Variation: How Evolution Learns from Past Environments To Generalize to New Environments. Department of Molecular Cell Biology, Weizmann Institute of Science
3. Hinton, G., Nowlan, S.: How learning can guide evolution. In: Adaptive Individuals in Evolving Populations, pp. 447–454 (1996)
4. Pellegrini, M., Marcotte, E., Thompson, M., Eisenberg, D., Yeates, T.: Assigning protein functions by comparative genome analysis: protein phylogenetic profiles. Proc. Natl. Acad. Sci. USA **96**, 4285–4288 (1999)
5. Suzuki, M.: A framework for the DNA protein recognition code of the probe helix in transcription factors: the chemical and stereo chemical rules. Structure **2**(4), 317–326 (1994)
6. Smith, D., Bullmore, E.: Small-World brain networks. Neuroscientist **12**, 512–523 (2007)
7. Sporns, O., Chialvo, D., Kaiser, M., Hilgetag, C.: Organization, development and function of complex brain networks. Trends Cogn. Sci. **8**(9), 418–425 (2004)
8. Leshno, M., Spector, Y.: Neural network prediction analysis: the bankruptcy case. Neurocomputing **10**(2), 125–147 (1996)
9. Chen, W., Du, Y.: Using neural networks and data mining techniques for the financial distress prediction model. Expert Syst. Appl. **36**, 4075–4086 (2009)
10. Kara, Y., Acar, M., Kaan, Ö.: Predicting direction of stock price index movement using artificial neural networks and support vector machines: the sample of the Istanbul Stock Exchange. Expert Syst. Appl. **38**, 5311–5319 (2011)
11. Guresen, E., Kayakutlu, G., Daim, T.U.: Using artificial neural network models in stock market index prediction. Expert Syst. Appl. **38**, 10389–10397 (2011)
12. Zhang, G., Hu, M., Patuwo, B., Indro, D.: Artificial neural networks in bankruptcy prediction: general framework and cross-validation analysis. Eur. J. Oper. Res. **116**, 16–32 (1999)
13. Kohara, K., Ishikawa, T., Fukuhara, Y., Nakamura, Y.: Stock price prediction using prior knowledge and neural networks. Intell. Syst. Account. Fin. Manag. **6**, 11–22 (1997)
14. Sheta, A., Ahmed, S., Faris, H.: A comparison between regression, artificial neural networks and support vector machines for predicting stock market index. Int. J. Adv. Res. Artif. Intell. **4**(7), 55–63 (2015)
15. Khuat, T., Le, M.: An application of artificial neural networks and fuzzy logic on the stock price prediction problem. Int. J. Inform. Visual. **1**(2), 40–49 (2017)
16. Naeini, M., Taremian, H., Hashemi, H.: Stock market value prediction using neural networks. In: International Conference on Computer Information Systems and Industrial Management Applications, pp. 132–136 (2010)
17. Iuhasz, G., Tirea, M., Negru, V.: Neural network predictions of stock price fluctuations. In: International Symposium on Symbolic and Numeric Algorithms for Scientific Computing, pp. 505–512 (2012)
18. Nicholas, A., Zapranis, A., Francis, G.: Stock performance modeling using neural networks: a comparative study with regression models. Neural Netw. **7**(2), 375–388 (1994)
19. Bahrammirzaee, A.: A comparative survey of artificial intelligence applications in finance: artificial neural networks, expert system and hybrid intelligent systems. Neural Comput. Appl. **19**, 1165–1195 (2010)
20. Coakley, J., Brown, C.: Artificial neural networks in accounting and finance: modeling issues. Int. J. Intell. Syst. Account. Fin. Manag. **9**, 119–144 (2000)

21. Fadlalla, A., Lin, C.: An analysis of the applications of neural networks in finance. Interfaces **31**(4), 112–122 (2001)
22. Huang, W., Lai, K., Nakamori, Y., Wang, S., Yu, L.: Neural networks in finance and economics forecasting. Int. J. Inf. Technol. Decis. Mak. **6**(1), 113–140 (2007)
23. Li, Y., Jiang, W., Yang, L., Wu, T.: On neural networks and learning systems for business computing. Neurocomputing **275**, 1150–1159 (2018)
24. Duarte, V.: Macro, Finance, and Macro Finance: Solving Nonlinear Models in Continuous Time with Machine Learning. Massachusetts Institute of Technology, Sloan School of Management, pp. 1–27 (2017)
25. Stefani, J., Caelen, O., Hattab, D., Bontempi, G.: Machine learning for multi-step ahead forecasting of volatility proxies. In: Workshop on Mining Data for Financial Applications, pp. 1–12 (2017)
26. Fischer, T., Krauss, C.: Deep learning with long short-term memory networks for financial market predictions. FAU discussion Papers in Economics, vol. 11, pp. 1–32 (2017)
27. Hasan, A., Kalıpsız, O., Akyokuş, S.: Predicting financial market in big data: deep learning. In: International Conference on Computer Science and Engineering, pp. 510–515 (2017)
28. Arifovic, J.: Genetic algorithms and inflationary economies. J. Monetary Econ. **36**, 219–243 (1995)
29. Kim, K., Han, I.: Genetic algorithms approach to feature discretization in artificial neural networks for the prediction of stock price index. Expert Syst. Appl. **19**, 125–132 (2000)
30. Ticona, W., Figueiredo, K., Vellasco, M.: Hybrid model based on genetic algorithms and neural networks to forecast tax collection: application using endogenous and exogenous variables. In: International Conference on Electronics, Electrical Engineering and Computing, pp. 1–4 (2017)
31. Hossain, D., Capi, G.: Genetic algorithm based deep learning parameters tuning for robot object recognition and grasping. Int. Sch. Sci. Res. Innov. **11**(3), 629–633 (2017)
32. Tirumala, S.: Implementation of evolutionary algorithms for deep architectures. In: Artificial Intelligence and Cognition, pp. 164–171 (2014)
33. David, O., Greental, I.: Genetic algorithms for evolving deep neural networks. In: ACM Genetic and Evolutionary Computation Conference, pp. 1451–1452 (2014)
34. Gelenbe, E.: Random neural networks with negative and positive signals and product form solution. Neural Comput. **1**, 502–510 (1989)
35. Gelenbe, E.: Learning in the recurrent random neural network. Neural Comput. **5**, 154–164 (1993)
36. Gelenbe, E.: G-Networks with triggered customer movement. J. Appl. Probab. **30**, 742–748 (1993)
37. Gelenbe, E.: A class of genetic algorithms with analytical solution. Robot. Auton. Syst. **22**(1), 59–64 (1997)
38. Gelenbe, E.: Steady-state solution of probabilistic gene regulatory networks. Phys. Rev. E **76**(1), 031903 (2007). Also in Virtual Journal of Biological Physics Research, 15 September 2007
39. Gelenbe, E., Liu, P., Laine, J.: Genetic algorithms for route discovery. IEEE Trans. Syst. Man Cybern. B **36**(6), 1247–1254 (2006)
40. Gelenbe, E.: Dealing with software viruses: a biological paradigm. Inf. Secur. Tech. Rep. **12**, 242–250 (2007)
41. Gelenbe, E.: Network of interacting synthetic molecules in equilibrium. Proc. Royal Soc. A (Math. Phys. Sci.) **464**, 2219–2228 (2008)
42. Kim, H., Gelenbe, E.: Anomaly detection in gene expression via stochastic models of gene regulatory networks. BMC Genom. **10**(Suppl 3), S26 (2009). https://doi.org/10.1186/1471-2164-10-S3-S26

43. Kim, H., Gelenbe, E.: Stochastic gene expression modeling with hill function for switch-like gene responses. IEEE/ACM Trans. Comput. Biol. Bioinform. **9**(4), 973–979 (2012). https://doi.org/10.1109/tcbb.2011.153. ISSN 1545-5963
44. Kim, H., Gelenbe, E.: Reconstruction of large-scale gene regulatory networks using Bayesian model averaging. IEEE Trans. NanoBiosci. **11**(3), 259–265 (2012). https://doi.org/10.1109/tnb.2012.221
45. Gelenbe, E.: Natural computation. Comput. J. **55**(7), 848–851 (2012)
46. Kim, H., Park, T., Gelenbe, E.: Identifying disease candidate genes via large- scale gene network analysis. IJDMB **10**(2), 175–188 (2014)
47. Gelenbe, E., Yin, Y.: Deep learning with random neural networks. In: International Joint Conference on Neural Networks, pp. 1633–1638 (2016)
48. Yin, Y., Gelenbe, E.: Deep Learning in Multi-Layer Architectures of Dense Nuclei. CoRR abs/1609.07160, pp. 1–10 (2016)
49. Yin, Y., Gelenbe, E.: Single-cell based random neural network for deep learning. In: International Joint Conference on Neural Networks, pp. 86–93 (2017)
50. Gelenbe, E.: G-Networks: a unifying model for neural nets and queueing networks. In: Modelling Analysis and Simulation of Computer and Telecommunications Systems, pp. 3–8 (1993)
51. Fourneau, J., Gelenbe, E., Suros, R.: G-Networks with multiple class negative and positive customers. In: Modelling Analysis and Simulation of Computer and Telecommunications Systems, pp. 30–34 (1994)
52. Gelenbe, E., Timotheou, S.: Random neural networks with synchronized interactions. Neural Comput. **20–9**, 2308–2324 (2008)
53. Serrano, W., Gelenbe, E.: An intelligent internet search assistant based on the random neural network. In: Iliadis, L., Maglogiannis, I. (eds.) AIAI 2016. IAICT, vol. 475, pp. 141–153. Springer, Cham (2016). https://doi.org/10.1007/978-3-319-44944-9_13
54. Serrano, W.: A big data intelligent search assistant based on the random neural network. In: Angelov, P., Manolopoulos, Y., Iliadis, L., Roy, A., Vellasco, M. (eds.) INNS 2016. AISC, vol. 529, pp. 254–261. Springer, Cham (2017). https://doi.org/10.1007/978-3-319-47898-2_26
55. Serrano, W., Gelenbe, E.: Intelligent search with deep learning clusters. In: Intelligent Systems Conference, pp. 254–267 (2017)
56. Serrano, W., Gelenbe, E.: The deep learning random neural network with a management cluster. In: Czarnowski, I., Howlett, Robert J., Jain, Lakhmi C. (eds.) IDT 2017. SIST, vol. 73, pp. 185–195. Springer, Cham (2018). https://doi.org/10.1007/978-3-319-59424-8_17
57. Kasun, L., Zhou, H., Huang, G.: Representational learning with extreme learning machine for big data. IEEE Intell. Syst. **28**(6), 31–34 (2013)

Can Artificial Neural Networks Predict Psychiatric Conditions Associated with Cannabis Use?

Daniel Stamate[1], Wajdi Alghamdi[1(✉)], Daniel Stahl[2],
Alexander Zamyatin[3], Robin Murray[4], and Marta di Forti[5]

[1] Data Science and Soft Computing Lab, Department of Computing,
Goldsmiths, University of London, London, UK
map01wa@gold.ac.uk
[2] Department of Biostatistics and Health Informatics, Institute of Psychiatry,
Psychology and Neuroscience, King's College London, London, UK
[3] Faculty of Informatics, Department of Applied Informatics, National Research
Tomsk State University, Tomsk, Russia
[4] Department of Psychosis Studies, Institute of Psychiatry, Psychology
and Neuroscience, King's College London, London, UK
[5] MRC Social, Genetic and Developmental Psychiatry Centre, Institute
of Psychiatry, Psychology and Neuroscience, King's College London, London, UK

Abstract. This data-driven computational psychiatry research proposes a novel machine learning approach to developing predictive models for the onset of first-episode psychosis, based on artificial neural networks. The performance capabilities of the predictive models are enhanced and evaluated by a methodology consisting of novel model optimisation and testing, which integrates a phase of model tuning, a phase of model post-processing with ROC optimisation based on maximum accuracy, Youden and top-left methods, and a model evaluation with the k-fold cross-testing methodology. We further extended our framework by investigating the cannabis use attributes' predictive power, and demonstrating statistically that their presence in the dataset enhances the prediction performance of the neural network models. Finally, the model stability is explored via simulations with 1000 repetitions of the model building and evaluation experiments. The results show that our best Neural Network model's average accuracy of predicting first-episode psychosis, which is evaluated with Monte Carlo, is above 80%.

Keywords: Machine learning · Neural networks · Prediction modelling
ROC optimisation · Monte carlo · Computational psychiatry · Cannabis
Psychosis

1 Introduction

Policy changes and the legalisation of cannabis across countries, especially the Netherlands, Uruguay and some states in the USA, indicate that cannabis is gaining greater global acceptance. It has been reported that cannabis has been the most popular

L. Iliadis et al. (Eds.): AIAI 2018, IFIP AICT 519, pp. 311–322, 2018.
https://doi.org/10.1007/978-3-319-92007-8_27

illicit drug in the world in the last decade, with an estimated 183 million annual users [1]. However, studies show that countries with higher cannabis consumption also have higher proportions of people seeking treatment for psychotic disorders, including first-episode psychosis, schizophrenia, anxiety and substance use disorders [2]. This makes it imperative to understand the likely consequences of cannabis use, even if these consequences affect only a minority of users. Therefore, the link between cannabis consumption and the risk of experiencing psychotic disorders must be thoroughly scrutinised.

Recent researches have attempted to understand whether specific patterns of cannabis use, such as potency or age, are associated with a higher risk of developing psychotic disorders. One study concluded that nearly a quarter of all new psychosis patients in South London (UK) could be associated with the use of high-potency, skunk-like cannabis [3]. Another study [4] estimated that a person who uses cannabis daily for more than six months has a 70% likelihood of suffering from psychotic disorders.

Few studies have used risk prediction modelling or advanced machine learning algorithms to establish a link between cannabis use and first-episode psychosis. In fact, apart from our recent work [4], we are not aware of the existence of any such studies. Most prior studies have relied solely on explanatory research strategies and been based on various conventional statistical techniques, such as hypothesis formulation and verification via statistical tests, logistic regression modelling, etc. These methods are well-recognised and widely used in medical research, but they rarely match the high potential of machine learning methods. The domain of machine learning has continued to develop for many years, and advanced predictive techniques have been expanded and improved constantly. These advanced predictive techniques, in turn, are prompting extensive usage of computers and artificial intelligence techniques in many domains, such as medicine [5, 6]. Artificial neural networks have proven their remarkable ability to detect predictive patterns in different types of datasets of various complexities, and often showed their superiority compared with other machine learning techniques.

Artificial neural networks are computational models that simulate the way biological neural networks process information in the human brain [7]. They are usually composed of several highly interconnected groups of artificial neurons that work together to solve specific problems. These computational models are typically used to model complex relationships between inputs and outputs, such as those in prediction models. Just like learning in biological neural networks, artificial neural networks process information by 'tuning' existing connections among neurons in order to process information.

While techniques involving support vector machines are still popular within the machine learning community [4, 8], artificial neural networks are gaining considerable attention again. Recently, artificial neural networks have been successfully used in understanding the heterogeneous manifestations of asthma [9], diagnosing tuberculosis [10], classifying leukaemia [11], detecting heart conditions in electrocardiogram (ECG) data [12], etc. These studies show that neural networks are capable of handling complex medical data, such as ambiguous ECG signal data, and achieving outstanding results not yet produced by other methods.

In this study, we offer a novel machine learning approach that uses neural networks to develop predictive models for the onset of first-episode psychosis. The dataset on which we based our study was collected by psychiatry practitioners and has been used in previously conducted studies, such as [3, 4]. It comprises an extensive set of variables, including demographic, drug-related and other variables, with specific information on participants' histories of cannabis use, as seen in Table 1.

Table 1. Cannabis use attributes in the analysed dataset [4].

Attribute	Description
lifetime_cannabis_user	Ever used cannabis: yes or no
age_first_cannabis	Age upon the first use of cannabis: 7 to 50
age_first_cannabis_under15	Age less than 15 when first used cannabis: yes, no or never used
age_first_cannabis_under14	Age less than 14 when first used cannabis: yes, no or never used
current_cannabis_user	Current cannabis user: yes or no
cannabis_fqcy	Pattern of cannabis use: never used, only on weekends or daily
cannabis_measure	Cannabis usage measure: none, hash less than once per week, hash on weekends, hash daily, skunk less than once per week, skunk on weekends, skunk daily
cannabis_type	Cannabis type: never used, hash or skunk
duration	Cannabis use duration: 0 to 41 (months)

Our paper proposes a novel data-driven computational psychiatry and machine learning approach to developing predictive models for the onset of first-episode psychosis, based on feed-forward artificial neural networks. The performance capabilities of the predictive models are enhanced and evaluated by a methodology consisting of model optimisation and testing, which integrates a phase of model tuning, a phase of model post-processing with ROC optimisation based on maximum accuracy, Youden and top-left methods, and a model evaluation with the k-fold cross-testing methodology. We further extend our framework by investigating the cannabis use attributes' predictive power, and demonstrating statistically that their presence in the dataset enhances the prediction performance of the neural network models. Finally, the model stability is explored via simulations with 1000 repetitions of the model building and evaluation experiments. The results show that our best models' accuracies in predicting first-episode psychosis in intensive Monte Carlo simulation fall between 75.03% and 85.13%, with an average of about 81%.

The rest of the paper is organised as follows. Section 2 presents our methodology for predicting the first-episode psychosis, based on experimenting with artificial neural networks, and our novel methodology for model optimisation and post-processing, and evaluation with optimized cut-off point selection on the ROC curve. The section also investigates the outcomes of the extensive Monte Carlo simulations in order to study the variation of the models' performance. In Sect. 3, we build optimised prediction models without the cannabis attributes to study if there is a statistically significant difference with respect to the performances of the models using the cannabis attributes. Finally, the conclusion and the directions for future work are presented in Sect. 4.

2 Building Prediction Models

2.1 Data Preparation

The data we used to build our predictive models were a part of a case-control study [3]. The clinical data comprise 1106 records divided into 489 patients, 370 controls and 247 unlabelled records. The patients were individuals who presented with first-episode psychosis to the inpatient units of the South London & Maudsley Mental Health National Health Service (NHS) Foundation Trust. The controls were healthy people recruited from the same area served by the Trust. The control samples were similar to the patient samples in age, gender, ethnicity, educational qualifications and employment status.

Each record in the data refers to a participant in the study and has 255 possible attributes divided into four groups. The first group consists of demographic attributes, which represent general features like gender, race and level of education. The second group of drug-related attributes contains information on the use of non-cannabis drugs, such as tobacco, stimulants and alcohol. The third group contains genetic attributes. These were removed from the analysis for the purposes of this study. The final group contains cannabis-related attributes, such as the duration of use, initial date of use, frequency, cannabis type, etc. (see Table 1).

The goal of this stage is to perform a high-level simplification of the dataset and to prepare the dataset for use in our novel approach to predict first-episode psychosis. This stage involved several steps. First, records that were missing critical data were removed from the dataset. This included both records with missing labels and records with missing values on all cannabis-related variables. Second, certain variables were removed from the dataset. This primarily included variables that were deemed to be irrelevant to the study (e.g. those related to the individual IDs of the study participants) and variables that fell outside the scope of the study (e.g. certain gene-related variables). In addition, any numeric predictors with zero or near-zero variance were dropped. Third, we sought to standardise the encoding of missing values across the dataset. Prior to this step, values including 66, 99 and −99 all represented cases with missing values; thus, we replaced all such indicators with a consistent missing value indicator: NA. Fourth, some variables were re-labelled to provide more intuitive descriptions of the data they contained. In multiple situations, some variables had similar meanings but also records with missing values. Therefore, we conducted an imputation process to effectively combine the information from all the related variables into one. For example, two variables described alcohol use, but were inconsistently present and presented missing values across the records. These were combined in a way that created one single variable with consistent values that were as complete as possible. This process was used to generate value-reacher and value-consistent variables related to alcohol use, tobacco use, employment history and age.

Finally, any attribute that had more than 50% missing values was removed from the study. We then dropped any record for which more than 70% of the remaining attributes contained missing values. The resulting dataset, after the transformations above, contained 783 records and 78 attributes. The records are divided into 451 patients and 332 controls. A summary of some of these fields—specifically, those that relate to cannabis use, such as type, the age of first use and duration—can be seen in Table 1.

2.2 Missing Values Treatment

Although the data set was pre-processed and attributes with more than 50% missing values were removed, the final dataset still contained several missing values. Of the 783 records, only 22.8% were complete cases. This volume of missing information makes modelling more challenging but is often the reality of medical and social research.

The predictive power of the data may depend significantly on the way that missing values are treated. Some machine learning algorithms, such as decision trees [7], have the capability to handle missing data outright. However, most of machine learning algorithms do not have the capability to handle missing data. In many situations, missing values are imputed using a supervised learning technique, such as k-Nearest Neighbour (KNN. These imputation techniques do not have theoretical formulations but are often applied in practice [4, 6]. Several imputations techniques, such as the KNN imputation, the tree bagging imputation from the *caret* package [7] and the random forest imputation from the *randomForest* package [13] were considered in this work. The last method, although it was the most computationally expensive, produced the best results regarding the performance of the final predictive models.

2.3 Training and Tuning Feed-Forward Artificial Neural Networks

To develop optimised predictive models for first-episode psychosis, we controlled the values of the parameters for each of the considered algorithms using chosen grids. Predictive models have been fitted in a five-fold cross-validation procedure, on each training set after pre-processing techniques were applied on the same training set, and have been tested on each test set. Models based on single-layer and multi-hidden-layer neural networks were optimised (tuned) to maximise AUC, the area under the ROC curve.

To avoid overfitting, the single-layer neural networks were tuned over 10 values for the size (i.e. the number of hidden units) and 10 values for the decay (i.e. the weight decay), which is the parameter in the penalisation method for model regularisation. This approach is like the penalisation method in ridge regression and is based on the L2 norm [7]. The optimal values were 17 and 0.01, respectively. Multi-layer neural networks were tuned over 10 values for each of the three hidden layers (i.e. 10 values for the number of hidden units in each layer) and over 10 values for the decay. The optimal values were 10, 10 and 10 for the three layers and 0.001 for the decay.

2.4 Treating Unbalanced Classes

When there is a priori knowledge of a class imbalance, one direct method to reduce the imbalance's influence on model training is to select training set samples with roughly equal event rates [7]. Treating data imbalances usually leads to better prediction models and a better trade-off between sensitivity and specificity.

In this study, we considered three sampling approaches to sub-sample the training data in a manner that mitigated the imbalance problem. The first approach was down-sampling, in which we sampled (without replacement) the majority class to be the same size as the minority class. The second method was up-sampling, in which we sampled (with replacement) the minority class to be the same size as the majority class. The last approach was the synthetic minority over-sampling technique (SMOTE) [14]. SMOTE selects a data point randomly from the minority class, determines the K nearest neighbours to that point and then uses these neighbours to generate new synthetic data points using slight alterations. Our analysis used five neighbours. The results show that the up-sampling procedure yielded no real improvement in the AUC or the accuracy performances. A simple down-sampling of the data also had no positive effect on the model performances. However, SMOTE with neural networks models led to an increase in both the AUC and the accuracy.

As mentioned, data balancing supports a good trade-off between sensitivity and specificity. Another method that helps to balance sensitivity and specificity, or a good trade-off between the two performances, is model post-processing through the determination of new cut-off points on the ROC curves [7]. Our framework used three such methods, which can be seen as post-processing optimisations of the models. The first method found the point on the ROC curve closest to the top-left corner of the ROC plot, which represents the perfect model (100% sensitivity and 100% specificity). The second method is Youden's J index [15], which corresponds to the point on the ROC curve farthest from the main diagonal of the ROC plot. The third method, which is "maximum accuracy" found the cut-off, which is the point with the highest accuracy.

In order to further improve the model performance, a specially designed post-processing procedure and model evaluation were adapted in our modelling procedure. First, the dataset is stratified splattered randomly into in 60% training data and 40% evaluation data. Then, the training data is used for training and for optimising the model, as explained in Subsect. 2.3, in a cross-validation fashion, with AUC as optimisation criterion, with and without class balancing. Different pre-processing methods such as missing values imputation and sampling methods that we have explained above were appropriately integrated into the cross-validation. The optimal model obtained on the training data was then applied to the evaluation dataset in a specially designed post-processing procedure, which we call the *k-fold cross-testing method*.

In the *k-fold cross-testing method*, we produce k post-processed model variants of the original optimised model. First, we create k stratified folds of the evaluation dataset. Then, k-1 folds are used to find an alternative probability cut-off on the ROC curve with one of the three specific methods presented above (top-left, Youden, and largest accuracy), obtaining a post-processed model variant. The remaining one-fold is scored with the post-processed model variant based on the newly found cut-off point. Finally, the whole procedure is repeated until all folds are used for scoring at their turn, then the predictions are integrated, and the model performance is measured on the whole evaluation dataset. We note here as an essential remark that in each such iteration of the procedure, the ROC optimisation data (the k-1 folds) and the scored data (the remaining fold) are always distinct, so the data for model post-processing and the data for scoring are always distinct.

2.5   Increasing Model Performance via Optimized Cut-off Point Selection on the ROC Curve

The ROC curve is a graphical technique for evaluating the ability of a prediction model to discriminate between two classes, such as patients and controls. ROC curves allow visual analyses of the trade-offs between a predictive model's sensitivity and specificity regarding various probability cut-offs. The curve is obtained by measuring the sensitivity and specificity of the predictive model at every cutting point and plotting the sensitivity against 1-specificity. The left image in Fig. 1 shows the ROC curves obtained for both the single-layer neural networks and the multi-layer neural networks. The curve shows that multi-layer neural network performs better regarding the evaluation dataset.

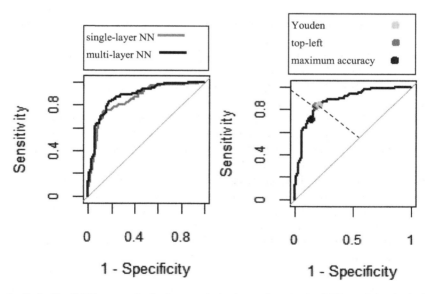

Fig. 1. Left: The ROC curves for 2 of our optimised neural networks (NN) models: single-layer NN and multi-layer NN. Right: ROC optimisation post-processing of the multi-layer NN model, with 3 optimal cutting points: maximum accuracy, Youden and top-left methods. (Color figure online)

Numerous methods exist for finding a new cut-off. First, one can find the point on the ROC curve that is closest to the perfect model (100% sensitivity and 100% specificity), which is the point with shortest distance value from the point (0,1) as shown in the left image in Fig. 1. To find the shortest distance, $[(1 - \text{sensitivity})^2 + (1 - \text{specificity})^2]$ was calculated and minimised [16]. Another approach for finding an optimal cut-off point on the ROC curve is finding the largest distance from the diagonal to the ROC curve as shown in the right image in Fig. 1. This is the point with the largest value for the Youden index which is defined as (sensitivity + specificity -1) [15]. These are the two most popular methods for establishing the optimal cut-off [7, 17]. We used both of these methods, as well as the maximum accuracy approach, which determines the point on the ROC curve corresponding to the greatest accuracy (the red point in Fig. 1, right). In our analysis, the optimal cutting point was derived from independent sets, rather than from the training set or the evaluation sets, as shown previously. This is particularly important, especially, for small datasets.

2.6   Monte Carlo and Models' Stability

Due to the uncertainties introduced by the missing values in the data and due to expected variations of the predictive models' performance, depending on the datasets that were chosen for training and testing, we perform extensive Monte Carlo simulations to study the performances' variations and the models' stability. The simulations for each NN consisted of 1,000 iterations of the proposed procedure. The models' performances concerning accuracy, sensitivity, specificity and kappa were evaluated for each iteration on separate a testing dataset. The aggregation of all iterations yielded various distributions of the concerned performance measures. These distributions were then visualised using box plots in Fig. 2 to capture the models' performance capability and stability. The subfigures in Fig. 2 were grouped by their performances' measures into four subfigures. Each subfigure contained sex box plots for single-layer and multi-layer neural networks with several optimized cut-off points on the ROC curve such as top-left, Youden index and the maximum accuracy. Also, estimations of the predictive neural networks' performances regarding means and standard deviation (SD) are shown in Table 2. The results as shown in Table 2 are regarding the models' performances when applied with the ROC optimisation techniques.

On the one hand, single-layer neural networks with ROC optimisations based on Youden or top-left scored a mean accuracy of 0.76. The performance of the single-layer neural networks slightly improved when a ROC optimisation based on maximum accuracy was applied, resulting in a mean accuracy of 0.79 (95% CI [0.75, 0.83]) and a mean sensitivity of 0.83 (95% CI [0.76, 0.9]). On the other hand, the multi-layer neural networks with an ROC optimisation based on top-left cutting point achieved the best results with a mean accuracy of 0.81 (95% CI [0.77, 0.86]) and a mean sensitivity of 0.84 (95% CI [0.77, 0.88]), comparable to the results achieved by multi-layer neural networks with Youden and maximum accuracy.

This procedure is very computationally costly; therefore, a robust framework was essential. Parallel processing was performed on a data analytics cluster of 11 servers with Xeon processors and 832 GB fast RAM. We used the R software with some packages, including *caret, pROC, e1071, randomForest, ggplot2, plyr, DMwR, Applied Predictive Modeling* and *doParallel* [18].

In general, we detect that the proposed models have good predictive power and stability, based on an acceptable level of variation in their performance measures

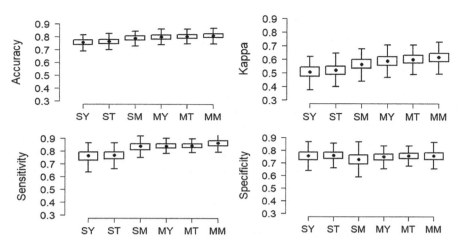

Fig. 2. 1000 Monte Carlo simulation for artificial neural networks. Where "SY" is single-layer NN with Youden cutting point, "ST" is single-layer NN with top-left cutting point, SM" is single-layer NN with maximum accuracy cutting point, "MY" is multi-layer NN with Youden cutting point, "MT" is multi-layer NN with top-left cutting point, and "MM" is multi-layer NN with maximum accuracy cutting point.

Table 2. Estimations of the predictive neural networks' performances.

Model	Accuracy		Kappa		Sensitivity		Specificity	
	Mean	SD	Mean	SD	Mean	SD	Mean	SD
Single-layers NN (Youden)	0.76	0.03	0.52	0.05	0.76	0.05	0.75	0.05
Single-layers NN (top-left)	0.76	0.02	0.52	0.05	0.77	0.04	0.76	0.04
Single-layers NN (max accuracy)	0.79	0.02	0.56	0.05	0.83	0.04	0.73	0.05
Multi-layers NN (Youden)	0.8	0.02	0.59	0.05	0.84	0.02	0.75	0.04
Multi-layers NN (top-left)	0.81	0.02	0.61	0.04	0.84	0.02	0.76	0.03
Multi-layers NN (max accuracy)	0.80	0.08	0.59	0.13	0.87	0.04	0.74	0.08

evaluated across extensive Monte Carlo experiments. However, the results indicate that the performance differences between the two types of neural networks with different methods for selecting the ROC cutting points are not significant regarding the 4 performances.

3   Cannabis Use Attributes' Predictive Power

After performing the Monte Carlo simulations, we further investigated the predictive models in order to better comprehend the predictive power of the cannabis-related attributes over first-episode psychosis. Moreover, we investigated the association between cannabis-related attributes and first-episode psychosis via statistical tests and attribute-ranking techniques.

3.1 Student's t-Test

In this subsection, we comprehend the predictive power of the cannabis-related attributes over first-episode psychosis via statistical tests by re-fitting our performing models but with the cannabis-related attributes, represented in Table 1, removed from the dataset. Then, we compared the performances with and without the cannabis-related attributes using Student's t-test. We thereby demonstrated the predictive value of cannabis-related attributes with respect to first-episode psychosis by showing that there is a statistically significant difference between the performances of the predictive models built with and without the cannabis variables.

Our analysis also showed that the accuracy decreased by 5% for single-layer neural networks and by 6% for the multi-neural networks, if the cannabis-related attributes were removed from the process of building the predictive models. Then, we compared the accuracies of the single-layer neural networks models built on the data sets with and without the cannabis-related attributes using one-tailed t-test. The p-value obtained for the t-test was 5.51×10^{-195}. As for the multi-layer neural networks models built on the data sets with and without the cannabis use attributes, the p-value obtained for the one-tailed t-test was and 2×10^{-16}. This means that the predictive models with cannabis attributes have higher predictive accuracy than the models that were built without the cannabis attributes. In other words, the additional cannabis variables jointly account for predictive information over first-episode psychosis. These results are consistent with findings from [4].

3.2 Ranking Attributes' Importance with the ROC Curve Approach

This subsection proposes the use of the ROC curves to determine the relevant variables affecting first-episode psychosis as introduced in [7]. We measure the individual importance of every attributes in the dataset to discover the attributes that yield significant improvements in the model predictivity power. To do so, the ROC curve is considered on each attribute. Then, a series of cutoffs is applied to the data to predict the class. The sensitivity and specificity are calculated for each cutoff, and the ROC curve is computed. Finally, the area under the curve is used as a measure of variable importance. Table 3 shows the top 10 attributes ranked by the ROC curve approach.

The results in Table 3 support prior evidence that cannabis attributes, such as the type of the cannabis used and the frequency of usage, have significant power in predicting first-episode psychosis. For example, the results in Table 3 support findings from [3] by associating the type of cannabis, especially high-potency cannabis, with the onset of psychosis. In addition, *bindur.3* in Table 3, which represents the duration of cannabis use, is consistent with findings from [4].

Table 3. ROC curve attribute importance

Attribute	Importance
typefreq. 1	100.00
cantype2.1	90.38
type_use.hash	88.53
totfreq. 1	87.74
bindur.3	85.84
education.university.professiolqualifications	85.55
frequenc.2	84.24
bullying.no	78.55
white	72.89
homeless.1	72.86

4 Conclusion and Future Work

This paper proposes a novel machine learning approach to developing predictive models for the onset of first-episode psychosis using artificial neural networks. We explored two types of artificial neural networks, each of which was able to recognise patterns differentiating patients from controls at an acceptable level. We based our approach on a novel methodology for optimising and post-processing predictive models. We also proposed several sampling methods and several methods for choosing the optimal cutting point on the ROC curve to improve the prediction models' performances. The models were then further tested using Monte Carlo experiments, and they consistently yielded adequate predictive power and stability.

The best-performing models were multi-layer neural networks, which achieved accuracies as high as 88% in some cases and an average accuracy of 81% in Monte Carlo simulations with 1000 repetitions. The scored performances were above all performances achieved in previous studies such as [3]. This paper extends on previous work as [3] by proposing a new machine learning framework based on a novel methodology in which models are post-processed based on optimized cut-off point selection on the ROC curve and evaluated with the recent method of k-fold cross testing which we adapt after [8]. Moreover, in this new framework, we developed optimized models with other powerful techniques such as artificial neural networks not addressed in [3]. Also, the predictive power of cannabis-use attributes was tested via statistical tests and ranking methods to demonstrate statistically that their presence in the dataset enhances the prediction performance of the neural network models. The proposed approach proves the high potential applicability of machine learning and, particularly, artificial neural networks in psychiatry and enables researchers and doctors to predict and evaluate risks for first-episode psychosis.

One possible direction for future work is to further investigate how this prediction performance variation evolves by limiting the uncertainty in the data, represented by the high proportion of missing values. The second possible work direction is redefining the predictive modelling approach by considering more high-dimensionality data, such as genotype data. A third future work direction, which we are currently investigating, involves enhancing the power to predict first-episode psychosis using deep learning approaches.

References

1. United Nations Office on Drugs and Crime, World Drug Report, United Nations publication, Sales No. E.16.XI.7 (2016)
2. Radhakrishnan, R., Wilkinson, S., Dsouza, D.: Gone to pot: a review of the association between cannabis and psychosis. Front. Psychiatry **5** (2014)
3. Di Forti, M., Marconi, A., et al.: Proportion of patients in South London with first-episode psychosis attributable to use of high potency cannabis: a case-control study. Lancet Psychiatry **2**(3), 233–238 (2015)
4. Alghamdi, W., Stamate, D., et al.: A prediction modelling and pattern detection approach for the first-episode psychosis associated to cannabis use. In: 15th IEEE International Conference on Machine Learning and Applications, pp. 825–830 (2016)
5. Zhou, H., Tang, J., Zheng, H.: Machine learning for medical applications. Sci. World J., **20**, 1 (2015)
6. Iniesta, R., Stahl, D., McGuffin P.: Machine learning, statistical learning and the future of biological research in psychiatry, psychological medicine (2016)
7. Kuhn, M., Johnson, K.: Applied Predictive Modelling. Springer (2013)
8. Katrinecz, A., Stamate, D., et al.: Predicting psychosis using the experience sampling method with mobile apps. In: 16th IEEE International Conference on Machine Learning and Applications (2017)
9. Belgrave, D., Cassidy, R., Stamate, D., et al.: Predictive modelling strategies to understand heterogeneous manifestations of asthma in early life. In: 16th IEEE International Conference on Machine Learning and Applications (2017)
10. Elveren, E., Yumuşak, N.: Tuberculosis disease diagnosis using artificial neural network trained with genetic algorithm. J. Med. Syst. **35**, 329–332 (2011)
11. Adjouadi, M., Ayala, M., et al.: Classification of leukaemia blood samples using neural networks. Ann. Biomed. Eng. **38**(4), 1473–1482 (2010)
12. Yan, Y., Qin, X., et al.: A restricted Boltzmann machine based two-lead electrocardiography classification. In: Proceedings of 12th International Conference on Wearable Implantable Body Sensor Networks (2015)
13. Liaw, A., Wiener, M.: Classification and regression by random forest. R News **2**(3), 18–22 (2002)
14. Qazi, N., Raza, K.: Effect of feature selection, SMOTE and under sampling on class imbalance classification. In: 2012 UKSim 14th International Conference on Computer Modelling and Simulation, pp. 145–150 (2012)
15. Bohning, D., Bohning, W., et al.: Revisiting Youden's index as a useful measure of the misclassification error in a meta-analysis of diagnostic studies. Stat. Methods Med. Res. **17**, 543–554 (2008)
16. Pepe, M.: The Statistical Evaluation of Medical Tests for Classification and Prediction. Oxford University Press, New York (2003)
17. Perkins, N., Schisterman, F.: The inconsistency of "optimal" cutpoints obtained using two criteria based on the receiver operating characteristic curve. Am. J. Epidemiol. **163**(7), 670–675 (2006)
18. Cran.r-project.org.: The Comprehensive R Archive Network (2018). https://cran.r-project.org/. Accessed 2 Jan 2018

Cost-Sensitive Decision Making for Online Fraud Management

Mehmet Yigit Yildirim$^{(\boxtimes)}$, Mert Ozer, and Hasan Davulcu

Arizona State University, Tempe, AZ 85281, USA
{yigityildirim, mozer, hdavulcu}@asu.edu

Abstract. Every online transaction comes with a risk and it is the merchant's liability to detect and stop fraudulent transactions. Merchants utilize various mechanisms to prevent and manage fraud such as automated fraud detection systems and manual transaction reviews by expert fraud analysts. Many proposed solutions mostly focus on fraud detection accuracy and ignore financial considerations. Also, highly effective manual review process is overlooked. We propose Profit Optimizing Neural Risk Manager (PONRM), a decision maker that (a) constitutes optimal collaboration between machine learning models and human expertise under industrial constraints, (b) is cost and profit sensitive. We suggest directions on how to characterize fraudulent behavior and assess the risk of a transaction. We show that our framework outperforms cost-sensitive and cost-insensitive baselines on three real-world merchant datasets.

Keywords: Fraud detection · Cost-sensitive learning · Risk management
E-commerce

1 Introduction

In 2016, card fraud cost businesses over \$20 billion and it is still continuing to grow dramatically [4]. Around 60% of this loss was caused by online transactions, as e-commerce fraud rates have doubled since last year. E-commerce fraud magnitude is estimated to reach \$71 billion during the next five years due to the steady rise in cost per fraudulent transaction while fraud rates continue to increase [13].

During fraud management, merchants are generally liable for paying for the fraud costs in the e-commerce ecosystem. They suffer the losses arising from shipped merchandise, shipping and handling costs alongside chargeback fees issued by the card processor [17]. Lexis Nexis reports that for every dollar of loss, merchants end up losing \$2.40 on average as fraud management costs [14]. When aggregated, they lose around 1.5% of their total revenue to fraud today - three times increase during the last 3 years. So, they implement various strategies to fight fraud from automated fraud prevention systems to manual order reviews by expert fraud analysts [6].

Electronic supplementary material The online version of this chapter (https://doi.org/10.1007/978-3-319-92007-8_28) contains supplementary material, which is available to authorized users.

One may think that manual reviews will be going away with advances in artificial intelligence; however, they remain very much relevant to the industry thanks to their accuracy. According to CyberSource, manual review is an established mechanism for fraud prevention with adoption by 79% of North American businesses [7]. Despite all efforts to fight fraud, significant improvements can still be made by investigating and answering the following questions: What are the most important characteristics of a fraudulent transaction that a merchant can capture without causing friction? As state-of-the-art machine learning algorithms are not perfect how should a merchant use them? What is the cost optimal role of expert manual reviews in this process?

Improving fraud prevention is not as straightforward as increasing fraud detection accuracy due to several factors: firstly, rejecting a legitimate order and approving a fraudulent transaction do not incur the same cost, secondly, transaction amount varies greatly by order, thus affecting profitability of a sale. Hence, merchants need to implement cost and profit sensitive fraud prevention strategies.

In this work, we introduce Profit Optimizing Neural Risk Manager (PONRM), a cost-sensitive decision maker for e-commerce fraud management. Our framework infers the risk of a transaction being fraud and combines it with the transaction amount to make an optimal decision regarding its fraud management strategy (i.e. automated accept, reject or manual review). The main contributions of our work are:

- A cost-sensitive decision making framework to manage fraud while maximizing profits and minimizing costs;
- A transaction risk model incorporating fraud characteristics and financial constraints relevant to a merchant;
- An optimal collaboration strategy between human experts and machine learning models for fraud management.

2 Related Work

Fraud detection has been an active area for data mining researchers since 1994 [10]; however, it has not been extensively studied due to private and confidential nature of financial data. Despite these limitations, researchers managed to conduct studies with industry partners on proprietary datasets. Major studies focusing on credit card fraud include: [3, 16, 21]. In related areas, product review fraud detection work [12] have also received attention. Theoretical contributions focusing on fraud detection applications such as [24, 25] are also made. Survey papers on fraud detection methods include [18, 20].

Although fraud loss is an enormous problem for e-commerce merchants, there is only a pair of studies [5, 11] investigating this problem from a merchant's perspective. However, these works aim to improve the accuracy of fraud detection alone, instead of developing a profit and loss aware fraud management strategy.

Fraud prevention teams must take various complications that arise from allowing or rejecting a transaction into account. Declining a legitimate transaction would often result in a loss of that customer's business whereas approving a fraudulent transaction would force the merchant to cover the fraud costs. Simply training a machine learning classifier by overlooking various costs leads to a less than optimal fraud management strategy. Researchers have been developing cost-sensitive learning frameworks including [2, 8, 9, 15, 22].

In [5], the role of manual reviews in fraud prevention process is recognized; however, authors do not provide a systematic analysis on how to integrate machine learning based detection with manual reviews under cost and capacity constraints. In this paper, we develop a cost-sensitive fraud management framework incorporating all relevant capacities, costs and evaluate its financial impact with real-world merchant datasets.

3   Problem Definition

Every online transaction comes with a risk of being fraudulent. As merchants are responsible for detecting fraud, they must take this risk into account or they would suffer from losses due to fraud. So, when a merchant receives an order it can accept, reject or manually review that transaction based on their risk assessment of that transaction. Brief explanation of each decision is as follows:

Accept: Accepting a transaction means that merchant approves the transaction and processes the payment. Accepting a legitimate transaction yields some profit. If the transaction turns out to be fraudulent, merchant becomes responsible for the dispute handling and losses.

Reject: Rejecting a transaction means that merchant declines the transaction and payment does not go through. In this case, sale does not happen, so they will not be earning a profit even if the order was legitimate. However, rejecting a legitimate transaction may cause the loss of lifetime value of the customer.

Review: In the case of sending the transaction to manual review, merchant halts the order and sends the transaction details to an expert fraud analyst for investigation. Fraud analyst would confirm the legitimacy of the order by manually analyzing the transaction details and by following-up with the consumer directly before approving or rejecting it. For the sake of our modeling, we assume that manual review always leads to correct decisions. However, expert fraud analysts are scarce and expensive resources and should be utilized wisely.

We refer to these decisions made for a set of transactions as the *fraud management strategy*. We define the task of finding an optimal fraud management strategy as follows: Given a streaming set of transactions, determine the accept, reject, and review populations to maximize profits by accepting most of the legitimate transactions; and achieve this objective by minimizing customer insults, fraud losses, and costly manual reviews.

4   Methodology

Figure 1 presents an overview of our system. It consists of two learning and a pair of data manipulation components. The workflow starts with a data preprocessing and feature extraction task. 2nd component of the system carries out the task of inferring the probability of each transaction being fraudulent. 3rd component of the system generates cost-sensitive labels. 4th and final component of the system learns a function to maximize the profit based on a criteria incorporating the transaction amount and its fraud risk probability. We call this component as Profit Optimizing Neural Risk Manager (PONRM). Each following subsection explains one component of our system in detail and their order is aligned with the numbering in Fig. 1.

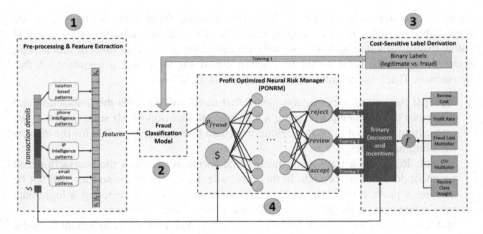

Fig. 1. System overview

4.1   Feature Extraction

Identifying consumer behavior to detect fraud is a delicate task. Businesses are hesitant to implement multi-factor authentication systems since it can be a source of friction and collecting invasive information such as cookie mining and device fingerprinting may damage the merchant's reputation. However, it may be possible to develop fraud prevention models without above options since merchants already have access to a rich source of information about their customers: the order form. Customers provide their personal and contact information to ensure the delivery of their order, so these can be leveraged by the fraud teams to build models. We present 4 types of patterns that merchants can reproduce:

Location Based Patterns: We measure the distance between IP geolocation and physical addresses. We create risk profiles for zip codes based on historical fraud behaviors observed from corresponding districts.

Phone Intelligence Patterns: Usage of VOIP, prepaid, spoofed, or invalid phone number is detected and may indicate malicious intent. Area code of a phone number is used to verify the (in-)consistency with the physical address.

IP Intelligence Patterns: An IP address coming through a proxy or an anonymous network could indicate risky behavior. We also profile the risk based on historical fraudulent behavior observed from blocks of IPs.

Email Address Patterns: We create email domain related attributes such as existence, disposability, anonymity, tenure, and category. Informed by [23], we derive features directly from the email handle (i.e. different email address characteristics such as character diversity, typing efficiency, proportion of numbers, etc.) to determine if an email address has been created with malicious intent.

By normalizing, profiling and combining these patterns, we come up with a set of 102 features that is used in our fraud classification model.

4.2 Fraud Classification Model and Risk Score Calculation

Risk score constitutes the input of the proposed model, PONRM. It is composed of a pair of elements: first element is the transaction amount (\$) and second element is a probability score of the transaction being fraudulent given its features. We propose using any supervised learner (θ) providing a robust posterior probability for fraud probability estimation such as:

$$\mathbf{f}_i = P(\mathbf{Y}_{i2} = 1 | \mathbf{X}_i; \theta)$$

where $\mathbf{f} = \{\mathbf{f}_i; \mathbf{f}_i \in [0, 1] \wedge i = 1 \ldots N\}$. As given in Equation [eq:f], $\mathbf{f}$ is assigned with the probability of a transaction being fraudulent. Finally, the risk score matrix $\mathbf{R}$ is built by concatenating $\mathbf{f}$ and the transaction amount (\$) as;

$$\mathbf{R} = [\mathbf{f}, \$]$$

4.3 Cost-Sensitive Label Derivation

The 3rd component is concerned with the training labels that PONRM will use. Cost-sensitive models require a pair of entities to be trained with: ground-truth decisions and cost-sensitive incentives for those decisions (Elkan 2001). Possible decisions are to *accept*, *review*, and *reject* a transaction. Incentives are determined based on earnings and losses that may arise from accepting, reviewing, or rejecting.

From Binary Labels to Trinary Ground-Truth Decisions: In the ideal binary decision making process, the model would accept all legitimate and reject all fraudulent transactions. However, models often fall short in performance compared to time consuming expert manual reviews in reality. To optimally integrate highly accurate but costly manual reviews into a decision making framework, a translation from binary to trinary decisions is necessary. Weight of the review decisions should be manipulatable based on the review capacity of a merchant. Following these constraints, we translate binary (legitimate, fraudulent) labels to trinary (accept, review, reject) decisions as $[\mathbf{Z}_{i1}, \mathbf{Z}_{i2}, \mathbf{Z}_{i3}]$. After the translation, legitimate transactions become $\mathbf{Z}_i = [1, r, 0]$ while fraudulent transactions become $\mathbf{Z}_i = [0, r, 1]$ as ground-truth decisions. r is a parameter for tuning the number of review decisions vs. accept/reject decisions, proportionally.

Computing Cost-Sensitive Decision Incentives: By following the fraud management strategy considerations from Sect. 3, we incentivize our decisions with 4 parameters, namely: *profit rate* (*pr*), *lifetime value multiplier* (*ltv*), *fraud loss multiplier* (*flm*), and *review cost* (*rc*). *Profit rate* is defined as the percentage of the transaction amount the merchant is earning as profit. *Lifetime value multiplier* simply models the lost opportunity due to losing customer's future business when a legitimate transaction is rejected (customer insult). *Fraud loss multiplier* weights the losses due to fraudulent activity to represent associated legal and chargeback costs. Finally, *review cost* is the compensation expert manual reviewers are paid per transaction. Derivation of the incentives for each decision is presented in Table 1. Although rejecting a fraudulent transaction does not provide any benefit, it is still the most desirable decision for a fraudulent transaction. From an information theoretic perspective, there is a need for a positive scalar to incentivize the learning process. To stay truthful to the initial incentives but represent most desirable decisions we offset the incentives: we add the initial incentive of accepting a fraudulent transaction to every decision incentive for fraudulent transactions. We add the initial incentive of rejecting a legitimate transaction to every decision incentive for legitimate transactions.

Table 1. Incentives for accepting, reviewing or rejecting a transaction

	Decision incentives		
	Accept	Review	Reject
Legitimate	$pr * \$_i$	$pr * \$_i - rc$	$-pr * \$_i * ltv$
Legitimate - Offset	$(1 + ltv) * pr * \$_i$	$(1 + ltv) * pr * \$_i - rc$	0
Fraudulent	$-flm * \$_i$	$-rc$	0
Fraudulent - Offset	0	$flm * \$_i - rc$	$flm * \$_i$

4.4 Profit-Optimizing Neural Risk Manager

Many of the off-the-shelf classification models are cost-insensitive; thus are sub-optimal for our task. Cost of accepting a fraudulent transaction and cost of rejecting a legitimate transaction can vary largely in different settings. While these costs differ between legitimate and fraudulent cases, they are also dependent on the transaction amounts. Moreover, off-the-shelf classification tools are not very adaptable for the expert opinion to intervene when necessary.

Hence, we formally define Profit Optimizing Neural Risk Manager (PONRM) which produces decisions as accept, review, or reject for transactions according to each transaction's risk score. PONRM mostly mimics a multilayer perceptron structure with sigmoid activation functions;

$$\mathbf{R}_i = [\mathbf{f}_i, \$_i]$$
$$\mathbf{H}^{(0)} = \sigma\left(\mathbf{W}^{(0)}\mathbf{R} + \mathbf{b}^{(0)}\right)$$
$$\mathbf{H}^{(i)} = \sigma\left(\mathbf{W}^{(i)}\mathbf{H}^{(i-1)} + \mathbf{b}^{(i)}\right) \qquad \text{for } i = 1,\ldots,l$$
$$\hat{\mathbf{Z}} = softmax\left(\mathbf{W}^{(l+1)}\mathbf{H}^{(l)} + \mathbf{b}^{(l+1)}\right)$$

where $\mathbf{R} \in \mathbb{R}_+^{N \times 2}$ is the risk score matrix. Each $\mathbf{H}^{(i)} \in \mathbb{R}^{N \times \sqrt{L}}$ is a higher dimensional ($\sqrt{L}$) internal representation of the risk score in the multilayer perceptron. It outputs the decisions for each transaction in the output layer $\hat{\mathbf{Z}} \in [0,1]^{N \times 3}$. To learn the parameters of the model, we use log loss multiplied by cost sensitive incentives and minimize the loss function by tuning $\mathbf{W}^{(i)}$, $\mathbf{b}^{(i)}$:

$$Loss = -\frac{1}{N}[\sum_{i=1}^{N}\sum_{c=1}^{3}\overbrace{\left[\mathbf{Z}_{ic}\log\hat{\mathbf{Z}}_{ic}\right]}^{log-loss}\overbrace{\mathbf{B}_{ic}}^{incentive}] + \overbrace{\sum_{i=1}^{l}\alpha_i\|\mathbf{W}^{(i)}\|_2^2}^{regularization}$$

where N is the number of transactions. $\mathbf{Z}_{ic}$ quantifies the weight of assignment of the ground-truth decision c to the transaction i. $\hat{\mathbf{Z}}_{ic}$ is the predicted assignments by the PONRM model for transaction i and decision c. $\mathbf{B} \in \mathbb{R}^{N \times 3}$ and $\mathbf{B}_{ic}$ quantifies the incentive of assigning the ith transaction to decision c. We use L-BFGS quasi-newton optimization implementation of ScipyOptimizer interface of Tensorflow to minimize the proposed loss function [1].

5 Experiments

Here, we evaluate the performance of our framework in various settings. In the first experiment, we present the effectiveness of PONRM in comparison to other cost-sensitive and cost-insensitive approaches. Next, we evaluate the performance of our system alongside baseline risk managers under different manual review capacities. Finally, we explore how fraud classification models perform with and without risk managers.

5.1 Evaluation Metrics

We introduce a new metric, named profit gain (PG), to measure the performance of our framework and the baseline models in a financially sound way. We normalize this metric using two extreme fraud management strategies:

No Fraud Management: A merchant can choose not to interfere with any orders and accept all transactions as if they were legitimate. Then, it would suffer the maximum loss from fraudulent orders but not from any customer insults. We refer the total profit this company makes as $\$_{nofraudmanagement}$.

Oracle: If a merchant could model the fraud characteristics perfectly, it would be accepting all legitimate orders and rejecting the fraudulent ones. In this case, its fraud and customer insult loss would be zero. It would earn the profit from all the legitimate transactions. We refer its total profit as $\$_{oracle}$.

To robustly measure the financial performance gain with a standardized scoring mechanism, we introduce *profit gain* as:

$$profit\ gain = \frac{\$_m - \$_{no\ fraudmanagement}}{\$_{oracle} - \$_{no\ fraudmanagement}}$$

where $\$_m$ is the profit of the model under experimentation. While calculating the profits, not-offset decision incentives in Table 1 is used. Also, we use *F-measure* to evaluate our fraud detection performance. As we assume perfect decisions by reviewers, review decisions are treated as accept for legitimate and reject for fraudulent transactions in calculation of F-measure. Each experiment is run 16 times and the average performance is reported for each parameter setting. For each parameter configuration, the best performing setting in terms of PG is reported as the representative performance of a model.

5.2   Dataset and Parameter Settings

We work with online transactions of three e-commerce merchants; an online travel agency, a physical goods store, and a digital goods store. We sample 1 month of transactional data for each company (October 2017), and remove transactions that do not include a transaction amount. Since some of the transactions have different currencies than USD, all the transaction amounts are converted to USD equivalent. Next, features are extracted as described in Sect. 4.1 for all datasets. Categorical features are one-hot encoded to ensure compatibility across different classifiers. Missing values are imputed with mean-values for the numeric, with 'Category-other' for the categorical variables. We estimate each merchant's manual review capacity according to [7]. Table 2 presents the datasets' descriptive statistics.

Table 2. Descriptive statistics

	OTA	PGS	DGS
Transactions	22,203	36,783	39,784
Fraudulent transactions	349 (1.57%)	253 (0.69%)	1,536 (3.86%)
Transaction amount mean (μ)	$622.25	$177.22	$75.61
$\mu_{fraudulent} / \mu_{legitimate}$	1.06	0.84	0.87
Manual review capacity	30%	20%	10%

We use the first 80% of the transactions as the training dataset, and the rest as the test dataset. To calculate the decision incentives, we set profit rate (pr) to 5%, lifetime value multiplier (ltv) to 3, fraud loss multiplier (flm) to 2.4, and review cost to $3 based on estimates from the merchants. For fraud classification models, we experiment with logistic regression (LR), gradient boosting machine (GBM), multilayer perceptron (MLP), and random forests (RF).

5.3   PONRM vs. Cost-Sensitive and Cost-Insensitive Baselines

In this experiment set, we investigate PONRM's performance in different settings in comparison with baseline cost sensitive and cost insensitive approaches.

Experimental Setup: Among all fraud classification models multilayer perceptron (MLP) resembles a similar structure to PONRM, hence, we report its performance characteristics alongside PONRM.

Baselines: We introduce the following baseline architectures:

- **MLP** is the multilayer perceptron classifier. We train a cost insensitive MLP classifier to detect legitimate and fraud detections. Transactions classified as legitimate are given *accept*, and those as fraudulent are given *reject* decisions.
- **CostMLP** is a cost sensitive binary classification model. It uses MLP as its learning component. Incentives of rejecting and accepting are given alongside with binary transaction labels. As in MLP, transactions classified as legitimate are given *accept*, and fraudulent are given *reject* decisions.
- **CostMLPwithR** is a cost sensitive trinary classification model. It uses MLP as its learning component. Incentives are given alongside trinary ground-truth decisions. Practically, it is the same as feeding transaction features to PONRM directly and bypassing the fraud classification model.
- **MLP+PONRM** is our proposed framework. It uses MLP as its fraud classification model component and PONRM as the risk manager.

We use profit gain (PG) and F-Measure to evaluate performances of above listed models. A grid search with $l = [0, 1, 2, 3]$ and $\alpha = [0, 0.0001]$ is performed for each MLP based model. First layer's layer size (L) is set to 300 in PONRM and other MLP based models. Each consecutive layer's size is calculated by square-rooting the previous layer's size.

Results: MLP+PONRM framework shows superior performance in terms of both performance metrics. Models with review decision options (CostMLPwithR, MLP+PONRM) also achieve superior results than models without review decision options (MLP, CostMLP). Cost sensitive approaches (CostMLP, CostMLPwithR) perform better than their cost insensitive counterpart (MLP) for maximizing the profit gain and increasing F-Measure. One exception is the F-Measure performance in PGS dataset where having the smallest average fraudulent transaction amount leads to lower gains in decision incentives biased for rejecting fraudulent transactions. Thus, CostMLP performs worse than MLP.

Our proposed framework MLP+PONRM consistently overperforms Cost-MLPwithR. Even in CostMLPwithR's best performing case, MLP+PONRM achieves 20% greater profit gain and 24% better F-Measure overall (Table 3).

Table 3. Comparison between PONRM and cost sensitive and insensitive baselines

	OTA		PGS		DGS	
	PG	F-Meas	PG	F-Meas	PG	F-Meas
MLP	0.1207	0.2769	0.0170	0.3115	0.1727	0.4143
CostMLP	0.0325	0.2874	0.0673	0.3048	0.2100	0.4222
CostMLPwithR	0.5954	0.7599	0.5280	0.7510	0.4541	0.5021
MLP+PONRM	**0.8113**	**0.8690**	**0.6514**	**0.8523**	**0.5876**	**0.6661**

5.4 PONRM vs. Risk Managers Under Different Review Capacities

In our third experiment set, we aim to show the efficacy of PONRM in comparison with other baseline risk managers in maximizing profit gain. We also explore the performance under different review capacities to ensure robust execution of our framework under various financial settings.

Baselines: Coupled with RF fraud classification model, we introduce 2 baseline fraud management strategies to compare with PONRM as follows:

- **Naive Risk Manager (NRM):** This model assigns accept/reject decisions based on a fraud classification model. If fraud classification model classifies the transaction as legitimate, it accepts, and if as fraudulent, it rejects. Next, it selects transactions randomly based on the review capacity and converts their decisions to review.
- **Price Prioritized Risk Manager (PPRM):** Similar to NRM, this risk manager uses a fraud classification model to produce initial decisions as *accept* or *reject*. Next, it assigns the transactions having the highest transaction amounts to review considering the capacity under experimentation. To achieve this, it first finds a transaction amount threshold based on the observed historical data, then sends the transactions exceeding this threshold until the specified review capacity is filled.

Experimental Setup: To be able to compare the performance of different risk managers, we fix the fraud classification model. Due to the space constraints, we only report the experiments with RF and others can be found in the supplementary material.[1] RF is chosen due to its superior performance. We explore different parameters of RF as number of trees being $n = [10, 50, 100, 200]$.

We run experiments with review ratios of 10%, 20%, 30%, and 40% and report their profit gain accordingly. Since there is no standard setting to enforce PONRM to produce any of the review ratios of 10%, 20%, 30% or 40%, we experiment with different values of the parameter *review class weight* (r) between 0.4 and 1.1 with 0.05 increments. According to the review ratio each PONRM experiment produces, we chunk them into bins of 10%, 20%, 30% or 40% review rates. We pick the best average performance of PONRM in the bins as the representative performance of the corresponding bin. Setting the review ratios for NRM and PPRM is straightforward.

---

[1] http://www.public.asu.edu/ ~ myildir3/cost_supp.pdf.

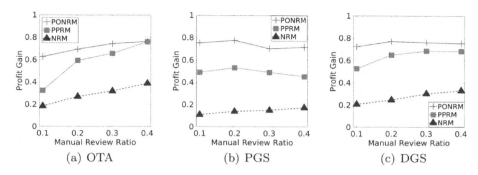

Fig. 2. Performance of Risk Managers under Different Review Capacities

Results: Fig. 2 shows PONRM's performance in terms of Profit Gain when manual review capacity of the user is tweaked between 0.1 and 0.4. At first sight, it is clear that PONRM performs superior to the two baseline risk managers. Some other key findings are given as follows:

- Profit gain improves when manual review capacity is increased in OTA Dataset. For most of its transactions, review cost is negligible compared to the expected loss or profit, thus, when given maximum capacity, sending as much transactions as possible to review makes sense.
- Sending most transactions to manual review may not be a sound strategy for PGS and DGS datasets due to lower transaction amounts. Each merchant must identify the optimal manual review ratio and implement its model accordingly. This would also let the merchant save time and resources by automating the process more.
- When manual review capacity is 10%, PONRM performs up to **3 times** better than PPRM and **4 times** better than NRM. However, PPRM slowly catches up when the manual review ratio is unrealistically high.
- PPRM's constantly superior performance compared to NRM asserts that consideration of the transaction amount is crucial for risk management.

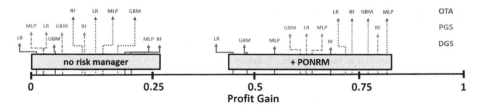

Fig. 3. Profit gain of fraud classification models with and without risk managers

5.5   Which Classifier to Use as the Fraud Classification Model

Posterior probability distribution based on the selected classifier may greatly affect the performance of PONRM. Thus, we experiment with four previously mentioned supervised learners to demonstrate their effects in the framework. Experimental setup and parameter settings are explored as in Sect. 5.4 and results with best parameter combinations are reported here for the sake of brevity. More detailed parameter analysis and guidance can be found in the supplementary material.

Results: Fig. 3 demonstrates the performance of fraud classification models with and without PONRM. Some major findings are given as follows:

- RF based fraud classification model with no risk manager often produces better results than the others with no risk manager. Especially its effectiveness in terms of profit gain contributes significantly to the RF+PONRM's performance, hence RF +PONRM generally gives the best performance.
- MLP+PONRM performs well on all datasets. Specifically, on OTA, it is marginally the best model where MLP uses only one hidden layer. There is a negative correlation between MLP+PONRM performance and number of layers in the MLP fraud classification model as it does not represent uncertainty accurately when complex.
- GBM+PONRM does not perform well as GBM is known to distort its posterior probabilities [19]. Since PONRM relies on the representation power of posterior probabilities, GBM is not an appropriate choice for our purposes.
- As a heuristic, profit gain of the fraud classification model can be used for model selection due to its positive correlation with PONRM's profit gain.

6   Conclusion and Future Work

In this study, we propose a cost-sensitive decision making framework and demonstrate its effectiveness in fraud management. We reveal how human expertise can be combined with machine learning to make decisions under risk and cost considerations. Future work includes developing a novel metric to characterize the relationship between fraud classification models and PONRM performances. Also, we plan to investigate the generalizability of our framework to other domains such as loan evaluation and healthcare decision support.

Acknowledgements. We thank Amador Testa and Ozgun Baris Bekki from Emailage Corp. for providing the datasets and their valuable industry insights.

References

1. Abadi, M., et al.: TensorFlow: Large-Scale Machine Learning on Heterogeneous Systems (2015). https://www.tensorflow.org/
2. Abe, N., Zadrozny, B., Langford, J.: An iterative method for multi-class cost-sensitive learning. In: Proceedings of the Tenth ACM SIGKDD International Conference on Knowledge Discovery and Data Mining, pp. 3–11. ACM (2004)
3. Bolton, R.J., Hand, D.J.: Statistical fraud detection: a review. Stat. Sci. JSTOR 17, 235–249 (2002)
4. Card Fraud Losses Reaches $21.84 Billion. Whitepaper. The Nilson Report (2016)
5. Carneiro, N., Figueira, G., Costa, M.: A data mining based system for credit-card fraud detection in E-Tail. Decis. Support Syst. 95, 91–101 (2017)
6. CyberSource: 2016 North America online fraud benchmark report. Report. CyberSource Corporation (2016)
7. CyberSource: 2017 North America online fraud benchmark Report. Report. CyberSource Corporation (2017)
8. Domingos, P.: Metacost: a general method for making classifiers cost-sensitive. In: Proceedings of the Fifth ACM SIGKDD International Conference on Knowledge Discovery and Data Mining, pp. 155–64. ACM (1999)
9. Elkan, C.: The foundations of cost-sensitive learning. In: International Joint Conference on Artificial Intelligence, vol. 17, pp. 973–78. Lawrence Erlbaum Associates Ltd. (2001)
10. Ghosh, S., Reilly, D.L.: Credit card fraud detection with a neural-network. In: Proceedings of the Twenty-Seventh Hawaii International Conference on System Sciences, vol. 3, pp. 621–30. IEEE (1994)
11. Halvaiee, N.S., Akbari, M.K.: A novel model for credit card fraud detection using artificial immune systems. Appl. Soft Comput. 24, 40–49 (2014)
12. Hooi, B., et al.: Fraudar: bounding graph fraud in the face of Camouflage. In: Proceedings of the 22nd ACM SIGKDD International Conference on Knowledge Discovery and Data Mining, pp. 895–904. ACM (2016)
13. Juniper: Online Payment Fraud: Emerging Threats, Key Vertical Strategies & Market Forecasts 2017-2022. Whitepaper. Juniper Research (2017)
14. KS&R: 2016 LexisNexis true cost of fraud study. Report. LexisNexis Risk Solutions (2016)
15. Ling, C.X., Sheng, V.S.: Cost-sensitive learning. In: Sammut, C., Webb, G.I. (eds.) Encyclopedia of Machine Learning, pp. 231–235. Springer, New York (2011)
16. Maes, S., Tuyls, K., Vanschoenwinkel, B., Manderick, B.: Credit card fraud detection using Bayesian and neural networks. In: Proceedings of the 1st International Naiso Congress on Neuro Fuzzy Technologies, pp. 261–270 (2002)
17. Montague, D.A.: Essentials of Online Payment Security and Fraud Prevention, vol. 54. Wiley, Hoboken (2010)
18. Ngai, E.W.T., et al.: The application of data mining techniques in financial fraud detection: a classification framework and an academic review of literature. Decis. Support Syst. 50(3), 559–569 (2011)
19. Niculescu-Mizil, A., Caruana, R.: Obtaining calibrated probabilities from boosting. In: UAI, p. 413 (2005)
20. Phua, C., Lee, V., Smith, K., Gayler, R.: A comprehensive survey of data mining-based fraud detection research. arXiv Preprint arXiv:1009.6119 (2010)
21. Van Vlasselaer, V., et al.: APATE: a novel approach for automated credit card transaction fraud detection using network-based extensions. Decis. Support Syst. 75, 38–48 (2015)

22. Zadrozny, B., Langford, J., Abe, N.: Cost-sensitive learning by cost-proportionate example weighting. In: Third IEEE International Conference on Data Mining, ICDM 2003, pp. 435–42. IEEE (2003)
23. Zafarani, R., Liu, H.: 10 Bits of surprise: detecting malicious users with minimum information. In: Proceedings of the 24th ACM International on Conference on Information and Knowledge Management, pp. 423–31. ACM (2015)
24. Zhang, S., et al.: HiDDen: hierarchical dense subgraph detection with application to financial fraud detection. In: Proceedings of the 2017 SIAM International Conference on Data Mining, pp. 570–78. SIAM (2017)
25. Zhou, D., et al.: A local algorithm for structure-preserving graph cut. In: Proceedings of the 23rd ACM SIGKDD International Conference on Knowledge Discovery and Data Mining, pp. 655–664. ACM (2017)

Echo State Network for Classification of Human Eye Movements During Decision Making

Petia Koprinkova-Hristova[1]([⊠]) [iD], Miroslava Stefanova[2],
Bilyana Genova[2], and Nadejda Bocheva[2] [iD]

[1] Institute of Information and Communication Technologies, Bulgarian
Academy of Sciences, Sofia, Bulgaria
pkoprinkova@bas.bg
[2] Institute of Neurobiology, Bulgarian Academy of Sciences, Sofia, Bulgaria
{mirad_st,b.genova}@abv.bg, nadya@percept.bas.bg

Abstract. The paper develops further a recently proposed author's approach for classification of dynamic data series using a class of Recurrent Neural Network (RNN) called Echo state network (ESN). It exploits the Intrinsic Plasticity (IP) tuning of ESN reservoir of neurons to fit their dynamics to the data fed into the reservoir input. A novel approach for ranking of a data base of dynamic data series into groups using the length of the multidimensional vector of reservoir state achieved after consecutive feeding of each time series into the ESN is proposed here. It is tested on eye tracker recordings of human eye movements during visual stimulation and decision making process. The preliminary results demonstrated the ability of the proposed technique to discriminate dynamic data series.

Keywords: Echo state network · Time series · Classification · Eye tracking

1 Introduction

In previous author's work [1] a novel approach for unsupervised clustering of static multidimensional data sets using a class of RNNs called Echo state networks [2, 3] was proposed. Next it was successfully tested on numerous practical examples and the results were summarized in [4]. In [5] the approach was upgraded and applied for classification of dynamic data series too.

The core of the approach, proposed first in [1], was to use the ESN to extract more informative features from multidimensional data sets. For this aim equilibrium states of the ESN reservoir neurons corresponding to every multidimensional data item presented to the ESN input were used. As it was shown in [6], the fitting of the ESN reservoir dynamics to reflect the input data structure can be achieved by an approach for ESN reservoir tuning called Intrinsic Plasticity (IP) [7, 8] that is aimed at achieving the desired distribution of the ESN reservoir output.

Since the number of the new extracted features depends on the size of the ESN, question how to choose the most proper among them is still under investigation.

L. Iliadis et al. (Eds.): AIAI 2018, IFIP AICT 519, pp. 337–348, 2018.
https://doi.org/10.1007/978-3-319-92007-8_29

Initially [1, 4] it was proposed to choose only two of all possible neurons steady states based on their distribution in one- or two-dimensional space [4]. Next in [9] we tried to extend the number of representative neurons until the accuracy of data clustering increases. However, this approach increased computational burden too much. That is why here another approach was proposed: to use the geometric size of the vector of all reservoir states and then to rank the time series data based on that single feature.

The approach was tested on dynamic series of eye movements data collected during psycho-physiological experiments with humans observing specific visual stimuli and making decisions. The preliminary results demonstrated the ability of the proposed approach to rank the time series of human eye movements in dependence on their characteristics.

The paper is organized as follows: next chapter describes briefly the ESN structure and its IP tuning and the newly proposed feature extraction approach; next the experimental set-up and the collected time series data are described; the results from classification by the proposed algorithm are presented and discussed in section four; the paper finished with concluding remarks and directions for future work.

2   Clustering Algorithm

2.1   Echo State Network and IP Tuning

ESN, shown on Fig. 1, is a type of recurrent neural network that belongs to the novel and fast developing family of reservoir computing approaches [2, 3]. The ESN output for the current time instance k is the vector $out(k)$ with size n_{out}. It is a linear function f^{out} (usually identity) of the vectors of the current states of the input $in(k)$ (with size n_{in}) and the reservoir neurons $X(k)$ (with size n_X):

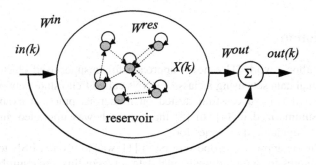

Fig. 1. Echo state network structure.

$$y(k) = f^{out}(W^{out}[in(k), X(k)])$$
(1)

Here W^{out} is a trainable $n_{out} \times (n_{in} + n_X)$ matrix. The neurons in the reservoir have a simple sigmoid output function f^{res} (usually hyperbolic tangent) that depends on both the ESN input $in(k)$ and the previous reservoir state $X(k-1)$:

$$X(k) = f^{res}\left(W^{in}in(k) + W^{res}X(k-1)\right) \tag{2}$$

Here W^{in} and W^{res} are $n_{in} \times n_X$ and $n_X \times n_X$ randomly generated weight matrices that are not trainable.

The main reason for development of such a type of RNN is to simplify their training algorithm. However, it appeared that although non-trainable weights can be random, there is need to tune them initially. For this aim different approaches were proposed [2, 3]. In [7, 8] an algorithm called intrinsic plasticity (IP) was proposed. Its aim was to increase the entropy of the reservoir neurons outputs by minimization of the Kullback-Leibler divergence:

$$D_{KL}(p(X), p_d(X)) = \int p(r) \log\left(\frac{p(X)}{p_d(X)}\right) \tag{2}$$

that is a measure for the difference between the actual $p(X)$ and the desired $p_d(X)$ probability distribution of reservoir neurons states X.

It was proven that for the commonly used hyperbolic tangent at the reservoir neurons output the proper target distribution has to be the Gaussian one. For this aim two additional reservoir parameters, gain a and bias b (both vectors with size n_X), were introduced in [8] as follows:

$$X(k) = f^{res}\left(diag(a)W^{in}in(k) + diag(a)W^{res}X(k-1) + b\right) \tag{3}$$

The IP training is gradient descent algorithm [8] minimizing the Kullback-Leibler divergence by adjustment of the vectors a and b.

2.2 Classification Approach for Dynamic Data Series

In [6] was demonstrated that besides its initial aim, the IP tuning also fits the reservoir connections matrix to the structure of the input data presented to the ESN. Moreover, the equilibrium states of reservoir neurons corresponding to each one of the input data items used during IP tuning reflect the overall data structure [1, 4]. Thus collected in this way features can be used for further classification or clustering.

In [5] it was demonstrated that the reservoir state $X(N)$ reached after feeding of non-constant (time varying) sequence of inputs from $in(0)$ to $in(N)$ to the IP tuned ESN:

$$\begin{aligned}
X(N) &= f^{res}(diag(a)W^{in}in(N) + diag(a)W^{res}X(N-1) + b) \\
X(N-1) &= f^{res}(diag(a)W^{in}in(N-1) + diag(a)W^{res}X(N-2) + b) \\
&\cdots \\
X(1) &= f^{res}(diag(a)W^{in}in(0) + diag(a)W^{res}X(0) + b)
\end{aligned} \tag{4}$$

depends on dynamic characteristics of the time series *in* and can be exploited as a set of classification features.

Since the choice of neurons whose states are the best feature set for each particular data subject to classification or clustering is non-trivial [4, 9], here we propose another approach: to calculate the size of the vector containing all collected reservoir neurons states:

$$R = \sqrt{\sum_{i=1}^{n_X} x_i(N)^2}, \quad X(N) = [\, x_1(N) \quad x_2(N) \quad \cdots \quad x_{n_X}(N) \,] \tag{5}$$

and to use it as single discriminating data feature.

3   Experimental Set-Up

The time series data used to test the idea described above were collected by eye tracking device that recorded the human eye movements during a behavioral experiment performed with the participation of volunteer human subjects observing series of visual stimuli.

Each stimulus is composed by a sequence of consecutive frames. A frame contains of 50 dots presented in a circular aperture with a radius of 7.5 cm in the middle of the computer screen. The dots were grouped in 25 pairs placed at 2 cm distance from each other. Each pair of dots had a limited lifetime of 3 frames. On every frame one-third of the pairs changed position. Each frame lasted 33 ms. The orientation of the virtual lines connecting the dots in 18 pairs intersected in a common point considered as the center of each frame, while the rest 7 pairs had random orientations. The mean position of the centers of all frames in a stimulus sequence determines its "imaginary" center. We generated 14 different types of stimuli having centers at 7 positions shifted left and 7 positions shifted right from the screen midpoint. All shifts were in horizontal direction and varied between 0.67 cm and 4.67 cm with step of 0.67 cm. Ten different patterns for each center position were generated.

The stimuli were presented on a gray screen with mean luminance 50 cd/m^2 using 20.1″ NEC MultiSync LCD monitor with NvidiaQuadro 900XGL graphic board at a refresh rate of 60 Hz and screen resolution 1280 × 1024 pixels. The experiments were controlled by a custom program developed under Visual C++ and OpenGl.

The subject sat at 57 cm from the monitor screen. Each stimulus presentation was preceded by a warning sound signal. A red fixation point with size of 0.8 cm appeared in the center of the screen for 500 ms. The stimuli were presented immediately after the disappearance of the fixation point. The Subject's task was to continue looking at the position where the fixation point was presented until he/she made a decision where the center of the pattern was and to indicate this position by a saccade (fast eye movement). The subjects also had to press the left or the right mouse button depending on the perceived position of the center - to the left or to the right from the middle of the screen. If the subject could not make a decision during the stimulus presentation (3.3 s for 100 consecutive frames), the stimulus disappeared and the screen remained gray until the subject made a response.

The eye movements of the participants in the experiment were recorded by a specialized hardware – Jazz novo eye tracking system (Ober Consulting Sp. Z o.o.). All recordings from all the sensors of the device for one session per person were collected with 1 kHz frequency and the information is stored in files. These include: the calibration information; records of horizontal and vertical eye positions in degrees of visual angle eye_x and eye_y; screen sensor signal for presence/absence of a stimulus on the monitor; microphone signal recording sounds during the experiment; information about tested subjects (code) and type of the experimental trail for each particular record.

The raw data were processed to extract only the records during presence of a stimulus on the screen. The data between the stimuli was excluded since it is not relevant to the eye movements during task performance.

Three age groups took part in the experiment: young (from 20 to 35 years), elderly (from 57 to 84 years) and middle age group (from 25 to 55 years). From all collected experimental data we observed big variety of eye movement behaviors varying not only between three age groups but also within each group. So it was very hard to classify test subjects only on the basis of this information. Hence we decided to try whether the proposed above dynamic data discrimination approach can yield some reasonable results.

The input to the ESN was two dimensional vector composed by the visual angles data series recorded during presence of a stimulus on the screen, i.e. $in(k) = [\, eye_x(k) \quad eye_y(k)\,]$. We tuned three ESNs with reservoir sizes 10, 50 and 100 neurons using the IP algorithm described above. The extracted in this way feature of each dynamic data series was R calculated according to the Eq. (5). Thus the tested subjects were ordered based on the obtained value of R from their recorded eye movement data series.

4 Classification Results and Discussion

First we selected a representative group of four experienced test subjects from different age groups. These subjects took part in experimental set-up preparation so they were able to perform the behavioral tasks strictly and their eye movement recordings were clear from outliers due to improper behavior like looking to the mouse before clicking when decision was taken or keeping fixation. Such noisy behavior was observed with other volunteer subjects especially during their first trails.

Figure 2 represents the eye movements' data series collected from these four "experienced" test subjects who performed first the described above experiment. Subject 1 is the youngest, subject 3 is middle aged and other two subjects (2 and 4) belong to the elderly group.

We can easily distinguish the middle aged subject while similarities between subjects 2 and 4 are not so obvious. From Fig. 3, representing the variances of the data series, we can conclude that age differentiation by this characteristic is also a hard task even for such small group.

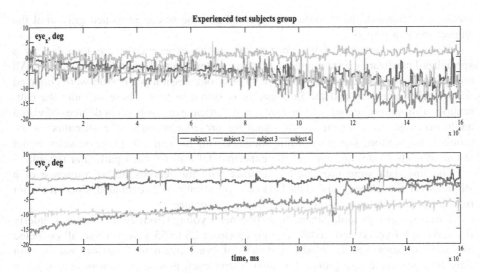

Fig. 2. Experienced 4 subjects' recordings from eye tracker.

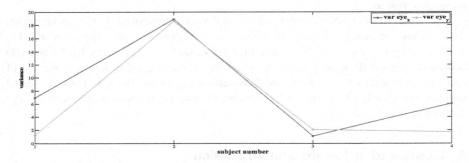

Fig. 3. Variances of eye movement coordinates from Fig. 2.

Then we applied described above classification approach to these data series. In order to prove the expected effect of IP tuning of the ESN reservoir, we compare the obtained feature value before (Fig. 4) and after (Fig. 5) its application to the three randomly generated ESN reservoirs containing 10, 50 and 100 neurons.

From Fig. 5 we can conclude that IP tuning definitely helps to classify our four subjects by their age no matter of the reservoir size.

As it was observed, the middle age subject was the best during experiments and his eye movements on Fig. 2 were significantly different from the other persons in the group. This was confirmed by our algorithm according to which the middle aged subject 3 is clearly differentiated from the other three experienced subjects of different ages. Moreover, the two elderly subjects 2 and 4 were classified as close to each other while the younger person 1 was clearly differentiated too.

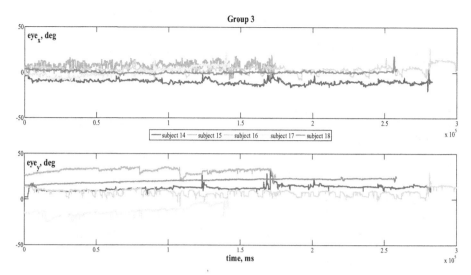

Fig. 8. Eye movements recorded from the elderly test subjects.

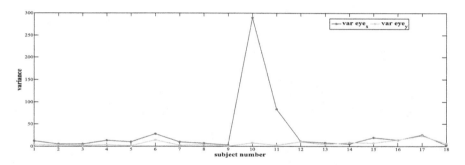

Fig. 9. Variances of eye movement coordinates for all test subjects.

Figure 11 represents the corresponding rank number of the subjects in dependence on the value of R from Fig. 10. The obtained subject order is similar for both ESN initial reservoirs. For most of the subjects two generations of ESN yielded the same rank. The same are the results from the ranking according to the mean value of R. The bigger differences are observed for the first and second subjects only.

However the obtained results showed that differentiation of tested subjects by age using only recorded eye movement behaviors is not possible since there are subjects from different age groups that received close ranks. Nevertheless, the approach seems promising for classification of types of eye movements during decision making that could be related to other psycho-physiological peculiarities of the tested subjects.

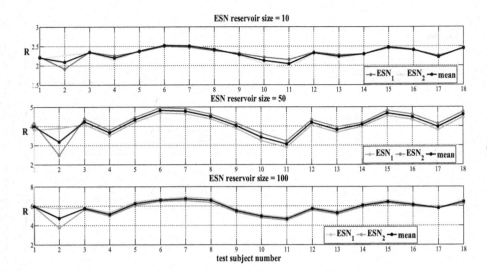

Fig. 10. Size of the reservoir state vector R for the three ESN reservoirs and all test subjects. ESN_1 and ESN_2 denote the results from the first and second ESN respectively; mean is the mean value between ESN_1 and ESN_2.

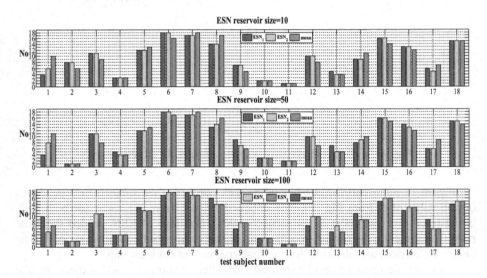

Fig. 11. Rank of the subjects according to the size of the reservoir vector R for the three ESN reservoirs and all test subjects. ESN_1 and ESN_2 denote the results from the first and second ESN respectively; mean is their mean value.

5 Conclusions

In conclusion, the proposed approach for classification of time series using the geometric size of the ESN reservoir vector state appears promising since it decreases significantly computational burden of the algorithm.

Concerning the classification of human subjects based on their eye movements, it is obvious that obtained ranking is not enough to separate the people into the groups related to their age. Since the achieved ranking of subjects remain stable using different initializations and sizes of ESN reservoir, we can search other similarities between tested subjects that this classification might reveal.

Another explanation of the reported results might be presence of outliers in the collected data since in these preliminary investigations the raw data was used. Hence further refinement of the collected experimental data base could help to reveal some age-related similarities of the recorded eye movements.

Another direction for future work can be inclusion of the additional information collected during the experiments like amplitude, velocity and acceleration of saccades performed during decision making as well as accuracy of the persons' response and the corresponding reaction time for each individual stimulus. All these characteristics can serve as features to support classification of test subjects in our future work.

Acknowledgment. The reported work is a part of and was supported by the project № DN02/3/2016 "Modelling of voluntary saccadic eye movements during decision making" funded by the Bulgarian Science Fund.

References

1. Koprinkova-Hristova, P., Tontchev, N.: Echo state networks for multi-dimensional data clustering. In: Villa, Alessandro E.P., Duch, W., Érdi, P., Masulli, F., Palm, G. (eds.) ICANN 2012. LNCS, vol. 7552, pp. 571–578. Springer, Heidelberg (2012). https://doi.org/10.1007/978-3-642-33269-2_72
2. Jaeger, H.: Tutorial on training recurrent neural networks, covering BPPT, RTRL, EKF and the "echo state network" approach. GMD Report 159, German National Research Center for Information Technology (2002)
3. Lukosevicius, M., Jaeger, H.: Reservoir computing approaches to recurrent neural network training. Comput. Sci. Rev. **3**, 127–149 (2009)
4. Koprinkova-Hristova, P.: Multi-dimensional data clustering and visualization via echo state networks. In: Kountchev, R., Nakamatsu, K. (eds.) New Approaches in Intelligent Image Analysis. ISRL, vol. 108, pp. 93–122. Springer, Cham (2016). https://doi.org/10.1007/978-3-319-32192-9_3
5. Koprinkova-Hristova, P., Alexiev, K.: Echo state networks in dynamic data clustering. In: Mladenov, V., Koprinkova-Hristova, P., Palm, G., Villa, A.E.P., Appollini, B., Kasabov, N. (eds.) ICANN 2013. LNCS, vol. 8131, pp. 343–350. Springer, Heidelberg (2013). https://doi.org/10.1007/978-3-642-40728-4_43
6. Koprinkova-Hristova, P.: On effects of IP improvement of ESN reservoirs for reflecting of data structure. In: Proceedings of the International Joint Conference on Neural Networks (IJCNN) 2015. IEEE, Killarney (2015). https://doi.org/10.1109/ijcnn.2015.7280703

7. Steil, J.J.: Online reservoir adaptation by intrinsic plasticity for back-propagation-decoleration and echo state learning. Neural Netw. **20**, 353–364 (2007)
8. Schrauwen, B., Wandermann, M., Verstraeten, D., Steil, J.J., Stroobandt, D.: Improving reservoirs using intrinsic plasticity. Neurocomputing **71**, 1159–1171 (2008)
9. Bozhkov, L., Koprinkova-Hristova, P., Georgieva, P.: Reservoir computing for emotion valence discrimination from EEG signals. Neurocomputing **231**, 28–40 (2017)

Medical Intelligence

Iliou Machine Learning Data Preprocessing Method for Stress Level Prediction

Theodoros Iliou[1], Georgia Konstantopoulou[2(✉)],
Ioannis Stephanakis[3], Konstantinos Anastasopoulos[4],
Dimitrios Lymberopoulos[4], and George Anastassopoulos[1]

[1] Medical Informatics Laboratory, Medical School,
Democritus University of Thrace, 68100 Alexandroupolis, Greece
{tiliou,anasta}@med.duth.gr
[2] Special Office for Health Consulting Services,
University of Patras, Patras, Greece
gkonstantop@upatras.gr
[3] Hellenic Telecommunication Organization S.A. (OTE),
99 Kifissias Avenue, 151 24 Athens, Greece
stephan@ote.gr
[4] Department of Electrical Engineer, Wire Communications Laboratory,
University of Patras, Patras, Greece
anastasofpv@gmail.com, dlympero@upatras.gr

Abstract. Data pre-processing is an important step in the data mining process. Data preparation and filtering steps can take considerable amount of processing time. Data pre-processing includes cleaning, normalization, transformation, feature extraction and selection. In this paper, Iliou and PCA data preprocessing methods evaluated in a data set of 103 students, aged 18–25, who were experiencing anxiety problems. The performance of Iliou and PCA data preprocessing methods was evaluated using the 10-fold cross validation method assessing seven classification algorithms, IB1, J48, Random Forest, MLP, SMO, JRip and FURIA, respectively. The classification results indicate that Iliou data preprocessing algorithm consistently and substantially outperforms PCA data preprocessing method, achieving 98.6% against 92.2% classification performance, respectively.

Keywords: Data preprocessing · Machine learning · Data mining
Classification algorithms · Stress · Anxiety disorder · Panic disorder

1 Introduction

Anxiety disorders are among the most prevalent mental disorders that may occur in the general population and they can lead to chronic characteristics, associated with significant percentages of mortality [3].

This paper is structured as follows: Sect. 2 describes the Diagnostic criteria, Sect. 3 presents the Cognitive models, Sect. 4 presents the Beck Anxiety Inventory (BAI), Sect. 5 describes our dataset, Sect. 6 presents the experimental results of this study, while Sect. 7 concludes this paper and describes future work.

© IFIP International Federation for Information Processing 2018
Published by Springer International Publishing AG 2018. All Rights Reserved
L. Iliadis et al. (Eds.): AIAI 2018, IFIP AICT 519, pp. 351–361, 2018.
https://doi.org/10.1007/978-3-319-92007-8_30

2 Diagnostic Criteria

According to DSM-5, anxiety of separation, selective mutism, specific phobia, social anxiety disorder (or social phobia), panic disorder, agoraphobia, generalized anxiety disorder, substance-induced or drug-induced anxiety disorder, anxiety disorder due to another physical state, another predetermined anxiety disorder and unspecified anxiety disorder fall in the category of anxiety disorders [10].

Panic attack is a sudden onset of intense fear or intense discomfort that culminates in minutes, during which can occur at least four of the following symptoms (abrupt onset may occur from calm situation or stressful situation): palpitations, heart "pounding", or accelerated heart rate, transpiration, trembling or intense fear, breathlessness or feeling of suffocation, choking feeling, pain or discomfort in the chest, nausea or abdominal discomfort, dizziness, instability or fainting, chills or feeling of warmth, hallucinations (numbness or tingling), derealization (feeling unreal) or depersonalisation (feeling posting by itself), fear of losing control or oncoming madness, fear of death.

Generalized anxiety disorder is characterized from feelings of excessive anxiety and worry (fearful expectation), which are present quite often and during a period of at least six days for a number of events or activities (such as work and school performance). The person feels that it is difficult to control his worry, while stress and anxiety are associated with at least three of the following symptoms (with some of the symptoms to be present for more days during the last six months) [1, 2, 10]: nervousness or anxiety or stress feeling, feeling of an unusual upset, difficulty in concentrating or feeling that the mind is emptied, irritability, muscle tension.

3 Cognitive Models

The theory of anxiety disorders through the cognitive-behavioral model has been the subject of extensive clinical research in recent years. Moreover, the use of this model in therapy has demonstrated so far promising indicators of high efficiency [4–15].

Hoehn-Saric and McLeod in 1988 [11], and also Freeman, in 1990 described stress as a globally known experience that function like a warning safety mechanism. This mechanism emits warning signals during hazardous conditions, associated with uncertainty, while it seems to malfunction in a number of cases, like for example when: (a) stress is too intense, (b) stress lasts also after the exposure to the risk (c) occurs in situations in which risk or threat are absent, or (d) occurs without any particular reason.

4 Beck Anxiety Inventory

Beck Anxiety Inventory (BAI), created by Aaron T. Beck and his colleagues, is a 21-item, multiple-choice, self-report inventory that is used to measure severity of anxiety in children and in adults [6]. BAI questions are associated with symptoms of anxiety that the subject experienced during the past week (including the day of the

BAI), such as numbness and tingling, sweating, and fear that the worst is going to happen. It can be administered to individuals over 17 years old and it takes around 5 to 10 min in order to be completed. Several studies have found BAI to be an accurate measurement of anxiety symptoms in children and adults [17].

Somatic subscale is more emphasized on the BAI, as there are 15 out of 21 items measuring physiological symptoms, while the rest of the items concern cognitive, affective, and behavioral components of anxiety. Therefore, BAI functions more adequately in anxiety disorders with a high somatic component, like for example panic disorder. On the other hand, BAI is not appropriate for disorders, such as social phobia or obsessive-compulsive disorder, which have a stronger cognitive or behavioral component. Many questions of the Beck Anxiety Inventory include physiological symptoms, such as palpitations, indigestion, and trouble breathing. Because of this, it has been shown to elevate anxiety measures in those with physical illnesses like postural orthostatic tachycardia syndrome, when other measures did not [18].

The Beck Anxiety Inventory (BAI) and the Anxiety Disorders Interview Schedule (ADIS-IV) were administered to 193 adults with a primary diagnosis of generalized anxiety disorder (GAD), specific or social phobia, panic disorder with or without agoraphobia, obsessive–compulsive disorder (OCD), and no psychiatric diagnosis, at a major Midwestern university recruited from an anxiety research and treatment center. The results of this study support previous findings that the strongest quality of the BAI is its ability to assess panic symptomatology and can be used as an efficient screening tool for distinguishing between individuals with and without panic disorder [16]. The study of Steer et al. (1995), administered the Beck Anxiety Inventory to 105 outpatients between 13 and 17 years old who were diagnosed with various types of psychiatric disorders and the results are supporting the use of the inventory for evaluating self-reported anxiety in outpatient adolescents [29].

The Beck Anxiety Inventory (BAI), created by Aaron T. Beck and other colleagues, is a 21-question multiple-choice self-report inventory that is used for measuring the severity of anxiety in children and adults. It is a reliable tool. The BAI contains 21 questions, each answer being scored on a scale value of 0 (not at all) to 3 (severely). Higher total scores indicate more severe anxiety symptoms. The standardized cutoffs are:

- 0–9: normal to minimal anxiety
- 10–18: mild to moderate anxiety
- 19–29: moderate to severe anxiety
- 30–63: severe anxiety

5   Data Collection

Questionnaires were completed by 103 students, aged 18–25, who were experiencing anxiety problems and had visited the Office of the Special Consulting Health Services, of Patras University, from the September 2014 until the June 2016.

A result between 0–21 indicates low levels of stress. Although this is usually positive, someone should consider whether the result is realistic or if the person is in refusal concerning its problems. A result between 22–35 indicates moderate stress levels, meaning that the body is trying to tell something. The person should look for patterns in relation to the appearance of symptoms. For example, whether symptoms appear before a specific activity (e.g., a business meeting) and must learn to manage the stress before this activity. No panic is needed, but certainly some technical manager stress will help. A result over 36 points shows high levels of stress and is certainly a reason to ask for supply management. Remember that a high level of anxiety is not a sign of weakness or personal failure. It is something that should be addressed in order to prevent the impact to the mental and physical level of someone [9].

Questionnaires were completed by 103 students, aged 18–25, who were experiencing anxiety problems and had visited the Office of the Special Consulting Health Services, of Patras University, from the September 2014 until the June 2016. It was performed by one person, the psychologist of the office. Though the BAI was developed to minimize its overlap with the depression scale as measured by the Beck Depression Inventory, a correlation of $r = .66$ ($p < .01$) between the BAI and BDI-II was seen among psychiatric outpatients, suggesting that the BAI and the BDI-II equally discriminate between anxiety and depression. Another study indicates that, in primary care patients with different anxiety disorders including social phobia, panic disorder, panic disorder with or without agoraphobia, agoraphobia, or generalized anxiety disorder, the BAI seemed to measure the severity of depression. This suggests that perhaps the BAI cannot adequately differentiate between depression and anxiety in a primary care population. We have uploaded the original data as well.

6 Data Preprocessing

The set of techniques used prior to the application of a data mining method are named as data preprocessing for data mining [19] and it is known to be one of the most meaningful issues within the famous Knowledge Discovery from Data process [20]. Since real world data are generally imperfect, incomplete (lacking attribute values, lacking certain attributes of interest, or containing only aggregate data), noisy (containing errors or outliers), inconsistent (containing discrepancies in codes or names) and contain redundancies, is not directly applicable for a starting a data mining process. We must also mention the fast growing of data generation rates and their size in business, industrial, academic and science applications. The bigger amounts of data collected require more sophisticated mechanisms to analyze it. Data preprocessing is able to adapt the data to the requirements posed by each data mining algorithm, enabling to process data that would be unfeasible otherwise. Data preprocessing mainly includes (Fig. 1):

(i)   Data cleaning: fill in missing values, smooth noisy data, identify or remove outliers, and resolve inconsistencies.
(ii) Data integration: using multiple databases or files.
(iii) Data transformation: normalization and aggregation.
(iv) Data reduction: reducing the features of the initial dataset but producing the same or similar analytical results.

Fig. 1. Data preprocessing techniques

(v) Data discretization: part of data reduction, replacing numerical attributes with nominal ones.

Indicatively, we describe the below data preprocessing methods:

- Principal component analysis (PCA) tries to find a rotation such that the set of possibly correlated features transforms into a set of linearly uncorrelated features [21]. The columns used in this orthogonal transformation are called principal components [22]. This method is also designed for matrices with a low number of features.
- Iliou Preprocessing method transforms the initial dataset into a completely new dataset with 4*m attributes (in big data, Iliou method achieves feature reduction), where m is the number of classes of the dataset output [23]. In this paper we modified our method in order to achieve better results and less complexity. Iliou method uses Statistics and Linear Algebra methods like the dot (inner) product of dataset vectors in conjunction with some descriptive statistics [24]. The new dataset achieves better classification performance comparing to other preprocessing methods. We used Iliou method for classification or prediction problems [24, 25]. Below follows the detailed description of the method:

Step 1
Let's assume that a dataset of a machine learning problem named dataset1 is chosen, with n instances (rows), k variables (columns) and m classes. Then, a new set (called from now-on Basic-Set or BS) is created randomly selecting 10% of data from dataset1, consisting of d instances and m classes. The remaining 90% of dataset1 is called Rest-Set.

Step 2
Afterwards, inner (dot) product of every Basic Set instance (row) with the remaining rows of the Basic Set is computed (An inner product is a generalization of the dot product. In a vector space, it is a way to multiply vectors together, with the result of this multiplication being a scalar). Then, follows the calculation of mean and median values of the inner product result for every instance of each class with the rest instances of its class (Mean_class$_m$_row$_x$ and Median_class$_m$_row$_x$ respectively, see Eqs. 1 and 2), producing totally m + m=2 m new variables, namely Total_Mean$_1$, Total_Mean$_2$,

..., Total_Mean$_m$ and Total_Median$_1$, Total_Median$_2$, ..., Total_Median$_m$. For each one of these variables, the method produces d values.

The Mean_class$_m$_row$_x$ and Median_class$_m$_row$_x$ values are calculated as shown in Eqs. (1) and (2) respectively, where m is the name of the class, x (ranges from 1 to d) is the row of the BS and m_1, m_2 ....m_k is the first, second...and last row of m class of the BS.

$$\text{Mean\_class}_m\_\text{row}_x = \sum_{i=1}^{k} \text{Mean } (\text{row}_x/\text{row}_i) \tag{1}$$

$$\text{Median\_class}_m\_\text{row}_x = \sum_{i=1}^{k} \text{Median } (\text{row}_x/\text{row}_i) \tag{2}$$

Apart from the above, the Total_Mean and Total_Median values are calculated based on Eqs. (3) and (4) respectively, where m is the name of the class and d is the sum of rows in the BS. Finally, m total_Mean and m total_MEDIAN values are generated, one for every class of the BS.

$$
\begin{aligned}
&\text{Total\_Mean}_m \\
&= \frac{(\text{Mean\_class}_m\_\text{row}_1 + \text{Mean\_class}_m\_\text{row}_2 + \ldots + \text{Mean\_class}_m\_\text{row}_d)}{d}
\end{aligned}
\tag{3}
$$

$$
\begin{aligned}
&\text{Total\_Median}_m \\
&= \frac{(\text{Median\_class}_m\_\text{row}_1 + \text{Median\_class}_m\_\text{row}_2 + \ldots + \text{Median\_class}_m\_\text{row}_d)}{d}
\end{aligned}
\tag{4}
$$

Step 3

Assuming that Rest-Set from step 2 has r instances (rows) and m classes, a similar to step 2 approach follows. Specifically, inner (dot) product of every single Rest-Set row with every single row of the Basic Set is performed. Then, the mean and median values of the inner (dot) product result of every row for each class are calculated (RS_Mean_class$_m$ _row$_j$ and RS_Median_class$_m$_row$_j$ respectively), producing new m + m=2 m variables for every row of the Rest Set. As a result, we have r values for RS_Mean_class$_m$_row$_j$, and r values for RS_Median_class$_m$_row$_j$.

Similarly to step 2, we compute mean and medial values (RS_Mean_class$_m$_row$_x$ and RS_Median_class$_m$_ row$_x$ respectively) for every class.

Apart from the above, the Final_Mean$_m$_row$_j$ and Final_Median$_m$_row$_j$ values are also calculated as shown in Eqs. (5) and (6) respectively (m is the name of the class and j (from 1 to r) is the row of the Rest set.

$$\text{Final\_Mean}_m\_\text{row}_j = \text{total\_Mean}_m \text{ (step 3)} - \text{RS\_Mean\_class}_m\_\text{row}_j \tag{5}$$

$$\text{Final\_Median}_m\_\text{row}_j = \text{total\_Median}_m \text{ (step 3)} - \text{RS\_Median\_class}_m\_\text{row}_j \tag{6}$$

Finally, m Final_Mean$_m$_row$_j$ and Final_Median$_m$_row$_j$ values result, one for every class m and every row j of the Rest set.

Step 4

The rows (variables) RS_Mean_class$_m$_row$_j$, RS_Median_class$_m$_row$_j$, Final_Mean$_m$_-row$_j$ and Final_Median$_m$_row$_j$ for every class are selected from previous step and then are placed in a new table.

The method ends with the transposition of the table we described in previous step and the final dataset is now ready to be forwarded in any classification schema. Concluding the description of the proposed method, it is evident that the final dataset consists of 4 variables, namely RS_Mean_class$_m$ _row$_j$, RS_Median_class$_m$ _row$_j$, Final_Mean$_m$_row$_j$ and Final_Median$_m$_row$_j$ for every class of the initial dataset. Thus, if the original dataset has m classes, the final dataset will have 4 * m variables

7   Experimental Results

The experiments conducted using seven classification schemes (Table 1): IB1 (Nearest-neighbour classifier), J48 (C4.5 algorithm implementation), Random Forest, MLP (Multilayer Perceptron), SMO (Support Vector Machines), JRip (Repeated Incremental Pruning to Produce Error Reduction) and FURIA (Fuzzy Unordered Rule Induction Algorithm), respectively. In order to estimate how accurately the above predictive models will perform in practice and to assess how the results will generalize to an independent data set, we used the repeated 10-fold cross validation technique [26]. The experiments conducted using WEKA 3.8 data mining software [27] by their default WEKA parameters. We evaluated the performance of the classification schemes using Precision, Recall, Kappa statistics, Weighted Avg ROC area, Weighted Avg Precision Recall Curve (PRC) area, Matthews correlation coefficient (MCC) and Root mean squared error metrics (Table 1) [28–31]. Hence, we evaluated the performance of Iliou preprocessing method by comparing against Principal Component Analysis (PCA) and initial data without preprocessing.

In literature, Galatzer-Levy, Isaac R. et al. (2014) they did experiments classifying trauma survivors according to their stress achieving classification performance 76–80% using SVM, AdaBoost and Random Forest classification algorithms [32]. Purnendu Shekhar Panday (2017) based on heart beat tried to predict whether a person is in stress or not achieving 68% accuracy in classification process [33]. In [34] a real-life, unconstrained study carried out with 30 employees within two organisations and the classification results using ensemble approach increased the accuracy by ≈10% to 71.58% compared to not using any transfer learning technique.

In Eqs. 7 and 8 the formulas for Precision and Recall metrics are presented. The True Positive (TP) is the number of items correctly labeled as belonging to the positive class. The items that correctly labeled as not belonging to the positive class, they are called True Negative (TN). In the case that items which were not labeled as belonging to the positive class by the classifier but should have been, they are called False Negatives (FN). Finally, the items incorrectly labeled as belonging to the class, they are

Table 1. Classification results

Original data

	Pre %	Rec %	k	ROC	PRC area	TP rate	FP rate	MCC	Root MSE
IB1	82.1	81.55	0.7	0.852	0.749	0.816	0.105	0.706	0.3455
J48	80.6	80.6	0.681	0.847	0.715	0.806	0.105	0.701	0.3493
Ran For	82.3	82.5	0.709	0.954	0.905	0.825	0.114	0.716	0.277
MLP	85.5	86.4	0.772	0.975	0.939	0.864	0.069	0.798	0.2388
SMO	92.4	**92.2**	0.872	0.955	0.888	0.922	0.034	0.887	0.3022
Jrip	73.5	71.8	0.54	0.796	0.705	0.718	0.165	0.555	0.4015
FURIA	67.1	68	0.45	0.788	0.664	0.680	0.222	0.468	0.4186

PCA

	Pre	Rec	k	ROC	PRC area	TP rate	FP rate	MCC	Root MSE
IB1	73.4	73.8	0.56	0.768	0.639	0.738	0.179	0.568	0.41
J48	87.3	87.4	0.79	0.901	0.836	0.874	0.077	0.797	0.27
Ran For	88.4	88.3	0.80	0.969	0.935	0.883	0.079	0.818	0.26
MLP	87.6	87.4	0.793	0.964	0.917	0.874	0.057	0.815	0.27
SMO	89.8	87.4	0.78	0.937	0.835	0.874	0.088	0.811	0.3196
Jrip	89.4	89.3	0.82	0.917	0.850	0.893	0.064	0.829	0.25
FURIA	90.5	**90.3**	0.84	0.953	0.906	0.903	0.056	0.843	0.2325

ILIOU method

	Pre	Rec	k	ROC	PRC area	TP rate	FP rate	MCC	Root MSE
IB1	98.7	**98.6**	0.97	0.990	0.977	0.986	0.002	0.981	0.09
J48	93.4	93.1	0.88	0.947	0.897	0.931	0.037	0.890	0.21
Ran For	94.5	94.4	0.9	0.998	0.996	0.944	0.035	0.908	0.14
MLP	97.4	97.2	0.95	1	1	0.972	0.014	0.957	0.09
SMO	98.7	**98.6**	0.97	0.993	0.979	0.986	0.002	0.981	0.27
Jrip	92.5	91.7	0.86	0.959	0.918	0.917	0.051	0.873	0.23
FURIA	93.2	93.1	0.88	0.985	0.972	0.931	0.047	0.887	0.17

called False Positives (FP). Thus, the number of true positives, true negatives, false negatives and false positives add up to 100% of the set.

$$\text{Precision} = (\text{true positives})/(\text{true positives} + \text{false positives}) \tag{7}$$

$$\text{Recall} = (\text{true positives})/(\text{true positives} + \text{false positives}) \tag{8}$$

As we can observe in Table 1, initial (raw) data have achieved the best classification results 92% with Support Vector Machines (SMO) algorithm, PCA transformed data achieved the best classification results 90% and 89% with FURIA and JRip algorithm respectively. Finally, Iliou method achieved 98% classification performance with SMO and IB1 algorithm (Fig. 2).

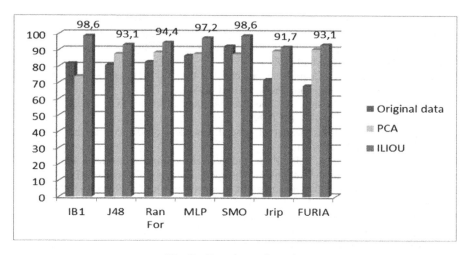

Fig. 2. Experimental results

8 Conclusions

In this paper we focused on stress level prediction using initial dataset without preprocessing and datasets being preprocessed by PCA and Iliou data preprocessing methods, respectively. Our experimental evaluation has shown that the Iliou data preprocessing algorithm consistently and substantially outperforms PCA data preprocessing method in classification performance. Moreover, Table 1 reveals that Iliou method achieved better classification results than initial dataset. In our point of view, Iliou method can be used for significantly improve classification algorithms performance in every stress level dataset.

In future work, it would be preferable to make the same experiments in larger datasets using more classifiers. In addition, Iliou data preprocessing method could be extended to classification algorithm.

References

1. American Psychiatric Association (APA): Diagnostic and Statistical Manual of Mental Disorders, 3rd edn - revised. American Psychiatric Association, Washington, DC (1987)
2. American Psychiatric Association (APA): Diagnostic and Statistical Manual of Mental Disorders, 4th edn. American Psychiatric Association, Washington, DC (1994)
3. Armstrong, K.A., Khawaja, N.G.: Gender differences in anxiety: an investigation of the symptoms, cognitions, and sensitivity towards anxiety in a nonclinical population. Behav. Cogn. Psychother. **30**, 227–231 (2002)
4. Bandura, A.: Self-efficacy: toward a unifying theory of behavioural change. Psychol. Rev. **84**, 191–215 (1977)
5. Beck, A.T., Emery, G.: Anxiety Disorders and Phobias. Basic Books, New York (1985). (with Greenberg, R.)

6. Beck, A.T., Epstein, N., Brown, G., Steer, R.A.: An inventory for measuring clinical anxiety: psychometric properties. J. Consult. Clin. Psychol. **56**(6), 893–897 (1988)
7. Blackburn, I., Davidson, K.: Cognitive Therapy for Depression and Anxiety. Blackwell Scientific Publications, Oxford (1990)
8. Clark, D.M., Beck, A.T.: Cognitive approaches. In: Last, C.G., Hersen, M. (eds.) Handbook of Anxiety Disorders. Pergamon Press, Oxford (1988)
9. Creamer, M., Foran, J., Bell, R.: The Beck Anxiety Inventory in a nonclinical sample. Behav. Res. Ther. **33**(4), 477–485 (1995)
10. Diagnostic and Statistical Manual of Mental Disorders (DSM -5), 5th edn. American Psychiatric Association (2013)
11. Hoehn-Saric, R., McLeod, D.R.: Panic and generalized anxiety disorders. In: Last, C.G., Hersen, M. (eds.) Handbook of Anxiety Disorders. Pergamon Press, Oxford (1988)
12. Kendall, P.C., Hollon, S.D.: Anxious self-talk: development of the anxious self-statements questionnaire. Cogn. Ther. Res. **13**(1), 81–93 (1989)
13. Kendall, P.C., Howard, B.L., Hays, R.C.: Self-referent speech and psychotherapy: the balance of positive and negative thinking. Cogn. Ther. Res. **13**(6), 583–598 (1989)
14. Kendall, P.C., Ingram, R.: The Future for Cognitive Assessment of Anxiety: Let's get Specific. Guilford Press, New York (1987)
15. Michelson, L., Ascher, L.M. (eds.): Anxiety and Stress Disorders: Cognitive-Behavioral Assessment and Treatment. The Guildford Press, London (1987)
16. Leyfer, O.T., Ruberg, J.L., Woodruff-Borden, J.: Examination of the utility of the Beck Anxiety Inventory and its factors as a screener for anxiety disorders. J. Anxiety Disord. **20**(4), 444–458 (2006)
17. Raj, S.R.: The Postural Tachycardia Syndrome (POTS): pathophysiology, diagnosis & management. Indian Pacing Electrophysiol. J. **6**(2), 84–99 (2006)
18. Pyle, D.: Data Preparation for Data Mining. Morgan Kaufmann Publishers, Los Altos (1999)
19. Balasubramanian, M., Schwartz, E.L.: The Isomap algorithm and topological stability. Science **295**(5552), 7 (2002)
20. Hall, M.A.: Correlation-based feature selection for machine learning. Waikato University, Department of Computer Science (1999)
21. Dunteman, G.H.: Principal Components Analysis. SAGE Publications, Thousand Oaks (1989)
22. Vafaie, H., Imam, I.F.: Feature selection methods: genetic algorithms vs. greedy-like search. In: Proceedings of International Conference on Fuzzy and Intelligent Control Systems (1994)
23. Iliou, T., Anagnostopoulos, C., Stephanakis, I., Anastassopoulos, G.: A novel data preprocessing method for boosting neural network performance: a case study in osteoporosis prediction. Inf. Sci. **380**, 92–100 (2017)
24. Iliou, T., Anagnostopoulos, C., Nerantzaki, M., Anastassopoulos, G.: A novel machine learning data preprocessing method for enhancing classification algorithms performance. In: Proceedings of the 16th International Conference on EANN, Article 11, 5 p. ACM (2015)
25. Kohavi, R.: A study of cross-validation and bootstrap for accuracy estimation and model selection. In: Proceedings of the Fourteenth International Joint Conference on Artificial Intelligence, vol. 2, no. 12, pp. 1137–1143 (1995)
26. Waikato Environment for Knowledge Analysis, Data Mining Software in Java. http://www.cs.waikato.ac.nz/ml/index.html. Accessed 11 Apr 2017
27. Matthews, B.W.: Comparison of the predicted and observed secondary structure of T4 phage lysozyme. Biochimica et Biophysica Acta (BBA) – Protein Struct. **405**(2), 442–451 (1975). https://doi.org/10.1016/0005-2795(75)90109-9

28. Lehmann, E.L., Casella, G.: Theory of Point Estimation, 2nd edn. Springer, New York (1998). ISBN 0-387-98502-6. MR 1639875
29. Powers, D.M.W.: Evaluation: from precision, recall and F-measure to ROC, informedness, markedness & correlation. J. Mach. Learn. Technol. 2(1), 37–63 (2011)
30. Steer, R.A., Kumar, G., Ranieri, W.F.: Use of the Beck Anxiety Inventory with adolescent psychiatric outpatients. Psychological Reports 76, 459–465 (1995). https://doi.org/10.2466/pr0.1995.76.2.459
31. Smeeton, N.C.: Early history of the Kappa statistic. Biometrics 41, 795 (1985). JSTOR 2531300
32. Galatzer-Levy, I.R., et al.: Quantitative forecasting of PTSD from early trauma responses: a machine learning application. J. Psychiatr. Res. 59, 68–76 (2014)
33. Purnendu Shekhar Panday: Machine learning and IOT for prediction and detection of stress. In: 2017 17th International Conference on Computational Science and Its Applications (ICCSA) (2017). https://doi.org/10.1109/iccsa.2017.8000018
34. Maxhuni, A., Hernandez-Leal, P., Sucar, L.E., Osmani, V., Morales, E., Mayora, O.: Stress modelling and prediction in presence of scarce data. In: Ambient Intelligence for Health, pp. 224–336. Springer, Puerto Varas, Chile (2015)

A Temporal-Causal Network Model for the Internal Processes of a Person with a Borderline Personality Disorder

Maria Hoţoiu[1], Federico Tavella[1,2], and Jan Treur[1(✉)]

[1] Behavioural Informatics Group, Vrije Universiteit Amsterdam,
Amsterdam, The Netherlands
mariahotoiu@gmail.com, federicotavella.7@gmail.com,
j.treur@vu.nl
[2] Department of Mathematics, University of Padua, Padua, Italy

Abstract. This paper presents a computational network model for a person with a Borderline Personality Disorder. It was designed according to a Network-Oriented Modeling approach as a temporal-causal network based on neuropsychological background knowledge. Example simulations are discussed. The model was verified based on Mathematical Analysis of stationary points.

Keywords: Borderline personality disorder · Temporal-causal network model

1 Introduction

Borderline Personality Disorder (often referred as BPD) is a psychiatric disorder characterized by a continuous pattern of swinging moods, self-image and behavior (NIH website 2017). People suffering from this disorder may also experience acute episodes of anger, depression and anxiety which can have different duration (typically from a few hours to days). These symptoms often lead to impulsive actions and problems in social interactions (Lis and Bohus 2013; Mellisa et al. 2017).

As for a relevant amount of mental disorders, people with borderline personality disorder may experience different symptoms based on disorder acuity and severity. In the case of BPD, two of the most common indicators are mood swings and display uncertainty about how they see themselves and their role in the world (NIH website 2017). People with borderline personality disorder also tend to view (i.e., interpret) things in a "dichromatic" way, such as all black or white. Consequently, their idea of other people can also change very quickly: an individual who is seen as a friend one day may be considered an enemy or traitor the day after. These fluctuating emotional states can lead to intense and unstable relationships. Other symptoms may include:

- A pattern of intense and unstable relationships with relatives, friends, and loved ones, often swinging from extreme closeness and love (idealization) to extreme dislike or anger (devaluation)
- Feelings of dissociation (Brand and Lanius 2014), such as feeling cut off from oneself, seeing oneself from outside one's body, or feelings of unreality

L. Iliadis et al. (Eds.): AIAI 2018, IFIP AICT 519, pp. 362–373, 2018.
https://doi.org/10.1007/978-3-319-92007-8_31

- Self-harming behavior and recurring thoughts of suicidal behaviors or threats;
- Difficulty imagining embodied others, i.e. different empathy levels (Haas and Miller 2015; Dammann et al. 2011)
- Inappropriate/intense anger or problems controlling anger
- Distorted and unstable self-image or sense of self (Dammann et al. 2011)

As previously mentioned, not all the subjects with borderline personality disorder experience every symptom. Some individuals experience only a few symptoms, while others have many. These symptoms can be triggered by everyday life events. Moreover, studies show that people with borderline personality disorder can have structural and functional changes in the brain (Soloff et al. 2017) specially in the areas that control impulses and emotional regulation (NIH website 2008). However, it is not clear whether these changes are risk factors for the disorder, or caused by the disorder.

This paper presents a computational network model for a person with borderline. It was designed as a temporal-causal network based on the Network-Oriented Modeling approach described in (Treur 2016). First in Sect. 2 some neuropsychological background is described. In Sect. 3 the model is introduced. Section 4 discusses some example simulations. In Sect. 5 it is described how the model was verified based on Mathematical Analysis.

2 Neuropsychological Background

The findings of numerous studies and research papers from Psychiatry, Cognitive and Social Neuroscience have been used to obtain a justifiable basis for the design of the computational model. The primary criteria for assessing the diagnosis of BPD according to (Hall et al. 2017; Ellison et al. 2016; American Psychiatric Association 2013) are (1) behavioral dysregulation, including impulsivity, excessive and inappropriate anger, self-harming and suicidality, (2) a history of failed relationships and feelings of "emptiness", (3) affective dysregulation including excessive mood lability, paranoia and fear of abandonment. One explanation offered by (De Meulemeester et al. 2017) for the interpersonal problems that these people experience is identity diffusion, fundamentally characterized by problems with self–other boundaries. According to the study, patients suffering from BPD displayed an instability in their sense of self and identity.

A factor contributing to the affective instability of BPD, according to a study by (Koenigsberg et al. 2009), is that, compared to healthy controls, patients with BPD do not engage the cognitive control regions when employing a distancing strategy to regulate emotional reactions. Anxiety and mistrust, as well as fear of other people's intentions are also common findings in the studies regarding BPD. One such study by (King-Casas et al. 2008) involved a mix sample of BPD patients and healthy controls playing a multi round economic exchange game. The findings suggest that BPD subjects express significantly lower levels of self-reported trust relative to healthy controls, as well as negative expectations of social partners, which was also implied by their decisions throughout the game. When studying the link between empathy and social attributions in BPD patients, (Homan et al. 2017) found that BPD patients display the tendency to attribute behavior to traits rather than context, meaning that they have a reduced empathic capacity.

The implications of these studies to the computational model are further discussed is Sects. 3 and 4.

3 The Temporal-Causal Network Model

In order to conceptualize the internal processes, as well as the interaction with an external person, of a person suffering from BPD, a temporal-causal network modelling approach was used, as described in (Treur 2016). Causal modelling, causal reasoning and causal simulation have a long tradition in AI; e.g., (Kuipers and Kassirer 1983; Kuipers 1984; Pearl 2000). The Network-Oriented Modelling approach based on temporal-causal networks described in (Treur 2016) on the one hand can be viewed as part of this causal modelling tradition, and on the other hand in the perspective of mental states and their causal relations as described in Philosophy of Mind; e.g., (Kim 1996). It is a widely usable generic AI modelling approach that distinguishes itself by incorporating a dynamic and adaptive temporal perspective, both on states and on causal relations. This dynamical perspective enables modelling of cyclic and adaptive networks, and also of timing of causal effects. This enables modelling by adaptive causal networks for connected mental states and for social interaction. Temporal-causal network models can be represented at two levels: conceptual and numerical. These is discussed subsequently in Sects. 3.1 and 3.2.

The following mechanisms based on different theories from the literature are incorporated in the model:

- mirror neuron systems (Iacoboni and Dapretto 2006; Iacoboni 2008)
- control neurons with self-other distinction and control function (Iacoboni 2008; Brass and Spengler 2009)
- emotion integration (Grèzes and de Gelder 2009; Grèzes et al. 2009)
- regulation of enhanced sensory processing sensitivity, in particular for face expressions (Neumann et al. 2006; Spezio et al. 2007; Baker et al. 2008; Corden et al. 2008)
- empathic responding using mirror neurons, self-other distinction and emotion integration (De Vignemont and Singer 2006; Singer and Leiberg 2009)

In order to have an adequate social interaction, all these mechanisms should function properly. Since they are correlated to one another, the malfunction of any one of them can lead to problems in the social functioning of the individual. People who suffer from BPD display faults in some of these mechanisms, as described in Sect. 2. They do not express the tendency to avoid stimuli, even if they are unpleasant, therefore no avoiding mechanism was included in the model. The manner in which these faults are translated into the model is described in Sect. 4.

3.1   The Conceptual Representation of the Network Model

Temporal-causal networks can be represented in a conceptual manner declaratively in either a graphical form or in a matrix form. The elements of a conceptual representation of a design are:

- the *states Y* of the network
- the *connections* between these states
- *connection weights* $\omega_{X,Y}$ which characterize the different strengths of these connections
- a *speed factor* η_Y for each state, expressing how fast this state can change
- for each state Y a *combination function* $c_Y(...)$ indicating how the multiple impacts from the states with outgoing connections to Y combine into a single impact on that state.

In the graphical conceptual representation, states are displayed as nodes and connections as arrows, the pointed end of the arrow indicating the direction of the causal impact. The graphical conceptual representation depicted in Fig. 1 describes the states and their connections in a person suffering from BPD. The above mentioned concepts connection weights, speed factors and combination functions are labels for the arrows (connection weights) and nodes (speed factors and combination functions) of this graph, so that a fully specified graphical conceptual representation gets the form of a labeled graph. There are six types of states in the presented model:

- world states ws, indicating an external stimulus, in this case ws_s for the stimulus s and ws_B for a person B
- sensor states ss_X (with $X = s$ or $X = B$) for the sensing of these two external stimuli
- sensory representation states srs_X (with $X = s$ or $X = B$) formed based on the sensor states, but also within the person itself and body states of aggression and anxiety
- preparation states ps_X for expressing the body states of anxiety $(X = anx)$ and aggression $(X = agg)$, as well as for communicating to person B $(X = B)$
- control states cs_X, which regulate the actual expression of anxiety and aggression $(X = self)$ as well the self-other distinction between the person and the other person $(X = B,s)$
- execution or expression states es_X for anxiety and aggression and execution state esc_X for communication to person B

Besides the connections described previously, there are also two loops: the *as-if body loops* between the preparation states for expressing anxiety and aggression and their sensory representation states, which adapt the internal body map, as described in (Treur 2016).

3.2   Numerical Representation of the Network Model

In order to obtain a basis for simulation and further mathematical analysis of the model, the conceptual representation can be transformed into a numerical representation in a systematic manner, as described in (Treur 2016), as follows:

- The value of each state Y at each time point t is denoted by $Y(t)$

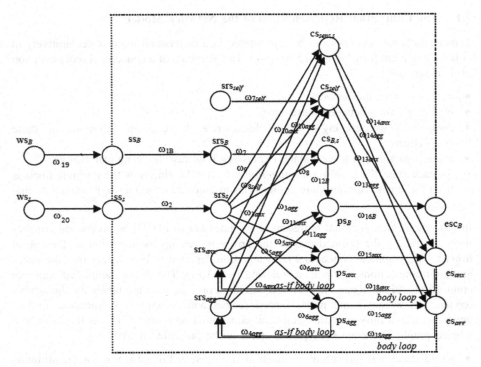

Fig. 1. The graphical conceptual representation of the temporal-causal network model

- The impact from any connection from a state X_i to a state Y at time point t is defined as

$$\mathbf{impact}_{X_i, Y}(t) = \omega_{X_i, Y} X_i(t) \tag{1}$$

where $\omega_{X_i, Y}$ is the weight of the connection from X_i to Y

- The total impact of all the connections $X_1, \ldots, X_k$ to a state Y at time t is

$$\mathbf{aggimpact}_Y(t) = \mathbf{c}_Y(\mathbf{impact}_{X_1, Y}(t), \ldots, \mathbf{impact}_{X_k, Y}(t)) \tag{2}$$

where $\mathbf{c}_Y(\ldots)$ is the combination function

- The change of the state Y from the time step t to the next time point $t + \Delta t$ is represented by the following difference equation:

$$Y(t + \Delta t) = Y(t) + \eta_Y[\mathbf{aggimpact}_Y(t) - Y(t)]\Delta t \tag{3}$$

where η_Y is the speed factor of the state Y, or by the following differential equation:

$$\mathbf{d}Y(t)/\mathbf{d}t = \eta_Y[\mathbf{aggimpact}_Y(t) - Y(t)] \tag{4}$$

As an example, by following the pattern described above based on formulae (1), (2), (3) and (4) the difference and the differential equation for ps_B are:

$$ps_B(t + \Delta t) = ps_B(t) + \eta_{ps_B} [c_{ps_B}(\omega_{11anx}\, srs_{anx}(t), \omega_{11agg}\, srs_{agg}(t), \omega_{12B}\, cs_{B,s}(t)) - ps_B(t)]\, \Delta t \tag{5}$$

$$\mathbf{d}ps_B(t)/\mathbf{d}t = \eta_{psB} [c_{ps_B}(\omega_{11anx}\, srs_{anx}(t), \omega_{11agg}\, srs_{agg}(t), \omega_{12B}\, cs_{B,s}(t)) - ps_B(t)]$$

Each state of the model, except for the world states which have no incoming connections, gets a difference and a differential equation assigned. The interaction between these equations describe the behavior of the model. For the model considered here there are 16 coupled difference and differential equations.

The combination function used for all the states with only one incoming impact is the identity function $\mathbf{id}(\dots)$ as described in (Treur 2016, Chap. 2): $c_Y(V) = \mathbf{id}(V) = V$. By using this combination function, based on (1) to (4) the difference and the differential equation for srs_B, for example, is the following:

$$srs_B(t + \Delta t) = srs_B(t) + \eta_{srs_B}[\omega_{1B}\, ss_B(t) - srs_B(t)]\Delta t$$
$$\mathbf{d}srs_B(t)/\mathbf{d}t = \eta_{srs_B}[\omega_{1B} ss_B(t) - srs_B(t)] \tag{6}$$

For the states which have multiple incoming impacts the combination function used was the advanced logistic sum combination function $\mathbf{alogistic}(\dots)$, described in (Treur 2016) as follows:

$$c_Y(V_1, \dots, V_k) = \mathbf{alogistic}_{\sigma, \tau}(V_1, \dots V_k)$$
$$= [(1/(1 + e^{-\sigma(V_1, \dots V_k - \tau)})) - 1/(1 + e^{\sigma\tau})]\,(1 + e^{-\sigma\tau}) \tag{7}$$

The parameters τ and σ of this advanced logistic function represent the threshold and the steepness. This function has the property that it maps 0 values to 0 and it also keeps the values between 0 and 1. With this combination function (7), based on (1) to (4) the following difference and differential equations for ps_B, for example, are obtained:

$$ps_B(t + \Delta t) = ps_B(t) + \eta_{ps_B}[\mathbf{alogistic}_{\sigma, \tau}(\omega_{11anx}\, srs_{anx}(t), \omega_{11agg}\, srs_{agg}(t), \omega_{12B}\, cs_{B,s}(t)) - ps_B(t)]\Delta t$$
$$\mathbf{d}ps_B(t)/\mathbf{d}t = \eta_{ps_B}[\mathbf{alogistic}_{\sigma, \tau}(\omega_{11anx}\, srs_{anx}(t), \omega_{11agg}\, srs_{agg}(t), \omega_{12B}\, cs_{B,s}(t)) - ps_B(t)] \tag{8}$$

4 Simulation Results

The numerical representation presented above was implemented in Matlab, in order to obtain a realistic picture of how the mechanisms discussed in Sect. 3 interact in the case of a person suffering from BPD. The traits presented in Sect. 2 are translated into the model by constraints of some of the parameters, as shown in Table 1, thus providing the data at the basis of the simulation.

Table 1. Connection weights and their values

Connection	Value	Connection	Value
ω_7	0.5	ω_{13anx}, ω_{13agg}	−0.2
ω_8	0.5	ω_{7self}, ω_{8self}	0.2
ω_{3agg}, ω_{3anx}	0.2	ω_{14anx}, ω_{14agg}	−0.2
ω_{10anx}, ω_{10agg}	0.2	ω_9	0.2

Following the reasoning presented in (Treur 2016, Chap. 10) a reduced self-other distinction means that the connections between srs_s and $cs_{B,s}$ and srs_B and $cs_{B,s}$ are weak, therefore the values of ω_7, ω_8 are low. The intensity of the anger and of the anxiety experienced by these people implicates that the connections between their corresponding sensory representations srs_{anx} and srs_{agg} and the control state for sensing $cs_{sens,s}$ are weak, as well as the connections between the control state for monitoring cs_{self} and srs_{anx} and srs_{agg} with ω_{10anx}, ω_{10agg}, ω_{3agg}, ω_{3anx} are low. The connection between the sensory representation srs_s of a stimulus s and the control state for sensing $cs_{sens,s}$ is also weak, with ω_9 low, since people suffering from BPD do not exhibit a distancing behavior.

The poor monitoring of emotions translates into weak connections between the sensory representations of the agent itself srs_{self}, as well as the sensory representation srs_s of stimulus s, and the control state for the agent itself cs_{self} with ω_{7self} and ω_{8self} low. Reduced self-control implicates that the connections coming from the control state $cs_{sens,s}$, as well as from cs_{self}, to the expression states es_{anx} and es_{agg} are weak, so ω_{13anx}, ω_{13agg}, ω_{14anx}, and ω_{14agg} are low. All the weights of the connections except for those in Table 1 are 1.

In order to incorporate the impulsivity trait in the implementation, the speed factors of the control states $cs_{sens,s}$, cs_{self} and $cs_{B,s}$ are adjusted as being lower than for the other states, for which it is 1. The speed factor of the states regarding communication, ps_B and esc_B are also a little lower than one, since verbalizing is a little difficult for people who suffer from BPD so it is most likely to happen after the body expressions of anxiety and aggression. The parameters for the advanced logistic sum combination function corresponding to each state are shown in Table 2.

The step size is set at $\Delta t = 0.5$. The initial values of the states are 0, except for the input states ws_B and ws_s which have either the value of 0.2 or 0, equivalent to no stimulus. The value of 0.2 is chosen so low in order to illustrate the strong impact a weak stimulus has on a person suffering from BPD. The results of the simulation for the values discussed above are shown in Fig. 2.

Table 2. Parameters for the combination function **alogistic**$_{\sigma,\tau}$(..) for each state

State	σ	τ	State	σ	τ
$cs_{sens,s}$	1	0.2	srs_{anx}	5	0.4
ps_B	4	0.2	ps_{anx}	5	0.4
$cs_{B,s}$	2	0.2	es_{anx}	5	0.4
srs_{agg}	5	0.4	ps_{agg}	5	0.4
es_{agg}	5	0.4	cs_{self}	1	0.2

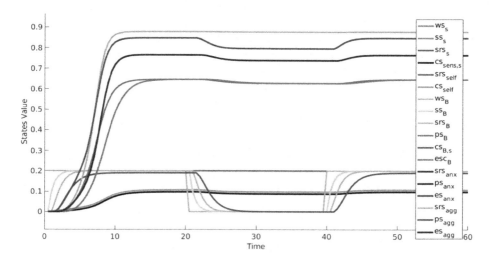

Fig. 2. Results of the simulation

In the first part of the simulation, all the values go up, first the values of the stimuli related states, ss_B and ss_s which are equal, so their graphical representations are overlapping, making only ss_B visible. The same is happening with srs_B and srs_s. Even though the value of the input is as low as 0.2, the values of the states for preparation ps_{anx} and ps_{agg} and expression es_{anx} and es_{agg} climb really fast to values as high as 0.8 and 0.9. This illustrates the power of a small stimuli, when self-control is not working correctly. Note that, since aggression and anxiety are expected to play an equal role in this model, their graphical representations are overlapping. The control states for emotion regulation and suppression and self-other distinction $cs_{sens,s}$, $cs_{B,s}$ and cs_{self} are always low, as expected. The preparation ps_B communication to person B esc_B happen after the expressions of anxiety and aggression, corresponding to the behavior previously described.

After the first 10 time steps, the stimuli go away, meaning that the values of ws_s and ws_B become 0. In a normal person, this would imply that the values of all the other states should decrease to 0, but here the states related to anger and anxiety drop only very little, as expected. The sensory representation states for anxiety srs_{anx} and aggression srs_{agg} are always high in value, illustrating the constantly disturbed inner

state people suffering from BPD experience. Since the value of the sensory representation state is high and the values of the control states are low, the expression of the
feelings is also high, even if there are no stimuli present. This process of stimuli/no
stimuli is repeated throughout the simulation a few times, with the same results.

5   Verification by Mathematical Analysis

In order to verify the implementation of the model, a mathematical analysis of the
equilibria was performed. A model is in equilibrium at a time point t if all the states of
the model have a stationary point at that time. A state Y has a stationary point at a
time t if $Y(t + \Delta t) = Y(t)$, for a small Δt. By considering the differential equation
representation for a temporal-causal network model (see (1) to (4) in Sect. 3.2), a state
Y has a stationary point a time t if and only:

$$Y(t) = c_Y(\omega_{X_1,Y} X_1(t), \ldots, \omega_{X_k,Y} X_k(t)) \tag{9}$$

where $c_Y()$ is the combination function for the state Y and $X_1,\ldots,X_k$ are the states which
have an impact on Y; see (Treur 2016, Chap. 12). Following this representation if we
consider the equilibrium equations for all the states X_i of the model, by leaving out the
t and denoting the values as constants $\underline{X}_i$, we get from (9) for all states Y that an
equilibrium is a solution $(\underline{X}_1,\ldots,\underline{X}_n)$ of the following n equations:

$$\begin{aligned}
\underline{X}_1 &= c_{X_1}(\omega_{X_1,X_1}\underline{X}_1, \ldots, \omega_{X_n,X_1}\underline{X}_n) \\
&\quad\cdots \\
\underline{X}_n &= c_{X_n}(\omega_{X_1,X_n}\underline{X}_1, \ldots, \omega_{X_n,X_n}\underline{X}_n)
\end{aligned} \tag{10}$$

The model discussed here has 18 states, out of which two are world states, therefore
16 equilibrium equations. For example, the equilibrium equation for the state ss_B,
which has the identity combination function, is:

$$\underline{ss}_B = \omega_{19}\underline{ws}_B \tag{11}$$

For the other states which use the identity combination function, the equilibrium
equations are similar. For the states which use the combination function $\mathbf{alogistic}_{\sigma,\tau}(..)$
(see (7) in Sect. 3.2), the equilibrium equations are similar to this one, which is for the
state ps_B:

$$\underline{ps}_B = \mathbf{alogistic}_{\sigma,\tau}(\omega_{11anx}\,\underline{srs}_{anx}, \; \omega_{11agg}\,\underline{srs}_{agg}, \; \omega_{12B}\,\underline{cs}_{B,s}) \tag{12}$$

Due to the 10 equations that include a logistic function, the equilibrium equations
cannot be solved analytically in an explicit manner, but they still can be used for
verification of the model. Since the model discussed here has an alternating presence of
the stimuli, the model reaches stationary points several times.

In order to be able to analyse the stationary points of the model, the number of time
steps for observation was increased from 120 to 1200, so that the values of the states

would be observed more often. The stimulus is removed and added again once every 200 time steps, so we would expect that the model reaches stationary points 6 times in the simulation. This type of pattern is called a limit cycle, with state values changing all the time. In a limit cycle, each state fluctuates between a minimum and a maximum value. When it reaches the time points for either a minimum or a maximum, each state should have a stationary point, which means that the equation for a stationary point can be verified. The stationary point equations were fulfilled for all the states of the model, with a very high accuracy, as can be seen in Table 3 which is evidence that the implemented model does what is expected.

Table 3. Overview of the outcomes of the verification of the stationary points

State	ss_B	srs_B	ss_s	srs_s	srs_{anx}	srs_{agg}	cs_{self}
Maxima							
Time point	196	196	196	196	196	196	196
Value	0.2	0.2	0.2	0.2	0.878487	0.878487	0.107426
Aggimpact	0.2	0.2	0.2	0.2	0.878487	0.878487	0.107426
Deviation	0	0	0	0	0	0	0
Minima							
Time point	406	406	406	406	406	406	406
Value	9.96e−61	1.97e−58	9.96e−61	1.97e−58	0.877405	0.877405	0.087503
Aggimpact	0	0	0	0	0.877405	0.877405	0.087503
Deviation	9.96e−61	1.97e−58	9.96e−61	1.97e−58	0	0	0

State	$cs_{B,s}$	$cs_{sens,s}$	ps_B	ps_{agg}	ps_{anx}	es_{anx}	es_{agg}	esc_B
Maxima								
Time point	196	196	196	196	196	196	196	196
Value	0.189974	0.097537	0.688646	0.848264	0.848264	0.848264	0.848264	0.646615
Aggimpact	0.189974	0.097537	0.688646	0.848264	0.848264	0.848264	0.848264	0.646615
Deviation	0	0	0	0	0	0	0	0
Minima								
Time point	406	406	406	406	406	406	406	406
Value	2.77e−37	0.087503	0.627566	0.796629	0.796629	0.739934	0.739934	0.627566
Aggimpact	0	0.087503	0.627566	0.796629	0.796629	0.739934	0.739934	0.627566
Deviation	2.77e−37	0	0	0	0	0	0	0

6 Discussion

In this paper a computational model of the internal processes of persons suffering from Borderline Personality Disorder was presented. The model was built as a temporal-causal network model according to the Network-Oriented Modelling approach presented in (Treur 2016), incorporating the characteristics described by neuropsychological findings from the literature. The Borderline Personality Disorder is a rather complex disorder, difficult to address. Such a computational model for the Borderline Personality Disorder is new, as far as the authors know.

Characteristics such as identity diffusion, the absence of a distancing mechanism, impulsivity, reduced emotion control and poor monitoring, low empathic capacity were incorporated in the model by setting specific values to the parameters concerning the underlying mechanisms, such as connection weights and speed factors. The model was verified by mathematical analysis, with satisfying results.

The model can be the basis for a virtual patient model application and used by therapists to perform what-if simulations to get insight in the borderline phenomenon. It may also be extended by therapies to simulate the effect of them. These can be next steps for future research.

References

American Psychiatric Association: Diagnostic and Statistical Manual of Mental Disorders. 5th edn. American Psychiatric Association, Arlington (2013)

Baker, A.E.Z., Lane, A.E., Angley, M.T., Young, R.L.: The relationship between sensory processing patterns and behavioural responsiveness in autistic disorder: a pilot study. J. Autism Dev. Disord. **38**, 867–875 (2008)

Brand, B.L., Lanius, R.A.: Chronic complex dissociative disorders and borderline personality disorder: disorders of emotion dysregulation? Borderl. Personal. Disord. Emot. Dysregul. **1**, 13 (2014)

Brass, M., Spengler, S.: The inhibition of imitative behaviour and attribution of mental states. In: Striano, T., Reid, V. (eds.) Social Cognition: Development, Neuroscience, and Autism, pp. 52–66. Wiley-Blackwell, Oxford (2009)

Corden, B., Chilvers, R., Skuse, D.: Avoidance of emotionally arousing stimuli predicts social-perceptual impairment in Asperger's syndrome. Neuropsychologia **46**, 137–147 (2008)

Dammann, G., et al.: The self-image in borderline personality disorder: an in-depth qualitative research study. J. Pers. Disord. **25**(4), 517–527 (2011)

De Meulemeester, C., Lowyck, B., Vermote, R., Verhaest, Y., Luyten, P.: Mentalizing and interpersonal problems in borderline personality disorder: the mediating role of identity diffusion. Psychiatry Res. **258**, 141–144 (2017)

De Vignemont, F., Singer, T.: The empathic brain: how, when and why? Trends Cogn. Sci. **10**, 437–443 (2006)

Ellison, W.D., Rosenstein, L., Chelminskil, I., Dalrymple, K., Zimmerman, M.: The clinical significance of single features of borderline personality disorder; anger, affective instability, impulsivity, and chronic emptiness in psychiatric outpatients. J. Pers. Disord. **30**(2), 261–270 (2016)

Grèzes, J., de Gelder, B.: Social perception: understanding other people's intentions and emotions through their actions. In: Striano, T., Reid, V. (eds.) Social Cognition: Development, Neuroscience, and Autism, pp. 67–78. Wiley-Blackwell, Oxford (2009)

Grèzes, J., Wicker, B., Berthoz, S., de Gelder, B.: A failure to grasp the affective meaning of actions in autism spectrum disorder subjects. Neuropsychologica **47**, 1816–1825 (2009)

Haas, B.W., Miller, J.D.: Borderline personality traits and brain activity during emotional perspective taking. Personal. Disord. Theory Res. Treat. **6**(4), 315–320 (2015)

Homan, P., et al.: Aberrant link between empathy and social attribution style in borderline personality disorder. J. Psychiatr. Res. **94**, 163–171 (2017)

Iacoboni, M.: Mirroring People: The New Science of How We Connect with Others. Farrar, Straus & Giroux, New York (2008)

Iacoboni, M., Dapretto, M.: The mirror neuron system and the consequences of its dysfunction. Nat. Rev. Neurosci. **7**, 942–951 (2006)

Kim, J.: Philosophy of Mind. Westview Press, Boulder (1996)

King-Casas, B., Sharp, C., Lomax-Bream, L., Lohrenz, T., Fonagy, P., Montague, P.R.: The rupture and repair of cooperation in borderline personality disorder. Science **321**, 806–810 (2008)

Koenigsberg, H.W., Fan, J., Ochsner, K., Liu, X., Guise, K.G., Pizzarello, S., Dorantes, C., Guerreri, S., Tecuta, L., Goodman, M., New, A., Siever, L.J.: Neural correlates of the use of psychological distancing to regulate responses to negative social cues: a study of patients with borderline personality disorder. Biol. Psychiatry **66**(9), 854–863 (2009)

Kuipers, B.J.: Commonsense reasoning about causality: deriving behavior from structure. Artif. Intell. **24**, 169–203 (1984)

Kuipers, B.J., Kassirer, J.P.: How to discover a knowledge representation for causal reasoning by studying an expert physician. In: Proceedings of the 8th International Joint Conference on Artificial Intelligence, IJCAI 1983, Karlsruhe, William Kaufman, Los Altos, CA (1983)

Lis, S., Bohus, M.: Social interaction in borderline personality disorder. Curr. Psychiatry Rep. **15**, 338 (2013). https://doi.org/10.1007/s11920-012-0338-z

Hall, M.A., Riedford, K.M.: Borderline personality disorder: diagnosis and common comorbidities. J. Nurse Pract. **13**(9), e455–e456 (2017)

Mellisa, A., Hall, Katherine M.: Riedford.Borderline Personality Disorder: diagnosis and common comorbidities. The J. Nurse Pract. - JNP. **13**(9), October (2017)

NIH Website https://www.nimh.nih.gov/health/topics/borderline-personality-disorder/index.shtml. https://www.nimh.nih.gov/news/science-news/2008/emotion-regulating-circuit-weakened-in-borderline-personality-disorder.shtml

Neumann, D., Spezio, M.L., Piven, J., Adolphs, R.: Looking you in the mouth: abnormal gaze in autism resulting from impaired top-down modulation of visual attention. Soc. Cognit. Affect. Neurosci. **1**, 194–202 (2006)

Pearl, J.: Causality. Cambridge University Press, Cambridge (2000)

Singer, T., Leiberg, S.: Sharing the emotions of others: the neural bases of empathy. In: Gazzaniga, M.S. (ed.) The Cognitive Neurosciences, 4th edn, pp. 973–986. MIT Press, Cambridge (2009)

Soloff, P., et al.: Structural brain abnormalities in borderline personality disorder: a voxel-based morphometry study. Psychiatry Res. **164**(3), 223–236 (2008, 2017)

Spezio, M.L., Adolphs, R., Hurley, R.S.E., Piven, J.: Analysis of face gaze in autism using 'Bubbles'. Neuropsychologia **45**, 144–151 (2007)

Treur, J.: Network-Oriented Modeling: Addressing Complexity of Cognitive, Affective and Social Interactions. Springer, Cham (2016). https://doi.org/10.1007/978-3-319-45213-5

Content Based Image Retrieval in Digital Pathology Using Speeded Up Robust Features

A. Kallipolitis and I. Maglogiannis[✉]

Department of Digital Systems, University of Piraeus, Piraeus, Greece
nasscall@yahoo.gr, imaglo@unipi.gr

Abstract. The recent expand in the utilization of Whole Slide scanners in Digital Pathology gave birth to a production of massive amount of data and the need of integration of Digital Pathology Systems (DPS's) into modern Laboratory Information Systems (LIS's). In this context, the problem of automatically retrieving a particular image from a large set of digital images that contains similar medical visual content has gained fruitful ground. This work investigates the fast and consistent properties of the Speeded-Up Robust Features (SURF) algorithm in order to search in the content of a digital pathology image, detect and find similarities for content-based image retrieval. An important aspect of this work is the diversity of Whole Slide Scanners. The proposed methodology that involves the process of the comparison of digital pathology images, mostly WSI, with the use of the SURF algorithm was proved robust to various condition changes.

Keywords: Digital pathology · Laboratory information system
Content based image retrieval (CBIR) · Speeded Up Robust Features (SURF)
Whole Slide Imaging (WSI)

1 Introduction

Digital Pathology was meant to solve many problems that physicians in this domain had faced in the earlier years, mainly associated with the management and preservation of tissue samples, the inability of conducting tele medical consultations and the lack of advanced computer based systems for diagnosis, analysis and education. Nevertheless, the transition to a new digital era of pathology brought up many new challenges. A vast amount of data is created every second as the digital image produced by a glass slide has a typical size of 3 GB along with its metadata. Analyzing such images in order to recognize patterns and similarities against images found in medical books and atlases have been proven tedious and time-consuming tasks for pathologists. There is an immense need for automated and fast book, database and storage systems screening. Furthermore, the variety of whole slide scanners vendors led to the building of a new "Babel" tower, where each DPS speaks a different language as far as hardware, operating systems, formats of digital images and communicating protocols are concerned [9]. To address these two challenges, the paper describes a system that, at first stage, is able to translate the different formats of WSI and, at second, detects similarities in pathology images. The system can also import medical books in pdf format and

L. Iliadis et al. (Eds.): AIAI 2018, IFIP AICT 519, pp. 374–384, 2018.
https://doi.org/10.1007/978-3-319-92007-8_32

extract the images found in them for storage and analysis along with whole slide images. A general overview of the system is shown in Fig. 1. Inputs to content based image retrieval system can be whole slides images, images extracted from digital pathology books (literature) and local storage or digital pathology databases. One of these images represents the query image and the others the test images. These inputs, digital images to their whole, are imported in the system, processed and the output of the process is the set of images that bear the greatest resemblance to the query image.

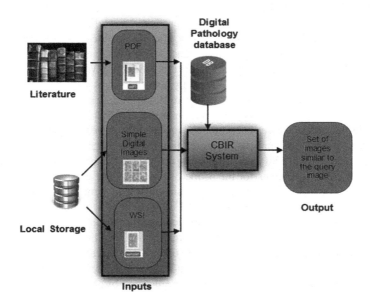

Fig. 1. General view of image retrieval system

The remainder of this paper is structured in 5 sections, as follows: Sect. 2 presents the related work, while Sect. 3 describes the proposed methodology for image retrieval. Section 4 describes the system in practice and Sect. 5 reports the experiments conducted and the corresponding results. Finally, Sect. 6 concludes the paper.

2 Related Work

The discipline of pathology has well accepted its "digital" character, since several years of evolution transforming the conventional LISs (Laboratory Information Systems) to their modern digital pathology version. This new version embodies several technologies such as Relational Database Management Systems (RDBMSs), Structured Query Language (SQL), eXtensible Markup Language (XML) and, most significantly, WSI (Whole Slide Imaging) [1]. The process of WSI is based on Whole Slide Scanners that produce Whole Slide Images and, more than often, participate in DPSs (Digital Pathology Systems), whose integration/cooperation within the LIS's have improved the functionality of the later in means of diagnostic assistance, educational tools and quality control [2]. Through DPSs and Whole Slide Scanners, glass slides that are used in light microscopes by pathologists to observe and examine specimens taken from surgery, are transformed into Whole Slide Images (digital slides). The digital slides can be read by viewing software in order to navigate into a vast range of standard magnifications of sectors of the specimen. However, the variety of manufacturers that are involved in the production of different whole slide scanners poses a complicity factor in the process of reading and viewing such images. This complicity factor is explained by the fact that each digital slide, which is produced by a brand scanner, has a certain format, different from all the other formats produced by other scanners. This lack of uniformity between formats of digital slides that are produced by different manufacturers will continue to exist despite the recent efforts for the creation of standards that will pose certain patterns and regulations in the process of WSI [3].

Apart from the difficult task of handling heterogeneous whole slide images, this paper proposes a solution to the problem of retrieving images from a dataset of digital images that are similar to a query image. Once the first technical task of deploying a universal digital image viewer is completed successfully, most formats of digital slides are available for preview, analysis, interpretation and handling. In the vast bank of data that digital images can provide, similarities are tracked and found between a query image and a dataset of images for the scope of retrieving the most similar image/s. For the purpose of detecting specific areas of interest where similarities can be found, a local feature representation, using the SURF algorithm [5], of the image is proposed due to the algorithm's promising properties concerning speed and robustness to variations. With the exploitation of SURF, interest points are, first, detected in an image and, then, the image is described by multiple 64d vectors, created in each interest point. Consequently, the image from the dataset that bears the most similarities with the query image is selected and retrieved. Similarities are defined by the score that is nominated to its image of the dataset when their interest points are compared with the interest points of the query image, not by the "naive" one-to-one comparison but by the implementation of the nearest neighbor algorithm with kd-trees.

The procedure of retrieving the image with the most similarities to the query image (best score) is explained in CBIR (Content Based Image Retrieval) methodology. For many years, image retrieval was based on text found in the meta-data attached to digital images. Text based image retrieval had faced several challenges from the early 70s up to today, mainly, concerning human effort to add annotations to images and inconsistencies between textual meta data information which describes visual content. These unsolved challenges lead to the advance of CBIR in the 80s, which has stepped forward to gain excessive terrain as a preferred method of solving image retrieval problems. In CBIR, images are indexed by their visual content automatically without the need of human intervention. CBIR can be performed in images that are represented either globally, or locally. As explained in [7], local feature representations can provide the localized information of interest from a small region of the whole slide image, whereas global feature representations fail to contribute to image retrieval due to the fact that the produced global signature depicts the whole image and not the small area of interest. In reference to relevant research work that has been conducted in CBIR and Digital Pathology, Mehta et al. in [6], retrieves sub-images from whole slide images using scale-invariant feature extraction algorithm SIFT (Scale Invariant Feature Transform). However, SURF algorithm has been proven to be fast, more accurate and reliable than SIFT. Velmurugan et al. in [8], used a combination of SURF and Color Moments to retrieve similar images of general context. The basic assumption to combine Color Moments in order improve the results of SURF algorithm lies on the fact that SURF is applied on gray scale images. In [9], Govindaraju and Ramesh Kumar propose a novel CBIR system using SURF and Bag of Words to detect resemblances in medical images. Results are compared with the use of both SIFT and SURF algorithms with the latter to prove better.

3   Methodology

The method, which is proposed in this paper to solve the image retrieval problem, consists of four (4) stages (illustrated in Fig. 2), as follows: (i) Image preprocessing, (ii) Image analysis, (iii) Feature extraction and (iv) Image retrieval.

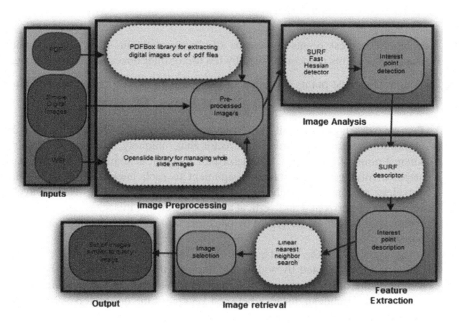

Fig. 2. Workflow diagram of the proposed methodology (Magenta boxes correspond to input/output, light green to processing steps and dark green refers to intermediate objects) (Color figure online)

Starting from the input of our system, they can be digital images downloaded from the Internet, selected regions of interest from whole slide images or images extracted from digital pathology atlases. One of these images represents the query image and all the others comprise the dataset from which the system will detect the image with the best similarity to the query image (output of the system). The following paragraphs discuss briefly the 4 stages.

(i) Image pre-processing. In this first stage the system creates the input images whether they take part in the search dataset, or they constitute the query image. It is important to note that not all images are ready to be analyzed by the system, as they may be contained in a PDF file or they need to be extracted from a whole slide image (being a part of it). In the case of handling.pdf files, the initial.pdf file is being processed by the system and all images are extracted in a folder by means of a java library called PDFBOX. Should a whole slide image be used, another java library called OPENSLIDE, reviewed in [10], offers its functionality in order for the whole slide images to be read, previewed, and processed. If the input image is a simple digital image the system's task is trivial. In the end of this stage all digital images are ready to be analyzed, as they enter the following stage of image analysis.

(ii) Image analysis. Each digital image is being analyzed and the interest points are detected using the fast Hessian detector of SURF algorithm. The detector function is divided in two basic steps:

1. Tracking of interest points by means of the determinant of the approximated Hessian Matrix. This is accomplished by the use of filter boxes and integral images.

2. Detection of interest points by means of the non-maximum suppression technique.

   In the end of this stage all interest points from all images are detected.

(iii) Feature extraction. Since all interest points are detected, the descriptor of SURF algorithm creates a 64-dimension vector that, uniquely describes each robust interest point of all images. The descriptor function is summarized in two basic steps, involving the orientation assignment to each interest point using Haar wavelets responses and the vector computation by adding Haar wavelets responses in horizontal and vertical axis. In the end of this stage each image has interest points that are described by 64-dimension vectors in a unique and robust manner.

(iv) Image retrieval. In the last stage the images with the highest score are selected. The score is calculated by adding the number of matches between the interest points of the query image and the candidate image. A match is found by calculating the Euclidean distance between vectors of the descriptors. This process is not accomplished in a naive way (one-by-one exhausting search), but by means of linear nearest neighbor search to avoid large computational cost. The results of the abovementioned methodology are influenced by the parameters of the SURF algorithm. In the following lines a laconic definition of the parameters of the parameters octaves and threshold is given in order to provide an understanding of their role in the implementation of SURF.

Hessian threshold: The minimum value of the determinant of the Fast Hessian Matrix for a feature point should be selected. This parameter is closely connected to the repeability of the algorithm, which means that by lowering the threshold the outcome is weaker feature points with less repeatability.

Octaves: A series of filter response maps obtained by convolving the same input image with a filter of increasing size. The Gaussian pyramid of the scale space is divided into octaves, which in turn are divided into layers. The increase of octaves detects larger features but costs in time.

Layers: The next level of division of the scale space.

Initial step: The initial sampling step, which is doubled for each next octave. This value determines how many pixels separate each pixel in the given pyramid octave.

In the next Section we discuss the usage scenarios of the implemented system.

4 The System in Practice

An application was development in java programming language utilizing the libraries Openslide (www.openslide.org), ImageJ Surf (www.labun.com/imagej-surf), and PDFBOX (www.pdfbox.apache.org). The GUI of the application, as depicted in Fig. 3, is divided in two panels, the screen panel and the control panel. Four basics buttons are provided on the upper section of the main menu, as follows:

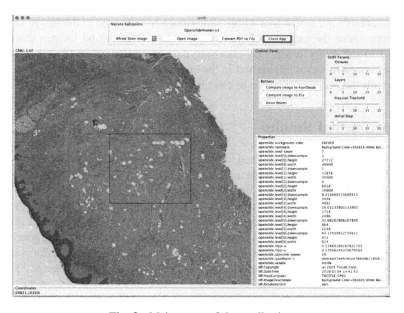

Fig. 3. Main menu of the application

- Simple Image/WSI
- Open Image
- Convert PDF to file
- Close App

The functionality of each button is briefly described below.

a. Simple Image/WSI. By pressing this button the type of the query image is selected. The user can choose between two options: Simple digital image or whole slide image.
b. Open Image. Selected query image is read and opened in order to be viewed and processed (for WSI).
c. Convert PDF to file. A digital pathology atlas can be selected and converted in a folder of digital images.
d. Close App. Self-explained.

Once a query image is selected, the requested image is visible in the screen panel section, as shown in Fig. 3. In this case the query image is a whole slide image produced by a Trestle whole slide scanner and its format is single-file pyramidal tiled TIFF (tagged image file format). In the control panel additional functionality appears by means of two new panels, SURF parameters and properties, and three buttons: compare image to handbook, compare image to folder and reset points. By using the SURF parameters panels the user can specify the parameters of the SURF algorithm for the detection and description of interest points. In the properties field the user can view the meta-data that are stored in a whole slide image in reference to the image attributes. The buttons serve the purpose of choosing the dataset of digital images that will be compared to the query image. By choosing dataset of images and query image, the process of image retrieval begins and in the end the result appears in the screen and the image/s with the most similarities to the query image is/are shown.

5   Experimental Results

A series of experiments is conducted by comparing a query image with another sample image. The images can be simple images (.jpg, .png, .bmp), whole slide images or images extracted from medical atlases in.pdf format. The query image is altered applying different brightness, rotation and scale transformations. Each time the SURF algorithm is applied and a number of matches between the query image and the image dataset are detected. Basic criteria of understanding the level of influence posed by the transformations is the number of interest points detected in each transformed image (test image) and the number of matches found between the query image and each test image.

The first set of conducted experiment uses the query image and a set of six variations of the query image from the brightest to the darkest one. Results are shown in Fig. 4.

The number of interest points increases as the image gets brighter and decreases as the image gets darken. However, the increase of the number of interest points does not

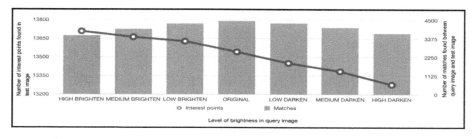

Fig. 4. Graph of matches found between query image and test image and interest points found in test image as the brightness changes

necessarily mean increase of the numbers of matches between the query and test image. The influence of the variations in brightness is slightly stronger when the pathology image gets darken (22% less matches) in respect to the brightest image (19% less matches).

The second set of experiments refers to rotation transformations. Results are illustrated in Fig. 5.

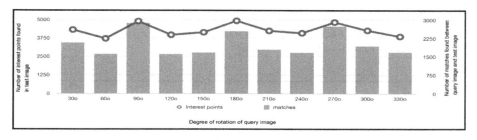

Fig. 5. Graph of matches found between query image and test image and interest points found in test image as the rotation changes

The worst case for the rotation transformations occurs at 120° (37% less matches), which is more intense that the worst case for brightness transformations. Transformations related with the scale up and down of the query image are also tried out to check the effect of these transformations to the function of SURF algorithm. The results are shown in Fig. 6.

As it is projected by the graph (Fig. 6) the effect of minimizing the query image is devastating more than any other transformation performed (97% less matches). Maximizing the image has a smoother impact to the algorithm with a 33% decrease on matches. Apart from the experiments performed with reference to the transformations of the query image, tests were conducted with the different values of the following parameters octaves, hessian threshold, explained earlier in Sect. 3, are assigned to check the influence of these variations.

The results for variations of the octaves and the threshold parameter are shown in Figs. 7 and 8.

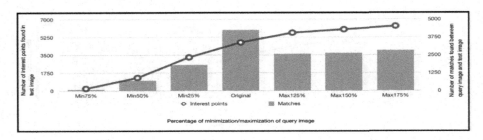

Fig. 6. Graph of matches found between query image and test image and interest points found in test image as the scale changes

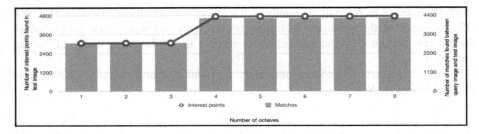

Fig. 7. Graph of matches found between query image and test image and interest points found in the query image as the octave parameter changes

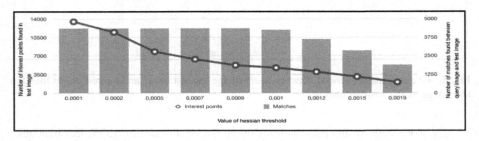

Fig. 8. Graph of matches found between query image and test image and interest points found in the query image as the threshold parameter changes

In Fig. 7 it is highlighted that the most matches are provided for four octaves and more, whereas in Fig. 8 the best results are given for a 0.00009 value of the parameter threshold, since this value ensures the most matches for the less interest points found.

One last experiment is conducted on 4 groups of similar images, which depict the effect of three different treatments (drug, radiation, drug and radiation) on cancer cells. The dataset, which is comprised by .jpg images, is described in [10]. This experiment proves the effectiveness of SURF algorithm on retrieving the most similar image/s even when the examined dataset is comprised by images that bear great resemblance. Using the application, the query image, selected from one the groups (control, drug, radiation, drug and radiation), is compared to each image of the dataset. Once the image with the greater similarity (best image) to the query image has been found, the query image is classified in the group of origin of the best image with success 67%, as illustrated in the confusion matrix below (Table 1).

Table 1. Confusion matrix of classification of 24 images in four classes (control, drug, radiation, drug n radiation)

Predicted class	Actual class			
	Control	Drug	Radiation	Drug and radiation
Control	5	0	0	1
Drug	0	4	1	1
Radiation	0	2	3	1
Drug and radiation	0	1	1	4

6 Conclusion

The retrieval of digital pathology images in references to similar images found in medical literature, storage systems and medical databases is the main goal of the work presented in this paper. The proposed methodology deploys a speeded up robust feature extraction technique along with a viewer that reads whole slide images. The experiments conducted confirm that the SURF algorithm fulfills the process efficiently and fast, mainly due to the small computational effort (integral images, box filters). To give a rough estimation of speed, the system compares 573 images (with the sized of 2.12 GB) extracted from a medical atlas called "Surgical Pathology of the Gastronomical System" in 5 min. The specific processing time refers to a desktop computer with a 3.06 GHz Intel "Core 2 Duo" Processor (E7600) and 4 GB RAM. Moreover, the robustness of SURF algorithm is verified to all brightness, rotation and scale up variations of the query image apart from the scale down transformation where the efficiency of the system is proven relatively low. Even in the worst case scenario (37% less matches) the final outcome of the system is not compromised, because the remaining matches are adequate for the system to correctly classify the query image in most cases. The initial goal of the system was the retrieval of specific images that bear resemblance to others. Nevertheless, results extracted from experiments, which are performed on cancer cells digital images, imply the capability of the system to classify an image to a certain class. A suggestion for future work would be to apply the Visual Bag of Words technique to create a single vector from each image and use the results for machine learning classification. Concluding, this work might be considered as a significant adjunct tool for pathologists in their everyday work, assisting them in searching atlases, electronic books and other electronic resources for similar cases to the one that they have in front of them. Additional evaluation with real users is required to validate this assumption.

References

1. Park, S.L., Pantarowitz, L., Sharma, G., Parwani, A.V.: Anatomic pathology laboratory information systems. Adv. Anatomic Pathol. Rev. 19(2), 81–96 (2012). https://doi.org/10.1097/pap.0b013e318248b787
2. Ellin, J., Haskitz, A., Premraj, P., Shields, K., Smith, M., Stratman, C., Wrenn, M.: Interoperability between Anatomic Laboratory Information Systems and Digital Pathology Systems. Digital Pathology Association. http://www.digitalpathologyassociation.org
3. Singh, R., Chubb, L., Pantarowitz, L., Parwani, A.: Standardization in digital pathology: Supplement 145 of the DICOM standards. J. Pathol. Inform. 2, 23 (2011)
4. Bay, H., Tuytelaars, T., Gool, V.G.: Speeded up robust features. Comput. Vis. Image Underst. 110(3), 346–359 (2008). https://doi.org/10.1016/j.cviu.2007.09.014
5. Mehta, N., Alomari, R.S., Chaudhary, V.: Content based sub-image retrieval system for high resolution pathology images using salient interest points. In: Annual International Conference of IEEE Engineering in Medicine and Biology Society, EMBC 2009 (2009)
6. Shyu, C. R., Brodley, C. E., Kosaka, A.C., Aisen, A., Broderick, L.: Local versus Global Features for Content-Based Image Retrieval. School of Electrical and Computer Engineering. Purdue University. Indiana University Medical Center
7. Velmurugan, K., Santhosh Baboo, S.: Content-based image retrieval using SURF and . Global J. Comput. Sci. Technol. 11(10), Version 1.0 (2011)
8. Govindaraju, S., Ramesh Kumar, G.P.: A novel content based medical image retrieval using SURF features. Int. J. Comput. Sci. Inf. Technol. 4(2), 242–245 (2016). https://doi.org/10.17485/ijst/2016/v9i20/89786
9. Goode, A., Gilbert, B., Harkes, J., Jukic, D., Satanarayanan, M.: Openslide: a vendor-neutral software foundation for digital pathology. J. Pathol. Inform. 4, 27 (2013)
10. Goudas, T., Maglogiannis, I.: An advanced image analysis tool for the quantification and characterization of breast cancer in microscopy images. J. Med. Syst. 39(3), 13 (2015). https://doi.org/10.1007/s10916-015-0225-3

An Investigation of Argumentation Theory for the Prediction of Survival in Elderly Using Biomarkers

Lucas Rizzo[1]([✉]), Ljiljana Majnaric[2], Pierpaolo Dondio[1], and Luca Longo[1]

[1] School of Computing, Dublin Institute of Technology, Dublin, Ireland
luca.longo@dit.ie
[2] Department of Family Medicine, School of Medicine,
University of Osijek, Osijek, Croatia

Abstract. Research on the discovery, classification and validation of biological markers, or biomarkers, have grown extensively in the last decades. Newfound and correctly validated biomarkers have great potential as prognostic and diagnostic indicators, but present a complex relationship with pertinent endpoints such as survival or other diseases manifestations. This research proposes the use of computational argumentation theory as a starting point for the resolution of this problem for cases in which a large amount of data is unavailable. A knowledge-base containing 51 different biomarkers and their association with mortality risks in elderly was provided by a clinician. It was applied for the construction of several argument-based models capable of inferring survival or not. The prediction accuracy and sensitivity of these models were investigated, showing how these are in line with inductive classification using decision trees with limited data.

Keywords: Biomarkers · Argumentation theory
Defeasible reasoning

1 Introduction

In the medical domain, biomarkers can be objectively defined as a medical condition which can be measured precisely and reproducibly. It has to be observed from outside the patient, contrarily to medical symptoms which are an indication of health recognized by the patients themselves [27]. Simple examples include blood pressure, pulse and waist circumference. It can also range to several diseases diagnostics or more complex laboratory tests of blood and other tissues. Over the past 50 years the advances in biological sciences have generated more than 30,000 candidate biomarkers from which less than a thousand might have clinical value [23]. There is a vital issue in determining the relationship between biomarkers and relevant clinical endpoints, such as survival, stroke and

L. Iliadis et al. (Eds.): AIAI 2018, IFIP AICT 519, pp. 385–397, 2018.
https://doi.org/10.1007/978-3-319-92007-8_33

myocardial infarction [27]. Data mining techniques incorporating machine learning algorithms have been used as a possible path for solving this problem [7,28]. However, these are usually suited for large amounts of data which are not always available due to the complexity of measurement and quantity of biomarkers. In such cases, it is argued that defeasible reasoning might be considered a possible resolution technique.

In formal logics a defeasible concept is built upon a set of interactive pieces of evidence that can become defeated by additional reasons [21]. Efforts have been made within the field of Artificial Intelligence (AI) to perform and analyze the act of reasoning defeasibly. Argumentation Theory (AT) is a computational approach which has been widely employed for modelling defeasible and non-monotonic reasoning [3]. It has been broadly applied in the field of health care [5,10] since data accounted in such problems is often uncertain, heterogeneous and incomplete. In this study the dataset employed follows this trend. It contains information of 93 patients and 51 different biomarkers collected in an European hospital from primary health care health records during the time span of five years. The survival of the patient is the dependent variable and indicates *survival* or *death*, while independent variables are both continuous and categorical. An initial investigation was performed and classification models such as decision trees could not provide accurate models, given the small amount of data. Thus, we proposed the investigation of computational argumentation theory for the prediction of survival in elderly. A knowledge-base constructed by a clinician was selected for examination. It adds dozens of rules and 7 different mortality risks. Its formalization was made by following the 5-layer modelling approach proposed by [16]. Finally, this schema was used for building a number of argument-based models with different parameters. Their accuracy and sensitivity (true positive rate) was subsequently computed for comparison purposes. The research question being investigated is: *to which extent can defeasible reasoning, implemented using formal argumentation theory, enhance the prediction of survival in elderly using information on biomarkers according to accuracy and sensitivity?*

The remainder of this paper is organized as follows. Section 2 presents related work on biomarkers and AT research, making the connection between the two areas. The design and methodologies of the study are detailed on Sect. 3. Section 4 provides the comparison against decision trees and subsequent discussion. Finally, Sect. 5 presents the conclusion and future work.

2   Related Work

Research on prognostic information for mortality in older adults is of significant importance on clinical decision-making, for instance when deciding for more advance care planning for higher risks patients [12]. Non-communicable diseases, such as cardiovascular, are the main cause of mortality among elderly individuals [13]. Hence, the increase of biomarkers research to obtain early prognostics. Examples include [1,6] which investigate possible biomarkers related to mortality. The predictive power of selected biomarkers is usually determined by a statistical analysis and so relies on data, not providing a complete explanation or a reasoning process. Recently, machine learning algorithms have also been used in this area of research [7,28]. Nonetheless, the validation of biomarkers as possible features of endpoints classification is still a concern on medical research [27]. It falls on the same issues as other medical fields. In these, different pieces of information taken into account might be in contradiction with each other, thus a method for resolving them is often necessary. Knowledge-based systems are approach to deal with uncertainty and potentially valid for overcoming such issues [24,25]. These are well established within AI and have been used in several domains such as the pharmaceutical industry, clinical trials and care planning [10,11,14,18,26]. However, despite the similarity of the previous areas, it appears, from literature, that there is no research that attempts to employ defeasible reasoning in the biomarker domain for the prediction of survival. Reasoning is defeasible when a conclusion can be retracted in the light of new evidence. It is argued here that the knowledge required for modelling and assessing mortality risk using biomarkers can be seen as defeasible. It contains inconsistent pieces of evidence supporting different risk levels that are also retractable in the light of new information. Let us consider the following example with arguments:

- *Arg 1: Increased mean cell volume of red blood cells (MCV) might lead to macrocytosis. Older people with macrocytosis are more likely to have poorer cognitive functioning and increased mortality.*
- *Arg 2: Deficiency of vitamin B12 is an indicator of increased MCV. If there is no vitamin B12 deficiency then MCV can not be increased.*

On one hand, in the first argument, a clinician may argue that there is evidence to infer an increased mortality risk, due to the increased measure of MCV which can lead to macrocytosis. In case there is no other evidence, increased mortality risk might be a reasonable conclusion. On the other hand, the second argument argues that if there is no deficiency of vitamin B12 then increased measure of MCV can not be taken into account. In this case the inference of an increased mortality risk no longer holds. This example illustrates how the set of conclusions does not increases monotonically and can be retracted in the light of new information. The next section explains how such arguments and conflicts can be represented and possible approaches to reach justifiable conclusions.

3   Design and Methodology

This section illustrates how a knowledge-base on mortality risk factors in elderly was translated into computational argument-based models following a 5-layer schema [15]. Due to space limitation the full knowledge-base is not shown here, but it can be found online[1]. It contains not only inference rules but also contradictions, preferences and a full description of all biomarkers utilized by the clinician, together with other 92 references used for the development of arguments (knowledge-base's rules).

---

[1] http://dx.doi.org/10.13140/RG.2.2.20905.49764.

3.1   Layer 1 - Definition of the Structure of Arguments

The first step on the argumentation process or the 5-layer schema is to define a set of *forecast* arguments. These can be represented like:

$$Forecast\ argument : premises \rightarrow conclusion$$

The objective is to determine a premise or set of premises from which a conclusion can be reasonably inferred (survival or not). Survival was deducted from mortality risks which were in turn based on natural language expressions utilized by the clinician. Expressions like "may affect survival", "strong mortality risk factor" and "increased mortality" are a few examples. These expressions were separated in seven different mortality risks: *no risk* (r_1), *low risk* (r_2), *medium low risk* (r_3), *medium risk* (r_4), *medium high risk* (r_5), *high risk* (r_6) and *extremely high risk* (r_7). From the initial set of 51 biomarkers, 44 had a natural language description employable for the inference of some mortality risk. Let us consider a description for chronic obstructive pulmonary disease (COPD) and the possible argument associated to it:

- *Description: COPD is a major cause of mortality and also a cardiovascular risk factor. There may be a survival benefit for treatment with new inhalatory drugs, however, conclusive data are currently lacking.*
- Arg: *presence of* COPD $\rightarrow$ **extremely high risk** (r_7)

From the knowledge-base's descriptions it is possible to infer some mortality risk for some biomarkers, but the deduction from risks to survival or death is not known. Because of these two approaches are selected for investigation:

- *Cautious*: all risks are considered as potential predictors. r_{1-3} are predictors for survival while r_{4-7} are predictors for death.
- *Skeptical*: only r_{1-2} are associated with survival and r_{6-7} with death. Arguments that support other conclusions (r_{3-5}) are no longer part of the reasoning process. Since risks r_{3-5} are in the medium range it might be argued that they do not provide strong evidence to infer survival or not.

3.2   Layer 2 - Definition of the Conflicts of Arguments

At this layer the relationship between arguments is defined. While the first layer allows the definition of the monological structure of arguments, the second layer allows the creation of dialogical structures of knowledge. The objective is to support the examination of invalid arguments that have the earmarks of being legitimate. According to [20] these can be referred to as *mitigating arguments*. Their internal structure is defined by a set of premises and an undercutting inference $\Rightarrow$ to an argument B (forecast or mitigating):

$$Mitigating\ argument : premises \Rightarrow B$$

A few classes of mitigating arguments can be found in [22]. However, only one of them, *undercutting attack*, is adopted in this research for the implementation of conflicts. An undercutting attack occurs when there is a special case, or a defeasible inference rule, that does not allow the application of the knowledge carried in some other argument. Examples include expressions such as:

– Arg: If `total cholesterol` is *high* then `hematocrite` (HTC) is not *low*.

Based on this description an undercutting attack to a forecast argument (or a mitigating argument) can be built, that assumes low HTC as one of its premises. For instance, consider a forecast argument F1 and an undercutting attack UC1:

– F1: `male` AND *low* `HTC` $\rightarrow$ `medium low risk` (r_3)
– UC1: *high* `total cholesterol` $\Rightarrow$ F1

Since it is known that HTC can not be low if total cholesterol is high, undercutting attack UC1 ensures that forecast rule F1 is not applied in this situation. A set of strict preferences among pairs of biomarkers for predicting survival are also provided by the clinician (expert) who was interviewed in this study. Such preferences can also be seen as undercutting attacks[2]. Consider the following preference P1, forecast arguments F2, F3 and an undercutting attack UC2:

– P1: `Hypertension` > `Age`   - F2: `Age` $\in [66, 70] \rightarrow$ `medium risk` (r_4)
– F3: *high* `Hypertension` $\rightarrow$ `high risk` (r_6)   - UC2: F3 $\Rightarrow$ F2

In the above example P1 suggests that hypertension is more important for inferring survival than age, thus forecast argument F3 should be considered instead of F2. Let us point out that forecast arguments F1 and F2 would not be defined according to the skeptical approach (layer 1) because their risks are not in the survival set (r_{1-2}) or death set (r_{6-7}), consequently UC1 and UC2 would also not be defined in this approach. Once layers 1 and 2 are finalized, the set or arguments and attacks can be seen now as a graph, or *argumentation framework* (AF). Figure 1 depicts AFs for cautions and skeptical approaches. Node labels follow the same names used for arguments in the full knowledge-base[3].

3.3   Layer 3 - Evaluation of the Conflicts of Arguments

Once an AF is constructed, it can be elicited with data[4]. Some of arguments will be activated and kept, while others will not be activated and discarded. For instance, F1 premises do not evaluate true for female individuals or individuals that do not have low HTC, hence it is not activated and is discarded. Activated arguments might be in conflict, according to attacks defined in layer 2. These can be evaluated employing different strategies such as the strength of argument, preferentiality and strength of attack relations [9]. Here attacks only present a form of a binary relation. In other words, once the arguments of an

---

[2] Note that preference among biomarkers is not the same as preferentiality of arguments, a notion mentioned on layer 3.

[3] http://dx.doi.org/10.13140/RG.2.2.20905.49764.

[4] http://dx.doi.org/10.13140/RG.2.2.17130.62402.

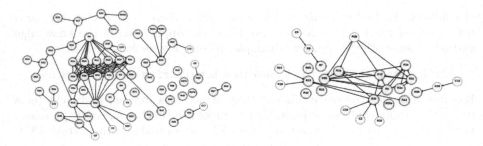

Fig. 1. Argumentation framework: graphical representation of cautious (left) and skeptical (right) knowledge-bases. Double circles represent forecast arguments supporting survival (blue) or death (red). Other nodes represent premises of undercutting attacks. Edges are directed and represent attacks from an argument to another argument, or from a forecast argument to another forecast argument. (Color figure online)

attack are activated, the attack is automatically considered efficacious. Activated arguments together with valid attacks form a *sub-argumentation framework* (sub-AF), that can now be evaluated against inconsistencies. Figure 2 depicts a sub-AF.

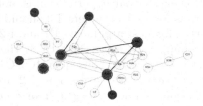

Fig. 2. Argumentation framework: an example of activated arguments (blue nodes inside) given one record of the dataset. Light nodes and edges are still part of the knowledge-base but are not considered for the next layers. (Color figure online)

3.4   Layer 4 - Definition of the Dialectical Status of Arguments

In order to accept or reject arguments, acceptability semantics are applied on top of each sub-AF. Note that each record in the dataset produces a different sub-AF, so semantics should be applied for each separated case. Most well known semantics, such as *grounded* and *preferred*, can be found in [8]. The goal in this layer is to evaluate not only if an argument is defeated but if the defeaters are defeated themselves. It is said that an argument A *defeats* argument B if and only if there is a valid attack from A to B. Dung's acceptability semantics [8] will generate one or more sets of *extensions* (conflict free sets of arguments). Each extension can be seen as a different point of view that can be used in a decision making process. At this stage the internal structure of arguments is not considered and in the literature this is known as an *abstract argumentation framework* (AAF). It is a pair $< Arg, attacks >$ where: Arg is a finite set of (abstract) arguments, $attacks \subseteq Arg \times Arg$ is binary relation over Arg. Given sets $X, Y \subseteq Arg$ of arguments, X *attacks* Y if and only if there exists $x \in X$ and $y \in Y$ such that $(x, y) \in attacks$. A set $X \subseteq Arg$ of argument is

- *admissible* iff X does not attack itself and X attacks every set of arguments Y such that Y attacks X;
- *complete* iff X is admissible and X contains all arguments it *defends*, where X *defends* x if and only if X attacks all attacks against x;
- *grounded* iff X is minimally complete (with respect to $\subseteq$);
- *preferred* iff X is maximally admissible (respect to $\subseteq$)

It is important to highlight that arguments with different conclusions (survival or death in this study), are not necessarily conflicting (given the expert's knowledge-base) and might be part of the same extension. This is because they are originally defined according to the set of mortality risks (r_{1-7}) and not survival, thus, unless some inconsistency is explicitly defined, they can coexist. Nonetheless, in order to minimize this inconsistency, ranking-based semantics were also applied. This class of semantics is capable of distinguishing arguments not only as accepted or rejected, but it also provides a mechanism to fully rank them, therefore defining a form of importance. Here, the *categorizer* semantic is employed [2]. It takes into consideration the number of direct attackers to compute the strength of an argument. In this sense, attacks from non-attacked arguments are stronger and are more impactful then attacks from arguments attacked several times. Given an $AAF = < Arg, attacks >$, and the set of direct attackers $att(a) \forall a \in Arg$, the categorizer function $Cat : Arg \rightarrow]0, 1]$ is given by:

$$Cat(a) = \begin{cases} 1 & \text{if } att(a) = \emptyset \\ \frac{1}{1 + \sum\limits_{c \in att(a)} Cat(c)} & \text{otherwise} \end{cases} \tag{1}$$

Finally, a ranking is given according to the value computed by Cat for each argument. Forecast arguments with different conclusions still might have the same ranking, for instance, if they are both not attacked. In this case another layer is required to accrue arguments and produce a final inference. Figure 3 illustrates *grounded* and *categorizer* semantics computed for the activated graph on Fig. 2. Note that forecast arguments attacked only by rejected arguments can still be rejected under the categorizer semantics.

3.5   Layer 5 - Accrual of Acceptable Arguments

The final step on the argumentation process of this study is to select one of the possible two outcomes: survival or death. As defined in layer 2 (Sect. 3.2), two types of arguments can be part of an extension or have the same ranking: forecast and mitigating. Mitigating arguments, by definition, do not support any conclusion and have already finalized their role attacking other arguments and

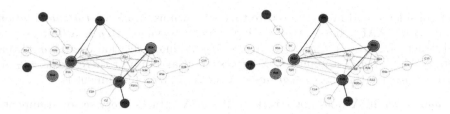

Fig. 3. Argumentation framework: acceptable arguments computed by the grounded semantics (left) and categorizer semantics (right). Blue nodes inside are activated but do not support a conclusion, so are not accepted neither rejected. Red and green nodes inside are forecast arguments rejected and accepted respectively. Double circles indicate whether forecast arguments support death (red) or survival (blue). (Color figure online)

contributing to the definition of the set of acceptable arguments. Thus, the final inference is given only by the forecast arguments. Three situations are possible:

1. If the set of acceptable forecast arguments support the same conclusion, then final inference coincides to that conclusion.
2. If both conclusions are supported we argue that the one with the highest number of supporters should be chosen. Preferences have already been taken into account, hence the amount of evidence, or number of arguments supporting a conclusion, may be seen as a possible reason for choosing one.
3. If there is still a tie (survival and death being supported by an equal number of acceptable forecast arguments), then logically there is no reason for the system to take any conclusion. This might reflect the uncertainty of the domain, in which the knowledge-base, as coded from the expert in this study, does not contain information for dealing with this type of situation. Nonetheless, because one conclusion is eventually required for comparison purposes, the preference goes to death making a skeptical inference.

Table 1 lists the constructed models, summarising their settings for each layer.

Table 1. Set up of each model investigated. For layers 1, 2 and 4 ($L1$, $L2$, $L4$) a parameter is set. Layers 3 and 5 are equal for all cases.

Model	Survival ($L1$)	AF ($L2$)	Semantics ($L4$)
M1	Cautious	Fig. 1 (left)	Grounded
M2	Cautious	Fig. 1 (left)	Categorizer
M3	Skeptical	Fig. 1 (right)	Grounded
M4	Skeptical	Fig. 1 (right)	Categorizer

4 Results

Collected data of 93 patients and 51 different biomarkers obtained from an European hospital from primary health care health records during the time span of five years[5] was used to instantiate the designed argumentation-based models (Table 1). In order to gauge the quality of the solutions an analysis was also performed using classification trees (CT) on the same dataset. Data was normalized and stratified 10-fold cross validation was applied for building CT models. The percentage of death and survival records is 39% and 61% respectively. The evaluation metrics selected were accuracy, obtained from each respective confusion matrix, and sensitivity or true positive rate. It is important to highlight that the comparison between argument-based inference (conducted case-by-case) and a learning technique (conducted on the whole dataset with CT) is not straightforward. In fact, argument-based models do not rely on data and consequently are not built on training sets. To be as fair as possible, oversampling could not be applied on the classification tree considering that synthetic data might be outside the knowledge-base capacity of understanding. The accuracy and sensitivity of each fold was computed across the argument-based models and the CT models (Figs. 4 and 5).

4.1 Accuracy

The accuracy of CT was higher than argument-based models in 4 folds, lower in 4 folds and equal in 2 folds. Given the size of the dataset, there is approximately 9 records on each fold, and because of that there is a large fluctuation in the accuracy percentage. Nonetheless, it is reasonable to say that, overall, tested approaches are nearly equivalent according to their accuracies (Fig. 4). Among the argument-based models, also no significant difference can be observed. This demonstrates a slight advantage of models M3-4 over M1-2, since the skeptical approach contain less information and could achieve similar results. Cautious models (M1-2) and skeptical models (M3-4) did not present any significant difference between them, suggesting that, given the topology of the argumentation frameworks (Fig. 1), grounded and categorizer semantics have no meaningful impact on inferences.

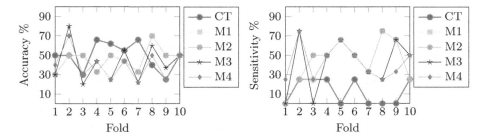

Fig. 4. Accuracy of classification tree (CT) and each model (M) by fold.

Fig. 5. Sensitivity of classification tree (CT) and each model (M) by fold.

---

[5] http://dx.doi.org/10.13140/RG.2.2.17130.62402.

4.2 Sensitivity

Argument-based models could outperform CT in all folds. Only model M3 had a lower sensitivity in one fold. This shows how the techniques are equivalent based on their accuracies but argument-based models have a better prediction capacity for death, which is highly important in this domain. Among argument-based models, folds 4 to 7 had the same sensitivity. Other folds presented a mixed prediction, sometimes having better results for models M1-2 and other times for models M3-4. Again, this suggests how the skeptical approach might be as predictive as the cautious one, making the use of medium risk biomarkers (by models M1-2) questionable for the prediction of survival.

4.3 Discussion

The analysis of accuracy of the investigated models demonstrates that the prediction capacity of survival by argument-based models is in line with the classification tree approach. Sensitivity, however, suggests that more precise inferences of death can be done by argument-based models. One can argue that learning algorithms might not be suited for the proportion of biomarkers by records in this problem (51 biomarkers and 93 records), thus another knowledge-base approach should be employed for comparison purposes. However, to the best of our knowledge, no other knowledge-base approach has been applied in the biomarker domain. In fact, the use of other knowledge-base techniques such as expert systems and fuzzy logic systems are mentioned as future work.

In line with this, it is important to mention the interest in pursuing explanation systems [4] in the health-care sector opposed to learning techniques where outcomes are not fully comprehended by humans. Defeasible reasoning and argument-based models allow a clearer reasoning process under uncertainty and incomplete data, are not based upon statistic or probability and allow the comparison of different knowledge-bases [19]. Efforts have already been made in order to apply argument-based systems in the medical field [17], so it is expected that this integration might be enhanced by this research. For instance, take the knowledge-base applied here. Although it presents a large set of biomarkers it is not completely clear how they interact with each other. It is also not clear how the deduction from mortality risk to survival should be made. However, these are questions that are possibly not known even by domain experts. Nonetheless, two models or interpretations of this knowledge-base (cautious and skeptical) could be investigated and hopefully shed some light on these questions. For example, skeptical and cautious models presented similar performance, demonstrating that medium risk biomarkers did not have a significant contribution in the prediction of survival. Furthermore, each record analyzed has its own sub-argumentation framework, its own set of acceptable arguments and its own set of successful attacks. Such information can also be used for additional reasoning and improvement of biomarkers understanding towards survival.

5   Conclusion and Future Work

This research investigated the use of defeasible reasoning, formally implemented via computational argumentation theory, for the prediction of survival in elderly built upon evidence on biomarkers. The motivation for applying this technique comes from the lack of other studies employing knowledge driven approaches in the biomarker domain and also from the small amount of available data. A 5-layer schema was used to translate an extensive expert's knowledge-base into arguments. These were used to infer death or survival of elderly patients. The main disadvantage of building argument-based models is the time required to translate a knowledge-base generally expressed in natural language terms, into formal rules. Findings suggest that argument-based models are a promising avenue for the investigation of the relationship between biomarkers and survival in elderly. A comparison between argument-based models, built upon this 5-layer schema, and a classification tree algorithm showed that the formers can achieve a similar accuracy than the latter but a better sensitivity. In addition, argument-based models are not based on statistic or probability and can reason with unclear and incomplete data. Future work will be focused on the application of different knowledge driven approaches, including expert systems and fuzzy logic. Moreover, given the uncertainty of the application (inference of survival of elderly using biomarkers) the same methodology of this study (5-layer schema) is going to be employed with different knowledge-bases designed by distinct experts.

Acknowledgments. Lucas Middeldorf Rizzo would like to thank CNPq (Conselho Nacional de Desenvolvimento Científico e Tecnológico) for his Science Without Borders scholarship, proc n. 232822/2014-0.

References

1. Barron, E., Lara, J., White, M., Mathers, J.C.: Blood-borne biomarkers of mortality risk: systematic review of cohort studies. PLoS ONE **10**(6), e0127550 (2015)
2. Besnard, P., Hunter, A.: A logic-based theory of deductive arguments. Artif. Intell. **128**(1–2), 203–235 (2001)
3. Bryant, D., Krause, P.: A review of current defeasible reasoning implementations. Knowl. Eng. Rev. **23**(3), 227–260 (2008)
4. Core, M.G., Lane, H.C., Van Lent, M., Gomboc, D., Solomon, S., Rosenberg, M.: Building explainable artificial intelligence systems. In: AAAI, pp. 1766–1773 (2006)
5. Craven, R., Toni, F., Cadar, C., Hadad, A., Williams, M.: Efficient argumentation for medical decision-making. In: KR (2012)
6. De Ruijter, W., Westendorp, R.G., Assendelft, W.J., den Elzen, W.P., de Craen, A.J., le Cessie, S., Gussekloo, J.: Use of framingham risk score and new biomarkers to predict cardiovascular mortality in older people: population based observational cohort study. BMJ **338**, a3083 (2009)
7. Dipnall, J.F., Pasco, J.A., Berk, M., Williams, L.J., Dodd, S., Jacka, F.N., Meyer, D.: Fusing data mining, machine learning and traditional statistics to detect biomarkers associated with depression. PLoS ONE **11**(2), e0148195 (2016)

8. Dung, P.M.: On the acceptability of arguments and its fundamental role in non-monotonic reasoning, logic programming and n-person games. Artif. Intell. **77**(2), 321–358 (1995)

9. García, D., Simari, G.: Strong and weak forms of abstract argument defense. In: Computational Models of Argument: Proceedings of COMMA 2008, vol. 172, p. 216 (2008)

10. Glasspool, D., Fox, J., Oettinger, A., Smith-Spark, J.: Argumentation in decision support for medical care planning for patients and clinicians. In: AAAI Spring Symposium: Argumentation for Consumers of Healthcare, pp. 58–63 (2006)

11. Hunter, A., Williams, M.: Argumentation for aggregating clinical evidence. In: 2010 22nd IEEE International Conference on Tools with Artificial Intelligence (ICTAI), vol. 1, pp. 361–368. IEEE (2010)

12. Lee, S.J., Lindquist, K., Segal, M.R., Covinsky, K.E.: Development and validation of a prognostic index for 4-year mortality in older adults. JAMA **295**(7), 801–808 (2006)

13. Lloyd-Jones, D., Adams, R., Carnethon, M., De Simone, G., Ferguson, T.B., Flegal, K., Ford, E., Furie, K., Go, A., Greenlund, K., et al.: Heart disease and stroke statistics-2009 update: a report from the American Heart Association Statistics Committee and Stroke Statistics Subcommittee. Circulation **119**(3), e21–e181 (2009)

14. Longo, L.: Formalising human mental workload as non-monotonic concept for adaptive and personalised web-design. In: Masthoff, J., Mobasher, B., Desmarais, M.C., Nkambou, R. (eds.) UMAP 2012. LNCS, vol. 7379, pp. 369–373. Springer, Heidelberg (2012). https://doi.org/10.1007/978-3-642-31454-4_38

15. Longo, L.: A defeasible reasoning framework for human mental workload representation and assessment. Behav. Inf. Technol. **34**(8), 758–786 (2015)

16. Longo, L.: Argumentation for knowledge representation, conflict resolution, defeasible inference and its integration with machine learning. In: Holzinger, A. (ed.) Machine Learning for Health Informatics. LNCS (LNAI), vol. 9605, pp. 183–208. Springer, Cham (2016). https://doi.org/10.1007/978-3-319-50478-0_9

17. Longo, L., Dondio, P.: Defeasible reasoning and argument-based systems in medical fields: an informal overview. In: 2014 IEEE 27th International Symposium on Computer-Based Medical Systems (CBMS), pp. 376–381. IEEE (2014)

18. Longo, L., Hederman, L.: Argumentation theory for decision support in healthcare: a comparison with machine learning. In: Imamura, K., Usui, S., Shirao, T., Kasamatsu, T., Schwabe, L., Zhong, N. (eds.) BHI 2013. LNCS (LNAI), vol. 8211, pp. 168–180. Springer, Cham (2013). https://doi.org/10.1007/978-3-319-02753-1_17

19. Longo, L., Kane, B., Hederman, L.: Argumentation theory in health care. In: 2012 25th International Symposium on Computer-Based Medical Systems (CBMS), pp. 1–6. IEEE (2012)

20. Matt, P.A., Morgem, M., Toni, F.: Combining statistics and arguments to compute trust. In: 9th International Conference on Autonomous Agents and Multiagent Systems, Toronto, Canada, vol. 1, pp. 209–216. ACM, May 2010

21. Pollock, J.L.: Defeasible reasoning. Cogn. Sci. **11**(4), 481–518 (1987)

22. Prakken, H.: An abstract framework for argumentation with structured arguments. Argument Comput. **1**(2), 93–124 (2010)

23. Pritzker, K.P., Pritzker, L.B.: Bioinformatics advances for clinical biomarker development. Expert Opin. Med. Diagn. **6**(1), 39–48 (2012)

24. Rizzo, L., Dondio, P., Delany, S.J., Longo, L.: Modeling mental workload via rule-based expert system: a comparison with NASA-TLX and workload profile. In: Iliadis, L., Maglogiannis, I. (eds.) AIAI 2016. IAICT, vol. 475, pp. 215–229. Springer, Cham (2016). https://doi.org/10.1007/978-3-319-44944-9_19
25. Rizzo, L., Longo, L.: Representing and inferring mental workload via defeasible reasoning: a comparison with the nasa task load index and the workload profile. In: 1st Workshop on Advances In Argumentation In Artificial Intelligence, pp. 126–140 (2017)
26. Slater, T., Bouton, C., Huang, E.S.: Beyond data integration. Drug Discovery Today **13**(13), 584–589 (2008)
27. Strimbu, K., Tavel, J.A.: What are biomarkers? Current Opin. HIV AIDS **5**(6), 463 (2010)
28. Swan, A.L., Mobasheri, A., Allaway, D., Liddell, S., Bacardit, J.: Application of machine learning to proteomics data: classification and biomarker identification in postgenomics biology. OMICS J. Integrative Biol. **17**(12), 595–610 (2013)

Recommender Systems

Reproducibility of Experiments in Recommender Systems Evaluation

Nikolaos Polatidis[1](✉), Stelios Kapetanakis[1,2], Elias Pimenidis[3], and Konstantinos Kosmidis[4]

[1] School of Computing, Engineering, and Mathematics,
University of Brighton, Brighton BN2 4GJ, UK
{N.Polatidis, S.Kapetanakis}@Brighton.ac.uk
[2] Gluru Research, Gluru, London WC2B 4HN, UK
stelios@gluru.co
[3] Department of Computer Science and Creative Technologies,
University of the West of England, Bristol BS16 1QY, UK
Elias.Pimenidis@uwe.ac.uk
[4] School of Computing and Engineering,
University of West London, London W5 5RF, UK
Konstantinos.Kosmidis@uwl.ac.uk

Abstract. Recommender systems evaluation is usually based on predictive accuracy metrics with better scores meaning recommendations of higher quality. However, the comparison of results is becoming increasingly difficult, since there are different recommendation frameworks and different settings in the design and implementation of the experiments. Furthermore, there might be minor differences on algorithm implementation among the different frameworks. In this paper, we compare well known recommendation algorithms, using the same dataset, metrics and overall settings, the results of which point to result differences across frameworks with the exact same settings. Hence, we propose the use of standards that should be followed as guidelines to ensure the replication of experiments and the reproducibility of the results.

Keywords: Recommender systems · Evaluation · Reproducibility
Replication

1 Introduction

Recommender systems are decision support systems found in online web services, mainly in e-Commerce for movies, music, videos or general item recommendation. During the last few years, research in recommender systems both in academia and in industry counts numerous publications found in the literature [1]. The popularity in recommender systems research has led to the increasingly important problem of reproducibility and replication of experiments during the evaluation of such systems. The valuation of recommendation algorithms is important for measuring the quality of the results and make objective comparisons among algorithms. A positive aspect found in the literature is the availability of papers that describe in detail their proposed recommendation algorithms, the evaluation methods, the settings and datasets used [2–4].

© IFIP International Federation for Information Processing 2018
Published by Springer International Publishing AG 2018. All Rights Reserved
L. Iliadis et al. (Eds.): AIAI 2018, IFIP AICT 519, pp. 401–409, 2018.
https://doi.org/10.1007/978-3-319-92007-8_34

In the research community, there are different recommendation frameworks that can be used for the evaluation of algorithms. These include, among others, the Apache Mahout [5], LensKit [6], MyMediaLite [7] and Recommender101 [8]. The first one has been developed by the Apache Foundation whereas the rest have been developed by researchers in academia. All these recommendation frameworks provide essentially the same portfolio of algorithms. However, substantial differences exist in the implementation of the algorithms, data management and evaluation methods and while all frameworks provide the same basic evaluation methods, differences in algorithm implementation makes it difficult to compare results across frameworks [1].

To assist towards the problem of reproducibility and replication of experimental results in recommender systems we:

- Provide a set of standards and best practices that can be used when performing experiments.
- Performed different experiments using a real dataset and different recommendation libraries with the results validating our approach.

The rest of the paper is organized as follows: Sect. 2 provides the required background, Sect. 3 is a comparison between recommendation libraries, real data and different settings, Sect. 4 delivers the proposed approach and Sect. 5 contains the conclusion and future work parts.

2   Background

In the literature, the progress of recommender systems algorithms can be measured using accuracy and classification evaluation methods. The most known and used accuracy methods are the Mean Absolute Error (MAE) and the Root Mean Square Error (RMSE), whereas the most known classification methods are Precision and Recall. State of the art works about the evaluation of recommender systems can be found in [3, 9]. Research papers that propose new recommendation algorithms will typically describe the experimental setup, the dataset used and the framework used and by reproducibility is meant the replication and validation of the results by third parties [1].

The four main problems that occur when evaluating recommender systems algorithms are [1, 10]:

1. The framework used for the generation of the recommendations and the evaluation should be mentioned and it should be publicly available.
2. The details of the algorithms should be clearly mentioned, such as the size of the neighborhood used.
3. The dataset used for the experiments, along with any possible version of it and it should be publicly available.
4. Details of how the dataset has been used. These must include training and test splits and if these have been randomly selected or if parameters have been used to select specific parts that will make the reproduction easier. Moreover, if k-folds have been used for cross-fold validation then details about the number of folds and how these have been selected should be available.

The problem of the replication of experiments and the reproducibility of the results has been an open issue in the research community with a workshop organized in 2013 [11]. The outcome of the joint community work identifies the key aspects of the reproducibility problem, although its future direction part is limited [12] since future directions are only theoretical towards the need of general guidelines to produce better results [10, 12–14]. One step further from the theoretical guidelines is RiVal [15], a toolkit that provides four stages in the recommendation process, data splitting, item recommendation, candidate item generation and performance evaluation. RiVal is not an evaluation framework since it pertains to three different frameworks, these of Apache Mahout, LensKit and MyMediaLite. The toolkit provides a user interface where the user will input the data splitting, item generation and recommendation and will select which framework will be used for the evaluation. Furthermore, there are different approaches to the problem with one found in [16], where the authors propose the use of a general framework for recommender systems and evaluation metric that operates over a set of sessions. Finally, another related metric available is the modified Reciprocal Hit Rand Metric (mRHR) proposed by [17], where the use of an alternative hit rank metric is proposed. However, in this work the problem of the average reciprocal hit rank (ARHR) is only tackled in the context of the evaluation of recommender systems.

3   Comparing Experimental Results Using Different Libraries

In this section we present a comparison of two recommendation libraries. Apache Mahout and Recommender101 based on the Pearson Correlation Similarity (PCC) and Jaccard similarity measurements and the Mean Absolute Error (MAE) error rating prediction metric.

3.1   Settings

The experimental evaluation took place on an Intel i7 with 8 GBs of RAM running Windows 10. The dataset used is the MovieLens 1 million [18], which contains 3952 movies, 6040 users and 1,000,209 ratings, with each user having at least 20 ratings. The dataset has been split in 80% for training and 20% for testing and the percentages have been randomly selected once for each library.

3.2   Recommendation Methods

For the experiments we have used PCC and Jaccard. PCC is defined in Eq. 1. In PCC the sum of ratings between two users is compared. Sim (a, b) is the similarity between users a and b, also $r_{a,p}$ is the rating of user a for product p, $r_{b,p}$ is the rating of user b for product p and $r'a$ and $r'b$ represent the user's average ratings. P is the set of all products. Moreover, in PCC the similarity value between users ranges from -1 to 1 and higher values represent a closer similarity between users. Additionally, Jaccard similarity which is defined in Eq. 2 and in this approach only the number of co-rated items is taken into consideration. In Jaccard a represents a user and b a second user. Then, Jaccard provides a similarity value between −1 and 1 by measuring the co-rated items and dividing the size of the intersection by the size of the union of the sets. Once again higher values represent better similarity.

$$PCC\,a,b = \frac{\sum p \in P(ra,p - r'a)(rb,p - r'b)}{\sqrt{\sum p \in P(ra,p - r'a)^2}\sqrt{\sum p \in P(rb,p - r'b)^2}} \qquad (1)$$

$$Jaccard\,a,b = \frac{|Ia\,Ib|}{|Ia\,Ib|} \qquad (2)$$

3.3   Accuracy Measure

For measuring the prediction accuracy, we have used MAE which is defined in Eq. 3 where pi is the predicted rating and ri is the actual rating in the summation. This method is used for the computation of the deviation between the predicted ratings and the actual ratings. It should also be noted that lower values are better. MAE has been widely used in previous research for predicting the accuracy of recommender systems [3, 19, 20].

$$MAE = \frac{1}{n}\sum_{i=1}^{n}|pi - ri| \qquad (3)$$

3.4   Results

The following tables describe the experimental results. Table 1 presents the results using the Apache Mahout library and Table 2 the results using the Recommender101 library. In both tables the values represent the rating prediction errors based on the MAE metric. It is shown in the tables that different values have been derived after using the same settings and evaluation metric for two different recommendation libraries.

Table 1. MAE results for Apache Mahout

	Number of k nearest neighbours used for evaluating MAE					
	60	80	100	200	300	400
PCC	0.843	0.835	0.827	0.802	0.789	0.785
Jaccard	0.798	0.802	0.775	0.790	0.799	0.786

Table 2. MAE results for Recommender101

	Number of k nearest neighbours used for evaluating MAE					
	60	80	100	200	300	400
PCC	0.870	0.862	0.841	0.811	0.785	0.761
Jaccard	0.724	0.718	0.717	0.715	0.710	0.715

4 Proposed Approach

In recommender systems evaluation to reproduce experiments it is recommended to follow a set of guidelines [1]. However, most researchers either do not follow them or do not explain in detail the settings of their research environment. Furthermore, the guidelines may vary across researchers and the need for their standardization in a form of framework is necessary. A major challenge in recommender system evaluation is that there are many different libraries for evaluating algorithms and the possibility of having one single library or making all the current libraries following a universal or standardized approach is rather impossible. Furthermore, scientists might decide they want to develop their own library for performing the evaluations. Thus, we list a set of guidelines in Sect. 4.1 that explain the differences in evaluation libraries and why the results are different and in Sect. 4.2 we propose how to replicate studies.

4.1 Guidelines

The following elements are the ones responsible for the reproducibility of results across libraries and within the same library.

Architecture. By this we mean the architecture of the recommendation library. For example, Apache Mahout has a different architecture when compared to Recommender 101. In the first library the *PearsonCorrelationSimilarity* class extends an *AbstractSimilarity* class but it implements Pearson, whereas in the second library there is a *NearestNeighbors* class implementing *AbstractRecommender,* which includes different neighborhood-based implementations including both Pearson and Cosine.

Main Recommendation Algorithm. The most widely used method for providing recommendations in e-Commerce and other online environments is Collaborative Filtering (CF) [4]. In CF, a user neighborhood is created based on previous common history between users based on a similarity function such as Pearson Correlation Coefficient (PCC) or Cosine similarity. However, small alterations on how CF works exist between frameworks.

Evaluation Settings. Some frameworks provide different settings whereas others do not.

For example, differences between Recommender101 and Apache Mahout include:

- Recommender101 provides options about the minimum number of ratings per user or per item whereas in Apache Mahout someone will have to manually edit the source code to do that. This parameter could lead to different results.
- Recommender101 provides settings for both the minimum and maximum rating value that should be taken into consideration during the evaluation, whereas Apache Mahout does not.

Hence, it is important for each framework to provide the same settings during the evaluation process. We believe that a framework such as Recommender101 that provides more options is more suitable for research and standardization development. A standard that defines all possible parameters for recommender system evaluation is necessary for reproducibility.

Dataset Settings. This is related to the evaluation settings and is necessary for users to follow them to make reproducibility easier. The standard should provide guidelines related to the percentage of training and test set. It should be clearly mentioned which part of the dataset has been used for training and which for testing and while pure random selection makes results more reliable affects the reproducibility. Furthermore, if k-folds have been used for cross-fold evaluation then details about which the folds are should be available. Furthermore, the dataset used should be explained in detail, including any possible version of it, its size and any other available parameters.

4.2 Replication

In Sect. 4.1 we discussed how the architecture, the algorithm implementation, the evaluation settings and the dataset settings are accountable for different results among different libraries or within the same library. However, the architecture of a library would be very difficult to change as well as the implementation of already established algorithms contained in libraries. Moreover, it would be dreadful to have different libraries behave the same. Thus, the main problem resides in reproducing the results of a study based on a proposed algorithm, the evaluation settings, the data used and the library the researchers have used to run the experiments.

Therefore, it is important to follow a set of guidelines or good practices to make the results reproducible. We have identified the following steps that if followed, will assist people reproducing the results using the same framework.

1. Explanation regarding the library and version you have used. If the library has been self-developed it should be available online.
2. Step by step explanation of the evaluation settings such as the number of user neighbors used, if ratings below a threshold have been removed, if users that have not rated a certain number of items have been removed, if items with few ratings or too many ratings have been removed and if from the user base satisfying the criteria a sample of the users have been used or if all the users in the dataset have been used.

Furthermore, other settings such as if there is a threshold for forming the user neighborhood or a threshold of common rated items should be mentioned. Finally, it should be noted that some of the settings available in a library might not be in another. All available settings of the library used should be mentioned.

3. In the dataset it should be made clear which dataset and version has been used, if the dataset has been split using test/train or whether a cross-fold validation has been used and how many folds have been used. In addition, it should be made clear which exact part has been used for training, which for testing and how the selection has been made to use the same training/testing parts in the reproduction of the experiments.

4. If the proposed algorithm extends a class of the library used or if it is a standalone file using the library for evaluation purposes.

Table 3 presents the results of replicating the tests that are presented in Table 2. The first two rows represent the first test where the exact same evaluation settings and data have been used as in Table 2. The two rows further down represent the second test run with a different random selection of 80% for training and 20% for testing. Finally, Table 4 contains results based on a 5-fold cross-fold validation and not on an 80-20 training/testing scale, which makes a difference because it produces the average of different MAE evaluations and this should be specified in the settings. In Table 4 Recommender101 and PCC have been used with 60 neighbors and with a different minimum number of ratings per user. Moreover, in Table 3 the 1st and 2nd tests of each method show that when the exact same settings are used but the training and testing parts of the dataset are randomly selected then there are differences in the output values and in Table 4 we show that if the number of minimum considered ratings that a user has submitted to be taken into consideration for the evaluation process is different then different results are derived.

Table 3. Reproducing the MAE results based on Recommender101

	Number of k nearest neighbours used for evaluating MAE					
	60	80	100	200	300	400
PCC (1st)	0.870	0.862	0.841	0.811	0.785	0.761
Jaccard (1st)	0.724	0.718	0.717	0.715	0.710	0.715
PCC (2nd)	0.868	0.860	0.841	0.810	0.784	0.760
Jaccard (2nd)	0.723	0.716	0.716	0.713	0.709	0.710

Table 4. 5-fold cross-validation with different settings MAE results based on Recommender101

Method used	Min number of ratings per user (30)	Min number of ratings per user (Not known and not specified – Default value used by the library)
PCC	0.872	0.890

5 Conclusions and Future Work

In this paper we have performed a comparative analysis and shown that it is difficult to reproduce evaluation results both across different libraries but also when the same library is used. The use of various settings and algorithm implementations lead to producing different results. For example, the selection of which data from datasets will be used for training and which for testing leads to different results, which in turn has an impact to the overall conclusion. Furthermore, we conclude that there are many different parameters that need to be considered by researchers when performing evaluation that it is very difficult to achieve a complete reproduction. Thus, we proposed a unified approach which can facilitate a common reference baseline for recommendation experiments across different frameworks and a set of guidelines to tackle a cross-industry challenge. This work is the first step towards an extensively broad validation framework for recommender systems and it aims to educate the community while collating feedback towards robust experimentation and comparison across recommender frameworks. The results show that when comparing results using the same settings with different libraries the output is not the same and within the same library small changes affect the output. This paper proposed a set of guidelines that can be followed to solve the problem. Furthermore, the results have been validated using two different libraries and real data.

In the future we aim to work towards the following research directions:

Tests for Information Retrieval Metrics such as Precision and Recall. Further validation will be necessary based on information retrieval metrics to examine the behavior of the libraries.

A Framework for the Reproduction of Experiments. A complete framework that will support researchers in the direction of reproducing experiments should be developed, used and possibly standardized.

A Universal Metric. The development of a universal metric that will make results comparable across libraries is essential.

Reproducibility in User Centric Studies. It is essential in the domain of recommender systems to have a set of guidelines in the form of a framework that will assist towards the direction of reproducing results in user centric studies. However, it will be difficult to reproduce studies when humans are involved, since it will be difficult to have the exact number of people with the same background and maintain a similar behavior.

References

1. Said, A., Bellogín, A.: Comparative recommender system evaluation. In: Proceedings of 8th ACM Conference Recommender Systems - RecSys 2014, pp. 129–136 (2014)
2. Jannach, D., Zanker, M., Felfernig, A., Friedrich, G.: Recommender systems: an introduction (2010)

3. Herlocker, J.L., Konstan, J.A., Terveen, L.G., Riedl, J.T.: Evaluating collaborative filtering recommender systems. ACM Trans. Inf. Syst. **22**, 5–53 (2004)
4. Polatidis, N., Georgiadis, C.K.: A multi-level collaborative filtering method that improves recommendations. Expert Syst. Appl. **48**, 100–110 (2016)
5. Owen, S., Anil, R., Dunning, T., Friedman, E.: Mahout in Action (2011)
6. Ekstrand, M.D., Ludwig, M., Konstan, J.A., Riedl, J.T.: Rethinking the recommender research ecosystem: reproducibility, openness, and LensKit. In: Proceedings of the Fifth ACM Conference on Recommender Systems, pp. 133–140. ACM, New York (2011)
7. Gantner, Z., Rendle, S.: MyMediaLite: a free recommender system library. In: Proceedings of Fifth ACM Conference Recommender Systems, pp. 305–308 (2011)
8. Jannach, D., Lerche, L., Gedikli, F., Bonnin, G.: What recommenders recommend–an analysis of accuracy, popularity, and sales diversity effects. In: User Modeling, Adaptation, and Personalization, pp. 1–13 (2013)
9. Shani, G., Gunawardana, A.: Evaluating recommendation systems. In: Ricci, F., Rokach, L., Shapira, B., Kantor, Paul B. (eds.) Recommender Systems Handbook, pp. 257–297. Springer, Boston, MA (2011). https://doi.org/10.1007/978-0-387-85820-3_8
10. Konstan, J.A., Adomavicius, G.: Toward identification and adoption of best practices in algorithmic recommender systems research. In: Proceedings of the International Workshop on Reproducibility and Replication in Recommender Systems Evaluation, pp. 23–28. ACM, New York (2013)
11. Bellogin, A., Castells, P., Said, A., Tikk, D.: Workshop on reproducibility and replication in recommender systems evaluation. In: Proceedings of the 7th ACM Conference on Recommender Systems - RecSys 2013, pp. 485–486 (2013)
12. Bellogin, A., Castells, P., Said, A., Tikk, D.: Report on the workshop on reproducibility and replication in Recommender Systems Evaluation (RepSys). SIGIR Forum. **48**, 29–35 (2014)
13. Beel, J., Breitinger, C., Langer, S., Lommatzsch, A., Gipp, B.: Towards reproducibility in recommender-systems research. User Model. User-adapt. Interact. **26**, 69–101 (2016)
14. Košir, A., Odić, A., Tkalčič, M.: How to improve the statistical power of the 10-fold cross validation scheme in recommender systems. In: RecSys RepSys 2013: Proceedings of the International Workshop on Reproducibility and Replication in Recommender Systems Evaluation, pp. 3–6 (2013)
15. Said, A., Bellogín, A.: RiVal – a toolkit to foster reproducibility in recommender system evaluation. In: RecSys 2014 Proceedings of 8th ACM Conference Recommender System, pp. 371–372 (2014)
16. Hernández del Olmo, F., Gaudioso, E.: Evaluation of recommender systems: a new approach. Expert Syst. Appl. **35**, 790–804 (2008)
17. Peker, S., Kocyigit, A.: mRHR: a modified reciprocal hit rank metric for ranking evaluation of multiple preferences in Top-N recommender systems. In: Dichev, C., Agre, G. (eds.) AIMSA 2016. LNCS (LNAI), vol. 9883, pp. 320–329. Springer, Cham (2016). https://doi.org/10.1007/978-3-319-44748-3_31
18. Harper, F.M., Konstan, J.A.: The MovieLens Datasets. ACM Trans. Interact. Intell. Syst. **5**, 1–19 (2015)
19. Polatidis, N., Georgiadis, C.K., Pimenidis, E., Mouratidis, H.: Privacy-preserving collaborative recommendations based on random perturbations. Expert Syst. Appl. **71**, 18–25 (2017)
20. Alshammari, G., Jorro-Aragoneses, J.L., Kapetanakis, S., Petridis, M., Recio-García, J.A., Díaz-Agudo, B.: A hybrid CBR approach for the long tail problem in recommender systems. In: Aha, D.W., Lieber, J. (eds.) ICCBR 2017. LNCS (LNAI), vol. 10339, pp. 35–45. Springer, Cham (2017). https://doi.org/10.1007/978-3-319-61030-6_3

Optimization

Advertiser Bidding Prediction and Optimization in Online Advertising

Panagiotis Spentzouris[1], Iordanis Koutsopoulos[1(✉)], Kasper Grud Madsen[2],
and Tommy Vestergaard Hansen[2]

[1] Athens University of Economics and Business Athens, Athens, Greece
pspentzouris@gmail.com, jordan@aueb.gr
[2] Intelligent Banker, Odense, Denmark
kaspergsm@gmail.com, tvhansen@gmail.com

Abstract. We study the problem of optimal bid selection across ads
and time, with the aim to maximize incoming click traffic to the advertiser's landing page, which is directly translated in maximizing revenue.
A major novelty of our approach lies in using Machine Learning (ML) to
build regression models out of available data for deriving for each ad the
relations, (i) cost-per-click (CPC) charged by the platform versus bid,
(ii) assigned ad position in the ad list versus bid value, and (iii) number of ad clicks versus its position. These regression models naturally
reveal hidden trends that would have been otherwise unavailable to the
advertiser, such as the bidding behavior of competing advertisers and
quality scores of their ads. We then incorporate these relations into a
convex optimization problem of budget allocation across ads and across
time, the solution of which is the optimal bidding strategy of the advertiser. We validate our approach with real data provided by an online
advertising company that is active in the banking sector. Our solution
leads to substantial increase in the amount of inbound click traffic to the
advertiser's landing page compared to other approaches that are either
heuristic and data-agnostic or employ simple statistics on data.

1 Introduction

Online Advertising has evolved into a thriving business, with an average annual
growth rate of 9.4%, and it is predicted to reach a total market size of \$142.5
billion by 2021. In web-search advertising, advertisers cast bids in order to have
their ads displayed in prominent positions in an ad list, next to organic results of
a search-engine platform. Each ad contains a number of keywords. Advertisers
set a budget they are willing to spend within a certain period of time, along
with their bid for each keyword. Then, an auction is run by the platform and
determines the ads to project and their ranking in the list, as well as relevant
charges to advertisers, in terms of a cost-per-click (CPC). The form of auction
that takes place is the Generalized Second-Price (GSP) one [7], and the rank
of an ad is determined by the product of its bid and quality score, the latter

© IFIP International Federation for Information Processing 2018
Published by Springer International Publishing AG 2018. All Rights Reserved
L. Iliadis et al. (Eds.): AIAI 2018, IFIP AICT 519, pp. 413–424, 2018.
https://doi.org/10.1007/978-3-319-92007-8_35

being a cumulative estimate of the quality of the ad, including its design, text, graphics and landing pages.

Contrary to the vast amount of existing literature which considers the point of view of the advertising platform, *we take the pragmatic viewpoint of an advertiser* and study the problem of optimal bid selection across ads and across time, with the aim to maximize incoming traffic to the advertiser's page in terms of number of clicks, while we recognize that having data about other advertisers is practically infeasible. Maximization of inbound click traffic in the landing page is directly analogous to advertiser revenue, since a portion of the click traffic will end up completing a transaction and will produce revenue for the advertiser through a lead.

Each advertiser may leverage historical data about a number of quantities that are directly available to her, either through the advertising platform (e.g. Google AdWords), or through simple measurements at the advertiser side. These quantities are (i), her bid values, i.e. how much the advertiser is willing to pay, (ii) the associated CPC values, i.e. what the advertiser actually pays in the end of the auction, (iii) the number of impressions of an ad, (iv) the average position of an ad in the auction over a certain time interval, and (v) the number of clicks received by the ad. The advertiser may then decipher the relationships between these measurable quantities and her bid. For example, the amount an advertiser actually pays for a certain ad position, i.e. the CPC value, depends on her bid, the quality score of the ad, as well as on the bids and quality scores of her competitors' ads. Also, the average position of an ad depends on its bid as well as the bids of competing ads. Finally, the number of clicks that an ad receives changes as a function of its average positions.

We capture the relations above by deriving regression models which may provide interesting insights, since they naturally contain in them hidden trends that would have been otherwise unavailable to the advertiser, such as the indirect impact of bidding behavior and quality scores of competing advertisers on the advertiser's ad position, CPC and number of clicks. The derived regression models provide the aforementioned relations in a simple analytic form that are then introduced to a convex optimization problem.

1.1 Our Contribution

Advertisers compete with each other for ad slots, over possibly several parallel auctions. Each advertiser has a set of ads, and each ad contains some keywords. For simplicity, we assume that each ad contains one keyword, and each keyword belongs to one ad. We study the problem of bid selection and allocation across ads and for different time intervals, in order to maximize the total incoming click traffic to the advertiser's landing page subject to a budget constraint (Fig. 1). The contributions of our work to the literature are as follows.

- We consider the pragmatic viewpoint of a single advertiser that aims to best utilize data available to her in order to tune her bids for ads so as to maximize incoming click traffic to her landing page.

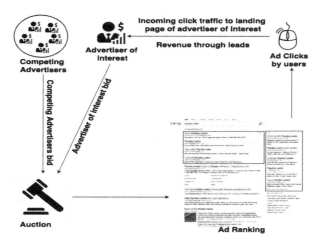

Fig. 1. A pictorial view of the sequence of steps in order for an ad to be projected and possibly clicked by users and produce revenue.

- We follow a data-driven approach, where we build linear regression models about the relations of position versus bid, and CPC versus bid, and number of clicks versus position for each ad. These regression models demonstrate hidden trends about the competitor's behavior for different ads and different time intervals.
- We incorporate the analytical expressions of the regression models into a convex optimization problem of bid selection across ads and across time, for maximizing the total number of ad clicks (and therefore the click traffic in the landing page), subject to a constraint on a maximum budget to be spent in a specific time period. The solution of the problem reveals interesting insights about the relation of the bid and the parameters of the regression models.
- We validate our approach using real data. Our approach is shown to outperform other approaches that are either heuristic and data-agnostic or employ simple statistics on the data.

To the best of our knowledge, our work is among the first to follow the sequence of steps needed for an ad to be projected and possibly clicked through search advertising, and it uses machine-learning-based generated models to find hidden relations between the core ad attributes that are involved in these steps. We then incorporate them into a convex optimization problem the solution of which is the optimal bidding strategy for the advertiser of interest (Fig. 2).

2   Model

2.1   Setup

We consider an advertising platform (e.g. Google AdWords) and a set of advertisers. We take the perspective of a single advertiser with a set $\mathcal{A}$ of N ads,

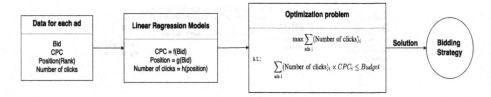

Fig. 2. Our methodology in order to find the optimal bidding strategy in terms of maximizing total click traffic for the advertiser.

where each ad has a quality score and contains some keywords. Without loss of generality, we assume that an ad includes exactly one keyword, so when we refer to an ad, we refer to its keyword. The advertiser has a budget B to be spent over a period of time for bidding for her ads. The advertiser decides on bid vector $\mathbf{b} = (b_1, \ldots, b_N)$, where b_i denotes the amount to bid for ad (keyword) i. The advertiser participates in different auction processes, one for each ad, and she competes with the same or similar keywords of other advertisers in order to have her ads displayed in as high a rank as possible in the lists. Each such auction takes as input the bids and quality scores of competing advertisers for the same or similar keywords and decides on the ranking of ads and the CPC to be paid by each ad. Finally, ads are displayed in the list, and they may be clicked by users who view the ad list next to organic search results. Once an ad is clicked, the user is taken to the landing page of the corresponding advertiser, from which a lead (i.e. a product purchase) might occur within some time interval. The advertiser thus earns a certain amount of revenue by each lead event.

For the advertiser of interest, let b_i denote her bid for ad i. We implicitly assume that the auction for ad i is run once, hence b_i is the amount that is bid for ad i. Let p'_i be the position of ad i in the ranked list. Although we know high positions in the ranked list have small absolute value, e.g. positions 1,2, we define the position in such a way that higher positions in the list are associated with high values. The position of each ad i in the list is equal to its negative, i.e. $p_i = -p'_i$. Thus, if ad i is ranked first in the list, then $p_i = -1$, if it is ranked second, then $p_i = -2$, and so on. Also let c_i be the cost-per-click (CPC) that is paid for ad i. Finally, let n_i be the number of user clicks on ad i within some time interval.

There exist hidden dependencies between these quantities that we seek to capture in the sequel. First, the CPC value for ad i, c_i, depends on bid value b_i, i.e. the amount of money that the advertiser declares she is willing to pay for ad i. We denote this relation as $c_i = f_i(b_i)$, where $f_i(\cdot)$ denotes a continuous, and non-decreasing function. Along the same lines, position p_i depends on the advertiser's bid b_i, and let $p_i = g_i(b_i)$ denote that relation, where $g_i(\cdot)$ is a continuous, non-decreasing function. Finally, the number of clicks n_i of ad i depends on its position, i.e. $n_i = h_i(p_i)$ where $h_i(\cdot)$ denotes again a non-decreasing function.

2.2   Dataset and Linear Regression Models

The dataset that is readily available at the advertiser's side for each ad i is of the form:

$$\mathcal{D}_i = \{(b_i^d, c_i^d, p_i^d, n_i^d) : d = 1, \ldots M_i\}, \tag{1}$$

where M_i is number of data points available in the dataset for ad i. For each ad i, we are interested in using dataset $\mathcal{D}_i$ so as to build models for approximating the relations $f_i(\cdot), g_i(\cdot), h_i(\cdot)$. We can use various machine-learning methods to derive models for the three relations above and then try to fit the models to the data in a way that reduces the total approximation error. Several methods are available, e.g. Neural networks, non-linear regression or linear regression models. In this work, we adhere to linear regression models, because our objective is to demonstrate the advantages of fitting a data-driven model in an optimization problem and extract the benefits of optimization, rather than comparing different ML methods. Further, linear regression models provide a simple means to have the relations above in an analytic form so as to feed them in the optimization problem, to be presented in the next section, and derive interesting insights about the solution. Hence we consider the following three models:

$$c_i = f_i(b_i) = \alpha_i b_i + \beta_i, \ \alpha_i \geq 0 \tag{2}$$

$$p_i = g_i(b_i) = \gamma_i b_i + \delta_i, \ \gamma_i \geq 0 \tag{3}$$

$$n_i = h_i(p_i) = \lambda_i p_i + \mu_i, \ \lambda_i \geq 0 \tag{4}$$

where (α_i, β_i), (γ_i, δ_i) and (λ_i, μ_i) are the parameters of the regression models to be computed from dataset $\mathcal{D}_i$ for each ad i. The approach can be clearly extended in case the dataset is of different form.

The functions $f_i(\cdot), g_i(\cdot), h_i(\cdot)$ above contain some hidden trends about the competing advertisers' bidding behavior as well. In the next section, we will include these models in an optimization problem that will give the optimal bid allocation policy in terms of total number of clicks for the ads of the advertiser.

3   Problem Statement and Formulation

3.1   Bidding for Maximizing Total Number of Clicks for Ads

We are interested in finding the bid allocation policy $\mathbf{b} = (b_1, b_2, ..., b_N)$ that maximizes the advertiser's total click traffic for all ads. This is a key objective for an advertiser, since a percentage of this traffic will end up completing a transaction and produce revenue through leads. Presumably the advertiser participates in several auctions, one for each ad, and that auctions are independent from each other. We formulate the optimization problem as follows:

$$\max \sum_{i=1}^{N} h_i(p_i), \tag{5}$$

subject to the constraint:

$$\sum_{i=1}^{N} h_i(p_i) f_i(b_i) \le B, \tag{6}$$

with $b_i \ge 0$ for $i = 1, \ldots, N$, where B is a fixed amount of budget to be spent over a specific period of time.

3.2 Solution

Since both the objective function and the function involved in the constraint are increasing over the vector bid $\mathbf{b}$, the constraint is satisfied with equality at the optimal solution $\mathbf{b}^*$. Thus, without loss of generality, it makes sense to consider the problem with an equality constraint. Let $\omega_i = \lambda_i \gamma_i \alpha_i$, and $\rho_i = \lambda_i(\gamma_i \beta_i + \delta_i \alpha_i) + \mu_i \alpha_i$.

This is a convex optimization problem, since both the objective function and the constraint are convex. Then we define the Lagrangian function, and after some algebraic manipulations we get the optimal solution as:

$$b_i^* = \frac{1}{2\nu a_i} - \frac{\rho_i}{2\omega_i} \tag{7}$$

Expression (7) shows that bid value b_i decreases as a_i (the slope of the straight line $c_i = f_i(b_i)$) increases. Thus, if the CPC value of an ad increases with a high rate, then our algorithm will raise the bids of alternative ads whose CPC value grows at a slower rate. On the other hand, as the parameter $\omega_i = \lambda_i \gamma_i \alpha_i$ increases, the bid value b_i increases. Parameter ω_i is the product of the slopes of the straight lines $c_i = f_i(b_i)$, $p_i = g_i(b_i)$, and $n_i = h_i(p_i)$. If an ad earns higher positions and its number of clicks increases at a high rate, then our algorithm will "promote" this ad and increase its bid value. A second observation is that the product $\lambda_i \gamma_i$ overpowers parameter α_i, which is inversely analogous to the bid value b_i. Therefore, the rate at which an ad's number of clicks increases or the rate at which it earns higher average positions weighs more in our algorithm than the rate at which the CPC value increases.

Remark 1: An alternative formulation could take into account the quality q_i for each ad $i \in \mathcal{A}$ and include that as a factor in the objective function, which will now become $\sum_{i=1}^{N} q_i h_i(p_i)$ and expresses the total weighted number of ads clicks, where the weight is the quality of each ad. By a similar reasoning as above, the optimal bid value for ad i is given as,

$$b_i^* = \frac{q_i}{2\nu a_i} - \frac{\rho_i}{2w_i} \tag{8}$$

which tells us that the bid value of an ad grows proportionally to its quality score.

Remark 2: The optimization problem above considers budget allocation only across ads. We can have an enhanced formulation that would allow the advertiser to spend different amounts of budget at different time intervals. For example, it is natural to assume that the auction structure (i.e the number of competing advertisers and their bids) and its outcome will be different at different times of the day or at different days of the week (e.g. week-days or week-ends) hence the bid would need to be adjusted as well. Let $t = 1, \ldots, T$ denote an index for different time intervals, where T is the total number for such time intervals. We will have another problem definition, where $b_i(t), p_i(t), c_i(t), n_i(t)$ denote the bid, position, CPC and number of clicks of ad i at time interval t. Then, the budget allocation policy is given by vector $(\mathbf{b}(t) : t = 1, \ldots, T)$, with $\mathbf{b}(t) = (b_1(t), \ldots, b_N(t))$. Hence, the optimization problem becomes one of deciding on the bid policy that maximizes the total number of clicks across ads and across time, subject to a budget constraint.

4   Data Experiments

4.1   Dataset and Regression Models

We use a real dataset that was provided to us by an advertiser. The dataset consists of data from Google AdWords, and among other metrics it contains the bid values, CPC values, average position, and number of clicks for all keywords of the company. These metrics are available per day, for a time period of 6 months between August 2016 and February 2017. In our experiments we use 5 popular keywords/ads from the dataset since we are interested in demonstrating the benefits of the optimal policy. The properties of this policy are expected to hold for a greater number of keywords as well.

For the optimization problem (5)–(6), we need 3 prediction models for each keyword and each time interval, i.e 30 regression models in total. The three regression models that we build for a keyword i and a time interval $t = 1, 2$ are, one for the estimation of the CPC $c_i = f_i(b_i)$, one for the estimation of the average position $p_i = g_i(b_i)$, and one for the estimation of the number of clicks $n_i = h_i(p_i)$.

In order to build the prediction models we used linear regression techniques from Machine Learning. Let us assume that our training dataset, for the regression model $c = f(b)$ of a specific ad and a specific time interval is $L = \{b_n, c_n\}_{j=1}^{M}$, where each b_j(bid) is the data input and c_j (CPC) the corresponding output, j is an index for each data point in the data set, and M is the size of the dataset, i.e. the number of different entries available to train each model. We will choose a polynomial of first degree as a model:

$$f(b_j, w_0, w_1) = w_0 + w_1 b_j, \tag{9}$$

and in order to find the parameters w_0, w_1 that minimize the approximation error, we minimize over $\mathbf{w}$ the cost function of least squares. We measure the performance of the model by means of Root-mean-square-error. Finally, we use cross-validation in order to choose an appropriate value for the reguralization parameter.

4.2 Results

We run our experiment and compare the results for 4 different policies. We use the same set of 5 keywords for each policy, and initialize all bids at the value 0.1. We run experiments for different values of budget $B = \{100, 200, 500, 1000, 1500, 2000\}$. The policies we study and compare are:

– **Random bid allocation policy** (Policy 1) is a baseline approach which allocates randomly a portion of the budget across ads, without taking into consideration any information about the performance of the ad. For this policy, we choose uniformly at random one of the five ads, and then we raise this ad's bid by 5%. We repeat this procedure until the portion of the budget is exhausted. We run experiments for portions equal to $10\%, 20\%$, and 30% of the budget. For each portion we run the experiment 10 times, and keep as result the average number of clicks from these runs.

– **Inversely proportional to CPC allocation policy** (Policy 2) allocates at each ad a portion of the budget that is inversely proportional to the average CPC value of ads, i.e. ads with high CPC get a smaller increase in their bids than ads with a lower CPC. Specifically, given the portion of the budget ϕ, which is the maximum amount of money that can be allocated across ads and across time without earning more clicks than the advertiser can pay, each ad's bid is raised by an amount $\frac{1/c_i}{\sum_i 1/c_i} \times \phi$.

– **Proportional to number of clicks allocation policy** (Policy 3) allocates a portion of the budget ϕ, which is the maximum amount of money that can be allocated across ads and across time without earning more clicks than the advertiser can pay, that is proportional to the average number of clicks that ads get, i.e. ads which get a large amount of clicks have their bids increased by a bigger amount than ads which get less clicks. The increase of each ad's bid is $\frac{n_i}{\sum_i n_i} \times \phi$.

– **Optimal policy** (Policy 4) which is the outcome of the optimization problem (5) and (6).

Comparison of Bid Allocation Policies. Figure 3 shows the total number of clicks to the advertiser's landing page under policy 1, for different budget amounts $B = \{100, 200, 500, 1000, 1500, 2000\}$, and different portions of the budget to be allocated across ads and across time equal to $10\%, 20\%$, and 30%. The total number of clicks seems to be an increasing function over budget B for all cases except when the portion of budget is equal to 20%. Due to the randomness of the allocation, for this case and different budget amounts $B = 1000$, and $B = 1500$, it seems that the advertiser could earn more clicks with the smaller budget. Also, because of the random fashion in which we allocate a portion of the budget across ads and across time, it occurs that for a smaller portion of the budget we could have a better bid allocation, which could result in a larger amount of clicks to the advertiser's landing page.

In Fig. 4, we depict the total number of clicks to the advertiser's landing page under three different policies. As expected, the total number of clicks seems to

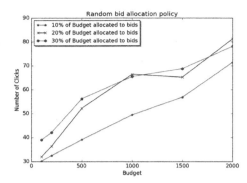
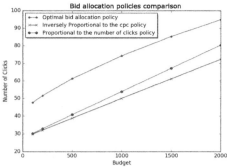

Fig. 3. Total number of clicks to the advertiser's landingpage under random bid selection policy, for 3 different portions of the budget to be allocated across ads and time.

Fig. 4. Total number of clicks to the advertiser's landing page under 3 different bidding policies.

	B = 500		B = 2000	
	Week-day	Week-end	Week-day	Week-end
keyword1	5.04	0.00	24.97	13.89
keyword2	19.63	19.99	41.49	43.12
keyword3	0.00	0.00	0.00	0.00
keyword4	22.13	0.00	41.31	15.57
keyword5	4.21	18.83	33.99	42.38

Fig. 5. Optimal bid selection for different amounts of budget B and different time intervals t.

be an increasing function over the budget B for all policies. We see that by building regression models about the relations and by integrating them into the optimization problem (5) and (6) we get the largest number of clicks, and thus larger revenue for the advertiser, compared to the other policies in the figure and the random policy in Fig. 3. In Fig. 5, we present the optimal bid selection for different amounts of budget $B = \{500, 2000\}$, and different time intervals $t = \{1, 2\}$, i.e. week-day and week-end.

We observe that policy 2 tries to balance bids across all ads, and as a result it increases the bad performing ads' bids as well. We also see that under policy 3, there may be some cases of ads that are not currently getting many clicks but they have the potential to get more with less money than the current top performing ads. Nevertheless, this policy will ignore them because of the better performing in terms of clicks, ads. Despite this fact, policy 3 seems to perform better than policy 2. Also, we notice that policy 1 is performing similarly to the two other policies.

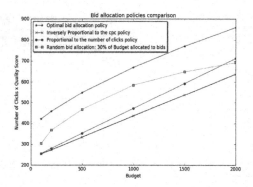

Fig. 6. Total number of clicks weighted by the quality score of each ad under 4 different bidding policies.

Bid Allocation Policies Weighted by Quality Score. In Fig. 6 we show the total number of clicks to the advertiser's landing page weighted by the quality score of each ad, under 4 different policies. The ads' quality scores are $9, 10, 8.8, 8$, and 10 respectively. We see that the optimal policy outperforms the other 3 policies. Further, due to randomness, the random allocation can be benefited from increasing the bids of the ads with the biggest quality score values and thus outperform policy 3. Nevertheless, as the budget gets bigger policy 2 closes the gap in performance and finally outperforms policy 1 for a budget amount larger than 1700. This shows that for small amounts of budget, it is possible for a quality score-agnostic policy to increase the bids of the non-top performing ads more than the bids of the top performing ones. If the budget is big enough though to increase the bids of all ads, all policies achieve better performance. Finally, policy 2 which tries to balance bids across all ads is again the worst performing policy.

Optimal Bid Allocation for Maximum Total ad Quality. Figure 7, depicts the optimal bid selection for different budget values $B = \{500, 2000\}$, and different time intervals $t = \{1, 2\}$, i.e. week-day and week-end, for the objective that wants to maximize the total ad quality for the advertiser. We observe that for a small

	Quality Score	B = 500		B = 2000	
		Week-day	Week-end	Week-day	Week-end
keyword1	9	10.76	0.00	24.03	12.84
keyword2	10	28.52	29.39	44.69	46.51
keyword3	8.8	0.00	0.00	0.00	0.00
keyword4	8	25.33	0.00	36.68	10.89
keyword5	10	16.32	28.38	38.39	45.75

Fig. 7. Optimal bid selection for different amounts of budget B and different time intervals t, for the objective that takes into account the quality score of ads.

budget value $B = 500$ all the ads' bid values are increased compared to their values in Fig. 5. However, for a bigger budget value $B = 2000$, the bid values of the ads with the best quality scores, i.e. the two ads with quality score $q = 10$, are significantly increased compared to their bid values in Fig. 5, while the bid values of the rest are decreased. As expected, the optimal bidding policy for the objective that wants to maximize the total ad quality, decides to increase the bids of the ads that have the highest quality scores, while bid less for the rest. Furthermore, we observe that keyword 3 has a bid value $b = 0$ in both Figs. 5 and 7. The main reason for that is the slope parameter λ of its regression model $n = \lambda p + \mu$, which show that keyword 3 gets clicks at a slower rate than the other keywords and thus our algorithm will not decide to increase its bid.

5   Related Work

Real-time bidding (RTB) represents the cutting-edge frontier of the computational advertising research, and an thriving research area in advertising together with the display ad network and search-based keyword advertising. In RTB, advertisers bid for an ad impression when a user visits a webpage. A repository with a nice taxonomy of recent works can be found at [1].

Budget and Bid Allocation. In the context of display advertising, the authors in [4], model the state transition via auction competition, and they build a Markov Decision Process framework for learning the optimal bidding policy to optimize the ads performance. In [6], the authors define a revenue maximization problem, on an account level, by incorporating a probabilistic model to approximate the probability of winning a position given a price, and then they convert it into an integer optimization programming one. In work [3] they study the problem of finding a bidding strategy in real time mobile advertising. First, they model the win rate using a logistic regression model, and then take the derivative of win rate estimation to generate the distribution of the winning price, and use the expected value of the distribution under the bid price as the winning price estimate. Then a bidding strategy is actually an optimization function that takes the input of expected revenue if winning the auction, win rate and winning price estimate, and generate the final bid price according to some pre-defined objective functions.

In another relevant work [5], the authors try to find the optimal bidding function that maximizes key performance indicator (KPI), i.e. the total number of clicks or revenue in Real Time Bidding (RTB) display advertising. They find a function that returns the probability of winning given a bid value, based on historic data, and then based on the form of the winning rate function they derive empirically a simple function that returns the bid value. Then, they feed these functions into an optimization problem that returns the optimal bid allocation for the advertiser. In a recent work [2], the authors try to use simple heuristic bidding policies to increase the number of clicks, and they set the bid for each ad impression proportionally to the increase of user's conversion rates.

6   Conclusion

We study the problem of bid selection for a single advertiser across ads, each of which is represented by linear regression models that are derived from real data. Our method showcases the benefit of feeding data-driven models into optimization problems, and to the best of our knowledge constitutes the major novelty of this paper.

Possible future steps in this work include studying the problem of maximizing advertiser's revenue across the whole path up to conversion, and pursuing sensitivity analysis to model and take into consideration the inaccuracy of the models.

References

1. Paper Collection of Real-Time Bidding, Weinan Zhang's github page. https://github.com/wnzhang/rtb-papers
2. Xu, J., Shao, X., Ma, J., Lee, K., Qi, H., Lu, Q.: Lift-based bidding in ad selection. In: Proceeding of the Association for the Advancement of Artificial Intelligence (AAAI) Conference (2016)
3. Li, X., Guan, D.: Programmatic buying bidding strategies with win rate and winning price estimation in real time mobile advertising. In: Tseng, V.S., Ho, T.B., Zhou, Z.-H., Chen, A.L.P., Kao, H.-Y. (eds.) PAKDD 2014. LNCS (LNAI), vol. 8443, pp. 447–460. Springer, Cham (2014). https://doi.org/10.1007/978-3-319-06608-0_37
4. Cai, H., Ren, K., Zhang, W., Malialis, K., Wang, J., Yu, Y., Guo, D.: Real-time bidding by reinforcement learning in display advertising. In: Proceedings of the ACM Web Search and Data Mining (WSDM) Conference (2017)
5. Zhang, W., Yuan, S., Wang, J.: Optimal real-time bidding for display advertising. In: Proceedings of the Knowledge Discovery and Data Minin (KDD) Conference (2014)
6. Zhang, W., Zhang, Y., Gao, B., Yu, Y., Yuan, X., Liu, T.: Joint optimization of bid and budget allocation in sponsored search. In: Proceedings of the Knowledge Discovery and Data Mining (KDD) Conference (2012)
7. Varian, H.: Online ad auctions. Am. Econ. Rev. **99**(2), 430–434 (2009)

A Multi-objective Data Mining Approach for Road Traffic Prediction

Ilias Kalamaras[✉], Anastasios Drosou, Konstantinos Votis,
Dionysios Kehagias, and Dimitrios Tzovaras

Information Technologies Institute, Centre for Research and Technology Hellas,
Thessaloniki, Greece
{kalamar,drosou,kvotis,diok,tzovaras}@iti.gr

Abstract. Road traffic prediction for the efficient traffic control has lately been in the focus of the research community, as it can solve significant urban issues, such as city evacuation plans, increased concentration of $CO2$ emissions and delays caused by extended traffic jams. The current paper proposes a novel approach for multi-variate data mining from past traffic data (i.e. average speed values per road), so as to dynamically detect all significant correlations between the road network components (i.e. the segments of the roads) by mapping the latter onto a low dimensional embedding. Multiple traffic-related features (e.g. speed correlation, spatial proximity, phase difference, etc.) are utilized in a multi-objective optimization framework, producing all Pareto-optimal embeddings, each one corresponding to a different trade-off between the objectives. The operator is provided with the option to interactively select among these Pareto-optimal solutions, so as to explore the most descriptive sets of road influences. The proposed method has been evaluated on real traffic data, while the evaluation of the forecasting performance of the multi-objective approach exhibited accuracy improvement with respect single-objective approaches.

Keywords: Data mining · Multi-objective optimization
Pareto-optimal solutions · Clustering · Graph-based representation

1 Introduction

Traffic conditions on road networks have grown to affect several aspects such as the amount of productivity and the lifestyle of the citizens in big urban centers. The optimization of transport, in terms of both individuals and/or fleets, has a serious socio-economic and environmental impact. The study towards the development of intelligent transportation systems (ITS) is constantly gaining attention by the research community. Although common traffic detectors could help alleviate certain traffic problems, the fact that traffic is a dynamic, constantly altering variable, poses new challenges in its confrontation. Consequently, the problem of forecasting traffic within short time intervals ahead of time has arisen as a crucial task, the satisfactory analysis of which is believed to result in more efficient and dynamic routing solutions.

Traffic may be interpreted in various ways through traffic descriptors, such as travel time and instantaneous vehicle speed, observed using GPS sensors. Traffic prediction

© IFIP International Federation for Information Processing 2018
Published by Springer International Publishing AG 2018. All Rights Reserved
L. Iliadis et al. (Eds.): AIAI 2018, IFIP AICT 519, pp. 425–436, 2018.
https://doi.org/10.1007/978-3-319-92007-8_36

techniques use this information, taking also into account the fact that the traffic in one region can affect the traffic in another. However, most techniques utilize a single notion of influence between roads, e.g. the correlation between their traffic time series. However, such influences are usually multi-dimensional, depending on more than one parameters, e.g. phase similarity of the corresponding time series, geographical proximity of the roads, etc.

In this paper, an approach for traffic prediction is proposed, which takes into account multiple types of influence among roads. The proposed method considers multiple notions of dissimilarity between roads, based on correlation, phase, geographical distance, etc. The dissimilarity measures are used in a multi-objective Multidimensional Scaling framework, for computing the influence between roads and using it for prediction. The multi-objective nature of the framework allows the selection of trade-offs among the dissimilarity measures, allowing data exploration by operators.

2 Related Work

Existing approaches used for **traffic prediction** are divided into parametric and non-parametric methods. *Parametric methods* are based on specific pre-determined models that are trained in order to deduce their parameters. Common parametric methods include the Auto-Regressive Integrated Moving Average (ARIMA) model [1], and its variations, such as the Auto-Regressive Moving Average (ARMA) model [2]. In contrast with the univariate analysis of the ARIMA model, its multivariate counterpart, the Space-Time ARIMA (STARIMA), first introduced in [3], takes into account several time series that are related to each other, introducing new parameters to account for spatial and temporal lags. A quite different line of parametric methods is the widely used Kalman Filters [4, 5], which are based on updating a state variable upon receiving each new measurement.

In *non-parametric methods*, the model is not known a-priori. Non-parametric methods can be categorized to memory-based ones, which retain historical samples in order to perform prediction, and model-based ones, which only need the extracted model, discarding historical data upon the training phase. The most typical example of a memory-based model is the k-Nearest Neighbor (kNN) method. Although simple in nature, kNN seems to produce satisfactory results [6], suggesting that performance lies mainly in the proper representation of the dataset features rather than the blind application of a robust algorithm. Model-based methods construct a model using training data. Typical examples include Random Forests (RFs) [7], Artificial Neural Networks (ANNs), such as Multi-Layered Perceptrons (MLPs) [8, 9], and Support Vector Machines (SVMs) [10, 11].

Multi-objective optimization deals with problems having many conflicting objectives [12, 13]. Such problems arise frequently, especially in engineering and economics, for instance maximizing speed while minimizing fuel consumption or maximizing profit while minimizing cost. A solution that is optimal for one objective is suboptimal for the other. One way to deal with this conflict is by scalarizing the objective functions, i.e. combining them in a single objective, which is then minimized with traditional optimization methods. Scalarization methods include using a weighted sum of the objectives [12], the ε-constraint method, where only one of the objectives is minimized, with the others used as constraints [12], or achievement function-based methods, that measure the distance of a solution from a reference one [14]. Scalarizing the objectives involves setting preferences for the multiple objectives, (e.g. the weights of a sum, or the reference point for achievement functions), which is not a trivial task. Another class of multi-objective optimization methods produce a set of solutions [12] instead of a single one, namely the *Pareto front*, containing different trade-offs among the objectives. Such an approach can often discover solutions that scalarization approaches cannot, e.g. solutions lying in concave parts of the Pareto front. The Pareto front is commonly calculated using genetic algorithms, since the fact that they maintain a population of solutions, instead of a single one, suits the goal of calculating multiple solutions [13, 15]. For the determination of the fitness function of the genetic process, different approaches have been followed [15], including weighted sums of the objectives with varying weights [16], alternating among the objectives [15] and using dominance relations [17].

Most of the existing methods for traffic prediction usually deal with one traffic-related characteristic (i.e. modality), e.g. speed velocity at a given time instant, travel time required to traverse a road, etc. However, traffic prediction is a multivariate problem and such approaches pose some information loss, since they restrict the cognitive understanding of the traffic to one dimension. In this respect, the current paper proposes a framework that is able to merge multiple variables on a common space via the utilization of Multi-Dimensional Scaling and multi-objective optimization, overcoming thus the so-called "curse of dimensionality", while a set of Pareto-optimal cases is provided to the traffic operator as possible choices for traffic prediction.

3   Motivation and Contribution

Existing research has shown that the choice of the data mining approach to use for traffic prediction can affect the capability traffic modeling. The work of [18] shows that just considering the flow of a road at previous times without considering the flow of neighboring roads discards information that is essential for producing more representative traffic models. Extending this further, the utilization of only a single notion of influence between roads, e.g. graph neighborhoods, may discard other types of influence that may lead to more accurate models. Influences among roads usually depend on more than one parameters, such as correlation between their traffic flow, flow phase similarity, geographical proximity, etc.

When multiple types of information are available, multi-modal processing techniques have proven useful in combining all available information, in order to produce outcomes that are more accurate than using each type of information separately. Combining multiple modalities has been especially useful in the field of multimedia analysis [19]. Multi-objective optimization has shown promising results in this field, for managing multiple modalities [20], as a generalization of other multimodal techniques, able to discover more solutions and to present the operator with a set of limited optimal trade-offs. Adapting this approach for combining multiple traffic-related characteristics seems promising for improving traffic prediction and allowing parameter exploration by the operator.

The contribution of this paper is the combination of multiple traffic-related features, using multi-objective optimization techniques, in order to measure the influence of one road to other roads of the network, and thus define different notions of "neighborhood", based on Multi-Dimensional Scaling, to be used in STARIMA traffic models. The proposed framework seems to produce promising results, and is adaptive to more traffic features and further notions of road similarity, providing space for further experimentation and research. From an application point of view, the operators are presented with a set of trade-offs among the multiple traffic features, allowing them to select the most important ones for prediction. Such interactivity facilitates the operator of an ITS in exploring the available data and making decisions.

4 Proposed Approach

The proposed approach proceeds as follows. Initially, traffic-related features (vehicle speed, etc.) are extracted for each road in order to compute pairwise distance matrices, using multiple notions of road distance. The distance matrices are used to construct objective functions, whose minimization leads to an embedding of the roads as points on the 2D plane. Multidimensional Scaling (MDS) is used to formulate these objectives, while multi-objective optimization techniques are used to compute a set of Pareto-optimal placement solutions. This way, a set of alternative placements of the roads are provided, that can be used to define neighborhoods of influence, for use in STARIMA [3] traffic prediction. The placement solutions can be interactively selected by the operators, with reference to the indicated current state of the selected road segment, while traffic prediction is visually annotated in real time on the map.

4.1 Problem Formulation

A set $O = \{R_1, R_2, \ldots, R_N\}$ of N road segments is considered. A road segment is the part of a road between two subsequent intersections. If there are two opposite lanes in the same road between two intersections, two separate road segments are considered, one for each lane. Without loss of generality, the road segments are hereby considered to be straight lines.

For a particular day, each road segment R_i, $i = 1 \ldots N$, is modeled as a set of certain attributes:

$$R_i = \{s_i, e_i, v_i\} \in P, \tag{1}$$

where $s_i \in R^2$ is the starting point of the segment, in map coordinates (latitude and longitude), $e_i \in R^2$ is similarly the ending point of the segment and $v_i \in R^M$ is a vector whose j-th element, $j = 1 \ldots M$, is the average speed of the vehicles traveling on the road segment at the j-th time interval, where the day has been split into M time intervals. The road segments R_i are considered to belong in the space P of all sets of these attributes.

The problem addressed hereby is, given the road segments and the vehicle speeds for a specific day, to discover which road segments are related to a selected road segment, in order to predict which segments will be influenced by a change in the vehicles' speed, e.g. denoting congestion, at the selected segment, on the same day another week.

4.2 Road Segment Distance Measures

The proposed approach is based on defining notions of distance among the road segments, which encode different types of influence among them. The following distance measures are used, covering various spatiotemporal characteristics, although others can be incorporated as needed. The distance measures are used to construct distance matrices among the data, containing the distances among each pair of road segments.

Cross Correlation Similarities. This metric stands for the cross correlation value between the sequences of speeds of two road segments. Given two road segments R_i and R_j, $i, j \in 1 \ldots N$, with their corresponding speed vectors v_i and v_j, the *correlation distance* d_{cor} is defined as follows:

$$d_{cor}\left(R_i, R_j\right) = \max_{k=-M\ldots M} \left| \frac{E\left[\left(v_{i,t} - \mu_i\right)\left(v_{j,t+k} - \mu_j\right)\right]}{\sigma_i \sigma_j} \right|, \qquad (2)$$

whereby $v_{i,t}$ is the t-th element of vector v_i, μ_i is the mean value of vector v_i, σ_i is the standard deviation of v_i and $E[\cdot]$ stands for the mean value of the enclosed values, for all values of t. The correlation value derives from the absolute value of the Pearson Product-Moment Correlation Coefficient (PPMCC), with the modification of considering a phase parameter k, in order to take all the possible alignments of the two time series, as in [21], since one of them may be delayed with respect to another due to time needed for traffic to pass from one segment to another.

Phase Similarities. The correlation value above considers the maximum value of the correlation coefficient for all possible alignments of the two time series. The *phase similarity* d_{phase} between two time series is hereby defined as the amount of sliding needed in order to achieve this maximum coefficient value. It is therefore defined as:

$$d_{phase}\left(R_i, R_j\right) = \left| \arg \max_{k=-M\ldots M} \left| \frac{E\left[\left(v_{i,t} - \mu_i\right)\left(v_{j,t+k} - \mu_j\right)\right]}{\sigma_i \sigma_j} \right| \right| \qquad (3)$$

Only the absolute value of the delay k is used, in order for the distance measure to be symmetric. However, the sign of the delay, i.e. whether the second segment precedes or follows the first, can be used in applications, in order to demonstrate which road segments will be influenced in the future.

Geographical Proximity. The *geographical distance* d_{geo} between two road segments is defined as the Euclidean distance between their midpoints:

$$d_{\text{geo}}(R_i, R_j) = ||\mathbf{m}_i - \mathbf{m}_j||, \tag{4}$$

where $\mathbf{m}_i = \frac{1}{2}(\mathbf{s}_i + \mathbf{e}_i)$ and $||\cdot||$ denotes the Euclidean norm.

Dynamic Time Warping Difference. Provided the strong dependence on temporal relations of the fluctuations in the recorded velocities during the day, another metric that has been utilized for the estimation of the intra-distances between the roads is the Dynamic Time Warping (DTW) algorithm [22] that sufficiently manages to capture the spatiotemporal characteristics of these signals. The DTW algorithm has been widely used in a series of matching problems, varying from speech processing [22] to biometric recognition applications. Its main advantages are its simple implementation and its satisfactory performance given the required processing time.

4.3 Multi-objective Multidimensional Scaling

The hereby proposed approach is, using the distance measures described in Sect. 4.2, to embed the road segments into a low dimensional space, where nearest neighbors can be calculated, given a selected segment. Formally, the goal is to find an embedding $\mathbf{p}_1, \mathbf{p}_2, \ldots, \mathbf{p}_N$, $\mathbf{p}_i \in \mathbb{R}^L$, for the N road segments $R_1, R_2, \ldots, R_N$, so that the distances among the points $\mathbf{p}_i$ in the low dimensional space $\mathbb{R}^L$ correspond to all the notions of distance between road segments which are defined in Sect. 4.2.

Multidimensional Scaling (MDS) [23] is a common technique used to find an embedding of a set of points, when only the distances among them are known. Let the known target distances be δ_{ij}, $i, j \in 1 \ldots N$. The desired embedding $P = (\mathbf{p}_1, \mathbf{p}_2, \ldots, \mathbf{p}_N) \in \mathcal{P}$ of the objects is one in which the target distances among points are best preserved in the embedding. Let $J : \mathcal{P} \to \mathbb{R}_{\geq 0}$ be a cost function (objective function), evaluating the capability of an embedding $p \in \mathcal{P}$ for preserving the target distances among the data. $\mathbb{R}_{\geq 0}$ is the set of non-negative real numbers. A commonly used objective function for MDS is the following:

$$J(\mathbf{p}_1, \mathbf{p}_2, \ldots, \mathbf{p}_N) = \sum_{i,j}^{N} \left(||\mathbf{p}_i - \mathbf{p}_j|| - \delta_{ij} \right)^2 \tag{5}$$

Since there are multiple notions of distance between two data points (Sect. 4.2), multiple objective functions for MDS can be defined, one for each distance measure used. This is handled as a *multi-objective optimization* problem [12], using genetic algorithms [17], resulting in a Pareto front of optimal trade-offs among the objectives. The genetic algorithms proceed by examining different placements of the N points on the 2D plane, so that there are $2N$ variables. Crossover strategies can combine two placements by randomly keeping, for each object, the corresponding point from either parent as the child's point. Mutation operates by adding random noise on the child's position. The initial population size can be chosen as multiple of the solutions that are kept to represent the final Pareto front, which can be in the order of 10–20, so that they are not overwhelming to the operator. The focus of this paper is more on the assessment of how the combination of multiple traffic characteristics can benefit prediction than on finding the optimal crossover/mutation functions and population size. Further work can use different optimization techniques, in order to achieve more representative Pareto fronts faster.

An example Pareto front for a problem of two objectives is illustrated in Fig. 1(a). The Pareto diagram depicts the Pareto optimal solutions as points, having the values of the objective functions as coordinates. The gray-shaded area represents the set of all feasible solutions, while the bold border in the lower left of the feasible area is the Pareto front. Point P_2 dominates P_1, as well as the whole hatched area, since both objectives have smaller values at P_2. On the other hand, points P_2 and P_3 are incomparable, since decreasing one objective leads to increasing the other one.

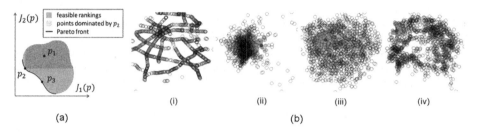

(a)   (b)

Fig. 1. (a) Example Pareto diagram. (b) Low-dimensional embeddings solely based on the (i) geographical proximity (ii) temporal proximity (iii) cross-correlation (iv) DTW-based modality.

The selection of a Pareto-optimal embedding to use for detecting roads with similar characteristics and making predictions is performed by a human user. The solutions of the Pareto set are presented to the user in the form of a Pareto diagram, such as the one in Fig. 1(a). By selecting among different trade-offs, the operator can focus on different aspects of traffic flow and be assisted in predicting future states. After the selection of a Pareto-optimal embedding, the road segments are represented by points in the 2D space (see Fig. 1(b)). Nearby points represent roads that are similar with respect to the distance measures used and the Pareto trade-off that has been selected. When an operator selects a road segment on the map, wishing to view the segments which are influenced by it, the nearest roads segments to the selected one in the embedding are found and presented on the map. The amount of closeness of a road segment can be depicted graphically on a map by e.g. controlling its color or opacity.

5   Evaluation of the Proposed Approach

5.1   Dataset Description

The proposed method has been tested on the so-called *Berlin dataset*, which was recorded from 18/03/2012 to 31/03/2012, using the open TomTom API [24]. The data contain real vehicle speed measurements from Berlin, collected from several road points using GPS locators. Each measurement contains the instantaneous speed at a specific road point, measured in millisecond intervals, and is accompanied by the map coordinates of the road location. However, due to the absence of speed values in many time moments, a preprocessing of the original data was performed, as described in [21]. The preprocessing procedure, for a day of measurements is as follows.

First, the measurement points were grouped in road segments, i.e. parts of a road between two subsequent intersections, resulting in about 7000 road segments, each associated with the speeds obtained for the road points inside it. Since each road segment may contain a different number of speed measurements, the raw measurements were grouped in five-minute intervals, considering the harmonic mean of the speed values at each interval. The size of the resulting speed vector assigned to a road segment was at most 288, the number of five-minute intervals in a day. This significantly reduced the size of the dataset and compensated for many missing values. However, there were still many intervals within a day with no measurements, so we kept a time period of 15 h that had a small overall number of missing values throughout the whole dataset. This truncated the speed vectors to 180 values. The remaining missing values were filled using cubic spline interpolation. Finally, in order to limit the experiments to busy, and thus interesting, roads, the road segments were further filtered by keeping only those within a radius of approximately 5 km from the city center. The final dataset consists of about 1300 road segments for each day of the week, each associated with a 180-dimensional speed vector (of average speed value 33.5 km/hour).

5.2   Experimental Results

The proposed method has been employed for the task of predicting the speed of a road segment at a future time interval. For evaluation purposes, it has been compared to the performance of methods which use a single objective to determine which road segments are influenced by the traffic of a selected segment. The model used for prediction is a simplified form of the STARIMA model, such as the ones used in [21]. For a selected road segment, the model is described by the following equation:

$$z_{t+1} = \phi_0 z_t + \phi_1 z_{t-1} + \phi_2 z_{t-2} + \psi_0 u_t + \psi_1 u_{t-1} \tag{6}$$

Hereby, z_{t+1} is the predicted value of the speed of the road segment at time interval $t+1$. This value is calculated as a weighted combination of the speed values of the same road at previous time intervals, as well as of roads that are influenced by the selected road segment. The values z_t, z_{t-1} and z_{t-2} in Eq. (6) are the speeds of the road segments at the current time interval, t, and at the two previous time intervals, $t-1$ and $t-2$, respectively. The parameters ϕ_0, ϕ_1 and ϕ_2 are used as weights to denote the importance of each previous speed value for the determination of the predicted one. The last two factors of Eq. (6) are related to the speeds of the road segments which are most influenced by the selected road segment. The parameter u_t is defined as:

$$u_t = \frac{1}{k} \sum_{R=\{s,e,v\} \in \mathcal{N}_k} v_t \tag{7}$$

The set $\mathcal{N}_k$ is the set of the k segments which are most influenced by the selected segment. The value of u_t is thus the mean value of the speeds at time interval t of the road segments which belong to the set $\mathcal{N}_k$. The determination of the most influenced road segments is hereby performed by selecting, in the 2-dimensional embedding, the k closest points to the point corresponding to the selected road segment. The most influenced road segments are thus determined by considering all notions of distance (Sect. 4.2) in a multi-objective manner, instead of using a single influence measure, as e.g. in the lag-based STARIMA model of [21].

In order to demonstrate the effectiveness of using multiple objectives, a comparison has been performed between two Pareto-optimal solutions. The first corresponds to a combination of the d_{cor} and d_{tim} distances measures, i.e. it is similar to the lag-based STARIMA method of [21], which uses correlation to find the roads that are most influenced, but also exploits time lags. The second Pareto point corresponds to a combination of the d_{cor}, the d_{tim} and the d_{geo} measures, i.e. it also includes geographical information. For each solution, the model of Eq. (6) is trained with data from a specific day of the week. The unknown model parameters ϕ_0, ϕ_1, ϕ_2, ψ_0 and ψ_1 are learned using a least-square error estimate. In order to test the model, predictions are made for the same day at another week. Given the current speed for a specific road segment, along with the previous speeds of the same segment and of the most influenced ones, the speed at the next time interval is calculated using Eq. (6).

Figure 2(a) illustrates the Root Mean Square Error (RMSE) between the predicted and the real values, for different time intervals. For each interval, the RMSE for the prediction of the next interval is depicted. The RMSE is defined as the square root of the mean of the squared error between the predicted and the real values, where the mean is taken over all road segments. The combination of the three measures results in generally smaller prediction errors than the combination of just two of them, especially at the beginning of the day by an improvement of 0.0301 in the RMSE. Figure 2(b) depicts similar results for another pair of sub-cases. Hereby, the first Pareto solution considers only the geographical distances among the roads, while the second solution

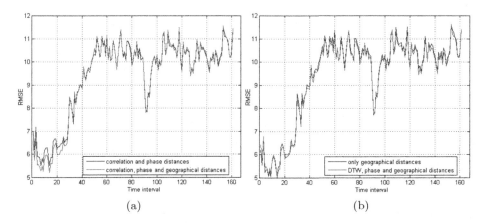

Fig. 2. Comparison of RMSE for predictions performed using: (a) a combination of d_{cor} and d_{tim} (blue curve) and a combination of d_{cor}, d_{tim} and d_{geo} (red curve), (b) only d_{geo} (blue curve) and a combination of d_{DTW}, d_{tim} and d_{geo} (red curve). (Color figure online)

considers a combination of the d_{DTW}, the d_{tim} and the d_{geo} measures of Sect. 4.2. Again the combination of three objectives outperforms the use of only one. The average improvements in the RMSE between the two curves is 0.0717.

The capabilities of the proposed approach have also been exhibited via a visualization application. Let us consider that, after the low-dimensional embedding has been performed and one of the Pareto-optimal solutions has been selected, an operator selects a specific road segment (blue line in Fig. 3(a)–(d)). The point in the 2D embedding that corresponds to the selected road segment is found and the road segments corresponding to nearby points in the embedding are colored on the map. The operator can thus have an overview of which roads are influenced by the traffic conditions of the selected road segment.

In Fig. 3(a)–(d), examples of different segment selections are depicted. When the operator selects a different segment, different roads are colored, denoting those which are mostly influenced by the selected segment. The color of the road segments is an indication of the direction of traffic. The faint red color corresponds to segments whose speed series precede the speed series of the selected segment, in terms of correlation, while segments with bright red color have speed series which follow the ones of the selected segment. As an example, in Fig. 3(d), the colors of the roads indicate that the general direction of traffic is towards the center of the city.

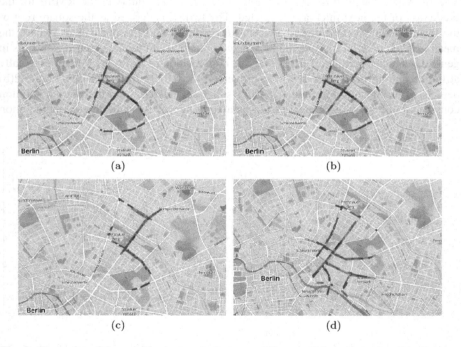

(a)   (b)

(c)   (d)

Fig. 3. Examples of the neighboring roads, in terms of "merged", low dimensionality distance. The brightest the red colored lines, the biggest is their phase difference in the future. (d) It can be noted that the traffic congestion in the next minutes will be moving towards the center of the city. (Color figure online)

6   Conclusions and Next Steps

In this study, the problem of forecasting traffic speeds was addressed, using a multi-objective framework that supports the combination of several traffic-related modalities via Multidimensional Scaling. The proposed approach facilitates increased flexibility and efficient human interaction, while exhibiting improved traffic prediction results when the broadly utilized STARIMA algorithm is applied. Furthermore, the proposed framework can form the basis for useful interactive applications, via suggesting only the (Pareto-) optimal solutions to the operator.

The potential for further improvement in the prediction accuracy of the proposed approach should be highlighted, since it supports the integration of an unlimited amount of additional traffic-related modalities. Apart from speed measurements, traffic volume measurements can also be exploited as additional modalities in the future. Traffic volume adds additional information, which, combined with traffic speed can lead to more accurate traffic prediction. The utilized distance measures can be extended by using geodesic distance measures, which exploit the graph-like structure of the road network, and may be more informative than actual geographic proximity. The graph-based structure can also be used to improve the distance measures already used, by adjusting the distance matrices, based on their geodesic proximity of the graph. Such improvements are the objectives of future extensions of the current work, with the goal of achieving more accurate traffic prediction.

Acknowledgments. This work was supported by the EU-funded projects RESOLUTE (H2020-DRS-2014, grant agreement no. 653460) and My-TRAC (H2020-S2RJU-OC-2017, grant agreement no. 777640).

References

1. Box, G.E.P., Jenkins, G.: Time Series Analysis, Forecasting and Control. Holden-Day, Incorporated, San Francisco (1990)
2. Brockwell, P.J., Davis, R.A.: Introduction to Time Series and Forecasting, 2nd edn. Springer, New York (2002). https://doi.org/10.1007/b97391
3. Pfeifer, P.E., Deutsch, S.J.: A three-stage iterative procedure for space-time modeling. Technometrics **22**(1), 35–47 (1980)
4. Kalman, R.E.: A new approach to linear filtering and prediction problems. J. Basic Eng. **82**(1), 35–45 (1960)
5. Okutani, I., Stephanedes, Y.J.: Dynamic prediction of traffic volume through Kalman filtering theory. Transp. Res. Part B: Methodol. **18**(1), 1–11 (1984)
6. Shen, W., Kamarianakis, Y., Wynter, L., He, J., He, Q., Lawrence, R., Swirszcz, G.: Traffic velocity prediction using GPS data: IEEE ICDM contest task 3 report. In: 2010 IEEE International Conference on Data Mining Workshops (ICDMW), pp. 1369–1371 (2010)
7. Breiman, L.: Random forests. Mach. Learn. **45**, 5–32 (2001)
8. Vlahogianni, E.I., Karlaftis, M.G., Golias, J.C.: Optimized and metaoptimized neural networks for short-term traffic flow prediction: a genetic approach. Transp. Res. Part C: Emerg. Technol. **13**(3), 211–234 (2005)

9. Innamaa, S.: Short-term prediction of travel time using neural networks on an interurban highway. Transportation **32**(6), 649–669 (2005)

10. Vapnik, V.N.: The Nature of Statistical Learning Theory. Springer-Verlag, New York (1995). https://doi.org/10.1007/978-1-4757-3264-1

11. Wu, C.-H., Ho, J.-M., Lee, D.T.: Travel-time prediction with support vector regression. Trans. Intell. Transport. Syst. **5**, 276–281 (2004)

12. Ehrgott, M.: Multicriteria Optimization, vol. 491. Springer, Heidelberg (2005). https://doi.org/10.1007/3-540-27659-9

13. Coello, C.A.C., Lamont, G.B., Van Veldhuizen, D.A., et al.: Evolutionary Algorithms for Solving Multi-objective Problems, vol. 5. Springer, New York (2007). https://doi.org/10.1007/978-0-387-36797-2

14. Wierzbicki, A.P.: On the completeness and constructiveness of parametric characterizations to vector optimization problems. Oper. Res. Spektrum. **8**(2), 73–87 (1986)

15. Zitzler, E., Laumanns, M., Bleuler, S.: A Tutorial on evolutionary multiobjective optimization. In: Gandibleux, X., Sevaux, M., Sörensen, K., T'kindt, V. (eds.) Metaheuristics for Multiobjective Optimisation. LNE, vol. 535, pp. 3–37. Springer, Heidelberg (2004). https://doi.org/10.1007/978-3-642-17144-4_1

16. Hajela, P., Lin, C.-Y.: Genetic search strategies in multicriterion optimal design. Struct. Optim. **4**(2), 99–107 (1992)

17. Zitzler, E., Laumanns, M., Thiele, L.: SPEA2: Improving the strength Pareto evolutionary algorithm, TIK-report, vol. 103 (2001)

18. Kamarianakis, Y., Prastacos, P.: Space-time modeling of traffic flow. Comput. Geosci. **31**, 119–133 (2005)

19. Atrey, P.K., Hossain, M.A., El Saddik, A., Kankanhalli, M.S.: Multimodal fusion for multimedia analysis: a survey. Multimed. Syst. **16**(6), 345–379 (2010)

20. Kalamaras, I., Drosou, A., Tzovaras, D.: Multi-objective optimization for multimodal visualization. IEEE Trans. Multimed. **16**(5), 1460–1472 (2014)

21. Diamantopoulos, T., Kehagias, D., König, F.G., Tzovaras, D.: Investigating the effect of global metrics in travel time forecasting. In Proceedings of 16th International IEEE Conference on Intelligent Transportation Systems (ITSC) (2013)

22. Sakoe, H., Chiba, S.: Dynamic programming algorithm optimization for spoken word recognition. In: Readings in Speech Recognition, pp. 159–165. Elsevier (1990)

23. Cox, M.A., Cox, T.F.: Multidimensional scaling. In: Handbook of data visualization. Springer Handbooks Comp.Statistics, pp. 315–347. Springer, Heidelberg (2008). https://doi.org/10.1007/978-3-540-33037-0_14

24. TomTom open maps API. https://developer.tomtom.com/online-traffic. Accessed 20 Mar 2018

A Simulation-Based Analysis
of Interdependent Populations
in a Dynamic Ecological Environment

Kristiyan Balabanov[1(✉)], Doina Logofătu[1], Costin Badica[2], and Florin Leon[3]

[1] Department of Computer Science and Engineering,
Frankfurt University of Applied Sciences, 60318 Frankfurt a.M., Germany
balabano@stud.fra-uas.de
[2] Department of Computer Sciences and Information Technology,
University of Craiova, 200285 Craiova, Romania
cbadica@software.ucv.ro
[3] Faculty of Automatic Control and Computer Engineering,
Gheorghe Asachi Technical University of Iaşi, 700050 Iaşi, Romania
florinleon@gmail.com

Abstract. With the ever increasing computational power of computers, simulation-based approaches have become a feasible testing technique that does not require investing valuable resources to create an actual prototype. Thus, design changes can be introduced and design errors can be fixed before it is too late, making simulation a cheaper, safer and often more acceptable from an ethical perspective approach. In our paper we summarize the results from the analysis with the help of a computational simulation of a simple, yet analytically intractable problem scenario from the field of ecology. Our main goal is to confirm that even with a seemingly simple agent-based model and simulation, one could obtain plausible results regarding a system's real life behavior. As a last point we propose a more efficient alternative for analysis, rather than the more expensive simulation.

Keywords: Population dynamics · Ecological simulation
Agent-based modeling · Predator-prey relation
Evolution-inspired optimization

1 Introduction

Simulation is a well-known and wide-spread method of system analysis, and a lot of different branches in industry/science make use of it due to the various advantages that it offers. As an example, it is more economical to test the aerodynamics of a car without the need of an actual prototype [12]. On the other hand, in some projects it is simply the most feasible approach with respect to effort-cost ratio, e.g. to simulate a space rover's mission to another planet [15].

© IFIP International Federation for Information Processing 2018
Published by Springer International Publishing AG 2018. All Rights Reserved
L. Iliadis et al. (Eds.): AIAI 2018, IFIP AICT 519, pp. 437–448, 2018.
https://doi.org/10.1007/978-3-319-92007-8_37

Certain phenomena occur at a rate either too fast or too slow to be efficiently observed in real-time, such as explosions or plant growth. Furthermore, a well-designed simulation can not only save time and money, but also spare lives, for instance when conducting air-bag tests or in any experiments with living organisms. One could refer to the latter as ecological simulation, which has become quite popular recently due to the numerous environmental issues resulting from globalization and industrialization. Despite still existing skepticism, it is evident by now that both have lead to a lot of changes in our environment, mostly negative and often irreversible. Species are becoming endangered or going extinct, which is bound to affect predator/prey chains in the respective ecosystems. With simulation means one could analyze the consequences of the resulting imbalance without involving actual animals and before it is too late.

In this paper we present the results we gathered when simulating a simple marine ecosystem on a micro level. We based our model on the one described in [1], but extended and formalized it according to the well known design of cellular systems and more precisely a *cellular automaton*. The main goals that we set for this project were to further confirm the statement introduced in [1] that even somewhat complex real world phenomena/events/scenarios can be simulated with a relatively simple abstract model, that, nevertheless, exhibits authentic behavior. Our emphasis, however, was on proving the strengths of computational simulation when considering analytically intractable problems. The tests that we present served not only the purpose to verify the accuracy of the extended model, but also to deliver useful insights regarding the problem under consideration, such as input/output relation, without the need of a complex formal description. Furthermore, we acknowledge the pitfalls of simulation-based analysis in terms of computational effort needed and shortly discuss a more efficient approach to optimize the given problem scenario with the use of an *evolutionary programming* technique.

2   Problem Description

In its core the problem scenario used for the experiments is a relatively simple one: a finite space populated with objects of certain type, that interact with one another according to predefined rules. A less abstract extension of this scenario would be any ecosystem and the species populating it. In our experiments we modeled a sea ecosystem and three marine species forming a food chain. For the concrete design we used the well-known Wa-Tor world described in Dewdney's work [3]. It is a torus-shaped world with no landmass, but only one great ocean inhabited by marine species. To simulate an actual ecosystem, each species has a specific behavior according to which it interacts with both the environment and members of other species'. The behavior consists of a set of rules, which reflect the real world equivalents of the respective species' to a certain degree. All rules are defined on a micro level, i.e. only an individual's current state and its direct neighbors are considered. Each rule can be easily modified to reflect any introduced change of both internal (evolution) or external (cataclysmic event) nature, as it happens in the real world, and then the potential impact on the environment can be observed. Originally Dewdney described a world inhabited by only two species forming a linear predator-prey relationship—sharks (predator) and fish (prey). Their interaction was pivotal for the environment's fate: sharks can survive only if there are enough fish to hunt, and fish can survive only if there are not too many sharks to hunt them to extinction. Fish feed on infinite plankton, which is not modeled for the sake of simplicity. Following the example of [1], we extended Dewdney's idea with an additional third species to create a slightly more complex food chain—whales, which hunt both sharks and fish, but have no enemy. This new species is partially theoretical as it does not depict the actual diet of real world whales.

Such a scenario related to ecology is a perfect example of a problem domain, that is well-nigh impossible to solve using real life resources for two major reasons: (a) constructing and populating or isolating an actual ecosystem would be insanely expensive, unless in a very small scale, which might not yield the desired authenticity and/or results; (b) experiments with animals in general raise a lot of questions regarding moral principles and are often reproached by modern society. On the other hand, formally specifying a mathematical model of the problem would prove to be as equally difficult simply due to its complexity— thousands of agents, each with its own characteristics, dispersed within the environment, randomly roaming and interacting. In other words, the given problem, although computationally solvable with finite resources in theory, can be seen as analytically intractable in practice. Therefore, developing a computer simulation using a moderately complex model is a viable approach to obtain valuable insights regarding the problem scenario, albeit not necessarily the optimal solution [5, 16, 17]. In our work we strove to confirm the accuracy of the model presented by [1] and its ability to self-sustain, but also tried to determine whether a relation between the input parameters and the ecosystem's ability to self-sustain exists. Moreover, we searched for an approach to efficiently find optimal input parameter combinations, i.e. such that do not cause an ecosystem collapse (species becoming extinct).

3   Implementation of the Problem

To test our ideas we developed a simple and robust software application. As more than 30 years have passed since Dewdney's initial publication, one can easily find various implementations of the Wa-Tor scenario. Proprietary software was excluded from consideration. After a brief evaluation of the *open-source* solutions according to the criteria *maturity* (how well developed is the product so far), *longevity* (what are the prospects of the software being further supported and developed) and *flexibility* (effort needed to integrate/modify the product) as suggested by [15] showed that neither was adequate enough, hence our initiative to design and implement an entirely new set of tools using Java.

3.1 Application Architecture and Representation

For the design of our application we chose a classic bio-inspired approach: an abstract cellular system. The idea is derived from biological tissues, where the fundamental unit is the cell. The cell is, indeed, a quite complex structure by itself [10], but when multiple cells cooperate even on a very basic local level, the outcome is a multicellular organism with unmatched capability compared to that of the individual cells building it. The human body is just one of countless examples in nature. This approach has already been widely used in design leading to the generalization of the resulting system type into the so called cellular systems. Essentially, such a system is a finite collection of basic units building a space. The units can be called cells and the space an organism accordingly. Each cell is identified by specific information about itself (e.g. an n-tuple of numerical values) and this information at a given time is called a *state*. The dynamics of such a system are expressed with the change in the cells' state depending on various factors. This *state transition* can depend on the current state of the cell, its past state and/or on the states of the surrounding cells. The collection of cells that can directly influence each other's state is called a *neighborhood*. Once the system is running, the cells update their states over time according to a predefined set of state transition rules and always reside in one from a finite set of possible states. A more detailed description of cellular systems is offered by [6, Chap. 2].

The most prominent advantage of cellular systems is that they offer a simple modeling approach on a micro level, which however, can still yield plausible insights regarding the global behavior of the model. In the case of our problem, it is much easier to model the behavior of separate individuals based on their direct neighbors, rather than model the behavior of the entire population as one complex object.

From the various kinds known today we adopted the relatively simple, but popular *cellular automaton* (CA), more precisely the 2-dimensional *game of life* CA, as the base architecture of our application. A vivid example is John Conway's Life Game [7,8]. Using Floreano et al.'s [6] decomposition of a cellular automaton into its components and their elaborate description, we modeled the Wa-Tor ecosystem scenario as a cellular automaton as follows:

Base Unit. The base unit is the cell represented as a square grid tile of certain color in the cellular space.

Cellular Space. The space is a 2-dimensional lattice of cells forming a rectangular grid with size 500×300 cells.

Time Variable. The state transitions in the system unfold along a discrete time axis with *cycle* as its base unit. One state transition happens per cell per cycle.

State and State Set. The state of each cell consists of the animal type that the cell represents together with its respective attributes tuple. Therefore, each cell can reside in one of four major states

$$\{Fish,\ Shark,\ Whale,\ Emptycell\}$$

and a multiple of sub-states defined by the numerical values of the respective species' attribute tuple.

State Transition Function. The transition from one state to another is represented by the actions that an individual can perform, such as moving, feeding, reproducing and dying. Both the major state of the neighbor cells and the instance of the attribute tuple of the considered cell influence the transition. It is not deterministic (e.g. a fish surrounded by empty cells could move to any one of it), and where more choices exist, their probability distribution is uniform.

Neighborhood. The *von Neumann* neighborhood is implemented, i.e. a cell's state is directly influenced only by neighbors at a *Manhattan distance* of 1 from it (its direct upward, downward, leftward and rightward neighbors).

Boundary Conditions. For practical reasons the cellular space cannot be infinitely large, hence the need of appropriate boundary conditions to ensure that the system has a homogeneous neighborhood (every cell has the same type of neighborhood). We chose *periodic* boundary conditions by connecting opposite ends of the grid and essentially eliminating the boundaries, i.e. transforming the 2-dimensional grid into a 2-dimensional toroid (torus).

Initial Conditions. The size of each species' population as well as the initial numerical values for each individual's attribute tuple (equal among all individuals of the same species). Both can be selected by the user before the start of the simulation. The distribution of the individuals over the cellular space is uniform.

Stopping Conditions. The simulation stops after 3000 cycles (user adjustable).

3.2 Defining the Simulation Model

For the purposes of our study we adopted the simplified model proposed by [3] and further described in [1]: the behavior of the animal species consists of the actions moving, feeding, reproducing and dying; an individual is represented as an n-tuple of quantifiable attributes. The fish class is the simplest one modeled as the 2-tuple

$$(C_{offs},\ A_{repr}),$$

consisting of the reproduction maturity age and the number of offspring created, which are positive natural numbers. Shark and whale objects are further identified by their life energy (a positive real number), that is constantly depleted and can be replenished only by killing prey, and by the energy gain from eating the prey (a positive natural number), which varies according to the prey type. Unlike fish, predators do not reproduce over a constant period, but do so only if a certain life energy level has been reached, thus their reproduction rate is directly related to the presence of prey. The shark class is modeled as the 4-tuple

$$(C_{offs},\ E_{repr},\ E_{life},\ E_{eat\_fish})$$

and the whale class as the 5-tuple

$$(C_{offs},\ E_{repr},\ E_{life},\ E_{eat\_fish},\ E_{eat\_shark}),$$

respectively. Each existing individual performs the aforementioned actions as defined in [1] in a specified order and a cycle in the simulation ends when all individuals have 'acted', after which the environment is updated. In terms of cellular automata the actions of an individual/cell can be seen as the state transition of that cell or/and one or more of its neighbors, whereas the various instantiations of the respective attribute tuples as the private information about the given individual/cell.

4   Performed Tests and Results Obtained

4.1   Model Accuracy

In the previous work on the topic [1] the simulation was run with different combinations of initial population sizes, repeating each combination multiple times to account for the not entirely deterministic behavior of the individuals. The obtained results did show similarities with real world population dynamics [2], e.g. predator overpopulation leads to the prey going extinct, vice versa with prey underpopulation and predators are more vulnerable than prey since they have to roam and search for food. Moreover, by plotting the change in the population sizes over the course of the simulation, it was shown that despite the simplicity of the model, successful initial population size combinations result in the system reaching an *equilibrium* state, and the populations exhibiting dynamics like those described by the Lotka-Volterra-Model [11].

4.2   Ecosystem's Capability to Self-Sustain

Since not every initial population size combination is favorable regarding the ecosystem's survival, and some combinations have only a partial success rate, a second series of experiments was aimed to (a) prove that there is an integral not empty solution space (initial population size combinations) for which the given model of the simulated ecosystem can reach the so called equilibrium state; and (2) to define its boundaries. For that purpose the system was run automatically over a long period of time with randomly generated initial population sizes from a specified domain for the three species. It was shown that the successful input combinations form a set in 3-dimensional space, which with enough runs would resemble an irregular *solid*. In other words a solution space exists and the ecosystem is with high probability capable to self-sustain given any input from the respective set.

4.3   Input/Output Relation

From the results discussed in Sects. 4.1 and 4.2 it is clear that the system has a high chance to reach equilibrium for some input combinations, and a very low chance for others, i.e. a relation between the input parameters and the outcome of the simulation presumably exists. This can be proven formally by finding a function $f(p_1, p_2, ..., p_n)$ that maps an instance of the input parameters $p_1, ..., p_2$ to the respective output. As already stated, however, the problem under consideration is in practice analytically intractable, thus such a function cannot be obtained with a reasonable amount of effort. Instead, in our approach we decided to reuse the *empirical* formula described in [1], which is based on the statistical data gained from the initial tests and on the observations made while analyzing it. The function is defined as $S(P_f[n_f], P_s[n_s], P_w[n_w])$, where S is the dependent variable (ecosystem stability), and $P_f[n_f], P_s[n_s], P_w[n_w]$ are the independent variables representing the probability with which the respective initial population sizes of fish, sharks and whales would survive. Moreover, from the already made conclusions it is known that some species are more vulnerable than others, and so their survival should be weighted more, e.g. sharks. As a result the stability of the system is defined as a function of the survival probability of each species, given its initial size, combined with a weighting factor based on the species' vulnerability:

$$S(P_f[n_f], P_s[n_s], P_w[n_w]) = P_f[n_f] \cdot 0.2 + P_s[n_s] \cdot 0.5 + P_w[n_w] \cdot 0.3 \ , \qquad (1)$$

where $P_x[n_x]$ is the survival probability of species x with initial size n_x in the respective test case. Using this approximation formula the ecosystem's stability factor was calculated for various initial predator population sizes within the range $[2, 50000]$ and two distinct fish population sizes: 5,000 and 50,000. The results are illustrated in Fig. 1 and show an obvious relation between the starting conditions and the simulation outcome. It is easy to see that an increasing predator population decreases the stability factor rapidly, indicated by the colors becoming darker towards the maximum values of the x- and y-axis. This is especially true for the whale population since the heat map darkens faster vertically (along the y-axis), rather than horizontally (along the x-axis). Ample quantities of fish prey also contribute for a better ecosystem stability (compare the visibly brighter heat map for the test cases involving an initial fish population of 50,000).

These results correspond to the conclusions made earlier about the accuracy of the model (see Sect. 4.1). Any combination representing a predator overpopulation resp. prey underpopulation is colored in dark. Additionally, the greater part of both heat maps is in blue/purple hue, indicating a value less than 0.3. In other words, in most test cases both predator species, but especially the sharks, went extinct before the stopping condition of the simulation was met. Nevertheless, a comparison with the results regarding the system's ability to self-sustain documented in [1] reveals a partial error in the solution space's bounds. It is our belief that this could be eliminated with a better approximation of the solution space boundaries (by performing more runs) as suggested in the corresponding section or a light modification of the weighting factors used in Eq. 1.

The last set of tests, that we conducted, were to determine a similar relation between the system's stability factor and the initial numerical values of a species' attribute tuple. For that purpose we repeated all test cases illustrated in Fig. 1 (left), while only changing the instance of the fish species' attribute tuple from

(2, 20) to (5, 20), i.e. increasing the maximum number of offspring a fish can spawn from 2 to 5. This yielded a definite increase in the ecosystem's chance to reach equilibrium, as highlighted by the considerably brighter coloring of the heat map even in predator overpopulation/prey underpopulation scenarios (see Fig. 2, right).

4.4   Approach to Efficiently Optimize Input Parameters

The final question we would consider during this work is how to optimize the entire set of input parameters, so that the outcome of the simulation is favorable. Up to now only the size of the initial populations was regarded, but when comparing the improvement of the system's stability by changing these as depicted on Fig. 1 with the improvement gained by modifying the attribute tuple of a species (see Fig. 2), one can quickly acknowledge the significantly better results of the latter approach. A major difficulty, however, is again the size of the input space. With sufficient knowledge in combinatorics it is easy to see that using the 3-tuple (*Fish*, *Sharks*, *Whales*) as input, where each element represents the respective species' population size within the range [10, 50000], yields a total of

$$44991^3 \approx 50000^3 = 1.25 \cdot 10^{14}$$

possible input combinations. In a similar way we can count the possible instances I for the attribute n-tuple of each species with Eq. 2:

$$I = \prod_{i=1}^{n} |A_i|, \tag{2}$$

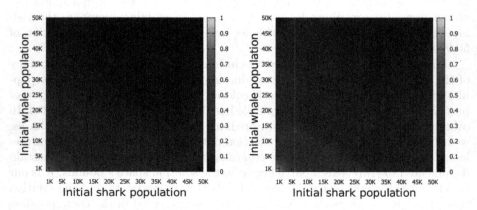

Fig. 1. Relation between the initial predator population sizes and the stability of the ecosystem obtained with Eq. 1. Two different fish population sizes have been used in the experiments: 5,000 (left) and 50,000 (right). Darker/colder colors represent lower stability factor. The stability factor ranges from 0.0 (no species survived any of the test cases) to 1.0 (every species survived all of the test cases).

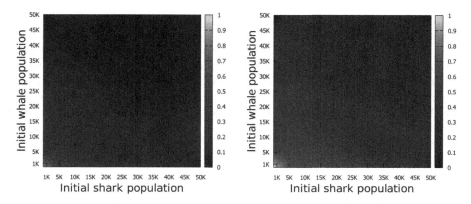

Fig. 2. Relation between the attribute 'offspring count' for the fish species and the stability of the ecosystem obtained with Eq. 1. Two different instances of the maximum offspring count have been used in the experiments: 2 (left) and 5 (right).

where $|A_i|$ is the number of distinct numerical values, that attribute A_i can take. For instance the 2-tuple of the fish species could have the following ranges for its elements

$$(C_{offs}, A_{reproduce}) \Rightarrow ([1,5], [1,100]),$$

yielding a total of $I_{fish} = 5 \cdot 100 = 500$ possible attribute instances. Analogously the shark 4-tuple and the whale 5-tuple could be defined as

$$(C_{offs}, E_{repr}, E_{life}, E_{eat\_fish}) \Rightarrow ([1,5], [51,100], [1,100], [1,10])$$

and

$$(C_{offs}, E_{repr}, E_{life}, E_{eat\_fish}, E_{eat\_shark}) \Rightarrow$$
$$([1,5], [101,200], [1,200], [1,10], [1,50]),$$

yielding $I_{shark} = 5 \cdot 50 \cdot 100 \cdot 10 = 250000$ and $I_{whale} = 5 \cdot 100 \cdot 200 \cdot 10 \cdot 50 = 50000000$ possible instances respectively. The total count of input parameter instances I_{total} is then

$$I_{total} = I_{fish} \cdot I_{shark} \cdot I_{whale} = 500 \cdot 250000 \cdot 50000000 = 6.25 \cdot 10^{15} .$$

Even though this number is not much greater than the number of population size combinations, there are 11 input parameters when summing the tuple elements of all three species, yielding an 11-dimensional input space respectively, unlike the 3-dimensional one for the population sizes. Therefore, applying the graphical solution approaches presented so far in the previous sections would be less than feasible. Moreover, the conclusions made were obtained using excessive testing at the cost of hundreds of hours of computational processing, and could be classified as good approximations at best, which is supported by the small contradiction between the results described in Sects. 4.2 and 4.3. This raises doubts regarding the efficiency of the simulation-based problem solving should problem complexity increase (e.g. more input parameters).

A more promising approach, that we would like to propose, is to combine the simulation-driven architecture of the cellular automaton as it is with an evolutionary search algorithm to traverse the input space for combinations that yield a stable ecosystem. Essentially, we would transform a simulation problem into an *optimization* one, where a model consisting of objects with specific characteristics and rules for their interaction is known, a desired output range is specified and the point of interest is the unknown set of input instances that yield an output within the desired range.

Inspired by biological evolution, hence their name, *evolutionary algorithms* (EA) have gained significant importance in the recent years, especially in the domain of optimization. Their use can be quite rewarding as an efficient alternative to traditional deterministic methods, more so in very complex and intractable problem scenarios. In the following a short summary of the basics is given, as well as an outline of the modifications needed to incorporate the evolutionary optimization technique in our application. It is our strong belief that the integration effort would not be considerable, but the obtained insights might prove to be of value. For a more comprehensive discussion on the topic of EA basics and application refer to [4,9,14].

Solution Candidate Space. As the name implies this is the set of all possible candidate solutions. It can be indefinitely large, but for practical reasons it has to be bounded. Candidate solutions can be anything from numerical values to entire objects. In the case of our Wa-Tor application, the candidate solution space consists of all attribute combinations for the three species (e.g. $6.25 \cdot 10^{15}$ if the aforementioned example is taken).

Genetic Operators. These operators are functions that randomly modify the existing collection of candidate solutions to increase diversity. Typical operators are (a) *mutation*—changing a random characteristic of a candidate solution; and (b) *recombination*—combining two or more solutions to produce new ones; Integrating this functionality in the existing Wa-Tor simulation can be done quite easily in the reproduction action of the animals, e.g. when offspring are spawned their attribute instance can be created by combining that of the parent with those of other existing individuals. Mutation can be implemented similarly as a random change in a spawned offspring's attribute instance inherited by the parent. Genetic operators modify only the genotype. The phenotype cannot be inherited, but is crucial for the fitness of the respective candidate.

Solution Candidate Encoding. A candidate solution is typically represented as a *phenotype-genotype* pair. Just like in biology the phenotype is comprised of a candidate's visible attributes that change over its lifespan due to interaction or external events. On the other hand the genotype is the entire information about the core structure of a candidate in some encoded form, e.g. DNA in real life and usually a binary string in software applications. In the Wa-Tor scenario the phenotype of an object would be its actual instance in the simulation, whereas an adequate genotype would be the information about the object's attributes received at its creation, that is immutable during the lifespan of the object, but inheritable by its offspring.

Fitness Function. The idea behind the fitness function is to decrease the population diversity by eliminating poor candidate solutions, but thus improve the overall quality of the candidate solution space (called 'survival of the fittest' or 'natural selection' in the field of biology). The fitness function in the Wa-Tor scenario is the simulated interaction between the individuals. Using the predefined interaction rules such as moving and feeding, individuals may survive or get killed by predators/die out of starvation. Certain genotype instances may have higher chances to prevail than others, e.g. individuals that can give birth to multiple offspring are more likely to pass down and spread their genotype in the respective population.

5   Conclusion and Future Work

The main goal of our project was to design and develop an application to test the strengths of a simulation-based analysis. A relatively simple and well-known problem domain was chosen, which, however, poses multiple challenges regarding its formal specification, hence the need of an alternative approach. An ecosystem and various species inhabiting it were modeled in the fashion of Dewdney's Wa-Tor [3]. Even though the created model is a fairly basic one, including only several interaction rules between the organisms within the simulation, and a handful of attributes to characterize them, no mathematical specification of the system can be derived without a significant amount of effort. Via simulation however, it was possible to define very simple rules on a micro level, and still obtain valuable insights regarding the global behavior of the environment and the populations inhabiting it.

We augmented previous work on the topic by performing extensive testing to gather enough data and visualize the relation between the inputs and the output of the system. For that an empirically derived formula (see Eq. 1) was used to calculate the system's output (stability factor) as a function of the probability that a species with a given population size would survive. The formula uses weight coefficients to discriminate between more robust and more vulnerable species. In Figs. 1 and 2 we showed the direct dependence of the ecosystem's stability on the initial population sizes and on a specific species' attribute—the number of created offspring after reproduction. In the final part of the paper the challenges of extensive testing were discussed and a new approach based on evolutionary programming was proposed as a possible more efficient alternative.

Future work would revolve around the expansion of the application to incorporate the described evolutionary technique and allow for the model (species' attributes) to change over the course of the simulation similar to the evolution of organisms in the real world. The potential optimization benefits of this approach are to be evaluated and compared to those of the extensive testing. Another interesting idea would be to model the predators' behavior using a space filling curve as a potentially more efficient roaming strategy when the prey is scarce [13].

References

1. Balabanov, K., Fietz, R.G., Logofătu, D.: Considerations in analyzing ecological dependent populations in a changing environment. In: Nguyen, N.T., Papadopoulos, G.A., Jędrzejowicz, P., Trawiński, B., Vossen, G. (eds.) ICCCI 2017. LNCS (LNAI), vol. 10448, pp. 223–232. Springer, Cham (2017). https://doi.org/10.1007/978-3-319-67074-4_22
2. Begon, M., Mortimer, M., Thompson, D.J.: Population Ecology: A Unified Study of Animals and Plants, 3rd edn. Wiley-Blackwell, Oxford (1996)
3. Dewdney, A.K.: Sharks and fish Wage an ecological War on the toroidal planet Wa-Tor. Sci. Am. **251**, 14–22 (1984)
4. Eiben, A.E., Smith, J.E.: Introduction to Evolutionary Computing, 2nd edn. Springer, Heidelberg (2015). https://doi.org/10.1007/978-3-662-05094-1
5. Farge, M.: Numerical experimentation: a third way to study nature. In: Kaneda, Y., Kawamura, H., Sasai, M. (eds.) Frontiers of Computational Science. Proceedings of the International Symposium on Frontiers of Computational Science 2005, pp. 15–30. Springer, Heidelberg (2007). https://doi.org/10.1007/978-3-540-46375-7
6. Floreano, D., Mattiussi, C.: Bio-Inspired Artificial Intelligence: Theories, Methods, and Technologies. MIT Press, Cambridge (2008)
7. Gardner, M.: The fantastic combinations of John Conway's new solitaire game "life". Sci. Am. **223**, 120–123 (1970)
8. Gardner, M.: On cellular automata, self-reproduction, the Garden of Eden and the game "life". Sci. Am. **224**, 112–117 (1971)
9. Gerdes, I., Klawonn, F., Kruse, R.: Evolutionäre Algorithmen: genetische Algorithmen - Strategien und Optimierungsverfahren - Beispielanwendungen. Vieweg, Wiesbaden (2004)
10. Harold, F.M.: The Way of the Cell. Oxford University Press, Oxford (2001)
11. Hoppensteadt, F.: Predator-prey model. Scholarpedia **1**, 1563 (2006)
12. Law, A.M.: Simulation Modeling and Analysis. McGraw-Hill Higher Education, New York (1997)
13. Logofătu, D., Sobol, G., Stamate, D., Balabanov, K.: A novel space filling curves based approach to PSO algorithms for autonomous agents. In: Nguyen, N.T., Papadopoulos, G.A., Jędrzejowicz, P., Trawiński, B., Vossen, G. (eds.) ICCCI 2017. LNCS (LNAI), vol. 10448, pp. 361–370. Springer, Cham (2017). https://doi.org/10.1007/978-3-319-67074-4_35
14. Michalewicz, Z.: Genetic Algorithms + Data Structures = Evolution Programs, 3rd edn. Springer, Heidelberg (2008)
15. Norris, J.S.: Mission-critical development with open source software: lessons learned. IEEE Softw. **21**, 42–49 (2004)
16. Rédei, M.: John von Neumann: Selected Letters. American Mathematical Society, Providence (2005)
17. Ulam, S.M.: Adventures of a Mathematician. Scribner, New York (1976)

Learning - Intelligence

Learning - Intelligence

The Hierarchical Continuous Pursuit Learning Automation for *Large* Numbers of Actions

Anis Yazidi[1], Xuan Zhang[2], Lei Jiao[3(✉)], and B. John Oommen[4]

[1] Department of Computer Science, Oslo and Akershus University College,
Pilestredet 35, Oslo, Norway
anis.yazidi@hioa.no

[2] Centre for Artificial Intelligence Research, University of Agder, Grimstad, Norway
xuan.z.jiao@gmail.com

[3] Department of ICT, University of Agder, Grimstad, Norway
lei.jiao@uia.no

[4] School of Computer Science, Carleton University, Ottawa K1S 5B6, Canada
oommen@scs.carleton.ca

Abstract. Although the field of Learning Automata (LA) has made significant progress in the last four decades, the LA-based methods to tackle problems involving environments with a large number of actions are, in reality, relatively unresolved. The extension of the traditional LA (fixed structure, variable structure, discretized, and pursuit) to problems within this domain cannot be easily established when the number of actions is very large. This is because the dimensionality of the action probability vector is correspondingly large, and consequently, most components of the vector will, after a relatively short time, have values that are *smaller* than the machine accuracy permits, *implying that they will never be chosen*. This paper pioneers a solution that extends the continuous pursuit paradigm to such *large*-actioned problem domains. The beauty of the solution is that it is hierarchical, where all the actions offered by the environment reside as leaves of the hierarchy. Further, at every level, we merely require a *two*-action LA which automatically resolves the problem of dealing with arbitrarily small action probabilities. Additionally, since all the LA invoke the pursuit paradigm, the best action at every level trickles up towards the root. Thus, by invoking the property of the "max" operator, in which, the maximum of numerous maxima is the overall maximum, the hierarchy of LA converges to the optimal action. Apart from reporting the theoretical properties of the scheme, the paper contains extensive experimental results which demonstrate the power of the scheme and its computational advantages. As far as we know, there are no comparable results in the field of LA.

X. Zhang—This author is also a *Data Analyst* in Confirmit AS, Norway.
B. J. Oommen—This author is also an *Adjunct Professor* with the University of Agder in Grimstad, Norway. The work of this author was partially supported by NSERC, the Natural Sciences and Engineering Council of Canada.

L. Iliadis et al. (Eds.): AIAI 2018, IFIP AICT 519, pp. 451–461, 2018.
https://doi.org/10.1007/978-3-319-92007-8_38

Keywords: Learning Automata (LA) · Pursuit LA
Estimator-based LA · Hierarchical LA
LA with large number of actions

1   Introduction

This paper deals with the well-trodden field of Learning automata (LA)[1]. For decades, this field, initiated by Tsetlin [10], has been studied as a typical model for learning in random environments, and has served as the precursor for the area of reinforcement learning. Unlike other fields of Artificial Intelligence (AI), an LA, by definition, operates in random environments, where the "Teacher" can respond differently and randomly, for the same query, at different time instances. More specifically, an LA is an adaptive decision-making unit that learns the optimal action from among a set of actions offered by the Environment that it operates in. Without loss of generality, to render the problem non-trivial, the Environment is stochastic. At each iteration (or time step), the LA selects one action and communicates it to the Environment. This, in turn, *stochastically* triggers either a reward or a penalty as a response from the Environment. Based on the response and the knowledge acquired in the past iterations, the LA, either deterministically or stochastically, adjusts its action selection strategy. This is done so as to make a "wiser" decision in the next iteration. Thus the LA, even though it lacks a complete knowledge about the Environment, is able to learn through repeated interactions with the Environment, and adapts itself, or "converges", to the optimal decision.

Although LA have been studied extensively [1,13–15,17] and been applied in many fields [4,9], designing LA when the number of actions involved, R, is large is extremely complex. The solution that we propose in this paper attempts to resolve this problem.

1.1   Contributions of the Paper

The contributions of this paper are the following:

1. We propose a hierarchical LA strategy which superimposes the learning process on a tree structure. Unlike the traditional hierarchical schemes, we do not resort to Fixed Structure Stochastic Automata (FSSA) or Variable Structure Stochastic Automata (VSSA) to achieve the learning.
2. We propose a novel learning process that involves multi-level two action Continuous Pursuit Algorithm (CPA) machines. The estimation and interaction with the real-world environment occur *only at the leaf level*.

---

[1] In the interest of brevity, we assume that the reader is fairly well-versed in the fundamental concepts of LA and their convergence properties. The review here is thus necessarily brief, although the intent is that it should also be comprehensive. However, excellent surveys of the field can be found in [5,8,9]. Also, due to the space limitations, the theoretical results about our new scheme are omitted here. They are included in [12].

3. We propose the process of trickling-up the estimates and accomplishing the learning by *only* invoking learning between a node and its sibling.
4. The scheme that we have proposed is novel in that it never involves action probabilities that are below machine accuracy. It also involves estimates whose accuracies can easily be attained.
5. The scheme that we have proposed is ϵ-optimal in all random environments [12].
6. The speed of the proposed scheme is *many* times faster than that of all the LA reported in the literature. It is thus the fastest and most accurate reported LA for environments with a large number of actions. As far as we know, no experiments have ever been done in the field of LA for environments when the number of actions was so large, and in that sense, this is truly a pioneering and ground-breaking venture, clearly proving the power of the scheme!

2   The HCPA LA

2.1   Rationale for Our Solution

The philosophy motivating our new scheme resorts to superimposing the actions onto a binary tree[2], in which, the leaves are the actual actions themselves. Further, each internal node represents the best action in the *entire subtree* below that node. By performing comparisons between the actions in a pairwise manner, i.e., at the leaves of the tree, only the superior actions are trickled up towards the root. By doing this, one always deals with 2-action LA. Here, however, unlike the work of previous researchers [2], we do not resort to FSSA or traditional VSSA, to differentiate between the various pairs of actions at the leaves. Rather, we shall use the 2-action continuous pursuit LA [16]. Since $R = 2$ at every level, the number of iterations required to achieve the estimation is considerably less. Further, the estimation that is achieved at the leaf level, is all that is required for the entire tree – no estimation operations are required at the internal nodes.

A notable attempt to devise hierarchical LA is due to Papadimitriou [7]. Before we comment on this work, we mention that the Pursuit concept can be used in a Continuous or Discretized paradigm, and that the action probabilities can be changed on Reward-Penalty (RP), Reward-Inaction (RI) and Inaction-Penalty (IP) scenarios. Consequently, we would have six Pursuit variants: CP_{RP}, DP_{RP}, CP_{RI}, DP_{RI}, CP_{IP} and DP_{IP}, and of these, Agache and Oommen [6] showed that the DP_{RI} is the most superior one. The author of [7] has precisely used this machine, and this is commendable. The differences between that work and the work that we have done here is, however, significant. First of all, this lies is in the way that we have modeled the tree along which the actions have been placed. Secondly, the strategy by which we have trickled up the "maximum" estimate at every node is quite unique and novel, and it does not require us to probe (query) the environment at every time instant, implying that these

---

[2] The tree is assumed to be binary only for the sake of convenience. In a more general setting, each node may have, for example, three children.

interactions with the Environment are only at the leaves. All of these lead to the superiority of our scheme over the recorded ones, demonstrated for experiments done for a much larger set than what has been reported in the literature[3]!

2.2   Construction of the Hierarchy

The search space for the binary tree alluded to above is constructed as follows. First of all, the hierarchy is organized as a balanced full[4] binary tree with maximal depth K. For the sake of convenience and in the interest of mathematical formalism, we will use the same notation adopted in [3,11], and index the nodes using both their depth in the tree and their relative order with respect to the nodes located at the same tree depth. The details of the hierarchy as described as follows.

1. **Root node:** The LA at the root of the hierarchy is the one at depth 0.
2. **The various LA:** At each node, we invoke a 2-action LA $\mathcal{A}$, whose actions are cited as 0 and 1.
3. **LA activations for K levels: from 0 to K-1:**
   - **The different LA at depth k:** The LA $j \in \{1, ..., 2^k\}$ at depth k, is referred to as $\mathcal{A}_{\{k,j\}}$, where $0 \leq k < K - 1$, and it has two actions $\alpha_{\{k+1,2j-1\}}$ and $\alpha_{\{k+1,2j\}}$.
     - Whenever the action $\alpha_{\{k+1,2j-1\}}$ is chosen, the LA $\mathcal{A}_{\{k+1,2j-1\}}$ is activated.
     - Whenever the action $\alpha_{\{k+1,2j\}}$ is chosen, the LA $\mathcal{A}_{\{k+1,2j\}}$ is activated.
     - We can informally say that $\mathcal{A}_{\{k+1,2j-1\}}$ and $\mathcal{A}_{\{k+1,2j\}}$ are the *Left Child* and *Right Child* of the parent LA $\mathcal{A}_{\{k,j\}}$ respectively.
   - **The LA at depth $K - 1$:** The LA at depth $K - 1$ (i.e., at the level *just* above the leaves) is responsible for choosing the action from the stochastic environment.
     - This LA has two actions $\alpha_{\{K,2j-1\}}$ and $\alpha_{\{K,2j\}}$.
     - At this level, there are 2^K actions: $\alpha_{\{K,j\}}$ where $j \in \{1, ..., 2^K\}$ at depth K.
     - Observe that $\alpha_{\{K,j\}}$ is attached to (or associated with) its "parent LA" $\mathcal{A}_{\{K-1,\lceil j/2 \rceil\}}$.
4. **At level K:** Finally, at depth K, i.e., at the maximal depth of the tree, the nodes do not have children.

---

[3] The author of [7] tested his scheme for a maximum of 64 actions. It was not possible to do a fair comparison between our scheme and the work done in [7]. This is because the author of [7] did not report the size of the ensemble of experiments that he conducted. In our case, the ensemble was of size 400, and we sought for the best parameter that yielded "absolute" convergence - i.e., convergence in every single experiment. However, the author of [7] should be given fair credit because of his result being the first reported hierarchical Pursuit-based LA strategy!.

[4] If the number of actions is less than 2^K, one can always add dummy actions whose reward probabilities are zero.

2.3   The Proposed Solution

At the bottom-most level, i.e., the level of the leaves, we invoke a two-action CPA to determine which is the superior action between two actions that are siblings at this level. To do this, we merely maintain running estimates of the reward probabilities of *these* two actions, and using this two-dimensional estimate vector and the corresponding two-action probability vector, the updating is achieved. The larger of these estimates is trickled to their common parent, and this estimate is now compared with the corresponding reward probability estimate of *its* sibling whose value was obtained from *its* children. This process is now recursively repeated, using the estimate of the reward probability at this level and the probability vector at this level, whence the updates are performed. The same process continues up the tree to the root itself.

2.4   The Algorithm of the Proposed Solution

Notation and Definitions. The notation that we shall use is as follows:

- The 2^K actions that interact with the Environment are elements from the set $\{\alpha_{\{K,1\}}, \ldots, \alpha_{\{K,2^K\}}\}$. Further, the actions $\{\alpha_{\{K,2j-1\}}, \alpha_{\{K,2j\}}\}$ are the two only actions that can be selected by the LA at level $K-1$, namely $\mathcal{A}_{\{K-1,j\}}$.
- Each LA $j \in \{1, ..., 2^k\}$ at depth k, called $\mathcal{A}_{\{k,j\}}$, where $0 \le k \le K-1$ has two actions, namely, $\alpha_{\{k+1,2j-1\}}$ and $\alpha_{\{k+1,2j\}}$.
- $P_{\{k,j\}} = [p_{\{k+1,2j-1\}}, p_{\{k+1,2j\}}]^T$ is the action probability vector of LA $\mathcal{A}_{\{k,j\}}$, where $0 \le k \le K-1$.

Begin Algorithm HCPA

Parameters:

λ: The learning parameter, where $0 < \lambda < 1$, where λ is close to zero.

$u_{\{K,2j-1\}}$, $u_{\{K,2j\}}$: The number of times $\alpha_{\{K,2j-1\}}$, $\alpha_{\{K,2j\}}$ have been rewarded *when* it has been selected.

$v_{\{K,2j-1\}}$, $v_{\{K,2j\}}$: The number of times $\alpha_{\{K,2j-1\}}$, $\alpha_{\{K,2j\}}$, has actually been selected.

$\hat{d}_{\{K,2j-1\}}$, $\hat{d}_{\{K,2j\}}$: The estimate of the reward probabilities of $d_{\{K,2j-1\}}$, $d_{\{K,2j\}}$, computed as:
$\hat{d}_{\{K,2j-1\}} = \frac{u_{\{K,2j-1\}}}{v_{\{K,2j-1\}}}$, $\hat{d}_{\{K,2j\}} = \frac{u_{\{K,2j\}}}{v_{\{K,2j\}}}$.

$\hat{D}$ is the vector of the estimates $\{\hat{d}\}$.

m: The index of the optimal action.

h: The index of the greatest element of $\hat{D}$.

R: The response from the Environment, where $R = 0$ corresponds to a Reward, and $R = 1$ to a Penalty.

T: A Threshold, where $T \ge 1 - \epsilon$.

Initialization: Traditional Pursuit algorithms require that we choose each action a few times to initialize the estimates of the reward probabilities. This step is really not so crucial and so we have avoided it and assumed that the estimate of the reward probabilities are initialized to 0.5.

Initialization:

$t = 0$

For i= 1 to 2^K Do:

$\quad u_{\{K,i\}}(0) = 1$

$\quad v_{\{K,i\}}(0) = 2$

$\quad \hat{d}_{\{K,i\}}(0) = \frac{u_{\{K,i\}}(0)}{v_{\{K,i\}}(0)}$

EndFor

Loop

1. $0 \leq k < K - 1$: **Levels 0 to $K - 1$**
   - LA $\mathcal{A}_{\{0,1\}}$ selects an action by randomly sampling as per the action probability vector $[p_{\{1,1\}}(t), p_{\{1,2\}}(t)]$.
   - Let $j_1(t)$ be the index of the chosen action where $j_1(t) \in \{1, 2\}$.
   - The next LA is activated $\mathcal{A}_{\{1, j_1(t)\}}$ which in turn chooses an action and activates the next LA at level '2'.
   - The procedure continues recursively until LA at level $K - 1$.
   - Let $\mathcal{A}_{\{k, j_k(t)\}}$ be the set of activated LA, where j_k denotes the activated LA at level k.

2. $k = K$: **Level K**
   - Update $\hat{D}_{\{K, j_K(t)\}}$ based on the response from the Environment at the leaf level, K:
   $$u_{\{K, j_K(t)\}}(t) = u_{\{K, j_K(t)\}}(t - 1) + (1 - R(t))$$
   $$v_{\{K, j_K(t)\}}(t) = v_{\{K, j_K(t)\}}(t - 1) + 1$$
   $$\hat{d}_{\{K, j_K(t)\}}(t) = \frac{u_{\{K, j_K(t)\}}(t)}{v_{\{K, j_K(t)\}}(t)}.$$

   - For all other "leaf actions", where $j \in \{1, ..., 2^k\}$ and $j \neq j_K(t)$,
   $$u_{\{K,j\}}(t) = u_{\{K,j\}}(t - 1)$$
   $$v_{\{K,j\}}(t) = v_{\{K,j\}}(t - 1)$$
   $$\hat{d}_{\{K,j\}}(t) = \frac{u_{\{K,j\}}(t)}{v_{\{K,j\}}(t)}.$$

3. Define the reward estimate for all other actions along the path from the root, $0 < k < K - 1$ in a recursive manner[5], where the LA at any one level inherits the feedback from the LA at the next level:
   $$\hat{d}_{\{k,j\}}(t) = max(\hat{d}_{\{k+1, 2j-1\}}(t), \hat{d}_{\{k+1, 2j\}}(t)).$$

4. Perform the probability updating for the corresponding vectors as follows:
   - By definition, each LA $j \in \{1, ..., 2^k\}$ at depth k, referred to as $\mathcal{A}_{\{k,j\}}$, where $0 \leq k \leq K - 1$, has two actions $\alpha_{\{k+1, 2j-1\}}$ and $\alpha_{\{k+1, 2j\}}$. Let $j^h(t) \in \{2j - 1, 2j\}$ be the larger of the elements between $\hat{d}_{\{k+1, 2j-1\}}(t)$ and $\hat{d}_{\{k+1, 2j\}}(t)$.
   - Let $\overline{j^h(t)} = \{2j - 1, 2j\} \setminus j^h(t)$ be the opposite action, i.e., the one that has the lower reward estimate.
   - Update $p_{\{k, j^h(t)\}}$ and $p_{\{k, \overline{j^h(t)}\}}$ using the estimates $\hat{d}_{\{k+1, 2j-1\}}(t)$ and $\hat{d}_{\{k+1, 2j\}}(t)$ as:

---

[5] More specifically, the LA at level $K - 2$, inherit the feedback from the LA at level $K - 1$ as:
$$\hat{d}_{\{K-2,j\}}(t) = max(\hat{d}_{\{K-1, 2j-1\}}(t), \hat{d}_{\{K-1, 2j\}}(t))$$
and so on. As a consequence, notice that *at every level*, the reward vector estimates of the actions of every LA, are composed of the respective *maxima* of the rewards of all the actions of the *entire* subtrees rooted at their children.

If $R(t) = 0$ **Then**
$$p_{\{k,\overline{j^h(t)}\}}(t+1) = (1-\lambda)p_{\{k,\overline{j^h(t)}\}}$$
$$p_{\{k,j^h(t)\}}(t+1) = 1 - p_{\{k,\overline{j^h(t)}\}}(t+1).$$
Else
$$p_{\{k,\overline{j^h(t)}\}}(t+1) = p_{\{k,\overline{j^h(t)}\}}(t)$$
$$p_{\{k,j^h(t)\}}(t+1) = p_{\{k,j^h(t)\}}(t).$$
EndIf

- For each $\mathcal{A}_{\{k,j\}}$, if either of its action probabilities $p_{\{k+1,2j-1\}}$ and $p_{\{k+1,2j\}}$ surpasses a threshold T, where T is a positive number that is close to unity, the action probabilities for this LA will stop updating, with its larger action probability jumping to unity.

5. $t = t + 1$

EndLoop
End Algorithm HCPA

The HCPA scheme proposed and described above has been shown to be ϵ-optimal in all random environments. The proofs are quite deep and intricate. However, due to the space limitations, these theoretical results are omitted here. They are included in [12].

3   Experimental Results

To evaluate the performance of the LA-based schemes, we carried out extensive simulations for environments with a "large" number of actions, where the total number of actions was set to various values. The main aspect that we intended to demonstrate was that if the learning problem was tackled using traditional VSSA, the convergence would be both less accurate and very slow. The reason for this, as mentioned earlier, is that if the number of actions is large, many of the action probabilities would be small, implying that these would be chosen seldom. Thus, even if we invoked estimator-based LA, it would be unreasonable to assume that each action would be chosen "a large number of times". Further, the estimates would be correspondingly inaccurate. The HCPA resolves both of these issues.

The simulations that we conducted were intended to capture two important metrics, namely, the accuracy of the convergence of HCPA, and its speed of the convergence. Our goal was also to compare its convergence with the existing LA.

3.1   The Data Sets for the Environment

The benchmark datasets reported in the existing literature had at most ten actions. In the absence of established benchmarks for larger numbers of actions, we have designed a set of Environments which can be used as benchmarks by other researchers. First of all, we determined the number of actions involved in the learning problem. To render the problem non-trivial, the total numbers of

Table 1. This table lists the reward probability of the 64 actions in our experiments. The reward probabilities for 16 and 32 actions are the corresponding 16 and 32 entries in the table, respectively.

A_1	A_2	A_3	A_4	A_5	A_6	A_7	A_8	A_9	A_{10}	A_{11}	A_{12}
0.3934	0.9902	0.4883	0.5768	0.2023	0.2390	0.5887	0.8894	0.0333	0.4323	0.6926	0.3474
A_{13}	A_{14}	A_{15}	A_{16}	A_{17}	A_{18}	A_{19}	A_{20}	A_{21}	A_{22}	A_{23}	A_{24}
0.6152	0.0900	0.0850	0.5652	0.7362	0.7603	0.5142	0.2273	0.6080	0.4791	0.9339	0.3808
A_{25}	A_{26}	A_{27}	A_{28}	A_{29}	A_{30}	A_{31}	A_{32}	A_{33}	A_{34}	A_{35}	A_{36}
0.02152	0.2399	0.7509	0.8773	0.4962	0.5649	0.9202	0.1335	0.6214	0.9777	0.4232	0.02773
A_{37}	A_{38}	A_{39}	A_{40}	A_{41}	A_{42}	A_{43}	A_{44}	A_{45}	A_{46}	A_{47}	A_{48}
0.1255	0.5650	0.1660	0.0148	0.0970	0.1319	0.1738	0.8901	0.3511	0.8945	0.6133	0.4813
A_{49}	A_{50}	A_{51}	A_{52}	A_{53}	A_{54}	A_{55}	A_{56}	A_{57}	A_{58}	A_{59}	A_{60}
0.2413	0.1714	0.8512	0.9791	0.7443	0.3469	0.8707	0.3863	0.4763	0.4446	0.9617	0.0329
A_{61}	A_{62}	A_{63}	A_{64}								
0.5004	0.3784	0.6553	0.9737								

actions was initially configured to be 16, 32 and 64. Once the number of actions was set, the actual reward probabilities associated with the different actions were uniformly distributed in the interval between zero and unity. Understandably, the difficulty the Environment increased with the number of actions. The reward probabilities associated with the configurations for 16 and 32 actions are the first 16 and 32 elements in Table 1, respectively. The reward probabilities of the configuration with 64 actions constitute the entire set given in Table 1.

3.2 Convergence of the HCPA Algorithm

If λ is sufficiently small, the HCPA will converge to the action with the maximum reward probability. To observe the convergence of the algorithm with a minimum number of iterations, our task was to determine the optimal value for λ for different configurations. The optimal λ value is the maximum λ value that will make the LA to *consistently* converge to the correct action. Obviously, for different configurations for the Environment, the value for optimal λ would vary. In this simulation, to find the optimal λ, we decreased the value of λ until we reached the one that provided the LA for the first 200 consecutive occurrences of convergence to the correct action.

Based on our simulations, for the configuration with 64 actions, the optimal λ was 0.000051. In other words, with this value of $\lambda \leq 0.000051$ system would consistently converge accurately. Similarly, the optimal values for λ for the configurations for 32 and 16 actions were 0.00085 and 0.0065 respectively. Understandably, the values of λ have an increasing trend when the environment becomes less challenging.

3.3   Average Convergence Iterations

To illustrate the average number of iterations before convergence, we present the simulation results of the experiments[6] in Tables 2. The standard deviation of the iterations are also included. To compare the HCPA with existing approaches, we include the simulation results for the L_{R-I} and CPA machines in the same environment. The λ values utilized in the HCPA are the ones shown in Sect. 3.2 while the ones in the CPA are the optimal values found based on the same approach explained in Sect. 3.2.

For each replication in HCPA, we register the number of iterations when all the LAs along the correct path had converged to the action probabilities which are greater than or equal to 0.99. Similarly, for each trial for the CPA and the L_{R-I}, we record the number of iterations when the LA had converged to the correct action with an action probability greater than or equal to 0.99. All the results presented in the table have been averaged over an ensemble of 400 independent replications using the optimal λ determined above.

Table 2. The simulation results obtained for various environments with different numbers of actions.

Number of Actions	16		32		64	
Parameters	Mean	SD	Mean	SD	Mean	SD
HCPA	904.5	103.6	6,812.3	614.6	115,295.5	11,346.2
CPA	1,584.2	62.3	7,260.0	529.1	156,616.3	6,985.0
L_{R-I}	3,920.8	1,629.2	28,618.2	7,911.3	644,234.0	20,0625.4

From Table 2, we can clearly see that HCPA outperforms CPA and L_{R-I} in general, especially when the number of actions is large. Thus, for example, for the 64-action environment, the L_{R-I} required 644,234 iterations. The HCPA required less than 18% of the number of iterations, namely 115,295. These results are typical. This confirms the efficiency of the hierarchical structure when the number of actions increases.

3.4   Environment with 128 Actions

The HCPA was also tested on environment with 128 actions, and as mentioned earlier, the testing of LA in environments with such a large number of actions is pioneering – it has been unreported in the literature. Rather than list the reward probabilities, we have plotted them in Fig. 1.

In the case of the first environment plotted in Fig. 1, the L_{R-I} required 734,474 steps for absolute convergence for an ensemble of 400 trials. The CPA,

---

[6] The experiments have been done for various randomly-generated environments. In the interest of brevity, we merely report the results from one such setting. This was representative of the results obtained for other settings.

Fig. 1. An example of an 128-action Environment.

on the other hand, required 543,529 steps - which represented a decrease of about 26%. Astonishingly, the HCPA needed only 266,257 steps. This implied an advantage of about 51% over the CPA and of almost 64% over the L_{R-I}. One can clearly see the advantage of the HCPA over the state-of-the-art.

4   Conclusions

In this paper, we have pioneered a new paradigm for designing and implementing Learning Automata (LA) when the number of actions is large. Learning in environments of this type is particularly hard because the dimensionality of the action probability vector is correspondingly large, and consequently, most components of the vector will, after a relatively short time, have values that are *smaller* than the machine accuracy, *implying that they will never be chosen*. This means that the traditional LA will be sluggish and inaccurate, and it would be unreasonable to assume that each action would be chosen "a large number of times" if we invoked estimator-based LA. In this paper, we have pioneered a solution that extends the Continuous Pursuit Algorithm's (CPA's) paradigm to such *large*-actioned problem domains. The salient feature of our new solution is that it is hierarchical, where all the actions offered by the environment reside as leaves of the hierarchy. Further, at every level, we merely require a *two*-action LA which automatically resolves the problem of dealing with arbitrarily small action probabilities. Most importantly, since all the LA invoke the pursuit paradigm, the best action at every level trickles up towards the root. Thus, by invoking the property of the "max" operator, in which, the maximum of numerous maxima is the overall maximum, the hierarchy of LA converges to the optimal action. The paper also reported experimental results that demonstrated the power of the scheme and its computational advantages.

References

1. Agache, M., Oommen, B.J.: Generalized pursuit learning schemes: new families of continuous and discretized learning automata. IEEE Trans. Syst. Man Cybern. Part B Cybern. **32**(6), 738–749 (2002)
2. Baba, N., Mogami, Y.: A new learning algorithm for the hierarchical structure learning automata operating in the nonstationary S-model random environment. IEEE Trans. Syst. Man Cybern. Part B Cybern. **32**(6), 750–758 (2002)
3. Granmo, O.C., Oommen, B.J.: Solving stochastic nonlinear resource allocation problems using a hierarchy of twofold resource allocation automata. IEEE Trans. Comput. **59**, 545–560 (2009)

4. Jiao, L., Zhang, X., Oommen, B.J., Granmo, O.C.: Optimizing channel selection for cognitive radio networks using a distributed bayesian learning automata-based approach. Appl. Intell. **44**(2), 307–321 (2016)
5. Obaidat, M.S., Papadimitriou, G.I., Pomportsis, A.S.: Learning automata: theory, paradigms, and applications. IEEE Trans. Syst. Man Cybern. Part B Cybern. **32**(6), 706–709 (2002)
6. Oommen, B.J., Agache, M.: Continuous and discretized pursuit learning schemes: various algorithms and their comparison. IEEE Trans. Syst. Man Cybern. Part B Cybern. **31**(3), 277–287 (2001)
7. Papadimitriou, G.I.: Hierarchical discretized pursuit nonlinear learning automata with rapid convergence and high accuracy. IEEE Trans. Knowl. Data Eng. **6**(4), 654–659 (1994)
8. Poznyak, A.S., Najim, K.: Learning Automata and Stochastic Optimization. Springer, Berlin (1997)
9. Thathacha, M.A.L., Sastry, P.S.: Networks of Learning Automata: Techniques for Online Stochastic Optimization. Kluwer Academic Publishers, Dordrecht (2004)
10. Tsetlin, M.L.: Finite automata and the modeling of the simplest forms of behavior. Usp. Matem Nauk **8**, 1–26 (1963)
11. Yazidi, A., Granmo, O.C., Oommen, B.J., Goodwin, M.: A novel strategy for solving the stochastic point location problem using a hierarchical searching scheme. IEEE Trans. Cybern. **44**(11), 2202–2220 (2014)
12. Yazidi, A., Zhang, X., Jiao, L., Oommen, B.J.: The hierarchical continuous pursuit learning automation: a novel scheme for environments with large numbers of actions. Unabridged version of this paper (2018)
13. Zhang, X., Granmo, O.-C., Oommen, B.J.: The Bayesian pursuit algorithm: a new family of estimator learning automata. In: Mehrotra, K.G., Mohan, C.K., Oh, J.C., Varshney, P.K., Ali, M. (eds.) IEA/AIE 2011. LNCS (LNAI), vol. 6704, pp. 608–620. Springer, Heidelberg (2011). https://doi.org/10.1007/978-3-642-21827-9_53
14. Zhang, X., Granmo, O.-C., Oommen, B.J.: Discretized Bayesian pursuit – a new scheme for reinforcement learning. In: Jiang, H., Ding, W., Ali, M., Wu, X. (eds.) IEA/AIE 2012. LNCS (LNAI), vol. 7345, pp. 784–793. Springer, Heidelberg (2012). https://doi.org/10.1007/978-3-642-31087-4_79
15. Zhang, X., Granmo, O.C., Oommen, B.J.: On incorporating the paradigms of discretization and Bayesian estimation to create a new family of pursuit learning automata. Appl. Intell. **39**, 782–792 (2013)
16. Zhang, X., Granmo, O.C., Oommen, B.J., Jiao, L.: A formal proof of the ϵ-optimality of absorbing continuous pursuit algorithms using the theory of regular functions. Appl. Intell. **41**(3), 974–985 (2014)
17. Zhang, X., Oommen, B.J., Granmo, O.C.: The design of absorbing Bayesian pursuit algorithms and the formal analyses of their ϵ-optimality. Pattern Anal. Appl. **20**(3), 797–808 (2017). https://doi.org/10.1007/s10044-016-0535-1

Speedup of Network Training Process by Eliminating the Overshoots of Outputs

Di Zhou[✉], Yuxin Zhao, Chang Liu, and Yanlong Liu

College of Automation, Harbin Engineering University,
Harbin 150001, HLJ, People's Republic of China
{zhoudi128, zhaoyuxin, liuchang407,
yanlong_liu}@hrbeu.edu.cn

Abstract. The overshoots between the expected and actual outputs while training network will slow down the training speed and affect the training accuracy. In this paper, an improved training method for eliminating overshoots is proposed on the basis of traditional network training algorithms and a suggestion of eliminating overshoot is given. Gradient descent is regarded as the training criterion in traditional methods which neglects the side effects caused by overshoots. The overshoot definition (OD) is combined with gradient descent. According to the overshoot suggestion, local linearization and weighted mean methods are used to adjust the parameters of network. Based on the new training strategy, a numerical experiment is conducted to verify the proposed algorithm. The results show that the proposed algorithm eliminates overshoots effectively and improves the training performance of the network greatly.

Keywords: Output overshoots · Local linearization · Weighted mean
Artificial neural network

1 Introduction

Artificial neural networks (ANNs) have developed rapidly and have been used wildly in many fields, such as speech recognition, computer vision, games and classification of skin cancer [1–4]. So far, the studies of ANNs can be divided into three aspects. The first aspect is the topology of network. The numbers of nodes and layers play a significant role in applications of networks. ANNs have developed multiple branch types, such as convolution neural network, recurrent neural network, extreme learning machine [5–7]. However, there is still no substantial instruction on the topology of network. The second aspect is to combine the neural network with other optimization algorithms. Since lots of optimization algorithms exist, this aspect is mainly used for special applications. In [8, 9], ANNs are combined with fuzzy and genetic theory to identify nonlinear system and a short-term load forecasting of natural gas. Network training algorithms are the third aspect and most popular aspect.

Training algorithms play a decisive role in the accuracy of ANNs. In general, a large number of historical data have to be used while training network. Therefore, how to handle big data efficiently and extract features accurately are the key to training network. In [10], Rumelhart proposed learning representations by back-propagating errors.

L. Iliadis et al. (Eds.): AIAI 2018, IFIP AICT 519, pp. 462–470, 2018.
https://doi.org/10.1007/978-3-319-92007-8_39

BP algorithm has good convergence property, however, it may lead to the problem of gradient vanishing. For the disadvantages of BP algorithm, ReLU is proposed to replace the sigmoid activation function [11]. In [12], dropout of nodes is proposed to prevent ANNs from overfitting. In addition, the parallel and online sequential learning algorithms are introduced to quicken the training process [13, 14].

Almost all existing algorithms focus on gradient while few studies take the overshoots of outputs into consideration. An eliminating overshoot method (EOM) is proposed to improve BP algorithm. An overshoot definition is given on the basis of traditional BP (TBP) algorithm. Meanwhile, local linearization and weighted mean algorithms are adopted to train ANNs. This paper is organized as follows. In Sect. 2, we briefly describe the overshoot definition and its mathematical method. Section 3 introduces the numerical simulation. Finally, the conclusion and the future work are summarized in Sect. 4.

2   The Overshoot Definition and Mathematical Method

In this study, the OD combines the outputs with gradient decent. The OD is given as all outputs must be on the same side of the excepted output with the output at the first iteration while training network. The purpose of training network is to adjust the parameters on the basis of a given set of samples to minimize the errors between the actual and expected outputs. Not only gradients but also outputs have to be considered while training networks. A cost function is defined to characterize the errors. At present, there are many kinds of cost functions. The Euclidean metric is used as the cost function in this study, which is defined as follows:

$$E = \frac{1}{2} \cdot (O - D)^T \cdot (O - D) \tag{1}$$

O is the actual output vector, D is the expected response output. T denotes transpose operation. E is the total instantaneous error energy.

The weight and threshold matrixes of the ith layer are defined as follows:

$$W_i = \begin{bmatrix} w_{i,1,1} & w_{i,1,2} & \cdots & w_{i,1,N_{i+1}} \\ w_{i,2,1} & w_{i,2,2} & \cdots & w_{i,2,N_{i+1}} \\ \vdots & \vdots & \ddots & \vdots \\ w_{i,1,1} & w_{i,1,1} & \cdots & w_{i,1,1} \end{bmatrix} \tag{2}$$

$$B^i = \begin{bmatrix} b_1^i \\ b_2^i \\ \vdots \\ b_{N_i}^i \end{bmatrix} \tag{3}$$

$w_{i,j,k}$ denotes the weight value between the jth node of the ith layer and the kth node of the $(i+1)^{th}$ layer. b_i^j denotes the threshold value of the jth node in the ith layer. N_i denotes the number of the nodes in the ith layer.

The output of the ith layer is defined as follows:

$$O^i = \begin{bmatrix} o_1^i \\ o_2^i \\ \vdots \\ o_{N_i}^i \end{bmatrix} \tag{4}$$

According to the Eqs. (2)–(4), the output of the $(i+1)^{th}$ layer can be expressed as follows:

$$O^{i+1} = F(W_i, B^i, O^i) \tag{5}$$

F is the action function.

The correction ΔW_i and ΔB_i are defined as follows:

$$\Delta W_i = -\eta \cdot \frac{dE}{dW_i} = -\eta \cdot \begin{bmatrix} \frac{\partial E}{\partial w_{i,1,1}} & \frac{\partial E}{\partial w_{i,1,2}} & \cdots & \frac{\partial E}{\partial w_{i,1,N_i+1}} \\ \frac{\partial E}{\partial w_{i,2,1}} & \frac{\partial E}{\partial w_{i,2,2}} & \cdots & \frac{\partial E}{\partial w_{i,2,N_i+1}} \\ \vdots & \vdots & \ddots & \vdots \\ \frac{\partial E}{\partial w_{i,N_i,1}} & \frac{\partial E}{\partial w_{i,N_i,2}} & \cdots & \frac{\partial E}{\partial w_{i,N_i,N_i+1}} \end{bmatrix} \tag{6}$$

$$\Delta B_i = -\eta \cdot \frac{dE}{dB^i} = -\eta \cdot \begin{bmatrix} \frac{\partial E}{\partial b_1^i} \\ \frac{\partial E}{\partial b_2^i} \\ \vdots \\ \frac{\partial E}{\partial b_{N_i}^i} \end{bmatrix} \tag{7}$$

In Eq. (7), $\frac{dE}{dB_i}$ is the jacobian matrix of E with respect to the threshold vector B^i denoted as J_i^B. The jacobian matrix can be calculated layer by layer.

$$J_i^B = \frac{dE}{dB^i} = \frac{dE}{dO^L} \cdot \frac{dO^L}{dO^{L-1}} \cdots \frac{dO^{i+1}}{dO^i} \frac{dO^i}{dB^i}, \tag{8}$$

Where $i = 1, 2, \cdots, L$.

In Eq. (8), $\frac{dE}{dO^L}$ denotes the jacobian matrix of E with respect to the actual output O^L. L denotes the number of all layers in network.

$$\frac{dE}{dO^L} = \begin{bmatrix} \frac{\partial E}{\partial O_1^L} & \frac{\partial E}{\partial O_2^L} & \cdots & \frac{\partial E}{\partial O_{N_L}^L} \end{bmatrix} = \begin{bmatrix} O_1^L - d_1^L & O_2^L - d_2^L & \cdots & O_{N_L}^L - d_{N_L}^L \end{bmatrix}. \tag{9}$$

d_i^L denotes the expected response.

$\frac{dO^{i+1}}{dO^i}$ denotes the jacobian matrix of the output of the $(i+1)^{th}$ layer O^{i+1} with respect to the output of the ith layer O^i.

$$\frac{dO^{i+1}}{dO^i} = \begin{bmatrix} \frac{\partial o_1^{i+1}}{\partial o_1^i} & \frac{\partial o_1^{i+1}}{\partial o_2^i} & \cdots & \frac{\partial o_1^{i+1}}{\partial o_{L_i}^i} \\ \frac{\partial o_2^{i+1}}{\partial o_1^i} & \frac{\partial o_2^{i+1}}{\partial o_2^i} & \cdots & \frac{\partial o_2^{i+1}}{\partial o_{L_i}^i} \\ \vdots & \vdots & \ddots & \vdots \\ \frac{\partial o_{L_{i+1}}^{i+1}}{\partial o_1^i} & \frac{\partial o_{L_{i+1}}^{i+1}}{\partial o_2^i} & \cdots & \frac{\partial o_{L_{i+1}}^{i+1}}{\partial o_{L_i}^i} \end{bmatrix} \tag{10}$$

$\frac{dO^i}{dB^i}$ denotes the jacobian matrix of O^i with respect to B^i.

$$\frac{dO^i}{dB^i} = \begin{bmatrix} \frac{\partial O_1^i}{\partial b_1^i} & \frac{\partial O_1^i}{\partial b_2^i} & \cdots & \frac{\partial O_1^i}{\partial b_{N_i}^i} \\ \frac{\partial O_2^i}{\partial b_1^i} & \frac{\partial O_2^i}{\partial b_2^i} & \cdots & \frac{\partial O_2^i}{\partial b_{N_i}^i} \\ \vdots & \vdots & \ddots & \vdots \\ \frac{\partial O_{N_i}^i}{\partial b_1^i} & \frac{\partial O_{N_i}^i}{\partial b_2^i} & \cdots & \frac{\partial O_{N_i}^i}{\partial b_{N_i}^i} \end{bmatrix} \tag{11}$$

According to the Eqs. (7)–(11), the initial correction ΔB^i can be obtained. The expression of the initial correction ΔW^i can be derived with the same method above. In this study, the sigmoid function is chosen as the action function. The output locates in the interval (0,1). It can be obtained from the Eq. (8) that the correction is determined by the errors of outputs directly.

Assuming that the overshoot arises at the nth iteration, it indicates the corrections exceed the range. Accordingly, the OD should be adopted to eliminate the overshoots for achieving the optimal solution as soon as possible. Since the traditional line search algorithm is time consuming, local linearization and weighted mean methods are used to adjust the parameters to eliminate overshoots in this paper. The local linearization method is based on the relationship between cost function and network parameters. When overshoots occur, the actual outputs of the latest two iterations locate on both sides of the excepted output, which are close to the expected output. In this situation, the error changes little, which is in line with the local linearization condition. The network parameters are regarded as the independent variables, while the cost function is the corresponding variable. Linear equations are established by the latest two iterations, which are defined as follows:

$$\begin{cases} E - E_n = \Delta B_n^i (\hat{B}_n^i - B_n^i) \\ E - E_{n-1} = \Delta B_{n-1}^i (\hat{B}_n^i - B_{n-1}^i) \end{cases} \tag{12}$$

ΔB_n^i is the gradient of E with respect to B^i at the nth iteration. $\overset{\wedge}{B_n^i}$ is the updated network parameters. E_n is the total error at the nth iteration.

The updated network parameters can be obtained by solving the equations when the gradients are nonzero. According to Eq. (12), the updated parameters can be divided into two cases. For the first case, if the cost function is a convex function between B_n^i and B_{n-1}^i, the updated parameters should locate in the interval $(\min(B_{n-1}^i, B_n^i), \max(B_{n-1}^i, B_n^i))$. Then the overshoot of the updated parameters is judged according to the OD. If overshoots are eliminated, the updated parameters are accepted and continue the next iteration. Otherwise, the above step has to be circulated until the overshoots are eliminated. For the second case, the cost function is a non-convex function between B_n^i and B_{n-1}^i. The updated parameters may not locate in the interval $(\min(B_{n-1}^i, B_n^i), \max(B_{n-1}^i, B_n^i))$. The weighted mean method is adopted to deal with this situation. The specific process is defined as follows:

$$\overset{\wedge}{B_n^i} = \frac{|\Delta B_n^i|}{|\Delta B_n^i| + |\Delta B_{n-1}^i|} \cdot B_{n-1}^i + \frac{|\Delta B_{n-1}^i|}{|\Delta B_n^i| + |\Delta B_{n-1}^i|} \tag{13}$$

Similarly to the first case, the updated parameters are accepted if the updated parameters satisfy the overshoot definition, or this step will continue to circulate until overshoots are eliminated.

3 Numerical Simulation and Result Analysis

In this section, a numerical simulation is conducted to verify the effectiveness and practicability of the EOM algorithm. A three layers feed-forward ANN is designed. The sigmoid function is chosen as the action function. The numbers of neurons in input, hidden and output layer are 22, 30 and 58. The input and output samples are selected from the solutions of the downwelling atmosphere monochromatic radiative transfer model equation (MonoRTM). Before training the network, all samples are normalized.

In order to avoid the denominator is 0, the network parameter is accepted when the absolute values of its gradients in the latest two iterations satisfy the overshoot definition and are both below 0.000001. This operation will also speed up the training process.

Similarly to the TBP methods, the OD is also introduced to train the network layer by layer. However, contrary to the direction the error propagates, the OD propagates forwardly. The parameters of the next layer are adjusted on the basis of no overshoot on the previous layers. The TBP algorithm is simulated to compare with the proposed method. The structure of network and initial parameters of the two methods are set to the same. The maximal number of iterations and the acceptable error are set to 50 and 0.000001.

The total instant error of all samples at each iteration is recorded and shown in Fig. 1. The blue and red curves represent the total error of the TBP and the EOM method respectively.

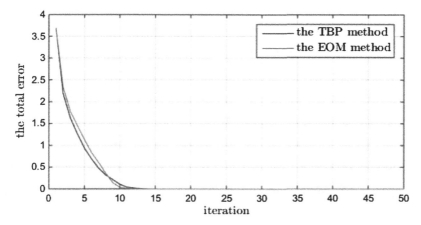

Fig. 1. The total errors of outputs of the EOM and BP methods. The red and blue lines represent the outputs of EOM and BP methods, respectively. (Color figure online)

As can be seen from the figure, the errors of the two methods almost overlap in the initial stage. This is mainly because no overshoot occurs at this stage. The network parameters meet the OD at each iteration which implies that they are not corrected again.

However, the error of the EOM method is reduced at a slower speed than the TBP method in the middle stage. The experimental data shows that errors of the most sample are still large, but overshoots appear at some sample points. In order to satisfy the OD, the parameters leading to overshoots are corrected again, resulting in that the error cannot reduce in the direction of the steepest descent. Therefore, the blue curve is lower than the red curve in the figure. However, the gradient of the blue curve slows down gradually while the red curve almost shows a linear decline trend.

In the final stage, the errors of the samples are small. Overshoots in many sample points lead to a slow speed of training network with traditional methods. However, the EOM method takes great advantage of the good suppression of overshoots and minimizes the error quickly. As shown in Fig. 1, it takes 14 iterations to achieve the optimal solution for the TBP method, however, only 11 for the EOM method.

An output sample point is selected randomly to study the elimination of overshoot detailedly. The actual outputs of the two methods are recorded and shown in Fig. 2. The red and blue curves are respective the actual output of the EOM and TBP method. The green curve is the excepted output.

It can be manifested from Fig. 2, no overshoot appears in the initial stage. It indicates the parameters satisfy the OD. The blue and red curves overlap each other which is consistent with the result in Fig. 1. The correctness of the results in Fig. 1 can be confirmed in this stage.

The blue curve implies the overshoot appears when training network with traditional BP method in the middle stage. In order to meet the OD, the parameters have to be corrected again by the local linearization and weighted mean methods. The red curve depicts the elimination of overshoots of outputs while training neural network. In

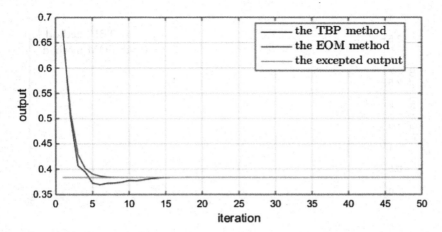

Fig. 2. The outputs of single sample of the EOM and BP methods. The red and blue lines represent the outputs of EOM and BP methods, respectively. The green line is the excepted output (Color figure online)

addition, the EOM method takes 8 iterations to approximate the excepted output which is half of that of the TBP method. Furthermore, the output curve of the EOM method is smoother than that of TBP method.

In order to illustrate the effectiveness of the proposed algorithm to eliminate overshoot intuitively, the training trajectories of 58 output samples of the two methods are shown in Figs. 3 and 4.

The blue points in Fig. 3 and green points in Fig. 4 represent the trajectories of the TBP and EOM method respectively. The red points in both figures are the excepted outputs. Overshoots appear at 90 percent of samples in Fig. 3. And overshoots are

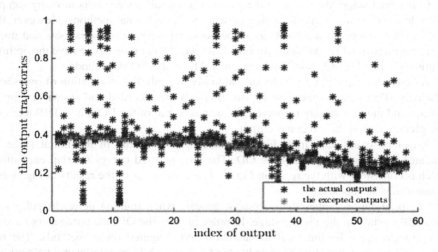

Fig. 3. The output trajectories of the TBP method. (Color figure online)

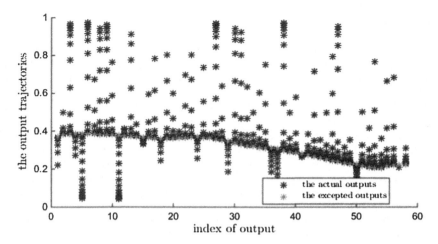

Fig. 4. The output trajectories of the EOM method. (Color figure online)

obvious especially when the initial error is around 0.15. However, no overshoot appears in Fig. 4 which is consistent with the results in Fig. 2. No overshoot for all samples indicates the proposed method is universal. And the OD is universal for other neural network model.

4 Conclusion

In this paper, an improved training method and the OD are proposed for eliminating the overshoots of outputs. The outputs and gradients of the network are taken into consider. The training process of neural network is derived in matrix form and the specific expressions are given. Local linearization and weighted mean methods are introduced to optimize training algorithm. In the final stage of training network, the proposed method eliminates all overshoots perfectly. The advantage of eliminating overshoot makes it possible to reach the optimal earlier than the traditional method. The simulation demonstrates effectiveness of the EOM method and its universality for all samples. Therefore, the EOM method is superior to the traditional method. In addition, a drawback of the EOM method is that it trains network at a slow speed in the middle stage. It is also the direction of our future work.

Acknowledgements. This paper is funded by the International Exchange Program of Harbin Engineering University for Innovation-oriented Talents Cultivation, National Natural Science Foundation of China (Grant Nos. 41676088) and the National Key Research and Development Project of China (2017YFC1404100).

References

1. Hinton, G., Deng, L., Yu, D., Dahl, G.E., Mohamed, A.R., Jaitly, N., Senior, A., Vanhoucke, V., Nguyen, P., Sainath, T.N., et al.: Deep neural networks for acoustic modeling in speech recognition: the shared views of four research groups. IEEE Sig. Process. Mag. **29**(6), 82–97 (2012)

2. Gould, S.: DARWIN: a framework for machine learning and computer vision research and development. J. Mach. Learn. Res. **13**, 3533–3537 (2012)

3. Silver, D., Huang, A., Maddison, C.J., Guez, A., Sifre, L., Van Den Driessche, G., Schrittwieser, J., Antonoglou, I., Panneershelvam, V., Lanctot, M., et al.: Mastering the game of go with deep neural networks and tree search. Nature **529**(7587), 484–489 (2016)

4. Esteva, A., Kuprel, B., Novoa, R.A., Ko, J., Swetter, S.M., Blau, H.M., Thrun, S.: Dermatologist-level classification of skin cancer with deep neural networks. Nature **542** (7639), 115–118 (2017)

5. Mahendran, A., Vedaldi, A.: Visualizing deep convolutional neural networks using natural pre-images. Int. J. Comput. Vision **120**(3), 233–255 (2016)

6. Weninger, F., Bergmann, J., Schuller, B.: Introducing CURRENNT: The munich opensource CUDA recurrent neural network toolkit. J. Mach. Learn. Res. **16**(1), 547–551 (2015)

7. Huang, G.B., Zhu, Q.Y., Siew, C.K.: Extreme learning machine: theory and applications. Neurocomputing **70**(1), 489–501 (2006)

8. Lin, Y.Y., Chang, J.Y., Lin, C.T.: Identification and prediction of dynamic systems using an interactively recurrent self-evolving fuzzy neural network. IEEE Trans. Neural Netw. Learn. Syst. **24**(2), 310–321 (2013)

9. Yu, F., Xu, X.: A short-term load forecasting model of natural gas based on optimized genetic algorithm and improved BP neural network. Appl. Energy **134**, 102–113 (2014)

10. Rumelhart, D.E., Hinton, G.E., Williams, R.J.: Learning representations by backpropagating errors. Nature **323**(6088), 533 (1986)

11. Dahl, G.E., Sainath, T.N., Hinton, G.E.: Improving deep neural networks for LVCSR using rectified linear units and dropout. In: 2013 IEEE International Conference on Acoustics, Speech and Signal Processing (ICASSP), pp. 8609–8613. IEEE (2013)

12. Srivastava, N., Hinton, G.E., Krizhevsky, A., Sutskever, I., Salakhutdinov, R.: Dropout: a simple way to prevent neural networks from overfitting. J. Mach. Learn. Res. **15**(1), 1929–1958 (2014)

13. Hinton, G.E., Osindero, S., Teh, Y.W.: A fast learning algorithm for deep belief nets. Neural Comput. **18**(7), 1527–1554 (2006)

14. Sutskever, I., Vinyals, O., Le, Q.V.: Sequence to sequence learning with neural networks. In: Advances in Neural Information Processing Systems, pp. 3104–3112 (2014)

Collective Intelligence for Decision-Making in Complex Environments: Literature Review

Daniela Rincón, Jhonatan Valdes, and Luz Bohórquez

Universidad Distrital Francisco José de Caldas, Bogotá D.C., Colombia
drincol@correo.uditrital.edu.co,
jdvaldesg@correo.udistrital.edu.co,
lebohorqueza@udistrital.edu.co

Abstract. The growing complexity of the environment makes explicit the fact that Human Social Systems must develop mechanisms that allow them to increase agility in decision-making. An alternative to achieve this is found in Collective Intelligence, which has been widely studied in Natural Social Systems, in Artificial Social Systems, and in Human Social Systems. Despite the research carried out in this last field, there is no clarity regarding the aspects that facilitate its understanding and emergency. This document identifies the structural and dynamic features in different Collective Intelligence models selected in the context of Human Social Systems. Finally, the possibility of proposing other features to be considered is discussed from the review of the factors that have explained the emergence of Collective Intelligence in Natural and Artificial Social Systems, and they are assessed in order to design Collective Intelligence models in future research.

Keywords: Collective Intelligence · Swarm Intelligence · Complex Systems
Human Social Systems

1 Introduction

Human Social Systems must develop ways that make possible to increase the agility to adapt to changing conditions in the environment, considering its increasing complexity. Adaptation is understood from the biological - evolutionary perspective, and involves variations that enable the system to provide solutions to survive in the environment [1].

Collective intelligence (CI), studied in Natural Social Systems (NSSs), in Artificial Social Systems (ASSs) and in Human Social Systems (HSSs), is an option to increase agility in adapting to changing environmental conditions. Research in NSSs has its origin in Swarm Intelligence (SI); term that was introduced for the first time by Beni and Wang [2], when they investigated the emergence of collective behaviors. This concept was later extended by Bonabeau et al. [3] including any effort to design algorithms for problem solving inspired by the collective behavior of social insects.

In human social systems, CI was formalized since the 1990s, by authors such as Lévy [4], Pór [5] and Malone [6]; and it is understood from the behaviors and decisions that arise from the crowds. CI appears as a mean to take advantage of the large volumes

© IFIP International Federation for Information Processing 2018
Published by Springer International Publishing AG 2018. All Rights Reserved
L. Iliadis et al. (Eds.): AIAI 2018, IFIP AICT 519, pp. 471–480, 2018.
https://doi.org/10.1007/978-3-319-92007-8_40

of information, which arise permanently on account of technological development, in the generation of new knowledge that acts as a society engine [4].

The different proposals of CI in HSSs have been oriented to the design of systems with capacities to solve problems in flexible, robust, adaptive, agile and resilient ways, allowing them to survive in highly changing environments [7]. However, a consensus regarding what are the structural and dynamic aspects that facilitate their understanding and emergence does not exist thus far.

2 Methodology

The literature available in CI, mainly in NSSs and ASSs, is extensive and has a broad trajectory. The study was carried out in three stages: S1 embraces wide database searches. Based on the results of S1, an emphasis in certain authors who are identified as relevant (Table 1) is given on S2, and finally, S3 focuses on the analysis of the obtained information.

Table 1. Main Databases, Journals and Authors consulted.

Collective intelligence review	Databases	Main journals	Main authors
Natural and Artificial Social Systems	ScienceDirect SpringerLink Scopus JSTOR World Scientific Elsevier IEEE	MIT Sloan Management Review Administrative Science Quarterly Philosophical Logic and Artificial Intelligence Artificial Intelligence Advances in Complex Systems Integrative and Comparative Biology	Bonabeau, E. (1999) Secundo G. (2012) Malone, T.W. (2010) Lévy, P. (1997) Atlee, T. (2000) Gerardo Beni (1993) Jing Wang (1993)
Human Social Systems	ScienceDirect SpringerLink Scopus APA PSYCNET	MIT Sloan Management Review Cognitive Systems Research Strategic management journal Advances in Complex Systems	Malone, T.W. (2008) Lévy, P. (2004) Pór G (1995) McHugh K.A. (2016)

The methodology proposed for the development of the present investigation was carried out in 4 stages indicated (Table 2).

Table 2. Stages of the methodology. Prepared by authors.

Stage	Definition
S1	CI literature review in NSSs and ASSs. CI literature review in HSSs
S2	Identification of the structural and dynamic features that different models applying CI in HSSs have in common. (Structural factors refer to features that the system structure should have. Dynamic factors focus on the features that emerge from the structure of the system
S3	Comparison of the NSSs and ASSs structural and dynamic factors with those of HSSs identified in S2, in order to recognize differences and similarities
S4	Structuring of new approaches and features that facilitate the emergence of CI in HSSs

3   Collective Intelligence in Natural and Artificial Social Systems

Research on collective behavior in NSS has its main background in Swarm Intelligence (SI). The expression Swarm Intelligence was introduced by Beni and Wang [2] when they studied decentralization and capacity for self-organization in the robotic systems context. The emergence of intelligent solutions presented by the colonies of ants, bees, termites, wasps, has surprised several researchers due to the high levels of robustness and flexibility [3].

4   Collective Intelligence in Human Systems

High levels of robustness, flexibility, adaptability, cooperation, Self-Organization and Collective Intelligence for environmental solution problems that NSSs and ASSs exhibit, has aroused the interest of various authors to design HSSs models [16]. The research conducted by McHugh [17] evidences that organizations with higher levels of CI present higher quality of decisions in terms of precision, agility [18] variety of knowledge [19], breadth and depth [20]. As mentioned by Alberts [21], even when an absence of agility does not represent a threat to existence, it is very expensive.

To date there are important investigations for CI in HSSs from different disciplines such as psychology [22], politics [18] and economics [23]. Table 3 presents some of the CI proposals in HSSs. The registered proposals cover different sectors (health, education, energy, among others) and are mainly oriented towards decision making.

Proposals registered in Table 3 provide the framework that enables the identification of structural and dynamic factors that explain the CI in the studied systems. In Table 3, each model is identified by an ID number that will be used to reference the model in some sections of the document.

Table 3. Models with CI Applications. Prepared by the Authors.

ID	PROPOSAL
1	Collective Intelligence and Online Learning Communities [24]. Gea, M., Soldado, R. M. and Lenguajes, D. (2011). New forms of non-formal learning skills in digital communities through Collective Intelligence
2	Collective intelligence for promoting changes in behavior: a case study on energy conservation [25]. Piccolo, L. S. G., Liddo, A. De, Burel, G., Fernandez, M. and Alani, H. (2017). Build knowledge in a collaborative manner around the conservation of energy
3	Collective Intelligence Meets Medical Decision-Making: The Collective Outperforms the Best Radiologist [26].Wolf, M., Krause, J., Carney, P. A., Bogart, A. and Kurvers, R. H. J. M. (2015). The proposal studies the way as certain established rules are used by a team of specialists in mammograms diagnosis and treatments
4	Fostering collective intelligence education [27] Meza, J., Monguet, J. M., Grimón, F. and Trejo, A. (2016). Teaching IC model using a virtual platform to promote shared learning between students and teachers
5	How common standards can diminish collective intelligence: a computational study. [28] Morreau, M. and Lyon, A. (2016) Create knowledge shared by a group of specialists through the collection of information and individual experiences to improve the medical diagnoses efficiency
6	Managing intellectual capital in entrepreneurial university: A collective intelligence approach. [29] Secundo, G., Passiante, G., Gianfreda, F. and Passabì, S. (2014, April). The proposal uses CI as a tool for the creation and administration of intellectual capital within an entrepreneurial university
7	Self-organized flexible leadership promotes collective intelligence in human groups. [30] Kurvers, R. H., Wolf, M., Naguib, M. and Krause, J. (2015). Demonstrate how roles are formed within a group to make a good decision when each of the members has different quality information
8	Using the Collective Intelligence for inventive problem solving: A contribution for Open Computer Aided Innovation. [31] Flores, R. L., Belaud, J. P., Le Lann, J. M. and Negny, S. (2015). Collaboration, interaction and use of knowledge between a company and the market for solving inventive problems in the industrial sector

5 Gap Between Natural and Artificial Systems Compared to Human Systems

The aim of this section is to identify the structural and dynamic features that facilitate the understanding of CI in NSSs and ASSs to enrich CI proposals in HSSs. In this research it is recognized that NSSs and ASSs do not have a specific and predetermined purpose as it happens in HSSs e.g. profitability. The pre-specification of the system's purpose can reduce the complexity this can absorb. In order to know how the HSSs could enhance their CI characteristics and improve decision-making in environments with high levels of uncertainty, it is necessary to contrast features they have in common with the NSSs and the ASSs. The structural and dynamic features identified in NSSs and ASSs, HSSs and the gap between Natural and Artificial Systems Compared to Human Systems are shown below (Table 4).

Table 4. Structural and dynamic features in NSSs and ASSs

NSSs and ASSs	HSSs	Gap
Structural Features		
Central Controller absence. The centrality is a structural attribute of the network nodes and not of the actors themselves, i.e. it is understood from the position occupied by an agent in the system [8]. Control is oriented to guarantee the fulfillment of the objectives or the development of tasks [9]. Diverse investigations have shown that the CI exhibited by social insects is characterized by the absence of a central controller and a hierarchical structure. [10]	**Autonomy**. It is described as multidisciplinary groups with self-organizing that operate with a decentralized authority [33]. For a collective to be intelligent, the autonomous perceptions of those who make up the group must be mobilized and respected: call for the active expression of singularities, creativities and competences. [34] In models 1, 2, 3 and 4 there is not a central node that makes decisions and exercises control over others, but, a decision is made according to a series of pre-established rules	**Decentralization and Autonomy**. While within NSSs and ASSs exist a full SO in the absence of a central controller to provide an agile solution to the group and environment needs, in HSSs there is not a complete decentralization. In NSSs, the division of labor is usually determined by morphological features. [3] From the analyzed models that use digital tools to fulfill their purpose (1, 2, 4, 6, and 8), platforms are means for cooperation between individuals with different roles and achieve a common goal, therefore, a central controller does not exist. **Direct/Indirect Communication, Information Processing, Shared Knowledge and Collaboration**. Communication in NSSs, ASSs and HSSs seeks to process information in an effective and agile way among the system agents. Nevertheless, agility in HSSs interactions cannot be considered as effective as in the
Direct Interaction. Some forms of direct communication in social insects are antennae, trophalaxis (feeding one another), mandibular contact, eye contact, chemical contact, among others [3]. Another example is birds attracted to sites where other birds already nest. This imitative behavior is a positive feedback process in which an individual follows the "I nest near where you nest" rule [11]	**Direct communication**. Gestures, language, context and prosody (pronunciation and accentuation) influence the interaction between agents [32]. Direct communication characterizes model 6 as soon as group decisions between agents were made face to face in the university facilities	NSSs. Authors such as Dale, Fusaroli, Duran and Richardson [32] propose the study of synchrony patterns between individuals. On the other hand, Barlow and Dennis [37] raise the importance of the medium in which the homogeneity in the signals interpretations is carried out to achieve coherent responses **Robustness**. In NSSs and ASSs it is observed that even though one of its components fails, the system has the ability to continue functioning as usual. In the models of HSSs using virtual media, despite identifying certain robustness, the characteristics of the human being (beliefs, thoughts, and feelings) can influence the collective performance. Models 3 and 5 may

(continued)

Table 4. (*continued*)

NSSs and ASSs	HSSs	Gap
Structural Features		
Indirect interaction. Refers to communication processes that arise through the modification of the environment. When termites build their nests, they send stimuli to others through pheromones and it causes other termites to build their nests close to the one previously placed [12]. Indirect interaction also called stigmergy by the French biologist Grassé [12] allows to understand the cooperative behavior that arises among insects	**Indirect communication.** Agents do not require to perceive the existence of others. However, the activities that are carried out in the system have consequences for all its actors [22]. In model 1, 2, 4, 8 the information exchange is generated through non-explicit assumptions in virtual media, without a face-to-face contact	be affected by the amount of people who make them up **Self-Organization**. SO describes the emerging responses to different situations that the environment may present. In HSSs information can condition the collective conduct. This idea can be identified in model 7, where, according to the quality information held by an agent, it could make decisions faster or slower according to the role. Models 1, 2 and 4 display how from the agents' opinions in real time some system conditions can be changed **Adaptability and Flexibility.** Different species and biological systems look for adapt agilely to changing and emerging environments. Some approaches have been made in the proposals that use virtual media as mechanisms to achieve the proposed intentions. In models that perform medical diagnoses using CI (3, 5) low level of adaptability is evidenced **Agility**. In model 2 and 8 technology is used to create an agile model with the aim of generating shared awareness around the environmental care and open innovation through the improvement of communication. Apparently, these models allow solutions to different cases in less time and with better results
Division of roles. It allows creating specialized groups that perform tasks better than if they were performed by a single agent [13], this ensure that if a member fails in the development of the labor, colony is still functioning through the work of other agents	**Distributed Information Processing.** Information is not concentrated on specific groups but rather integrates naturally to the entire human activities and returns to the hands of all. Collectives communicate transversally without a hierarchical structure. [34] In model 4 ideas are produced individually-collectively and are hierarchized; then, they are assessed	
Dynamic Features		
Self-organization (SO). It Is understood as the emergence of collective behaviors from interactions between agents [14] or as a set of dynamic mechanisms in which global-level structures appear from an interactions system among the components of different levels [15]	**Self-Organization.** Behavior patterns emerges from interaction. These patterns are formed and reformed spontaneously and continuously at multiple levels within the system. The objective is to understand how they are determined by the interactions of the agents to carry out the appropriate interventions in the system [35]. In models 1, 2 and 4 when an individual participates and contributes new ideas, the other agents are stimulated and actively participate	

(*continued*)

Table 4. (*continued*)

NSSs and ASSs	HSSs	Gap
Structural Features		
Adaptability. SO allows to explain adaptability as the capacity of modify and being modified as well as adjust itself to the changing environment	**Adaptability.** If a link is congested, the interconnection between agents must allow an alternative path to be used to reach its destination, whether it is information or a decision. [36]. In the model 4, the students feedback towards the proposed ideas changes according to the other students opinions	
Flexibility. Denotes the capacity of changing within the system	**Collaboration.** The capacity of a multi-agent system is not determined by a simple agent but by the intelligence shown by mutual coordination from the interactions that are generated in the system. [23] Information and Communication Technologies (ICTs) are used in model 8 as facilitators in the collaborative environments creation to gather resources and experts to relate existing knowledge	
Robustness. Refers to the ability to continue operating despite failures that occur at individual level [3]	**Shared knowledge.** One person can represent a source of knowledge enrichment for another one. By associating their competences, they demonstrate that they can do a better job together than apart. [22, 34]. The model 7 have two roles. Leaders have the most accurate information and decide quickly	

6 Discussions and Future Research Lines

The development of this article has allowed to understand and identify structural and dynamic features present in the NSSs, ASSs and HSSs. Within the features found in the HSSs models closest to the characterization in NSSs and in ASSs, are the absence of a central controller (NSSs) and autonomy (HSSs). Despite the similarity, the roles within the system are predefined. It is necessary that the function an actor plays within the system properly emerges from the interactions with the environment. On the other hand, proposals where virtual platforms are included, information processing presents a good approach to what is set in the NSSs; virtual media allows greater flexibility in the systems. However, quality of input information determines how agile the system can be and its capacity for self-organization; therefore, collaboration emerges as a possible response to avoid aspects such as opportunism and other characteristics of the human being that provide limited information and slow down the system.

A proposal for future research in the CI models design is to identify the range in which the number of participating actors should be found to decrease the influence of specific nodes, and ensure that it does not decrease the level of interactions between agents and the environment. The use of ICTs tools could improve the design of a CI model, creating information bases, supporting them on adaptive learning and leading the system to adapt itself to changes in the environment.

References

1. Bock, W.J.: The definition and recognition of biological adaptation. Am. Zool. **20**, 217–227 (1980). https://doi.org/10.1093/icb/20.1.217
2. Beni, G., Wang, J.: Swarm intelligence in cellular robotic systems. In: Dario, P., Sandini, G., Aebischer, P. (eds.) Robots and Biological Systems: Towards a New Bionics? NATO ASI Series (Series F: Computer and Systems Sciences), vol 102. Springer, Heidelberg (1993). https://doi.org/10.1007/978-3-642-58069-7_38
3. Boneabeau, E., Dorigo, M., Theaulaz, G.: Swarm Intelligence: From Natural to Artificial Systems (1999)
4. Lévy, P.: L'intelligence collective. Pour une anthropologie du cyberespace, vol. 246 (1997)
5. Pór, G.: The quest for collective intelligence. In: Community Building: Renewing Spirit and Learning in Business. California (1995)
6. Malone, T.W.: What is collective intelligence and what will we do about it? Collective Intelligence: Creating a Prosperous World at Peace (2008)
7. Alberts, D., Hayes, R.: Power to the edge: Command... control... in the information age. (CCRP) (2003)
8. Hossain, L., Wu, A.: Communications network centrality correlates to organisational coordination. Int. J. Proj. Manage. **27**(8), 795–811 (2009)
9. Simons, R.: Levers of control: How managers use innovative control systems to drive strategic renewal (1994)
10. Greene, M.J., Gordon, D.M.: Interaction rate informs harvester ant task decisions. Behav. Ecol. **18**, 451–455 (2007). https://doi.org/10.1093/beheco/arl105
11. Camazine, S.: Self-Organization in Biological Systems. Princeton University Press, Princeton (2003)

12. Grassé, P.P.: The automatic regulations of collective behavior of social insect and "stigmergy". J. Psychol. Norm. Pathol. (Paris) **57**, 1–10 (1959)
13. Park, J.C., et al.: Measures to take advantage of the collective intelligence of the Web 2.0 platform. Rev. Korean Soc. Internet Inf. **8**(2), 15–20 (2007)
14. Kauffman, J.M., Hallahan, D.P.: The illusion of full inclusion: a comprehensive critique of a current special education bandwagon (1995)
15. Bonabeau, E., Theraulaz, G., Deneubourg, J.L., Aron, S., Camazine, S.: Self-organization in social insects. Trends Ecol. Evol. **12**(5), 188–193 (1997)
16. Atlee, T., Por, G.: Collective Intelligence as a Field of Multi-disciplinary Study and Practice. Community Intell
17. McHugh, K.A., Yammarino, F.J., Dionne, S.D., Serban, A., Sayama, H., Chatterjee, S.: Collective decision making, leadership, and collective intelligence: tests with agent-based simulations and a Field study. Leadersh. Q. **27**, 218–241 (2016). https://doi.org/10.1016/j.leaqua.2016.01.001
18. Gilliland, S.W., Landis, R.S.: Quality and quantity goals in a complex decision task: Strategies and outcomes. J. Appl. Psychol. **77**(5), 672–681 (1992). https://doi.org/10.1037/0021-9010.77.5.672
19. Bantel, K.A., Jackson, S.E.: Top management and innovations in banking: does the composition of the top team make a difference? Strateg. Manage. J. **10**(S1), 107–124 (1989). https://doi.org/10.1002/smj.4250100709
20. Kraiger, K., Wenzel, L.H.: A framework for understanding and measuring shared mental models of team performance and team effectiveness. Salas, E., Brannick, M.T., Prince, C. (eds.) (1997)
21. Alberts, D.S.: The agility advantage: A Survival Guide for Complex Enterprises and Endeavors (2011)
22. Marsh, L., Onof, C.: Stigmergic epistemology, stigmergic cognition. Cogn. Syst. Res. **9**, 136–149 (2008). https://doi.org/10.1016/j.cogsys.2007.06.009
23. Guo, Q.L., Zhang, M.: Multiagent-based scheduling optimization for Intelligent Manufacturing System. Int. J. Adv. Manuf. Technol. **44**, 595–605 (2009). https://doi.org/10.1007/s00170-008-1858-x
24. Gea, M., Soldado, R.M., Gámiz, V.: Collective intelligence and online learning communities. In: 2011 International Conference Information Society (i-Society), pp. 336–340 (2011)
25. Piccolo, L.S.G., De Liddo, A., Burel, G., Fernandez, M., Alani, H.: Collective intelligence for promoting changes in behaviour: a case study on energy conservation. AI Soc. **33**, 15–25 (2017). https://doi.org/10.1007/s00146-017-0710-y
26. Wolf, M., Krause, J., Carney, P.A., Bogart, A., Kurvers, R.H.J.M.: Collective intelligence meets medical decision-making: The collective outperforms the best radiologist. PLoS ONE **10**, 1–11 (2015). https://doi.org/10.1371/journal.pone.0134269
27. Meza, J., Monguet, J.M., Grimón, F., Trejo, A.: Fostering Collective Intelligence Education, pp. 165–172 (2016). https://doi.org/10.1007/978-3-319-28883-3_21
28. Morreau, M., Lyon, A.: How common standards can diminish collective intelligence: a computational study. J. Eval. Clin. Pract. **22**, 483–489 (2016). https://doi.org/10.1111/jep.12585
29. Secundo, G., Passiante, G., Gianfreda, F., Passabì, S.: Managing intellectual capital in entrepreneurial university: a collective intelligence approach. In: 6th European Conference on Intellect Cap ECIC 2014, vol. 209–216 (2014)
30. Kurvers, R.H.J.M., Wolf, M., Naguib, M., Krause, J.: Self-organized flexible leadership promotes collective intelligence in human groups. R Soc. Open Sci. **2**, 150222 (2015). https://doi.org/10.1098/rsos.150222

31. Lopez Flores, R., Belaud, J.P., Le Lann, J.M., Negny, S.: Using the collective intelligence for inventive problem solving: a contribution for open computer aided innovation. Expert Syst. Appl. **42**, 9340–9352 (2015). https://doi.org/10.1016/j.eswa.2015.08.024
32. Dale, R., Fusaroli, R., Duran, N.D., Richardson D.C.: The Self-Organization of human interaction. In: Psychology of Learning and Motivation - Advances in Research and Theory, pp 43–95 (2014)
33. Ismail, S., Malone. M.S., Van Geest, Y.: Organizaciones Exponenciales. Bubok Publishing (2016)
34. Levy, P.: Inteligencia colectiva: por una antropología del ciberespacio. Centro Nacional de Información de Ciencias Médicas (INFOMED) (2004)
35. Eoyang, G.H.: Conditions for self-organizing in human systems. Futuries **28**, 10–59 (2004)
36. Peters, K., Johansson, A., Dussutour, A., Helbing, D.: Analytical and numerical investigation of ant behavior under crowded conditions. Adv. Complex Syst. **9**(04), 337–352 (2006). https://doi.org/10.1142/S0219525906000859
37. Barlow, J.B., Dennis, A.R.: Not as smart as we think: a study of collective intelligence in virtual groups. J. Manage. Inf. Syst. **33**, 684–712 (2016). https://doi.org/10.1080/07421222.2016.1243944

Quantile Estimation Based on the Principles of the Search on the Line

Anis Yazidi and Hugo Lewi Hammer$^{(\boxtimes)}$

Department of Computer Science, Oslo Metropolitan University, Olso, Norway

Abstract. The goal of our research is to estimate the quantiles of a distribution from a large set of samples that arrive sequentially. We propose a novel quantile estimator that requires a *finite memory* and is simple to implement. Furthermore, the estimator falls under the family of incremental estimators, i.e., it utilizes the previously-computed estimates and *only* resorts to the last sample for updating these estimates. The estimator estimates the quantile on a set of discrete values. Choosing a low resolution results in fast convergence and low precision of the current estimate after convergence, while a high resolution results in slower convergence, but higher precision. The convergence results are based on the theory of Stochastic Point Location (SPL). The reader should note that the aim of the paper is to demonstrate its salient properties as a novel quantile estimator that uses only *finite* memory.

Keywords: Discretized estimation · Learning automata
Stochastic Point Location · Quantile estimation

1 Introduction

An incremental estimator, by definition, resorts to the last observation(s) in order to update its estimate. This is especially true of quantile estimators because they work with the samples as they come from a stochastic distribution. The research on developing incremental quantile estimators is sparse. Probably, one of the outstanding early and unique examples of incremental quantile estimators is due to Tierney, proposed in 1983 [20], and which resorted to the theory of stochastic approximation. Applications of Tierney's algorithm to network monitoring can be found in [4]. A very limited number of studies have devised *incremental* quantile estimators including the Frugal estimator due to Ma et al. [10], the higher fidelity Frugal due to Yazidi et al. [26] and the DUMIQE estimator due to Yazidi and Hammer [25].

In order to appreciate the qualities of our estimator, we will present the estimator scheme proposed by Tierney [20]. Let X be a random variable. Let $x(n)$ be a concrete realization of X at time 'n'. $x(n)$ is drawn from the distribution of X, $f_X(x)$. The intention of the exercise is to estimate the q-th quantile, the number Q_q such that $F_X(Q_q) = q$. Tierney [20] achieved this by maintaining a

Published by Springer International Publishing AG 2018. All Rights Reserved
L. Iliadis et al. (Eds.): AIAI 2018, IFIP AICT 519, pp. 481–492, 2018.
https://doi.org/10.1007/978-3-319-92007-8_41

running estimate $\widehat{Q_q}(n)$ at time 'n'.

$$\widehat{Q_q}(n+1) = \widehat{Q_q}(n) + \frac{d_n}{n+1}(q - I(x(n) \le \widehat{Q_q}(n)))) \tag{1}$$

where $d_n = min(\frac{1}{f_n(Q_q)}, d_0 n^a)$. Here $0 < a < 1/2$, $d_o > 0$, and $f_n(Q_q)$ is an estimator of $f(Q_q)$ defined in [20]. The reason for invoking the min operation in the above expression of $d(n)$ is the fact that the estimated density must be bounded to prevent the correction factor from "exploding". In other words, f_n is current estimate of the density of X at the q-th quantile. This is usually done based on maintaining a histogram structure. However, requiring the incremental constructions of local approximations of the distribution function in the neighborhood of the quantiles increases the complexity of the algorithm. Our goal is to present an algorithm that does not involve any local approximations of the distribution function. Recently, a generalization of the Tierney's [20] algorithm was proposed by [5] where the authors proposed a batch update of the quantile, where the quantile is updated every $M \ge 1$ observations.

A body of research has been focused on quantile estimation from data streams without making any specific assumption on the distribution of the data samples. We shall first review some the related work on estimating quantiles from data streams. However, as we will explain later, these related works require some memory restrictions which renders our work to be radically distinct from them. In fact, our approach requires storing only one sample value in order to update the estimate. The most representative work for this type of "streaming" quantile estimator is due to the seminal work of Munro and Paterson [11]. In [11], Munro and Paterson described a p-pass algorithm for selection using $O(n^{1/(2p)})$ space for any $p \ge 2$. Cormode and Muthukrishnan [6] proposed a more space-efficient data structure, called the Count-Min sketch, which is inspired by Bloom filters, where one estimates the quantiles of a stream as the quantiles of a random sample of the input. The key idea is to maintain a random sample of an appropriate size to estimate the quantile, where the premise is to select a subset of elements whose quantile approximates the true quantile. From this perspective, the latter body of research requires a certain amount of memory that increases as the required accuracy of the estimator increases [21]. Examples of these works are [2, 7, 11, 21].

In [5], the authors proposed a modification of the stochastic approximation algorithm [20] in order to allow an update similar to the well-known Exponentially Weighted Moving Averages form for updates. This modification is particularly helpful in the case of non-stationary environments in order to cope with non-stationary data. Thus, the quantile estimate is a weighted combination of the new data that has arrived and the previously-computed estimate. Indeed, a "weighted" update scheme is applied to incrementally build local approximations of the distribution function in the neighborhood of the quantiles. In the experiments results that we report, we consider the cases when data are generated randomly from stationary and non-stationary distributions.

This paper introduces a novel discretized quantile estimator. While we have earlier solved the binomial estimation problem using discretized estimators [23], this is the first solution to the quantile estimation.

We submit that the entire phenomenon of utilizing the concepts of discretization in quantile estimation is unexplored, and it is precisely here that we have our primary contributions.

1.1 Legacy SPL Solutions

To place our work in the right perspective, we briefly review the state of the art of the SPL problem, whose formulation and solution is central to our approach. The SPL problem, in its most elementary formulation, assumes that there is a Learning Mechanism (LM) whose task is to determine the optimal value of some variable (or parameter), x. We assume that there is an optimal choice for x – an unknown value, say $x^* \in [0, 1)$. The SPL involves inferring the value x^*. Although the mechanism does not know the value of x^*, it was assumed that it has responses from an intelligent "Environment" (synonymously, referred to as the "Oracle"), Ξ, that is capable of informing it whether any value of x is too small or too big. To render the problem both meaningful and distinct from its deterministic version, we would like to emphasize that the response from this Environment is assumed "faulty." Thus, Ξ may tell us to increase x when it should be decreased, and *vice versa*. However, to render the problem tangible, in [14] the probability of receiving an intelligent response was assumed to be $p > 0.5$, in which case Ξ was said to be *Informative*. Note that the quantity "p" reflects on the "effectiveness" of the Environment. Thus, whenever the current $x < x^*$, the Environment correctly suggests that we increase x with probability p. It simultaneously could have incorrectly recommended that we decrease x with probability $(1 - p)$. The converse is true for $x \geq x^*$.

We can summarize the existing SPL-related literature as follows:

- Oommen [14] pioneered the study of the SPL when he proposed and analyzed an algorithm that operates on a discretized search space[1] while interacting with an informative Environment (i.e., $p > 0.5$). The search space was first sliced into N sub-intervals at the positions $\{0, \frac{1}{N}, \frac{2}{N}, \ldots, \frac{N-1}{N}, 1\}$, where a larger value of N ultimately implied a more accurate convergence to x^*. The algorithm then did a controlled random walk on this space by "obediently" following the Environment's advice in the discretized space. In spite of the Oracle's erroneous feedback, this discretized solution was proven to be ϵ-optimal.

---

[1] Some of the existing results about discretized automata are found in [1, 9, 12, 13, 15, 16, 19]. Indeed, the fastest reported LAs are the discretized pursuit, and discretized maximum likelihood and Bayesian estimator algorithms [1, 12, 16].

- An novel alternate *parallel* strategy that combined LA and pruning was used in [17] to solve the SPL. By utilizing the response from the environment, the authors of [17] partitioned the interval of search into three disjoint subintervals, eliminating at least one of the subintervals from further search, and by recursively searching the remaining interval(s) until the search interval was at least as small as the required resolution[2].
- In a subsequent work [18], Oommen *et al.* introduced the Continuous Point Location with Adaptive d-ARY Search (CPL-AdS) which was a generalization of the work in [17]. In CPL-AdS, the given search interval was sub-divided into d partitions representing d disjoint subintervals, where $d > 3$. In each interval, initially, the midpoint of the given interval was considered to be the estimate of the unknown x^*. Each of the d partitions of the interval was independently explored using an ϵ-optimal two-action LA, where the two actions were those of selecting a point from the left or right half of the partition under consideration. Thereafter, the scheme proposed in [18] eliminated at least one of the subintervals from being searched further, and recursively searched the remaining pruned contiguous interval until the search interval was at least as small as the required resolution of estimation. Again, this elimination process essentially utilized the ϵ-optimality property of the underlying LA and the monotonicity of the intervals to guarantee the convergence. By virtue of this property, at each epoch consisting of a certain number, N_∞, of iterations, the algorithm could "$(1 - \epsilon)$-confidently" discard regions of the search space.
- The authors of [8] proposed a rather straightforward modification of the latter CPL-AdS so as to also track changes in x^*. Indeed, to achieve the latter, the authors of [8] proposed to perform an *additional* parallel d-ARY search at each epoch on the original search interval. The limitation of this work is that the strategy proposed in [8] can only track x^* under certain conditions relative to the frequency of change in x^* and the length of an epoch. However, more importantly, the interesting facet of the solution presented in [18] is that it converges with an arbitrarily high accuracy even if the Oracle is a *stochastic compulsive liar* who is attempting to stochastically deceive the LM.
- Recently Yazidi *et al.* [22] proposed a *hierarchical* searching scheme for solving the SPL problem. The solution involves partitioning the line in a hierarchical tree-like manner, and of moving to relatively distant points, as characterized by those along the path of the tree. With regard to its advantages, this solution is an order of magnitude faster than the classical SPL solution [14]. The marginal drawback, however, is that it works under the premise that p is a constant whose value is larger than the golden ratio conjugate.

---

[2] The logic behind this is explained in the next item, when the authors generalized this scenario for the case when the number of partitions was $d > 3$.

2   Discretized Estimator

Let $Q_i = a + i.\frac{(b-a)}{N}$ and suppose that we are estimating the quantile in interval $[a, b]$, where $a > 0$. Note $Q_0 = a$ and $Q_N = b$. There is an implicit assumption that the true quantile lies in $[a, b]$. However, this is not a limitation of our scheme, the proof is valid for any bounded and probably non bounded function.

We suppose that the estimate at each time instant $\widehat{Q}(n)$ takes values from the $N + 1$ values $Q_i = a + i.\frac{(b-a)}{N}$, where $0 \leq i \leq N$.

According to whether q is lager or smaller than $1/2$, we will have two different estimation schemes.

- **Case 1:** $q < \frac{1}{2}$
  If $\widehat{Q}(n) \leq x(n)$ and $rand() \leq \frac{1}{2(1-q)}$

$$\widehat{Q}(n+1) \leftarrow Min(\widehat{Q}(n) + 1/N, b) \tag{2}$$

  Else

$$\widehat{Q}(n+1) \leftarrow Max(\widehat{Q}(n) - 1/N, a) \tag{3}$$

- **Case 2:** $q > \frac{1}{2}$
  If $\widehat{Q}(n) > x(n)$ and $rand() \leq \frac{1}{2q}$

$$\widehat{Q}(n+1) \leftarrow Max(\widehat{Q}(n) - 1/N, a) \tag{4}$$

  Else

$$\widehat{Q}(n+1) \leftarrow Min(\widehat{Q}(n) + 1/N, b) \tag{5}$$

where $Max(.,.)$ and $Min(.,.)$ denote the max and min operator of two real numbers while $rand()$ is a is a random number generated in $[0, 1]$.

Theorem 1. *We would like to estimate the q-th quantile to be estimated, i.e,* $Q^* = F_X^{-1}(q)$. *Applying the updating rules (2), (3), (4) and (5), we obtain:* $\lim_{n \to \infty} \lim_{N \to \infty} E(\widehat{Q}(n)) = Q^*$.

The proof of the theorem is quite involved and has been omitted here for the sake of space limitation. The full proof can be found in [24].

Remarks: A few remarks regarding our method for updating the estimates are not out of place. Indeed:

- First of all, it is pertinent to mention that although the rationale for updating is similar to that of the SSL algorithm [14], there are some fundamental differences. Unlike the latter, which explicitly assumes the existence of an "Oracle", in this case, our scheme simulates such an entity.

- Secondly, at this juncture, we emphasize that unlike the work of [14], the probability that the Oracle suggests the move in the correct direction, is not constant over the states of the estimator's state space. This is quite a significant difference, which basically reduces our model to a Markov Chain with state-dependent transition probabilities.

3   Experimental Results

We compare our estimator to the EWSA (Exponential weighted Stochastic Approximation) due to Chen et al. [5], which is a direct extension of the Stochastic Approximation based quantile estimator proposed by Tierney [20]. Note that both, our estimator and the EWSA are incremental estimators.

In this section, we compare both estimators for different distributions, under different resolution parameter and in stationary environments. The results are conclusive and demonstrate that the convergence of the algorithms conform to the theoretical results. We use different distributions namely:

- Uniform in $[0, 1]$
- Normal $N(0, 1)$
- Exponential distribution with mean 1 and variance 1
- Chi-square distribution with mean 1 and variance 2.

In all the experiments, we chose a to be -4 and b is fixed to 4. Note that whenever the resolution is N, the estimate is moving with either additive or subtractive step size equal to $\frac{b-a}{N}$. A larger value of the resolution parameter N implies a small step size, while a low value of the resolution parameter N results in a smaller step size.

Initially, at time 0, the estimates for the Discretized Quantile Estimator (DQE) are set to $Q_{N/2}$, while for the EWSA the initial value of the estimate is $(a + b)/2$.

The reader should note that the aim of the paper is to demonstrate its salient properties as a novel quantile estimator that uses only *finite* memory.

3.1   Comparison in Stationary Environments for Different Distributions

In this set of experiments, we examine a stationary environment. We used different resolutions namely $N = 30$, $N = 100$ and $N = 1000$ and as previously mentioned $[a, b] = [-4, 4]$. Given that the step size is obtained by the formula $\frac{b-a}{N}$, please note that the resulting step sizes of the resolutions $N = 30$, $N = 100$ and $N = 1000$ are $8/30$, $8/100$ and $8/1000$, respectively.

While for the EWSA, we use three different typical values, namely $\lambda = 0.01$, $\lambda = 0.05$, $\lambda = 0.1$, which illustrates the overall properties of this estimator. In fact, a low value of λ permits slow updates of the estimates and is convenient for a stationary environment, while a high value of λ for dynamic environment as it allows faster updates of the estimates.

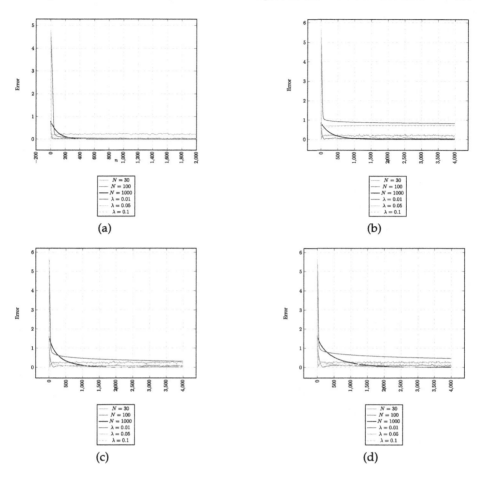

Fig. 1. This figure depicts the variation of the estimation error with time n for the quantile of 80% for the DQE ($N = 30$, $N = 100$ and $N = 1000$) and for the EWSA ($\lambda = 0.01$, $\lambda = 0.05$ and $\lambda = 0.1$) for (a) *uniform* distribution, (b) *normal* distribution, (c) *exponential* distribution, (d) *Chi − Square* distribution.

Figure 1 depicts the case of estimating the 80% quantile for the four different distributions: uniform, normal, exponential and Chi-square. We report the estimation error from an ensemble of 1000 experiments. We observe that our DQE approaches the true value for all the four distributions asymptotically over time. We observe that given a low resolution ($N = 30$), the error drops very fast but stabilizes on a value between 0.05 and 0.15. Using a higher resolution, the error drops slower, but asymptotically the error becomes much smaller compared to the low resolution alternative. A very intriguing characteristic of our estimator is that by choosing a sufficiently high resolution, we are able to estimate the quantile as precise as we want. This is not possible for traditional off line quantile

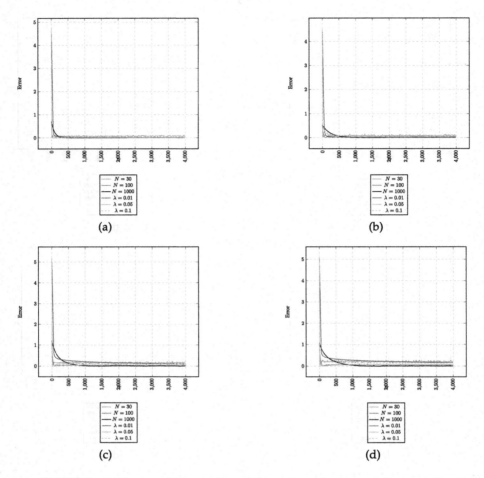

Fig. 2. This figure depicts the variation of the estimation error with time n for the quantile of 70% for the DQE ($N = 30$, $N = 100$ and $N = 1000$) and for the EWSA ($\lambda = 0.01$, $\lambda = 0.05$ and $\lambda = 0.1$) for (a) *uniform* distribution, (b) *normal* distribution, (c) *exponential* distribution, (d) *Chi − Square* distribution.

estimators without using an infinite amount of memory. Comparing the results of EWSA and DQE, it seems that the performance of the EWSA is highly dependent of λ which can be hard to choose. E.g. for the normal distribution EWSA ends up with high errors for all the three values chosen for λ. In comparison the convergence properties of the DQE is far more consistent.

A very intriguing characteristic of our estimator, as the resolution increases, the estimation error diminishes (asymptotically). In fact, the limited memory of the estimator does not permit to achieve zero error, i.e, 100% accuracy. As noted in the theoretical results, the convergence will be centred around the smallest interval $[Q_z, Q_{z+1}]$ containing the true quantile. Loosely speaking, a

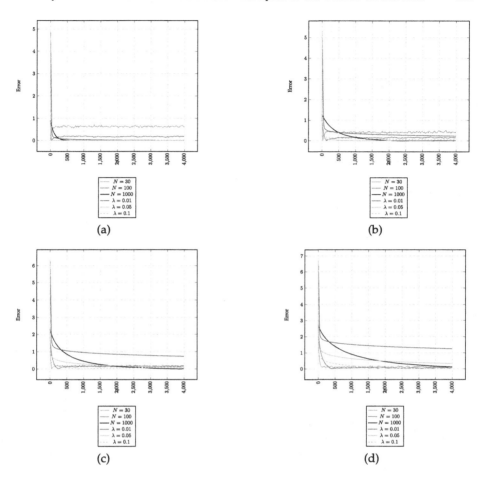

Fig. 3. This figure depicts the variation of the estimation error with time n for the quantile of 90% for the DQE ($N = 30$, $N = 100$ and $N = 1000$) and for the EWSA ($\lambda = 0.01$, $\lambda = 0.05$ and $\lambda = 0.1$) for (a) *uniform* distribution, (b) *normal* distribution, (c) *exponential* distribution, (d) *Chi − Square* distribution.

higher resolution increases the accuracy while a low resolution decreases the accuracy.

Figures 2, 3 and 4 depict the cases of estimating the 70%, 90%, 95% quantiles respectively for the same four different distributions. In the comparison of the results for the different values of N and for different values of λ for the EWSA scheme, the conclusions are as for the 80% quantile case described above.

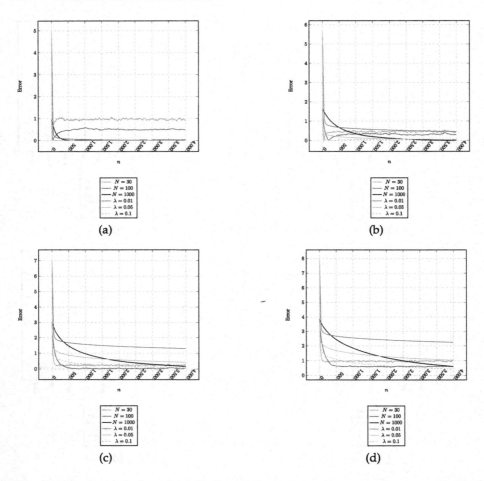

Fig. 4. This figure depicts the variation of the estimation error with time n for the quantile of 95% for the DQE ($N = 30$, $N = 100$ and $N = 1000$) and for the EWSA ($\lambda = 0.01$, $\lambda = 0.05$ and $\lambda = 0.1$) for (a) *uniform* distribution, (b) *normal* distribution, (c) *exponential* distribution, (d) *Chi − Square* distribution.

4   Conclusion

In this paper, we have designed a novel incremental discretized quantile estimator based on the theory of stochastic search on the line. We emphasize that the estimator can be easily implemented and that it is much simpler than the state of the art incremental estimator proposed by Tierney [20] as it does not require estimation of the density at the quantile. We have also extended our estimator in order to handle data arriving in a batch mode.

There are different extensions that can be envisaged for future work:

- We worked in finite Markov chain domain, and suppose that the true quantile lies in the interval $[a, b]$. As a future work, we plan to extend the proof to infinite state Markov chain.
- The existing algorithm for quantile estimation is designed for data elements that are added one by one. A possible extension is to generalize our algorithm to handle not only data insertions, but also dynamic data operations such as deletions and updates such as in [3].
- An interesting research direction is to simultaneously estimate more than a single quantile value. To achieve this, our present scheme will have to be modified so as to guarantee the monotonicity property of the quantiles, i.e, maintaining multiple quantile estimates while simultaneously ensuring that the estimates do not violate the monotonicity property.

References

1. Agache, M., Oommen, B.J.: Generalized pursuit learning schemes: new families of continuous and discretized learning automata. IEEE Trans. Syst. Man Cybern.-Part B Cybern. **32**(6), 738–749 (2002)
2. Arasu, A., Manku, G.S.: Approximate counts and quantiles over sliding windows. In: Proceedings of the Twenty-Third ACM SIGMOD-SIGACT-SIGART Symposium on Principles of Database Systems, pp. 286–296. ACM (2004)
3. Cao, J., Li, L., Chen, A., Bu, T.: Tracking quantiles of network data streams with dynamic operations. In: IEEE INFOCOM, pp. 1–5. IEEE (2010)
4. Chambers, J.M., James, D.A., Lambert, D., Wiel, S.V.: Monitoring networked applications with incremental quantile estimation. Stat. Sci. 463–475 (2006)
5. Chen, F., Lambert, D., Pinheiro, J.C.: Incremental quantile estimation for massive tracking. In: Proceedings of the Sixth ACM SIGKDD International Conference on Knowledge Discovery and Data Mining, pp. 516–522. ACM (2000)
6. Cormode, G., Muthukrishnan, S.: An improved data stream summary: the count-min sketch and its applications. J. Algorithms **55**(1), 58–75 (2005)
7. Greenwald, M., Khanna, S.: Space-efficient online computation of quantile summaries. In: ACM SIGMOD Record, vol. 30, pp. 58–66. ACM (2001)
8. Huang, D.-S., Jiang, W.: A general CPL-ADs methodology for fixing dynamic parameters in dual environments. IEEE Trans. Syst. Man Cybern. Part B Cybern. **42**(5), 1489–1500 (2012)
9. Lanctôt, J.K., Oommen, B.J.: Discretized estimator learning automata. IEEE Trans. Syst. Man Cybern. **SMC–22**(6), 1473–1483 (1992)
10. Ma, Q., Muthukrishnan, S., Sandler, M.: Frugal streaming for estimating quantiles. In: Brodnik, A., López-Ortiz, A., Raman, V., Viola, A. (eds.) Space-Efficient Data Structures, Streams, and Algorithms. LNCS, vol. 8066, pp. 77–96. Springer, Heidelberg (2013). https://doi.org/10.1007/978-3-642-40273-9_7
11. Munro, J.I., Paterson, M.S.: Selection and sorting with limited storage. Theor. Comput. Sci. **12**(3), 315–323 (1980)
12. Oommen, B., Agache, M.: Continuous and discretized pursuit learning schemes: various algorithms and their comparison. IEEE Trans. Syst. Man Cybern. Part B Cybern. **31**(3), 277–287 (2001)

13. Oommen, B.J.: Absorbing and ergodic discretized two-action learning automata. IEEE Trans. Syst. Man Cybern. **SMC–16**, 282–293 (1986)

14. Oommen, B.J.: Stochastic searching on the line and its applications to parameter learning in nonlinear optimization. IEEE Trans. Syst. Man Cybern. **SMC–27B**, 733–739 (1997)

15. Oommen, B.J., Hansen, E.: The asymptotic optimality of discretized linear reward-inaction learning automata. IEEE Trans. Syst. Man Cybern. **SMC-14**(3) (1986)

16. Oommen, B.J., Lanctôt, J.K.: Discretized pursuit learning automata. IEEE Trans. Syst. Man Cybern. **SMC–20**(4), 931–938 (1990)

17. Oommen, B.J., Raghunath, G.: Automata learning and intelligent tertiary searching for Stochastic Point Location. IEEE Trans. Syst. Man Cybern. **SMC–28B**, 947–954 (1998)

18. Oommen, B.J., Raghunath, G., Kuipers, B.: Parameter learning from stochastic teachers and stochastic compulsive liars. IEEE Trans. Syst. Man Cybern. **SMC–36B**, 820–836 (2006)

19. Thathachar, M.A.L., Oommen, B.J.: Discretized reward-inaction learning automata. J. Cybern. Inf. Sci. 24–29 (1979)

20. Tierney, L.: A space-efficient recursive procedure for estimating a quantile of an unknown distribution. SIAM J. Sci. Stat. Comput. **4**(4), 706–711 (1983)

21. Weide, B.: Space-efficient on-line selection algorithms. In: Computer Science and Statistics: Proceedings of the Eleventh Annual Symposium on the Interface, pp. 308–311 (1978)

22. Yazidi, A., Granmo, O., John Oommen, B., Goodwin, M.: A novel strategy for solving the Stochastic Point Location problem using a hierarchical searching scheme. IEEE Trans. Cybern. **44**(11), 2202–2220 (2014)

23. Yazidi, A., Granmo, O.-C., Oommen, B.J.: A stochastic search on the line-based solution to discretized estimation. In: Jiang, H., Ding, W., Ali, M., Wu, X. (eds.) IEA/AIE 2012. LNCS (LNAI), vol. 7345, pp. 764–773. Springer, Heidelberg (2012). https://doi.org/10.1007/978-3-642-31087-4_77

24. Yazidi, A., Hammer, H.: Dicsretized qunatile estimation using the SPL theory. Unabridged journal version of this paper, 2018. To be submitted for publication

25. Yazidi, A., Hammer, H.: Multiplicative update methods for incremental quantile estimation. IEEE Trans. Cybern. **PP**(99), 1–10 (2017)

26. Yazidi, A., Hammer, H.L., John Oommen, B.: A higher-fidelity frugal quantile estimator. In: Cong, G., Peng, W.-C., Zhang, W.E., Li, C., Sun, A. (eds.) ADMA 2017. LNCS (LNAI), vol. 10604, pp. 76–86. Springer, Cham (2017). https://doi.org/10.1007/978-3-319-69179-4_6

Heuristic approaches - Cloud

Improved Cuckoo Search with Luus-Jakoola Heuristics for the IFS Inverse Problem of Binary Self-Similar Fractal Images

Akemi Gálvez[1,2] and Andrés Iglesias[1,2(✉)]

[1] Department of Information Science, Faculty of Sciences, Toho University,
2-2-1 Miyama, Narashino Campus, Funabashi 274-8510, Japan
[2] Department of Applied Mathematics and Computational Sciences,
University of Cantabria, Avenida de los Castros s/n, 39005 Santander, Spain
iglesias@unican.es
http://personales.unican.es/iglesias

Abstract. This paper addresses the following problem: how to reconstruct a given binary self-similar fractal image through iterated functions systems. This means to obtain an iterated function system (IFS) whose attractor is a good approximation of the input image. This problem is known to be a very difficult multivariate nonlinear continuous optimization problem. To tackle this issue, this paper introduces a new hybrid method comprised of a modification of the original cuckoo search method for global optimization called improved cuckoo search (ICS) along with the Luus-Jakoola heuristics for local search. This hybrid methodology is applied to three fractal examples with 3, 4, and 26 contractive functions. Our experimental results show that the method performs very well and provides visually satisfactory solutions for the instances in our benchmark. The numerical values of the similarity index used in this work also show that the results are not optimal yet, suggesting that the method might arguably be further improved.

Keywords: Swarm intelligence · Hybrid methods
Improved cuckoo search algorithm · Luus-Jakoola heuristics
Iterated function systems · Self-similar fractal images

1 Introduction

Fractals are one of the most challenging and intriguing mathematical shapes ever defined. Basically, they are geometric figures created by repeating a simple process over and over so that it yields a self-similar pattern across different scales. Interestingly, in the case of fractals, the scale factor of this replicating pattern is not an integer number, but a real one. Such a number is called the *fractal*

© IFIP International Federation for Information Processing 2018
Published by Springer International Publishing AG 2018. All Rights Reserved
L. Iliadis et al. (Eds.): AIAI 2018, IFIP AICT 519, pp. 495–506, 2018.
https://doi.org/10.1007/978-3-319-92007-8_42

dimension and it is usually larger than the topological dimension of the fractal [3,9]. Fractals have become ubiquitous objects in popular culture, particularly since the 80s of last century, owing to the technological advances in hardware and software and the widespread availability of personal computers. They are also very popular in science due to their ability to describe many growing patterns and natural structures commonly found in real-life objects: branches of trees, river networks, coastlines, mountain ranges, and so on. Furthermore, fractals have found remarkable applications in computer graphics, scientific visualization, image processing, dynamical systems, telecommunications, medicine, biology, arts, and many other fields [1,3,9,11,12].

There are several methods described in the literature to obtain fractal images. They include the Brownian motion, escape-time fractals, finite subdivision rules, L-systems, strange attractors of dynamical systems, and many others [1,3]. One of the most popular methods is the *Iterated Function Systems* (IFS), originally conceived by Hutchinson [13] and popularized by Barnsley in [1]. Roughly, an IFS consists of a finite system of contractive maps on a complete metric space. It can be proved that the Hutchinson operator over the set of all compact subsets of this space has a unique non-empty compact fixed set for the induced Hausdorff metric, called the *attractor of the IFS*. The graphical representation of this attractor is (at least approximately) a self-similar fractal image. Conversely, each self-similar fractal image can be represented by an IFS. Obtaining the parameters of such IFS is called the *IFS inverse problem*. Basically, it consists of solving an image reconstruction problem: given a fractal image, compute the IFS whose attractor approximates the input image accurately.

This IFS inverse problem has shown to be extremely difficult. In fact, the general case is still unsolved and only partial solutions have been reached so far. In this paper we propose a new approach to address this problem for the case of binary fractal images. Our methodology consists of the hybridization of a bio-inspired metaheuristics based on the cuckoo search algorithm for global optimization and a local search procedure. In particular, we consider a modification of the original cuckoo search method called the *improved cuckoo search* (ICS), which is based on the idea of allowing the method parameters to change over the generations [16]. This method is hybridized with the *Luus-Jakoola* (LJ) heuristics, a search method aimed at improving the local search step to refine the quality of the solution.

The structure of this paper is as follows: Sect. 2 introduces the basic concepts and definitions about the iterated function systems and the IFS inverse problem. Then, Sect. 3 describes the original and the improved cuckoo search algorithms. Our proposed method is described in detail in Sect. 4, while the experimental results are briefly discussed in Sect. 5. The paper closes with the main conclusions and some ideas about future work in the field.

2 Basic Concepts and Definitions

2.1 Iterated Function Systems

An *Iterated Function System* (IFS) is a finite set $\{\phi_i\}_{i=1,\dots,\eta}$ of contractive maps $\phi_i : \Omega \longrightarrow \Omega$ defined on a complete metric space $\mathcal{M} = (\Omega, \Psi)$, where $\Omega \subset \mathbb{R}^n$ and Ψ is a distance on Ω. We refer to the IFS as $\mathcal{W} = \{\Omega; \phi_i, \dots, \phi_\eta\}$. For visualization purposes, in this paper we consider that the metric space (Ω, Ψ) is $\mathbb{R}^2$ along with the Euclidean distance d_2, which is a complete metric space. Note, however, that our method can be applied to any other complete metric space of any dimension without further modifications. In this two-dimensional case, the affine transformations ϕ_κ are of the form:

$$\begin{bmatrix} \xi_1^* \\ \xi_2^* \end{bmatrix} = \phi_\kappa \begin{bmatrix} \xi_1 \\ \xi_2 \end{bmatrix} = \begin{bmatrix} \theta_{11}^\kappa & \theta_{12}^\kappa \\ \theta_{21}^\kappa & \theta_{11}^\kappa \end{bmatrix} \cdot \begin{bmatrix} \xi_1 \\ \xi_2 \end{bmatrix} + \begin{bmatrix} \sigma_1^\kappa \\ \sigma_2^\kappa \end{bmatrix} \tag{1}$$

or equivalently: $\mathbf{\Phi}_\kappa(\mathbf{\Xi}) = \mathbf{\Theta}_\kappa.\mathbf{\Xi} + \mathbf{\Sigma}_\kappa$ where $\mathbf{\Sigma}_\kappa$ is a translation vector and $\mathbf{\Theta}_\kappa$ is a 2×2 matrix with eigenvalues $\lambda_1^\kappa, \lambda_2^\kappa$ such that $|\lambda_j^\kappa| < 1$. In fact, $\mu_\kappa = |det(\mathbf{\Theta}_\kappa)| < 1$ meaning that ϕ_κ shrinks distances between points. Let us now define a transformation called the *Hutchinson operator*, Υ, on the compact subsets of Ω, $\mathcal{H}(\Omega)$, by:

$$\Upsilon(\mathcal{B}) = \bigcup_{\kappa=1}^{\eta} \phi_\kappa(\mathcal{B}) \tag{2}$$

with $\mathcal{B} \in \mathcal{H}(\Omega)$. If all the ϕ_κ are contractions, Υ is also a contraction in $\mathcal{H}(\Omega)$ with the induced Hausdorff metric [1,13]. Then, according to the fixed point theorem, Υ has a unique fixed point, $\Upsilon(\mathcal{A}) = \mathcal{A}$, called the *attractor of the IFS*.

Consider a set of probabilities $\mathcal{P} = \{\omega_1, \dots, \omega_\eta\}$, with $\sum_{\kappa=1}^{\eta} \omega_\kappa = 1$. There exists an efficient method, known as *probabilistic algorithm*, for the generation of the attractor of an IFS. It follows from the result $\overline{\{\mathbf{\Xi_j}\}}_j = \mathcal{A}$ provided that $\mathbf{\Xi}_0 \in \Omega$, where: $\mathbf{\Xi}_j = \phi_\kappa(\mathbf{\Xi}_{j-1})$ with probability $\omega_\kappa > 0$, see [2]. Picking an initial point $\mathbf{\Xi}_0$, one of the mappings in the set $\{\phi_i, \dots, \phi_\eta\}$ is chosen at random using the weights $\{\omega_1, \dots, \omega_\eta\}$. The selected map is then applied to generate a new point, and the same process is repeated again with the new point and so on. As a result of this stochastic iterative process, we obtain a sequence of points that converges to the fractal as the number of points increases [1,10].

2.2 The Collage Theorem

The *Collage Theorem* basically says that any digital image $\mathcal{I}$ can be approximated through an IFS [1,10]. In particular, it states that given a non-empty compact subset $\mathcal{I} \in \mathcal{H}(\Omega)$, the Hausdorff metric $H(.,.)$, a non-negative real threshold value $\epsilon \geq 0$, and an IFS $\mathcal{W} = \{\Omega; \phi_i, \dots, \phi_\eta\}$ on Ω with contractivity factor $0 < s < 1$ (the maximum of the contractivity factors s_κ of maps ϕ_κ), if $H(\mathcal{I}, \Upsilon(\mathcal{I})) = H\left(\mathcal{I}, \bigcup_{\kappa=1}^{\eta} \phi_\kappa(\mathcal{I})\right) \leq \epsilon$ then $H(\mathcal{I}, \mathcal{A}) \leq \dfrac{\epsilon}{1-s}$, where $\mathcal{A}$ is the attractor of the IFS. That is: $H(\mathcal{I}, \mathcal{A}) \leq \dfrac{1}{1-s} H\left(\mathcal{I}, \bigcup_{\kappa=1}^{\eta} \phi_\kappa(\mathcal{I})\right)$.

2.3   The IFS Inverse Problem

Suppose that we are given an initial fractal image $\mathcal{F}^{\square}$. The *Collage Theorem* says that it is possible to obtain an IFS $\mathcal{W}$ whose attractor has a graphical representation $\mathcal{F}^{\blacksquare}$ that approximates $\mathcal{F}^{\square}$ accurately according to a similarity function $\mathcal{S}$, which measures the graphical distance between $\mathcal{F}^{\square}$ and $\mathcal{F}^{\blacksquare}$ [1]. Note that once $\mathcal{W}$ is computed, $\mathcal{F}^{\blacksquare} = \Upsilon(I^{\square})$ for any (not necessarily fractal) initial image $I^{\square}$. Mathematically, this means that we have to solve the optimization problem:

$$\underset{\{\Theta_{\kappa}, \Sigma_{\kappa}, \omega_{\kappa}\}_{\kappa=1,\ldots,\eta}}{minimize} \quad \mathcal{S}\left(\mathcal{F}^{\square}, \Upsilon(I^{\square})\right) \tag{3}$$

The problem (3) is a continuous constrained optimization problem, because all free variables in $\{\Theta_{\kappa}, \Sigma_{\kappa}, \omega_{\kappa}\}_i$ are real-valued and must satisfy the condition that the corresponding functions ϕ_{κ} have to be contractive. It is also a multi-modal problem, since there can be several global or local minima of the similarity function. The problem is so difficult that only partial solutions have been reported so far, but the general problem still remains unsolved to a large extent. In this paper we address this problem by using a hybrid approach based on the cuckoo search algorithm described in next paragraphs.

3   The Cuckoo Search Algorithms

3.1   Original Cuckoo Search (CS)

The *Cuckoo search* (CS) is a powerful metaheuristic algorithm originally proposed by Yang and Deb in 2009 [18]. Since then, it has been successfully applied to difficult optimization problems [5,14,17,19]. The algorithm is inspired by the obligate interspecific brood-parasitism of some cuckoo species that lay their eggs in the nests of host birds of other species to escape from the parental investment in raising their offspring and minimize the risk of egg loss to other species, as the cuckoos can distributed their eggs amongst a number of different nests.

This interesting and surprising breeding behavioral pattern is the metaphor of the cuckoo search metaheuristic approach for solving optimization problems. In the cuckoo search algorithm, the eggs in the nest are interpreted as a pool of candidate solutions of an optimization problem while the cuckoo egg represents a new coming solution. The ultimate goal of the method is to use these new (and potentially better) solutions associated with the parasitic cuckoo eggs to replace the current solution associated with the eggs in the nest. This replacement, carried out iteratively, will eventually lead to a very good solution of the problem.

In addition to this representation scheme, the CS algorithm is also based on three idealized rules [18,19]:

1. Each cuckoo lays one egg at a time, and dumps it in a randomly chosen nest;
2. The best nests with high quality of eggs (solutions) will be carried over to the next generations;

Table 1. Cuckoo search algorithm via Lévy flights as originally proposed in [18,19].

Algorithm. Cuckoo Search via Lévy Flights

> **begin**
>> Objective function $f(\mathbf{x})$, $\mathbf{x} = (x_1, \ldots, x_D)^T$
>> Generate initial population of n host nests $\mathbf{x}_i$ $(i = 1, 2, \ldots, n)$
>> **while** $(t < MaxGeneration)$ or (stop criterion)
>>> Get a cuckoo (say, i) randomly by Lévy flights
>>> Evaluate its fitness F_i
>>> Choose a nest among n (say, j) randomly
>>> **if** $(F_i > F_j)$
>>>> Replace j by the new solution
>>> **end**
>>> A fraction (p_a) of worse nests are abandoned and new ones
>>>> are built via Lévy flights
>>> Keep the best solutions (or nests with quality solutions)
>>> Rank the solutions and find the current best
>> **end while**
>> Postprocess results and visualization
> **end**

---

3. The number of available host nests is fixed, and a host can discover an alien egg with a probability $p_a \in [0, 1]$. In this case, the host bird can either throw the egg away or abandon the nest so as to build a completely new nest in a new location. For simplicity, this assumption can be approximated by a fraction p_a of the n nests being replaced by new nests (with new random solutions at new locations).

The basic steps of the CS algorithm are summarized in the pseudocode shown in Table 1. Basically, the CS algorithm starts with an initial population of n host nests and it is performed iteratively. The initial values of the jth component of the ith nest are determined by the expression $x_i^j(0) = rand.(up_i^j - low_i^j) + low_i^j$, where up_i^j and low_i^j represent the upper and lower bounds of that jth component, respectively, and $rand$ represents a standard uniform random number on the interval $(0, 1)$. With this choice, the initial values are within the search space domain. These boundary conditions are also controlled in each iteration step.

For each iteration t, a cuckoo egg i is selected randomly and new solutions $\mathbf{x}_i^{t+1}$ are generated by using the Lévy flight. According to the original creators of the method, the strategy of using Lévy flights is preferred over other simple random walks because it leads to better overall performance of the CS. The general equation for the Lévy flight is given by:

$$\mathbf{x}_i^{t+1} = \mathbf{x}_i^t + \alpha \oplus levy(\lambda) \tag{4}$$

where t indicates the number of the current generation, and $\alpha > 0$ indicates the step size, which should be related to the scale of the particular problem under study. The symbol $\oplus$ is used in Eq. (4) to indicate the entry-wise multiplication. Note that Eq. (4) is essentially a Markov chain, since next location at generation $t + 1$ only depends on the current location at generation t and a transition probability, given by the first and second terms of Eq. (4), respectively. This transition probability is modulated by the Lévy distribution as:

$$levy(\lambda) \sim t^{-\lambda}, \qquad (1 < \lambda \leq 3) \qquad (5)$$

which has an infinite variance with an infinite mean. From the computational standpoint, the generation of random numbers with Lévy flights is comprised of two steps: firstly, a random direction according to a uniform distribution is chosen; then, the generation of steps following the chosen Lévy distribution is carried out. The authors suggested to use the Mantegna's algorithm for symmetric distributions (see [19] for details), which computes the factor:

$$\hat{\phi} = \left(\frac{\Gamma(1 + \hat{\beta}).sin\left(\frac{\pi.\hat{\beta}}{2} \right)}{\Gamma\left(\left(\frac{1+\hat{\beta}}{2} \right).\hat{\beta}.2^{\frac{\hat{\beta}-1}{2}} \right)} \right)^{\frac{1}{\hat{\beta}}} \qquad (6)$$

where Γ denotes the Gamma function and $\hat{\beta} = \frac{3}{2}$ in the original implementation by Yang and Deb [19]. This factor is used in Mantegna's algorithm to compute the step length ς as: $\varsigma = \frac{u}{|v|^{\frac{1}{\hat{\beta}}}}$, where u and v follow the normal distribution of zero mean and deviation σ_u^2 and σ_v^2, respectively, where σ_u obeys the Lévy distribution given by Eq. (6) and $\sigma_v = 1$. Then, the stepsize ζ is computed as $\zeta = 0.01\,\varsigma\,(\mathbf{x} - \mathbf{x}_{best})$. Finally, $\mathbf{x}$ is modified as: $\mathbf{x} \leftarrow \mathbf{x} + \zeta.\mathbf{\Delta}$ where $\mathbf{\Delta}$ is a random vector of the dimension of the solution $\mathbf{x}$ and that follows the normal distribution $N(0, 1)$. The CS method then evaluates the fitness of the new solution and compares it with the current one. In case the new solution brings better fitness, it replaces the current one. On the other hand, a fraction of the worse nests (according to the fitness) are abandoned and replaced by new solutions so as to increase the exploration of the search space looking for more promising solutions. The rate of replacement is given by the probability p_a, a parameter of the model that has to be tuned for better performance. Moreover, for each iteration step, all current solutions are ranked according to their fitness and the best solution reached so far is stored as the vector $\mathbf{x}_{best}$.

3.2   Improved Cuckoo Search (ICS)

The *improved cuckoo search* (ICS) method was proposed in [16] to enhance the performance of the original CS. It is based on the idea of allowing its parameters p_a and α to change over the generations, as opposed to their fixed values in the original CS. In ICS the parameter p_a is modified as:

$$p_a^t = p_{a_M} - \frac{p_{a_M} - p_{a_m}}{\Lambda} t \qquad (7)$$

where the subscripts M and m are used to indicate the maximum and minimum values of the parameter respectively, and Λ indicates the total number of iterations. According to Eq. (7), the parameter p_a is now decreased linearly with the number of iterations from a maximum value p_{a_M} until a minimum one, p_{a_m}. At early iterations, its value is high to enforce the diversity of solutions in the algorithm. This diversity is decreasing over the time so as to intensify the search using the best candidates of the population in final iterations for a better fine-tuning of the solutions. The parameter α, also assumed constant in the CS, is primarily used to promote exploration of the search space. Therefore, it makes sense to modify it dynamically starting from a high value, α_M, to perform a extensive exploration and gradually reducing it until a low value, α_m, to promote exploitation and eventually homing into the optimum, in a rather similar way to the inertia weight in PSO. Consequently, it is modified as:

$$\alpha^t = \alpha_M \, Exp \left(\frac{Ln \left(\dfrac{\alpha_m}{\alpha_M} \right)}{\Lambda} t \right) \tag{8}$$

4 Proposed Approach

4.1 Hybrid ICS with Luus-Jakoola Heuristics

To address the IFS inverse problem described in Sect. 2.2, we propose a new hybrid scheme for proper balance between exploration and exploitation. Firstly, we consider the improved cuckoo search method for global optimization described in Sect. 3.2. This modified scheme is improved by its hybridization with a local search procedure. In particular, we apply the *Luus-Jaakola* (LJ) method, a gradient-free heuristics firstly proposed in [15] to solve nonlinear programming problems. LJ starts with an initialization step, where random uniform values are chosen within the search space by computing the upper and lower bounds for each dimension. Then, a random uniform value in-between is sampled for each component. This value is added to the current position of the potential solution to generate a new candidate solution, which replaces the current one only when the fitness improves; otherwise, the sampling space is multiplicatively decreased by a factor (usually of value 95%, but other values can also be used). In practice, we found that it is better to consider a self-adaptive size for this factor, with the effect of speeding up the convergence to the steady state. This process is repeated iteratively. With each iteration, the neighborhood of the point decreases, so the procedure eventually collapses to a point.

4.2 Application to the IFS Inverse Problem

Given a 2D self-similar binary fractal image $\mathcal{I}^\square$ comprised of η functions ϕ_κ, we apply our hybrid method to solve the IFS inverse problem. We consider an initial population of χ individuals $\{\mathcal{C}_i\}_{i=1,\dots,\chi}$, where each individual $\mathcal{C}_i = \{\mathcal{C}_i^\kappa\}_\kappa$ is a collection of η real-valued vectors $\mathcal{C}_\kappa^i$ of the free variables of Eq. (1), as:

$$\mathcal{C}_i^\kappa = (\theta_{1,1}^{\kappa,i}, \theta_{1,2}^{\kappa,i}, \theta_{2,1}^{\kappa,i}, \theta_{2,2}^{\kappa,i} | \sigma_1^{\kappa,i}, \sigma_2^{\kappa,i} | \omega_\kappa^i) \tag{9}$$

These individuals are initialized with uniform random values in $[-1, 1]$ for the variables in $\boldsymbol{\Theta}_\kappa$ and $\boldsymbol{\Sigma}_\kappa$, and in $[0, 1]$ for the ω_κ^i, such that $\sum_{\kappa=1}^\eta \omega_\kappa^i = 1$. After this initialization step, we compute the contractive factors μ_κ and reinitialize all functions ϕ_κ with $\mu_\kappa \geq 1$ to ensure that only contractive functions are included in the initial population. Before applying our method, we also need to define a suitable fitness function. In this paper we use the Hamming distance: the fractal images are stored as bitmap images of 0s and 1s for a given resolution defined by a mesh size parameter, m_s. Then, we divide the number of different values between the original and the reconstructed matrices by the total number of boxes in the image. This yields the *normalized similarity error rate* index between both images, denoted by $|\mathcal{S}|_\square^\blacksquare$, the fitness function used in this work.

Fig. 1. Example of the *rotated triangle* fractal: (left) original (top) and reconstructed image (bottom); (right) their different contractive functions with different colors. (Color figure online)

4.3   Parameter Tuning

It is well-known that the parameter tuning of metaheuristic methods is troublesome and problem-dependent. The cuckoo search is specially advantageous in this regard, as it depends on only two parameters: the population size, χ, set to $\chi = 100$, and the probability p_a, calculated taking: $p_{a_M} = 0.5$ and $p_{a_m} = 0.005$ in Eq. (7). Moreover, the method is executed for Λ iterations. In our simulations, we

Fig. 2. Example of the *Crystal* fractal: (left) original (top) and reconstructed image (bottom); (right) their different contractive functions with different colors. (Color figure online)

found that $\Lambda = 1500$ is enough to reach convergence in mp all cases. Our hybrid method also requires to define suitable values for α_M and α_m in Eq. (8). Similar to [16], in this work they are set to 0.5 and 0.01, respectively. Finally, our method requires to define the mesh size, ν, set to $\nu = 80$ in this work.

5   Experimental Results

Our method has been applied to several examples of fractals. Only three of them are included here because of limitations of space: rotated triangle, Crystal, and the *AIAI-2018* fractal (especially created for this paper). They are shown in Figs. 1, 2 and 3, respectively. The input fractal images are displayed twice in each figure, one in red and another with one color for each individual contractive function. As the reader can see, the three fractals are comprised of 3, 4, and 26 functions, respectively. The application of our method to these input images returns the IFS minimizing the $|\mathcal{S}|_{\square}^{\blacksquare}$ index, which are then used to render the reconstructed fractal images, shown in blue and with different colors as above.

As the reader can see, although the matching is not optimal, our method captures the underlying structure of the fractal images with good visual quality.

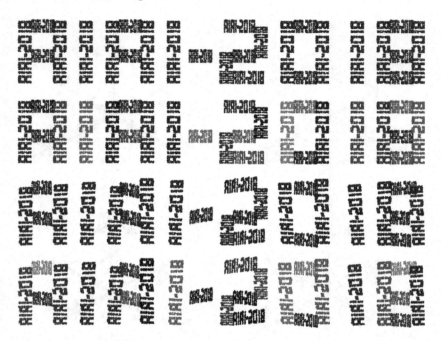

Fig. 3. Example of the *AIAI-2018* fractal (from top to bottom): original image in red, original image with different colors for each contractive function, reconstructed image in blue, and reconstructed image with different colors for each contractive function. (Color figure online)

This is a remarkable result because our initial population is totally random, meaning that their corresponding images at early generations are all totally different from the given image. Our method is able to obtain a final image that replicates well the input image and is also a self-similar fractal for all instances in our benchmark. Our graphical results indicate that our method performs very well, as it provides visually satisfactory solutions for the IFS inverse problem.

This good visual appearance is confirmed by our numerical results, reported in Table 2. For each fractal example (in rows), the table shows (in columns): number of contractive functions η, number of free variables of the optimization problem, and best and mean value of the $|\mathcal{S}|_{\square}^{\blacksquare}$ index for 20 independent executions of the method. As the reader can see, the similarity index for the best execution yields errors ranging from 20% to 30%, depending on the example. Although the reconstructed images are perfectly recognizable in all cases, this similarity error increases with the complexity of the model, with the third example exhibiting the larger value. This result is very reasonable because this example requires to solve an optimization problem with many more variables than the other two examples. In addition, the numerical values of the similarity index used in this work indicate that the results are not optimal yet, suggesting that the method might arguably be further improved.

Table 2. Numerical results of the best and mean values of the $|\mathcal{S}|_\square^\blacksquare$ index for the examples in Figs. 1, 2 and 3 with the proposed method.

Example	η	#free variables	$|\mathcal{S}|_\square^\blacksquare$ (best)	$|\mathcal{S}|_\square^\blacksquare$ (mean)
Rotated triangle fractal	3	21	0.1952	0.2113
Crystal fractal	4	28	0.2038	0.2194
AIAI-2018 fractal	26	182	0.2974	0.3125

All computations in this paper have been performed on a 2.6 GHz. Intel Core i7 processor with 16 GB of RAM. The source code has been implemented by the authors in the native programming language of the popular scientific program *Matlab version 2015a* and using the numerical libraries for fractals in [4, 6–8]. Regarding the CPU times, they depend on the complexity of the model and its number of contractive functions. In general, we noticed that the method is slow and time-consuming. For illustration, each single execution takes about 25–45 min for the first two examples, and more than 1 h for the third one.

6   Conclusions and Future Work

In this paper we introduced a new hybrid method to solve the following optimization problem: given any binary self-similar fractal image, the goal is to determine an IFS whose attractor is a good approximation of this input image. This problem, called the IFS inverse problem, is known to be a very difficult multivariate nonlinear continuous optimization problem. In this new hybrid method, a modification of the original cuckoo search method for global optimization called improved cuckoo search (ICS) is coupled with the Luus-Jakoola heuristics for local search. This hybrid methodology is applied to three fractal examples: *rotated triangle*, *crystal*, and the *AIAI-2018* fractal. The method replicates the input images very well, yielding visually satisfactory results in all cases.

The numerical results show however that our final solutions are not optimal yet, so the method might be improved in several ways. On one hand, we want to modify our fitness function to obtain a better measure of the quality of the reconstructed fractal. On the other hand, we would like to obtain automatically the optimal value of the number of contractive functions for the IFS. We also wish to extend our results to the cases of images that are neither binary nor self-similar. Reducing our CPU times is also one of our future goals in the field.

Acknowledgements. This research work has received funding from the project PDE-GIR of the European Union's Horizon 2020 research and innovation programme under the Marie Sklodowska-Curie grant agreement No 778035, the Spanish Ministry of Economy and Competitiveness (Computer Science National Program) under grant #TIN2017-89275-R of the Agencia Estatal de Investigación and European Funds FEDER (AEI/FEDER, UE), and the project #JU12, jointly supported by public body SODERCAN and European Funds FEDER (SODERCAN/FEDER UE). We also thank Toho University and the University of Cantabria for their support for this research work.

References

1. Barnsley, M.F.: Fractals Everywhere, 2nd edn. Academic Press, San Diego (1993)
2. Elton, J.H.: An ergodic theorem for iterated maps. Ergodic Theory Dynam. Syst. **7**, 481–488 (1987)
3. Falconer, K.: Fractal Geometry: Mathematical Foundations and Applications, 2nd edn. Wiley, Chichester (2003)
4. Gálvez, A.: IFS Matlab generator: a computer tool for displaying IFS fractals. In: Proceedings of ICCSA 2009, pp. 132–142. IEEE CS Press, Los Alamitos (2009)
5. Gálvez, A., Iglesias, A.: Cuckoo search with Lévy flights for weighted Bayesian energy functional optimization in global-support curve data fitting. Sci. W. J. **2014**, 11 (2014). Article ID 138760
6. Gálvez, A., Iglesias, A., Takato, S.: Matlab-based KETpic add-on for generating and rendering IFS fractals. In: Ślęzak, D., Kim, T., Chang, A.C.-C., Vasilakos, T., Li, M.C., Sakurai, K. (eds.) FGCN 2009. CCIS, vol. 56, pp. 334–341. Springer, Heidelberg (2009). https://doi.org/10.1007/978-3-642-10844-0_40
7. Gálvez, A., Iglesias, A., Takato, S.: KETpic Matlab binding for efficient handling of fractal images. Int. J. Future Gener. Commun. Netw. **3**(2), 1–14 (2010)
8. Gálvez, A., Kitahara, K., Kaneko, M.: *IFSGen4*LATEX: interactive graphical user interface for generation and visualization of iterated function systems inLATEX. In: Hong, H., Yap, Chee (eds.) ICMS 2014. LNCS, vol. 8592, pp. 554–561. Springer, Heidelberg (2014). https://doi.org/10.1007/978-3-662-44199-2_84
9. Gutiérrez, J.M., Iglesias, A.: A mathematica package for the analysis and control of chaos in nonlinear systems. Comput. Phys. **12**(6), 608–619 (1998)
10. Gutiérrez, J.M., Iglesias, A., Rodríguez, M.A.: A multifractal analysis of IFSP invariant measures with application to fractal image generation. Fractals **4**(1), 17–27 (1996)
11. Gutiérrez, J.M., Iglesias, A., Rodríguez, M.A., Burgos, J.D., Moreno, P.A.: Analyzing the multifractal structure of DNA nucleotide sequences. In: Chaos and Noise in Biology and Medicine, vol. 7, pp. 315–319. World Scientific, Singapore (1998)
12. Gutiérrez, J.M., Iglesias, A., Rodríguez, M.A., Rodríguez, V.J.: Generating and rendering fractal images. Mathematica J. **7**(1), 6–13 (1997)
13. Hutchinson, J.E.: Fractals and self similarity. Indiana Univ. Math. J. **30**(5), 713–747 (1981)
14. Iglesias, A., Gálvez, A.: Cuckoo search with Lévy flights for reconstruction of outline curves of computer fonts with rational Bézier curves. In: Proceedings of Congress on Evolutionary Computation-CEC 2016. IEEE CS Press, Los Alamitos (2016)
15. Luus, R., Jaakola, T.H.I.: Optimization by direct search and systematic reduction of the size of search region. Am. Inst. Chem. Eng. J. (AIChE) **19**(4), 760–766 (1973)
16. Valian, E., Tavakoli, S., Mohanna, S., Hahgi, A.: Improved cuckoo search for reliability optimization problems. Comput. Industr. Eng. **64**, 459–468 (2013)
17. Yang, X.-S.: Nature-Inspired Metaheuristic Algorithms, 2nd edn. Luniver Press, Frome (2010)
18. Yang, X.S., Deb, S.: Cuckoo search via Lévy flights. In: Proceedings of World Congress on Nature & Biologically Inspired Computing (NaBIC), pp. 210–214. IEEE Press, New York (2009)
19. Yang, X.S., Deb, S.: Engineering optimization by cuckoo search. Int. J. Math. Modelling Numer. Optim. **1**(4), 330–343 (2010)

A Scatter Search Based Heuristic for Reliable Clustering in Vehicular Ad Hoc Networks

Rejab Hajlaoui[1,2(✉)], Tarek Moulahi[2,3], and Hervé Guyennet[2]

[1] Community College, Hail University, Ha'il, Saudi Arabia
[2] FEMTO-ST Institute, Univ. Bourgogne Franche-Comté, Besançon, France
{rejab.hajlaoui,herve.guyennet,
tarek.moulahi}@femto-st.fr
[3] Faculty of Science and Technology, Sidi Bouzid, Sidi Bouzid, Tunisia

Abstract. Achieving a safe, comfort and autonomous driving in vehicular ad hoc networks (VANET) is the great interest of a large number of researchers and car manufacturers. Despite the variety of the proposed approaches and the development of communications technologies, there are no typical solutions. Indeed, several recent studies prove the practical advantages of heuristic method to solve various problems of optimization. Therefore, we used in this paper a Hybrid Scatter Tabu Search (HSTS) based heuristic approach to assign cluster members (CMs) to convenient cluster heads (CHs). We addressed in this work the cluster formation phase in our Weighted K-medoids Clustering Algorithm (WKCA) proposed recently. The main objective is to derive new solutions from the combination of previous one, including the network coverage as a special criterion. To achieve this objective and to locate the global minimum, we integrate the tabu search in the inner process of the scatter search. To the best of our knowledge, there is no study that uses the scatter search to perform clustering in VANET. By simulation, results show that our scheme improves the network stability in term of several metrics compared with prior approaches.

Keywords: Vehicular ad hoc network · Communication · Heuristic algorithm

1 Introduction

VANET is an extension of the Mobile Ad hoc NETwork (MANET), where the node movements are restricted by the topology of the street, traffic signals and obstacles [1]. The purpose of the Intelligent Transportation System (ITS) is to collect and to share information in order to improve the road safety and to provide comfort to travelers. Despite the fact that vehicles have high computing power and adequate storage capacity, the problem of delay and poor connectivity persists. On the other hand, due to the high mobility in highway scenario and the multitude of obstacles in the urban environments, the links can be broken frequently. In this case network maintenance has to be triggered automatically to ensure stability and to send messages within the deadlines. Under these constraints, keeping a high stability of network is an NP-Complete combinatorial optimization problem. It means that all exact algorithms

© IFIP International Federation for Information Processing 2018
Published by Springer International Publishing AG 2018. All Rights Reserved
L. Iliadis et al. (Eds.): AIAI 2018, IFIP AICT 519, pp. 507–519, 2018.
https://doi.org/10.1007/978-3-319-92007-8_43

require exponential execution time to resolve it. Thus, they are unsuitable in practice even for moderately large instances [2].

For these reasons, several heuristic based researches have been developed to find efficient and adaptable models for routing problems in high mobility networks. Although obtaining an optimal solution is not guaranteed, the use of heuristic methods gives competitive advantages, the most important of which are:

- Approximate the best solutions for the biggest instances.
- Define the right solutions within a reasonable calculation time.

Indeed, among the ways to improve the performance of an algorithm or to fill some of these gaps is to combine it with another method. This cooperation between approaches makes it possible to exploit their advantages in order to improve the overall performance and to minimize the convergence time. It is obvious that population-based methods are superior in identifying different areas in the search space, while trajectory methods are better in exploring a well-defined area in the search space [3]. In this context, we proposed a Hybrid Scatter Tabu Search model to improve the assignment of ordinary nodes to elected cluster heads. Indeed, the power of this contribution is to unify the advantage of population-based methods with the power of trajectory methods. In this way, there is less chance of missing a good solution compared to population-based methods.

In this work, we treated the nodes that exist in common area as shown in "Fig. 1". These nodes are covered by several CH and their assignments is a challenge in itself.

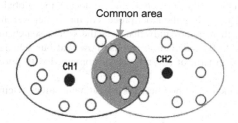

Fig. 1. Overlapping clusters.

Several simulations are conducted to understand and to analyze the performance of our model by comparing it against competitive protocols designed for the same objective.

The remaining of this paper is organized as follows. In Sect. 2, we presented some existing solutions. Sections 3 and 4 describe our proposal including the theoretical foundation. Section 5 discusses the simulation results. Finally, Sect. 6 concludes the paper and draws some directions for future work.

2 Prior Works

Due to the unbounded network size and the dynamic nature of vehicles, the intermittent connectivity is considered as the biggest challenge. Indeed, many researchers used the clustering technique to satisfy the VANET stability and to improve the network life time. For instance, in [4], authors proposed a multi-head clustering algorithm considering a data sharing application in vehicular network.

Each cluster contains a master CH (MCH), and several slave CHs (SCHs). The main goal of using more than one CH is to speed up the data downloading from multiple seed nodes (CHs) based on the bit-torrent downloading mechanism.

In the same context, Little et al. [5] used two CHs to extend the MOBIC (MOBIlity metrics Clustering) [6] into vehicular environments. The first CH is located at the head and the second is in the tail of a cluster. In [7], authors introduced a new clustering technique which uses velocity and distance to create a stable cluster structure. When more nodes converge to be cluster head, the Cuckoo Search algorithm [8] is triggered to select the super cluster-head which will be at an optimum distance, minimum delay, more network lifetime and high packet delivery ratio. In [9], Nasr et al. presented a novel VANET routing algorithm based on clustering technique (CBVRP). This protocol is appropriate for rugged environments, such as deserts scenarios. Indeed, the CBVRP used the vehicle's equipment, velocity and location in the cluster classifications and the CH election process. When the communication is inside a cluster, the CH selected the relay node which leads to the destination. In contrast, when the communication is between clusters, the CH uses the flooding mechanism towards its cluster members in order to find the nearest vehicles able to communicate with the outside. This route is kept until the cluster structure changes. In [10], Hassanabadi et al. presented a novel model called "Affinity PROpagation for VEhicular networks" (APROVE). It uses the Affinity Propagation algorithm in a distributed manner to maximize the similarity $s(i, j)$ between the data point i and its chosen exemplar j. In this algorithm, nodes exchanged two types of messages to make decision on independent clustering:

- Responsibility message $r(i, j)$: sent from i to candidate exemplar j. It indicates how well suited j is to be i's exemplar.
- Availability message $a(i, j)$: sent from candidate exemplar j back to i. It indicates j's desire to be an exemplar for i based on supporting feedback from other data points.

In [11], authors developed a new distributed algorithm to build a stable multi-hop cluster suitable for vehicular networks. With minimum number of cluster head, this model contains three techniques that depend only on the positions of both receiver and transmitter nodes. When the GPS signal is lost, the proposed algorithms switched to use the RSS (Received Signal Strength) of the packet received to decide if the packet should be retransmitted. Given the continuing research in this area, several clustering solutions, including mobility-based clustering, cluster-based MAC protocols, topology-based clustering, weight-based clustering and energy-based clustering, have been proposed [11–13].

3   Theoretical Foundation of the Proposed Model

3.1   Weighted k-Medoids Clustering Approach (WKCA)

The WKCA is a novel clustering algorithm proposed recently [14]. This model based on the k-medoids clustering approach provides an automatic switching from small to large cluster depending on the road conditions. It generates small clusters in dense zone in order to avoid the network congestion, whereas in sparse zone it generates large clusters to ensure large coverage.

A node becomes a cluster head if it has the highest weight based on a several metrics (direction, transmission range, speed and node disconnection frequency). Periodically, each node calculates and sends its weight to the CH. Then, the node having a weight greater than that of the current CH will be announced as the new coordinator.

Consequently, the cluster maintenance phase will be triggered immediately. Finally, if a node leaves the coverage area of its CH, it has to join another one. Otherwise, it announces itself as a new cluster head to start its own cluster formation. Indeed, two main phases distinguish this model.

Phase 1: Cluster Formation
A vehicle V is assigned to cluster C according to its similarity value (SV).
Where

$$SV = (w_1 * D) - (w_2 * \Delta S) + (w_3 * \Delta P) \tag{1}$$

- D: Boolean variable. It indicates the direction of the node compared to the CH.
- ΔS: difference in speed (compared to the CH).
- ΔP: proximity to CH.

In which w_1, w_2 and w_3 reflect the relative importance of D, ΔS and ΔP.

Phase 2: Cluster Head Switching
A vehicle V is elected as a new CH if its weight (W) is greater than the weight of the current CH, provided that its behavior in the past was not wobbling or suspicious.

Indeed, the weight (W) is calculated based on four metrics (direction, transmission range, speed and node disconnection frequency).

3.2   Scatter Search (SS)

The Scatter Search is a population-based metaheuristics. It is suitable to solve a wide range of optimization problems including Routing Protocol, Traveling Salesman Problem (TSP), and clustering [15, 16]. Recent studies demonstrate the practical advantages of this approach compared to similar heuristics. The most important is that the SS used an adaptive and an associated memory to be adapted to particular contexts [15, 17]. Basically, the SS starts with a set of feasible solutions. At the next step, some of these solutions are extracted and combined. The resulted offspring solutions will be enhanced according to an improving procedure. By the end, these new feasible solutions are evaluated according to some criteria to be included or not in the collections. These steps are presented in the Basic Scatter Search Algorithm below [18].

Basic Scatter Search Algorithm

Input: population of the problem.
Output: the best of solutions.
(1) Initialize the population Pop using a Diversification Generation Method.
(2) Apply the Improvement Method to the population.
(3) Reference Set Update Method (Good solutions for RefSet1 and Diversity solutions for RefSet2).
(4) **While** (itr < MaxItr) **do**
(5)   **While** (Reference set is changed) **do**
(6)   Subset Generation Method
(7)   **While** (subset-counter < > 0) **do**
(8)   Solution Combination Method.
(9)   Improvement Method.
(10)   Reference Set Update Method;
(11)   **End while**
(12)   **End while**
(13)   **End while**
(14) Return the best of solutions

3.3   Tabu Search (TS)

Proposed by Glover in 1986, the tabu search is a local search heuristic used to solve complex and large problems. It is an iterative approach starting with an initial feasible solution. Then, from a given position the procedure moves step by step to explore the neighborhood and to select the one that minimizes the objective function. At each iteration, the algorithm chooses the best neighbor not tabu, even if it degrades the cost function. For this reason, the tabu research is known as an aggressive method. The process continues until stopping criteria is met. Unlike other methods, the TS overcomes the problem of local optima using adaptive memory. The basic idea is to save the solutions that are temporarily forbidden to avoid cyclic movements [19].

4   Proposed Model

The proposed solution that we have developed is based on the clustering technique. The main challenge is to find the most appropriate cluster for all node in the common area. Indeed, at an instant "t", a vehicle V has to be assigned only to one cluster head.

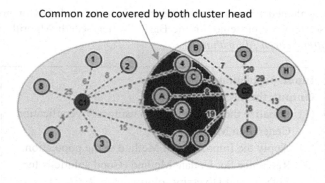

Fig. 2. Clusters representation

In this work, each cluster is described as a graph G(V, E), as shown in "Fig. 2".

- V: represents the set of vehicles defined by an index i, i ∈ {1, 2, 3, ..., N}.
- C: represents the set of cluster heads defined by an index j, j ∈ {1, 2, 3,., M}.
- E: represents the set of edges. Each edge Eij designs the similarity value (SV) of the node i to the cluster head j.

The goal is to maximize the similarity within clusters. It is calculated by the summation of the costs of all edges. In our case, for all pairs of nodes {i, j}, the cost's SVji and SVij are equal, then the problem is said to be symmetric.

4.1 Initialization (by User)

At the beginning, the user has to define values of the starting parameters

- NI: Number of Iterations.
- NII: Number of Iterations without Improvement.
- NIS: Number of Initial Solutions.

4.2 Reference Set Generation

This method is the first step in the SS process. Indeed, the set of starting solutions are not randomly generated, but obtained from the WKCA model detailed in Sect. 3.1.

4.3 Evaluation

To know the quality of any potential solution, we used the fitness function (F). It indicates how similar the nodes of a cluster are compared to their cluster head.

$$F = \sum_{j=1}^{M} \sum_{i=1}^{N} SVij \tag{2}$$

4.4   Subset Generation

Several methods are used in the literature to generate the subsets. In our solution, we treated the nodes that can be assigned to more than one cluster as shown in "Fig. 2".

- Let B1 the best solution obtained by the WKCA algorithm.

C1	1	2	3	4	5	6	7	8
C2	A	B	C	D	E	F	G	H

- Let B2 the feasible solution very different from the solution B1. (B2 is obtained by switching the nodes of cluster 1 of common area to the cluster 2 and vice versa).

C1	1	2	3	6	8	A	C	D
C2	4	5	7	B	E	F	G	H

- Set diff: the difference between the two solutions. It represents the average of nodes switched from C1 to C2, and vice versa.

$$Diff = number\ of\ permuted\ nodes/total\ number\ of\ nodes = 6/16 = 38\%$$

4.5   Combination Method

This method is used to combine the elements of the subsets in order to form new solutions. In our case, we used the Path-Relinking combination method (PR) [17] to generate new trial solutions. By applying the PR method, each node in the common area is evaluated comparing to all reachable cluster heads. Then the best assignment with high similarity value is selected. To maintain a fair distribution, the density of the two clusters has to be very close and the difference should not exceed a given value "μ". In other words, we avoid having dense clusters compared to other one, resulting in poor bandwidth exploitation and frequent collisions.

For instance, based on the similarity values of border nodes as shown in "Fig. 3", it is more suitable to assign node 4 to cluster C2 instead of cluster C1. Likewise, it is better to move the node D from cluster C2 to cluster C1.

After applying the PR combination method to all nodes, we get C1* and C2* from C1 and C2, as shown in "Fig. 4".

4.6   Improvement Method

In this step, we used the tabu search to transform the solutions obtained by the combination method into more efficient solutions. In our implementation, the TS treated the border nodes. If the improved solution increases the global similarity within the cluster, then it will be included in the reference set, otherwise, it will be ignored. To avoid the loss of time in case of large number of neighborhood, the selected number of iterations

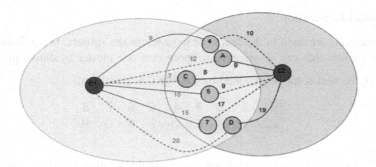

Fig. 3. Similarity values of border nodes

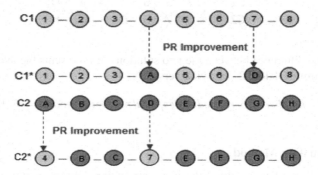

Fig. 4. Solutions generated by combination method

does not exceed 10. Indeed, the "Fig. 5" resumes the steps of the proposed Scatter Tabu Search model as well as the methods associated with it (Path Relinking, WKCA, TS, SV).

5   Experimental Results and Analysis

5.1   Simulation Setup

To evaluate the performance of our algorithm, simulations have been carried out using NS3 [20]. We have set experimentations in highway scenario by varying the density from 40 to 240 vehicles per km and the speed from 20 to 120 kmph. Table 1 below provides the used simulation parameters.

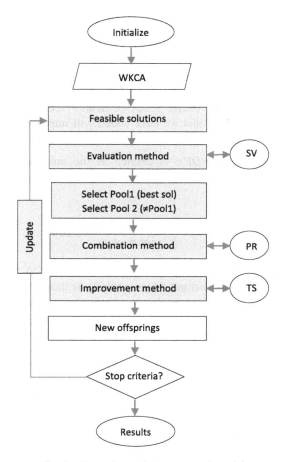

Fig. 5. Flow chart of the proposed model.

Table 1. Simulation setup.

Parameters	Values
Simulator	NS3
Scenario	Highway
Nb of lanes	Two-lanes
Number of vehicles	40 .. 240
Speed	20–120 Kmph
Vehicle distribution	Randomly
Transmission range	200 m, 300 m and 500 m
Simulation time	1500 s
MAC protocol	DSRC
Data type	Constant Bit Rate (CBR)

5.2 Simulation Results

In order to evaluate the improvement given by the Hybrid Scatter Tabu Search in vehicular networks (HSTS), we have performed a careful analysis according to several metrics [21]. Our contribution is compared with the basic Weighted K-medoid Clustering Algorithm (WKCA). Indeed, as we have explained before, the output of the WKCA is used as the initial Reference Set of the Scatter Search. This comparison will show us if the additional work that we have added will improve the results obtained, especially in terms of delay.

a. Packet delivery ratio (PDR): is defined as the ratio of packets successfully delivered to the destination compared to the number of packets sent out by the source

$$PDR = \frac{\sum received\ packets}{\sum sent\ packets} * 100 \tag{3}$$

As observed in "Fig. 6", the HSTS outperforms the WKCA in term of PDR for different densities. The reason behind this superiority is that the obtained clusters are highly similar. Therefore, there is less chance of route failure and the data reaches the destination without any shortage. Indeed, for both models, the high density will create a flood of data to find the appropriate route from source to destination. This broadcast storm will lead to congestion and some packets will be dropped by the master node. For instance, the abandoned packets by the WKCA reached 35% in dense zone. Whereas, the HSTS maintains its performance regardless of the network status and the average of dropped packet does not exceed 22%. Therefore, about 80% of packets reach the destination even in bad traffic condition.

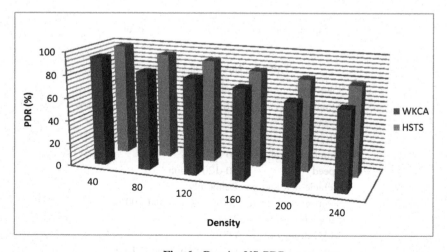

Fig. 6. Density VS PDR

b. End-to-end Delay: is defined as the needed time to send packet from source to destination.

$$Delay = \frac{\sum (PRT - PTT)}{\sum RP} * 1000 \qquad (4)$$

- PRT: Packet Reception Time.
- PTT: Packet Transmission Time.
- RP: Received Packet.

"Figure 7" presents a comparison between the HSTS and the WKCA protocols in term of E2ED. The result shows that our enhanced model provides less time amount of propagation delay whether for high or low density. Indeed, when the similarity of nodes within clusters is not optimized, the linking path between the source and the destination will contain more relays. This excess number of nodes causes more delay with high bandwidth usage. For example, with low density (40), when the speed reaches 120 kmph, the delay decreases significantly to reach 20 ms for all approaches. However, when the speed decreases and the density becomes the main challenge

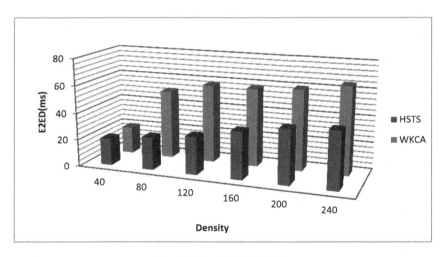

Fig. 7. Density VS E2ED

(240), the delay in the WKCA increases dramatically to reach 67 ms. While the HSTS maintains a high performance and the delay does not exceed 42 ms in the worst case.

c. Throughput: is defined as the rate of successful data delivered over a communication channel.

$$Throughput = \frac{\sum Packet\ successfully\ received\ by\ destination}{Unit\ time} \qquad (5)$$

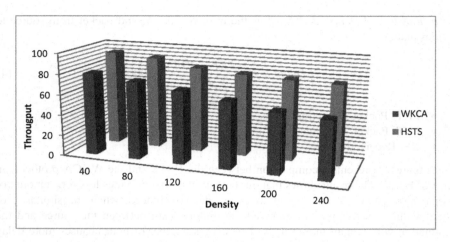

Fig. 8. Density VS Throughput

"Figure 8" compares the impact of the density on the throughput for all schemes. Indeed, the WKCA protocol has the lowest throughputs especially in dense situation due to the inability of the available bandwidth to cope with the large volume of control packets. To deal with this challenge of density, the HSTS formed clusters with high similarity. This procedure will create direct paths with minimum number of relays. Therefore, the throughput has been improved with the scatter search. Mostly, the traffic crowding is a nonlinear function. Thus, any reduction in traffic stream reduces the collisions and allows a significant rise in throughput. With the best road condition, the situation changes rapidly and the rate of successful delivered messages over a communication channel increases gradually. For instance, by reducing the density from 120 to 80 vehicles, the throughput of both HSTS and WKCA is improved by respectively 10% and 7%.

6   Conclusion

Due to the diversity of routing environments (residential, urban, highway,…) and the high mobility of vehicles, constructing stable networks seems to be the basic challenge. To tackle this problem, we improved the weighted k-medoid clustering algorithm (WKCA) proposed recently. We used a hybrid scatter tabu search to maximize the intra-cluster similarities. We treated the overlapping clustering where a node can simultaneously belong to more than one cluster. As shown in Sect. 5, the proposed model (HSTS) outperforms the basic WKCA in term of PDR, E2ED and throughput in all situations. Finally, we can conclude that the greater the similarity within a cluster, the better the network stability. As a future work, we plan to improve the behavior of our model based on the Cuckoo Search heuristic especially in urban scenario with the existence of intersections and obstacles.

References

1. Hajlaoui, R., Guyennet, H., Moulahi, T.: A survey on heuristic-based routing methods in vehicular ad-hoc network: technical challenges and future trends. IEEE Sens. J. **16**(17), 6782–6792 (2016)
2. Aadil, F., Bajwa, K.B., Khan, S., Chaudary, N.M., Akram, A.: CACONET: Ant Colony Optimization (ACO) based clustering algorithm for VANET. PLoS ONE **11**(5), e0154080 (2016)
3. Talbi, E.G.: A taxonomy of hybrid metaheuristics. J. Heuristics **8**(2), 541–564 (2002)
4. Shou-Chih, L., Lin, Y.-J., Gao, J.-S.: A multi-head clustering algorithm in vehicular ad hoc networks. Int. J. Comput. Theor. Eng. **5**(2), April 2013
5. Little, T.D.C., Agarwal, A.: An information propagation scheme for VANETs. In: IEEE Intelligent Transportation Systems Conference, pp. 155–160, September 2005
6. Basu, P., Khan, N., Little, T.D.C.: A mobility based metric for clustering in mobile ad hoc networks. In: International Conference of Distributed Computing Systems Workshop, pp. 413–418, April 2001
7. Malathi, A., Sreenath, N.: An efficient clustering algorithm for Vanet. Int. J. Appl. Eng. Res. **12**(9), 2000–2005 (2017)
8. Yang, S.: Deb: Cuckoo search via Le′vy flights. In: IEEE Proceedings of World Congress on Nature & Biologically Inspire Computing, India, pp. 210–214 (2009)
9. Nasr, M.M.M., Abdelgader, A.M.S., Wang, Z.-G., Shen, L.-F.: VANET clustering based routing protocol suitable for deserts. Sens. J. **16**(4), 478 (2016)
10. Hassanabadi, B., Shea, C., Zhang, L., Valaee, S.: Clustering in vehicular ad hoc networks using affinity propagation. Ad Hoc Netw. J. **13**, 535–548 (2014)
11. Shea, C., Hassanabad, B., Valaee, S.: Mobility-based clustering in VANETs using affinity propagation. In: The 28th IEEE Conference on Global Telecommunications (2009)
12. Mammu, A.S.K., Hernandez, U., Sainz, N.: Cluster based MAC in VANETs for safety applications. In: International Conference on Advances in Computing, Communications, Informatics (ICACCI), pp. 1424–1429 (2013)
13. Moniruzzaman, A.B.M., Rahmann, M.S.: Analysis of topology based routing protocols for Vehicular Ad-Hoc Network (VANET). Int. J. Comput. Appl. (2014)
14. Hajlaoui, R., Moulahi, T., Guyennet, H.: A weighted k-medoids clustering algorithm for effective stability in vehicular ad hoc networks. In: 19th International Conference on Communication Systems, Applications, Venice, Italy (2017)
15. Scheuerer, S., Wendolsky, R.: A scatter search heuristic for the capacitated clustering problem. Eur. J. Oper. Res. **169**, 533–547 (2006)
16. Yamashita, D.S., Armentano, V.A., Laguna, M.: Scatter search for project scheduling with resource availability cost. Eur. J. Oper. Res. **169**(2), 623–637 (2004)
17. Glover, F., Laguna, M., Marti, R.: Fundamentals of scatter search and path relinking. Control Cybern. J. **39**, 653–684 (2000)
18. Laguna, M., Martí, R.: Scatter Search: Methodology, Implementations. Kluwer Academic Press, Boston (2003)
19. Glover, F., Taillard, E., Laguna, M., de Werra, D.: Tabu search. Ann. Oper. Res. **41**, 1–28 (1993)
20. The Network Simulator. https://www.nsnam.org/
21. Agrawal, J., Singhal, A., Yadav, R.N.: Multipath routing in mobile ad-hoc network using meta-heuristic approach. In: IEEE International Conference on Advances in Computing, Communications, Informatics (ICACCI), India (2017)

Providing Mission-Critical Services over 5G Radio Access Network

Rubén Solozabal[1(✉)], Aitor Sanchoyerto[1(✉)], Miren Cava[1(✉)],
Bego Blanco[1(✉)], Hicham Khalife[2(✉)], Mathieu Bouet[2(✉)],
Damien Lavaux[2(✉)], and Emmanouil Kafetzakis[3(✉)]

[1] University of the Basque Country (UPV/EHU),
Pl. Ingeniero Torres Quevedo 1, Bilbao, Spain
{ruben.solozabal,aitor.sanchoyerto}@ehu.eus
[2] Thales Communications,
4 Avenue des Louvresses, 92230 Gennevilliers, France
[3] Orion Innovations, Aminokleous 43, 117 44 Athens, Greece

Abstract. 5G is called to introduce a major transformation in communication network architectures with its transition to cloud native networks. This transformation will enable new unique service capabilities that will drive the development of innovative applications. But, for 5G being successful in this task, the identification of the vertical sectors' requirements is of outmost importance in order to map them into the design of the network architecture. This paper proposes a novel Cloud-Enabled Radio Access Network (CE-RAN) architecture to support Public Safety services at the edge of the network. This proposal leverages Network Functions Virtualisation, Software Defined Networking and Mobile Edge Computing principles to provide Mission-Critical services through an isolated network slice. We suggest a CE-RAN architecture with two levels of cloudification to bring the service closer to the end user.

Keywords: Mobile edge computing · 5G
Cloud-Enabled Radio Access Network · CUPS · IOPS

1 Introduction

Even though 5G is obviously the natural evolution of current mobile broadband networks, it is called to make a disruptive change in communication network architectures, becoming the broader transition to cloud native networks. 5G is expected to bring new unique network and service capabilities, becoming a key enabler for emerging, revenue-generating 5G applications.

With this aim, the design of 5G is based on three main pillars: the flexibility of Network Functions Virtualisation (NFV), the programmability of Software Defined Networking (SDN) and the proximity to users of Mobile Edge Computing (MEC). The application of these trending technologies enables the creation of isolated service slices over the same physical network, allowing to adapt the network in order to meet the requirements of specific services.

© IFIP International Federation for Information Processing 2018
Published by Springer International Publishing AG 2018. All Rights Reserved
L. Iliadis et al. (Eds.): AIAI 2018, IFIP AICT 519, pp. 520–530, 2018.
https://doi.org/10.1007/978-3-319-92007-8_44

All these forthcoming capabilities encourage the development of new applications and vertical industries. Consequently, it is also decisive for the success of 5G to identify the key vertical sectors' requirements and map them into the design of the network architecture. On this point, from Release 11 onwards 3GPP is considering the requirements of Mission-Critical (MC) communications as a central topic to address the key requirements of the next generation broadband Public Safety (PS) networks. There is a clear trend towards different forms of network sharing models as opposed to building out dedicated legacy PS networks.

In order to support the demanding set of requirements of the new verticals, 5G standardisation bodies aim to define a new Radio Access Network (RAN) architectural framework that leverages NFV and SDN to provide a complete virtualised ecosystem suitable for the execution of Virtual Network Functions (VNF). To this aim, we consider that the most appropriate place to build 5G infrastructure foundations is the edge of the network, in order to relieve the core network from the traffic that can be efficiently processed and served closer to the end user and, thus, to reduce the response time. We use Small Cell-as-a-Service (SCaaS) paradigm to build a highly flexible and scalable platform, able to support new business models and revenue streams by creating a neutral host market that reduces the operational costs by providing new opportunities for ownership, deployment, operation and amortisation.

The technical approach for exploiting the benefits of the centralisation of RAN functions is based on a two-tier architecture: a first distributed tier for providing low latency services and a second centralised tier with high processing power for access network control applications. Decoupling the control and user planes of the Radio Access Network (RAN) frees from the enormous fronthaul latency restrictions. The use of end-to-end network slicing mechanisms will allow sharing the infrastructure among multiple operators/vertical industries and customising its capabilities on a per-tenant basis.

This paper is organised as follows: Sect. 2 defines the use case for Public Safety applications, a vertical sector that is attracting appreciable interest in the latest years. Next, in Sect. 3 we describe the 5G Cloud-Enabled RAN with edge computing capabilities to support the defined used case. Then Sect. 4 proposes a solution that exploits MEC capabilities to provide MC services. Finally, Sect. 5 concludes this paper.

2 Description of the Public Safety Use Case

The current trends in the Public Safety ecosystem lead towards a future Mission-Critical (MC) communications framework based on standardised commercial technologies. In the recent years, several worldwide administrations have collaborated in the 3GPP to create the first operational solution in Release 13, named Mission Critical Push to Talk (MCPTT). This solution defines the service and network level specifications to provide mission-critical services over 4G LTE technologies. Currently, Release 14 evolved the solution towards a more mature state, including also other mission-critical services such as video and data. The adoption of the solution for future 5G networks will be specified during Release 15 normative work (scheduled for 2018).

In order to provide MC services the network provider must guarantee the required levels of QoS, security/privacy and resiliency.

This use case considers one or several Public Safety organisations using the resources provided by a third-party dense small cell deployment, which could be owned by the mobile network operator or by a venue owner such as the case of a stadium. In this case, the owner will exploit the proposed two-tier cloud edge platform to provide the required network slicing capabilities with dedicated characteristics to different types of tenants.

The public safety use case presented in this paper is organised in three main stages:

Stage 1. In a first step, the small cell deployment owner is providing the required network slices to the different tenants (Fig. 1). Each network slice is composed by a volume of radio data rate over a coverage area (which is mapped by the edge cloud RAN Controller to a volume of small cell radio resources) and a volume of edge service capabilities (which is mapped to a volume of processing power in the lower level distributed cloud).

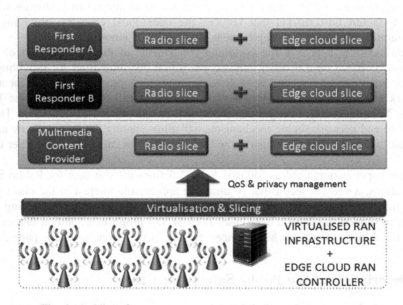

Fig. 1. Public safety use case stage 1 – default service agreement.

For the case of Public Safety organisations, normal operations may require a certain number of group communications supported in the area of the SC cluster. This requirement can be mapped to a number of radio KPIs in the SCs and the deployment of edge group communication service instances at the edge (i.e., MCPTT Application Servers deployed at the edge) to enhance the responsiveness of the service.

In addition to the QoS guarantees for each tenant, the deployment owner has to assure the required levels of isolation in the provisioning of the different network slices.

Stage 2. In case there is an incident in the area, the Orchestrator has to be able to react to the new service requirements (illustrated on Fig. 2). A Public Safety organisation may require additional service capacity in the geographical area, in order to cope with increased number of first responders or additional types of service such as mission-critical video transmissions. Based on pre-arranged or on-demand service scaling policies, the Orchestrator would implement the new resource allocation scheme taking into account both radio (for the access connections) and cloud resources (for deploying more resource-consuming edge services).

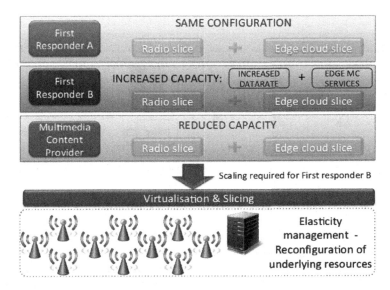

Fig. 2. Public safety use case stage 2 – incident demanding extended capacity.

The deployment of edge service instances serves a twofold objective: first, it enables close-to-zero delay in the mission-critical services; second, it allows maintaining the operability even when the backhaul connection is damaged.

Stage 3. Addresses the potential need for coverage extension (Fig. 3). The typical situation is that a Public Safety organisation decides to use a deployable system, e.g. to mitigate the damage of a macro base station. In the proposed use case, the deployable system also offers an (evolved) LTE connectivity to the first responders in the field, consolidating the interoperability requirements.

In order to better orchestrate the radio transmissions, the deployable system will be considered as a new small cell that can be dynamically added to the cluster. In this way, the enhanced SON and RRM features of the platform can be applied to the coverage extension unit. The connectivity of the deployable unit with the SC cluster would be made through a wireless backhauling technology.

Once the Public Safety use case has been outlined, the next section describes the architecture proposed to provide PS services at the edge of the cloud-based RAN.

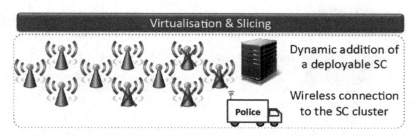

Fig. 3. Public safety use case stage 3 – breakdown demanding extended coverage.

3 5G Cloud-Enabled RAN with MEC Capabilities

It is estimated that the user traffic volume over the mobile network will increase on the order of several magnitudes in the coming decade [1]. In addition, with the advent of Internet of Things (IoT) devices, outsourcing tasks to powerful clouds is becoming a trend due to the lack power of these devices. Nevertheless, traditional cloud services may end in a high-latency not compatible with real-time services. To overcome these problems, service providers can take advantage of MEC [2].

MEC allows bringing computation and network management to the edge of the mobile network, within the Radio Access Network (RAN), allowing service providers to deploy applications closer to the end-user. MEC reduces service latency as well as the bandwidth consumption since the core network is not or at least less involved in traffic between UEs and application servers. The relocation of the services on the edge of the mobile network will be of outmost importance in order to achieve technological expectations of 5G with an end-to-end latency of one milliseconds, over one million connections per square kilometre, and traffic rates ten times higher than in 4G.

Currently, MEC deployments are limited due to the lack of flexibility on the mobile network. In order to overcome these barriers, 5G will leverage NFV and SDN technologies to bring a cloud execution platform at the edge of the network [3].

For all these reasons, 5G will have to face architectural changes in the RAN. ENodeBs based on specific hardware will be aggregated in centralised cloud centres within the RAN, concentrating resources to simplify its deployment and management. RAN functions will be virtually executed and ideally connected to the remote radio heads through optical fibre fronthauls, as high fronthaul delays may degrade the performance of certain novel edge services that require close-to-zero latencies as prescribed by 5G objectives, As a consequence, this execution platform will be able to provide the computational power at the edge not only to virtualise network functionality but also third-party services.

The evolution of the current RAN to that envisioned in 5G represents a great effort for network operators. Therefore, intermediary solutions as [4] adopt the aforementioned principles to propose a novel distributed CE-RAN architecture evolving the traditional commercial Small Cells eNodeB (SCeNB) to Cloud Enabled Small Cells eNodeB (SCeNBce). These solutions rely on currently installed Physical Network Functions (PNF) and complement them along with a virtualised platform that supports the execution of innovative edge services as Virtual Network Functions (VNFs).

Proposals as [5] envision the coexistence of both centralised and edge cloud. This two-tier cloud-enabled RAN forms which is known as a hybrid cloud in which both centralised and edge clouds will cooperate to take advantage of the resulting peculiarities of the architecture, ending in the benefits described below.

The First-tier is the Edge Cloud. It remains distributed over a SCeNBce cluster for providing close-to-zero service latency directly from the networks' edge. The edge cloud is used to support the executions of VNFs as deep packet inspection, GTP encapsulation or distributed SON. The Edge Cloud will reduce the cost of high bandwidth fronthaul over long distances to centralised data centres while being able to provide close-to-zero latency services.

The edge cloud consists in a Multi-RAT 5G small cell cluster with its standard backhaul interface. It allows multiple core network operators to provide its services sharing the same physical infrastructure. In this environment, the small cell is the termination of the GTP-User Plane which communicates with each of the core networks.

The Second-tier is a high-scale cloud. The Central Cloud will provide high processing power for computing intensive network applications. It will benefit from its global vision of the underlaying infrastructure so as to be able to compute efficient scheduling algorithms. The central cloud hosts the RAN controller, which makes control plane decisions for all radio elements in the geographical area of the cluster, security, traffic engineering, mobility management, etc.

Both these clouds will be conceived as an integrated hybrid cloud infrastructure from the upper layers. In this context, a single orchestrator will coordinate a variety of both, being able to deploy VNFs along them in a unified manner.

3.1 Network Slicing Within the Radio Access Network

5G will enable logical network slicing, with which, a single physical network is partitioned into multiple virtual networks being able to personalize it for each type of services. With this technology, slices can be optimized to guarantee multiple characteristics for specific services including latency or bandwidth requirements.

In order to provide an end-to-end service, network slicing is required not only in the operator's core network but also within the RAN. Service slices must be achieved over the same physical infrastructure. Therefore, computational and radio resources need to be shared and isolated between different services and tenants. In this context,

Mission-Critical (MC) services must be provided over a prioritised slice, guaranteeing the access to the needed end infrastructure. As a result, resources are delivered in an elastic manner based on on-demand service and the scaling policies applied.

The envisioned neutral RAN is an infrastructure shared between multiple virtual network mobile operators and content service providers. Guaranteeing resource isolation in a cloud environment is the key element in order to obtain an architecture capable of hosting multiple virtual network operators and vertical industries providing their services using the same infrastructure.

3.2   Radio Resource Management Within the Radio Access Network

Currently, radio resource allocation remains inadequate, especially in urban areas, where, due to the increased in traffic and limited spectrum, operators may have to decrease the size of the cells. The dense deployment of small cells leads to interferences among neighbouring base stations. In order to solve this, a separation between control from data plane of the Radio Resource Management (RRM) is proposed. This way, the radio controller could be allocated in the Central Cloud, benefiting from the overall view of the underlying architecture and making decisions to the whole distributed data plane on how to operate, and reducing interference in a centralised manner and increasing the spectrum utilisation efficiency.

Therefore, the RAN evolves not only to provide multi-operator radio access, but also to achieve an increase in the capacity and the performance.

3.3   Management and Orchestration of Edge Services

The approach for network control centralisation does not only remain for radio interfaces, but also for service managing and orchestration. The management and orchestration (MANO) will operate at multiple SCeNBces clusters at multiple point-of-presence, transforming them in a uniform virtualised environment, enabling the creation of optimization algorithms that would act over the whole deployment. The main part is the Network Function Virtualization Orchestrator (NFVO). It composes service chains and manages the deployment of VNFs over the edge cloud. The NFVO delegates the management of VNF lifecycle to the VNFM, which oversees the instantiation, update and overall scaling and termination of VNFs.

Inside the MANO an important part is the Element Management System (EMS). It provides end-user functions for management of both PNFs and VNFs. It is responsible for set the management functionalities that other entities as the Network Management System of each operator will see.

The MANO also encompasses telemetry and analysis to capture relevant indicators of the network operation, since it is responsible for the SLA agreements.

4 Deploying Mission-Critical Service on MEC Infrastructure

Nowadays, 5G core architecture standardization is in an early stage [6]. It is envisioned that 5G New Radio will be first implemented using 4G EPC, give rise to what is known as 5G Non-Standalone. Therefore, the core nodes we are going to refer to belong to the legacy EPC core architecture.

The isolation that will be achieved in 5G enables the network to meet the specific requirements of services as Mission-Critical (MC) communications. As a reference, Mission-Critical Push-to-Talk (MCPTT) is an IP-based MC service that can benefit from the MEC infrastructure. This kind of service requires of a Session Initiation Protocol (SIP) core such as IP Multimedia Subsystem (IMS) to operate. An IMS aims to reach interoperability for session control in all-IP Next Generation Networks and currently are implemented as a centralized subsystem attached to the Evolved Packet Core (EPC) of each operator.

We propose to distribute MC services near the end-user, making use of MEC capabilities obtained throughout the virtualisation of the RAN. Distributing the User Plane (UP) in the proximities of the end-user benefits first responders from mouth-to-ear latency reduction. Thanks to NFV, it also enables service providers to scale the user plane on demand in specific locations straightforwardly.

Distributing the service demands bringing the UP of the IMS and EPC to the edge of the mobile network. The deployment of an "IMS as a Service" (IMSaaS) and an "EPC as a Service (EPCaaS)" at the edge enables the necessary infrastructure to provide over-the-top services that otherwise would be located behind the operator's core network. As it will be discussed in the following section, it is common that none of the IMS nodes manage user data. And therefore, it will not be necessary to ensure with this layer near the user, service application located at the edge will be directly connected to the local EPC.

On the other hand, we propose to leave the Control Plane (CP) centralized due the complications that entails the synchronization of a distributed control.

4.1 Distributing Core Operator Infrastructure at the Edge of the Network

Extending the current EPC infrastructure next to the edge allows reducing latency, enables scaling the service horizontally in specific locations and reduces traffic over the central core network. Nevertheless, the standardized EPC by 3GPP was never designed for a centralised network architecture, where the EPC nodes are part of the Core Network: Mobility Management Entity (MME), the Home Subscriber Server (HSS), the Serving Gateway (SGW) and the Packet Data Network Gateway (PGW). Recently, 3GPP has addressed an initiative called CUPS (Control and User Plane Separation) [7] with the aim to study possibilities for a separation of S/PGW functionality into user plane functions and control plane functions, so that the user plane functions can be placed flexibly at the edge while the control plane functions could still remain centralized.

Local edge nodes are able to manage user data plane functions of SGW (SGW-U) and PGW (PGW-U) (illustrated on Fig. 4). Nevertheless, the replication of the EPC at the edge entails some limitations. Providing a stable data path to terminals changing their point of attachment to the network is the essential issue that will drive the new architecture design. In the legacy network architectures, a terminal's user traffic is always routed through a centralised node in the core network. This centralised node acts as an anchor point for the data path and ensures that IP packets reach the terminal irrespective of its point of attachment. Mobile networks need to adopt the distributed nature of routing IP providing mobile data path management on top of a distributed architecture because, in case of unmanaged IP mobility, the transmission could be disrupted. Nevertheless, there is a way to achieve application session continuity managed in upper functional layers. For example, a session that has been established using the SIP can survive IP address changes using the mobility management support built into those protocols.

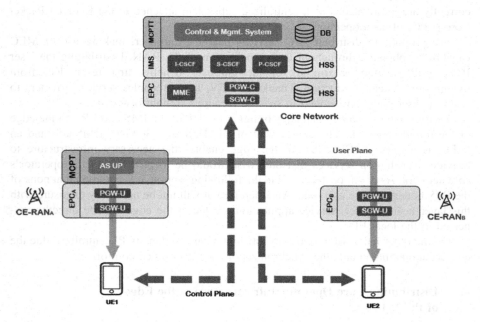

Fig. 4. Distributed MCPTT user plane at the edge.

In the same way that the EPC has been partially re-located at the edge, IMS shall be replicated as well. Nevertheless, 3GPP has not specified yet how the separation between the CP/UP of the IMS would be handled.

As mentioned before, an IMS is a signalling core, it's main operation is controlling. There are some nodes in the IMS architecture that manage UP (e.g. the Media Resource Function), yet these nodes are dispensable in a basic configuration. For this reason, the IMS do not appear as layer of the UP we are deploying at the edge. And service communication with IMS centralized nodes only will take place during control operations (e.g. during communication establishment).

Therefore, an EPCaaS at the edge entails the necessary infrastructure to provide over-the-top services with independent user plane without relying in the core network, being the appropriate host MC services as MCPTT.

4.2   Isolated E-UTRAN Operation for Public Safety

A specific scenario in which public safety communications can take advantage of MEC is in case of network failure. As defined in 3GPP technical specification 22.346 [8], isolated E-UTRAN aims to restore the service of an eNodeB or a set of interconnected eNodeBs without backhaul connectivity. The goal of Isolated E-UTRAN Operation for Public Safety (IOPS) is to maintain the maximum level of communication for first responders when the connectivity with the EPC is either unavailable or non-ideal.

In an emergency scenario, the execution platform located in the edge of the network could be used not only to bring the core UP near end-users but also to provide the CP, resulting in a fully capable local Core able to provide MC services within the isolated zone. In that direction, policies of backhaul disconnection must be agreed, as well as a methodology to change between a fully connected eNodeB to an isolated situation.

5   Conclusions

Considering the envisioned disruptive capabilities of forthcoming 5G communications and the highly demanding requirements of the services that will be supported, a radical RAN paradigm change is foreseen. It is also expected that this transformation will leverage NFV, SDN and MEC technologies as key enablers of this philosophy turnaround.

We rely on the two-tier Cloud-Enabled RAN as the platform to execute the virtualised services in end-user proximity. This architecture benefits the network operator from CAPex/OPex reduction, but also provides the necessary infrastructure to share the point-of-presence between multiple operators and third-party service providers.

We present the benefits of transferring the user data plane close to the end user, both in terms of QoS and from an operation prospective. To achieve this goal a separation between user and control planes throughout the vertical infrastructure is needed. In this paper, a use case of a Mission-Critical service on MEC is described. Enabling the deployment of user plane over at the edge of the mobile network benefits the service latency, but also facilitates the deployment and scaling on demand from the operators' perspective. In future work, we will analyse the impact of applying these MEC architecture principles over key performance indicators (KPI) for a Mission-Critical service.

We conclude highlighting the opportunities of the edge architecture in an emergency scenario. Under exceptional circumstances, in which the interconnections with the operators' core or even between base stations is damaged, a complete service deployment on the described architecture is able to maintain the service locally, at the expense of service restoration.

Acknowledgement. The research leading to these results has been supported by the EU funded H2020 5G-PPP project ESSENCE (Grant Agreement N° 761592) and the Spanish Government's MINECO project 5GRANVIR (TEC2016-80090-C2-2-R).

References

1. Chen, S., Zhao, J.: The requirements, challenges, and technologies for 5G of terrestrial mobile telecommunication. IEEE Commun. Mag. **52**(5), 36–43 (2014). https://doi.org/10.1109/MCOM.2014.6815891
2. Tran, T.X., Hajisami, A., Pandey, P., Pompili, D.: Collaborative mobile edge computing in 5G networks: new paradigms, scenarios, and challenges. IEEE Commun. Mag. **55**(4), 54–61 (2017). https://doi.org/10.1109/MCOM.2017.1600863
3. Blanco, B., Fajardo, J.O., Giannoulakis, I., Kafetzakis, E., Peng, S., Pérez-Romero, J., Trajkovska, I., Khodashenas, P.S., Goratti, L., Paolino, M., Sfakianakis, E.: Technology pillars in the architecture of future 5G mobile networks: NFV, MEC and SDN. Comput. Stand. Interf. **54** (2017). https://doi.org/10.1016/j.csi.2016.12.007
4. Fajardo, J.O., et al.: Introducing mobile edge computing capabilities through distributed 5G cloud enabled small cells. Mob. Netw. Appl. (2016). https://doi.org/10.1007/s11036-016-0752-2
5. Ku, Y.J., et al.: 5G Radio Access Network Design with the Fog Paradigm: Confluence of Communications and Computing. IEEE Commun. Mag. **55**(4), 46–52 (2017). https://doi.org/10.1109/MCOM.2017.1600893
6. GPP: Technical specification group services and system aspects; system architecture for the 5G system. 3rd Generation Partnership Project (3GPP), TR 23.501, July 2017
7. GPP: Architecture enhancements for control and user plane separations of EPC nodes. 3rd Generation Partnership Project (3GPP), TR 23.214, July 2017
8. GPP: Isolated E-UTRAN operation for public safety. 3rd Generation Partnership Project (3GPP), TS 22.346, March 2017

Fuzzy

A Study of Heuristic Evaluation Measures
in Fuzzy Rule Induction

Ashraf A. Afifi[1,2(✉)]

[1] Department of Engineering, Design and Mathematics, Faculty of Environment
and Technology, University of the West of England, Bristol, UK
Ashraf.Afifi@uwe.ac.uk
[2] Industrial Engineering Department, Faculty of Engineering,
Zagazig University, Zagazig, Egypt

Abstract. The rule induction process could be conceived as a search process, and hence an evaluation metric is needed to estimate the quality of rules found in the search space and to direct the search towards the best rule. The evaluation measure is the most influential inductive bias in rule learning. It is therefore important to investigate its influence on the induction process and to compare the behaviour of different evaluation measures. Many different evaluation measures have been used to score crisp rules. For some of these measures, fuzzy variations have been designed and used to score fuzzy rules. This paper examines the most popular crisp evaluation measures and demonstrates how they can be adapted into the fuzzy domain. The paper also studies the performance of these measures on a large number of data sets when used in a recently developed fuzzy rule induction algorithm. Results show that there are no universally applicable evaluation measures and the choice of the best measure depends on the type of the data set and the learning problem.

Keywords: Fuzzy rule induction · Heuristic evaluation measures
Fuzzy sets

1 Introduction

Rule induction has proven to be a valuable tool for description, classification and generalisation of data. A variety of methods exist for rule learning using crisp sets [1–4]. Fuzzy sets are a generalisation of crisp sets providing increased expressive power and comprehensibility. A number of fuzzy rule induction algorithms have been developed as an extension of crisp rule learners [5, 6]. Recently, Afify [7] introduced a novel fuzzy rule induction method called FuzzyRULES (for Fuzzy RULe Extraction System). FuzzyRULES is based on the learning strategy used in the RULES-6 [8] crisp rule induction algorithm, previously developed by the author. FuzzyRULES preserves all the advantages of RULES-6 such as good comprehensibility and high classification accuracy. Moreover, it incorporates approximate reasoning offered by fuzzy representation, which allows better dealing with inconsistent, inexact, subjective, or noisy data.

© IFIP International Federation for Information Processing 2018
Published by Springer International Publishing AG 2018. All Rights Reserved
L. Iliadis et al. (Eds.): AIAI 2018, IFIP AICT 519, pp. 533–545, 2018.
https://doi.org/10.1007/978-3-319-92007-8_45

Rule induction algorithms typically use an evaluation measure to score the performance of rules found during the learning process, and to select the best rules for further exploration. Therefore, the evaluation measure as a search heuristic is very important as it determines to a large extent the performance of the learning algorithm. The selection of the most appropriate evaluation measure for any particular learning algorithm is a critical and difficult task, which is usually carried out empirically. This paper examines the role of several well-known crisp evaluation measures and how they address the specific requirements of the rule forming process. The paper also studies the performance of the fuzzy variants of these measures when applied to fuzzy rule induction algorithms. The aim is to identify the most appropriate measures to be applied in fuzzy rule induction algorithms, especially in FuzzyRULES.

The layout of the paper is as follows. Section 2 reviews the FuzzyRULES algorithm. Section 3 introduces the evaluation measures, and demonstrates the adaptation of these measures to the fuzzy set domain. Section 4 gives an empirical evaluation of the different evaluation measures when used in FuzzyRULES. Section 5 concludes the paper and provides suggestions for future work.

2   FuzzyRULES

The recently developed FuzzyRULES fuzzy rule induction algorithm will be used in this study to assess the performance of several heuristic evaluation measures. FuzzyRULES is based on the RULES-6 crisp rule induction algorithm. RULES-6 broadly follows the approach of AQ-like [2] learning algorithms. It employs heuristic search techniques with different learning biases and rule-space pruning strategies that significantly reduce the proportion of the search space examined during the learning process, resulting in substantial performance benefits.

FuzzyRULES follows the so-called *separate-and-conquer* or *covering* strategy of rule induction algorithms. It creates the rule set one rule at a time. Each rule explains (covers) a part of the training instances. After a rule is generated, the instances covered by it are removed (separated) from the training data set before subsequent rules are learned. The remaining instances are conquered using the same induction procedure until all the instances are covered by at least one rule in the rule set. Figure 1 provides a simplified description of the FuzzyRULES algorithm. A detailed description of the algorithms can be found in [7].

3   Evaluation Measures

A typical objective of a rule induction algorithm is to find rules that optimise a rule evaluation measure that takes both training accuracy and rule coverage into account so that the rules learned are both accurate and general. Many different measures for evaluating and assigning a score to crisp rules have been proposed in the literature [9]. For some of these measures, fuzzy variations have been designed and used to score fuzzy rules [10]. In this section, the most commonly used rule evaluation measures are discussed and the adaptation of these measures into the fuzzy domain is demonstrated.

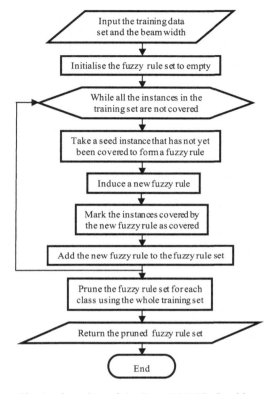

Fig. 1. Overview of the FuzzyRULES algorithm.

To derive fuzzy evaluation measures, the cardinality and α-cut operators [11] will be used to describe the instances matched by the rules. Let $A => C$ denote a candidate rule R, where A is the rule antecedent (a conjunction of conditions) and C is the rule consequent (the value predicted for the goal attribute). The set of instances in the training set T that are covered by a rule R can be defined using the cardinality measure $M(A)$, also referred to as the sigma count, as follows:

$$M(A) = \sum_{I \in T} \mu_R(I) \tag{1}$$

where $\mu_R(I)$ represents the degree of match of a particular instance I with the antecedent of a rule R. For each instance, this degree is computed by a fuzzy AND of the degree of matching between each attribute value in the instance and the corresponding fuzzy condition in the rule. The conventional definition of the fuzzy AND has been used as the minimum operator.

In practice, many of the instances can match a rule antecedent to a small degree, and the summation of all these small degrees of membership can give the false impression that the rule is good, which can undermine the reliability of the evaluation measure. To prevent such instances from being covered, a user-defined α-cut threshold can be applied to the instance memberships. The membership of an instance to a rule, $\mu_R(I)$, is defined to be zero when it lies below the α-cut threshold value. When the value of $\mu_R(I)$ is greater than or equal to the specified value of α, rule R is said to α-cover instance I. Using the α-cut operator, the set of instances in the training set T that are α-covered by a rule R can be expressed by redefining Eq. (1) as follows:

$$M(A) = \sum\nolimits_{I \in R_\alpha(T)} \mu_R(I) \tag{2}$$

where $R_\alpha(T) = \{I \in T | \mu_R(I) \geq \alpha\}$ contains all instances in the training set T that have a membership grade in R greater than or equal to the specified value of α.

The evaluation measures include different parameters that assess the coverage of the rules. For a particular rule R, the parameters P and N denote the total number of positive instances (instances belonging to the target class) and negative instances (instances not belonging to the target class) in the training set, $p(n)$ the number of positive (negative) instances covered by rule R, and $p'(n')$ the number of positive (negative) instances covered by rule R', the predecessor (parent) of rule R.

3.1 Purity

This measure is utilised in GREEDY3 [12] and SWAP-1 [13] algorithms. It gives the ratio between the number of positive instances covered by a rule and the total number of covered instances. In the crisp case, the purity measure of a rule R is given by:

$$P(R) = \frac{p}{p+n} \tag{3}$$

The purity measure attains its optimal value when no negative instances are covered. Also, it does not aim to cover many positive instances. As a result, this metric tends to select very specific rules covering only a small number of instances. This is undesirable since rules covering few instances are unreliable, especially where there is noise in the data. The accuracy of these rules on the training data does not adequately reflect their true predictive accuracy on new test data.

The purity measure can be fuzzified using the cardinality and α -cut operators as follows:

$$P(R) = \frac{M(A \cap C)}{M(A)} = \frac{\sum_{I \in R_\alpha(P)} \mu_R(I)}{\sum_{I \in R_\alpha(T)} \mu_R(I)} \tag{4}$$

where $M(A \cap C)$ is the fuzzification of the number of positive instances covered by a rule R (p), $M(A)$ is the fuzzification of the number of instances covered by the rule $(n + p)$, and $R_\alpha(P) = \{I \in P | \mu_R(I) \geq \alpha\}$, $R_\alpha(T) = \{I \in T | \mu_R(I) \geq \alpha\}$ are the sets of positive instances and total instances that are α-covered by rule R, respectively.

3.2 Information Content

The information content function measures the amount of information contained in the classification of the covered instances. It is originally used in the PRISM inductive learner [14], and its crisp version is given by:

$$IC(R) = -\log_2\left(\frac{p}{p+n}\right) \tag{5}$$

The best rule is the one that minimises Eq. (5). The information content function is basically equivalent to the purity measure and its main advantage is that using a logarithmic scale tends to assign higher penalties to rules with low coverage.

The fuzzy version of the information content function can be expressed as:

$$IC(R) = -\log_2\left(\frac{M(A\cap C)}{M(A)}\right) = -\log_2\left(\frac{\sum_{I\in R_\alpha(P)}\mu_R(I)}{\sum_{I\in R_\alpha(T)}\mu_R(I)}\right) \tag{6}$$

3.3 Entropy

The entropy measure is adopted in the original version of the CN2 algorithm [15]. It is the weighted average of the information content of the positive and negative classes. The entropy measure of a rule R is given by (the lower the entropy, the better the rule):

$$E(R) = -\left(\frac{p}{p+n}\log_2\frac{p}{p+n} + \frac{n}{p+n}\log_2\frac{n}{p+n}\right) \tag{7}$$

The entropy measure suffers from similar deficiencies as purity and information content measures. Also, it does not consider whether the majority of instances are positive or not. For example, a rule that covers 100 positive and 10 negative instances is considered of equal quality to another rule that covers 10 positive and 100 negative instances. To assign higher scores to rules with higher positive coverage, the following function is adopted [10].

$$E(R) = -\frac{n}{p}\left(\frac{p}{p+n}\log_2\frac{p}{p+n} + \frac{n}{p+n}\log_2\frac{n}{p+n}\right) \tag{8}$$

Equation (8) can be adapted to the domain of fuzzy sets as follows:

$$
\begin{aligned}
E(R) &= -\frac{M(A\neg C)}{M(A\cap C)}\left(\frac{M(A\cap C)}{M(A)}\log_2\frac{M(A\cap C)}{M(A)} + \frac{M(A\neg C)}{M(A)}\log_2\frac{M(A\neg C)}{M(A)}\right) \\
&= -\frac{\sum_{I\in R_\alpha(N)}\mu_R(I)}{\sum_{I\in R_\alpha(P)}\mu_R(I)}\left(\frac{\sum_{I\in R_\alpha(P)}\mu_R(I)}{\sum_{I\in R_\alpha(T)}\mu_R(I)}\log_2\frac{\sum_{I\in R_\alpha(P)}\mu_R(I)}{\sum_{I\in R_\alpha(T)}\mu_R(I)} + \frac{\sum_{I\in R_\alpha(N)}\mu_R(I)}{\sum_{I\in R_\alpha(T)}\mu_R(I)}\log_2\frac{\sum_{I\in R_\alpha(N)}\mu_R(I)}{\sum_{I\in R_\alpha(T)}\mu_R(I)}\right)
\end{aligned} \tag{9}
$$

where $M(A \neg C)$ is the fuzzification of the number of negative instances covered by rule R (n), and $R_\alpha(N) = \{I \in N | \mu_R(I) \geq \alpha\}$ is the set of negative instances that are α-covered by rule R.

3.4   Information Gain

The information gain measure is originally used in the FOIL relational learner [16]. It computes the reduction of the information content in a rule when a new condition is added to it. More precisely, it calculates the difference in the information content of the current rule R and its parent R', multiplied by the number of covered positive instances as a bias for generality. In the crisp case, it is given by:

$$IG(R) = p \cdot (IC(R') - IC(R)) = p \cdot \left(-\log_2\left(\frac{p'}{p'+n'}\right) + \log_2\left(\frac{p}{p+n}\right) \right) \tag{10}$$

The goal is to maximise this measure.

The fuzzy information gain can be computed as follows:

$$
\begin{aligned}
IG(R) &= M(A \cap C) \cdot \left(-\log_2\left(\frac{M(A' \cap C)}{M(A')}\right) + \log_2\left(\frac{M(A \cap C)}{M(A)}\right) \right) \\
&= \left(\sum\nolimits_{I \in R_\alpha(P)} \mu_R(I) \right) \cdot \left(-\log_2\left(\frac{\sum_{I \in R'_\alpha(P)} \mu_{R'}(I)}{\sum_{I \in R'_\alpha(T)} \mu_{R'}(I)}\right) + \log_2\left(\frac{\sum_{I \in R_\alpha(P)} \mu_R(I)}{\sum_{I \in R_\alpha(T)} \mu_R(I)}\right) \right)
\end{aligned}
\tag{11}
$$

where $M(A' \cap C)$ is the fuzzification of the number of positive instances covered by rule R' (p'), $M(A')$ is the fuzzification of the number of instances covered by the rule $(p' + n')$, and $R'_\alpha(P) = \{I \in P | \mu_{R'}(I) \geq \alpha\}$, $R'_\alpha(T) = \{I \in T | \mu_{R'}(I) \geq \alpha\}$ are the sets of positive instances and total instances that are α-covered by rule R', respectively.

3.5   Accuracy

This metric is employed in I-REP [17]. It is the proportion of positive instances that are covered (p) and negative instances that are not covered $(N - n)$, in all instances $(P + N)$. In the crisp case, the accuracy measure for a rule R is given by:

$$A(R) = \frac{p + (N - n)}{P + N} \tag{12}$$

The accuracy measure favours high coverage and scores rules in the range $[-\infty, \infty]$, with higher scores given to better evaluations. The problem of the accuracy measure is that this measure sometimes does not lead to a satisfactory behaviour. For example, it favours a rule that covers 2000 positive and 1000 negative instances over another rule that covers 1000 positive and only 1 negative instance.

A fuzzy variant of the accuracy measure can be defined as:

$$A(R) = \frac{M(A \cap C) + (N - M(A \neg C))}{P + N} = \frac{\sum_{I \in R_\alpha(P)} \mu_R(I) + (N - \sum_{I \in R_\alpha(N)} \mu_R(I))}{P + N} \quad (13)$$

3.6 Laplace

The Laplace estimate penalises rules with low coverage and it is used in CN2 [1] and several other algorithms due to its simplicity and efficiency. The Laplace estimate of a rule R is given by:

$$L(R) = \frac{p + 1}{p + n + k} \quad (14)$$

where k is the number of classes. Rule induction algorithms learn multi-class concepts by learning one class at a time. Thus, k is always 2.

The Laplace estimate has the desirable property of taking into account both accuracy and coverage when estimating rule accuracy. However, it has a problem when learning rules with less than 50% training accuracy. The Laplace estimate does not satisfy the requirement that the rule quality value should rise with increased coverage. Another problem is that the Laplace accuracy estimate is often unrealistic, especially in multi-class decision problems [18]. This occurred because of the assumption that underlies Laplace accuracy estimate, namely, that the *a priori* distribution is uniform.

A fuzzy variant of the Laplace estimate can be given by:

$$L(R) = \frac{M(A \cap C) + 1}{M(A) + 2} = \frac{\sum_{I \in R_\alpha(P)} \mu_R(I) + 1}{\sum_{I \in R_\alpha(T)} \mu_R(I) + 2} \quad (15)$$

3.7 *m*-estimate

The *m-estimate* [18] is a more general version of the Laplace measure and it is defined as follows:

$$M(R) = \frac{p + m * P/(P + N)}{p + n + m} \quad (16)$$

where $P/(P + N)$ is the *a priori* probability of the target class and m is a domain dependent parameter. The value of m is related to the amount of noise in the domain. m can be small if little noise is expected and should increase if the amount of noise is substantial. m is usually set to k, where k is the number of classes.

The m-estimate is a good choice because it is based on strong theoretical foundations and it meets the requirements of a good evaluation function. The Laplace measure can be obtained from the m-estimate when m is set to 2 and the *a priori* probability is assumed to be uniform. It should be noted that the m-estimate generalises the Laplace measure so that rules that cover no instances will be evaluated with the *a priori* probability instead of the value 1/2, which is more flexible and convenient.

The fuzzy variant of the m-estimate can be defined as follows:

$$M(R) = \frac{M(A \cap C) + k * P/(P+N)}{M(A) + k} = \frac{\sum_{I \in R_\alpha(P)} \mu_R(I) + k * P/(P+N)}{\sum_{I \in R_\alpha(T)} \mu_R(I) + k} \tag{17}$$

3.8   *H* Measure

This measure is applied in RULES-5 [3]. It is the product of the accuracy (first part) and generality (second part) of a rule.

$$H(R) = \sqrt{\frac{p+n}{P+N}} \left(2 - 2\sqrt{\frac{p}{p+n} \cdot \frac{P}{P+N}} - 2\sqrt{(1 - \frac{p}{p+n})(1 - \frac{P}{P+N})} \right) \tag{18}$$

The H measure can be fuzzified as follows:

$$
\begin{aligned}
H(R) &= \sqrt{\frac{M(A)}{P+N}} \left(2 - 2\sqrt{\frac{M(A \cap C)}{M(A)} \cdot \frac{P}{P+N}} - 2\sqrt{(1 - \frac{M(A \cap C)}{M(A)})(1 - \frac{P}{P+N})} \right) \\
&= \sqrt{\frac{\sum_{I \in R_\alpha(T)} \mu_R(I)}{P+N}} \left(2 - 2\sqrt{\frac{\sum_{I \in R_\alpha(P)} \mu_R(I)}{\sum_{I \in R_\alpha(T)} \mu_R(I)} \cdot \frac{P}{P+N}} - 2\sqrt{(1 - \frac{\sum_{I \in R_\alpha(P)} \mu_R(I)}{\sum_{I \in R_\alpha(T)} \mu_R(I)})(1 - \frac{P}{P+N})} \right)
\end{aligned}
\tag{19}
$$

3.9   AQ18 Measure

This measure was introduced in AQ18 [2] and it aims to combine completeness, consistency and consistency gain. This is done by allowing changes in the relative importance of completeness (first part) or consistency gain (second part) and also by changing the value of the parameter $w \in [0, 1]$.

$$Q(R) = \left(\frac{p}{P}\right)^w \cdot \left(\left(\frac{p}{p+n} - \frac{P}{P+N}\right) \cdot \frac{P+N}{N} \right)^{(1-w)} \tag{20}$$

The fuzzy version of the AQ18 measure can be expressed as:

$$
\begin{aligned}
Q(R) &= \left(\frac{M(A \cap C)}{P}\right)^w \cdot \left(\left(\frac{M(A \cap C)}{M(A)} - \frac{P}{P+N}\right) \cdot \frac{P+N}{N} \right)^{(1-w)} \\
&= \left(\frac{\sum_{I \in R_\alpha(P)} \mu_R(I)}{P}\right)^w \cdot \left(\left(\frac{\sum_{I \in R_\alpha(P)} \mu_R(I)}{\sum_{I \in R_\alpha(T)} \mu_R(I)} - \frac{P}{P+N}\right) \cdot \frac{P+N}{N} \right)^{(1-w)}
\end{aligned}
\tag{21}
$$

The aforementioned evaluation measures have been developed alongside specific algorithms and their performances have not been compared to other metrics when applied to the same rule induction algorithm. As part of this work, the performance of these measures when used in the FuzzyRULES algorithm is evaluated experimentally in the following section.

4 Experimental Evaluation

This section presents an empirical evaluation of the nine fuzzy heuristic evaluation measures discussed in the previous section. Experimental tests were carried out using the FuzzyRULES algorithm, without applying any pruning procedures because such post processing could mask the real effect of using one or another heuristic. Three criteria were used to evaluate the results, namely, classification accuracy, rule set complexity, and the number of rules examined to obtain the rule set. The complexity of a rule set is measured by the total number of conditions in that rule set. Tests were performed on 30 data sets from the UCI repository of machine learning databases [19]. The selected data sets either have only continuous attributes or a mixture of nominal and continuous attributes. The hold-out approach was used to partition the data into training and test data [20]. FuzzyRULES was run with the default settings, and the default value of 0.5 was used for the parameter w of the AQ18 measure.

Table 1 shows the classification accuracies obtained with each of the nine evaluation measures. Bold numbers indicate the best performance for a specific data set among the tested measures. In the last row, the total performance over all data sets is shown. A number of results are notable. First, the accuracy obtained with the m-estimate measure over all the data sets was in total higher than that produced with all the other measures. Also, the m-estimate measure produced the best classification results for 14 out of the 30 data sets. The Laplace and information content measures had a very similar total accuracy, but the Laplace measure had the best results overall for a higher number of data sets. The entropy and purity measures yielded the next best total accuracy, followed by the H and AQ18 measures. The accuracy and information gain measures obtained the lowest total accuracy. Second, every evaluation measure obtained the best results overall for some data sets, and the best performing measures had a notable worse performance for some other data sets. This suggests that there will not be a universal solution to all learning problems. The best result is obtained by choosing the evaluation measure that best fits the requirements of a particular learning problem.

Table 1. Classification accuracies for each evaluation measure when used in FuzzyRULES.

Data set name	Purity	Entropy	Information content	Information gain	Accuracy	Laplace	m-estimate	H measure	AQ18
Abalone	23.0	24.2	23.0	15.8	21.6	22.9	23.9	**25.0**	18.8
Adult	**82.0**	79.4	81.9	79.8	77.1	81.9	81.8	79.4	80.1
Anneal	99.0	87.3	**99.3**	82.3	84.7	97.7	97.7	96.3	84.7
Australian	80.4	**87.0**	83.0	86.5	86.5	85.7	85.2	80.3	86.5
Auto	**72.5**	65.2	68.1	62.5	59.4	59.4	65.2	62.9	44.9
Balance-scale	64.6	64.6	64.6	56.9	66.0	64.6	**69.6**	65.0	66.0
Breast	**95.3**	94.8	94.0	92.7	92.7	92.3	94.3	91.9	92.7
Cleve	75.2	74.3	75.2	74.3	79.2	**82.2**	**82.2**	77.3	72.3
Crx	74.0	81.0	75.0	**83.0**	**83.0**	74.5	81.0	80.0	**83.0**
Diabetes	64.5	75.0	64.5	72.3	69.5	64.5	**75.2**	68.2	74.6
German	70.3	71.2	72.1	69.4	66.0	70.0	**75.6**	73.1	67.9
German-organisation	68.5	71.8	66.7	70.9	66.0	69.4	**76.4**	67.0	71.5
Glass	52.8	51.4	58.3	49.4	58.3	50.0	**64.7**	63.9	58.3
Glass2	78.2	**83.6**	76.4	76.4	76.4	**83.6**	**83.6**	72.7	81.5
Heart-disease	73.3	67.8	76.7	73.3	72.2	**80.0**	78.9	73.3	75.6
Heart-Hungarian	73.5	76.5	**98.5**	78.6	74.5	76.5	78.6	72.4	**75.5**
Hepatitis	80.8	82.7	78.8	73.1	**88.5**	86.5	84.8	82.7	**88.5**
Horse-colic	70.6	82.4	70.6	65.0	79.4	76.5	**83.5**	76.2	80.9
Hypothyroid	**96.0**	98.1	96.0	**98.8**	97.0	98.4	97.9	94.8	98.7
Ionosphere	93.2	88.5	92.3	87.8	95.3	92.3	92.3	88.9	**95.7**
Iris	96.0	94.0	**96.0**	94.0	94.0	**96.0**	**96.0**	96.0	**96.0**
Letter	80.5	76.4	82.2	53.2	71.1	**82.1**	66.1	60.7	58.3
Lymphography	74.0	**84.0**	78.0	56.0	68.0	78.0	76.0	78.0	64.0
Satimage	81.2	80.6	83.2	60.4	76.3	**86.0**	84.0	81.8	67.1
Segment	80.9	82.1	87.7	77.4	80.8	84.8	**89.5**	88.4	79.0
Shuttle	97.6	95.4	95.9	94.8	94.8	**98.4**	**98.4**	95.9	94.8
Sick-euthyroid	92.0	90.4	91.8	90.9	9.6	91.9	**96.4**	91.6	90.4
Sonar	70.0	70.0	**80.0**	74.3	77.1	80.0	**80.0**	68.6	61.4
Tokyo	91.5	91.3	92.3	91.9	87.3	**92.5**	92.1	91.4	90.8
Vehicle	63.1	48.3	63.5	51.7	61.3	64.5	**66.0**	61.7	53.2
Total	2314.4	2319.2	2365.6	2193.2	2213.8	2363.0	**2416.8**	2305.2	2252.8

Table 2 shows the total number of conditions generated with each of the evaluation measures. Bold numbers indicate the smallest number of conditions per rule set for a particular data set. The information gain measure produced significantly fewer conditions in total than the other measures. In addition, it obtained the smallest rule sets for 29 out of the 30 data sets. However, the over-general rule sets created resulted in a deteriorated classification accuracy for most data sets. The AQ18 measure also found simple rule sets but again had poor accuracy performance. The accuracy, m-estimate, H, entropy and Laplace measures created general rules without sacrificing accuracy for most data sets. These measures prefer rules covering more instances, which often helps the learning algorithm to prevent overfitting. The purity and information content measures generated the most complex rule sets, which might be an indication of overfitting. This is most likely due to that these measures prefer more consistent rules and do not favour rules with high coverage.

Table 2. Total number of conditions for each evaluation measure when used in FuzzyRULES.

Data set name	Purity	Entropy	Information content	Information gain	Accuracy	Laplace	m-estimate	H measure	AQ18
Abalone	105	56	103	**12**	325	108	53	36	15
Adult	814	137	1134	8	**7**	286	128	179	30
Anneal	60	24	47	**6**	33	49	39	36	63
Australian	222	6	207	2	**2**	126	118	52	**2**
Auto	69	59	62	7	32	62	48	67	39
Balance-scale	33	18	33	2	11	33	29	30	14
Breast	121	9	92	3	12	30	27	22	12
Cleve	103	30	78	5	10	52	52	47	17
Crx	173	17	159	5	13	141	151	50	13
Diabetes German	50	34	48	**6 7**	9	39	32	26	9
German-organisation	536	338	471	**4**	175	222	219	312	45
Glass	142	79	124	7	34	104	60	96	14
Glass2	59	11	48	**4**	6	20	20	27	10
Heart-disease	136	16	63	3	6	106	60	47	15
Heart-Hungarian	82	4	72	2	12	42	38	34	16
Hepatitis	65	13	46	4	12	27	24	51	24
Horse-colic	135	16	104	3	8	121	107	134	13
Hypothyroid	89	20	61	5	25	52	49	7	18
Ionosphere	43	9	34	2	13	32	29	41	28
Iris	9	**3**	**5**	3	**3**	5	5	5	5
Letter	7863	3248	5434	**31**	1997	2573	1073	1307	517
Lymphography	76	17	61	7	9	54	29	63	17
Satimage	1844	395	1442	**24**	220	816	521	678	128
Segment	621	412	499	**13**	192	286	121	372	68
Shuttle	419	61	846	**19**	36	151	98	76	30
Sick-euthyroid	163	18	162	**9**	31	76	53	21	11
Sonar	49	15	34	2	16	32	31	26	17
Tokyo	89	13	74	**9**	15	82	55	77	28
Vehicle	406	204	402	**9**	169	360	158	150	61
Total	14978	5407	12297	**223**	3506	6282	3600	4410	1320

Table 3 presents the size of the search space examined for each evaluation measure. The bold numbers indicate the smallest search per data set. The number of rules explored during the search process is often directly linked to the rule set complexity. Therefore, the fewer and more general rules created by the information gain measure made it to examine the least number of rules. It investigated 98% less rules than the purity method, which inspected the most rules. The amount of search required by the other evaluation measures is also related to the rule set complexity of these measures.

Table 3. Total number of rules explored for each evaluation measure when used in FuzzyRULES.

Data set name	Purity	Entropy	Information content	Information gain	Accuracy	Laplace	m-estimate	H measure	AQ18
Abalone	1527	449	1500	**231**	3882	1560	936	752	424
Adult	38136	2920	30074	**643**	288	12639	14091	10543	1197
Anneal	2669	955	2089	**1320**	1898	2944	2310	2715	3659
Australian	4843	116	4393	**64**	53	3198	2938	2421	95
Auto	3195	2819	2812	**657**	1321	2802	2149	3507	1798
Balance-scale	179	92	179	**28**	59	177	161	157	67
Breast	1736	85	1216	**49**	127	400	364	239	135
Cleve	2683	730	2089	**174**	227	1539	1531	1529	352
Crx	5998	564	5619	**326**	333	4120	4496	1092	450
Diabetes	558	357	526	**181**	230	497	426	384	241
German	18651	6245	13952	**1156**	3836	8343	8475	12666	3210
German-organisation	28988	9890	25034	**934**	11778	14123	13134	17819	4644
Glass	2327	1434	2053	**198**	568	1807	977	1884	278
Glass2	753	134	636	**103**	103	291	294	449	143
Heart-disease	2390	395	1659	**101**	138	1559	1626	1595	329
Heart-Hungarian	1787	48	1671	**71**	181	1074	987	1084	406
Hepatitis	2186	406	1562	**207**	257	576	468	1817	653
Horse-colic	7338	540	6353	**216**	285	5841	4974	6370	560
Hypothyroid	2625	821	1948	964	1059	1533	1431	**399**	802
Ionosphere	2578	266	2029	**185**	687	1328	1207	1399	1098
Iris	50	**12**	30	12	**12**	23	23	23	18
Letter	326494	162820	241125	**2445**	114189	192745	77979	101101	19991
Lymphography	2678	531	2119	369	**325**	1947	687	2411	665
Satimage	163604	60538	128661	**1676**	14699	50811	37315	46844	9496
Segment	14062	10600	12389	**507**	5855	7077	4247	9308	2256
Shuttle	5548	755	11391	**165**	403	2412	1420	1033	270
Sick-euthyroid	4911	1666	4868	**963**	1655	3405	2849	1496	1046
Sonar	2906	1250	1292	**181**	735	1144	1038	979	849
Tokyo	7572	682	6633	**581**	629	5764	3231	5201	1387
Vehicle	14091	9633	14079	**705**	5555	13854	7082	8995	2209
Total	673063	277753	529981	**15412**	171367	345533	198846	246212	58728

5   Conclusions and Future Work

This paper has examined the influence of different crisp evaluation metrics and analysed their role during the rule forming process. It has also proposed fuzzy variants of these measures and examined their performance when used in a recently developed fuzzy rule induction algorithm. The paper has demonstrated the strong effect of the evaluation measures on the performance of the learning algorithm. Evaluation measures that prefer more general over more specific rules helped the learning algorithm to determine the correct models for many data sets. However, over-generalisation may also deteriorate performance in problems that require a very specific concept description. The performance of additional evaluation measures, in particular those balancing the complexity and the accuracy of a particular induced model, could be studied on more data sets and other fuzzy rule induction algorithms.

Acknowledgements. The author wishes to thank the Department of Engineering, Design and Mathematics, University of the West of England for providing a good environment, facilities and financial means to complete this paper.

References

1. Clark, P., Boswell, R.: Rule induction with CN2: some recent improvements. In: 5th European Conference on Artificial Intelligence, Porto, Portugal, pp. 151–163 (1991)
2. Michalski, R.S., Kaufman, K.A.: A measure of description quality for data mining and its implementation in the AQ18 learning system. In: ICSC Symposium on Advances in Intelligent Data Analysis, The Rochester Institute of Technology, USA, pp. 22–25 (1999)
3. Pham, D.T., Bigot, S., Dimov, S.S.: RULES-5: a rule induction algorithm for problems involving continuous attributes. Proc. Inst. Mech. Eng. Part C J. Mech. Eng. Sci. **217**(12), 1273–1286 (2003)
4. Pham, D.T., Afify, A.A.: SRI: a scalable rule induction algorithm. Proc. Inst. Mech. Eng. Part C J. Mech. Eng. Sci. **220**(5), 537–552 (2006)
5. Hühn, J., Hüllermeier, E.: FURIA: an algorithm for unordered fuzzy rule induction. Data Min. Knowl. Discov. **19**, 293–319 (2009)
6. Afify, A.A.: A novel algorithm for fuzzy rule induction in data mining. Proc. Inst. Mech. Eng. Part C J. Mech. Eng. Sci. **228**(5), 877–895 (2014)
7. Afify, A.A.: A fuzzy rule induction algorithm for discovering classification rules. J. Intell. Fuzzy Syst. **30**(6), 3067–3085 (2016)
8. Pham, D.T., Afify, A.A.: RULES-6: a simple rule induction algorithm for handling large data sets. Proc. Inst. Mech. Eng. Part C J. Mech. Eng. Sci. **219**(10), 1119–1137 (2005)
9. Fürnkranz, J., Flach, P.A.: An analysis of rule evaluation metrics. In: 20th International Conference on Machine Learning, Washington, DC, USA, pp. 202–209 (2003)
10. van Zyl, J., Cloete, I.: Heuristic functions for learning fuzzy conjunctive rules. In: IEEE International Conference on Systems, Man and Cybernetics, The Hague, The Netherlands, pp. 2332–2337 (2004)
11. Klir, G.J., Yuan, B.: Fuzzy Sets and Fuzzy Logic: Theory and Applications. Prentice-Hall, Upper Saddle River (1995)
12. Pagallo, G., Haussler, D.: Boolean feature discovery in empirical learning. Mach. Learn. **3**, 71–99 (1990)
13. Weiss, S., Indurkhya, N.: Reduced complexity rule induction. In: 12th International Joint Conference on Artificial Intelligence, Sydney, Australia, pp. 678–684 (1991)
14. Cendrowska, J.: PRISM: an algorithm for inducing modular rules. Int. J. Man-Mach. Stud. **27**, 349–370 (1987)
15. Clark, P., Niblett, T.: The CN2 induction algorithm. Mach. Learn. **3**, 261–284 (1989)
16. Quinlan, J.R.: Learning logical definitions from relations. Mach. Learn. **5**, 239–266 (1990)
17. Fürnkranz, J., Widmer, G.: Incremental reduced error pruning. In: 11th International Conference on Machine Learning, New Brunswick, NJ, USA, pp. 70–77 (1994)
18. Cestnik, B.: Estimating probabilities: a crucial task in machine learning. In: 3rd European Conference on Artificial Intelligence, Stockholm, Sweden, pp. 147–149 (1990)
19. Blake, C.L., Merz, C.J.: UCI Repository of Machine Learning Databases. http://www.ics.uci.edu/~mlearn/MLRepository.html. Accessed 1 June 2017
20. Efron, B., Tibshirani, R.: An Introduction to the Bootstrap. Chapman & Hall, Boca Raton (1993)

A Visual Quality Index for Fuzzy C-Means

Aybüke Öztürk$^{(\boxtimes)}$, Stéphane Lallich, and Jérôme Darmont

Université de Lyon, Lyon 2, ERIC EA 3083 5 avenue
Pierre Mendès France, 69676 Bron Cedex, France
{aybuke.ozturk,stephane.lallich,jerome.darmont}@univ-lyon2.fr

Abstract. Cluster analysis is widely used in the areas of machine learning and data mining. Fuzzy clustering is a particular method that considers that a data point can belong to more than one cluster. Fuzzy clustering helps obtain flexible clusters, as needed in such applications as text categorization. The performance of a clustering algorithm critically depends on the number of clusters, and estimating the optimal number of clusters is a challenging task. Quality indices help estimate the optimal number of clusters. However, there is no quality index that can obtain an accurate number of clusters for different datasets. Thence, in this paper, we propose a new cluster quality index associated with a visual, graph-based solution that helps choose the optimal number of clusters in fuzzy partitions. Moreover, we validate our theoretical results through extensive comparison experiments against state-of-the-art quality indices on a variety of numerical real-world and artificial datasets.

Keywords: Fuzzy clustering · Fuzzy C-Means · Quality indices
Visual index · Elbow Rule

1 Introduction

Clustering refers to the assignment of unlabeled data points into clusters (groups) so that the points belonging to the same cluster are more similar to each other than those within different clusters. There are various types of clustering strategies, including crisp and fuzzy clustering. In crisp (or hard) clustering, a data point can belong to one and only one cluster, while in fuzzy clustering [1], a data point can belong to several clusters. Fuzzy clustering is very useful in many applications, e.g., the text categorization of various news into different clusters: a science, a business, and a sport cluster; where an article containing the keyword "gold" could belong to all three clusters. Furthermore, it is also possible to open discussions with domain experts when using fuzzy clustering.

Clustering algorithms behave differently for different reasons. The first reason relates to dataset features such as geometry and the density distribution of clusters. The second reason is the choice of input parameters such as the fuzziness

L. Iliadis et al. (Eds.): AIAI 2018, IFIP AICT 519, pp. 546–555, 2018.
https://doi.org/10.1007/978-3-319-92007-8_46

coefficient m ($m = 1$ indicating that clustering is crisp and $m > 1$ that clustering becomes fuzzy).

These parameters all affect the quality of clustering. To study how the choice of parameters impacts clustering quality, we need a quality criterion. For instance, when the dataset is well separated and has only two variables, a scatter plot can help determine the number of clusters. However, when the dataset has more than two variables, a good quality index is needed to compare various cluster configurations and choose the appropriate number of clusters.

Achieving a good clustering involves both minimizing intra-cluster distance (compactness) and maximizing inter-cluster distance (separability). A common issue in this process is that clusters are split up while they could be more compact. Many cluster quality indices have been proposed to address this problem for hard and fuzzy clustering, but none of them is always highly efficient [2].

Moreover, there is no real-life golden standard for clustering analysis, since various experts may have different points of views about the same data and express different constraints on the number and size of clusters. Thanks to a visual index, different solutions can be presented with respect to the data. Thus, experts can make a trade-off between their opinion and the best local solutions proposed by the visual index.

Hence, in this paper, we first review existing quality indices that are well-suited to fuzzy clustering, such as [3–8]. Then, we propose an innovative, visual quality index for the well-known Fuzzy C-Means (FCM) method. Moreover, we compare our proposal with state-of-the-art quality indices from the literature on several numerical real-world and artificial datasets.

The remainder of this paper is organized as follows. Section 2 recalls the principles of fuzzy clustering. Section 3 surveys quality indices for fuzzy clustering. Section 4 details our visual quality index. Section 5 reports on the experimental comparison of our quality index against existing ones on different datasets. Finally, we conclude this paper and provide research perspectives in Sect. 6.

2 Principles of Fuzzy Clustering

Fuzzy inertia is a core measure in fuzzy clustering. Fuzzy inertia FI (Eq. 1) is composed of fuzzy within-inertia FW (Eq. 2) and fuzzy between-inertia FB (Eq. 3). Membership coefficients u_{ik} of data point i to cluster k are usually stored in a membership matrix U that is used to calculate FW, FB and FI. Note that $FI = FW + FB$. Moreover, FI is not constant because it depends on u_{ik}. When FW changes, the values of FI and FB also change.

$$FI = \sum_{i=1}^{n} \sum_{k=1}^{K} u_{ik}^{m} d^2(x_i, \overline{x}) \tag{1}$$

$$FW = \sum_{i=1}^{n} \sum_{k=1}^{K} u_{ik}^{m} d^2(x_i, c_k) \tag{2}$$

$$FB = \sum_{i=1}^{n}\sum_{k=1}^{K} u_{ik}^{m} d^2(c_k, \bar{x}) \tag{3}$$

where n is the number of instances, K is the number of clusters, m is the fuzziness coefficient (by default, $m = 2$), c_k is the center of the kth cluster $\forall 1 \le k \le K$, $\bar{x}$ is the grand mean (the arithmetic mean of all data – Eq. 4), and function $d^2()$ computes the squared Euclidean distance.

$$\bar{x} = \frac{1}{n}\sum_{i=1}^{n} x_i \tag{4}$$

FCM is a common method for fuzzy clustering that adapts the principle of the K-Means algorithm [9]. FCM, proposed by [10] and extended by [11], applies on numerical data. Since numerical data are the most common case, we choose to experiment our proposals with FCM.

The aim of the FCM algorithm is to minimize FW. It starts by choosing K data points as initial centroids of the clusters. Then, membership matrix values u_{ik} (Eq. 5) are assigned to each data point in the dataset. Centroids of clusters c_k are updated based on Eq. 6 until a termination criterion is reached successfully. In FCM, this criterion can be a fixed number of iterations t, e.g., $t = 100$. Alternatively, a threshold ϵ can be used, e.g., $\epsilon = 0.0001$. Then, the algorithm stops when $FW_{K+1}/|FW_{K+1} - FW_K| < \epsilon$.

$$u_{ik} = \frac{1}{\sum_{j=1}^{K}\left(\frac{\|x_i - c_k\|^2}{\|x_i - c_j\|^2}\right)^{\frac{1}{m-1}}} \tag{5}$$

$$c_k = \frac{\sum_{i=1}^{n} u_{ik}^{m} x_i}{\sum_{i=1}^{n} u_{ik}^{m}} \tag{6}$$

3   Fuzzy Clustering Quality Indices

According to Wang et al. [12], there are two groups of quality indices. Quality indices in the first group are based only on membership values. They notably include partition coefficient index V_{PC} [3] (Eq. 7; $\frac{1}{K} \le V_{PC} \le 1$; to be maximized) and Chen and Linkens' index V_{CL} [4] (Eq. 8; $0 \le V_{CL} \le 1$; to be maximized). V_{CL} takes into consideration both compactness (first term of V_{CL}) and separability (second term of V_{CL}).

$$V_{PC} = \frac{1}{n}\sum_{i=1}^{n}\sum_{k=1}^{K} u_{ik}^{2} \tag{7}$$

$$V_{CL} = \frac{1}{n}\sum_{i=1}^{n} max_k(u_{ik}) - \frac{1}{c}\sum_{k=1}^{K-1}\sum_{j=k+1}^{K}\left[\frac{1}{n}\sum_{i=1}^{n} min(u_{ik}, u_{ij})\right], \tag{8}$$

where $c = \sum_{k=1}^{K-1} k$.

Quality indices in the second group associate membership values to cluster centers and data. They include an adaptation of the Ratio index V_{FRatio} to fuzzy clustering [5] (Eq. 9; $0 \leq V_{FRatio} \leq +\infty$; to be maximized), Fukuyama and Sugeno's index V_{FS} [6] (Eq. 10; $-FI \leq V_{FS} \leq FI$; to be minimized), and Xie and Beni's index V_{XB} [7,13] (Eq. 11; $0 \leq V_{XB} \leq FI/n * min\|x_j - v_k\|^2$; to be minimized).

$$V_{FRatio} = FB/FW \tag{9}$$

$$V_{FS} = FW - FB \tag{10}$$

$$V_{XB} = \frac{\sum_{k=1}^{K} \sum_{i=1}^{n} u_{ik}^m \|x_i - v_k\|^2}{n * min_{j,k}\|v_j - v_k\|^2} \tag{11}$$

When the number of clusters increases, the value of quality indices mechanically increases, too. Then, the important question is: how useful is the addition of a new cluster? To answer this question, the most common solutions are penalization and the Elbow Rule [14].

The first way to penalize a quality index is to multiply it by a quantity that diminishes the index when the number of clusters increases. In this case, the main difficulty is to choose the penalty. For instance, the penalized version of V_{FRatio} is Calinski's V_{FCH} [5] (Eq. 12; $0 \leq V_{FCH} \leq +\infty$; to be maximized), where the penalty is based on both the number of clusters and data points.

$$V_{FCH} = \frac{FB/(K-1)}{FW/(n-K)} = \frac{n-K}{K-1}\frac{FB}{FW} \tag{12}$$

The second way to penalize a quality index is to evaluate index evolution relatively to the number of clusters, by considering the curve of the index' successive values. The most appropriate value of K can be determined visually by help of the Elbow Rule or algebraic calculation [15].

To construct a visual determination of the Elbow Rule, K is represented on the horizontal axis and the considered quality index on the vertical axis. Then, we look for the value of K where there is a change in the curve's concavity. This change represents the optimal number of clusters K. To construct an algebraic determination, let i_K being the index value for K clusters. The variation of i_K before K and after K are compared. In case of a positive Elbow, the second difference $min_K((i_{K+1} - i_K) - (i_K - i_{K-1}))$ is minimized. Yet, since the values before K and after K are used for calculation, the Elbow Rule can be applied to more than two clusters only.

Among all the above-stated quality indices, there is no single quality index that gives the best result for any dataset. Thus, there is room for a new quality index that is specifically tailored for fuzzy validation and helps the user choose the value of K.

4   An Index Associated with a Visual Solution

Building a new quality index, we first consider FW to evaluate compactness and FB to evaluate separability. We can choose to calculate either $FB - FW$, which is similar to V_{FS} except for the sign, or $FB \div FW$, which is similar to V_{FRatio}. Unfortunately, $FI = FB + FW$ is not constant and $FB - FW \in [-FI, +FI]$. To take this particularity of fuzzy clustering into account, we propose to standardize $FB - FW$ by considering the *Standardized Fuzzy Difference SFD* $= (FB - FW) \div FI$ instead. Then, $SFD \in [-1, +1]$.

Adding a new cluster often improves clustering quality mechanically. Thus, many authors penalize the quality index with respect to K (the smaller n is, the greater the penalty), e.g., V_{FCH} (Sect. 3). To obtain a penalized index, SFD is first linearly transformed in an index belonging to $[0, 1]$, obtaining the *Transformed Standardized Fuzzy Difference TSFD* (Eq. 13; $TSFD \in [0, 1]$; to be maximized). Finally, by penalizing $TSFD$ as V_{FCH}, we obtain the *Penalized Standardized Fuzzy Difference PSFD* (Eq. 14; $PSFD \in [0, (n - K)/(K - 1)]$; to be maximized).

$$TSFD = \frac{1 + SFD}{2} = \frac{FB}{FI} \tag{13}$$

$$PSFD = TSFD * \frac{n - K}{K - 1} = \frac{FB - FW}{FI} * \frac{n - K}{K - 1} \tag{14}$$

Instead of penalizing the quality index, another solution is to visualize the search for the best number of clusters K. First solution is to apply the Elbow Rule to $TSFD$. $TSFD$ is plotted with respect to K in Fig. 1(a). The drawback of this method is that the horizontal axis corresponds to an arithmetic scale of K values, which is not satisfying. To fix this problem, we suggest to plot FB with respect to FI, which we call *Visual TSFD*. Our aim is not to give an automatic solution, but to help the user visually choose the most appropriate K value. The visualization we propose is shown in Fig. 1(b), where the blue line plots $TSFD$ with respect to K, the full red line is the diagonal that corresponds to the best solutions ($FB = FI$) such that $TSFD = 1$, and the dashed red line connects the origin to each point associated with K values. The smaller the angle between the full red line and the dashed red line, the better is the solution. As the value of K increases, the angle between the dashed red line and the diagonal decreases. Then, we choose the value of K beyond which the decrease becomes negligible. This value is considered as the optimal number of clusters. For example, in Fig. 1(b), a first solution could be $K = 4$, a better solution $K = 6$, and it is not very interesting to consider $K > 6$.

5   Experimental Validation

In this section, we compare our proposals $TSFD$, $PSFD$, *Visual TSFD* and the use of the Elbow Rule to state-of-the-art clustering quality indices for FCM-like clustering algorithms, i.e., V_{PC}, V_{CL}, V_{FCH}, V_{FS} and V_{XB} (Sect. 3).

In our experiments, the FCM algorithm is parameterized with its default settings: termination criterion $\epsilon = 0.0001$ and default fuzziness coefficient $m = 2$. All clustering quality indices are coded in Python version 2.7.4.

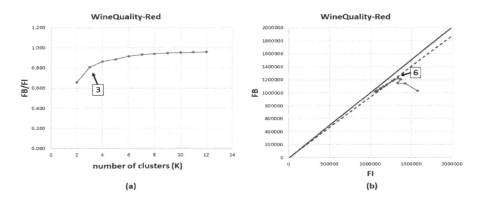

Fig. 1. Comparison of Elbow Rule (a) and *Visual TSFD* (b) on the WineQuality-Red dataset (Table 1)

5.1 Datasets

Quality indices are compared on ten real-life datasets (Table 1; IDs 1–10) from the UCI Machine Learning Repository[1] and seven artificial datasets (Table 1; IDs 11–17). In real-life datasets, the true number of clusters is assimilated to the number of labels. Although using the number of labels as the number of clusters is debatable, it is acceptable if the set of descriptive variables explains the labels well. In artificial datasets, the number of clusters is known by construction. Moreover, we created new artificial datasets by introducing overlapping and noise to some of the existing datasets, such as E1071-3 [16], Ruspini [1] and E1071-5 [16] (Table 1; IDs 12–14). To create a new dataset, new data points are introduced, and each must be labeled. To obtain a dataset with overlapping, we modify the construction of the E1071 artificial datasets [16]. In the original datasets, there are three or five clusters of equal size (50). Cluster i is generated according to a Gaussian distribution $N(i; 0.3)$. To increase overlapping in the three clusters while retaining the same cluster size, we only change the standard deviation from 0.3 to 0.4. Then, there is no labeling problem. To introduce noise in a dataset, we add in each cluster noisy points generated by a Gaussian variable around each label gravity center. Noisy data are often generated by distributions with positive skewness. For example, in a two-dimensional dataset, for each label, we add points that are far away from the corresponding gravity center, especially on the right-hand side, which generally contains the most points. Then, we draw a random number r between 0 and 1. If $r \leq 0.25$, the point is attributed to the left-hand side. Otherwise, the point is attributed to the right-hand side. This method helps obtain noisy data that are $^1/_4$ times smaller and $^3/_4$ times greater, respectively, than the expected value for the considered label. This process is applied to the Ruspini dataset [1].

---

[1] http://archive.ics.uci.edu/ml/.

5.2 Experimental Results

In our experiments, all validation indices (Sects. 3 and 4) are applied on all the datasets from Table 1. Moreover, since presenting all the results would take too much space, we retain only the best results for each index (even excluding *PSFD*).

Table 1. Quality Indices Experiment Results with Different Datasets

ID	Datasets	# of data points	# of clusters	V_{PC}	V_{CL}	FB	V_{FCH}	V_{FS}	V_{XB}	Elbow V_{TSFD}	Visual V_{TSFD}
1	Wine	178	3	2	2	8	12	8	2	**3**	5
2	Iris	150	3	2	2	**3**	**3**	**3**	2	**3**	**3**
3	Seeds	210	3	2	**3**	**3**	**3**	**3**	2	**3**	**3**
4	Glass	214	6	2	2	12	12	12	2	4	5,7
5	Vehicle	846	4	2	2	2	2	5	2	3	4,5
6	Segmentation	2310	7	2	4	4	4	12	12	3	**7,8**
7	Movement Libras	360	15	2	18	16	16	18	2	14	14,16
8	Ecoli	336	8	2	3	3	3	12	3	3	3,7
9	Yeast	1484	10	2	2	5	2	12	2	4	7,8
10	WineQuality-Red	1599	6	2	2	**6**	7	**6**	2	3	**6**
11	Bensaid [17]	49	3	**3**	**3**	9	11	11	**3**	**3**	5
12	E1071-3 [16]	150	3	**3**	**3**	**3**	**3**	**3**	**3**	**3**	**3**
13	Ruspini [1]	75	4	**4**	**4**	**4**	**4**	**4**	**4**	3	**4**
14	E1071-5 [16]	250	5	2	**5**	4	**5**	**5**	2	3	**5**
15	E1071-3- overlapped	150	3	2	**3**	**3**	2	**3**	2	**3**	**3**
16	Ruspini_noised	95	4	**4**	12	**4**	**4**	**4**	**4**	**4**	**4**
17	E1071-5- overlapped	250	5	2	2	4	**5**	4	2	3	**5**
# of wins for real-life datasets				0	1	3	2	3	0	3	**5**
# of wins for artificial datasets				4	5	4	5	5	4	4	**6**
Total # of wins				4	6	7	7	8	4	7	**11**

As shown in Table 1, it is more difficult to predict an appropriate number of clusters for real-life datasets than for artificial datasets. Considering all indices, the average rate of success is indeed 21% in the case of real data, against 66% in the case of artificial data. Whatever the type of data, *Visual TSFD* outperforms the other indices, with 5 wins out of 10 in the case of real datasets, and 6 wins out of 7 in the case of artificial datasets. The worst results are obtained with V_{PC} and V_{XB} (0/10 and 4/7 wins each). The other indices achieve intermediary results. In addition, when the value given by *Visual TSFD* is erroneous, it is quite close to the expected K, in contrast to V_{FS}, our closest competitor (Table 1; Wine, Glass, Segmentation, Ecoli and Bensaid). For example, the optimal number of clusters should be 6 for the Glass dataset. $V_{FS} = 12$, *Visual TSFD*'s results are 5 and 7. Furthermore, we compare in Figs. 2 and 3 *Visual TSFD* and the plot obtained with the Elbow Rule (which is labeled Elbow *TSFD*) with respect to K, on a sample of both real-life and artificial datasets bearing different characteristics, i.e., Glass, Vehicle, Ecoli, Ruspini, Ruspini_noised and E1071-5-overlapped

(Table 1). As is clearly visible from Figs. 2 and 3, *Visual TSFD* gives a better visual idea than Elbow *TSFD*. Elbow *TSFD* indeed highlights K values of 3 or 4, while the *TFSD* blue plot systematically indicates larger K values.

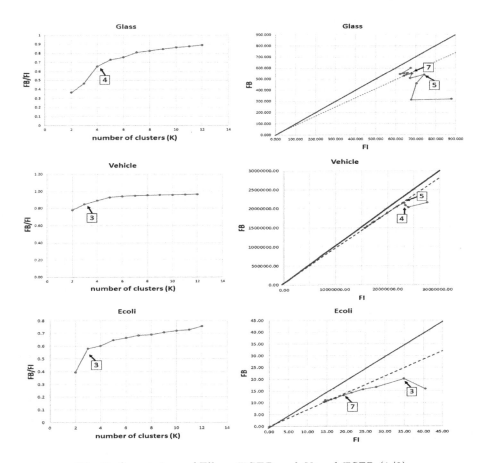

Fig. 2. Comparison of Elbow *TSFD* and *Visual TSFD* (1/2)

Eventually, since our work aims at real-life datasets, there is no ground truth or golden standard for clustering analysis. In such a context, *Visual TSFD* has the advantage of providing options to experts instead of outputting a single K value. This makes our method more flexible that the existing ones in real-life scenarios.

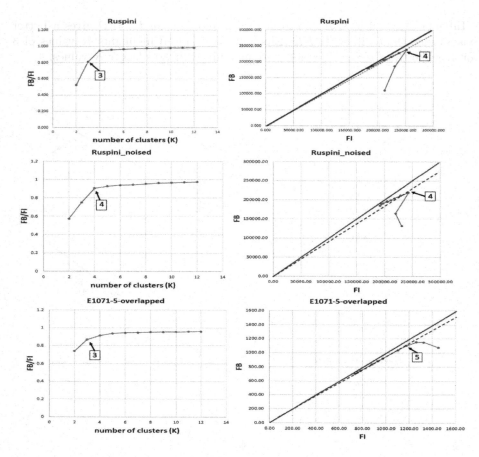

Fig. 3. Comparison of Elbow *TSFD* and *Visual TSFD* (2/2)

6   Conclusion and Perspectives

In this paper, we propose a novel quality index for FCM called *Visual TSFD*, which provides an overview of fuzzy clustering with respect to the number of clusters. We compare *Visual TSFD* to several clustering quality methods from the literature and experimentally show that it outperforms existing methods on various datasets. Furthermore, *Visual TSFD* can also be used in the case of categorical data with Fuzzy K-Medoids [18]. Thus, *Visual TSFD* allows to deal with heterogeneous datasets, which makes our method a simple but noteworthy contribution, in our opinion. As a result, our next step is to design an ensemble fuzzy clustering method based on *Visual TSFD* that would deal with both numerical and categorical data.

Acknowledgments. This project is supported by the Rhône Alpes Region's ARC 5: "Cultures, Sciences, Sociétés et Médiations" through A. Öztürk's Ph.D. grant.

References

1. Ruspini, E.H.: Numerical methods for fuzzy clustering. Inf. Sci. **2**(3), 319–350 (1970)
2. Pal, N.R., Bezdek, J.C.: Correction to "on cluster validity for the fuzzy c-means model" [correspondence]. IEEE Trans. Fuzzy Syst. **5**(1), 152–153 (1997)
3. Bezdek, J.C.: Cluster validity with fuzzy sets (1973)
4. Chen, M.Y., Linkens, D.A.: Rule-base self-generation and simplification for data-driven fuzzy models. In: The 10th IEEE International Conference on Fuzzy Systems, vol. 1, pp. 424–427. IEEE (2001)
5. Caliński, T., Harabasz, J.: A dendrite method for cluster analysis. Commun. Stat. Theory Methods **3**(1), 1–27 (1974)
6. Fukuyama, Y., Sugeno, M.: A new method of choosing the number of clusters for the fuzzy c-mean method. In: Proceedings of 5th Fuzzy System Symposium, pp. 247–250 (1989)
7. Xie, X.L., Beni, G.: A validity measure for fuzzy clustering. IEEE Trans. Pattern Anal. Mach. Intell. **13**(8), 841–847 (1991)
8. Zhang, D., Ji, M., Yang, J., Zhang, Y., Xie, F.: A novel cluster validity index for fuzzy clustering based on bipartite modularity. Fuzzy Sets Syst. **253**, 122–137 (2014)
9. MacQueen, J., et al.: Some methods for classification and analysis of multivariate observations. In: Proceedings of the Fifth Berkeley Symposium on Mathematical Statistics and Probability, Oakland, CA, USA, vol. 1, pp. 281–297 (1967)
10. Dunn, J.C.: A fuzzy relative of the isodata process and its use in detecting compact well-separated clusters (1973)
11. Bezdek, J.C., Ehrlich, R., Full, W.: FCM: the fuzzy c-means clustering algorithm. Comput. Geosci. **10**(2–3), 191–203 (1984)
12. Wang, W., Zhang, Y.: On fuzzy cluster validity indices. Fuzzy Sets Syst. **158**(19), 2095–2117 (2007)
13. Pal, N.R., Bezdek, J.C.: On cluster validity for the fuzzy c-means model. IEEE Trans. Fuzzy Syst. **3**(3), 370–379 (1995)
14. Cattell, R.B.: The scree test for the number of factors. Multivar. Behav. Res. **1**(2), 245–276 (1966)
15. Dimitriadou, E., Dolničar, S., Weingessel, A.: An examination of indexes for determining the number of clusters in binary data sets. Psychometrika **67**(1), 137–159 (2002)
16. Meyer, D., Dimitriadou, E., Hornik, K., Weingessel, A., Leisch, F., Chang, C.C., Lin, C.C., Meyer, M.D.: Package 'e1071'. Version 1.6-8 (2017)
17. Bensaid, A.M., Hall, L.O., Bezdek, J.C., Clarke, L.P., Silbiger, M.L., Arrington, J.A., Murtagh, R.F.: Validity-guided (re) clustering with applications to image segmentation. IEEE Trans. Fuzzy Syst. **4**(2), 112–123 (1996)
18. Park, H.S., Jun, C.H.: A simple and fast algorithm for k-medoids clustering. Expert Syst. Appl. **36**(2), 3336–3341 (2009)

Evaluation of the Linked Open Data Quality Based on a Fuzzy Logic Model

Esteban Arias Caracas$^{(\boxtimes)}$ (ID), Daniel Fernando Mendoza López$^{(\boxtimes)}$ (ID),
Paulo Alonso Gaona-García$^{(\boxtimes)}$ (ID),
Jhon Francined Herrera Cubides$^{(\boxtimes)}$ (ID),
and Carlos Enrique Montenegro-Marín$^{(\boxtimes)}$ (ID)

Faculty of Engineering, Universidad Distrital Francisco
José de Caldas, Bogotá, Colombia
{eariasc,dfmendozal}@correo.udistrital.edu.co,
{pagaonag,jfherrerac,cmontenegrom}@udistrital.edu.co

Abstract. Linked Open Data has been one of the most widely used online data publishing methods in recent years. This growth means that the quality of this data is required for the benefit of consumers and people who wish to use this data. There are approaches based on classical mathematical models, however, most of these results are too linear; that is, they use conventional evaluators to define both quality aspects and results. In response, a new approach based on fuzzy logic is constructed as an application, which aims to complement and compare traditional models without the need to restrict the quality aspects with which it can be measured. As a methodology, it is done by obtaining data from each dataset through the SPARQL Endpoints provided by high category datasets, classifying them within accessibility and trust dimensions, represented in 4 values: response time, scalability, trustworthiness and timeliness. This analysis is done internally for the values within the accessibility dimension, and externally for the values within the confidence dimension. In this way, it is possible to know or determine a better general quality approximation of the Linked Open Data according to a large number of quality evaluation variables, or even parameterize its own aspects in the model as a complement to the already established models, through the concept of fuzzy logic.

Keywords: Linked open data · Fuzzy logic · Quality measurement

1 Introduction

Linked Open Data has been one of the most recent changes in information in recent years, specifically the way in which data is published, distributed and consumed [1]. These data can easily be uploaded and updated by any type of organization, be it individuals, small groups of people, educational organizations, social networking sites and even government agencies [2]. This upload process in the data management platforms allows an agile data publication, and with few restrictions to the end user, through a simple web interface. On the other hand, if a developer or researcher, it is required to query or download their Dataset, these platforms offer an API interface that interacts with different tools, offers a variety of services, and allows to carry the

© IFIP International Federation for Information Processing 2018
Published by Springer International Publishing AG 2018. All Rights Reserved
L. Iliadis et al. (Eds.): AIAI 2018, IFIP AICT 519, pp. 556–567, 2018.
https://doi.org/10.1007/978-3-319-92007-8_47

required processes [18]. Due to this large number of people, which can upload data to the Web, this model has grown exponentially, from 12 datasets in 2007, to approximately 300 in September 2011, and 9,960 datasets in 2016 [3], taking into account that this number is accumulated from the data catalogs: data.gov, publicdata.eu and data-hub.io [4]; three of the main collections of datasets available to the public.

This growth in Linked Open Data requires methods or tools that can handle this data, to make it "secure, stable, fast and accurate; in other words, have a better quality," [5]. However, quality is a very complex concept; defining what is good quality or not is very subjective and cannot be defined in one way or by a simple judgment [2, 6].

For this reason, many researchers have been looking for methods to complement the quality of the data and administer them for later evaluation. Some of these researchers have created software that can evaluate quality with mathematical procedures, such the quality measurement software, "Luzzu" [6]. However, much of these results are extracted from classical or conventional mathematical models. This causes the calculated quality to possess a certain degree of uncertainty. Therefore, a formulated problem is generated: How to calculate the quality of Linked Open Data in a more precise way, with a considerable amount of quality variables to take into account?

As a new solution to the previous problem, modeling based on fuzzy logic is a solution that can provide the measurement of quality, taking into account the tolerance of intermediate values between conventional evaluators [7]. To cover the complexity of quality, it has approached the classification of quality through dimensions [8]. The proposed model covers 2 dimensions, of which four aspects will be represented in order to evaluate the quality of the linked open data, which will help to show the capacity of the fuzzy logic model when supporting a large number of quality aspects, and obtain a more accurate approximation of quality.

2 Theoretical Background and Related Work

2.1 Quality Dimensions

Datasets can be analyzed and classified through different dimensions, which can be contextual, trustworthy, intrinsic, among others [8]. These dimensions are classifications of groups of different variables or data quality measurement values or variables. For this model, the trust and accessibility dimensions were the most appropriate approaches to analyze the model.

The reason why these dimensions were chosen resides in the importance of each dimension can generate and the relationship between factors linked to the opinion of the client and linked to the functionality of the data set. The combination of both factors can arrive at a closer approximation to correctly measure the quality of the data, as well as to build the model as comprehensible to the user as possible.

But each dimension has different values or variables to work with. As an example, intrinsic dimensions classify variables such as accuracy, consistency or conciseness [8]. These dimensions can be defined differently for each author, however, they share similar approaches and characteristics. For this model, it is defined by the values of Response Time, Scalability, Trustworthiness and Timeliness.

The classification of each concept to its respective dimension results in the grouping of the response time and scalability in the dimensions of accessibility and the Trustworthiness and Timeliness in the confidence dimension.

2.2 Fuzzy Logic

The need to specify the fuzzy logic as the model to work was justified by the importance of changing the paradigm of mathematical results during studies during the last years. In classical mathematical concepts, variables can only be represented in 0 or 1, true or false, among others. In the measurement of quality, this type of results is ambiguous, since quality cannot exist or not exist. It is a value that can be partially good or partially bad, partially true or partially false [9]. Quality, for example, is something that cannot be described in a classic model of good or bad so easily; leads to ambiguous results and inaccurate results, but Fuzzy Logic, considering that it uses
rules that define quality in segments and results that can be represented in more than two ways or variables, can adequately define a better approximation of the Data Quality evaluation.

2.3 Related Work

It is worth noting that both the fuzzy logic, which is the model used, and the open data are quite recent concepts and both have a very strong affinity, as well as a greater use during the last years [10]. Due to this reason, there are very few previous works similar to the one in this article.

The union of these two concepts arises from their compatibility and innovation. The representation of the rules that define the quality in segments of more than two answers can adequately define a better approximation of the evaluation of Data Quality, without the need of great requirements both for its main design and its portability, thus allowing to add more quality variables and more dimensions to work, for later calculation of quality more accurately.

The most outstanding works to take into account are the one by Daniel Lewis and Trevor Martin about the use of fuzzy logic for the analysis of ontologies and vocabularies within of Linked OpenData [11]; and the other one by Herrera-Cubides et al., about the description, modeling, implementation and analysis of a fuzzy system type I based on logical rules, oriented to the decision making about the uncertainty of trust levels in the consumption LOD Datasets [17].

3 The Proposed Methodology

As a modeling of the methodology, it was decided to use a quasi-experimental empirical study, which allows estimating the impact of the different aspects of quality to obtain a global quality, without the use of random variables in the process, as shown in Fig. 1.

Type of Investigation Quasi-Experimental Methodology	Population SPARQL Endpoint opendata.cz	Sample 100 associated datasets to opendata.cz
Variables Response Time, Scalability, Trustworthiness, Timeliness	Instruments for the collection of information Query SPARQL with result in JSON format	Result Analysis Graphs, Statistic Tests

Fig. 1. Methodological design graphic, source: own elaboration

As a population the dataset of opendata.cz is taken into account, which has its own RDF Query Language (SPARQL) Endpoint, by which query type queries are carried out. As a sample, 100 datasets were taken associated with the main dataset opendata.cz, located in the Czech Republic. The SPARQL Endpoint corresponding to the opendata.cz dataset was used as instruments for data collection, and a JSON file for its subsequent analysis within the model was obtained as a result of a query to this endpoint. As a model analysis plan, it has been decided to compare quality values between the two cases raised for the visualization of the effect of more or less variables included within the fuzzy logic model. In turn, it was decided to show the comparative graphs between both cases for the values resulting from the evaluated quality, at the same time to visualize by means of tables statistical tests such as the deviation and the standard error.

The modeling for the evaluation of data quality in Linked Open Data can be built with a fuzzy logic approach, defining whether the quality is low, medium or high. Due to the represented model that uses a centroid method, since the need to improve previous models of data quality with a considerable number of inputs or quality criteria, allows us to obtain a percentage approximation value. As a percentage that is represented between a range and this truth value is more extended than the classical mathematical values of 0 and 1, the established ranges represent values of real life, such as low, medium or high (Fig. 2).

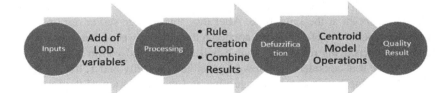

Fig. 2. Structure graph of fuzzy logic, Source: Own elaboration

The fuzzy logic model requires the evaluation of each of the four quality measurement channels, also known as the background of the model, through a series of rules, to then evaluate the output to determine if the quality of the data is high, medium or low. Two cases are evaluated: for the first case all four aspects are taken and the quality is measured with them. In the second case, 2 of the aspects are taken and redefined in their worst possible values and evaluate the quality of the data in a similar way to the first case. The main objective of these cases is to evaluate and compare the results considering that one case has many more factors than the other, and therefore is more accurate [8].

The first entry to evaluate is the Response Time, in which it can be calculated using the capacity in which the analyzed dataset is available and can respond to requests, because it is defined as "a data set can work well only if It is available and has a low response time" [12]. As a model definition within a range between 0 and 1, the response time is 1 if a response is received when requesting internal data from each dataset and the value is 0 otherwise. (Figure 3).

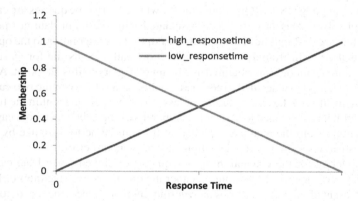

Fig. 3. Fuzzy logic model for the first case, response time. Source: Own elaboration

The second input to be measured in the model is scalability. Scalability measures the ability to respond to multiple users or requests at the same time [8]. The evaluation of this concept is taken by the concept of concurrency that supports the service that exposes the endpoint. As a methodology, it is measured by one and four users towards each of the datasets, performing a simulation in which each of these users makes a query towards the endpoint at the same time. After this, the average server response time is calculated for each user case and then applied a division between each average time of one and four users. This response variable will be expressed within a range [0,1], in which the value 0 is considered the lowest possible scalability and 1, the highest.

The relationship between the average time and the generation of the formula was based on the formula of the Timeliness assessment model of Olaf Hartig [13]. In his work, due to the similarity and the evaluation method used, which allowed to verify mathematically in a range, adaptable to this model of fuzzy logic.

The third entry to analyze in the model is Trustworthiness. The reliability allows to evaluate if the information and the data are classified as true and correct within the needs of each user of them. The Trustworthiness is measured in an interval [−1,1] that considers −1 as absolute distrust and 1 as absolute confidence.

The fourth entry of the model is Timeliness. This concept defines the moment in which the datasets were updated or modified for the last time. As a measurement, Timeliness is defined in an interval [0,1] in which 0 represents uncertainty and the result 1 represents certainty.

Each case of the fuzzy logic model has three specific rules, one defining each possible case of quality within each dimension. It is necessary to clarify that, the output value called Quality within each rule for each dataset is according to the dimension in which the rule is classified, but not to the global quality. This is for the purpose of measuring global quality taking into account all the proposed rules and not only one or two that are met, at the same time to associate each aspect with its related ones and not to mix them, since comparing non-related metrics does not have a lot of logic. According to Fig. 3 and thanks to the software MATLAB and the tool Fuzzy Logic Toolbox, the rules for the Accessibility Dimension (from number 1 to number 6) and the rules for the Trust Dimension (from number 7 to number 10) are:

It is necessary to emphasize that the relationship that has the response time and the scalability shown in Fig. 4, is mainly the performance that both variables specify when evaluating the dataset. Scalability successively measures the response time of each dataset, so the result of the response time will directly affect the scalability result. The relationship that maintains Trustworthiness and Timeliness sown in Fig. 4, is mainly from the internal analysis of each dataset. Both Trustworthiness and Timeliness take internal data from the dataset as date of creation, authors, dataset of origin, among others, which internally define the confidence dimension for obtaining the quality of the data.

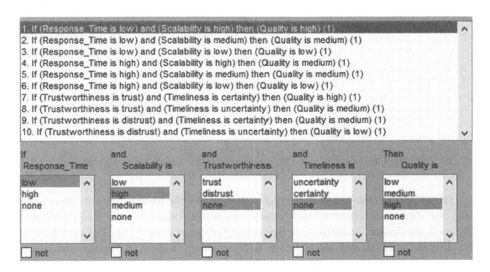

Fig. 4. Fuzzy logic model for the first case, response time. Source: Own elaboration

Regarding the output result, the model will take into account the generated rules and produce an interval percentage between 0% and 100%, 0% representing the worst possible quality and 100% representing the best possible quality.

4   The Infrastructure of the Implemented Model

The capture of the data (or the population to be taken into account in the research) was done through the SPARQL Endpoint of the data set "opendata.cz", known for its interest in "building an open data infrastructure that allows access to public data in the Czech Republic" [14]. Within this Endpoint, the number of data sets that the SPARQL query displays is 100, taking it as the investigative sample of the process. It is necessary to emphasize that the approach used requires both the internal data of the SPARQL query and external data, taken mainly to measure the values of Response Time and Scalability within the framework.

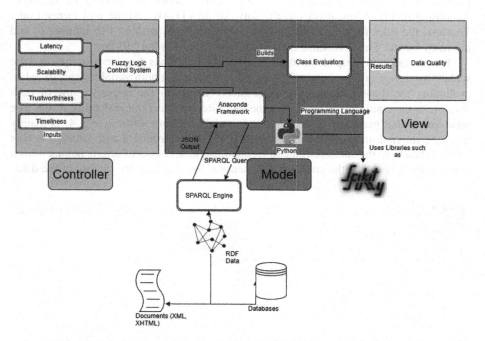

Fig. 5. Infrastructure of the Implemented Model. Source: Own elaboration

The SPARQL query used in the test model obtains the metadata results: the dataset title, the dataset description, the dataset creator (important for the Trustworthiness analysis), the dataset's contributors (important for the analysis of the Trustworthiness), the date of creation and modification of the dataset (important for the analysis of Timeliness), these grouped within a JSON file for later addition to the model. These are designed for the standards of the Semantic Web of RDF and the Vocabularies dcterms (Dublin Core Terms) and foaf (Friend Of A Friend).

As shown in the Fig. 5, the analysis of the data is done through Anaconda Framework, driven by the Python programming language, which allows to evaluate the data of a JavaScript Object Notation (JSON), which is a light interchangeable structured result of data generated by SPARQL Endpoints through the open server VIRTUOSO. As a note, the SPARQL query that obtains information shows the associated datasets, defining their relationship, point of origin and internal data such as the dataset author or the creation date of the dataset [4]. Mechanically, both the response time and the scalability are calculated by making requests based on HTTP/1.1 of the SPARQL query, to obtain response times and calculate an average.

After obtaining the main data, the model proceeds to use controllers and evaluators defined for each antecedent as part of the structure in its programming, each with its specific function; the controllers allow the JSON data to be extracted and divided into segments, defined by the four dimensions of the quality of the data, and the evaluators execute the operations on the data to prepare them for processing in the model. Within the fuzzy logic model, the entries are updated and proceeds to compare the results with the 6 previously defined rules, and allow to obtain an output result per dataset.

5   Results

The data collection was successful for the 100 datasets to be analyzed, obtained in a JSON file as a result. To show results not extensive to the reader, only four sample datasets from the list of 100 datasets obtained from the SPARQL Endpoint of the dataset "opendata.cz" are shown in this section.

For the Response Time case, the average response time calculated as 43.73 ms was compared to each time calculated. This procedure was executed approximately 50 times more and then the average of those times was obtained, in which it gave the result of 48.32 ms. It was possible to verify that each of the datasets analyzed within the study gave results within the JSON of the given request, that is, no null values or no response were obtained from the datasets, so the response time value for each of these datasets is 1 (Table 1).

Table 1. Examples of results of response times, Source: Own.

Dataset name	Calculated response time
Czech municipalities	48.1128183467
Job applicants in regions of Czech Republic	47.8042141867
Institutional research plans	49.1565653333
R&D Programmes	47.9116424533

In the case of Scalability, the procedure to follow was a SPARQL request to extract internal data from each dataset, used within the cases of Trustworthiness and Timeliness. This process was executed an amount of 50 times more, obtaining as a result response times for one and four users separately, for a total added of 250 times. As a next step, each of the four user times were added, obtaining data from a single response time group, which were then compared with a user's data, using the average time of both groups. With this, the formula proposed above is applied and the average scalability result equals 0.900363599953. As a reference, this value is between a range of [0,1] (Table 2).

Table 2. Examples of scalability results. Source. Own elaboration

Dataset name	Calculated scalability result
Czech municipalities	0.917890563599
Job applicants in regions of Czech Republic	0.891315467557
Institutional research plans	0.937077953964
R&D Programmes	0.921803070866

In the case of Trustworthiness, the natural way to measure this case is to take the author and collaborator values of each dataset and evaluate if these data are present (without null value). However, due to the empirical status of the study for the 100 sample datasets, the Trustworthiness was statically evaluated as 1, considering that all datasets contain authors and contributors verified by Datahub, a platform designed by the Open Knowledge Foundation.

In the case of Timeliness, the date of each dataset was taken into account as regards its creation and last modification. In order to specify and generalize the calculation of this factor, only the current year of this article (2017) was taken into account to compare both dates. As a result, you get a range between 0 and 1 per data set.

Taking into account the analysis plan previously proposed in the Methodology section, as a first step we studied the standard deviation and the error of the results of the model both for the quality cases and for the Response Time and Scalability due to the use of its average values to execute the model. The standard deviation of both quality cases is quite small, which can define the high precision of the calculated data, due to the low dispersion range between the mean and the values obtained [15]. It is worth noting that Case 2 has a larger Standard Deviation because taking only Timeliness and Response Time as factors that fluctuate the result, but all other variables are still present within the same values as Case 1, so a correlation between both cases exists and has similar standard deviation results, and, therefore, defining a high precision in the output results of the fuzzy logic model.

At the same time, the addition of the standard error confirms the fact that the sample of the data taken does not have a high discrepancy. Specifically, with the result of the quality in case 1, which contains all four quality variables, it is important to know that this discrepancy decreases, and thus allows recognizing that the model can support a greater number of quality variables without fluctuation much discrepancy found (Figs. 6 and 7).

In relation to the results of the quality of the results for both cases, it is observed that the first case has a higher percentage than the second case due to having a better score in two of the dimension values, however, it is observed that both cases have peaks that mean higher quality. The main reason for this phenomenon is that Timeliness and Response Time fluctuate the results. In a real scenario, the peaks are represented by values that do not have a high Timeliness, proven by not having the best possible value in the interval, 1.

In the comparison of the Luzzu framework, although the modeling of both frameworks are different, it can be seen that their growth in terms of processing and speed based on the execution time of the models are linear. However, it is noted that the

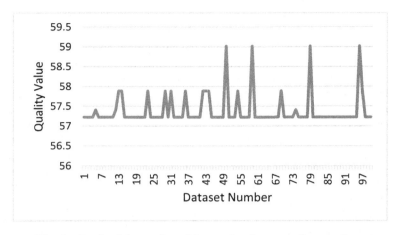

Fig. 6. Graph of the quality of the results, first case. Source: Own.

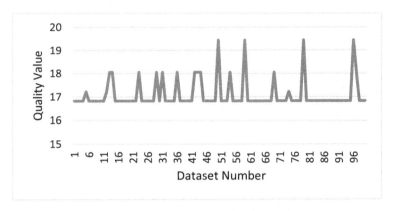

Fig. 7. Graph of the quality of the results, second case. Source: Own.

fuzzy logic model has a faster amount of time executed for the processing in comparison to Luzzu, making it have a better performance.

As an added value to this model, although it uses mathematical formulas similar to those of this model for the calculation of data [6, 12], Luzzu uses classic modeling to process data in a percentage way, without the advantages that fuzzy logic generates to obtain a more precise result, such as the establishment of rules according to dimensions.

6 Conclusion and Discussion

Linked Open Data has been growing exponentially in recent years, and will continue to grow more and more due to the full capacity for everyone to publish data on the web freely to share information. However, that only makes quality more and more important towards the future as shown in reviews of the state of the Web of the data made by authors such as Herrera-Cubides et al. [16]. An approach through fuzzy logic is a solution that has many advantages, such as the ability to mathematically define quality and focus on it deeply, rather than classical mathematical approaches. However, as an example, its full potential has not been proven; in this case, the same endpoint was evaluated, which means that quality aspects were similar, apart from facts such as the need to add more and more quality dimensions and, therefore, the use of more rules and operations. Another aspect that this model must consider is a greater inclusion of the user in the evaluation of quality, due to the need to evaluate the model personally and with the help of feedback, allowing the model to be even more precise. In turn, as seen in the comparison with other recent frameworks, there are limitations both of this fuzzy logic model, and of these frameworks, which can be mitigated or complemented. It is possible to find results that allow us to verify the main functionality of this concept, that is, in the definition of relative results, instead of absolutes, as in the case of "if it has quality or does not have quality" scenario.

In summary, the key contribution of the fuzzy logic model is the capacity of the quality calculation of Linked Open Data, related within the datasets, in a precise and controlled manner with a large number of variables and dimensions of quality to measure. As future work, we mainly seek to add a greater number of dimensions to achieve a global quality of the data, while adapting this model to other research techniques within the LOD field with different means and alternatives, according to the evolution of these data.

References

1. Hu, B., Rodrigues, E.M., Viel, E.C.: Proceedings of the 16th International Conference on Information Integration and Web-based Applications & Services - iiWAS 2014, pp. 217–223. ACM Press, New York (2014). https://doi.org/10.1145/2684200.2684336
2. Bonatti, P.A., Hogan, A., Polleres, A., Sauro, L.: Robust and scalable linked data reasoning incorporating provenance and trust annotations. Web Semant. Sci. Serv. Agents World Wide Web 9(2), 165–201 (2011). http://aidanhogan.com/docs/saor_ann_final.pdf
3. Auer, S., Ermilov, I., Lehmann, J., Martin, M.: LODStats - 9960 datasets (2016). http://stats.lod2.eu/. Accessed 14 Aug 2017
4. Ermilov, I., Lehmann, J., Martin, M., Auer, S.: LODStats: the data web census dataset. In: International Semantic Web Conference, pp. 38–46 (2016). http://jens-lehmann.org/files/2016/iswc_lodstats.pdf
5. Thakkar, H., Endris, K. M., Gimenez-Garcia, J. M., Debattista, J., Lange, C., Auer, S.: Are linked datasets fit for open-domain question answering? A quality assessment. In: Proceedings of the 6th International Conference on Web Intelligence, Mining and Semantics - WIMS 2016, pp. 1–12. ACM Press, New York (2016). https://doi.org/10.1145/2912845.2912857
6. Debattista, J., Auer, S., Lange, C.: Luzzu—a methodology and framework for linked data quality assessment. J. Data Inf. Qual. 8(1), 1–32 (2016). https://doi.org/10.1145/2992786
7. Hellmann, M.: Fuzzy Logic Introduction. Universite de Rennes, pp. 1–9 (2001). http://citeseerx.ist.psu.edu/viewdoc/download?doi=10.1.1.85.9757&rep=rep1&type=pdf

8. Zaveri, A., Rula, A., Maurino, A., Pietrobon, R., Lehmann, J., Auer, S.: Quality assessment methodologies for linked open data a systematic literature review and conceptual framework, Undefined(1), pp. 1–5 (2012). http://www.semantic-web-journal.net/system/files/swj414.pdf
9. Stella-vagaska Alena, H.: Application of fuzzy principles in evaluating quality of manufacturing process. WSEAS Trans. Power Syst. 7(2), 1–10 (2012)
10. Dernoncourt, F.: Introduction to Fuzzy Logic, pp. 1–21. Massachusetts Institute of Technology (2013). http://aisii.azc.uam.mx/mcbc/Cursos/IntCompt/Lectura15.pdf
11. Lewis, D.J., Martin, T.P.: Managing vagueness with fuzzy in hierarchical big data. Procedia Comput. Sci. 53, 19–28 (2015). https://doi.org/10.1016/j.procs.2015.07.275
12. Zaveri, A.: Linked Data Quality Assessment and its Application to Societal Progress Measurement. University of Leipzig (2015). https://core.ac.uk/download/pdf/35206278.pdf
13. Hartig, O., Zhao, J.: Using web data provenance for quality assessment. In: Proceedings of the First International Conference on Semantic Web in Provenance Management, vol. 526, pp. 29–34 (2009). http://ceur-ws.org/Vol-526/paper_1.pdf
14. Nečaský, M., Klímek, J., Chlapek, D., Kučera, J., Mynarz, J., Svátek, V. OpenData.cz (2015). https://opendata.cz/. Accessed 5 Sept 2017
15. DataStar Inc.: How to Interpret Standard Deviation and Standard Error in Survey Research (2013). www.surveystar.com. Accessed 7 Sept 2017
16. Herrera-Cubides, J.F., Gaona-Garcia, P.A., Sánchez-Alonso, S.: The web of data: past, present and future? In: XI Latin American Conference on Learning Objects and Technology (LACLO), San Carlos, Costa Rica, pp. 1–8 (2016). https://doi.org/10.1109/LACLO.2016. 7751802. https://ieeexplore.ieee.org/document/7751802/. Accessed 3 Sept 2017
17. Herrera-Cubides, J.F., Gaona-García, P.A., Alonso-Echeverri, J.I., Riaño Vargas, K.A., Gómez- Acosta, A.C.: A Fuzzy Logic System to Evaluate Levels of Trust on Linked Open Data Resources. Revista Facultad de Ingeniería, 86 (2018). http://aprendeenlinea.udea.edu. co/revistas/index.php/ingenieria/article/view/328937, Universidad de Antioquia, Colombia, ISSSN 0120-6230. Accessed 1 Feb 2018
18. Herrera-Cubides, J.F., Gaona-García, P. A., Gordillo-Orjuela, K.: A view of the web of data. case study: use of services CKAN. Revista Ingeniería, 22(1) (2017). https://revistas. udistrital.edu.co/ojs/index.php/reving/article/view/10542, Universidad Distrital Francisco José de Caldas, ISSN 0121-750X, E-ISSN 2344-8393. Accessed 2 Sept 2017

A Hybrid Fuzzy Regression-Based Methodology for Normal Distribution (Case Study: Cumulative Annual Precipitation)

M. Spiliotis$^{(\boxtimes)}$ (iD), P. Angelidis (iD), and B. Papadopoulos (iD)

Department of Civil Engineering, Democritus University of Thrace,
Kimmeria Campus, 67100 Xanthi, Greece
m.spiliotis@gmail.com

Abstract. An advantage of the probabilistic approach is the exploitation of the observed probability values in order to test the goodness-of-fit for the examined theoretical probability distribution function (pdf). Since in fact, the interest of the engineers is to determine the hydrological variable which corresponds to a selected return period, a fuzzy linear relation between the standardized normal variable Z and the examined hydrologic random variable is achieved in condition that the hydrological variable is normally distributed. In this work, for the first time, the implementation of the fuzzy linear regression of Tanaka is proposed, to achieve a fuzzy relation between the standardized variable Z and the annual cumulative precipitation. Thus, all the historical data are included in the produced fuzzy band. The proposed innovative methodology provides the opportunity to achieve simultaneously a fuzzy assessment of the mean value and the standard deviation based on the solution of the fuzzy linear regression. The suitability test of the examined theoretical pdf is founded on the comparison of the spread of the fuzzy band and the distance between the achieved central values of the mean value and the standard deviation with the unbiased statistical estimation of the same variables.

Keywords: Fuzzy linear regression · Fuzzy sets
Empirical probability function · Normal distribution
Cumulative annual precipitation

1 Introduction

During the hydraulic design and management the first step is the assessment of the hydrological variables. Unfortunately, these cannot be treated with crisp values. There is plenty of academic works and engineering experience about the probabilistic implementation of the hydrological variables. However, the couple between the statistic and theoretical probability distributions is not without problems.

Thus, in this article, for first time, a hybrid model is proposed to improve the matching between the sample and the normal probability distribution function. This hybrid approach treats the couple between the normal distribution density function and the observed probabilities enhanced by the using of fuzzy linear regression.

© IFIP International Federation for Information Processing 2018
Published by Springer International Publishing AG 2018. All Rights Reserved
L. Iliadis et al. (Eds.): AIAI 2018, IFIP AICT 519, pp. 568–579, 2018.
https://doi.org/10.1007/978-3-319-92007-8_48

An advantage of the probabilistic approach as a choice to treat the uncertainty is the exploitation of the cumulative empirical (observed) probability distribution in order to test the goodness-of-fit for a theoretical probability distribution with respect to the historical sample. In this article, a hybrid methodology is developed so that, both the concepts of the observed probability and the flexibility of the fuzzy approach can be used.

More specifically, the main idea is to express the probabilistic parameters as fuzzy numbers and thus, the flexibility of the fuzzy arithmetic and other concepts of the fuzzy sets can be exploited.

Mainly, in contrast with the traditional approaches, the proposed hybrid, fuzzy enhanced methodology produces a fuzzy relation which can be seen as a fuzzy band, which contains all the observed data, that is, all the pairs between the observed hydrological values and the observed probability. This fuzzy relation (it can be seen as a fuzzy band) is modulated based on the fuzzy linear regression model of Tanaka (1987). Therefore, the thresholds of fuzziness are modulated with respect to the observed data, by following a constraining optimization problem, and not by following an a- priori information as in several cases of the fuzzy optimization problems.

Fuzzy linear regression may be a useful tool to express functional relationships between variables, especially when the available data are not sufficient (Ganoulis 2009). For instance, Kitsikoudis et al. (2016) employed a fuzzy regression to produce a lower and an upper limit for the critical dimensionless shear stress. Thus, we avoid the ambiguity of selecting a threshold for the initiation of motion, and hence, the model provides a smoother transition to the state of general movement.

More generally, for studying complex physical phenomena such as the interconnection between adjacent watersheds (Tsakiris et al. 2006), the rainfall-runoff process without all the involved parameters, the use of fuzzy models should be investigated. In contrast to the statistical regression, fuzzy regression analysis has no error term, while the uncertainty is incorporated in the model by means of fuzzy numbers (Spiliotis and Bellos 2016; Papadopoulos and Sirpi 2004).

In brief, the proposed methodology can be divided into three steps: modulation of the data (an analysis based on the conventional statistical approach), application of the fuzzy linear regression (which concludes to a constrained optimization problem) and finally evaluation of the solution achieved where the assumption of the considered *pdf* is tested. The proposed methodology concludes to a fuzzy relation between the probability and the hydrological variables simultaneously with the fuzzy assessment of the mean value and the standard deviation. In this work, the methodology is developed for normal distributed annual cumulative precipitation.

2 Basic Notions

Let a historical sample. The rank order method involves ordering the data from the largest hydrological value to the smallest hydrological value, assigning a rank of 1 to the largest value and a rank of N to the smallest value. Based on the Weibull empirical distribution (which is widely used in the Greek regions) to compute the plotting position probabilities, the cumulative exceedance probability can be calculated as follows (e.g. Chow et al. 1988):

$$Prob(P \geq p) = \frac{m}{N+1} \tag{1}$$

where m is the rank of the value in a list ordered by descending magnitude (Chow et al. 1988). As P many hydrological random variables can be considered. In this work we focus on the *annual cumulative precipitation*.

It is evident that the cumulative probability of non-exceedance can be calculated as follows based on the exceedance probability (given that that P is a continuous random variable and according to the common practice in hydrology):

$$Prob(P \leq p) = 1 - \frac{m}{N+1} \tag{2}$$

The return period of an event, T, of a given magnitude may be viewed as the average recurrence length of time (usually years) between events equaling or exceeding a specified magnitude (Chow et al. 1998):

$$Prob(P \leq p) = 1 - \frac{1}{T} \tag{3}$$

In case of the normal distribution, based on the calculated unbiased estimation of the mean and the standard deviation with respect to the available historical sample, $\bar{p}, s$, correspondingly, it holds:

$$Prob(P \leq p_T) = \left(1 - \frac{1}{T}\right), \tag{4}$$

$$\left. \begin{array}{l} Prob(P \leq p_T) = \left(1 - \frac{1}{T}\right) = \Phi(Z_T) \\ Z_T = \frac{p_T - \bar{p}}{\sigma} \end{array} \right\} \Rightarrow \frac{p_T - \bar{p}}{\sigma} = Z_T \Rightarrow p_T = \bar{p} + \sigma Z_T \tag{5}$$

where Z is the standardized normal variable and p_T is the magnitude of the event having a return period T.

A used technique in hydrology is to investigate a linear relation between the standardized normal variable Z and the hydrological variable (here the cumulative annual precipitation), instead of the probability plot. Similarly with the probability plot, the calculation of the normal variable Z is based on the empirical probability of the sample which corresponds to each pair between the standardized normal variable and the examined hydrological variable:

$$p_T = a_0 + a_1 Z_T \tag{6}$$

It is desirable, that the coefficients α_0 and α_1 to be close to the unbiased estimation of the mean value and the standard deviation of the sample, $\bar{p}$ and s respectively, as it occurs in the case of the crisp formulation. In the past, the graphical method with specified paper plots were used in order to rather manually identify the proper curve and the corresponding parameters. Also the conventional regression can be used to determine the parameters α_0 and α_1.

The main proposal of this article is the application of the fuzzy linear regression to determine the parameters α_0 and α_1. That is,

$$\tilde{p}_T = \tilde{a}_0 + \tilde{a}_1 Z_T \tag{7}$$

An interesting point is that additionally, a fuzzy approach for the mean value and the standard deviation can be achieved. The proposed methodology is graphically presented in Fig. 1 and it will be presented bellow more analytically. As aforementioned, the produced fuzzy band will contain all the observed data and this is one significant advantage of the proposed methodology.

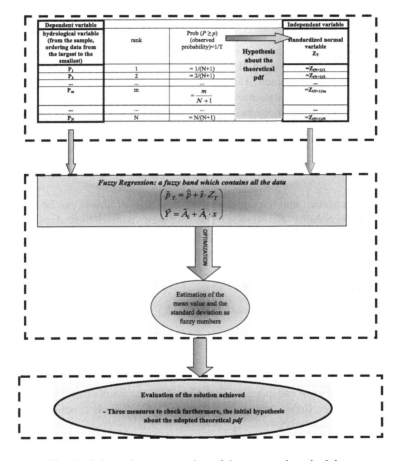

Fig. 1. Schematic representation of the proposed methodology.

3 Proposed Methodology

The aim of the proposed methodology is to provide a fuzzy relation between the standardized normal variable Z and the examined hydrological variable simultaneously with a fuzzy estimation of the mean value and the standard deviation. The proposed methodology is based on the observed probabilities of the sample and thereafter the fuzzy regression is used. However, the proposed method holds is the hypothesis of normal distributed random variable holds. Next the main three steps of the proposed methodology are presented.

3.1 Modulating the Independent and Dependent Variables

Firstly, the data are ordered from the largest hydrological value to the smallest hydrological value, assigning a rank. Then, based on the Weibull 1939 empirical distribution, the cumulative non-exceedance probability is calculated. Subsequently, a hypothesis must be made about the theoretical probability distribution. Here, the normal distribution is examined. Hence, the standardized normal variable Z can be determined for each pair of data based on the empirical probabilities.

As aforementioned the independent variable is the Z_T term. To determine the Z_T term the following two assumptions must be made:

$$Z_T = \Phi^{-1}\left(1 - \frac{m}{N+1}\right) \tag{8}$$

It should be clarified that the standard statistical tests of fitness can be used only to predispose the probability distribution. The proposed methodology does not use the standard statistical tests of fitness. Furthermore, the evaluation of the solution achieved is based on the fuzzy solution and not on any conventional statistical test.

3.2 Applying Fuzzy Regression

Fuzzy linear regression model proposed by Tanaka (1987) has the following form:

$$\tilde{Y}_j = \tilde{A}_0 + \tilde{A}_1 x_{1j} + \ldots \tilde{A}_i x_{ij} + \ldots + \tilde{A}_N x_{Nj}$$
$$\text{with } j = 1, \ldots, M, \ i = 1, \ldots, N \tag{9}$$

where N is the number of independent variables, M is the number of data, and $\tilde{A}_i = (a_i, c_i)_L$ are symmetric fuzzy triangular numbers selected as coefficients (Fig. 2) (Papadopoulos and Sirpi 2004):

In case of normally distributed annual cumulative precipitation, the following fuzzy linear regression model is examined:

$$\tilde{p}_{Tj} = \tilde{\bar{p}} + \tilde{s} \cdot Z_{T,j}$$
$$(\tilde{Y}_j = \tilde{A}_0 + \tilde{A}_1 \cdot x_{1j}) \tag{10}$$

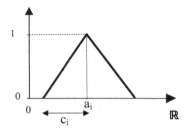

Fig. 2. Fuzzy triangular symmetrical number.

where $\tilde{P}_{Tj}$ is the fuzzy assessment of the hydrological magnitude of the event (dependent variable) having a return period T for the jth set of data.

With respect to Eq. 10, the mean and the standard deviation $\tilde{\bar{p}}, \tilde{s}$ respectively, are the fuzzy coefficients (fuzzy symmetrical triangular numbers in this application). The fuzzy coefficients are determined based on the Tanaka fuzzy linear regression method. The standardized normal variable is the independent variable, which takes only crisp values as well as the dependent variable which is the annual cumulative precipitation.

Thus, the proposed methodology can produce a fuzzy estimation of the mean value and the standard deviation. This fuzzy estimation is based on the fuzzy regression and hence, it is founded with the respect to the data. However, we highlight that the fuzzy estimation of the mean value and the standard deviation is related with the assumption of the normal distribution.

In this point it should be referred, that many problems of fuzzy logic, as the fuzzy arithmetic, the fuzzy linear regression e.t.c. are formulated with the aim of *a-cuts*. The α-*cuts* could be characterized as the bridge between the fuzzy and the crisp (conventional) sets. The α–*cut* set of the fuzzy number A (with $0 < \alpha \leq 1$) is defined as follows:

$$[A]_{\alpha} = \{x | \mu_A(x) \geq \alpha\} \tag{11}$$

Note that the α–*cut* set is a crisp set determined from the fuzzy set according to a selected value of the membership function and, alternatively, a fuzzy set can be practically decomposed to a significant number of α–*cut sets*. In case of α= *0*, the above definition (Eq. 14) can be modified without the equality in order to describe the *zero-cut* (Kitsikoudis et al. 2016; Spiliotis and Bellos 2016; Buckley and Eslami 2002).

The concept of inclusion can be defined with respect to the *a-cut*. The inclusion of a fuzzy set A to the fuzzy set B with the associated degree $0 \leq h \leq 1$ (it is a critical point, that the inclusion property is based on a selected *h-cut* between all the other α-*cuts*) is defined as follows:

$$[A]_h \subseteq [B]_h \tag{12}$$

The constraints of the problems are modulated based on the concept of inclusion. Thus, all the data (which are crisp numbers) must be included in the produced fuzzy band:

$$p_j \in \left[p_{h,j}^L, \ p_{h,j}^R \right] \tag{13}$$

By taking into account the fuzzy arithmetic, for a selected level h, the inclusion constraints in case the decision variables are selected to be symmetrical triangular numbers, are equivalent to:

$$\begin{cases} \textit{Inclusion Constraints} \\ \left(\bar{p} + s \cdot Z_{T,j} \right) - (1-h) \left(w_{\bar{p}} + w_s \left| Z_{T,j} \right| \right) = p_{h,j}^L \leq p_j \\ \left(\bar{p} + s \cdot Z_{T,j} \right) + (1-h) \left(w_{\bar{p}} + w_s \left| Z_{T,j} \right| \right) = p_{h,j}^R \geq p_j \\ w_{\bar{p}}, \ w_s \geq 0 \end{cases} \tag{14}$$

Since the fuzzy regression leads to a constrained optimization problem, the assessment of the fitness is based on the produced fuzzy band. The smaller the fuzzy band, the more proper the fuzzy model becomes. Hence, Tanaka (1987) suggested the minimization of the sum of the produced fuzzy semi-spreads for all the data (Spiliotis and Bellos 2016; Kitsikoudis et al. 2016; Papadopoulos and Sirpi 2004):

$$Min \, J \left(= \sum_{j=1}^{M} w_{pj} = \left\{ M \cdot w_{\bar{p}} + w_s \sum_{j=1}^{M} \left| Z_{T,j} \right| \right\} \right) \, (objective \, function) \tag{15}$$

The above measure is the sum of all the produced semi-spreads (from the fuzzy band) for all the observed data.

Therefore, in brief, based on the Tanaka methodology, the parameters of the fuzzy coefficients, that is, the centers and the widths of the fuzzy coefficients, are determined by solving a constrained optimization problem (Eqs. 14 and 15). In the examined problem, these fuzzy coefficients can be viewed as an estimation of the mean value and the standard deviation. The objective function is selected to be the total semi-spread of the fuzzy outputs.

3.3   Evaluation of the Solution Achieved

In fact, every fuzzy regression problem based on Tanaka formulation will have a solution, and hence, the magnitude of the produced fuzzy band could be a criterion about how successful is the proposed fuzzy linear transformation. A large semi-spread, J, indicates that the axis of the standardized normal variable Z must be changed and hence, other probability distribution could be examined (Spiliotis and Papadopoulos 2017).

Another measure to test the suitability of the examined probability distribution is proposed, F which is the Euclidean distance between the central values of the mean value and the standard deviation with the unbiased (usual statistical) estimation of the same variables, $\hat{\mu}$, $\hat{\sigma}$:

$$F = \sqrt{(\bar{p} - \hat{\mu})^2 + (s - \hat{\sigma})^2} \tag{16}$$

4 Application in Case of Annual Rainfall Time Series

The meteorological station of Aldeia Nova de São Bento belongs to the National Information System for the Water Resources (SNIRH) of Portugal. The station is located inside the area of Guadiana between the Guadiana River and the Portugal – Spain border, as shown in Fig. 3 (Angelidis et al. 2012). The data cover a large time span, from 1931 up to 2007. The proposed methodology was applied to express the annual cumulative rainfall with respect to the for normal distributed rainfall.

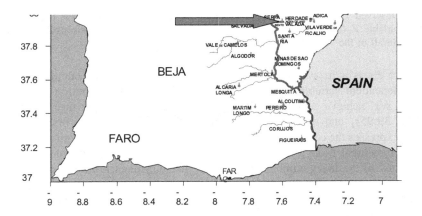

Fig. 3. Location of the Aldeia Nova de São Bento rain station.

Indeed, by using the statistical test of Kolmogorov-Smirnov (K-S) with an interval confidence $(1-\alpha) = 0.80$, the result indicates that the normal distribution can be used to express the annual rainfall in Aldeia Nova de São Bento. As aforementioned the statistical test is not used directly in the proposed methodology, but it simply indicates a proper algebraic transformation.

Fuzzy regression is applied for a selected $h = 0$ whilst fuzzy symmetrical triangular numbers were selected as fuzzy coefficients. Finally, based on the above assumptions, the problem of fuzzy regression leads to a linear programming problem. All in all, the following fuzzy curve between the standard normal random variable Z and the annual rainfall is produced through the constrained optimization problem according to Eqs. 14 and 15 (Fig. 4):

$$\tilde{P}_T = (161.96, \ 3.58)_L \cdot Z_T + (551.50, \ 39.95)_L \tag{17}$$

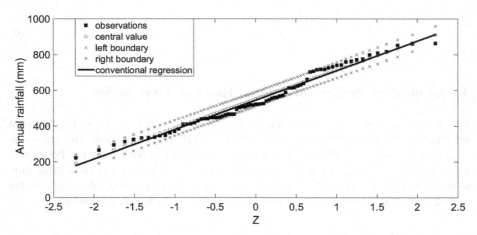

Fig. 4. Observed data, fuzzy and conventional (crisp) regression between the standardize normal variable Z (based on the observed cumulative non-exceedance probabilities) and the annual rainfall of the sample.

where $\tilde{P}_T$ is a fuzzy number which represents the estimated cumulative annual runoff (dependent variable). Hence, by adopting the normal distribution, according to Eq. 17, we achieve simultaneously a fuzzy assessment of the mean value $(551.50, 39.95)_L$ and the standard deviation $(161.96, 3.58)_L$. The first term in the bracket expresses the central value (Fig. 2) and the second term, the semi-width of each fuzzy symmetrical triangular number. In general, a fuzzy symmetrical number is Q special case of the fuzzy number. In general, a fuzzy symmetrical number is Q special case of the fuzzy number.

The objective function of the fuzzy regression problem which expresses the total uncertainty is equal to:

$$J_N = 75 \cdot 39.95 + 3.58 \sum_{j=1}^{75} |Z_{Tj}| = 3,202.8 \tag{18}$$

In addition, from the fuzzy curve (Eq. 17), it is easy to see that the central values of the fuzzy coefficients, which can be seen as a fuzzy approximation of the mean value and the standard deviation, are very close to their unbiased estimation based on the historical sample ($\hat{\mu} = 545.50$, $\hat{\sigma} = 159.91$). Indeed, the Euclidean distance between the central values of the mean value and the standard deviation with the unbiased (usual statistical) estimation of the same variables, $\hat{\mu}$, $\hat{\sigma}$ has a rather small value:

$$F = \sqrt{(545.50 - 551.50)^2 + (161.96 - 159.91)^2} = 6.34\,\text{mm} \tag{19}$$

The values of both the objective function (Eq. 18) and the proposed measure F (Eq. 19) indicate that the fuzzified normal distribution can be used to express the annual cumulative rainfall in Aldeia Nova de São Bento. Therefore, from the application, it is evident that the objective function and the proposed measure of suitability,

F, provide us the opportunity to test the suitability of the initial hypothesis about the use of the normal distribution as the theoretical probability distribution.

Another interesting perspective to discuss is the proposed methodology in relation with the statistic test of Kolmogorov–Smirnov. The statistic test of Kolmogorov–Smirnov involves the absolute values of the distance between the observed probability and the probability value from the adopted theoretical cumulative distribution function for all the sample. By applying the proposed methodology, all the data, that is, each pair which includes the value of the hydrological value and the corresponding non-exceedance empirical probability is included in the produced fuzzy band at least to some degree (Fig. 4).

An interesting point is that the proposed fuzzy estimation of the mean value and the standard deviation is more founded to fuzzy logic and without subjective choices which must be made by the user, compared with Sfiris et al. 2014 approach. According to Sfiris et al. 2014, the mean value and the standard deviation are estimated as fuzzy numbers starting from the conventional probabilistic confidence interval. However, a confidence interval must be selected from the user, in order to move from the probabilistic approach to the fuzzy approach. In addition, the transition from the asymptotic to non asymptotic membership function was done by selecting a suitable function. According to the new methodology, the mean value and the standard deviation are estimated as fuzzy numbers based on the observed data by following a fuzzy regression approach without specific considerations from the user. Furthermore, two measures to test the validity of the method are proposed.

It should be clarified also that the proposed methodology is based on the probabilistic model with crisp data whilst the fuzziness arises from the matching between the theoretical probability distribution function and the observed probabilities. The method should not be confused with either methods which are based on fuzzy data (fuzzy sample, e.g. Viertl 2011) or methods with starting from a probabilistic approach conclude to a fuzzy approach (e.g. Sfiris and Papadopoulos 2014).

Another interesting point for further investigation is the use of several theoretical distributions. Then, the use of the suitability measure F and the value of the objective function J can be seen as the criteria according to which the selection of the suitable theoretical probability distribution can be done. Spiliotis and Papadopoulos 2017 have already studied a similar methodology in case of lognormal theoretical probability distribution. In general, the proposed methodology could be expanded based on the frequency factor method which includes also the proposed analysis based on the standardized variable Z for normal probability distribution.

As aforementioned in case that a significant fuzzy band is produced, then the first think will be the change of the theoretical pdf and this can be seen as the main challenge for further investigation. However, the use of new techniques of fuzzy regression should also be investigated. For instance, it could be investigated the use of more sophisticated objective functions which will contain both the centers and the widths of the fuzzy coefficients. Hence, a new objective function could try either to increase the possibility of equality between the observations and fuzzy intervals (Shakouri et al. 2017) or could incorporate simultaneously with the fuzzy spreads the sum of possibility grade in the objective function (Yabuuchi 2017). Alternatively, ideas from goal programming could be applied in order to reduce the impact of outliers (Kitsikoudis et al. 2016) and hence, the objective function is changed accordingly.

5   Concluding Remarks

A hybrid combination between the problem of coupling between the observed probabilities and the normal distribution with the aim of fuzzy linear regression analysis is proposed in this article. According to the proposed methodology, the exploitation of the empirical probability function can be achieved together with a fuzzy approach. The key of the proposed methodology is the application of the fuzzy linear regression model of Tanaka in order to achieve a linear relation with fuzzy numbers as coefficients. In addition, based on the proposed fuzzy regression, the mean value and the standard deviation are determined as fuzzy coefficients.

Hence, the proposed innovative methodology provides the opportunity to achieve simultaneously a fuzzy assessment of the mean value and the standard deviation based on the solution of the fuzzy linear regression. In contrast, the application of the conventional crisp regression products crisp numbers as coefficients, which differ from the unbiased estimation of the mean value and the standard deviation. The proposed fuzzy estimation of the mean value and the standard deviation is desirable to include the unbiased estimation of the mean value and the standard deviation.

Indeed, the measure of the distance between the central values of the mean value and the standard deviation with the unbiased (usual statistical) estimations together with its fuzziness, are proposed also as measures of suitability in order to test the validation of the method and consequently the selected probability pdf.

Another interesting property of the proposed methodology is that the proposed fuzzy band includes all the data at least at some degree. In general, the proposed methodology improves the matching between the sample of the hydrological variable and the used probability distribution.

References

Tanaka, H.: Fuzzy data analysis by possibilistic linear models. Fuzzy Sets Syst. **24**, 363–375 (1987)

Ganoulis, J.: Risk Analysis of Water Pollution. Wiley-VCH Verlag GmbH & Co. KGaA (2009)

Kitsikoudis, V., Spiliotis, M., Hrissanthou, V.: Fuzzy regression analysis for sediment incipient motion under turbulent flow conditions. Environ. Process. **3**(3), 663–679 (2016)

Tsakiris, G., Tigkas, D., Spiliotis, M.: Assessment of interconnection between two adjacent watersheds using deterministic and fuzzy approaches. Eur. Water **15**(16), 15–22 (2006)

Spiliotis, M., Bellos, C.: Flooding risk assessment in mountain rivers. Eur. Water **51**, 33–49 (2016)

Papadopoulos, B., Sirpi, M.: Similarities and distances in fuzzy regression modeling. Soft. Comput. **8**(8), 556–561 (2004)

Chow, V., Maidment, D., Mays, L.: Applied Hydrology. International editions. McGraw-Hill, New York (1988)

Spiliotis, M., Papadopoulos, B.: A hybrid fuzzy probabilistic assessment of the extreme hydrological events. In: 15th International Conference of Numerical Analysis and Applied Mathematics (ICNAAM 2017), 25–30 September, Thessaloniki, Greece (2017, in Press)

Buckley, J., Eslami, E.: An Introduction to Fuzzy Logic and Fuzzy Sets, Advances in Soft Computing, vol. 13. Springer, Heidelberg (2002)

Angelidis, P., Maris, F., Kotsovinos, N., Hrissanthou, V.: Computation of drought index SPI with alternative distribution functions. Water Resour. Manag. **26**(9), 2453–2473 (2012)

Sfiris, D., Papadopoulos, B.: Non-asymptotic fuzzy estimators based on confidence intervals. Inf. Sci. **279**, 446–459 (2014)

Viertl, R.: Statistical Methods for Fuzzy Data, p. 256. Wiley, Hoboken (2011)

Shakouri, H., Nadimi, R., Ghaderi, S.-F.: Investigation on objective function and assessment rule in fuzzy regressions based on equality possibility, fuzzy union and intersection concepts. Comput. Ind. Eng. **110**, 207–215 (2017)

Yabuuchi, Y.: Possibility grades with vagueness in fuzzy regression models. Procedia Comput. Sci. **112**, 1470–1478 (2017)

Fuzzy Approach for Bibliometric Analysis of Publication Trends on Intragastric Balloon as a Minimally Invasive Procedure for Weight Loss in Obese Individuals

Trasanides George[2], Tsaousi Georgia[1], Adjenughwure Kingsley[2],
Kotzampassi Katerina[1], Kapanidis Konstantinos[1],
and Papadopoulos Basil[2(✉)]

[1] Department of Surgery, Faculty of Medicine,
Aristotle University Thessaloniki, University Campus,
54006 Thessaloniki, Greece
[2] Department of Civil Engineering, Democritus University of Thrace,
Komotini, Greece
papadob@civil.duth.gr

Abstract. In this paper, we perform Bibliometric assessment of research output that has been carried out pertaining to the literature on intragastric balloon (IGBs) as a treatment modality of morbid obesity. To do this, we conducted a bibliometric analysis on this topic using the growth of publications, publication trends over time, annual research productivity and authors' activity as main outcome points. Furthermore, we validate the comparable applicability of Lotka's law among authors with a single publication and those with multiple ones using a fuzzy approach. The analysis shows that publication trend follows Price's law. The extracted trend is exponential and in accordance with what is found in other studies. Lotka's formula using one and two publications, is found to hold but for mean $x = 3.025$.

Keywords: Fuzzy estimators · Bibliometric analysis · Fuzzy sets
Bariatric Surgery · Intragastric balloon · Lotka's law

1 Introduction

Obesity constitutes a worldwide epidemic socio-economic entity incurring serious repercussions on health status and exacerbation of obesity-related comorbidities (Laing et al. 2017; Flegal et al. 2010). These seem to exert an adverse impact on both life quality and expectancy of obese individuals, all leading to spiralling health costs (Cawley and Meyerhoefer 2012).

Although, lifestyle/behavioural and diet modification assisted by physical exercise is recommended as a first line approach to weight loss, yet numerous studies failed to support a sustainable effectiveness for the vast majority of those who attempted such practice (Norris et al. 2005). As to pharmacotherapy, which is considered as the second

L. Iliadis et al. (Eds.): AIAI 2018, IFIP AICT 519, pp. 580–591, 2018.
https://doi.org/10.1007/978-3-319-92007-8_49

line approach, a modest efficacy associated with significant side-effects has been documented (Yanovski and Yanovski 2014).

Thus, bariatric surgery emerges as the most reliable treatment modality for the management of severe obesity, with long-term efficacy in weight loss (Colquitt et al. 2014; Buchwald and Oien 2013). Nonetheless, the substantial cost and non-negligible surgical morbidity and mortality render bariatric surgery as a less attractive option for obese patients to pursue (Jirapinyo and Thompson 2017; Buchwald and Oien 2013).

To fill the void, minimally invasive non-surgical options for weight loss are gaining popularity; the intragastric balloon (IGB) being the most widely applied in clinical practice (Laing et al. 2017; Yorke et al. 2016). The fundamental concept of an IGB is the attainment of a continuous sensation of satiety owing to mechanical gastric distension caused by an artificial gastric bezoar, thereby facilitating decreased food intake and maintenance of a low-calorie diet (Kumar et al. 2017; Laing et al. 2017; Yorke et al. 2016). Its versatility, low invasiveness, ease of retrieval and relative safety has resulted in the broad acceptance of its use with thousands of devices placed globally each year (Yorke et al. 2016). Consequently, numerous publications have assessed the applicability of various types of IGBs from their inception to clinical practice up to nowadays (Laing et al. 2017; Yorke et al. 2016; Kotzampassi et al. 2012; Kotzampassi et al. 2014).

Bibliometric analysis incorporates statistical and mathematical methods with a view to provide a quantitative and qualitative analysis of scientific evidence, as well as the course of research performance and productivity on a certain scientific topic and period of time (Ellegaard and Wallin 2015; Mishra et al. 2016; Thompson and Walker 2015). Bibliometric indicators have been extensively used in various medical disciplines to outline research trends, suggest future research ideas and challenge public health issues (Khan et al. 2014; Sweileh et al. 2015; Zyoud et al. 2015).

In the recent literature, several bibliometric analyses have attempted to elucidate publication productivity regarding the implementation of bariatric surgery as a treatment modality of severe obesity (Aminian et al. 2015; Ozsoy and Demir 2017; Dabi et al. 2016) or to comparably assess bariatric procedures in terms of their popularity (Ozsoy and Demir 2018).

To the best of our knowledge, no bibliometric assessment of research output has been carried out pertaining to the literature on IGBs as a treatment modality of morbid obesity, for the 25-year period (1982 to 2017) this technique has come into clinical effect.

Thus, we conducted this bibliometric analysis on this topic using the growth of publications, publication trends over time, annual research productivity and authors' activity as main outcome points. Furthermore, we aimed to validate the comparable applicability of Lotka's law among authors with a single publication and those with multiple ones using a fuzzy approach.

2 Materials and Methods

2.1 Data Source and Description

The data used in this study were sourced from Scopus database. The terms Bintragastric balloons^ and Bobesity ^ with Band^ as Boolean term were used as keywords entered into the Scopus engine to retrieve data related to the objectives of this study.

A search of these terms was confined to the article title, abstract and keywords of document search. The accuracy of search query was achieved with quotation marks.

Documents from all subject areas, with no time period limitation and language restriction, were retrieved. Only articles published as an erratum were excluded. Search was accomplished on 20 December 2017 to avoid any bias addressed to the daily updating of the database.

Data on overall scientific production regarding the use of IGBs for obesity management were analysed for the overall growth of publications, annual research productivity, authors' activity, etc. To verify Lotka's law, a fuzzy approach was used.

A total of 569 articles were retrieved and further analyzed. Published articles on the use of IGBs for obesity management assessed in this study cover a time-period between 1982 up to the end of 2017. Temporal distribution of production of publications is presented in Fig. 1.

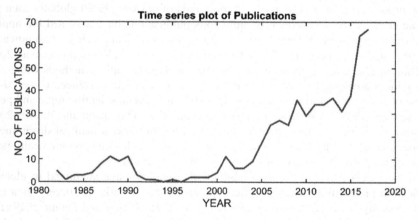

Fig. 1. Timeseries of New Publications per year in the domain

Analysis of authors' productivity revealed that a total of 2001 authors contributed to the published articles. The average number of authors per article was 3.41. Detailed data on authors' activity is provided in Table 1.

Table 1. Authors' activities

No of authors	No of articles	Percentage%
1533	1	76,7
466	>1	23,3
290	2	14,5
73	3	3,65
95	4 to 9	4,75
8	>10 11 to 27	0,4

Ethical approval of this study was not deemed necessary since no human subjects or data were involved.

2.2   Data Analysis Techniques

This analysis has two parts, first we look at the publication trend by analysing the time series of publications. The trend is extracted from the original series using the singular spectrum analysis technique (Golyandina et al. 2001; Hassani 2007). Singular Spectrum Analysis (SSA) is a relatively new technique for time series decomposition, reconstruction and prediction. The SSA is a two-stage process.

The first stage is the *decomposition* of the series and the second stage is the *reconstruction* of the decomposed series to get the original series. The decomposition of the series is done in two steps namely: *embedding* and *Singular Value Decomposition* (SVD). The reconstruction of the original series is done by *diagonal averaging* of the resulting matrix after and optional *grouping* of the eigenvalues step has been completed. The mathematical description of all the steps mentioned above is presented in (Golyandina et al. 2001; Hassani 2007).

This technique is chosen, because it allows the time series to be divided into a sum of many time series with different periods and extract noise. There is no need to specify the shape of the trend beforehand.

In the second part of analysis, we try to verify, if the number publication pattern follows Lotka's law. $n_i = n_1/i^x$. Where n_i is the number of authors with i publications and n_1 is the number of authors with one publication and x is a positive real number usually assumed to be 2. In the analysis, we focus on authors with one and two publications. For this surgical procedure, there were not enough number of authors with more than 2 publications. Thus, we chose to verify $n_2 = n_1/2^x$. In contrast to other studies, we do not assume that the number of publications is deterministic but we assume them to be stochastic in nature. This is a valid assumption, since we do not expect the number of publications to exactly follows Lotka's law. So, we assume that n_1, n_2 and x are random variables whose sampling distribution follows a normal distribution. These assumptions allow us to calculate the 95% confidence interval for n_1, n_2 and x using the sample estimate for the means and standard deviations of these variables. To correctly propagate the error in estimation, a fuzzy approach is adopted. In this approach, all confidence intervals, are converted to fuzzy numbers using the procedure described in (Buckley 2005; Sfiris and Papadopoulos 2014). A description of the fuzzy theory and fuzzy estimators is presented in (Buckley 2005; Sfiris and Papadopoulos 2014).

3   Results and Discussion

3.1   Time Series Components

We split the time series into a sum of 15 series. This is to enable us detect any seasonality in the publications. As can be seen from the Fig. 2 below, there is strong 5 years seasonality where publication number increase and decrease every 5 years.

Apart from this, there are no other strong seasonality. It can be concluded that the time series is made of an increasing trend and a 5 year-periodic trend.

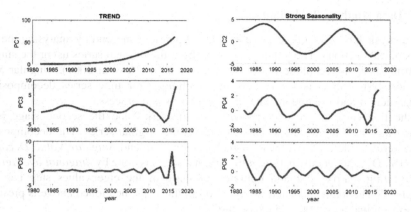

Fig. 2. First 6 Timeseries components as extracted by SSA technique

3.2   Trend Extraction and Fitting

The SSA technique was used to extract the trend of the original time series without specifying its form. The only parameter needed for the extraction is the window length, L which was chosen to be 15 (procedure for choosing the lag is explained in the (Golyandina et al. 2001; Hassani 2007). The extracted trend shows an exponential increase in number of publications as expected following Price's law. An exponential function is fitted to the observed data. The fitted function is in line with Prices' law and corresponds to those results found in (Dabi et al. 2016) (Fig. 3).

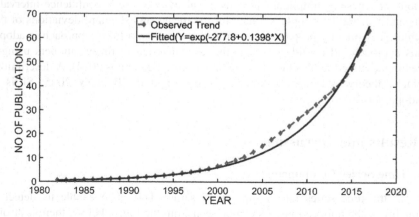

Fig. 3. Price's Law exponential fitting of publication trend

3.3   Verification of Lotka's Law with Fuzzy Estimators

To verify Lotka's law, we assume that the number of authors with 1 and 2 publications is stochastic. Since we do not know the true distribution, we use the sampling distribution and assume that it follows a t-distribution since the sample mean and unbiased sample standard deviation are used.

We construct the 95% confidence interval for n_1 and n_2, and transform the intervals to fuzzy numbers using the approach described in (Buckley 2005; Sfiris and Papadopoulos 2014). (Please see appendix for description of method). We then use the formula $n_2 = n_1/2^x$ to calculate x. Then the 95% confidence interval for x is also calculated and transformed to a fuzzy number. The goal is to check whether for the estimated x

$$\frac{n_1}{n_2} - 2^x = 0$$

We perform the α-cut operation on the equation above as follows (see (Buckley 2005; Sfiris and Papadopoulos 2014) for arithmetic on alpha-cuts):

$$\frac{{}^\alpha \tilde{n}_1}{{}^\alpha \tilde{n}_2} - 2^{{}^\alpha \tilde{x}} = 0$$

Where $\tilde{n}_1$, $\tilde{n}_2$, $\tilde{x}$ are fuzzy numbers
The resulting fuzzy numbers are shown below (Figs. 4, 5, 6, 7, 8 and 9):

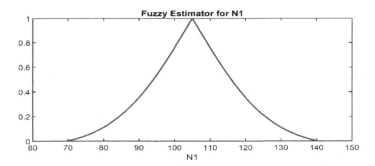

Fig. 4. Fuzzy estimation for number of authors with one publication (mean value has a truth value of 1)

The fuzzy estimator for the error in Lotka's formula shows that, publication trend indeed follows the given formula but with average x = 3.0208. Using this value of x, then the formula is considered accurate to a degree of 0.95. This is a pretty high truth value which verifies that it can be used to predict number of authors with two publications. From the fuzzy number of x, it can be concluded that x = 2 is highly unlikely, since its truth value equals zero. Thus, the usual Lotka's formula where x = 2 does not hold in this case (Fig. 10).

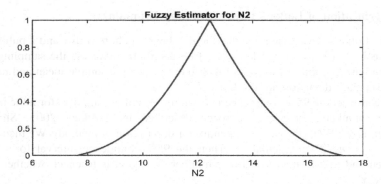

Fig. 5. Fuzzy estimation for number of authors with two publications (mean value has a truth value of 1)

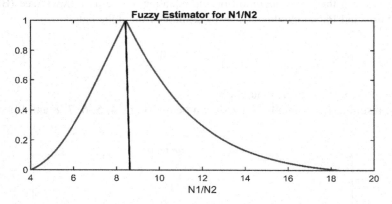

Fig. 6. Fuzzy estimation for the ratio of number of authors with one publication to the number of authors with two publications (mean value has a truth value of 1)

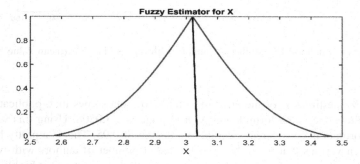

Fig. 7. Fuzzy estimation for the estimated parameter x (mean value has a truth value of 1)

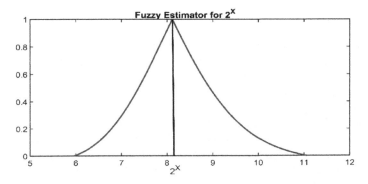

Fig. 8. Fuzzy estimation for the exponent 2^x (mean value has a truth value of 1)

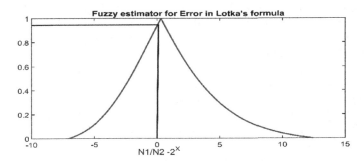

Fig. 9. Fuzzy estimation for the error in Lotka's formula (possibility of error zero is approximately 0.95)

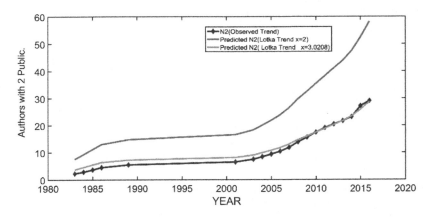

Fig. 10. Publication trend for authors with 2 publications showing observed and estimated trend for x = 2, and x = 3.0208

4 Conclusion

As the prevalence of serious obesity is constantly increased, there is a growing pressure on medical research for the evolvement of less-permanent procedures, as alternatives to surgical ones, aiming to achieve a sustainable weight loss effect that outweighs the morbidity associated with bariatric surgery.

Use of IGBs emerges as a technically easier and of minimal-risk procedure ensuring a significant weight loss in selected obese patients (Kotzampassi et al. 2012). IGBs being currently in practice are delivered endoscopically into the stomach to reduce gastric capacity and inflated with either saline or air. It has been advocated as an effective method of inducing adequate weight loss in non-morbid obesity for whatever reason or aesthetic purposes, prior to a more definitive treatment through bariatric surgery in an attempt to minimize complication rates and technical difficulties of surgery or as an adjunct to conservative treatment in the morbidly obese denied anaesthesia and/or surgery (Fernandes et al. 2007; Kotzampassi and Eleftheriadis 2006; Kotzampassi and Shrewsbury 2008). Typically, IGB devices are removed after 6 months, as the risk of balloon deflation and possible migration is heightened substantially beyond this time-period (Papavramidis et al. 2012).

Bibliometric analysis is regarded as one scientometry tool used to assess the scientific activities, according to the four major domains of published articles, such as authors, citations, references and publications. In the present study we decided to evaluate both the trend of publications and alos verify Lotka's law using a fuzzy approach. The analysis shows that publication trend follows Price's law. The extracted trend is exponential and in accordance with what is found in other studies. Lotka's formula using one and two publications, is found to hold but for mean x = 3.025. Thus using the original value x = 2 will grossly over-estimate number of authors with two publications. Further analysis is needed to verify, if this hold for higher number of publications also. The proposed approach also has some limitations regarding the calculations with alpha-cuts. Since the exact membership functions are not known, the membership values are approximated.

Appendix

Let X be a universal set. A fuzzy set is defined as any function of the form $A: X \rightarrow [0, 1]$. $A(x)$ is the membership degree of x in the fuzzy set A. The α-cuts of a fuzzy set A are defined as the sets:

$$^{\alpha}A = \{x \in R : A(x) \geq \alpha\}, \alpha \in (, 0, 1]$$

The α-cuts of a fuzzy number A can written as intervals of the form $^{\alpha}A = [A_1(\alpha), A_2(\alpha)]$ where $A_1(\alpha), A_2(\alpha)$ can be regarded as functions on [0, 1].

1. $A_1(\alpha)$ is left continuous and non-decreasing
2. $A_2(\alpha)$ is right continuous and non-increasing
3. $A_1(\alpha) \leq A_2(\alpha)$

Non-asymptotic Fuzzy Estimators

Buckely (2005) introduced fuzzy estimators. Papadopoulos and Sfiris (2014) generalize fuzzy estimators and showed new ways to construct them.

Let $X_1, X_2, \ldots X_n$ be a random sample of size n from a distribution with unknown parameter θ and let $[\theta_1(\alpha), \theta_2(\alpha)]$ denote the $(1 - \alpha)100\%$ confidence intervals for θ. Using any monotonic, continuous and onto function:

$h(\alpha) \colon (0, 1] \to \left[\frac{\gamma}{2}, 0.5\right]$, $\gamma \in (0, 1)$, then a family of fuzzy estimators is derived by the following super-imposed intervals:

$$^{\alpha}\tilde{\theta}_{\gamma} = [\theta_1(2h(\alpha)), \theta_2(2h(\alpha))], \alpha \in (0, 1]$$

It is shown that these fuzzy estimators are non-asymptotic and proper fuzzy numbers with compact support. Note that the explicit membership function can also be derived as:

$$\tilde{\theta}_{\gamma}(u) = min\left\{\theta_1^{-1}(u), -\theta_2^{-1}(-u), 1\right\}$$

For the confidence interval of the mean, this membership function can be derived as:

$$A_{\mu}(x) = \begin{cases} \frac{2}{1-\gamma}F\left(\frac{x-\bar{x}}{\sigma/\sqrt{n}}\right) - \frac{\gamma}{1-\gamma}, & \bar{x} - \frac{\sigma}{\sqrt{n}}\Phi^{-1}\left(1 - \frac{\gamma}{2}\right) \leq \bar{x} \\ \frac{2}{1-\gamma}F\left(\frac{\bar{x}-x}{\sigma/\sqrt{n}}\right) - \frac{\gamma}{1-\gamma}, & \bar{x} \leq \bar{x} + \frac{\sigma}{\sqrt{n}}\Phi^{-1}\left(1 - \frac{\gamma}{2}\right) \\ 0, & otherwise \end{cases}$$

The α-cut of this fuzzy number is:

$$^{\alpha}A = \left[\bar{x} - \frac{\sigma}{\sqrt{n}}z_{h(\alpha)}\bar{x} + \frac{\sigma}{\sqrt{n}}z_{h(\alpha)}\right] \text{ where } h(\alpha) = \left(\frac{1}{2} - \frac{\gamma}{2}\right)\alpha + \frac{\gamma}{2}$$

For unknown σ, $\sigma/\sqrt{n} = \frac{s}{\sqrt{n}}$ and $z_{h(\alpha)} = t_{h(\alpha)}$ where $t_{h(\alpha)}$ is the T-distribution with $n - 1$ degrees of freedom.

The arithmetic operations can be performed on the alpha-cuts (see Papadopoulos and Sfiris 2014).

References

Laing, P., Pham, T., Taylor, L.J., Fang, J.: Filling the void: a review of intragastric balloons for obesity. Dig. Dis. Sci. **62**(6), 1399–1408 (2017)

Flegal, K.M., Carroll, M.D., Ogden, C.L., et al.: Prevalence and trends in obesity among US adults, 1999–2008. JAMA **303**(3), 235 (2010)

Jirapinyo, P., Thompson, C.C.: Endoscopic bariatric and metabolic therapies: surgical analogues and mechanisms of action. Clin. Gastroenterol. Hepatol. **15**(5), 619–630 (2017)

Cawley, J., Meyerhoefer, C.: The medical care costs of obesity: an instrumental variables approach. J. Health Econ. **31**, 219–230 (2012)

Norris, S.L., Zhang, X., Avenell, A., Gregg, E., Schmid, C.H., Lau, J.: Long-term non-pharmacological weight loss interventions for adults with prediabetes. Cochrane Database Syst. Rev. **18**, CD005270 (2005)

Yanovski, S.Z., Yanovski, J.A.: Long-term drug treatment for obesity: a systematic and clinical review. JAMA **311**, 74–86 (2014)

Colquitt, J.L., Pickett, K., Loveman, E., Frampton, G.K.: Surgery for weight loss in adults. Cochrane Database Syst. Rev. **8**, CD003641 (2014)

Buchwald, H., Oien, D.M.: Metabolic/bariatric surgery worldwide 2011. Obes. Surg. **23**, 427–436 (2013)

Yorke, E., Switzer, N.J., Reso, A., Shi, X., de Gara, C., Birch, D., Gill, R., Karmali, S.: Intragastric balloon for management of severe obesity: a systematic review. Obes. Surg. **26** (9), 2248–2254 (2016)

Kumar, N., Bazerbachi, F., Rustagi, T., McCarty, T.R., Thompson, C.C., Galvao Neto, M.P., et al.: The influence of the Orbera intragastric balloon filling volumes on weight loss, tolerability, and adverse events: a systematic review and meta-analysis. Obes. Surg. **27**, 2272–2278 (2017)

Kotzampassi, K., Grosomanidis, V., Papakostas, P., Penna, S., Eleftheriadis, E.: 500 intragastric balloons: what happens 5 years thereafter? Obes. Surg. **22**(6), 896–903 (2012)

Kotzampassi, K., Shrewsbury, A.D., Papakostas, P., Penna, S., Tsaousi, G.G., Grosomanidis, V.: Looking into the profile of those who succeed in losing weight with an intragastric balloon. J. Laparoendosc. Adv. Surg. Tech. A **24**, 295–301 (2014)

Ellegaard, O., Wallin, J.A.: The bibliometric analysis of scholarly production: how great is the impact? Scientometrics **105**, 1809–1831 (2015)

Mishra, L., Pattnaik, P., Kumar, M., Aggarwal, S., Misra, S.R.: A bibliometric analysis of two PubMed-indexed high-impact factor endodontic journals: a comparison of India with other countries. Indian J. Dent. **7**(3), 121–125 (2016)

Thompson, D.F., Walker, C.K.: A descriptive and historical review of bibliometrics with applications to medical sciences. Pharmacotherapy **35**, 551–559 (2015)

Khan, N.R., Thompson, C.J., Taylor, D.R., Venable, G.T., Wham, R.M., Michael 2nd, L.M., Klimo Jr., P.: An analysis of publication productivity for 1225 academic neurosurgeons and 99 departments in the United States. J. Neurosurg. **120**(3), 746–755 (2014)

Sweileh, W.M., Zyoud, S.H., Al-Jabi, S.W., Sawalha, A.F.: Worldwide research productivity in emergency contraception: a bibliometric analysis. Fertil. Res. Pract. **1**, 6 (2015)

Zyoud, S.H., Al-Jabi, S.W., Sweileh, W.M.: Worldwide research productivity of paracetamol (acetaminophen) poisoning: a bibliometric analysis (2003–2012). Hum. Exp. Toxicol. **34**, 12–23 (2015)

Kotzampassi, K., Eleftheriadis, E.: Intragastric balloon as an alternative procedure for morbid obesity. Ann. Gastroenterol. **19**, 285–288 (2006)

Kotzampassi, K., Shrewsbury, A.D.: Intragastric balloon: ethics, medical need and cosmetics. Dig. Dis. **26**, 45–48 (2008)

Fernandes, M., Atallah, A.N., Soares, B.G.O., et al.: Intragastric balloon for obesity. Cochrane Database Syst. Rev. **1**, CD004931 (2007)

Papavramidis, T.S., Grosomanidis, V., Papakostas, P., Penna, S., Kotzampassi, K.: Intragastric balloon fundal or antral position affects weight loss and tolerability. Obes. Surg. **22**, 904–909 (2012)

Golyandina, N., Nekrutkin, V., Zhigljavsky, A.: Analysis of Time Series Structure: SSA and Related Techniques. Chapman & Hall/CRC, New York, London (2001)

Hassani, H.: Singular spectrum analysis: methodology and comparison. J. Data Sci. **5**(2), 239–257 (2007)

Buckley, J.J.: Fuzzy statistics: hypothesis testing. Soft. Comput. **9**(7), 512–518 (2005)

Sfiris, D.S., Papadopoulos, B.K.: Non-asymptotic fuzzy estimators based on confidence intervals. Inf. Sci. **279**, 446–459 (2014)

Dabi, Y., Darrigues, L., Katsahian, S., Azoulay, D., De Antonio, M., Lazzati, A.: Publication trends in bariatric surgery: a bibliometric study. Obes. Surg. **26**(11), 2691–2699 (2016)

Aminian, A., Brethauer, S.A., Schauer, P.R.: Citation analysis in bariatric surgery. Obes. Surg. **25**, 2417–2418 (2015)

Ozsoy, Z., Demir, E.: The evolution of bariatric surgery publications and global productivity: A Bibliometric Analysis. Obes Surg. **28**, 1117–1129 (2017) https://doi.org/10.1007/s11695-017-2982-1

Dabi, Y., Darrigues, L., Katsahian, S., Azoulay, D., De Antonio, M., Lazzati, A.: Publication trends in bariatric surgery: a bibliometric study. Obes. Surg. **26**, 2691–2699 (2016)

Ozsoy, Z., Demir, E.: Which bariatric procedure is the most popular in the world? A bibliometric comparison. Obes Surg. (2018, in press). https://doi.org/10.1007/s11695-018-3163-6

Temporal Modeling of Invasive Species' Migration in Greece from Neighboring Countries Using Fuzzy Cognitive Maps

Konstantinos Demertzis[1], Vardis-Dimitris Anezakis[2],
Lazaros Iliadis[1(✉)], and Stefanos Spartalis[3]

[1] Lab of Mathematics and Informatics (iSCE), Department of Civil Engineering,
School of Engineering, Democritus University of Thrace, University Campus,
Kimmeria 67100 Xanthi, Greece
kdemertz@fmenr.duth.gr, liliadis@civil.duth.gr
[2] Democritus University of Thrace, 193 Pandazidou st., 68200 Orestiada, Greece
danezaki@fmenr.duth.gr
[3] Lab of Computational Mathematics, School of Engineering,
Department of Production and Management Engineering,
Democritus University of Thrace, V. Sofias 12, Prokat,
Building A1, 67100 Xanthi, Greece
sspart@pme.duth.gr

Abstract. A serious side effect of climate change is the spread of invasive species (INSP), which constitute a serious and rapidly worsening threat to ecology, to the preservation of natural biodiversity, to the protection of flora and fauna and it can even threaten human population health. These species do not seem to have particular morphological differences, despite the intense variations in their biological characteristics. This often makes their identification very difficult. The need to protect the environment and to safeguard public health requires the development of sophisticated methods for early and valid identification which can lead to timely rational management measures. The aim of this research is the development of an advanced Computational Intelligence (COIN) system, capable to effectively analyze the conditions that influence and favors spreading of invasive species, due to the problem of climate change. Fuzzy Cognitive Maps (FCM) have been used to determine the specific temporal period (in years) in which the rapidly changing average temperature and precipitation in Greece, will become identical to the respective values of the neighboring countries for the period 1996–2015. This climatic evolution will cause spread of INSP met in these Mediterranean countries, to Greece. Separate analysis has been done for several cases of invasive species. The whole analysis is based on climate change models up to 2100.

Keywords: Fuzzy cognitive maps · Invasive species
Species distribution model · Soft Computing Techniques · Bioclimatic data
Climate change scenarios · Greece

© IFIP International Federation for Information Processing 2018
Published by Springer International Publishing AG 2018. All Rights Reserved
L. Iliadis et al. (Eds.): AIAI 2018, IFIP AICT 519, pp. 592–605, 2018.
https://doi.org/10.1007/978-3-319-92007-8_50

1 Introduction

1.1 Invasive Species

The potential impacts of climate change are evident at various levels of biological organization and particularly in the disturbances of biodiversity, in the biodegradability of organisms and the emergence of invasive species [15]. The Invasive species are entering new foreign habitats and they can stifle natural flora or fauna and harm the environment. They can even have negative social and economic impact on human health, agriculture, fisheries and food production. The usual reason for the movement of these species is search of colder climates, either because their natural environment does not meet the range of temperatures they can survive, or because they follow different species of plants or organisms that migrate to colder ecosystems. Although not all alien species are harmful, it is imperative to draw up a management plan according to their degree of risk. Control or eradication of these species and restoration of the ecosystems affected by them is necessary. Timely identification of INSP can slow down the uncontrolled expansion of the problem and it can increase the likelihood of eliminating the phenomenon before it is widely established and ultimately avoid the need for costly and long-term control efforts.

1.2 Related Literature - Innovations of the Proposed Methodology

There are some studies in the literature using statistical approaches and only a few employing Soft Computing Techniques to model the spread of invasive species in other countries. However, none of them aims in INSP expansion projection into the future, by estimating specific time intervals using fuzzy cognitive maps.

Coro et al. [5] constructed and produced an overall habitat suitability map and an effective geographical spread map for L. sceleratus at Mediterranean scale by using cloud computing-based algorithms to merge seven machine learning approaches. The results suggest that without an intervention, L. sceleratus will continue its rapid spread and will likely have a high impact on fisheries. Paini et al. [12] using global presence/absence data of insect crop pests employed a self-organizing map (SOM) to categorize regions based on similarities in species assemblages. This technique enabled them to generate a list of species and rank them based on an index of the risk of establishment. Gevrey and Worner, [6] predicted the worldwide distribution of two pest species based on climatic factors. They used an artificial neural network, the multilayer perceptron, trained using the backpropagation algorithm, to model the distribution of each species. Capinha et al. [4] calculated consensus predictions for current conditions and 3 future time periods (2030, 2050 and 2080) under low and high scenarios of greenhouse gas emissions, from an ensemble of forecasts generated by 5 distinct algorithms (generalized linear models, artificial neural networks, support vector machines, random forests and alternating decision trees). Sadeghi et al. [16] used support vector machines (SVMs) methods in order to predict distribution pattern of Azolla filiculoides. Various structural habitat and physico-chemical variables were used as inputs and 3 classes (low, medium and high) of cover percentage of Azolla were served as output for the models. Gras et al. [7] presented an individual-based predator-prey model in which each agent behavior is modeled by a fuzzy cognitive map and allows its evolution through the epochs of the simulation. Ramsey and Norbury, [14] used a method to assist decision making using FCM. Their approach took into account interactions between pests and conservation assets in complex food webs. Also, there are some research efforts on the expansion and distribution of INSP due to climate change [8–10, 13, 20] but none of them for the neighboring area of Greece.

This paper proposes an innovative system that performs analysis of the climate features that favor the expansion of five invasive species to Greece from neighboring countries. Also, it proposes a model of medium and long-term forecasting of temporal periods related to the potential future identification of these INSP in Greece, due to severe changes in the country's climate til 2100. Initially, the countries in which the five INSP have been listed and their climatic conditions for the period 1996–2015 have being explored. Correlation Analysis of 12 parameters for the above time-period has been performed by using values recorded in Greece. Finding the values of the positive and negative correlations and their fuzzy Linguistics, contributes to their comprehensive representation in the modeling process of the FCM. The fuzzy values of the positive and negative correlations are introduced as weights into the FCM, thereby specifying the degree of interaction of a parameter's change to the other interconnected parameters. The future climatic AVTE and AVPRE of Greece, have been formulated on the basis of the projections of a variety of climatic models and scenarios of the latest project CMIP5 (Coupled Model Inter-comparison Project Phase5) for the period up to 2100.

1.3   Description of Data

Correlation analysis of twelve bioclimatic parameters with values from Greece was performed for the period 1996–2015 [13], in order to make a symbolic representation of the complex associations of the climatic conditions with the FCM approach. Totally, five (5) INSP were studied in this research. The four of them are included in the 100 most dangerous species of the planet and they are: *Trogoderma granarium* (Insect) the *Acacia mearnsii* (Shrub) the *Trachemys scripta elegans* (Reptile) and the *Acridotheres tristis* (Bird) [11]. The fifth is known as *Eupatorium cannabinum* (Herb) and it is the most frequently recorded in 10 neighboring countries (NECO). The average temperature (AVTE) and precipitation (AVPRE) values of the 11 NECO (where the above INSP were identified) were taken into consideration.

The estimation of the future AVTEM and AVPRE values in Greece for the period 2020–2099 was based on the consideration of sixteen timely and reliable climate models of the project CMIP5.

2   Theoretical Frameworks and Methodology

2.1   Correlation Analysis

The relativity analysis with the Pearson(r) parametric correlation coefficient method was used to test the existence of a linear relationship between the parameters.

The Pearson linear correlation coefficient of two variables X and Y is defined based on a sample of n pairs of observations (x_i, y_i) $i = 1, 2, ..., n$, and it is denoted as $r(X, Y)$ or simply as r.

The variables $\bar{x}$ and $\bar{y}$ are the averages of (xi, yi). The r is the covariance $(\text{Cov } X, Y)$ of the two variables divided by the product of their standard deviations (sx, sy). It is given by the following Eq. 1:

$$r = \frac{s_{xy}}{s_x s_y} = \frac{\sum_{i=1}^{v}(x_i - \bar{x})(y_i - \bar{y})}{\sqrt{\sum_{i=1}^{v}(x_i - \bar{x})^2}\sqrt{\sum_{i=1}^{v}(y_i - \bar{y})^2}} = \frac{\sum_{i=1}^{v} x_i y_i - v\bar{x}\bar{y}}{\sqrt{\sum_{i=1}^{v} x_i^2 - v\bar{x}^2}\sqrt{\sum_{i=1}^{v} y_i^2 - v\bar{y}^2}}$$

(1)

The correlation coefficient is a pure number in the closed interval $-1 \leq r \leq 1$. More specifically, when $0 < r \leq 1$, then X, Y are positively linearly correlated. When $-1 < r < 0$, then X, Y are negatively linearly correlated. When $r = 0$, there is no correlation at all [3].

2.2 Fuzzy Cognitive Maps

In the fuzzy cognitive map models, the nodes are interconnected with edges and each edge connecting two nodes, describes the variation of the *state activation* value of the one node, in the configuration of the *state activation* value of the interconnected node. The direction of the edge implies which node affects which, where the sign of the causality relationship is positive, if there is a direct relationship of influence, negative if there is an inverse relation of influence and zero if the two nodes are uncorrelated. Relations of causality usually defined by specialists are described using fuzzy linguistic variables, and they are fuzzified by using membership functions in the interval $[-1,1]$ [17, 19].

Unlike the majority of complex dynamic systems characterized by non-linearity and great uncertainty, FCM utilize advanced learning techniques to select appropriate weights for causal interrelationships between the variables examined.

This feature helps them to capture the problem in question with absolute realism. FCM cover the need of comparing and characterizing reference sets, solving and modeling complex problems for which there is no exact mathematical model. This is achieved by employing the theoretical background of fuzzy logic. FCM are an efficient tool in modeling multiparametric problems which call for long term decisions [1, 2].

2.3 Climate Change Scenarios Employed

Our research team has already modeled complex systems concerning climate change and its direct impact which is the increased concentration of atmospheric pollutants [1, 2]. The Intergovernmental International Panel on Climate Change (IPCC) has published five reports to date. The objective of the program (CMIP5) set in the Fifth Assessment Report on Climate Change (IPCC-AR5, Assessment Report 5) was the planning of climate simulations, which aim at assessing future climate changes in both the short and the long term.

The goal is achieved using Earth System Models (ESM) and global Atmospheric-Ocean General Circulation Models (AOGCMs). In the last report (AR5) significant improvement was found in temperature and precipitation modeling mechanisms, in the study of anthropogenic effects on the environment and in the study of biochemical cycles. According to this report, four future scenarios of Green House Gases (GHGs) concentrations in the atmosphere have been developed, which are known as the Representative Concentration Pathways (RCPs).

According to the RCP2.6 scenario, a small increase in greenhouse gas emissions by the middle of the decade, would result in radiation increase to 3 W/m^2 by 2050, followed by a decrease to 2.6 W/m^2 by the year 2100. Based on the RCP4.5 and RCP6.0 scenarios, moderate increases in greenhouse gas emissions, would result in a standard increase of the radiation values. Based on the RCP4.5, the radiation values will be stabilized at about 4.5 W/m^2 before 2100, while based on the RCP6.0 they will be stabilized at 6.0 W/m^2 after 2100. Finally, according to the most extreme scenario (RCP8.5) which includes a rapid and continuous increase in greenhouse gas concentrations, the radiation will increase above 8.5 W/m^2 and it will continue to have an increasing trend for a certain period after 2100. The following climate models *bcc_csml_1, bcc_ csml_1_m, ccsm4, cesml_cam5, csiro_mk3_6_0, fio_esm, gfdl_cm3, gfdl_esm2 m, giss_e2_h, giss_e2_r, ipsl_cm5a_mr, miroc_esm, miroc_esm_chem, miroc5, mri_cgcm3, noresml_m* included in the project CMIP5, were employed in this research as the most timely and reliable ones for the estimation of temperature and precipitation future fluctuations for the period 2020–2099 [18].

3   Description of the Proposed Methodology

The basic methodology aims in modeling the occurrence of invasive species in Greece and moreover in predicting the time-period required for the Greek average temperature and precipitation values to become equal to the ones of the neighboring countries. It includes 4 distinct algorithmic stages (Modeling, Grid, Scenarios and Forecasting).

In the first step (modeling) all associated parameters are added and named. They are interconnected with synapses in order to develop the causative negative or positive correlations (Fig. 1) .

The Fuzzification of the obtained correlations is related to the description of any interconnections between features, with Linguistic terms. This has been implemented by selecting the following six terms: Low Positive (denoted in the FCM as +), Moderate Positive (++), High Positive (+++)), Negative (denoted as −), Moderate Negative (−−), High Negative (−−−)). These linguistics, represent the Fuzzy weights (see Table 1).

The description of the algorithmic steps is done in the next paragraph:

Step 1 (Modeling): Application of Correlation Analysis for the calculation of the degree of correlation between the variables under consideration (for Greece): absolute air humidity (aah), air temperature (airtemp), frost days frequency (fd), potential evapotranspiration (pet), relative humidity (rh), soil moisture (sm),

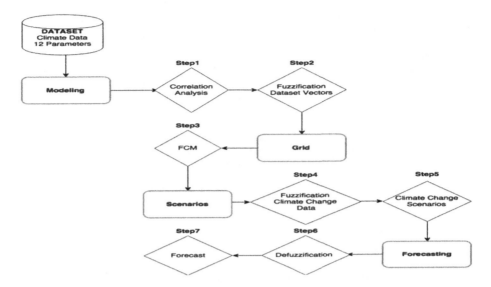

Fig. 1. Flowchart of the proposed model

Table 1. Linguistics describing the effect and their corresponding fuzzy weight value

Effect	Value
High Positive (+++)	1
Moderate Positive (++)	0.5
Low Positive (+)	0.25
Low Negative (−)	−0.25
Moderate Negative (−−)	−0.5
High Negative (−−−)	−1

sunshine fraction (sf), water vapor pressure (wvp), Water vapor saturation pressure (wvsp), wet days frequency (wd), wind speed (ws) and Precipitation (P).

Step 2: Classification of the negative and positive correlations between the parameters used, by fuzzifying their crisp numerical values. This is achieved by employing three Triangular Fuzzy Membership functions (TRIMF Eq. 2) to classify the types of correlations into the following fuzzy sets "Low Correlation" Moderate Correlation" and "High Correlation". The following Eq. 2 corresponds to a triangular fuzzy membership function (FMF) where a, b, c are the boundary values defined by the developer.

$$f(x; a, b, c) = \max\{\min[(x - a)/(b - a), (c - x)/(c - b)], 0\} \qquad (2)$$

The following Table 2 includes the Fuzzy Classification of the correlations among the features of interest.

Table 2. Fuzzification of the correlation with corresponding Linguistics

	aah	airtemp	fd	pet	P	rh	sm	sf	wd	ws	wvp	wvsp
aah	1	+++	---	+++	--	---	--	+++	---	-	+++	+++
airtemp	+++	1	---	+++	--	---	--	+++	---	+	+++	+++
fd	---	---	1	---	++	+++	++	---	++	+	---	---
pet	+++	+++	—	1	-	-	-	+++	-	+	+++	+++
P	--	--	++	--	1	++	++	--	++	-	--	--
rh	---	---	+++	---	++	1	++	---	+++	--	---	---
sm	--	--	++	--	++	++	1	--	++	++	--	--
sf	+++	+++	---	+++	--	---	--	1	---	+	+++	+++
wd	---	---	++	---	++	+++	++	---	1	-	---	---
ws	-	+	+	+	-	--	++	+	-	1	-	+
wvp	+++	+++	---	+++	--	---	--	+++	---	-	1	+++
wvsp	+++	+++	---	+++	--	---	--	+++	---	+	+++	1

Step 3 (Grid): This step simulates the interactions between the FCM nodes. This is done by employing an iterative process, which calculates the updated value of each node. This value depends on the ones of the starting edges that point to it, and on the weight assigned to the acne that joins them. Transfer functions are used to transform the result of the sum of the Products of node activation values. A new node value is calculated and the corresponding weight of the connecting edge is estimated and assigned. This is practically the case that transfers the actual value of each variable in the closed interval $[-1,1]$. The negative type of influence is shown in orange and the positive in blue. The degree of influence depends on the thickness of each line. The greater the effect, the thicker the line is, as shown in Fig. 2 (Table 3). The parameters used in the correlation analysis and in the development of the fuzzy cognitive map, are related to Greek data vectors for the period 1996–2015. The degree of influence between involved variables is depicted in Fig. 2. Mental Modeler provides some details regarding to the architecture of the grid. The number of ordinary concepts (nodes) is 12 and the connections per component are 11. So, the number of total connections between the concepts is $11 * 12 = 132$.

Temperature and precipitation changes due to climate change for the period 2020 to 2099 have been fuzzified and proper linguistics have been developed. The whole process was based on sixteen climatic models as well as on extensive testing of a variety of climate scenarios for Greece (RCP2.6, RCP4.5, RCP6.0, RCP8.5). At this stage the mean average temperature value and the mean average precipitation for Greece (1996–2015) were estimated to be 15.66 $^{\circ}$C and 45.81 mm respectively.

Step 4 (Scenarios): Step 4 performs classification of the parameters based on the future changes of the average temperature and precipitation of Greece, as they were estimated by the sixteen climate models. Four overlapping TRIMF and eight Semi-TRIMF were employed to fuzzify the crisp values of the parameters involved.

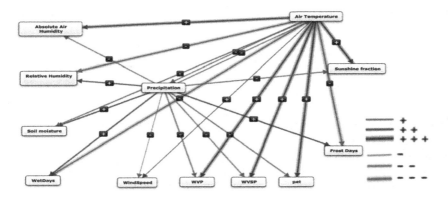

Fig. 2. The developed FCM connecting air temperature and precipitation with other variables

Regarding the period 2020–2099 two TRIMF and four Semi-TRIMF were applied on the crisp values of the average monthly temperature (AVTE) values that ranged in the closed interval $[-0.98°, +8.93°]$. The 1st Semi-TRIMF, the first TRIMF and the 2nd Semi-TRIMF were applied on the reduction of the AVTE in the interval $[-0.98°, 0°]$. These FMF correspond to the following fuzzy Linguistics: Low Negative (−), Moderate Negative (−−), and High Negative (−−−) with the last containing values close to the highest estimated reduction.

The next Semi-TRIMF, the TRIMF and the last Semi_TRIMF were used for the increase of the AVTE. These FMF correspond to the Low Positive (+), Moderate Positive (++), High Positive (+++), with the late being close to the maximum temperature increase. In the same way, two TRIMF and four Semi-TRIMF were developed for the precipitation (Table 4).

Step 5: It includes extensive testing on various scenarios based on potential changes in average temperature and precipitation and their effect on other parameters.

Step 6 (Forecasting): The fuzzy Linguistics generated by considering the mentioned climate change scenarios are de-fuzzified in order to produce crisp future values related to all interconnected parameters. In this way a future projection regarding the appearance of invasive species in Greece (due to climate change) can be achieved.

For the defuzzification the centroid function was used which estimates the center of gravity of the fuzzy set distribution.

$$x = \frac{\int x \cdot \mu(x)dx}{\int \mu(x)dx} \tag{3}$$

Table 3. Degree of influence of the average Temperature (airtemp) and average Precipitation to the other climatic variables

	aah	airtemp	fd	pet	P	rh	sm	sf	wd	ws	wvp	wvsp
airtemp	+++	1	---	+++	--	----	--	+++	---	+	+++	+++
P	--	--	++	--	1	++	++	--	++	-	--	--

Table 4. TRIMF and Semi-TRIMF boundary values for the Average Monthly Temperature and Precipitation in Greece.

Fuzzy sets corresponding to average monthly temperature and monthly precipitation changes	TRIMF and Semi-TRIMF boundaries (AVTE in C degrees)	TRIMF and Semi-TRIMF boundaries (Precipitation mm)
--- (Semi-TRIMF)	[−0.98 −0.588]	[−29.98 −17.99]
-- (TRIMF)	[−0.882 −0.49 −0.098]	[−26.98 −14.99 −2.998]
- (Semi-TRIMF)	[−0.392 0]	[−11.99 0]
+ (Semi-TRIMF)	[0 3.572]	[0 20.91]
++ (TRIMF)	[0.893 4.465 8.037]	[5.232 26.15 47.06]
+++ (Semi-TRIMF)	[5.358 8.93]	[31.38 52.29]

Step 7: The index of the magnitude of change for the other correlated parameters is calculated based on the amount of relative change of each parameter as it is given in Eq. 4.

$$Relative\ Change = \frac{FutureValue - InitialValue}{InitialValue} \tag{4}$$

4 Results and Discussion

The following Table 5 presents the changes of the average temperature and average precipitation in Greece (for the four future periods A, B, C, D) based on the historical values of the period 1996–2015. Based on climate changes models, there are five countries where the Combination of Average Temperature and Precipitation (CATEP) (for the period 1996–2015) will become identical with the future respective values for Greece (2020–2099) namely: Cyprus, Italy, Lebanon, Portugal and Israel (Tables 5, 6 and 7).

The future CATEP intervals for Greece were fuzzified in order to estimate the temporal intervals for the appearance of specific Invasive Species. A variety of scenarios have been examined. Based on them and on the application of two climate models, the species *Acacia mearnsii* is expected to appear in the country during the period 2020–2039. This could be caused by the combination of a small increase +0.1 °C in the Average Temperature (AVTE) denoted as (+) with a High increase (+++) of the Average Precipitation (AVPRE) by +41.22 mm. The combined effect of a small

Table 5. The intervals of the average monthly Temperature and Precipitation changes in Greece, for four future temporal periods till 2099

Future periods	Boundaries of future average monthly temperature change (in Celcium degrees)	Boundaries of future average monthly precipitation change (mm)
1996–2015	15.66 °C	45.81 mm
A 2020–2039	[−0.98 0] [0 +4.2]	[−21.95 0], [0 +49.18]
B 2040–2059	[−0.75 0] [0 +5.55]	[−24.19 0], [0 +52.29]
C 2060–2079	[−0.7 0] [0 +6.84]	[−27.37 0], [0 +49.26]
D 2080–2099	[−0.8 0], [0 +8.93]	[−29.98 0], [0 +48.78]

Table 6. Average monthly Temperature and Precipitation changes in Greece for the period 2020–2099. It determines the expansion of 5 INSP (recorded in 11 countries)

Countries	Crisp values of temperature change (Greece 2020–2099)	Crisp values of precipitation change (Greece 2020–2099)	Countries	Crisp values of temperature change (Greece 2020–2099)	Crisp Values of Precipitation change (Greece 2020–2099)
Cyprus	+4.29 °C	+15.52 mm	Spain	−3.63 °C	−8.29 mm
Israel	+3.91 °C	−28.09 mm	Turkey	−5.36 °C	+2.12 mm
Italy	+0.1 °C	+41.22 mm	Albania	−2.49 °C	+18.33 mm
Lebanon	+3.44 °C	−15.51 mm	Bulgaria	−4.04 °C	+13.85 mm
Portugal	−0.23 °C	+12.98 mm	Syria	+3.15 °C	−35.27 mm
			Egypt	+6.73 °C	−41.41 mm

Table 7. Presentation of: (a) Changes in CATEP (b) Estimated temporal period for the invasive species appearance in Greece

Species-Countries 1996–2015	Appearance in Greece	Crisp values of temperature change and fuzzy linguistics	Crisp values of precipitation change and fuzzy linguistics
Am-Italy	2020–2039	+0.1 (+)	+41.22 (+++)
Am-Portugal	2020–2039	−0.23 (−)	+12.98 (+)
Am-Israel	2080–2099	+3.91 (++)	−28.09 (−−−)
At-Israel	2080–2099	+3.91 (++)	−28.09 (−−−)
Ec-Italy	2020–2039	+0.1 (+)	+41.22 (+++)
Ec-Lebanon	2020–2039	+3.44 (++)	−15.51 (−)
Ec-Portugal	2020–2039	−0.23 (−)	+12.98 (+)
Ec-Cyprus	2040–2059	+4.29 (++)	+15.52 (++)
Ec-Israel	2080–2099	+3.91 (++)	−28.09 (−−−)
Tse-Italy	2020–2039	+0.1 (+)	+41.22 (+++)
Tse-Israel	2080–2099	+3.91 (++)	−28.09 (−−−)
Tg-Italy	2020–2039	+0.1 (+)	+41.22 (+++)
Tg-Lebanon	2020–2039	+3.44 (++)	−15.51 (−)
Tg-Portugal	2020–2039	−0.23 (−)	+12.98 (+)
Tg-Cyprus	2040–2059	+4.29 (++)	+15.52 (++)

Acacia mearnsii = Am, Acridotheres tristis = At, Eupatorium cannabinum = Ec, Trachemys scripta elegans = Tse, Trogoderma granarium = Tg decrease (−) of the AVTE (−0.23 °C) with a small increase (+) of the AVPRE (+12.98 mm) would have similar result. The future values for these parameters in Greece from 2020 to 2039 will be identical to the corresponding values of Italy and Portugal for the period 1996–2015 (Table 7). The species Acacia mearnsii which appeared in Israel from 1996 to 2015 is expected to appear in Greece during the period 2080–2099, due to the combined Moderate increase (++) of the AVTE (+3.91 °C) and the Moderate decrease of AVPRE (−−−) (−28.09 mm) (Table 7). For the Acacia mearnsii the combined AVTE and AVPRE values (1996–2015) of the three countries (Italy, Portugal, Israel) will be identical with the corresponding values for Greece for the period 2080–2099 (Table 8).

Table 8. Countries where invasive species have been recorded 1996–2015

Species	Countries										
Acacia mearnsii	I	Is	P	Sp							
Acridotheres tristis		Is		Sp	T						
Eupatorium cannabinum	I	Is	P	Sp	T	A	B	C	L	S	
Trachemys scripta elegans	I	Is		Sp							
Trogoderma granarium	I		P	Sp	T		B	C	L	S	E

*Italy = I, Israel = Is, Portugal = P, Spain = Sp, Turkey = T,
Albania = A, Bulgaria = B, Cyprus = C, Lebanon = L, Syria = S,
Egypt = E

The Acacia mearnsii has been recorded (for the period 1996–2015) in four Mediterranean countries (Italy, Portugal, Spain, Israel). The species Eupatorium cannabinum (Ec) and Trogoderma granarium (Tg) are expected to appear in Greece from 2020–2039 because during these 20 years the Average Temperature and Precipitation (ATE_PR) in the country will become identical to the respective ones related to the time interval 1996–2015 in Lebanon, Italy and Portugal. The Eupatorium cannabinum (Ec) will increase the likelihood of appearance in Greece for the period 2080–2099, since at that time its ATE_PR will be similar to the ones of the 1996–2015 period, in 5 out of 10 countries (Tables 6 and 7). The Trogoderma granarium (Tg) will have an increased likelihood to migrate in Greece in the temporal zone 2040–2059. The Trachemys scripta elegans (Tse) will be migrating to Greece from 2080–2099 due to the very close similarity between Greece's ATEPR (during these 20 years) and the ones of Italy and Israel for the period (1996–2015) (Table 9).

The combination of the small temperature increase (+) with the high increase of precipitation mm (+++) results in the highest fluctuations for all interconnected parameters. On the other hand, the combination of Moderate average temperature increase (++) and the highest precipitation decrease in mm (−−−) causes mainly changes in the soil moisture. Overall, the highest positive relative change is observed in the soil moisture (+0.08) which is mainly determined by the mm of precipitation (+++).

Table 9. Related changes of the involved climate parameters as a result of the changes in the AVTE and AVPRE for the period 2080-2099

Climate parameters	Fuzzification of temperature (+) and precipitation change (+++)	Fuzzification of temperature (++) and precipitation change (−−−)
Aah	−0.02	0
fd	0.01	0
pet	−0.02	0
rh	0.01	0
sm	0.08	0.01
sf	−0.02	0
wd	0.01	0
ws	−0.09	0.03
wvp	−0.02	0
wvsp	−0.02	0

5 Conclusions and Future Work

This paper proposes an innovative Soft Computing approach that estimates the temporal period in which five invasive species will be migrating to Greece. It is predicting the temporal period of their appearance based on the expected changes in average temperature and precipitation values in the country by 2100 due to climate change. Correlation Analysis has been performed with data from Greek repositories, related to twelve parameters for the period 1996–2015. The correlations have been fuzzified and the obtained Fuzzy Linguistics enabled the development of FCM. The model calculated the time-period during which the five most dangerous INS will expand in Greece. The projection of the AVPRE and AVTE of the country to the future, was based on sixteen well known and accepted climate models from today till 2100. In the near future we wish like to employ optimization methods like Genetic Algorithms and to combine them with heuristic approaches. Such hybrid modelling could enhance the dynamics of the system offering more effective and reliable results.

References

1. Anezakis, V.-D., Dermetzis, K., Iliadis, L., Spartalis, S.: Fuzzy cognitive maps for long-term prognosis of the evolution of atmospheric pollution, based on climate change scenarios: the case of Athens. In: Nguyen, N.-T., Manolopoulos, Y., Iliadis, L., Trawiński, B. (eds.) ICCCI 2016. LNCS (LNAI), vol. 9875, pp. 175–186. Springer, Cham (2016). https://doi.org/10.1007/978-3-319-45243-2_16
2. Anezakis, V.D., Demertzis, K., Iliadis, L., Spartalis, S.: Evolving systems (2017). https://doi.org/10.1007/s12530-017-9196-6
3. Asuero, A.G., Sayago, A., Gonzalez, A.G.: The correlation coefficient: an overview. Crit. Rev. Anal. Chem. **36**(1), 41–59 (2006). https://doi.org/10.1080/10408340500526766

4. Capinha, C., Anastácio, P., Tenedório, J.A.: Predicting the impact of climate change on the invasive decapods of the Iberian inland waters: an assessment of reliability. Biol. Invasions **14**(8), 1737–1751 (2012). https://doi.org/10.1007/s10530-012-0187-z
5. Coro, G., Vilas, L.G., Magliozzi, C., Ellenbroek, A., Scarponi, P., Pagano, P.: Forecasting the ongoing invasion of Lagocephalus sceleratus in the Mediterranean Sea. Ecol. Model. **371**, 37–49 (2018). https://doi.org/10.1016/j.ecolmodel.2018.01.007
6. Gevrey, M., Worner, S.P.: Prediction of global distribution of insect pest species in relation to climate by using an ecological informatics method. J. Econ. Entomol. **99**(3), 979–986 (2006)
7. Gras, R., Devaurs, D., Wozniak, A., Aspinall, A.: An individual-based evolving predator-prey ecosystem simulation using a fuzzy cognitive map as the behavior model. Artif. Life **15**(4), 423–463 (2009). https://doi.org/10.1162/artl.2009.gras.012
8. Hoveka, L.N., Bezeng, B.S., Yessoufou, K., Boatwright, J.S., Van der Bank, M.: Effects of climate change on the future distributions of the top five freshwater invasive plants in South Africa. S. Afr. J. Bot. **102**, 33–38 (2016). https://doi.org/10.1016/j.sajb.2015.07.017
9. Jung, J.M., Lee, W.H., Jung, S.: Insect distribution in response to climate change based on a model: Review of function and use of CLIMEX. Entomol. Res. **46**(4), 223–235 (2016). https://doi.org/10.1111/1748-5967.12171
10. Jung, J.M., Jung, S., Ahmed, M.R., Cho, B.K., Lee, W.H.: Invasion risk of the yellow crazy ant (Anoplolepis gracilipes) under the Representative Concentration Pathways 8.5 climate change scenario in South Korea. J. Asia Pac. Biodivers. **10**(4), 548–554 (2017). https://doi.org/10.1016/j.japb.2017.08.004
11. Lowe, S., Browne, M., Boudjelas, S., De Poorter, M.: 100 of the world's worst invasive alien species: a selection from the Global Invasive Species Database. Published by The Invasive Species Specialist Group (ISSG) a specialist group of the Species Survival Commission (SSC) of the World Conservation Union (IUCN), Auckland, New Zealand (2000)
12. Paini, D.R., Worner, S.P., Cook, D.C., De Barro, P.J., Thomas, M.B.: Using a self-organizing map to predict invasive species: sensitivity to data errors and a comparison with expert opinion. J. Appl. Ecol. **47**(2), 290–298 (2010). https://doi.org/10.1111/j.1365-2664.2010.01782.x
13. Qin, Z., Zhang, J.E., DiTommaso, A., Wang, R.L., Liang, K.M.: Predicting the potential distribution of Lantana camara L. under RCP scenarios using ISI-MIP models. Clim. Change **134**(1–2), 193–208 (2016). https://doi.org/10.1007/s10584-015-1500-5
14. Ramsey, D.S.L., Norbury, G.L.: Predicting the unexpected: Using a qualitative model of a New Zealand dryland ecosystem to anticipate pest management outcomes. Aust. Ecol. **34**(4), 409–421 (2009). https://doi.org/10.1111/j.1442-9993.2009.01942.x
15. Robert, I.C., Hugh, J.M.: A neutral terminology to define 'invasive' species. Divers. Distrib. **10**(2), 135–141 (2004). https://doi.org/10.1111/j.1366-9516.2004.00061.x
16. Sadeghi, R., Zarkami, R., Sabetraftar, K., Van Damme, P.: Use of support vector machines (SVMs) to predict distribution of an invasive water fern Azolla filiculoides (Lam.) in Anzali wetland, southern Caspian Sea, Iran. Ecol. Model. **244**, 117–126 (2012). https://doi.org/10.1016/j.ecolmodel.2012.06.029
17. Salmeron, J.L., Froelich, W.: Dynamic optimization of fuzzy cognitive maps for time series forecasting. Knowl. Based Syst. **105**, 29–37 (2016). https://doi.org/10.1016/j.knosys.2016.04.023
18. Scafetta, N., Willson, R.C.: ACRIM total solar irradiance satellite composite validation versus TSI proxy models. Astrophys. Space Sci. **350**(2), 421–442 (2014). https://doi.org/10.1007/s10509-013-1775-9

19. Vidal, R., Salmeron, J.L., Mena, A., Chulvi, V.: Fuzzy cognitive map-based selection of TRIZ trends for eco-innovation of ceramic industry products. J. Clean. Prod. **107**, 202–214 (2015). https://doi.org/10.1016/j.jclepro.2015.04.131

20. Wang, C.J., Wan, J.Z., Zhang, Z.X.: Expansion potential of invasive tree plants in ecoregions under climate change scenarios: an assessment of 54 species at a global scale. Scand. J. For. Res. **32**(8), 663–670 (2017). https://doi.org/10.1080/02827581.2017.1283049

An Approach to Modelling User Interests Using TF-IDF and Fuzzy Sets Qualitative Comparative Analysis

Dimitris K. Kardaras[1(✉)], Stavros Kaperonis[2],
Stavroula Barbounaki[3], Ilias Petrounias[4], and Kostas Bithas[2]

[1] Athens University of Economics and Business,
Patission str. 76, 10434 Athens, Greece
Kardaras@aueb.gr, dkkardaras@yahoo.co.uk
[2] Panteion University of Social and Political Sciences,
Syggrou ave. 136, 17671 Athens, Greece
skap@panteion.gr, kbithas@eesd.gr
[3] Merchant Marine Academy of Aspropyrgos, 10559 Athens, Greece
sbarbounaki@yahoo.gr
[4] The University of Manchester, Oxford Rd, Manchester M13 9PL, UK
ilias.petrounias@manchester.ac.uk

Abstract. Modelling and understanding user interests are particularly important tasks for designing services and building systems for customized solutions in web personalization and recommender systems. User generated content (UGC) constitutes a significant source of information for capturing user interests. This paper, suggests an approach to user profiling that analyses the Term Frequency (TF) and the Inverse Document Frequency (IDF) of selected tourism services by utilising the Fuzzy set Qualitative Comparative Analysis (FsQCA). It analyses a sample of customer reviews that are collected from tourism web sites. This paper considers the amount of money that customers spent during their hotel stay, as the outcome set in the FsQCA analysis. The results produce causal combinations of services that are necessary and sufficient for building customer interests models that best lead to the outcome and argue for the applicability of the FsQCA in modelling user interests.

Keywords: User interests · Fuzzy sets Qualitative Comparative Analysis
TF · IDF

1 Introduction

Recommender systems RC utilise techniques spreading from statistics, to AI and machine learning in order to capture user interests, build user and products/services profiles and suggest the most appropriate products or services to them. RC draw on several methods for developing user references models, with user-generated-content (UGC) to represent a source with rich customer information [1, 2]. Since social media platforms allow users to exchange experience, feedbacks, opinions, complaints, etc., they provide significant information for capturing and understanding user interests [3].

© IFIP International Federation for Information Processing 2018
Published by Springer International Publishing AG 2018. All Rights Reserved
L. Iliadis et al. (Eds.): AIAI 2018, IFIP AICT 519, pp. 606–615, 2018.
https://doi.org/10.1007/978-3-319-92007-8_51

Web personalisation is another area where user profiling is necessary for developing customised web interfaces, supporting personalised search [4] that allow users to retrieve search results according to their personal needs.

2   User Profiling in Tourism

Building user interests models has also been the focus of e-tourism research studies. Drawing on behavioural, socio-economic and demographic data analysis several researchers shed light into understanding people's travel behaviour [3]. Indeed, surveys on travellers' preferences have shown that the travel selection process is complex depending among others, on personality and mood related factors, service quality issues, the Word-Of-Mouth (WOM) and the eWOM. Customers often express their experience by publishing their reviews. Sentiment analysis of user reviews provides the means for capturing and modelling users' preferences, emotions and attitudes, thus refining market segregation by grouping customers with similar needs and incentives and predicting customers' travel behaviour more precisely [5].

Collantes and Mokhtarian [6] claim that a variety of personality factors such as: personality traits, travel-related behaviours, lifestyle characteristics, and travel trends, determine the subjective assessment of travelling and tourism services. Other researchers have noticed that travel behaviour is influenced by travel experiences and feelings [7, 8]. It is also argued that it is important to analyse human behaviour characteristics in order to understand how customers react to alternative transport policies [9]. Other travel research studies have analysed environmental factors that influence travel and tourism. Stradling and Anable [10], argue that environmental characteristics, such as workplace, shops and site topography affect travel choices.

Several approaches have been proposed for building user interests models. Kim and Chan [11], have proposed a hierarchical model for representing user interests. The user profile is constructing by analysing documents that users have visited on the web. The documents' analysis yields a list of user interests, which subsequently are grouped upon their similarity on the hierarchical interests' model. It is argued that there exist four classes of information contexts that need to be specified when attempting to understand user interests [12]. The *general information class* that refers to personal characteristics such as name, contact details, demographics of the user. The *event class* represents user's activities. The *preference class* refers to user's interests. *The social network class* explains user's connections and interactions with other users. The preference class is usually discovered by analysing various sources such as relevant documents that the user has published [12, 13].

Several representational approaches have been proposed for representing user interests. Most frequently though there are three different formats namely: keywords, semantic networks and concept-based representations [14, 15]. Keywords representing domains of interests are associated with weights indicating the strength of user interests for a particular topic. Polysemy and Synonymy are problems associated with keywords. Semantic networks, address these problems, by representing keywords with nodes that are connected with each other, including co-occurrences. Concept-based representations resemble semantic networks in structure but they differ in having nodes to represent abstract topics rather than keywords [14, 15]. User profiles can be used in various ways such as: during personalised information retrieval, that is when a system detects relevant documents and information according to users' interests, during re-evaluating the relevance of documents taking into consideration what documents a user has retrieved and during query processing, when a user query can be modified based on user interests [16].

It is argued that filtering and clustering techniques are very useful in reducing the number of concepts that are found on the web in order to be used in formulating user profiles. However, [16], argues that these techniques lack effectiveness for they produce the same structure of interests for users with different needs. Research show that while many systems produce and use user profiles, e.g. in web personalisation, recommender systems there exists no definite procedure for deriving user interests [16–19]. This paper addresses the need for investigating alternative ways of developing user interests' models and suggests the analysis of the TF-IDF with the FsQCA.

3   Methodology

The aim of the paper is to identify the causal combinations that are necessary and sufficient to represent customer interests. This paper utilises the FsQCA in order to analyse the TF and IDF of UGC and produce causal combinations that best lead to an outcome. The FsQCA is particularly important for investigating intertwined relationships between multiple factors that affect a dependent variable or contribute to the realisation of certain outcome [20]. The FsQCA analyses the sets of relationships among causes. In FsQCA variables are modelled as sets. The FsQCA models allow a detailed analysis of how alternative conditions of causes combine and contribute to high membership scores of the outcome [21]. FsQCA may detect multiple paths, i.e. alternative causal combinations that can lead to high levels of the same outcome [20, 22]. Data in this paper is collected from customer reviews published on hotel web sites. Causal combinations may be represented by tourism services terms such as room, view, cleanliness, etc., in the set of selected documents. The outcome set in this paper, is represented by the *large amount of money spent by the customer*. Other outcome sets can also be considered. Thus, this paper aims to identify the combinations of customer hotel services interests that best reflect customer's spending. A sample of the data collected is analysed in this paper. The steps of the methodology are shown below:

1. Select documents published by user (u_i).
2. Identify the terms that will constitute the causal combinations and specify the term that will represent the outcome set.
3. Calculate the (TF) and the (IDF) for each identified term.
4. Calculate the weight of each term (t_k) using the following formula:

$$W_{tk} = TF_{tk} * \log\left(\frac{N_i}{d_{tk}}\right) \text{ [23]} \tag{1}$$

where, W_{tk}, represents the weight of term (t_k), TF_{tk}, is the term frequency for term (t_k), N_i, is the total number of documents published by user (u_i) and d_{tk}, represents the number of documents that contain term (t_k).

5. Apply the FsQCA and produce User Interests causal combinations.
   a. Produce the truth table of all possible permutations of the terms considered. Each permutation is a possible causal combination.
   b. Calculate membership degrees for each combination. Its calculation is performed drawing on the fuzzy sets operations theory. Assume two fuzzy sets $\tilde{A}$ and $\tilde{B}$ then:

The fuzzy union, is defined as

$$\mu_{(A \cup B)} = \max(\mu_A, \mu_B), \tag{2}$$

The fuzzy intersection is defined as

$$\mu_{(A \cap B)} = \min(\mu_A, \mu_B) \tag{3}$$

and the fuzzy complement is calculated as

$$\mu_{\neg A} 1 - \mu_A \tag{4}$$

6. Calculate the consistency and the coverage of the solutions using formulas (2) and (3) respectively.

$$Consistency(X \prec Y) = \frac{\sum \min(X, Y)}{\sum X} \quad [24] \tag{5}$$

$$Coverage = \frac{\sum \min(X, Y)}{\sum Y} \quad [24] \tag{6}$$

where (X) is the membership degree of each causal combination and (Y) is the membership degree of the outcome set.

7. Identify best combinations, by selecting the combinations that exhibit a consistently rate above a threshold (in this paper is set at 0.8) and the highest possible coverage. Simplify solutions into the final set of causal combinations.

The final causal combinations indicate the hotel services that customers who spend large amount of money consider as the most important.

4 Data Analysis: Illustrative Example

This paper analyses reviews collected from five (5) hotel customers. Then, for simplicity reasons, five (5) terms representing hotel services are selected from the total set of terms identified in the reviews. The outcome set *large amount of money spent* (LMSp) by each user during his/her hotel stay is represented as triangular fuzzy numbers (TFN). The membership function $f_A(x)$ of TFN $\tilde{A}(a, m, b)$ can be calculated according to the following equation [25]:

$$
f_A(x) = \begin{cases} \frac{x-a}{m-a}, & a \leq x \leq m, \ m \neq a \\ \frac{x-b}{m-b}, & m \leq x \leq b, \ m \neq b \\ 0, & otherwise \end{cases} \tag{7}
$$

where a, m, b are real numbers. The linguistic scales which are used and their corresponding TFNs adopted in this study are shown in Table 1.

Table 1. Linguistic scales and corresponding TFNs for large amount of money-spent fuzzy sets

Linguistic scale	Triangular fuzzy scale	Mean of fuzzy numbers
Very high	(0.75, 1.00, 1.00)	1.00
High	(0.50, 0.75, 1.00)	0.75
Medium	(0.25, 0.50, 0.75)	0.50
Low	(0.00, 0.25, 0.50)	0.25
Very low	(0.00, 0.00, 0.25)	0.00

The linguistic scales represent indicate to what extent a customer is included to the set of those who spend large amount of money during their hotel stay. The TF and IDF scores (step 3) are calculated by using the KNIME tool, for all documents published by each user (u_i). Then, the weights for each term result from using formula (1). The results are shown in Table 2.

Table 2. The term weights and the membership degree for money spent for each Customer

Large amount spent membership degree outcome set (Y)	Customer	Terms' weights W_{tk} based on TF-IDF for each customer				
		Quietness	Sea view	Staff friendliness	Cultural activities	Restaurant
0.50	1	0.30	0.50	0.40	0.70	0.70
0.70	2	0.30	0.70	0.60	0.70	0.90
0.1	3	0.10	0.30	0.20	0.60	0.50
0.7	4	0.50	0.70	0.40	0.50	0.70
0.9	5	0.30	0.70	0.60	0.70	0.70

Table 3. The truth table (part of) show all possible permutations of the terms

Causal combination	Quietness	Sea view	Staff friendliness	Cultural activities	Restaurant
1	0	0	0	0	0
2	0	0	0	0	1
3	0	0	0	1	0
4	0	0	0	1	1
5	0	0	1	0	0
6	0	0	1	0	1
7	0	0	1	1	0
8	0	0	1	1	1
9	0	1	0	0	0
10	0	1	0	0	1
11	0	1	0	1	0
12	0	1	0	1	1
13	0	1	1	0	0
14	0	1	1	0	1
15	0	1	1	1	0
16	0	1	1	1	1
17	1	0	0	0	0

Next the FsQCA is applied. The truth table is developed. Since there are 5 terms to consider the number of permutations is $2^5 = 32$. Table 3 shows part of the truth table.

The cells in the truth table take the value (1) or (0) representing true or false. Thus, permutation number 3 is read (*Quietness = false, Sea View = false, Staff Friendliness = false, Cultural Activities = true, Restaurant = false*). Next the membership degrees for all combination for each user are calculated drawing on the fuzzy sets operations theory. Table 4 shows the membership degrees for the first 17 combinations.

The membership degree of combination number 3 μ_{C3}, for customer-1, see framed cell in Table 4, is calculated as follows by using formulas (3) and (4):

Consider combination number 3 membership degree $\mu_{C3} = \mu(Quietness = false \cap Sea View = false \cap Staff Friendliness = false \cap Cultural Activities = true \cap Restaurant = false) = \mu(not (Quietness), not (Sea View), not (Staff Friendliness), Cultural Activities, not (Restaurant)).$

The $\mu(Quietness = false) = \mu(1 - \mu(Quietness)) = (1 - 0.3) = 0.7$. Similar calculations are performed for all terms thus, $\mu_{C3} = min(0.7; 0.5; 0.6; 0.3) = 0.3$. After all membership degrees are calculated the consistency and coverage degrees are determined. Table 5 shows the results for the first 17 combinations.

The consistency for combination number 3 is calculated, by applying formula (5) as follows: Consider the outcome column (Y) shown in Table 2 and the membership degrees (X) of combination number 3, for all users as shown in Table 4. Then,

Table 4. Membership degrees for combinations for each customer

Causal combination	Customer 1	Customer 2	Customer 3	Customer 4	Customer 5
1	0.3	0.1	0.4	0.3	0.3
2	0.3	0.3	0.4	0.3	0.3
3	**0.3**	0.1	0.5	0.3	0.3
4	0.5	0.3	0.5	0.3	0.3
5	0.3	0.1	0.2	0.3	0.3
6	0.3	0.3	0.2	0.3	0.3
7	0.3	0.1	0.2	0.3	0.3
8	0.4	0.3	0.2	0.3	0.3
9	0.3	0.1	0.3	0.3	0.3
10	0.3	0.3	0.3	0.5	0.3
11	0.3	0.1	0.3	0.3	0.3
12	0.5	0.4	0.3	0.5	0.4
13	0.3	0.1	0.2	0.3	0.3
14	0.3	0.3	0.2	0.4	0.3
15	0.3	0.1	0.2	0.3	0.3
16	0.4	0.6	0.2	0.4	0.6
17	0.3	0.1	0.1	0.3	0.3

Table 5. Causal combinations' consistency and coverage

Causal combination	Consistency	Coverage
1	0.785714286	0.379310345
2	0.8125	0.448275862
3	0.733333333	0.379310345
4	0.789473684	0.517241379
5	0.916666667	0.379310345
6	0.928571429	0.448275862
7	0.916666667	0.379310345
8	0.933333333	0.482758621
9	0.846153846	0.379310345
10	0.882352941	0.517241379
11	0.846153846	0.379310345
12	**0.904761905**	**0.655172414**
13	0.916666667	0.379310345
14	0.933333333	0.482758621
15	0.916666667	0.379310345
16	**0.954545455**	**0.724137931**
17	1	0.379310345

$$\sum \min(X, Y) = \min\{\min(0.3; 0.5) + \min(0.1; 0.7) + \min(0.5; 0.1) + \min(0.3; 0.7)$$
$$+ \min(0.3; 0.9) = \min(0.3 + 0.1 + 0.1 + 0.3 + 0.3) = 1.1.$$
$$\sum X = (0.3 + 0.1 + 0.5 + 0.3 + 0.3) = 1.5.$$

Therefore the consistency for combination number 3 = 0.733.

Regarding the coverage, by applying formula (6), $\sum \min(X, Y) = 1.5$ and $\sum Y = 2.9$ thus coverage = 0.37.

According to FsQCA the best causal combinations should exhibit as high as possible consistency and coverage. However, the higher the consistency is the lower the coverage. Assuming a threshold value of 0.8 for the consistency firstly and then the higher possible coverage, the analysis results into two causal combinations; the combinations number 12 and 16 extracted from Table 3, are shown in Table 6.

Table 6. The two necessary and sufficient causal combinations

Causal combination	Quietness	Sea view	Staff friendliness	Cultural activities	Restaurant
16	0	1	1	1	1
12	0	1	0	1	1

A closer look at the combinations reveals that "quietness" is not within the customers interests at all. It is not a necessary service. Thus, restructuring the causal combination the analysis results that customers who spend a large amount of money, show interest in

- (Sea View) AND (Staff friendliness) AND (Cultural activities) AND (Restaurant) OR
- (Sea View) AND (Cultural activities) AND (Restaurant).

In order to simplify the causal combinations, the "staff friendliness" could be omitted for it does not appear on both combinations.

5   Conclusions-Future Research

This study suggests that the FsQCA can be used for modelling users' interests. Data selected from customer reviews is analysed by utilising the TF and the IDF. The application of the FsQCA results into useful insights that can be used to understand customer priorities and build customer profiles. Future research can focus on examining the applicability of the FsQCA to handle multiple outcome sets and to specify terms' priorities. When applying the FsQCA method in large data sets with a long list of factors, the truth table and the set of possible causal combinations can become cumbersome to analyse. Thus, future research can focus on combining the FsQCA analysis with other techniques that will be used in pruning the size of the truth table and reduce the causal combinations to manageable size.

References

1. Martínez-Garcia, E., Ferrer-Rosell, B., Coenders, G.: Profile of business and leisure travelers on low cost carriers in Europe. J. Air Transp. Manag. **20**, 12–14 (2012)
2. Baka, V.: The becoming of user-generated reviews: looking at the past to understand the future of managing reputation in the travel sector. Tour. Manag. **53**, 148–162 (2016)
3. Hunecke, M., Haustein, S., Böhler, S., Grischkat, S.: Attitude-based target groups to reduce the ecological impact of daily mobility behavior. Environ. Behav. **42**, 3–43 (2010)
4. Zhang, Z., Lin, H., Liu, K., Wu, D., Zhang, G., Lu, J.: A hybrid fuzzy-based personalized recommender system for telecom products/services. Inf. Sci. (Ny) **235**, 117–129 (2013). https://doi.org/10.1016/j.ins.2013.01.025
5. Wedel, M., Kamakura, W.A.: Market segmentation: Conceptual and methodological foundations. Springer Science & Business Media (2012)
6. Collantes, G.O., Mokhtarian, P.L.: Subjective assessments of personal mobility: what makes the difference between a little and a lot? Transp. Policy **14**, 181–192 (2007)
7. Handy, S., Weston, L., Mokhtarian, P.L.: Driving by choice or necessity? Transp. Res. Part A Policy Pract. **39**, 183–203 (2005)
8. Sheller, M., Urry, J.: The new mobilities paradigm. Environ. Plan. A. **38**, 207–226 (2006)
9. Schade, J., Schlag, B.: Acceptability of urban transport pricing strategies. Transp. Res. Part F Traffic Psychol. Behav. **6**, 45–61 (2003)
10. Stradling, S.G., Anable, J.: Individual transport patterns (2008)
11. Kim, H.R., Chan, P.K.: Learning implicit user interest hierarchy for context in personalization. In: Proceedings of the 8th International Conference on Intelligent User Interfaces, pp. 101–108. ACM (2003)
12. Joung, Y., El Zarki, M., Jain, R.: A user model for personalization services. In: Fourth International Conference on Digital Information Management, ICDIM 2009, pp. 1–6. IEEE (2009)
13. Bakalov, F., König-Ries, B., Nauerz, A., Welsch, M.: A hybrid approach to identifying user interests in web portals. In: IICS, pp. 123–134 (2009)
14. Gauch, S., Speretta, M., Chandramouli, A., Micarelli, A.: User Profiles for personalized information access. In: Brusilovsky, P., Kobsa, A., Nejdl, W. (eds.) The Adaptive Web. LNCS, vol. 4321, pp. 54–89. Springer, Heidelberg (2007). https://doi.org/10.1007/978-3-540-72079-9_2
15. Michlmayr, E., Cayzer, S.: Learning user profiles from tagging data and leveraging them for personal(ized) information access (2007)
16. Saleheen, S., Lai, W.: UIWGViz: An architecture of user interest-based web graph vizualization. J. Vis. Lang. Comput. **44**, 39–57 (2018)
17. Magnini, B., Strapparava, C.: Improving user modelling with content-based techniques. In: Bauer, M., Gmytrasiewicz, Piotr J., Vassileva, J. (eds.) UM 2001. LNCS (LNAI), vol. 2109, pp. 74–83. Springer, Heidelberg (2001). https://doi.org/10.1007/3-540-44566-8_8
18. Lehmann, S., Schwanecke, U., Dörner, R.: Interactive visualization for opportunistic exploration of large document collections. Inf. Syst. **35**, 260–269 (2010)
19. Bastian, M., Heymann, S., Jacomy, M.: Gephi: an open source software for exploring and manipulating networks. In: ICWSM, vol. 8, pp. 361–362 (2009)
20. Chari, S., Tarkiainen, A., Salojärvi, H.: Alternative pathways to utilizing customer knowledge: a fuzzy-set qualitative comparative analysis. J. Bus. Res. **69**, 5494–5499 (2016)
21. Rihoux, B., Ragin, C.C.: Configurational Comparative Methods: Qualitative Comparative Analysis (QCA) and Related Techniques. Sage Publications, Los Angeles (2008)

22. Skarmeas, D., Leonidou, C.N., Saridakis, C.: Examining the role of CSR skepticism using fuzzy-set qualitative comparative analysis. J. Bus. Res. **67**, 1796–1805 (2014)
23. Chen, K., Zhang, Z., Long, J., Zhang, H.: Turning from TF-IDF to TF-IGM for term weighting in text classification. Expert Syst. Appl. **66**, 245–260 (2016)
24. Korjani, M.M., Mendel, J.M.: Fuzzy set qualitative comparative analysis (fsQCA): challenges and applications. In: 2012 Annual Meeting of the North American Fuzzy Information Processing Society (NAFIPS), pp. 1–6. IEEE (2012)
25. Lin, H.-Y., Hsu, P.-Y., Sheen, G.-J.: A fuzzy-based decision-making procedure for data warehouse system selection. Expert Syst. Appl. **32**, 939–953 (2007)

Human & Computer Interaction - Sound - Video - Processing

Spatial-Temporal Neural Networks for Action Recognition

Chao Jing[1,2], Ping Wei[1(✉)], Hongbin Sun[1], and Nanning Zheng[1]

[1] Institute of Artificial Intelligence and Robotics, Xi'an Jiaotong University,
Xi'an, China
pingwei@xjtu.edu.cn
[2] State Key Laboratory of Mathematical Engineering and Advanced Computing,
Wuxi, China

Abstract. Action recognition is an important yet challenging problem in many applications. Recently, neural network and deep learning approaches have been widely applied to action recognition and yielded impressive results. In this paper, we present a spatial-temporal neural network model to recognize human actions in videos. This network is composed of two connected structures. A two-stream-based network extracts appearance and optical flow features from video frames. This network characterizes spatial information of human actions in videos. A group of LSTM structures following the spatial network describe the temporal information of human actions. We test our model with data from two public datasets and the experimental results show that our method improves the action recognition accuracy compared to the baseline methods.

Keywords: Action recognition · Spatial-Temporal structure · LSTM

1 Introduction

Action recognition is to predict an action category label for an input video. It is an important problem in many applications, such as video search, security surveillance, and human-machine interaction.

Recognizing actions in daily-activity videos is a challenging problem. First, some different action categories have similar appearance and motion features. For example, the actions *drinking* and *eating* are very similar in motion features. Second, motion noise in videos increases the difficulty of action recognition. Third, the unrelated background or scene features often make the model unable to capture the key information of action recognition.

In this paper, we present a spatial-temporal neural network model to recognize human actions in videos. This network is composed of two connected structures - the spatial structure and the temporal structure, as shown in Fig. 1. The spatial structure is a Two-Stream Network [1], which extracts appearance and optical flow features from video frames. Following the spatial network, the temporal structure is a group of LSTM networks [23] which represent the temporal and transition information of human actions. With these two structures, our model can deeply mine and utilize the spatial and temporal features in videos for action recognition. We test our model with data

© IFIP International Federation for Information Processing 2018
Published by Springer International Publishing AG 2018. All Rights Reserved
L. Iliadis et al. (Eds.): AIAI 2018, IFIP AICT 519, pp. 619–627, 2018.
https://doi.org/10.1007/978-3-319-92007-8_52

from two challenging datasets - MSR DailyActivity 3D [2] and UCF101 [3]. The experimental results show that our method improves the action recognition performance compared to other baseline methods.

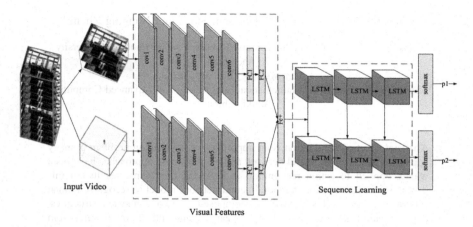

Fig. 1. Illustration of our spatial-temporal network model. The left side is a two-stream model and the right side with LSTM describes the temporal information of human actions.

1.1 Related Work

Traditional action recognition methods generally consist of two key parts: feature extraction and feature classification. For feature extraction, most approaches are based on appearance, geometric, or motion features of human bodies, such as skeleton features [4, 5], optical flow features [6]. These methods extract features from human bodies and can achieve satisfactory results in most scenes. However, in complex scenes with cluttered backgrounds, it is difficult to compute the accurate positions of human body parts, the action recognition accuracy is drastically depressed. Similar to HOG (Histogram of oriented gradient) [7] and SIFT (Scale-invariant feature transform) [8] in images, multi-scale feature extraction algorithms with prior knowledge were proposed. For example, some approaches extracted action features around the spatial-temporal interest point [9–11]. In complex scenes or backgrounds, such kinds of methods have achieved impressive improvements in action recognition accuracy. With the extracted features, various classifiers are learned to recognize actions, such as Support Vector Machine (SVM) [12].

Recently, neural networks and deep learning techniques [13–15] have been widely used in action recognition and achieved impressive performance [16–21]. Compared with static image classification, the temporal components of videos provide additional and important recognition clues - motion information [1, 22]. In the early stage, action recognition based on single CNNs model was adopted [16]. Although this method improves action recognition performance compared with traditional methods, the characteristics of time series was not deeply processed. Later, two-stream networks [1] which utilize appearance and optical flow CNNs have significantly improved action recognition performance compared with the single CNNs model. After that, the Long Short-Term Memory (LSTM) models [23] and other Recurrent Neural Network (RNN) models are applied to action recognition tasks [24–26]. LSTM and RNN models incorporate the temporal information of videos into spatial features and therefore remarkably improve the recognition accuracy compared with previous neural network architectures.

Inspired by those models, our spatial-temporal network model is a hybrid architecture of the two-stream network [1] and the LSTM network [23–25]. From data pre-processing to network structures, it extracts local and global features, combines multi-feature learning, and is consistent with the sequential-data-based action recognition.

2 Spatial-Temporal Neural Network Model

A video frame containing appearance and geometric information of human actions is the smallest feature unit of the video sequence [24–28]. The temporal and motion information between successive frames is also essential for distinguishing different actions. Inspired by the previous convolutional network and LSTM methods [1, 23–25, 29], we present a spatial-temporal neural network model to jointly describe the spatial information in single frames and the temporal information between successive frames, as shown in Fig. 1.

This network is composed of two connected structures - the spatial structure and the temporal structure, as shown in Fig. 1. The spatial structure is a two-stream network [1], which extracts appearance and optical flow features from video frames. Following the spatial network, the temporal structure is a group of LSTM networks [25] which describe the temporal and motion information of human actions. With these two structures, our model can deeply mine and utilize the spatial and temporal features in videos for action recognition.

For a complete video, we first carry out the frame pre-processing (Sect. 3). One stream of the spatial structure extracts RGB features and another stream extracts optical flow features. The main structures of each stream are 6 convolutional layers and two dense layers [29]. The size of each channel input to the first convolutional layer (conv1) is 227 * 227 * 8. Through the feature extraction of the convolutional layer (conv1 to conv6), the dimension of our FC1 and FC2 layers is 4096. We use two layers of dense layer to prevent over fitting. Through this part, we obtain the feature in Fe+ layer with dimension of 4096 * 2L.

The temporal structure is a sequential 6 layers LSTM network. By dynamically inputting the obtained Fe+ features into the sequence learning module, it can learn the temporal feature of the video sequence.

3 Data Processing

Data preprocessing is the process to convert the original video sequence into the actual input data of the network model. In this section, we will address the problem of multi-frame inputs and introduce how to calculate multi-frame optical flows.

3.1 RGB Multi Frame Sequence Input Processing

We adopt a pre-processing method to take into account the feature expression of single frame RGB data and multi-frame RGB data. The basic idea is that for a complete video sequence, we take into account the connectivity of a video segment when we divide video into multiple segments. In the process, every 8 frames are used as a unit fragment. A sliding window is defined with 4 frames per step. It slides from the video start to the end. This process method is shown in Algorithm 1.

Algorithm 1. Multi-frame preprocessing algorithm.

Multi-frame preprocessing algorithm.
1: **for** i = 1; i < L; i + + do
2: N + +;
3: **end for**
4: **for** i = 1; i < N; i + + **do**
5:     **for** w = 1; w < 8; w + + **do**
6:         F($f_1, f_2, ..., f_n$);
7:     **end for**
8: **end for**
9: **while**(4n + 8 ≤ N) *and* (n ≥ 2) **do**
10:     F_n ∈ [4n, 4n + 8];
11: **end while**

3.2 Multi Optical Flow Calculation

In this section, we introduce how to calculate optical flow features in videos. Optical flow is an important feature of videos and it is widely used in the task of action recognition [1, 22, 30]. The optical flow contains the motion information of targets and is used to describes the video frame changes. In video sequence data, the instantaneous speeds of pixels can be used to characterize the correlations between pixel sequences in time domain, as shown in Fig. 2.

We adopt the similar method with two-stream network [1] to calculate the optical flow features in videos. For a video segment with L frames, we extract the optical flow information along the X and Y axes in each two adjacent frames. Then the optical flow feature of the video segment is an encapsulation of all the frame optical flow features. It is a vector with a dimension of w * h * 2L [1], where w * h is the dimension of the single optical flow.

Fig. 2. Illustration of optical flow in human actions. (a) and (b) show a pair of successive video frames with human body motion. (c) shows the motion area.

4   Experiments

We use the action recognition accuracy to evaluate the performance of different methods. The action recognition accuracy is defined as the ratio of correctly labeled video numbers to all testing video numbers. We train the model under the caffe framework [31] and use the hardware CUDA plus GPU to deal with the floating-point matrix operation of the network. We test the models on the MSR DailyActivity 3D dataset [2] and the data samples from the UCF101 datase [3].

For the convolutional network component, we use video frames and optical flows to fine-tune a pre-trained AlexNet model [32]. We set the learning batch size as 32. The learning rate starts at 0.001 and is divided by 10 after every 30 k iterations. For all experimental settings, we set the dropout regularization ratio as 0.5 to reduce complex co-adaptations of neurons in nets.

For the LSTM part, the output of Fe+ is used as the input to the LSTM. The momentum and weight decay are set as 0.9 and 0.0005, respectively. The learning rate starts at 0.01 and is divided by 10 after every 30 k iterations. The output dimension of the softmax layer is 16.

4.1   Action Recognition on MSR DailyActivity 3D Dataset

The MSR DailyActivity 3D dataset [2] is captured using a Kinect camera. There are 16 action classes: *drinking water, eating, reading, calling, writing on paper, using notebooks, vacuuming, waking up, sitting, throwing paper, playing games, lying on the sofa, walking, playing guitar, standing up, sitting down.* There are ten subjects in total and two types of actions in each subject. One type action is at a standing position and one at a sitting position. The depth frames, the 3D skeletons of human bodies, and the RGB frames are recorded.

We compare our method with seven other approaches: Dynamic Temporal Warping [33], Actionlet Ensemble on Joint Features [34], HDMM+3ConvEets [35], 4DH [36], 4DHOI [36], Proposed method with Spatial Structure, and Proposed method with Temporal Structure. Proposed method with Spatial Structure only uses the Two-Stream Network component, and Proposed method with Temporal Structure uses the LSTM component. Table 1 shows the overall action recognition accuracy comparison, and Fig. 3 (a) shows the accuracy of each action category.

Table 1. Action recognition comparison on MSR DailyActivity 3D Dataset.

Method	Accuracy
Dynamic Temporal Warping [33]	0.54
Actionlet Ensemble on Joint Features [34]	0.74
HDMM+3ConvNets [35]	0.82
4DH [36]	0.74
4DHOI [36]	0.8
Spatial Structure Method	0.74
Temporal Structure Method	0.78
Proposed Method (Spatial + Temporal)	**0.87**

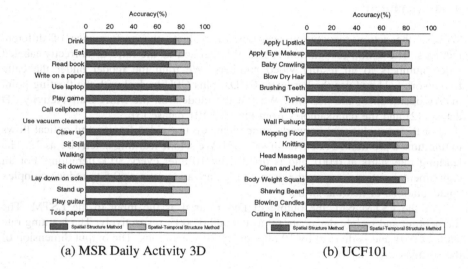

(a) MSR Daily Activity 3D   (b) UCF101

Fig. 3. Accuracy of each action of MSR DailyActivity 3D and UCF101 recognition on the network.

Our method achieves an accuracy of 0.87, which outperforms other baseline approaches. Table 1 also shows that our method outperforms the spatial structure method and temporal structure method by a considerable margin, which proves the effectiveness of joint spatial-temporal network.

4.2   Action Recognition on UCF101 Dataset

UCF101 [3] is a large-scale dataset of realistic action videos. It has 101 action categories. UCF101 dataset has the largest diversity in terms of actions and with large variations in camera motion, object appearances, poses, scales, viewpoints, cluttered backgrounds, illumination conditions, etc. It is one of the most challenging datasets to date. We choose 16 categories of indoor actions in the dataset for our experiments.

These 16 categories are: *Apply Eye Makeup, Apply Lipstick, Baby Crawling, Blow Dry Hair, Brushing Teeth, Typing, Jumping Jack, Wall Pushups, Mopping Floor, Knitting, Head Massage, Clean and Jerk, Body Weight Squats, Shaving Beard, Blowing Candles, Cutting In Kitchen*. Each category consists of 25 groups and each group has 4 videos, with a total of 100 videos per category. The videos from the same group may share some common features, such as similar background, similar viewpoint, etc.

We compare our approach with the spatial structure method of two-stream network and the temporal structure method of LSTM. Table 2 shows the accuracy comparison and Fig. 3(b) shows the accuracy of each action class. Our method achieves an accuracy of 0.85. The results show that our method outperforms the comparison methods by a large margin, which proves the strength and effectiveness of our method.

Table 2. Action recognition comparison with UCF101 data.

Method	Accuracy
Spatial Structure Method	0.72
Temporal Structure Method	0.75
Proposed Method (Spatial + Temporal)	**0.85**

5   Conclusions

This paper presents a spatial-temporal neural network model to recognize human actions in videos. Our model jointly uses temporal and spatial dimension features of video sequences. With spatial and temporal structures, our model can deeply mine and utilize the spatial and temporal features in videos for action recognition. We test our model on two challenging datasets. The experimental results show that our methods improve the performance compared to other baseline methods.

Our future work will focus on complex neural network models on action recognition and video understanding.

Acknowledgement. This work is supported by National Natural Science Foundation of China 61503297, National Key Research and Development Program of China 2016YFB1000903, National Natural Science Foundation of China 61790563, and the Open Project Program of State Key Laboratory of Mathematical Engineering and Advanced Computing.

References

1. Simonyan, K., Zisserman, A.: Two-stream convolutional networks for action recognition in videos. Adv. Neural. Inf. Process. Syst. **1**(4), 568–576 (2014)
2. Wang, J., Liu, Z., Wu, Y., Yuan, J.: Learning actionlet ensemble for 3D human action recognition. In: IEEE Conference on Computer Vision and Pattern Recognition, pp. 1290–1297 (2012)
3. Soomro, K., Zamir, A.R., Shah, M.: Ucf101: a dataset of 101 human actions classes from videos in the wild. In: Computer Science (2012)

4. Fujiyoshi, H., Lipton, A.J.: Real-time human motion analysis by image skeletonization. In: Proceedings, Fourth IEEE Workshop on Applications of Computer Vision, WACV 1998, p. 15 (2002)
5. Wei, P., Zheng, N., Zhao, Y., Zhu, S.C.: Concurrent action detection with structural prediction. In: International Conference on Computer Vision, pp. 3136–3143 (2013)
6. Chaudhry, R., Ravichandran, A., Hager, G., Vidal, R.: Histograms of oriented optical flow and binet-cauchy kernels on nonlinear dynamical systems for the recognition of human actions. In: IEEE Conference on Computer Vision and Pattern Recognition, CVPR 2009, pp. 1932–1939 (2009)
7. Dalal, N., Triggs, B.: Histograms of oriented gradients for human detection. In: IEEE Computer Society Conference on Computer Vision and Pattern Recognition, CVPR 2005, pp. 886–893 (2005)
8. Lowe, D.G.: Object recognition from local scale-invariant features. In: Proceedings of the International Conference on Computer Vision (1999)
9. Sch, C., Laptev, I., Caputo, B.: Recognizing human actions: a local SVM approach. In: International Conference on Pattern Recognition, pp. 32–36 (2004)
10. Wang, H., Kläser, A., Schmid, C., Liu, C.L.: Action recognition by dense trajectories. In: IEEE Conference on Computer Vision and Pattern Recognition, pp. 3169–3176 (2011)
11. Kläser, A., Marszalek, M., Schmid, C.: A spatio-temporal descriptor based on 3D-gradients. In: The British Machine Vision Conference (2008)
12. Cortes, C., Vapnik, V.: Support-vector networks. Mach. Learn. **20**(3), 273–297 (1995)
13. Schmidhuber, J.: Deep learning in neural networks: an overview. In: Neural networks: the Official Journal of the International Neural Network Society, vol. 61, p. 85 (2014)
14. Goodfellow, I., Bengio, Y., Courville, A.: Deep Learning. MIT Press (2016)
15. Lecun, Y., Bengio, Y., Hinton, G.: Deep learning. Nature **521**, 436–444 (2015)
16. Ji, S., Xu, W., Yang, M., Yu, K.: 3d convolutional neural networks for human action recognition. IEEE Trans. Pattern Anal. Mach. Intell. **35**(1), 221–231 (2012)
17. Chen, X., Weng, J., Lu, W., Xu, J., Weng, J.: Deep manifold learning combined with convolutional neural networks for action recognition. IEEE Trans. Neural Netw. Learn. Syst. (99), 1–15 (2017)
18. Li, C., Sun, S., Min, X., Lin, W., Nie, B., Zhang, X.: End-to-end learning of deep convolutional neural network for 3D human action recognition. In: IEEE International Conference on Multimedia & Expo Workshops, pp. 609–612 (2017)
19. Rahmani, H., Mian, A., Shah, M.: Learning a deep model for human action recognition from novel viewpoints. IEEE Trans. Pattern Anal. Mach. Intell. **40**(3), 667–681 (2018)
20. Husain, F., Dellen, B., Torras, C.: Action recognition based on efficient deep feature learning in the spatio-temporal domain. IEEE Robot. Autom. Lett. **1**(2), 984–991 (2016)
21. Mora, S.V., Knottenbelt, W.J.: Deep learning for domain-specific action recognition in tennis. In: Computer Vision and Pattern Recognition Workshops, pp. 170–178 (2017)
22. Papenberg, N., Bruhn, A., Brox, T., Didas, S., Weickert, J.: Highly accurate optic flow computation with theoretically justified warping. Int. J. Comput. Vis. **67**(2), 141–158 (2006)
23. Hochreiter, S., Schmidhuber, J.: Long short-term memory. Neural Comput. **9**(8), 1735–1780 (1997)
24. Donahue, J., Hendricks, L.A., Guadarrama, S., Rohrbach, M., Venugopalan, S., Darrell, T., Saenko, K.: Long-term recurrent convolutional networks for visual recognition and description. In: Computer Vision and Pattern Recognition, pp. 677–691 (2015)
25. Baccouche, M., Mamalet, F., Wolf, C., Garcia, C., Baskurt, A.: Sequential deep learning for human action recognition. In: Salah, A.A., Lepri, B. (eds.) HBU 2011. LNCS, vol. 7065, pp. 29–39. Springer, Heidelberg (2011). https://doi.org/10.1007/978-3-642-25446-8_4

26. Ng, Y.H., Hausknecht, M., Vijayanarasimhan, S., Vinyals, O., Monga, R., Toderici, G.: Beyond short snippets: deep networks for video classification. In: Computer Vision and Pattern Recognition, CVPR 2015, pp. 4694–4702 (2015)
27. Graves, A.: Supervised sequence labelling with recurrent neural networks. In: Springer Berlin Heidelberg (2012)
28. Barbu, A., Bridge, A., Burchill, Z., Coroian, D., Dickinson, S., Fidler, S., Michaux, A., Mussman, S., Narayanaswamy, S., Salvi, D., Schmidt, L., Shangguan, J., Siskind, J.M., Waggoner, J., Wang, S., Wei, J., Yin, Y., Zhang, Z.: Video in sentences out. In: The Conference on Uncertainty in Artificial Intelligence, UAI 2012, pp. 102–112 (2012)
29. Yuan, Z.W., Zhang, J.: Feature extraction and image retrieval based on AlexNet. In: Eighth International Conference on Digital Image Processing (2016)
30. Baker, S., Roth, S., Scharstein, D., Black, M.J., Lewis, J.P., Szeliski, R.: A database and evaluation methodology for optical flow. In: IEEE International Conference on Computer Vision, pp. 1–31 (2007)
31. Jia, Y., Shelhamer, E., Donahue, J., Karayev, S., Long, J., Girshick, R., Guadarrama, S., Darrell, T.: Caffe: convolutional architecture for fast feature embedding, pp. 675–678 (2014)
32. Krizhevsky, A., Sutskever, I., Hinton, G.E.: Imagenet classification with deep convolutional neural networks. Adv. Neural. Inf. Process. Syst. **25**, 1097–1105 (2012)
33. Müller, M., Röder, T.: Motion templates for automatic classification and retrieval of motion capture data. In: ACM SIGGRAPH/EUROGRAPHICS Symposium on Computer Animation, SCA 2006, Vienna, Austria, September, pp. 137–146 (2006)
34. Wang, J., Liu, Z., Wu, Y., Yuan, J.: Learning actionlet ensemble for 3d human action recognition. IEEE Trans. Pattern Anal. Mach. Intell. **36**(5), 914 (2014)
35. Wang, P., Li, W., Gao, Z., Zhang, J., Tang, C., Ogunbona, P.: Deep convolutional neural networks for action recognition using depth map sequences. In: Computer Science (2015)
36. Wei, P., Zhao, Y., Zheng, N., Zhu, S.C.: Modeling 4D human-object interactions for joint event segmentation, recognition, and object localization. IEEE Trans. Pattern Anal. Mach. Intell. **39**(6), 1165–1179 (2017)

Building Trust Between Users and Telecommunications Data Driven Virtual Assistants

Marta Perez Garcia$^{(\boxtimes)}$ ⓘ and Sarita Saffon Lopez

Telefonica R&D, Madrid, Spain
{marta.perezgarcia, sarita.saffonlopez}@telefonica.com

Abstract. When we think about traditional technology services, such as the Internet and popular smartphone apps, interaction or experience related words tend to come to our mind. However, when we shift to more disruptive and breakthrough technologies, such as big data, IoT or Artificial Intelligence (AI), trust and security become a key challenge as the environments in which the personal information is stored and used to extract value changes in ways that are difficult to understand for normal users. This study explores the current challenges to trust and rely on a Virtual Assistant and establishes a series of constructs to build trust in a Telecoms Data Driven Virtual Assistant by considering aspects from an embryonic idea of the AI to its final articulation as a digital service. It examines a series of multi-methodology research interactions to help shape and refine the service, not only to build trust in the AI but also in the organisation behind it.

Keywords: Artificial intelligence · Data driven virtual assistants
Trust · Human computer interaction · Telecommunications

1 Introduction

Since ancient times, humans have had the curiosity to explore their own cognitive capacities, also referred to as *intelligence*, and how to replicate them in their own inanimate creations [1]. Literature, myths and history itself prove this; from Von Kempelen's "Turk" automaton playing chess with Napoleon, to Mary Shelly's Frankenstein, to Alan Turing's code deciphering machine, until the development of Data Driven Virtual Assistants (DDVA) [2, 3]. The relationship between the human mind and machines has grown so strong that the language used to refer to both is almost analogous, with terms such as memory, hard drive, sensors, neurons, and so on. This discipline then, of studying the human cognitive competences and trying to replicate them, has become a science called Artificial Intelligence (AI). From competing in games such as chess [4]; to being part of strategic war weapons [5], to being able to recognize speech [6], and now to current uses in industries such as logistics, retail, education and financial services [7]. Furthermore, the future uses of AI are expected to apply to diverse areas, such as medicine, where surgeries might be done by automatons [8]. After briefly reviewing AI's past, present and future, it is clear that it has become part of our lives, even though humans continue to doubt, and even fear the power that AI may reach. This assertion is supported by Pega Systems global 6.000 consumer study [9] where 70% of the participants reported that they feared AI and 24% are worried about robots taking over the world.

2   What Does Trust Mean and Why Is It Important?

Trust is defined as someone's willingness to become susceptible regarding a certain issue, context or information [10]. This is the reason why trust is of special importance when it comes to human-computer interaction, where users need to trust and rely on the digital agents or virtual assistants because they have to act on their behalf [11]. In the context of online versus offline, Corritore et al. [10] identified three core aspects that need to be built in order to generate trust: ease of use, risk involved and technology credibility. Sas and Khairuddin [12] go beyond this, establishing there are two different types of trust when it comes to people interacting with technology: (1) trust between users and technology itself; and (2) trust between users who interact with technology. In the case of Virtual Assistants, trust is more focused on the first one, trust between users and technology, as it is a one-to-one relationship and there is no communication or information sharing with other party. In fact, when it comes to this information sharing between the user and the AI technology, it becomes obvious that not all of the information is of the same quality and usefulness, so allowing a system to dissect it is the first step towards trust [13]. Ultimately, the objective would be to enable these artificial intelligence virtual assistants to take care of issues with no intervention or supervision of the user [14]. Many articles have been written arising this trust issue between users and artificial intelligence but there is however little work done on the investigation of their key constructs needed to generate trust between these parties.

3   Key Challenges in Trusting an AI

Northstar Research Partners [15] carried out a survey study that explored the awareness and acceptance of AI from a consumer perspective. It highlights three concerns that participants reported around the subject of AI, which constitute the focus of building and maintaining trust.

3.1   A Lack of Knowledge of AI Does not Help Build Reliance

By definition, there are two types of AI: weak and strong [16]. On one hand, only weak AI exists currently, which is based on programmed response-powered algorithms. Therefore, this is a supervised process that does not comprehend the commands it receives, but classifies them according to a pre-set data base of responses, and only simulates a human-like experience. On the other hand, strong AI, not yet created but in the process, has a mind of its own, hence it creates clusters and associations in order to provide a response. However, do users know this? Are they aware of how artificial intelligence works? Pega Systems study [9] reports that more than 50% of its

6,000-customer base are not aware of ever interacting with AI technology. This fact highlights the massive gap between people's perceptions, awareness and conscience around AI. Most information about AI users have is what they have seen in futuristic science fiction movies where machines take over the world, so it becomes crucial to create support, coordination, explanation groups and initiatives [11] to make people knowledgeable of the benefits and potential of AI to enrich their lives. As MIT professors Erik Brynjolfsson and Andrew McAfee [17] explain, AI is the base of what they refer to as the second machine age, resembling a new industrial revolution, where "computers and other digital advances are doing for mental power…what the steam engine and its descendants did for muscle power." (pp. 7–8). The process towards trusting this technology will require exposure and experience, such as it did in the 18th century with the Industrial Revolution. In summary, people mistrusted machines at the beginning of the Industrial Revolution like people mistrust AI today because, as the Pega Study [9] shows, they do not even know what AI actually is.

3.2 Mistrusting AI to Solve Complex Problems

Every customer is different and as such, their problems have very diverse contingencies. How can a DDVA be smart enough to understand all the details, specifics of thousands and millions of customers? Research shows that existing AI relies on human monitoring, a best practice referred to as *Human-in-the-Loop* [18], which is based on generating machine learning models that, in case of uncertainty or in contexts with a low level of confidence, yields the decision making to a human mind. This feedback is used to learn and improve algorithms over time. AI is not currently taking over the complex functions but the easy ones, while real people still work on the hard functions. This case is illustrated in current automatic pilot commercial planes like the Boing 777 [19] and self-driving cars as the Tesla autopilot mode in their models X, S and 3 [20], where a human is always in the driving seat to take control if needed. When the AI systems need autonomy to perform tasks and make decisions on behalf of users, it becomes essential to develop trust on the AI actions in order to use them and adopt them as assistants in people's daily lives [21]. Currently, a human is always there controlling cases of doubt or ambiguity, for no machine is perfect, as no human is [22], so there is no need to separate AI from humans, since various trials such as with Centaur Chess [23] and IBM Watson [24] proved that human minds and machines work better together than separately [25].

3.3 Managing and Handling Personal and Private Data

Other concern that increases distrust on AI is the uncomfortable necessity of sharing our personal data with an AI system, and not being sure of the ethical guidelines that it follows [26]. For instance, to assure ethical guidelines, it is important AI developers address the three AI factors suggested in The Cambridge Handbook of Artificial Intelligence [27]: (1) being transparent to inspection, (2) being predictable and (3) being non-operable, with the objective of becoming trust-generating features. This could be done by explaining the algorithms behind the system to support the transparency and predictability of the system [28]. Banavar [29] also proposes various tasks in order to achieve trust and reassurance. For example, before launching an AI system, he suggests to run field testing for ethics-related design issues, and continue to elicit user feedback throughout the deployment to monitor other potential ethical problems. When considering a product or service for a DDVA, ethics programs should be embedded in the AI system so they can reduce the risks and guide the system into values and principles in which it has to base its own behaviour [29]. These guidelines require research and interdisciplinary teams of professionals in ethics and in AI development, to find a common language that will ensure the proper and practical implementation of ethical program in the machines [30]. For ensuring that these best practices are respected and enforced, current players in the AI field (Amazon, Google, Facebook, IBM, etc.) have already formed an alliance, in which they pursue various ethical topics, and develop new ones to safeguard the transparency and safety of data used by AIs [31].

4   Best Practices in AI: What to Do and What to Avoid

Trust building in any part of people's lives is affected by first impressions [32]. With DDVA, it is no different. According to psychologist Albert Mehrabian [33], 38% of first impressions depend on the tone of voice, and only 7% on the words used. This includes using silences between sentences so that the person listening has time to process the information given, and having fillers just like "mmm" or "well", all to create the feeling of talking to a human being and therefore developing trust [34]. A second aspect that has to be considered is the gender of the DDVA, some key players in this area, such as Apple, Google or Amazon, have ensured that the device not only has a human-like tone of voice but a female one, as they are perceived as warmer [35], more trustworthy [36], easier to understand [37], in summary, easier to like. However, the human like aspect of the DDVAs cannot go to an extreme. Dr. Masahiro Mori [38] developed in 1970 the theory of the Uncanny Valley, which states that as the AI becomes more human-like there is an increase in the levels of acceptability and affinity with the device, but if it resembles too much human, there is a dramatic decrease of approval reaching even negative likeness and unsettling feelings [38]. This is the reason why many organisations are now going into the opposite direction, trying to avoid this Uncanny Valley. For instance, newly competitors have shifted from previous DDVA trend of naming their devices with human-like names as Alexa or Cortana, to more neutral and unbiased names like Bixby by Samsung and Tmall by Alibaba. Even though these best practices are being published, implemented and protected by the DeepMind Alliance, a well-established AI research organisation, there exist various cases of AI failures from where other learnings can rise. An example is Microsoft's Tay, an AI chatbot which used people's Twitter conversations to generate her own, and was tricked by users to learn and produce racist and other harmful tweets. Additionally, Tay was modelled as a teenager girl, pushing the feminisation of the AI, worsening the situation [39]. Another example of a not so successful outcome is Facebook's AI robots, Alice and Bob, which were disconnected because, while performing a nego-tiation between them, they generated a language that was incomprehensible for human beings [40]. These cases represent examples that feed fears inherent in the human mind, and inhibits them from trusting AI systems.

5 The Context

This research study takes place within a multinational telecoms organisation because it reflects rather clearly two challenges the literature review has highlighted around trusting AI: (1) AI taking over complex points of interaction between users and humans where problem solving is essential; and (2) the aversion towards an AI handling personal data (consumption of services, behaviours, habits, etc.). A Telecoms DDVA could work as an artefact to save time and effort, helping users make the most of their hired services and improve overall customer experience satisfaction [41]. The principles that appear in the findings section of this paper are being applied to Telefonica (trading as Movistar, Vivo and O2 in more than twenty countries) and its cognitive intelligence Aura. However, the study has been carried out as an exploratory study and has been conducted in general terms, evaluating the results as a category (not associating it to a specific brand) and recruiting participants from all the major Telecoms providers in Spain.

6 Methodology and Sample

To explore and tackle the issues highlighted in the literature, two ad-hoc user-centred research activities in Spain were conducted:

1. Sixteen in-depth interviews to find out perceptions around the concept, the value proposal and use cases. This was tested with a sample of six current DDVA users, six ex users and four aware but not current users. Two people of three age ranges (25–35, 36–45, 46–55) formed each of the groups.
2. Five hundred online questionnaires to explore the personality of current DDVAs and future interests, of which two hundred and nine participants were current users of DDVAs, a hundred and one ex users, and hundred and one aware but not current users. In each of these groups there was a mix of ages: 16–24, 25–34, 35–44 and 45–54 years old.

All participants were of medium- high socio economic level, living in capital cities and in proportion of 50% men and 50% women. The reason behind all these recruitment parameters was to understand habits, expectations, fears and perceptions of different segments with different approaches and usage of technology.

7 Findings

These different research activities that took place during this exploratory study helped identify a series of key aspects in the development of trust with a telecoms DDVA:

7.1   How Should a Telecoms Data Driven Virtual Assistant Be?

After identifying a suitable name for the DDVA, this study sought to understand the personal qualities it should have in order to emotionally connect with users. In the quantitative phase of this study, the 500 questionnaires, users were presented with a series of characters, skills and personality aspects to determine current and future perception of VAs. This helped understand the relationship between functional and emotional benefits users experiment with this type of Artificial Intelligence. In terms of characters, users were given a wide range of options to articulate the way they would perceive a Telco DDVA. Among these options, 60% of current 299 VA users agreed that they would interact with a robot-like character, contrasted by the 0% and 11% that chose mother or friend, respectively. This remote expectation of a personified human-like DDVA and instead an expectation of a pure technological, digital and artificial machines, confirms once more the Uncanny Valley theory of not humanising AI in excess [38]. In terms of personality traits, users expect DDVAs to be precise, especially when serving them information and answers. A suggested future improvement of DDVA personality is creativity, which is something they currently lack. Users also desire a Telecoms DDVA to be proactive, able to make intelligent suggestions and teach them how to make the most out of their services. However, users also expressed that they still lack the trust in AI to handover decision making, so we believe the proactivity of DDVAs must have a clearly defined scope. In summary, the personality traits (precision, creativity, proactivity) users expect and desire from a Telecoms DDVA have the potential of fostering positive connotations that could influence the perception of the Telecommunication Organization itself.

7.2   Transferring Human Roles to AI

The in-depth individual interviews explored the different aspects regarding the concept and value proposal of the DDVA. Within this context, users highlighted the fact that one of the DDVA objectives should be to improve customer experience and customer care with a Telecoms provider. This led to two major findings: (i) Users considered this would represent a massive change for customer care experience and many of them felt, *a priori,* reluctant to change. However, after a first moment of doubt, most users started balancing pros and cons of current situation and the proposed one and considered the optimisation of time and resources that a DDVA would have for them resulted on a more positive perceived customer care relationship; (ii) Secondly, users also would like to have a backup person to talk to when the DDVA is not able to solve their problem, following the *Human In-The-Loop* practice [18]. These findings point out to the fact that people do not consider the DDVA will satisfy all their requests, and consider that they would not remain unsolved when combining human and AI forces [25]. This led to a higher level of satisfaction of the DDVA concept proposed, while establishing a potential scenario to merge both worlds in order to enhance customer service and strengthen the value proposition.

7.3   The Importance of the Decision-Making Process

In this case, users were given a series of stimulus data in the form of different use cases the DDVA could carry out in order to improve their relationship with the Telecoms provider. This led to a discussion around the articulation of these scenarios, exploring the role the DDVA would play. The results of this study showed users are very interested in a DDVA that is proactive, makes suggestions and has a didactic function for users in order to learn the possibilities it offers. They showed an interest in receiving alerts about anomalies in their hired telco services. However, a key insight that was identified was the importance of the decision-making process in this type of scenarios. Users implied that even when a DDVA could potentially solve a problem with their services, they expect the DDVA to alert them and ask for permission to start sorting out the incidence. This suggests users are at a very early stage within the trust path towards independent DDVAs and still want to ensure they have the power and authority to control them. They are not interested yet in a DDVA that is able to make independent decisions on their behalf, even if this is for their own good. This takes the results back to perception of the DDVA as a robot or servant exposed previously.

7.4   Gathering and Handling Personal Data

The literature has highlighted how personal data handling is one of the main challenges when trusting AI [15]. This was a core aspect in this study as the Virtual Assistant is driven by the data gathered in the Telecoms organisation and the data that the user keeps generating when making use of its telecoms services. The interviews with users have helped identify two moments of truth around this issue: (1) The first one happens when a person realises the quantity of data the Telecoms has about its customers, which generates a sense of surprise and agitation, however, after this brief moment, users tend to have (2) the second moment of truth, by which they understand that information is already within their service provider, it is acceptable they have it. This thought calms them down as they realise nothing bad has ever happened to them around data handling with their telecoms provider.

8   Conclusions

Building trust is a complex task, as it rests on a combination of several characteristics or features. The different research activities have helped identify a series of aspects that are essential to the start building trust between a user and a Telecoms DDVA, so the learnings from the different experiments are currently being applied to Aura, Telefonica's Data Driven Virtual Assistant. Firstly, when building a DDVA, a series of characteristics to shape its personality are required. This study has pointed out the importance of being precise in the information offered and the level of quality in the results the DDVA shows. In the future, a more creative personality could be built on top of efficiency. These personality qualities, are currently being applied to Aura, so the team is working on the efficiency and precision with which Aura can answer a series of given questions to users. Furthermore, deepening the knowledge around these attributes is key to build the desired personality and that works with the mother brand. A second issue that has emerged is the articulation of the decision-making process, which the qualitative interviews have shown is placed on the user. Even when dealing with a contingency or problem, users are not yet prepared for the DDVA to make decisions on its own. This study highlighted the importance that having control has for the user so Aura will notify users of any abnormality so that the user is the one with the power, the control over his own telecoms services and it is the one who makes the decisions. This is something that could evolve in the future, as these type of products and services become increasingly integrated in everyday life, but not yet at this early stage. Consequently, when this type of DDVA adoption evolves, Aura's team would like to test if users trust her enough to enable her to make decisions on her own (benefiting the user). In terms of the implications of the DDVA taking over certain interactions in the customer experience, specially its potential implementation in customer care, users have shown an interest toward the time and effort saving the DDVA could bring them in this type of situation, improving their level of satisfaction with the telecoms organisation. The trade-off they require is to be redirected to a person when the DDVA is not able to solve the issue they are trying to sort out. As for privacy and security of personal data, this study has suggested that the brand equity of the organisation providing the DDVA plays a key role in addressing this challenge. An organisation that is not able to build trust and confidence in its customers will probably not be able to generate trust in a DDVA, no matter the value proposition.

References

1. Villena, J., Crespo, R., García, J.: Inteligencia en Redes de Comunicaciones - 01 Historia de la Inteligencia Artificial. Universidad Carlos III de Madrid, Madrid (2012)
2. McCorduck, P., Minsky, M., Selfridge, O., Herbert, S.: History of artificial intelligence. In: IJCAI, pp. 951–954. AAAI Press, Cambridge (1977)
3. Bolter, D.: Turing's Man: Western Culture in the Computer Age. UNC Press Books, Chapel Hill (2014)
4. DeCoste, D.: The future of chess-playing technologies and the significance of kasparov versus deep blue. In: Proceedings of the 4th AAAI Conference on Deep Blue Versus Kasparov: The Significance for Artificial Intelligence, pp. 9–13. AAAI Press (1997)
5. Teuscher, C.: Alan Turing: Life and Legacy of a Great Thinker, 1st edn. Springer, Heidelberg (2004)
6. Kuligowska, K., Lasek, M.: Virtual assistants support customer relations and business processes. In: 10th International Conference on Information Management, Gdańsk, pp. 155–164 (2011)
7. Bahrammirzaee, A.: A comparative survey of artificial intelligence applications in finance: artificial neural networks, expert system and hybrid intelligent systems. Neural Comput. Appl. **19**(8), 1165–1195 (2010)
8. Grace, K., Salvatier, J., Dafoe, A. Zhang, B., Evans, O.: When will ai exceed human performance? Evidence from AI Experts. ArXiv e-prints (2017)
9. Pega Systems. What consumers really think about AI: A Global Study. https://www.pega.com/ai-survey. Accessed 18 Jan 2018

10. Corritore, C., Kracher, B., Wiedenbeck, S.: On-line trust: concepts, evolving themes, a model. Int. J. Hum Comput Stud. **58**(6), 738–758 (2003)
11. Castelfranchi, C.: The role of trust and deception in virtual societies. Int. J. Electron. Commer. **6**(3), 55–70 (2002)
12. Sas, C., Khairuddin, I.: Design for trust: an exploration of the challenges and opportunities of bitcoin users. In: Proceedings of the 2017 CHI Conference on Human Factors in Computing Systems, pp. 6499–6510. ACM, New York (2017)
13. Marsh, S.: Trust and reliance in multi-agent systems: a preliminary report. In: MAAMAW 1992, 4th European Workshop on Modelling Autonomous Agents in a Multi-Agent World, Rome (1992)
14. Castelfranchi, C., Falcone, R.: Social trust: a cognitive approach. In: Castelfranchi, C., Tan, Y.H. (eds.) Deception, Fraud and Trust in Virtual Societies. Kluwer, Dordrecht (2001)
15. Northstar Research Partners. AI today, AI tomorrow: Awareness, acceptance and anticipation of AI: A global consumer perspective. http://pages.arm.com/rs/312-SAX-488/images/arm-ai-survey-report.pdf. Accessed 21 Jan 2018
16. Kerns, J.: What's the difference between weak and strong ai. Machine Design. http://www.machinedesign.com/robotics/what-s-difference-between-weak-and-strong-ai. Accessed 21 Jan 2018
17. Erik Brynjolfsson, E., McAfee, A.: The Second Machine Age: Work, Progress, and Prosperity in a Time of Brilliant Technologies. WW Norton & Company, New York (2014)
18. Dautenhahn, K.: The art of designing socially intelligent agents: science, fiction, and the human in the loop. Appl. Artif. Intell. **12**(7–8), 573–617 (1998)
19. Sha, S., Bumataria, R., Choudhary, A., Bandhnia, G: Primary flight control of boeing-777. Int. J. Adv. Res. Eng. Sci. Technol. (IJAREST) **2**(5) (2015)
20. Tesla: Full Self-Driving Hardware on All Cars. https://www.tesla.com/autopilot. Accessed 2 Sept 2017
21. Glass, A., McGuinness, D., Wolverton, M.: Toward establishing trust in adaptive agents. In: Proceedings of the 13th International Conference on Intelligent User Interfaces, pp. 227–236. ACM, New York (2008)
22. Negnevitsky, M.: Artificial Intelligence: A Guide to Intelligent Systems, 2nd edn. Pearson Education Limited, Essex (2005)
23. Scharre, P.: Centaur warfighting: the false choice of humans vs. automation. Temple Int. Comp. Law J. **30**(1), 151 (2016)
24. Rachlin, H.: Making IBM's computer, Watson, human. Behav. Anal. **35**(1), 1–16 (2012)
25. Bunch, L., Bradshaw, J., Hoffman, R., Johnson, M.: Principles for human-centered interaction design, part 2: can humans and machines think together? IEEE Intell. Syst. **30**(3), 68–75 (2015)
26. Abascal, J., Colette, N.: Moving towards inclusive design guidelines for socially and ethically aware HCI. Interact. Comput. **17**(5), 484–505 (2005)
27. Frankish, K., Ramsey, W. (eds.): The Cambridge Handbook of Artificial Intelligence. Cambridge University Press, Cambridge (2014)
28. Gibb, J.: T-Group Theory and Laboratory Method: Innovation in Re-Education Climate for Trust Formation. Wiley, New York (1964)
29. Banavar, G.: Learning to trust artificial intelligence systems. IBM Research. https://www.research.ibm.com/software/IBMResearch/multimedia/AIEthics_Whitepaper.pdf. Accessed 23 Aug 2017
30. Anderson, M., Leigh Anderson, S.: Machine Ethics. Cambridge University Press, Cambridge (2011)
31. Industry Leaders Establish Partnership on AI Best Practices. IBM News. https://www-03.ibm.com/press/us/en/pressrelease/50668.wss Accessed 29 Aug 2017

32. Yu, M., Saleem, M., Gonzalez, C.: Developing trust: first impressions and experience. J. Econ. Psychol. **43**, 16–29 (2014)
33. Mehrabian, A.: Silent Messages: Implicit Communication of Emotions and Attitudes, 2nd edn. Wadsworth, Belmont (1981)
34. Kedem, A.: Is Siri lying to you? Knowing when a bot sounds trustworthy is the next step in digital security. https://qz.com/928201/is-siri-lying-to-you-knowing-when-a-bot-sounds-trustworthy-is-the-next-step-in-digital-security/. Accessed 18 Jan 2018
35. Mitchell, W., Ho, C., Patel, H., MacDorman, K.: Does social desirability bias favour humans? Explicit–implicit evaluations of synthesized speech support a new HCI model of impression management. Comput. Hum. Behav. **27**(1), 402–412 (2011)
36. Siegel, M., Breazeal, C., Norton, M.: Persuasive robotics: the influence of robot gender on human behaviour. In: IEEE/RSJ International Conference on Intelligent Robots and Systems, IROS 2009, pp. 2563–2568. IEEE (2009)
37. Sokhi, D., Hunter, M., Wilkinson, I., Woodruff, P.: Male and female voices activate distinct regions in the male brain. Neuroimage J. **27**(3), 572–578 (2005)
38. Mori, M.: The Uncanny Valley. Energy **7**(4), 33–35 (1970)
39. Neff, G., Nagny, P.: Automation, algorithms, and politics | talking to bots: symbiotic agency and the case of tay. Int. J. Commun. **10**, 17 (2016)
40. Bradley, T.: Facebook AI creates its own language in creepy preview of our potential future. https://www.forbes.com/sites/tonybradley/2017/07/31/facebook-ai-creates-its-own-language-in-creepy-preview-of-our-potential-future/#473aba81292c. Accessed 18 Jan 2018
41. Perez, M.: The potential of data-driven virtual assistants to enhance customer experience in the telecommunications industry. In: 9th Interaction South America Conference, Floripa (2017)

Voice Separation in Polyphonic Music: Information Theory Approach

Michele Della Ventura[⊠]

Department of Technology, Music Academy "Studio Musica", Treviso, Italy
dellaventura.michele@tin.it

Abstract. Voice Separation is a delicate stage in a music information retrieval process intended to be used in the automated music analysis processes through textual segmentation or for the indexation of a music score. This article presents a method that is capable of separating polyphonic music, considered in its symbolic aspect, into its individual parts (or voices). This method considers every single note as an individual entity and assigns it to the part (or voice) where the information content that it assumes in relation to the already-existing notes of the same score is maximum. The algorithm may separate the voices identifying them even in the points that intersect. The algorithm was tested against a handful of musical works that were carefully selected from the repertoire of Bach and of Mendelssohn.

Keywords: Entropy · Information · Music segmentation
Overlapping musical notes · Voice separation

1 Introduction

Computerized music analysis is a constantly-changing discipline, both thanks to the consequences originating from technology research and to the ongoing influences deriving from the study of cognitive sciences. Focusing on the comprehension of the brain processes involved in the musical activities [1, 2], the latter may assume a decisive role in the analysis of the computerized music analysis.

This kind of approach is important to musicians and to IT developers alike. To musicians it provides an innovative means to obtain the composing elements of a composition (pre-thematic elements, themes/melodies, rhythmic cells,...) [3, 4, 5, 6]. To IT developers, these techniques are used to perfect the text segmentation systems in order to improve the capacities of a search engine in the identification of the information on the web [7]. The amount of information on the web is growing fast as well as the number of new users lacking experience in the art of web searching. The automated search engines based on the correspondence of keywords usually deliver too many low-quality matches. In general, the more precise the collection of data to be analyzed is, the better the results of the elaborations will be. The starting point is therefore the reading of the notes that is carried out from a MIDI file or from the more recent XML file.

In case of a polyphonic composition (Fig. 1), which entails a simultaneous ensemble of several voices on several pitches and in parallel or opposite directions, data

L. Iliadis et al. (Eds.): AIAI 2018, IFIP AICT 519, pp. 638–646, 2018.
https://doi.org/10.1007/978-3-319-92007-8_54

(sound) reading and their proper assignment to a certain voice rather than to another voice becomes vital: both in case of the analysis of the musical text and in case of the information retrieval by the search engine.

Fig. 1. Polyphonic composition

The analysis of a score is usually carried out by the main algorithms through a process of segmentation that considers the sounds of the various voices, one after another (Fig. 2).

Fig. 2. Representation of the score for the segmentation process

In polyphonic music and, in particular, in the FUGUE form, there are many examples where a voice intersects another voice (Fig. 3).

Fig. 3. Overlapping musical notes.

In these cases an incorrect reading of the data would lead the segmentation processes (which precede the analyses described above) to rather inaccurate and, in certain cases, even erroneous results. In the example from Fig. 4 the "subject" of the FUGUE is no longer recognizable.

Fig. 4. Representation of the score for the segmentation process

In recent years various methods have been proposed for the separation of the voices of a polyphonic composition.

Some works include algorithms which are capable of separating the voices based on specific preset rules [9, 10, 11]: the computer does not learn these rules and develop its own knowledge, but rather simply uses the knowledge provided by the human analysis.

In other cases the algorithm is able to autonomously learn the rules [12, 13, 14]: parameters that are trained on music already labeled with voice information.

Some algorithms [9] take on the problem of overlapping musical notes, even if the results are not always satisfying. These are systems that take into consideration the sound vicinity concept. A marked improvement is the study by Gray and Bunescu [15], a neural model for voice separation in symbolic music that assigns notes to active voices using a greedy ranking approach, or the study by Guiomard-Kagan [16], which taking inspiration from the method of Chew and Wu [9] that defines what contigs to connect and how to connect them, improved these connections by using musical parameters such as the average pitch difference between neighbor contigs.

This article presents a method that, drawing inspiration from the preceding studies, is able to reconstruct the various voices of a polyphonic composition, by reading the sounds from a MIDI file: every single note is considered as an individual entity and inserted into the voice where the information content that it assumes in relation to the already-existing sounds in the same score is maximum. It is a system based on two clearly distinct principles: a musical one, related to the structure of the thematic material (interval structure - distance between various sounds) and a mathematical-statistical one, derived from the Information Theory elaborated by Weaver and Shannon [8], tied to the possibility of transition from one interval to the other.

This paper is organized as follows.

Section 2 describes the information theory. Section 3 describes the analysis of the musical message. Section 4 shows some experimental tests that illustrate the effectiveness of the proposed method. Finally, conclusions are drawn in Sect. 5.

2 Information Theory

The analysis based on the Information Theory, considers the audio message as a linear process endowed with a syntax formulated not on the basis of preset rules, but on the probability of occurrence of each element of the audio message in relation to the element preceding it [17, 18]. From the definition of a "message" as a chain of discontinuous speech "units of meaning" [17], there follows that the speech "units of meaning" coincide with the minimum events of an audio message. Any event of a chain built in this fashion requires a prevision in relation to the event that will follow it [19]. In a communication happening by means of a given alphabet of symbols, the information is associated to every single transmitted symbol [17]. Information, therefore, may be defined as *the reduction of the uncertainty that might have been, a priori, present on the transmitted symbol*. The ampler the range of messages that the source may transmit (and the larger the uncertainty of the receiver in relation to the possible message), the larger the quantity of transmitted information is – and, along with it, its own measure: *the entropy* [19]. In the Information Theory, the *entropy* measures the quantity of uncertainty or of information existing in a random signal. If every message has the probability p_i of being transmitted, the entropy is obtained as the sum of all the set of functions $p_i \log_2 p_i$, each of them being related to a message, i.e.:

$$H(X) = E[I(x_i)] = \sum\nolimits_{i=1}^{n} I(x_i) \cdot P(x_i) = \sum\nolimits_{i=1}^{n} P(x_i) \cdot \log_2 \frac{1}{P(x_i)}$$

3   The Voice Separation Model

To separate the voices of a score starting from a musical input, the sounds must be, first of all, divided into movements, according to the beat of the composition (Fig. 5a), thus obtaining chords (i.e. the simultaneous overlapping of several sounds). Bear in mind that every voice may be even made up by several sounds within the same movement (Fig. 5b). The assignment of the notes to the various voices is therefore performed in chronological order, from the left to the right, beginning with the first movement: every note of the first movement is considered in itself as sound of a voice.

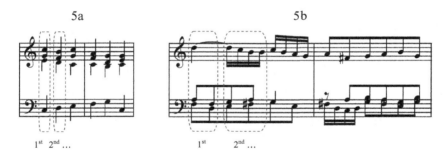

Fig. 5. Subdivision of the scores into movements.

Subsequently, the algorithm determines all the possible musical segments obtainable by combining the sounds of a voice with the sounds of the other voices of the movement following the analyzed one (Fig. 6).

Finally, the information value is calculated for every identified segment: the segment having the larger value will represent the succession of the sounds for the specific voice (Fig. 7).

To compare various segments among them, in order to determine which is more important, each entropy is calculated: the less the entropy value, the greater the information carried by the sound [18]. In order to calculate the entropy it is necessary to take into consideration a specific alphabet: the alphabet is language – specific [19] and, as it may be immediately deduced from the formula (based on the probability of certain

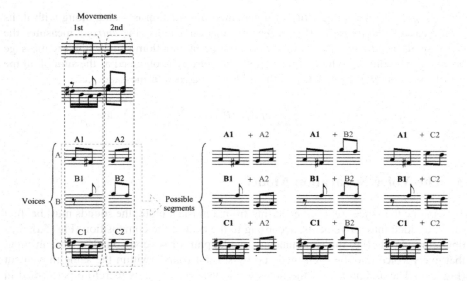

Fig. 6. Possible segments between two consecutive movements.

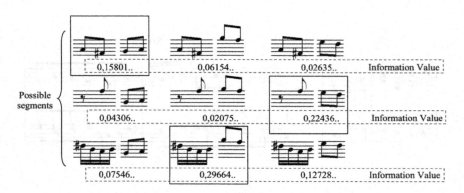

Fig. 7. Constitution of the voices.

symbols rather than other symbols to be transmitted) it demonstrates to be associated to language.

For the **melodic analysis** the various melodic intervals were classified as symbols of the alphabet [18]. For every single musical piece a table, which represents its own alphabet, is filled in: in the melodic analysis every interval has been considered for its ascending or descending trend (Table 1). A peculiarity of the proposed method is related to the fact that only the sounds of the initial subject of the FUGUE are taken into consideration to define the alphabet table.

The definition of the alphabet is not enough in order to calculate the entropy of a musical segment: it is necessary to consider the manner in which the sound succeeds one another inside the musical piece.

Table 1. Example of alphabet.

Sound	Number
Fa	1
Mi	1
Re	1
Do	4
Si	
La	3
Sol	
Fa	2

In order to do this, the Markov process (or Markov's stochastic process) is used: we chose to deduce the transition probability that determines the passage from a state of the system to the next uniquely from the immediately preceding state [14, 18]. On the base of the above considerations, the transition matrix is created. It consists of the transition probabilities between the states of the system (conditional probability). In our case, the matrix represents the probabilities for a sound to resolve to another sound (Table 2).

Table 2. Transitions matrix drawn about the melodic segment of Table 1.

		Fa		La		Do		Re		Mi		Fa	
		a	d	a	d	a	d	a	d	a	d	a	d
Fa	a					1							
	d				1								
La	a	2											
	d						1						
Do	a			2									
	d							1					
Re	a												
	d										1		
Mi	a												
	d											1	
Fa	a				1								
	d												

4 Obtained Results

The method presented in this article was tested by analyzing some musical compositions written in the form of a FUGUE, carefully selected from the repertoire of Johann Sebastian Bach (48 fugues of the well-tempered clavier) and of Felix Mendelssohn

(6 fugues op. 35). Both cases regard polyphonic compositions that include from 2 to 5 voices and some of them even have overlapping musical notes.

The algorithm, realized on purpose, does not provide any limitation with respect to the dimensions of the table representing the alphabet and the matrix of transitions that will be automatically dimensioned in every single analysis on the basis of the characteristics of the analyzed musical piece. This allows conferring generality to the algorithm and specificity to every single analysis (Strength). Furthermore, the algorithm does not entail any limitation as to the number of possible voices to be extracted (Strength).

The analysis of the time needed for every single elaboration was not taken into consideration inasmuch as the objective of the study was solely to separate the voices of a polyphonic composition to further improve potential subsequent segmentations for analyses of a different nature: musical or web indexation.

The larger the number of decimals used to express the information content value of every segment, the more precise the results of the elaborations. The larger the number of decimals, the smaller the error risk.

Some examples of the obtained results are given below (Figs. 8 and 9) as well as examples related to the specific moments in which the voices were intersecting. The first stave shows the subject of the FUGUE, presented in the first 2/3 beats; the second stave shows a segment of the FUGUE where the parts intersect; the third stave shows the final result with the various separated voices.

Fig. 8. J.S. Bach: fugue No.6 of "The Well-Tempered Clavier" (BWV 851).

Fig. 9. F. Mendelssohn: fugue No. 2 op. 35.

5   Discussion and Conclusions

This article described an approach to the separation of the voices of a polyphonic musical composition, considered on their symbolical level, based on the Information concept.

The algorithm was applied to musical compositions in the form of FUGUE by authors such as Bach, Frescobaldi and Mendelssohn.

The results show on the one hand how the musical fabric of a composition is characterized by a strong structural uniqueness; on the other hand how this method represents a solution for the problem of voice separation, even if the voices intersect.

This method represents an alternative approach in the applications of computational methods to the voices separation problem: the high degree of complexity of musical phenomena imposes certain forms of achievement that must be adequate and that, for completeness' sake, must cope with the problems under a sufficiently large number of angles.

References

1. Deliège, I., McAdams, S.: La musique et le sciences cognitives (1989). Liegi-Bruxelles, P. M. (Editeur)
2. De Poli, G., et al.: Reti neuronali per il controllo delle deviazioni temporali nell'esecuzione musicale. In: Camurri, A., Canepa, C. (a cura di), Atti del IX Colloquio di Informatica Musicale, Genova, 13–16 novembre 1991, Genova, AIMI/DIST (1991)
3. Pancini, M.: Problematiche e modelli formali per la segmentazione automatica/interattiva di partiture musicali simboliche, Rapporto Tecnico CNR-PFBC-MUS-TR (2000)
4. Ventura, M.D.: Analysis of algorithms' implementation for melodic operators in symbolical textual segmentation and connected evaluation of musical entropy. In: Proceedings 1st Models and Methods in Applied Sciences, Drobeta Turnu Severin, pp. 66–73 (2011)
5. Ventura, M.D.: Rhythm analysis of the "sonorous continuum" and conjoint evaluation of the musical entropy. In: Proceedings Latest Advances in Acoustics and Music, Iasi, pp. 16–21 (2012)
6. Ventura, M.D.: The influence of the rhythm with the pitch on melodic segmentation. In: Abraham, A., Jiang, X.H., Snášel, V., Pan, J.-S. (eds.) Intelligent Data Analysis and Applications. AISC, vol. 370, pp. 191–201. Springer, Cham (2015). https://doi.org/10.1007/978-3-319-21206-7_17
7. Hui, K., Berberich, K.: Selective labeling and incomplete label mitigation for low-cost evaluation. In: Iliopoulos, C., Puglisi, S., Yilmaz, E. (eds.) SPIRE 2015. LNCS, vol. 9309, pp. 137–148. Springer, Cham (2015). https://doi.org/10.1007/978-3-319-23826-5_14
8. Weaver, W., Shannon, C.: The Mathematical Theory of Information. Illinois Press, Urbana (1964)
9. Chew, E., Wu, X.: Separating voices in polyphonic music: a contig mapping approach. In: Computer Music Modeling and Retrieval: Revised Papers, Esbjerg, Denmark (2005)
10. Karydis, I., Nanopoulos, A., Papadopoulos, A., Cambouropoulos, E.: VISA: the voice integration/segregation algorithm. In: ISMIR, Austria (2007)
11. Madsen, S., Widmer, G.: Separating voices in MIDI. In: ISMIR, Canada (2006)
12. Kirlin, P., Utgoff, P.: Voise: learning to segregate voices in explicit and implicit polyphony. In: International Conference on Music Information Retrieval (ISMIR) (2005)
13. Jordanous, A.: Voice separation in polyphonic music: a data-driven approach. In: Proceedings of the International Computer Music Conference, Belfast, Ireland (2008)
14. de Valk, R., Weyde, T., Benetos, E.: A machine learning approach to voice separation in lute tablature. In: Proceedings of the 14th International Society for Music Information Retrieval Conference, pp. 555–560, Curitiba, Brazil (2013)
15. Gray, P., Bunescu, R.: A neural greedy model for voice separation in symbolic music. In: International Society for Music Information Retrieval Conference + (ISMIR 2016), pp. 782–788 (2016)
16. Guiomard-Kagan, N.: Traitement de la polyphonie pour l'analyse informatique de partitions musicales, Informatique [cs], Université de Picardie-Jules Verne (2017)
17. Angeleri, E.: Information, Meaning and Universalit. UTET, Turin (2000)
18. Lerdhal, F., Jackendoff, R.: A Grammatical Parallel between Music and Language. Plenum Press, New York (1982)
19. Nattiez, J.J.: Fondements d'une sémiologie de la musique. Union Générale d'Éditions, Paris (1975)

Author Index

Printed in the United States
By Bookmasters